Energy Systems

Series Editor:

Panos M. Pardalos, University of Florida, USA

For further volumes:
http://www.springer.com/series/8368

Roger L. Conkling

Energy Pricing

Economics and Principles

Springer

Dr. Roger L. Conkling
University of Portland
School of Business Administration
North Willamette Boulevard 5000
Portland 97203-5798, Oregon
USA
conklingr@comcast.net

ISSN 1867-8998　　　　　　　　　e-ISSN 1867-9005
ISBN 978-3-642-15490-4　　　　　e-ISBN 978-3-642-15491-1
DOI 10.1007/978-3-642-15491-1
Springer Heidelberg Dordrecht London New York

© Springer-Verlag Berlin Heidelberg 2011

This work is subject to copyright. All rights are reserved, whether the whole or part of the material is concerned, specifically the rights of translation, reprinting, reuse of illustrations, recitation, broadcasting, reproduction on microfilm or in any other way, and storage in data banks. Duplication of this publication or parts thereof is permitted only under the provisions of the German Copyright Law of September 9, 1965, in its current version, and permission for use must always be obtained from Springer. Violations are liable to prosecution under the German Copyright Law.

The use of general descriptive names, registered names, trademarks, etc. in this publication does not imply, even in the absence of a specific statement, that such names are exempt from the relevant protective laws and regulations and therefore free for general use.

Cover illustration: Cover art is designed by Alex Kaufmann

Cover design: WMXDesign GmbH, Heidelberg

Printed on acid-free paper

Springer is part of Springer Science+Business Media (www.springer.com)

To
April 4, 1941,
the wedding day that brought Meta,
beautiful, gracious, and caring

We have celebrated 4/4 annually
for sixty-nine years since

Acknowledgments

The author is most grateful to Brother Donald J. Stabrowski, C.S.C., Provost of the University of Portland, and to Robin D. Anderson, Dean and Franz Chair in Entrepreneurship of the Dr. Robert B. Pamplin, Jr. School of Business Administration, for permitting the use of the University's facilities for the completion of this book.

The author is also grateful to Gwynn Klobes, Erica Jones, and Kathleen Staten for their supervision of the typing by students of the final draft of the manuscript. Also deserving mention are student-typist Olga Mosiychuk, for overcoming the obstacles of last-minute changes, and next-door neighbor, Tim O'Hearn, for outsmarting his intractable computer.

He owes thanks to Leonard A. Girard, General Council and Secretary, Portland General Electric Company (retired), and Thomas E. Bottorff, Senior Vice President, Regulatory Relations, Pacific Gas and Electric Company, for their encouragement in the early stages.

But greatest of all is his debt of appreciation and gratitude to his wife, Meta, and to his daughter, Beth, for their help and understanding throughout the writing process.

Contents

1	**Introduction**			1
	1.1	Distinguishing Between Cost and Price		1
	1.2	Cost and Price in Our Daily Vocabulary		2
	1.3	The Credibility of Cost		3
	1.4	Total Cost of the Operation as a Whole		4
	1.5	Joint-Product Costs		7
	1.6	Price Relationships: The Baker Revisited—The Quantity Discount		11
	1.7	The Economics of Fixed (Overhead) Costs		13
		1.7.1	Production Within the Capability of Existing Plant	14
		1.7.2	Where Plant Expansion Is Required	15
	1.8	A Closer Look at Two-Part Pricing		17
	1.9	Competitive Pricing (Value to the Purchaser)		18
	1.10	From Wonderland to Reality		18
		1.10.1	The Baker	19
		1.10.2	The Utility	19
		1.10.3	A Broader Horizon	20
		1.10.4	Benefits vs. Costs	20
	1.11	Cost and Price-A Primer		20
	1.12	Conclusions, If Any		22
2	**The Cost Approach to Pricing: The Direction of Cost**			25
	2.1	Preface		25
	2.2	Fixed and Variable Costs		27
		2.2.1	The "Readiness to Serve" Concept	28
		2.2.2	The "Use of Service (Product)" Concept	29
		2.2.3	Relative Proportion of Fixed and Variable Costs	29
	2.3	Decreasing, Constant, and Increasing Costs Conditions		29
	2.4	Decreasing Costs		30
		2.4.1	The Static Hypothesis	30
		2.4.2	The Dynamic Hypothesis	33
	2.5	The Base System		34

	2.6	Future Additions	37
		2.6.1 Decreasing Fixed-Cost Scenario	38
		2.6.2 Constant Fixed-Cost Scenario	40
		2.6.3 Increasing Fixed-Cost Scenario	40
	2.7	The Small Base-Load Plant	42
	2.8	The Peaking or Firming-Up Plant	46
	2.9	Power Purchases by Electric Utilities from Non-utility Sources, Bypass, and Discounts	50
		2.9.1 Purchase by a Utility	50
		2.9.2 Construction by the Utility of Its Own Plant	51
		2.9.3 Purchase of IPP Power	51
		2.9.4 Bypass of the Utility	53
		2.9.5 An Alternative to Bypass: A Discounted Price	55
		2.9.6 Arrested or Contracted Output	56
		2.9.7 Summary of Findings	57
	2.10	Variable Costs	59
		2.10.1 The Dominance of Variable Costs	61
		2.10.2 The Uncertainty of Variable Costs	61
		2.10.3 High Capital/Low Operating Costs vs. Low Capital/High Operating Costs	62
	2.11	Matters of Judgment	63
	2.12	A Note on Generating Plants	66
	2.13	A Note on the Level of Costs	66
3	**The Cost Approach to Pricing: Joint Cost Allocations**		**69**
	3.1	Direct and Joint/Common Costs	69
	3.2	Cost Causation	71
		3.2.1 The Classification of Customers	71
		3.2.2 The Classifications of Services	71
		3.2.3 The Classification of Costs	71
	3.3	Utility Cost Allocation Theory	73
	3.4	The Functionalization of Costs	74
	3.5	Methods of Allocation	74
		3.5.1 The "Coincident Demand Peak-Responsibility" Method	74
		3.5.2 The "Non-coincident Demand Peak-Responsibility" Method	76
		3.5.3 Other Peak-Responsibility Methods	77
		3.5.4 Various Other Methods	77
		3.5.5 The "Phantom Customer" Method	78
		3.5.6 The Nordin Proposal	78
		3.5.7 Edison's Improvements	79
	3.6	Distribution	80
	3.7	Rate Schedule Divisions of Cost	81
		3.7.1 Demand Costs	81

	3.7.2	Customer Costs	81
	3.7.3	Commodity Costs	82
	3.7.4	The "Perfect" Rate	82
3.8	Suballocations		82
3.9	The Total Cost and Incremental Cost Methods		83
	3.9.1	Marginal Costs	84
	3.9.2	Use of the Incremental Cost Method	84
3.10	The Separable Costs-Remaining Benefits Method of Cost Allocation in Federal Multi-purpose Projects		85
3.11	Limits on the Ascertainment of Costs		87
3.12	Definitions of Cost		89

4 The Cost Approach to Pricing: The Tenneco Pattern — 93

4.1	Tenneco Pattern		93
4.2	The Issues		94
4.3	The Regulatory Scheme in Brief		95
4.4	Assignment of Fixed and Variable Costs		95
	4.4.1	The Seaboard Formula	96
	4.4.2	The United Formula	100
	4.4.3	The Modified Fixed–Variable (MFV) Formula	100
	4.4.4	The Straight Fixed–Variable (SFV) Formula	103
	4.4.5	Comparison of the Formulae	104
4.5	The Demand Charge		105
4.6	Zoning		106
	4.6.1	A "Postage-Stamp" Approach	107
	4.6.2	The Zoning Alternatives	107
	4.6.3	Which Alternative Is the Best?	108
	4.6.4	The Legal Standards	108
	4.6.5	The Commission's Appraisal Yardsticks	108
	4.6.6	Commission Precedents	109
	4.6.7	The Commission's Findings and Orders	109
4.7	A Resume		110
4.8	The Minimum Bill		111
4.9	Tenneco Allocations for Rate Design		112
	4.9.1	Step 1: The Company-Wide Cost of Service	112
	4.9.2	Step 2: Functionalization of the Cost of Service	113
	4.9.3	Step 3: Classification of Functional Costs as Fixed or Variable	116
	4.9.4	Step 4: Classification of Costs as Demand or Commodity	120
	4.9.5	Step 5: Classification of Transmission Sector Costs	122
	4.9.6	Step 6: Distance-Related Costs	122
	4.9.7	Step 7: The New York Zone	125
	4.9.8	Step 8: Per-Unit Rate Elements	125

	4.9.9	Step 9: Total System Costs Revisited	128
	4.9.10	Closing Reminders	130

5 The Value Approach to Pricing: Demand Influence — 131

5.1	Preface	131
5.2	Value of Service Defined	131
5.3	Cost vs. Value in Juxtaposition	132
5.4	The "Upper and Lower Limit of Rates" Concept	133
5.5	Economic Demand	136
5.6	Direct and Derived Demand	136
5.7	Option Demand	136
5.8	The Price Elasticity of Demand	137
5.9	The Crucial Importance of Price Elasticity	139
	5.9.1 Electric—Washington Public Power Supply System (WPPSS)	140
	5.9.2 Gas—Producer-Pipeline Take-or-Pay Contracts	142
5.10	The Revenue Effects of Elasticity	143
5.11	Immediate, Short-Run and Long-Run Price Elasticities of Demand	146
5.12	Repression and Stimulation	147
5.13	The Principle of Diminishing Utility	148
5.14	Economics of Pricing on a Value of Service Basis	149
5.15	Monopoly Pricing	149
5.16	The Theory of Class Price	151
	5.16.1 Price Differentiation	152
	5.16.2 Reasonable Price Differences	152
	5.16.3 Determination of Rate Classifications Under Value and Combined Cost-Value Approaches	155
	5.16.4 Combined Value and Cost Bases	156
5.17	Bases of Rate Classes	157
5.18	The Cost and Value Approaches Compared	162
5.19	Unreasonable Discrimination	164
	5.19.1 The FERC Lists	165
	5.19.2 Statutory Prohibitions	165
5.20	Predatory Pricing	168
5.21	Is There a Problem?	169
5.22	Concluding Observations on Cost vs. Value	170
5.23	Marketing and Advertising	173
	5.23.1 Civic Participation	173
	5.23.2 Marketing	173
	5.23.3 Giveaways	174
	5.23.4 Advertising	175

6 The Value Approach to Pricing: Planning for Demand — 177

6.1	Units of Measurement	177
6.2	Procedure	178

	6.3		Planning: Short-Run Demand Forecasts	178
		6.3.1	Natural Gas	179
		6.3.2	Electric	179
		6.3.3	Common Issues	179
	6.4		Planning: Long-Range Demand Forecasts	180
		6.4.1	The Purpose of the Forecast	182
		6.4.2	The Strategic Plan	182
		6.4.3	The Supply Forecast	183
		6.4.4	Matching Supply and Demand	183
		6.4.5	The Input Assumptions	184
		6.4.6	Other Market Share Considerations	186
		6.4.7	Availability and Reliability	186
		6.4.8	Finally, the Factor of Governmental Policy	187
	6.5		Final Results	187
		6.5.1	The Single Forecast vs. a Range	188
		6.5.2	The Components of the Forecast	189
		6.5.3	Testing the Forecast	189
		6.5.4	Reliance on Forecasts	191
	6.6		Public Policy Forecasts	192
		6.6.1	Errors in Public Policy	192
		6.6.2	Omissions in Public Policy	193
	6.7		Concluding Comments	193
		6.7.1	Conflicting Forecasts	194
		6.7.2	Guidelines	194
		6.7.3	A Personal Note	195
		6.7.4	Alternative Forecasts	195
		6.7.5	Resolving Forecasting Conflicts	196
7	**The Public Policy/Social Engineering Approach to Pricing**			**197**
	7.1		California's Lifeline/Baseline Rate	197
		7.1.1	The California Lifeline Philosophy	198
		7.1.2	The Lifeline/Baseline Rate Schedule	198
		7.1.3	Pricing Procedure	200
	7.2		Cost Components of Rates	202
	7.3		Timed Pricing	203
		7.3.1	Prior to 2000	203
		7.3.2	Real-Time Pricing (RTP)	204
		7.3.3	Now	204
	7.4		The Color GREEN	205
		7.4.1	Comparisons	206
		7.4.2	Electric Utilities: Clean-Energy Programs	207
		7.4.3	From the Printed Media	207
	7.5		Venture into Marginal Cost Regulation	212
		7.5.1	Marginal Cost Defined	213
		7.5.2	The Steppingstone	213

		7.5.3	The Proxy, a Combustion Turbine	214
		7.5.4	Levelization Out, RECC In	214
		7.5.5	EPMC Adopted, EDP Dropped	214
		7.5.6	Energy Reliability Index (ERI) Established	215
		7.5.7	Excess Generating Capacity and the ERI	215
		7.5.8	The Resource Plan and the ERI	216
		7.5.9	Long-Run vs. Short-Run and the ERI	216
		7.5.10	The Capacity Response Ratio (CRR)	216
		7.5.11	VOS In, ERI Out	216
		7.5.12	The Abrupt Halt	216
	7.6	Wind Rates on an Integrated Electric System	217
		7.6.1	A Primer on Wind and the Electric Grid	217
		7.6.2	Amount of Wind Generation	219
		7.6.3	Wind and Planning	219
		7.6.4	Planning: Wind Generators	219
		7.6.5	Planning: Persistence Models	220
		7.6.6	The Generation Reserves	221
		7.6.7	Costs	222
		7.6.8	Balancing Measures	223
		7.6.9	Points of Contention	224
		7.6.10	Services Offered	224
		7.6.11	Rate Design	224
		7.6.12	Physical Specifications	227
		7.6.13	What's Left Out	227
8	**Introduction to Rates**			229
	8.1	The Unregulated Marketplace		229
	8.2	The Marketplace Under Regulation		230
	8.3	The Customer Viewpoint		230
	8.4	The Management Viewpoint		231
	8.5	The Public Viewpoint		232
		8.5.1	The California PUC	233
		8.5.2	The Federal Energy Regulatory Commission	234
	8.6	Related Objectives		236
	8.7	Some Expert Opinions		236
	8.8	Definitions		237
9	**Elements of Rate Design**			241
	9.1	Frequent Features		241
		9.1.1	Minimums	241
		9.1.2	Ratchets	243
		9.1.3	Adjustment Clauses	244
		9.1.4	Penalties and Discounts	245
		9.1.5	"Frozen" Rates	246
		9.1.6	Caps and Floors	246
	9.2	The "Blocking" Principle		247
	9.3	"Postage Stamp" vs. Zone Rates		250

9.4		All-Purpose vs. Special-Purpose Rates: Unbundling	252
9.5		Seasonal vs. Year-Round Rates	254
9.6		Rolled-in vs. Incremental Pricing/Old Customer vs. New Customer Rates	254
9.7		Rate-Level Changes Across-the-Board	257
9.8		The "Fine-Print" Provisions	259
9.9		Nota Bene	260

10 Traditional Types of Rate Forms ... 261

10.1		Introduction	261
10.2		Rate Elements Defined Again	262
10.3		Single-Part Rate Forms	262
	10.3.1	Flat Rates	262
	10.3.2	Metered Commodity Rates (Also Called Straight-Line Commodity Rates)	264
	10.3.3	Metered Demand Rates	265
	10.3.4	Single-Part Rate Forms and Rate Theory	266
10.4		Two-Part Rate Forms	272
	10.4.1	The Hopkinson Rate	272
	10.4.2	The Wright Rate	279
	10.4.3	Comparison of Hopkinson and Wright Rate Forms	281
	10.4.4	Two-Part Rate Forms and Rate Theory	282
10.5		Three-Part Rate Forms	287
	10.5.1	The Doherty Three-Part Rate	287
	10.5.2	The Lester Special-Investment Three-Part Rate	288
	10.5.3	The Zanoff Three-Part Gas Pipeline Rate	289
10.6		Modifications of Rate Forms and Special Applications	290
	10.6.1	Promotional, Incentive-Type Rates	290
	10.6.2	The Objective Rate	290
	10.6.3	Additions to Standard Rate Forms	291
10.7		Miscellany	292
	10.7.1	A 1946–1950 Case History with Overtones for Today	292
	10.7.2	Rate Forms and Rate Comparisons	294
	10.7.3	A 1971 Gas Distributor and Pipeline Tariff	295
	10.7.4	Some Concluding Observations	299

11 Tools of the Trade ... 301

11.1		Introduction	301
11.2		Knowing the Market: Load Curves	302
	11.2.1	Load/Demand Curve	302
	11.2.2	Season Usage Patterns	303
	11.2.3	Duration Curve	305
	11.2.4	Planning	306
11.3		Gauging the Market: Analysis Factors	308
	11.3.1	Diversity and Diversity Factor	309
	11.3.2	Load Factor	315

11.4		Capacity Factor	321
11.5		Utilization Factor	322
11.6		Demand Factor	322
11.7		Power Factor	323
11.8		A Note to the Rate maker	324
12	**Matters of Judgment**	**325**
12.1		Part 1: Dubious Accounting	326
12.2		Earlier Accounting Results	326
12.3		Current Accounting Results	327
	12.3.1	Overstatements	328
	12.3.2	Understatements	328
	12.3.3	Special Issues	329
	12.3.4	Potpourri	330
	12.3.5	Three Tidbits over 10 Years	331
	12.3.6	Debt Concealment	332
	12.3.7	At the Borderline	332
12.4		An Appraisal	333
12.5		Difference: Utility and General Corporate Accounting	333
	12.5.1	Lack of Uniformity	334
	12.5.2	The Question of Prudence	336
	12.5.3	AFUDC	337
	12.5.4	Deferred Income Taxes	338
12.6		Part 2: The California Energy Crisis	339
12.7		1996: Assembly Bill 1890	340
12.8		Optimism Reigns: No Doubts (1996)	341
12.9		The Lull Before the Storm (1997–1999)	342
	12.9.1	FERC's Approval	343
	12.9.2	Sales of California Generation Capacity	343
	12.9.3	The California PX	344
	12.9.4	Acquisitions of Generating Capacity Beyond California	345
	12.9.5	Other Notes of the Majors	347
	12.9.6	Rate Reduction Bonds	348
12.10		The Storm Hits: The Energy Crisis (2000–2001)	348
	12.10.1	PG&E Corporation and Edison International	349
	12.10.2	Other Activities of PG&E Corporation and Edison International	352
	12.10.3	The Special Case of Sempra Energy, Parent of San Diego Gas and Electric Company	354
12.11		Chronology: The Crisis and Its Aftermath (to Early 2002)	356
	12.11.1	November 1999	357
	12.11.2	August 2000	357
	12.11.3	January 2001	361
	12.11.4	February 2002	382

12.12	Comments		389
	12.12.1	The Fatal Contradiction	389
	12.12.2	Regulatory and Economic Failures	390
	12.12.3	The Divestiture of Generating Capacity by California Utilities	391
	12.12.4	The Issue of Long-Term Contracts	392
	12.12.5	The Uniform-Price Auction	393
	12.12.6	The Neglect of Costs	393
12.13	From Storm to Turmoil		394
12.14	P.S. – 2009		394
	12.14.1	Pacific Gas and Electric Company	394
	12.14.2	Edison International	395
	12.14.3	Sempra Energy	396
	12.14.4	Statutory Changes	396
	12.14.5	CPUC Actions	396
12.15	Part 3: The 2008–2009 Recession		397
12.16	Toxic Assets in Action: The Beginning		398
	12.16.1	The Securitization Process in Detail	398
	12.16.2	The CDS	399
	12.16.3	The CMBS	399
	12.16.4	A Bond Called Jupiter	400
12.17	Disregarded History		400
12.18	Earlier Bailouts		400
12.19	The Financial Crisis		400
12.20	The Bailouts		401
12.21	A Conducive Environment		402
12.22	Causes		403
12.23	The Dow from September 10 to October 10, 2008		404
12.24	The Paths of the Giants		404
12.25	Regulation		404
12.26	2008 Statistics		405
12.27	Epilogue		406
12.28	Acronyms and Definitions		406

Index 407

List of Figures

2.1	Average fixed costs under decreasing cost conditions (static plant)	32
2.2	Average total costs under decreasing cost conditions (static plant)	33
2.3	Base system dependable capacity vs. output (sales)	34
2.4	Base system fixed costs per kilowatt-hour	37
5.1	Residential price vs. consumption	148
7.1	"Make the choice for renewable power today"	206
7.2	BPA's Wind Generation Capacity	218
7.3	BPA Wind Rates	225
11.1	Sample Daily Load Curves	303
11.2	PG&E's summer and winter peakday loads, 1990* (in megawatts)	304
11.3	PG&E's load duration curve, 1990 net system load* (in megawatts)	305
11.4	Northwest Natural Gas Company rate schedule 24 - residential - all gas seasonal usage pattern - 1993	308
11.5	Northwest Natural Gas Company rate schedule 23 - interruptible seasonal usage pattern - 1993	309
11.6	Diversity of energy demand in PG&E's electric power system, 1990* (in megawatts)	310
11.7	Coincident (Peak) demand (in thousands of megawatts)	311
11.8	Daily ridership of the One-bus One-route Transit Line, Lake Woebegon, MN. - permanent schedule	318
11.9	Daily ridership of the One-bus One-route Transit Line, Lake Woebegon, MN. - condensed schedule	319

List of Tables

1.1	Incremental and average cost	4
1.2	Relative utilization of oven	8
1.3	Investment costs	9
1.4	Allocation of indirect costs	10
1.5	Regular and club prices compared (small package)	12
1.6	Regular and club price (large package)	12
1.7	Unit cost at varying outputs	14
2.1	Illustration of the operation of fixed and variable costs (Static Plant)	31
2.2	Base system plants	34
2.3	Base three-plant generating system: fixed costs by plant	35
2.4	Base three-plant generating system: fixed costs in total and per kWh	36
2.5	Millions of dollars of annual fixed costs per one million kWh of annual output (in constant dollars)	38
2.6	Comparative fixed costs at selected capacity factors: decreasing fixed costs	39
2.7	Decreasing fixed-cost scenario	39
2.8	Comparative fixed costs at selected capacity factors: constant fixed costs	40
2.9	Constant fixed-cost scenario	41
2.10	Comparative fixed costs at selected capacity factors: increasing fixed costs	42
2.11	Increasing fixed-cost scenario	43
2.12	The small base-load plant (increasing fixed costs)	44
2.13	Comparison of costs of large and small plant systems (Tables 2.11 and 2.12)	45
2.14	Cost differences between large and small plants	46
2.15	Annual sales capability with and without interruptible	48
2.16	Comparative results of firm and split outputs	48
2.17	Output and costs with peaking plant	49
2.18	Fixed cost revenue requirement for firm service with peaking	49

2.19	Range of competitive costs	51
2.20	Utility-owned new plant	52
2.21	Purchase of IPP power	52
2.22	Comparative costs of generation alternatives	52
2.23	Results of bypass opportunities	54
2.24	A discounted price to industrial customer(s) to prevent bypass	56
2.25	Decline in fixed costs with improvement in utilization	58
2.26	Decline in costs with decline in investment	58
2.27	Increase in costs with increase in investment	59
2.28	Typical central station costs	62
2.29	Sensitivity of costs of combined-cycle generating plant to fluctuations in the price of gas	63
3.1	Examples of peak-responsibility methods of joint cost allocations	75
3.2	Illustrative analysis of allocation of project costs by separable costs-remaining benefits method	86
3.3	Comparison of costs of multiple purpose and single purpose projects	87
4.1	Comparison of fixed-variable allocation formulae	105
4.2	STEP 1 The company-wide cost of service (take-off point for rate design)	112
4.3	Recapitulation of expenses	113
4.4	STEP 2 Functionalization of the cost of service	115
4.5	Relative size of functionalized physical components	115
4.6	STEP 3 Classification of functional costs as fixed or variable	116
4.7	Relative size of fixed and variable expenses	116
4.8	Unadjusted sales and storage rates	117
4.9	Adjusted comparative rates – straight fixed variable	117
4.10	Adjusted comparative rates – seaboard	118
4.11	Adjusted comparative rates – united	118
4.12	Adjusted comparative rates – modified-fixed variable	119
4.13	Comparative demand and commodity components of allocation methods	119
4.14	STEP 4 Classification of fixed and variable costs as demand or commodity with transfers for market area rate design -- Transmission sector --	121
4.15	STEP 5 Classification of transmission sector costs as distance sensitive and non-distance sensitive (Administrative and General)	122
4.16	STEP 7 Allocation of costs to sales zones -- Allocation of transmission sector costs to New York zone --	126
4.17	STEP 8 Assignment of costs to per-unit rate elements -- New York zone transmission sector costs --	127

List of Tables

4.18	STEP 9 The system as a whole (Base, Net system cost of service) ($1,589,967,000) = $1,000	129
4.19	Confirmation of fixed costs to be borne by demand charges	130
5.1	Price increases with elastic and inelastic demands	144
5.2	Price deceases with elastic and inelastic demands	145
5.3	Monopoly pricing	150
7.1	Simplified illustration of calculation of baseline and nonbaseline rates for season	201
7.2	Example of lifeline/baseline rate	202
7.3	BPA's forecast of reserve requirements	222
7.4	Illustration of balancing transaction	223
9.1	Illustration of fish-hook blocking	249
9.2	Domestic rates of pacific gas and electric company, vintage 1950	252
9.3	Base blocked rate-light consumption	257
9.4	Base rate increased by alternative methods–light consumption	257
9.5	Industrial rate increased by alternative methods–high consumption	258
9.6	Relationship of class rates before and after rate increase	258
10.1	Costs by rate elements	268
10.2	Energy consumption by rate blocks	269
10.3	Cost/Price assignment to rate blocks	269
10.4	Annual contributions to demand costs by rate blocks (in $)	269
10.5	Blocked and unblocked customer bills	269
10.6	Revenues from blocked and unblocked customer bills	270
10.7	The customer charge–monthly bills with unblocked rates	271
10.8	The customer charge–monthly bills with blocked and unblocked rates	271
10.9	Base Hopkinson blocked rate–demand and commodity components in total and percent	274
10.10	Base Hopkinson unblocked rate–demand and commodity components in total and percent (equivalent at 50% Load factor to blocked rate)	275
10.11	Hopkinson rate–doubled volumes	275
10.12	Base Hopkinson blocked rate–the impact of size components in total and percent	275
10.13	Base Hopkinson unblocked rate–the impact of size components in total and percent	276
10.14	The Hopkinson rate–increased demand component	277
10.15	The Hopkinson rate–restated volumes	277
10.16	The Hopkinson rate–the impact of size–per kWh charges in total and percent with increased demand costs	277
10.17	The Hopkinson rate–decreased demand component	278

10.18	The Hopkinson rate–the impact of size: per kWh charges in total and percent with decreased demand charges	278
10.19	Standby wright rate	281
10.20	Wright and Hopkinson rates–restated volumes	282
10.21	Wright and Hopkinson rates–comparative charges	282
10.22	Base Hopkinson Rate with Tilt toward Demand	285
10.23	The Zanoff rate	289
10.24	Characteristics of tariff of Northwest Natural Gas Company, January 1971	296
10.25	Pipeline prices to distributors	299
11.1	Timing of peak loads	310
11.2	Monthly home consumptions of electricity and natural gas	316
12.1	Producer accounting: alternative approaches to dry hole costs	336
12.2	Rate reduction bonds of utility companies	348

Chapter 1
Introduction

Abstract This chapter adopts the mundane activities of a lowly baker to portray one of the most fundamental functions of the economy—the determination of cost and price. The baker computes his costs as the sum of the prices he pays for his ingredients and other inputs. He sets his prices to recover these costs plus a profit. This is simple in broad concept, but becomes elusive in the real world. The baker produces a variety of products—doughnuts, pies, and cakes, as well as bread—to each of which he must assign a portion of his costs, a process called cost allocation. This process in most cases is involved and subjective. And, finally, the baker may be faced with competition. He must then adjust his several prices to meet the prices of his competitors, either directly or by distinguishing his product from theirs (product differentiation).

1.1 Distinguishing Between Cost and Price

The whole of this chapter is a struggle to define and understand two terms, "cost" and "price." We ask, what is cost? What is price? And, what is the economic relationship of cost to price?

This struggle of definition and understanding is akin to the efforts of philosophers to define "mind" and "matter," and the interrelation of the two, in that branch of philosophy known as epistemology. The kinship gives little comfort. Philosophers, from Socrates to the present, have for more than 2000 years attempted to arrive at unequivocal definitions, and straightforward relationships, without final success. Many have argued exhaustively, and some convincingly, but a final conclusion as to what is mind and what is matter, and as to the link between them, remains to be reached. Perhaps our dilemma can be summed up in Pilate's question, "what is truth?"[1]

This chapter has no hope, and makes no pretense, of contributing to economics any new or definitive explanations of cost and price, and of how the two mesh. It

---

[1] Saint John's Gospel, Chapter 18, 37–38.

simply strives, like the epistemologist to philosophy, to lead to a better comprehension of two central terms which are elusive to grasp in their complexities of different meanings and interpretations.

Whether the effort will contribute to economics in general is unlikely. That is not its aim. Its purpose is to help put into a broader perspective the succeeding chapters, which later sketch out in more pragmatic terms the translation of cost to price as developed under governmental price regulations and anti-trust enforcement.

1.2 Cost and Price in Our Daily Vocabulary

In and of themselves, cost and price are not obscure terms. They are used daily by laymen, accountants, and professional economists alike with apparently clear-cut meanings.[2] We seek a loaf of bread from the bakery. The price of the loaf is $2.00. We buy the loaf, paying the $2.00 price. Having bought the loaf, its cost to us is $2.00. To us, as buyer, cost and price are identical.

But there is a distinction. The terms vary in their meaning depending upon whether one speaks from the buyer's viewpoint or the seller's.

The buyer: When the buyer buys an item, the *price* he pays for that item is its *cost* to him. In this context, price and cost are interchangeable.

The Seller: To the seller, *price* is the amount at which he is willing to dispose of an item and which buyers are willing to pay.[3] Such price may be higher than, or equal to, or below, the cost to him of producing (or offering) that item. The seller's price is not interchangeable with the seller's cost.

But the seller is also a buyer. He must purchase some of the ingredients or services which he needs to produce and/or market the item he intends to sell. So the seller-cum-buyer's cost includes a variety of purchases for which his cost is the price he has paid to his suppliers. The seller's cost also includes, however, a variety of expenditures which he has incurred so as to add value to the item he sells over

---

[2]*Webster* does little to clarify the distinction between the two terms. The primary definition of cost makes that term equivalent to price: "1. (a) the amount of money or the like asked or paid for a thing; price." The secondary definition is completely different "1. (b) the amount spent in producing or manufacturing a commodity." Broader definitions are "2. (a) the amount of money, time, effort, etc. required to achieve an end; 2. (b) loss, sacrifice, detriment."

The primary definition of price also makes that term equivalent to cost: "1. the amount of money, etc. asked or given for something; charge." Again, the secondary definition is different: "2. value; worth," synonyms are charge, cost, expense, expenditure, outlay, value, and worth.

At the level of "our daily vocabulary," economics texts also give little clarification. The texts tend to give too much rather than too little. Paul A. Samuelson's *Economics*, perhaps the most widely read of all texts, lists in its index under COST (S): accounting; average (fixed, long-run, marginal, minimum, short-run, variable); constant; decreasing; increasing; least; and total, together with other subdivisions. His index under PRICE is even longer.

[3]The seller may attach a price to an item which is too high, in which event the item will not sell. The item must be priced at an amount which buyers are willing to pay. This is why we define price in a twofold sense: the amount offered by the seller and accepted by the buyer.

and above the sum of the values of his purchases from others. The seller's cost of an item is the aggregate or sum of the seller's individual elements of cost.[4]

1.3 The Credibility of Cost

> Alice, returning to Wonderland, asks the Queen of Hearts, "What is Cost?"
> "Cost," the Queen replies, "is what I say it is."
> (With apologies to Lewis Carroll)

The concept of cost is disarmingly simple. We tend to take for granted that cost is easily and accurately computed. And so it is, in many cases. For a young couple, the cost of rent is definite. So is the cost of groceries actually bought, although the buyer has many choices as to which products to buy. Beyond such simple illustrations, cost becomes more and more elusive. Let us follow our young couple a step or two further.

They are fortunate enough to be blessed with a beautiful baby girl. What is the cost to them of this wonderful child? The first thought that may occur to them is of a monetary benefit, not a cost. They will be able to take an exemption for the baby on their federal income tax. Of course, the actual benefit of the exemption in dollars will depend on their income in the year under consideration. What figure should they use as an offset against the cost of their baby girl: the benefit in the year of her birth, the benefit in some later year, or the benefit over an average of years?

Now let us turn to rent. Present accommodations may suffice to house the new arrival, so the rent remains the same as before. But should the child be given a rent-free ride, or should one-third of the rent be considered a part of the child's cost? Or, it may turn out that the accommodations which earlier were quite sufficient for the young couple alone are no longer large enough for a family of three.

So the couple seeks different quarters, and must pay an additional $100.00 per month in rent for their new housing. Here they are confronted with a real choice in their accounting. They may take an *incremental* cost approach, and assign to the child only the added cost of rent, $100.00; or they may take an *average* cost approach, and assign to the child one-third of the total new rent. The choice is simple, but the results can be radically different. Assume two cases: in case 1, the present rent is $100.00 per month; in case 2, $500.00 per month. The new rent is $100.00 more in both cases (Table 1.1). In practice, these choices are unimportant for the young couple, for no one really computes the cost of a baby.

But, as we shall see, such seemingly simple choices are of vast importance to businesses, such as the utilities, whose prices are regulated so as to be oriented to cost.

---

[4]This definition does not include societal or externality costs, which represent detriments to the economy as a whole resulting from the manufacturing or marketing of the item, but which are not compensated for by the seller either as a payment or a tax. A current controversy in utility regulation is whether the utility and/or its customers should be required to compensate society for such costs through its rates.

Table 1.1 Incremental and average cost

Present rent	$100.00	$500.00
Added rent	$100.00	$100.00
New rent	$200.00	$600.00
Incremental costing	$100.00	$100.00
Average costing	$67.00	$200.00

In case 1, average cost is about 2/3 of incremental cost. In case 2, it is double.

1.4 Total Cost of the Operation as a Whole

Now let us return to the bakery for a somewhat more realistic example. For some of his costs, the baker's accounting is easy. He adds up what he pays for ingredients—flour, sugar, milk, yeast, shortening—the wages of his employees, heat, light, telephone bills, building maintenance, etc. to determine his operating costs.[5] These costs represent cash outlays for the baker. He must pay for them in cash. If he rents the space he uses, rent is added to these costs. Rent must also be paid in cash. But if he owns the building, what is the cost of the building? He may assign an estimated rental as this cost, an uncertain figure, or he may calculate the cost of ownership, which also involves uncertainty. Each of these would require a combination of cash and non-cash payments.

If the baker's decision is to assign an estimated rental as his cost, he must divide the total estimated rent between property taxes (which as owner he must pay in any event as a cash payment) and the balance of the rent estimate (which is a non-cash cost since there is no landlord to whom it must be paid).

It may be helpful to emphasize the difference between costs which must be paid in cash and those which, while equally real, do not require a cash outlay. The former, cash costs, may be regarded as "hard" costs, in the sense that they are precise and must be covered on a dollar-for-dollar basis by cash payments. The latter may be seen as "soft" costs, since a cash payment is not required; the dollar amounts of soft costs are dependant upon subjective judgments; they may be deferred or otherwise adjusted from year to year; they are *not* intangible, but they are variable within broad limits.

Stating this concept differently, soft costs are soft because they are flexible; hard costs are hard because they are not.

We return to the baker, who does not rent his land and building; he is the owner. Therefore, he calculates the cost of ownership.

---

[5] An apology to Thomas Bowdler, pioneer in sanitizing our language, and to Random House's new *Webster's College Dictionary*. When the writer drafted his first pencil version of the adventures in cost-land of our baker, he wondered if the baker should be a he or she, and the bakery his or hers. Revealing a cowardly streak, that first draft was neutral on the matter. It was him or her making decisions, etc. Even for a coward, a few paragraphs proved gender-neutralism to be too much of a good thing. Therefore, this chapter returns to the old *Webster* on the subject of gender. "His" bakery refers to ownership by "Mr." Baker, "Mrs." Baker, or "Ms." Baker, without differentiation to whether his or her birth certificate notes "M" or "F" under "sex."

1.4 Total Cost of the Operation as a Whole

The baker's records show his investment in the land and the building: this is a definite figure. His records show the amount of his mortgage, the rate of interest he pays on the mortgage, and his total annual interest payments: these also are definite figures.

The baker knows he is entitled to consider depreciation on the building and its equipment as a part of his investment costs, but at what rate? If he is entitled to a rapid rate of depreciation, his yearly depreciation cost is higher, but he recovers his investment in a short span of years; if he is entitled only to a slow rate of depreciation, his yearly cost is lower, but it will take longer for him to recoup his invested dollars. What rate is appropriate? The rate and the total amount of annual depreciation expense are uncertain. Perhaps the Internal Revenue Service has a standard depreciation rate for bakeries which he can use and avoid an IRS tax controversy, but at the risk that a standard rate is not appropriate for his particular plant. Or he may make his own estimate of a proper rate. If he does, should he consider the full life expectancy of a plant such as his, or should he assume that technology changes in bakery plants might render his plant (building, ovens and other baking equipment, or both) obsolete, short of the life expectancy of the structure and equipment themselves? Whatever he chooses, his choice is judgmental to a degree. The depreciation expense in his aggregation of cost is a figure which cannot claim absolute certainty. And, whatever the figure may be, it is a soft, non-cash item of expense, less precise than a payment in cash.

He also knows that he is entitled to a return on the undepreciated portion of his investment, which is not covered by the mortgage—his equity. His own funds are tied up. He is entitled to earn on these funds, just as much as if he had invested them in other ways. But at what rate? Should he earn only at a rate comparable to a bank savings account, where the savings are guaranteed? Obviously no, for his investment in the bakery is not guaranteed. He is subject not only to the vagaries of a changing market for bakery goods, but also to the onslaughts of competitors. He has made a risky investment, and is entitled to a rate of return commensurate with that risk. The principle is clear, but the rate itself is clouded. Whatever rate he chooses to use as a basis for his costs, it is also a figure which cannot claim absolute certainty. The baker's return on equity is the product of the rate of return times his equity. Like depreciation, it is a soft, non-cash item.[6] Not so are the income taxes which the baker must pay on his equity return. This is as hard a cost as the baker is likely to encounter—one that must be paid in cash. (We beg the question as to whether the income taxes due actually mesh with the baker's chosen rate of return.

---

[6] Return on equity often is referred to rather loosely as "profit." This is unfortunate for it leads to the erroneous conclusion that cost does not include a return on invested capital, as if capital were free: thus, we hear the phrase, "cost plus profit." There is a cost of capital: if one doubts this, try to acquire an interest free loan. The uncertainty lies in trying to pin down just what that cost is for an enterprise having its own unique circumstances and degree of risk. Cost-based utility regulation attempts to determine a rate or return which is appropriate to the circumstances and risk of the given utility, which rate is then applied to the depreciated equity investment.

They may or may not. Here, to avoid undue complexity and incursions into tax law, we merely accept income taxes on actual profit as a given.) The baker's mortgage interest also is a hard cost, to be paid in cash.

Above we have identified in terms of our baker two of the uncertainties which exist in the determination of the costs of a regulated utility: the rate of depreciation on the physical plant and the rate of return on the owner's equity.

We mention one further uncertainty, unique to our baker illustration. The baker acts not as employee, but as an owner, an entrepreneur. What is the amount to which the baker is entitled for his management of the enterprise? He forgoes the wages he could earn by working for another. Instead, he devotes time, perhaps his entire time, to the job of running the bakery. This is a job requiring skill and judgment—above the skills and judgment required of his employees. Whatever the amount may be, it too is a speculative figure and it too is a soft cost. (The baker actually may earn more or less than the total of his cash and non-cash costs, inclusive of entrepreneurial wages, but he cannot gauge whether or not he has done so without knowledge of what this total is.)

To this point, we have observed the steps the baker might take to determine the total cost of running his bakery. If a bakery were a regulated electric or natural gas utility company, the baker would be entitled to receive in revenue only an amount which did not exceed such total cost. In fact the first step in utility regulation is to determine the utility's total cost of operations, which total cost establishes a ceiling on the total revenues the utility is entitled to receive. But, as we have just observed, cost, even in an overall context and even with reference to a basic operation such as a bakery, is elusive and indefinite in many respects.

The second step in utility regulation is to determine the prices (rates) which the utility may charge for the individual products (classes of service) which it offers—residential, commercial, etc.—within the revenue ceiling established by the total cost finding. These prices must be "non-discriminatory." They must be cost-based.

In most respects, the costs of a utility are joint or common in an economic sense, in that very few of the costs of individual components of a utility system can be traced directly to any particular service and that service only; most of the costs benefit more than one class of service and thus are joint or common with other classes. For example, the costs of an electric generating plant are joint since the power from that plant will flow to residences, businesses, and industries, not just a single class. This means that most costs must be apportioned (or allocated) to the specific services which give rise to their incurrence. The apportionment (or allocation) is based upon some scheme which seems rational and appropriate at the time under the circumstances then existing. In almost every instance, an equally rational and appropriate scheme could be chosen in the alternative. The derived cost of the joint service will vary, sometimes radically, depending upon the allocation method which is used. Yet, price discrimination often is defined as "a difference in price not based upon a difference in cost."

We now turn to the determination of the costs of individual services, which costs for a regulated utility would set the prices which can be charged for each service and establish whether these prices are discriminatory or not. We continue to turn to our baker to illustrate the process.

1.5 Joint-Product Costs

The baker does not offer only identical loaves of bread. He also sells doughnuts, Danish rolls, pies and cakes, and similar delicacies. He varies his base loaf with one which is smaller to suit the smaller family and one which is larger to court the larger family. The baker may be able to approximate with a high degree of reliability his *direct* costs for flour, eggs, sugar, milk, and other ingredients; for a standard size loaf of bread and a smaller or larger loaf; for bread and for each of his other products. (Here we have introduced an important term: direct costs. These are the costs which can be linked by association with a given product, and no other.) It takes "x" pounds of flour to knead up a day's production of bread, a bit less than the average per loaf for the smaller loaves, a bit more than the average for the larger loaves, "y" pounds to make a dozen doughnuts, etc. Taking all ingredients into account, the costs of the components add up to the sum of the direct costs of the individual several products.

A good cook often offers her recipes in general terms: we add a pinch of salt here, a splash of dressing there . . . . These recipes generally prove to be amazingly right. We grant the same intuitive accuracy to our baker. We do not imply that meticulous accuracy in the sense of repeated, refined measurements is required of him. We are willing to accept his judgment as to the relative amounts of ingredients which should enter into his calculations of the direct costs of each of his products.[7]

We cannot be quite as lenient concerning his *indirect* costs, i.e., those costs which are *joint* or common to all of his products, such as lighting of the bakery, heat for the ovens (which are likely to bake several products at the same time), wages of bakers and sales personnel, etc., as well as other *overhead* costs such as the cost of plant (depreciation, interest on borrowed funds, and return on the equity investment together with associated income taxes), property taxes, and our baker-entrepreneur's own salary. (Here we again introduce important terms: *indirect* costs, namely those costs arising from the *joint* or *common* production of several products, often referred to interchangeably in a non-technical sense as indirect, joint, common, or *overhead* costs. These are costs which cannot be assigned to a single product because they are incurred in the production of multiple products.)[8]

Let us try to parallel our baker's reasoning when confronted with the issue of this division of indirect/joint/common/overhead costs among joint products—the issue of cost allocation. How should these costs be divided among the products?

The baker's first reaction is, "No problem. I will make the allocation on the basis of the revenues I receive from each of my products. Sixty percent of my receipts are from bread, 7% from doughnuts, and so on." However, if there is a price regulator looking over his shoulder, he will be told, "No, no, that won't do. You cannot use your present prices as the foundation for the computation of the costs upon which

---

[7]In the real world of utility regulation, broad estimates of direct costs normally would not be acceptable. "Refined measurement" would be the rule not the exception.

[8]There are differences between these terms when used on a more stringent analytical basis, as is done in later chapters.

your future prices will be based. This would be circular reasoning. Your method would use a price basis (per unit prices times units sold equals revenue) to determine prices. To the contrary, you are expected to delineate costs independently of prices."

Well, then, what? Our baker has an illuminating idea. My ovens are at the heart of my bakery. I will measure the hours of use of my ovens for bread, doughnuts, Danish rolls, and whatever, and assign to each product as its portion of the joint cost the ratio of hours during which that product is in the ovens to the total of the oven-hours of use for all products. Since several products may be in the ovens at the same time, it is necessary under this allocation theory to aggregate the baking hours for all products. To illustrate: Assume that the ovens are heated over a 9-hour span, from 10 p.m. to 7 a.m. (one 8-hour shift for the bakers, plus a staggered 1-hour meal break). During this period the several products are in the ovens, as follows (Table 1.2).

Table 1.2 Relative utilization of oven

	Total hours in oven	% of total
Bread	9	45
Doughnuts	4	20
Danish rolls	2	10
Pie and cakes	3	15
Other pastries	2	10
Total	20	100

Joint costs would be allocated to products in accordance with the foregoing percentages. This should be fair he concludes, since what would a bakery be without its ovens?

Don't be so self-satisfied, the regulator tells the baker. It is true that your apportionment of joint costs based upon the relative use of your ovens may make sense for your manufacturing activities, but it doesn't make sense for the other side of your operation, your sales activities. You should first segregate the joint costs of heating your ovens, mixing dough, packaging, and other manufacturing work. When you have isolated the joint manufacturing costs, you may apply your hours-of-oven-use allocation to those joint costs, but only to those costs. You must use a different standard to allocate the remainder of your joint costs, those related to actually selling your bakery goods.

By this stroke, the regulator has made the baker's joint cost allocation problem materially more complex and judgmental. The baker had proposed distributing the entirety of his joint costs among his joint products according to the single yardstick of relative oven use. Now he must not only use more than one yardstick for each product: he must divide his joint costs between yardsticks.

The regulator is not without helpful advice. Why not use some sort of space measurement as your second yardstick, he suggests.

By this time, our befuddled baker realizes that he needs an accountant, introducing a new cost which also must be allocated. The accountant he selects is, fortunately, imaginative and an expert at approximations.

1.5 Joint-Product Costs

First, the joint costs related primarily to manufacturing must be identified. To manufacturing he assigns the wages of all of the bakers and packers. He assigns a portion of the bill for natural gas on the basis of an estimate of the Btu's used in the ovens (derived as the excess of the total Btu's billed over the Btu's which might be used for space heating in a building of comparable size which has no ovens).[9]

He also assigns a portion of the investment costs and property taxes to manufacturing. As used here, investment costs include hard and soft (cash and non-cash) costs, as follows (Table 1.3). He makes this assignment on the basis of the purchase costs of the ovens, and of the dough mixing and packaging equipment, as a percentage of the total purchase costs of the building, plus additional improvements.[10]

Table 1.3 Investment costs

Hard costs	Soft costs
Interest on the mortgage	Depreciation
Income taxes on equity return	Return on equity
Property taxes	

To sales he assigns joint costs which seem reasonably related to that activity: primarily, the wages of the sales personnel and the balance of the investment costs. These sales-related investment costs include investment in the display cases and other non-segregated investment, such as that for the open space in the front of the store which is used as an entry point for customers, space used as traffic corridors within the structure, and the parking area outside.

As a yardstick for the assignment of sales costs, relative display space seems as good as any, since the several bakery products are exposed in the display cases to tempt the buying public.

If the baker is consistent in the amount of display space he allows for bread vis-à-vis rolls, vis-à-vis cakes, etc., the percentage of display space to be assigned to each product can be a fairly definite figure. If not—woe to the certitude of cost—the baker or his accountant must make an "informed" guess. The percentages of the total display space occupied by each product are used as the allocation yardstick for the joint sales costs.

To this point, three allocation yardsticks have been adopted: *purpose of the investment* for investment costs; *relative oven utilization* for joint costs which are assigned as being primarily related to the manufacturing function of the bakery; and *relative display space*, for joint costs which are primarily related to sales. Several joint costs which have defied classification as either primarily manufacturing or

---

[9] We regard this as only a basis for estimation, short of a yardstick for allocation.

[10] In effect, this is a yardstick or allocation method for the assignment of investment costs: *purpose of the investment*.

primarily sales remain unassigned. Fitting into neither category are such costs as janitorial wages (the janitor cleans both the manufacturing and sales spaces); lighting and telephone bills (which are equally necessary for both functions); general space heating (non-oven heating being required to conduct either operation); the wages due the owner-entrepreneur (who is equally concerned about the success of his manufacturing and sales functions); and taxes other than property taxes and income taxes associated with the return on equity. To what kind of a yardstick should these joint costs be subjected?

With apologies to the Federal Power Commission/Federal Energy Regulatory Commission, we unabashedly borrow from precedents set by these agencies. As they sometimes do, we solve this insolvable dilemma in a most pragmatic fashion. We will divide these costs 50/50. One-half we will assign to manufacturing, allocating to products per the relative-oven-use yardstick; the other half we will assign to sales, allocating pursuant to the relative-display-space yardstick.

At this juncture it may be helpful to summarize the chain of decisions on joint cost allocations enumerated above (Table 1.4).

Table 1.4 Allocation of indirect costs

Indirect costs	Allocation to products
Joint manufacturing costs 　Wages of bakers 　Wages of packers 　Oven heating 　Investment costs for ovens, dough mixing, and packaging equipment[a]	Relative-oven-use
Joint sales costs 　Wages of sales personnel 　Investment costs for items other than those included under manufacturing[a]	Relative-display-space
Joint–joint manufacturing/sales costs 　Janitorial wages 　Lighting bills 　Telephone bills 　General (non-oven) heating 　Taxes not included as investment costs 　Owner-entrepreneur's base wages (but not associated income taxes)	50% Relative-oven-use 50% Relative-display-space

[a] Allocated pursuant to the purpose-of-the-investment yardstick.

Recall that all direct costs are assigned to each product, in addition to its allocated portion of indirect costs. The addition of direct and indirect costs results in the total cost figure for each product.

Every reader will have a different view of the foregoing allocation approach—agreeing or disagreeing on the yardsticks and/or each cost item as the case may be. That is just the point: allocation of the cost of joint products is a subjective process. Who is to say that one method is better or worse than another? The reliability of the final cost for each product rests entirely upon a judgment as to whether the allocation steps are or are not logical. By the same token, the allocated final cost for each product can be taken, at best, as only an approximation. We cannot say "x" *is* the cost of a loaf of bread and "y" *is* the cost of a dozen doughnuts. Nonetheless, assertions that an allocated cost *is* the cost of a product will, like the leitmotif in a Wagnerian opera, reoccur over and over again.

The foregoing exercise in which our innocent baker has played so conspicuous a role is designed to illustrate that a figure entitled "cost" in a joint cost situation is a myth, even in a relatively simple business environment, if that term is supposed to mean a definite and unarguable amount in the same sense as "five" is the sum of two plus three. Cost has a multiple not a single dimension.

This undoubtedly will fall short of being a "politically correct" view to many in both academia and business. After all, how can a "cost" finding be imprecise in a world of highly sophisticated accounting? It might be argued that the baker analogy is designed for eighth-grade students, not accounting or financial professionals. To this argument, we respond "guilty," for if a proposition is logical the logic should be as apparent to the neophyte as to the Ph.D. It also might be argued that we have resorted to an oversimplified and outmoded description of cost, much as Adam Smith's descriptions of the economy in "The Wealth of Nations" might seem to be oversimplified and outmoded by today's standards, for we ignore, or at least downgrade, the refinements in costing which have been made. To this also we plead "guilty." Our explanation admittedly is elementary. But the analogies are valid.

1.6 Price Relationships: The Baker Revisited—The Quantity Discount

Price is a tricky subject once we advance beyond the point where "the seller's price is the buyer's cost." This section does not attempt to sketch out the economic theory of price. We now attempt to explore in an elementary fashion some relationships between cost and price, and the uncertainties that exist even with respect to the interpretation of that mundane term, price.

At the outset of our discussion of the baker we saw price as a simple matter, being couched solely on a "per loaf" basis. The price of a loaf was $2. Therefore, the price of two loaves would be $4, etc. But suppose the baker's price is stated differently: first loaf, $2.10; additional loaves, $1.90 each. Here we pay the same $4 for two loaves, but what is the price *per loaf* if we buy two: $2.10 for the one and $1.90 for the other? "Elementary, my dear Watson." We paid $4 in total for the two loaves, so the cost per loaf is the *average* price of the two, namely $2.

Now let us suppose a more intricate price scheme: first loaf, $2.10; second loaf, $2; third and additional loaves, $1.90. If a housewife[11] buys three loaves, her total bill is $6, or the same $2 per loaf on average. But if she buys only two loaves, her total bill is $4.10, an average of $2.05 per loaf; or if she buys six loaves, her total bill becomes $11.70, or $1.95 per loaf on average. As she increases her purchases from six loaves to a higher number, her total bill increases with each additional loaf, but her *average* cost per loaf declines, coming closer to an average of $1.90 with

---

[11] For balance, we now reverse gender and adopt the feminine for our example.

each additional loaf. Her *incremental* cost per loaf—the out-of-pocket cost of the last loaf—remains constant regardless of how many loaves she buys.

Finally, we suppose that the baker wishes to emulate the discount store club appeal. "Better-but-Cheaper Bakery Club" memberships are offered at $50 per year. All club members, having paid $50 for membership, will be able to buy at 20% below prices for non-members. In other words, the baker offers a year-round 20% discount from his regular prices if the housewife is willing to pay $50 annually for the privilege.

If the housewife makes only one purchase of six loaves during the year, the aggregate of the prices she pays—i.e., the cost to the buyer—is shown in Table 1.5.

Table 1.5 Regular and club prices compared (small package)

	Regular price		Club price	
	Per loaf ($)	Total ($)	Per loaf ($)	Total ($)
First loaf	2.10	2.10	1.68	1.68
Second loaf	2.00	2.00	1.60	1.60
3rd, 4th, 5th, and 6th	1.90	7.60	1.52	6.08
		11.70		9.36
Membership fee		–0–		50.00
Total annual bill		11.70		59.36

When a buyer purchases only six loaves per year, a 20% discount on those loaves will not induce any buyer to pay a $50 annual membership fee. The membership becomes attractive only for a volume purchaser. We examine below a situation where the housewife purchases the entire bread appetite of her hungry family from the baker, averaging six loaves per week. In this situation, the annual non-club price compares with the club membership price, as shown in Table 1.6.

Table 1.6 Regular and club price (large package)

	Regular price ($)	Club price ($)
Bread purchases (312 loaves)	608.40	486.72
Membership fee	0	50.00
Total annual bill	608.40	536.72
Savings		71.68

During the year, the housewife has bought 52 loaves at the "first loaf" price, another 52 loaves at the "second loaf" price, and 208 loaves at the lowest "additional loaves" price. She has bought either at the regular price or at the special club price. At the regular price she would have paid an average price of $1.95 per loaf; at the club price, $1.72 per loaf. The latter, however, is comprised of two elements: $1.56 average per loaf for the bread, plus 16 cents average per loaf for the club membership. The housewife accountant can choose for herself what figure or combination of figures she will choose to enter in her accounts as her club cost/price of bread. Which will it be: $1.56, $1.72, or separately $1.56 for bread and 16 cents for the membership?

These simplified examples have a purpose. All examples (both club and non-club) incorporate a declining per loaf price as added loaves are bought, and thus illustrate the quantity-discount principle of pricing which has been followed extensively in the electric and natural gas utility industries throughout most of their history. Recently, energy conservation has dampened the adoption of discounts in utility rates where such could be interpreted as promoting higher utilization of energy.

The last example, the club membership, also illustrates the same quantity-discount pricing principle, but with the introduction of an additional feature: a two-part pricing scheme, the membership fee plus a quantity-discounted price per loaf. Two-part pricing is also common in the utility industries.

We address first the quantity-discount principle in general.

The quantity discount in pricing has obvious parallel purposes: (1) to serve as an incentive to the buyer to increase her volume of purchases, and (2) to increase the sales volume of the seller.

We cannot simply assume as valid the seller's motivation to increase volume. Is it a logical reaction to economic facts of life, or merely an impulse to be bigger—growth for growth's sake, as it were?[12]

1.7 The Economics of Fixed (Overhead) Costs[13]

In our prior discussion of costs, we found that a classification of costs as either direct or common was a necessary first step in computing individual costs for each of different joint products. The second step was the apportionment or allocation of common costs to the individual products. The prices for each product would be set to cover the sum of its direct and allocated joint costs. But what should be the form and direction of their prices?

The specifics of a price—its form and direction—flow from the characteristics of its originating production operations. In this text we deal primarily with the utility industries, which are capital intensive, with prices which must bear the burden of major plant investments.

Setting prices for a capital-intensive operation requires a breakdown of costs into fixed and variable classifications. Fixed (or overhead) costs are those which do not vary with changes in output; variable costs are those which fluctuate as output rises or falls.

Fixed costs, such as investment costs and other overheads, remain constant (or relatively so) in total over a given period, but vary per unit. On the other hand, variable costs remain relatively constant per unit but vary in total.

---

[12] We beg the question as to whether the discount incentive to the buyer in our examples is sufficient to overcome the buyer's aversion to buying more than is immediately needed, a weeks supply at one time rather than from day to day. That is a question which only trial-and-error discounts of varying amounts will answer.

[13] For an earlier but brilliant discussion of this subject, see J. Maurice Clark, "Studies in the Economics of Overhead Costs," 1923.

Fixed costs per unit decline as production expands (although they remain constant in total), while variable costs increase or decrease in total as production rises or falls (while they remain constant per unit). To illustrate this, assume an enterprise having a total of fixed (overhead) costs of $1 million, with an output capability of 10 units, each unit having a variable cost of $100,000. Costs at three stages of production, at 50% of output capacity, at 80%, and at 100%, are computed in Table 1.7.

Table 1.7 Unit cost at varying outputs

At 50% output, or 5 units, costs are:		
Fixed	$1 million total	(per unit, $200,000)
Variable	$500,000 total	(per unit, $100,000)
Total	$1,500,000 total	(per unit, $300,000)
At 80% output, 8 units, costs are:		
Fixed	$1 million total	(per unit, $125,000)
Variable	$800,000 total	(per unit, $100,000)
Total	$1,800,000 total	(per unit, $225,000)
At full production, 10 units, costs are:		
Fixed	$1 million total	(per unit, $100,000)
Variable	$1,000,000 total	(per unit, $100,000)
Total	$2,000,000 total	(per unit, $200,000)

As production progresses from 50 to 100% of capability, fixed costs per-unit decline from $200,000 to $100,000, although they remain constant at a total of $1 million, while variable costs increase from $500,000 to $1 million although they remain the same per unit. In terms of pricing on a unit cost basis, with each unit bearing its full fixed and variable costs, the total price per unit would change downward by a third from $300,000 to $200,000.

This is why a quantity discount in price to promote additional purchases is justified where large fixed costs are present. The discount takes advantage of the decreases in unit costs which accompany increases in volume—an inverse relationship.

Timing and other specifics may be important in determining whether a cost is fixed or variable. Returning to our baker as an example, take the cost in question to be his employees and their wages. If his business is stable throughout the year, he may employ a given number of people steadily over the period, their wages being fixed for price determination. On the other hand, if he has seasonal peaks and valleys in his operations, he may employ more or fewer people as his seasonal output changes, thus making wages a variable cost.

1.7.1 Production Within the Capability of Existing Plant

In summary, with a manufacturing plant of a given size—in our illustration, a bakery—cost per unit will decline as production moves from partial to full utilization of the plant's facilities. The bakery is there in any event. So, the fixed overhead costs of the bakery can be spread over a larger number of loaves as the bakery produces more loaves, up to its maximum capacity. This means a decreasing overhead cost per loaf as production expands. Stated another way, the fixed costs of the bakery can be spread over a broader base, with a resultant smaller apportionment of fixed cost to each loaf as the number of loaves increases.

In passing we note that variable costs per unit, such as the cost of a pound of flour, may also fluctuate somewhat with the volume of production rather than remaining constant. They may decline as more pounds are bought, since the bakery's suppliers of flour or sugar may also find that they can sell additional pounds at a lesser cost per pound as their own fixed costs are spread over more and more pounds. Variable costs also may increase a bit, but again, they may not. Therefore, we consider only fixed costs as we continue our examination of declining costs per unit.

1.7.2 Where Plant Expansion Is Required

The premise that fixed costs per-unit decline as production increases is, in one respect, a rebuttable conclusion. Assume that our bakery is already at or close to producing at the limit of its capability, so that additional sales will require a second tier of ovens, i.e., an expansion of its existing plant. The second tier may, or may not, be cheaper per unit of production (per loaf) than the initial tier.[14] Technological advances may have produced ovens which are more efficient, *or* new safety measures may be greater in cost than the technological cost savings. In one circumstance the new tier of ovens is cheaper than the original; in the second, the new tier is more expensive. In the first circumstance, continuation of quantity discounts would make economic sense; in the latter, such discounts might not.

But quantity discounts might make sense even in the latter case, even where the second tier of ovens is more expensive per unit than the first. When the second tier of ovens initially comes on line, it will not be fully used. The transition from one tier to two tiers will not see a monumental increase in sales sufficient to jump production levels at one fell swoop from full production of the one tier to full production of both. Lacking some miraculous increase in sales volumes, the second tier will be only partially used at the outset. Here we are presented with precisely the same situation as when the fist tier was only partially used. If we can improve the utilization of the second tier, each step in the improvement means the same spreading of a total amount of fixed costs over a greater number of loaves of bread, and therefore a lesser burden of fixed costs to be borne by each loaf. Hence, the continuing incentive on the part of the baker to offer volume-discounted prices for increased takes by consumers. The discount may be different, reflecting two tiers in operation instead of one, but the incentive to discount the price to increase volume remains.

The unit cost–price linkage remains the same as three, five, or seven additional tiers of ovens are added. The quantity-discount incentive changes only in degree as the additional tiers are added at a lower or higher per-unit fixed cost than prior tiers.

---

[14] Assuming constant dollars; i.e., disregarding any changes in the value of money due to inflation.

This leads to the conclusion that whenever production capability is greater than sales volume, per-unit costs savings for additional sales provide a rationale for price discounts to increase sales.[15] However, this generality applies only where a major portion of the total costs of the seller are related to the fixed expense of paying for the seller's investment in expensive plant—a fully equipped bakery as in our illustration. If we look to the famed haberdashery of President Truman's pre-political days, we do not find a huge fixed investment which must be paid for by current revenues. We have, instead, the relatively minor costs of rental or ownership of a store, where fixed costs are small in relation to total costs—the bulk of which are for buying the merchandise, paying a flexible number of salespeople, etc. Here considerations other than fixed costs come into play in the sellers' price decisions. We do not explore these, since our concern with the electric and gas utilities involves circumstances where the cost of facilities to provide service to consumers is a major portion of total costs. The utilities are industries where capital costs are enormous and, therefore, where the fixed costs exercise a tremendous influence upon pricing.[16]

Therefore, we restate with qualifications, our conclusion given a few paragraphs ago. *Where the costs of production capability*—i.e., of the facilities necessary to render the seller's service or to provide the seller's product—*are high and incapable of ready reduction, then per-unit costs savings resulting from additional sales provide an economic incentive which supports price discounts for additional sales* to the benefit of both seller (who achieves a better utilization of his plant) and buyer (who benefits from a lower price per unit).

Now we change course 180 degrees. Having explored why quantity discounts might make sense even when the second tier of ovens entails higher per-unit costs than the first tier, we also must discuss why such discounts might *not* make sense. To do so, we must move back in time to the point where the baker still has substantial excess producing capacity in his first tier of ovens. Looking forward, he realizes that if he keeps on promoting a higher volume of sales, a second tier at a higher per-unit fixed cost will have to be added to his plant. For one reason or another, he does not want to make the addition. To mitigate or postpone the need, he may reduce or eliminate his present quantity discounts if the prices of his competitors permit. Thus, the question: could the baker in the face of competition settle for reduced sales and under-utilization of this present plant in return for a constant or higher present unit price and delay in the time when he must expand? In the baker's case, this is unlikely.

---

[15]From the seller's point of view, this cost rationale has an opposite side. Discounts lower the price for current sales as well as for induced added sales. Therefore, the *revenue* from current sales declines as a certainty, while the *additional revenue* from added sales is speculative. Discounts place the future cost-to-revenue balance at risk.

[16]It is safe to say that quantity-discount pricing by the electric and gas utilities has a solid economic basis since the utilities normally operate under conditions of declining unit costs. We develop this basis in chapter 2 on the Cost Approach to Pricing, so we mention only the highlights here.

But in the case of the regulated utility, such a response is not hypothetical. *Inverted* electric and gas rates—i.e., first loaf, $1.90, second loaf $2.00, and additional loaves, $2.10, an inversion of discount pricing—have been strongly advocated at times by proponents of energy conservation, and sometimes have been adopted to postpone the need for new energy supplies.[17]

1.8 A Closer Look at Two-Part Pricing

A two-part price scheme for the unregulated retailer has related but different objectives and results than the two-part rate of a utility.

For the retailer, the club membership fee provides a revenue offset to the seller for the higher discounts given to the buyer, while at the same time inducing the shopper to buy as many items as possible so as to take maximum advantage of the discount which comes with the fee. Other considerations being equal, the buyer will tend to gravitate toward the store to which a membership fee has been paid.

The two-part rate of a utility usually is designed with a variety of different aims in mind, which we summarize only broadly at this point. From the cost-responsibility point of view, certain costs of the utility are incurred completely irrespective of the customer's purchase volume—the costs of meters, meter reading, accounting and billing, collecting bills, etc. These are essentially the same whether the customer uses little energy or a great deal. Also, essentially the same irrespective of customer usage, are the investment-related costs arising from the necessity for the utility to have capacity to permit lights to go on at the flick of the switch or the furnace to respond to a higher thermostat level. These are the "readiness to serve" costs, since they arise whether the lights or the furnace are used intermittently or full time. In a two-part rate some portion of these fixed or non-variable costs are reflected in a separate charge, which does not vary with customer usage. Thus, a customer's bill may include two separate elements, a fixed "customer charge" and a variable "energy-used charge" (per kilowatt-hour or per-therm actually taken by the customer).

Now we come to the question as to how utility practice does or does not relate to quantity-discount pricing via a two-part rate. We call attention to the obvious. The price attached to the customer charge must be paid by the customer regardless of the volume of the customer's actual usage of energy. Therefore, the charge per unit of use is less with a separate customer charge than if the total cost were to be recouped through only the energy charge—in the same fashion as the baker with a club membership fee can charge a lower price per loaf. To this extent, then, the two-part utility rate is mildly promotional since the *average* price of each unit of consumption declines as more energy is used.

---

[17] Similarly, energy conservation objectives have pointed to the substitution of *energy saving devices* (such as double glazing of windows in homes) for added capacity which otherwise would have to be installed by utilities.

This tendency toward a declining average total price to the buyer may be accelerated if energy charges themselves are shaped according to the quantity-discount principle—or, to parallel our baker (first loaf, $2.10, second loaf, $2.00, additional loaves, $1.90), the first 100 units of energy at "x" price, the next 100 units, at a price of "x − y," and additional units at a price of "x − (y + z)."

Alternatively, if the conservation ethic rules, savings to the buyer for a higher volume of purchases may be reversed under an inverted price structure for the energy charges: first 100 units at a price of "x" per unit, the next 100 units at a price of "x + y," and additional units at a price of "x + y + z."

In spite of the differences between the unregulated retailer and the regulated utility, there are similarities in pricing motivation. Both provide a degree of revenue stability. Both the club fee and its counterpart in the two-part utility rate provide a revenue offset, which reduces the level of the other charges. In both, the fixed price element allows the seller a greater degree of flexibility in per-unit-of-sales pricing than otherwise would be practicable. The flexibility may be exercised to promote volume or, as in the case of inverted prices of a utility, to discourage (penalize) higher volume.

1.9 Competitive Pricing (Value to the Purchaser)

We have examined the baker who initially has a single tier of ovens, and the same baker who must, to keep apace with demand for his bread, add a second tier. We have explored the bakers approach to pricing under these two circumstances. But we have not yet considered the circumstance where the bakery co-exists in close proximity to another, or to more than one other. Let us hypothesize a number of bakeries of different sizes in the same market area. One has one tier of ovens in operation; another two, and others from three to ten. Our illustrative single baker operating alone in his locality could set the price of bread at whatever level he saw fit because no competitors would undercut him. *Now, he must keep his price in line with the prices of others.* The economics of cost of a single baker no longer set his minimum price, i.e., a price which would cover his costs. Competition (competitive economics)—an entirely different matter—now sets the price. In terms relevant to this text, we have left the field of monopoly or semi-monopoly regulated pricing dominated by cost to enter into the arena of competitive pricing dominated by value. We do not now pursue this departure at length, for that is aside from the thrust of this chapter. We merely point it out here. Competitive pricing for utilities is discussed in some detail in chapter 5 on the Value Approach to Pricing (chapters 5 and 6).

1.10 From Wonderland to Reality

We cannot leave our baker in limbo. Having devised a scheme by which he can derive a cost for each of his several bakery products, does he care?

1.10 From Wonderland to Reality

1.10.1 The Baker

Since the prices the baker charges for his several products are unregulated, it is highly unlikely that he will be interested in a full cost calculation for each (or even in *any* cost calculation for each). At most, he may be concerned only that he charges enough for one product as to compensate for the *direct* costs of that product. In economic parlance (if he be rational as the economist usually sees rationality), he must recoup in his price for a dozen doughnuts at least the *direct* cost of the doughnuts (their incremental direct or out-of-pocket cost). Otherwise he would be better off not to sell the doughnuts and thus avoid a loss on their sale.

Or would he be better off? Not necessarily. Maybe he knows his market better than the "rational" economic convention. If he does not offer doughnuts at a somewhat lesser price than direct incremental cost, he may lose customers and therefore suffer a reduction in his sales of bread and his other products, for an overall loss in net revenue. He may rationally price his doughnuts at less than his direct incremental cost so as to preserve his market over all. (The "loss leader" in non-price regulated marketing, but a "no-no" for a regulated utility.)

So much for price vs. cost in the unregulated market for joint products. *The unregulated entrepreneur must price his products at a competitive level, regardless of any computation of cost for the individual product.* Of course, his revenue—the aggregate of his prices—must be enough to cover the aggregate of his costs, or eventually he must abandon his business. But the price for any single product is governed by the competition, not by his computation of cost for that product.

1.10.2 The Utility

This is not so—or at least, not necessarily so—in the regulated market, although the trend toward market-based pricing is becoming increasingly evident in long-distance telecommunications, natural gas and electric transmission, and large-scale industrial sales by electric and gas distribution companies. For the regulated utility, generally the attempt is to require a price for each of the several joint products which will equate to cost. The *minimum* price level is that which will cover at least the direct incremental cost of the product, and this minimum level is allowed only under circumstances where the specific incrementally priced product lowers the cost burden which otherwise would have to be borne by other products.

Given the incremental cost exception, a cost, an average cost, must be determined for each product. Direct costs are no problem, since they can be directly linked to the individual product. However, for utilities the indirect, joint, common, or overhead costs are a significant (and sometimes an overwhelming) part of total costs. The objective of making the price for each product equate to (or reasonably resemble) the specific cost for that product requires that the total cost of the individual product be determined. The indirect costs by some rational theory (sometimes approaching legerdemain) must be divided up among the various products so that in the final result all costs will have been apportioned in a non-discriminatory fashion.

1.10.3 A Broader Horizon

Our discussions of joint-product costing, highlighting the uncertainties of cost allocations, are included in this text to demonstrate the problem in relation to utilities. But the reader should not dismiss the matter as solely a utility issue. Any business may be called upon to render a cost figure for one of its joint products. Such rendering requires a cost allocation. Most allegations of "dumping," or selling below cost, involve joint costs and mandate a cost finding by both accuser and accused. The same is likely to be true for "predatory pricing." But the arena goes beyond these conspicuous examples. An illustration in a different business area appeared in a recent suit against the Bank of America. The Bank charged a fee of $3 for each bad check written by its customers. It was alleged that this charge was excessive and an "unfair business practice." The trial court agreed, ordering the Bank not to collect more than $1.75 per check. The court cited evidence that it cost the Bank anywhere from 24 to 60 cents to process a returned check.[18] (Notice the extreme range of the cost estimates.) A moments thought will suffice to convince the reader of the complexity of attempting to establish a cost for a bounced check amid the numerous interlocking functions of a large bank.

1.10.4 Benefits vs. Costs

Current economic and political thought tends to be increasingly concerned with a comparative evaluation for any proposed project of its benefits vs. its costs. An evaluation may be via the comprehensive structure of an environmental impact statement or something less formal. In any event, a comparison of benefits and costs, by definition, requires a quantification of each of these two elements. A benefit–cost evaluation may entail the additional complexity of distinguishing between those who must pay the costs and those who receive the benefits.

We point out that most if not all of the uncertainties which exist in a determination of cost are paralleled in a determination of benefits. Almost as surely as for costs, allocation of benefits among joint beneficiaries will be unavoidable parts of the benefit-determination procedure. And benefit allocations will be fully as indeterminate and speculative as cost allocations. We point this out in passing to suggest that allocation theories and procedures are broader in scope than the joint cost issue, and extend beyond the costing of joint utility services.

1.11 Cost and Price-A Primer

In spite of our subsequent chapters on the cost and value approaches to pricing, we would be remiss if we did not attempt to capsulize at this juncture the teachings of economics relative to price and cost.

---

[18]See Faludi, S.C., "Judge Orders Bank of America to Slash Fee Charged Firms for Bounced Checks," *The Wall Street Journal*, July 9, 1991.

1.11 Cost and Price-A Primer

Economics suggests that for conditions of *perfect* competition over the long haul—i.e., *in the long run*—the aggregate of the prices which producers are able to charge must be equal to the aggregate of their costs. If the prices of an individual producer fall short, that producer eventually will become bankrupt, to be replaced by a more efficient operator. If prices on average exceed costs, some producers will achieve a windfall (or excessive) profit, which will lure other producers to enter the market. These new producers will undercut the prices of the pre-existing producer group, thus forcing the industry price level down to cost. So equilibrium—or balance—theoretically is achieved. Prices in the aggregate will equate to costs in the aggregate in the long run.[19]

Thus, economics recognizes that different producers confront different costs. Some, with lower costs, will be able to sell in the competitive marketplace at more favorable margins than the industry-wide average level of cost would show to be necessary. Others, with higher costs, cannot sell and remain solvent at prices which are sufficient only to cover the industry-wide average level of cost. Each year high cost producers go deeper into the hole financially, and finally are forced to succumb. New, more efficient, producers take their place. The entry and exit from the market of individual firms over time drives the prices of ongoing producers up or down toward the theoretical cost level which just suffices to keep them in business—healthy financially, but no more.

But these generalities presuppose an economic environment which rarely, if ever, actually is found in the real world. Even under perfect competition, seldom would any given phase of the economy be in absolute equilibrium.

Examples of perfect competition are rare to non-existent. Even farming, often cited as coming closest to the perfectly competitive ideal, falls short, by reason of innumerable constraints for some farmers and privileges for others, imposed or given by reason of governmental policy.

But most of the economy falls outside of the concept of perfect competition. Competition is "imperfect" (to use Joan Robinson's term) or "monopolistic" (as described by Edward Chamberlin), both terms meaning the same—something short of the offering of identical products. Sellers attempt to distinguish their products from the products of competing sellers by introducing differences which are directed toward establishing a unique appeal for their own brands. One toothpaste manufacturer may market its brand by alleging tarter control, another a pleasant taste, etc. Brands establish "product differentiation" so that competition will not be guided by price alone, but also by consumer preferences stimulated by advertising and like means. The rule that price matches cost in the long run becomes obscured in the actuality of the imperfectly competitive marketplace.

---

[19] Samuelson and other economists might disagree with the above. In his *Economics*, Samuelson states categorically: "Competitive price and quantity are determined by supply and demand," noting that this declaration says little about "competitive price being determined by cost of production." He asks and responds as follows: "Should not this be listed as a third factor in addition to supply and demand? Our answer is firmly, 'No.'" (Samuelson, Paul A., *Economics*, Eleventh Edition, p. 366).

Monopoly, oligopoly, and varying degrees of each, beyond imperfect competition itself, introduce other exceptions to the general rule. However, monopoly is obstructed by the anti-trust laws and is legally tenable only during the limited life of exclusive patents or copyrights.

This leads us to the thought that the only certain cost–price relationship is for the individual firm. No firm can stay in business unless its prices in the aggregate are sufficient to cover its costs. If the firm is a multi-product supplier, it is not necessary that each product be priced to cover the individual costs of that product, *even if such costs could reliably be calculated.* It is necessary only that the sum of all prices—i.e., revenues—be sufficient to meet the sum of all costs. Economics is full of qualifications, so we must qualify even the foregoing statement. Recall our baker. Even in the simplest case, overall costs are subject to subjective judgments—the rate of depreciation and the rate of return, being those cited in the example. However, a firm may lower its apparent (reported) cost of operations by lengthening out depreciation periods, accepting a lower rate of return or by other measures not mentioned earlier, such as deferring maintenance and replacements.

Beneath the level of overall or total costs, in the unregulated market the prices of the several joint products need bear no necessary relation to the allocated costs of these products, suffice only that there not be "predatory pricing," "dumping," or the like. This leads to a conclusion which need not be qualified: *cost for a joint product in the unregulated market, however, calculated, does not necessarily translate into the price of that product.*

1.12 Conclusions, If Any

This chapter was introduced with the hope that it might enlarge, or at least clarify, our understanding of cost and price, and of their relationship.

An attempt has been made to illustrate that "cost," even in the broadest sense of the total cost of doing business for a business enterprise as a whole, is illusive and indeterminate. We have further attempted to illustrate that the cost of any one of a group of joint products of an individual firm is even more illusive and indeterminate, due to the inherent uncertainties of allocating joint costs to joint products.

Still further, we have attempted to point out that the uncertainty and indeterminate nature of a cost figure exists whether is it calculated for a simple operation, such as a bakery, or via the most sophisticated modern accounting techniques embraced by the largest multi-billion dollar corporation.

Our purpose in so doing is not complicated. We suggest only that cost results as reported in financial statements, or as calculated by regulators, be observed with a degree of skepticism. And we assert that the costs of joint operations—and of joint products—are valid only to the extent that the allocation theories upon which they are based are valid.

Re price, we have suggested that even such a presumably precise figure is susceptible of a number of different interpretations, depending not only on what has

1.12 Conclusions, If Any

been paid, but also upon the price scheme pursuant to which the payment has been made.

Concerning the relationship between cost (however derived) and price (however set forth), we have suggested that value—except in a monopoly, non-competitive situation—is a more relevant consideration than cost. We support this reasoning on the premise that a given product must be competitive in price with another alternative product if it is to sell in the marketplace. Whether costs are in line with prices is irrelevant at any given point in time.[20]

We state this irrelevance with a major qualification, however. The cost-to-price relationship is irrelevant only at the moment (which moment may be a day, a month, a year, or a period of years). Over the longer haul, *in the long run*, prices must be such as to cover costs.

Utility pricing under regulation strives to require that current prices approximate current revenue requirements (i.e., match costs). And this is all to the good provided that the regulated prices are not out-of-sync with the prices of currently competitive alternatives. If a shift from cost-based prices to value-based prices is necessary to enable the regulated utility to compete, our final suggestion is that competitive pricing takes precedence over cost-based pricing.

---

[20]On this point, at least, Samuelson would agree. WG: Energy Pricing/Conkling/text in word/Chapter1

Chapter 2
The Cost Approach to Pricing: The Direction of Cost

Abstract Two elements enter into the determination of the price of every component exchanged in the economy: the costs of producing, transporting, and delivering it, on the one hand, and its value to the buyer, on the other hand. Under price regulation, these two individual elements are the subject of highly developed formal processes and strictures, particularly as to costs. Chapters 2, 3, and 4 explore the economics of various aspects of the cost approach. Chapter 2 emphasizes one central principle–that prices tend to follow the direction of costs. To determine this direction, costs are examined from their fundamental role as either fixed or variable, and whether in combination they lead to decreasing, constant, or increasing per-unit costs. For capital-intensive industries, such as the energy utilities, the direction of unit costs is downward as plant is utilized more extensively with growth. Comparative scenarios are presented which analyze growth in its several stages, even or erratic, constant or interrupted, with resulting changes in the firm's prognosis.

2.1 Preface

Cost of service is the first of three basic approaches to utility pricing theory and practice. Under this approach, price determination is viewed from the supply side of the economic spectrum. The regulatory objective is that rates charged to customers will approximate the costs of rendering the service to these customers as closely as possible.

Cost analyses, consistent with standard accounting and economic analytical procedures, provide the foundation for the cost of service approach. In addition, these more or less standardized procedures are augmented and refined by the specialized tools and concepts peculiar to the energy utilities, which are explained in Chap. 11.

Henry Ford is credited with having introduced the concept of mass production into the American economy. If a product can be manufactured in quantity, Ford reasoned, the cost of each item produced can be cut to a minimum. So, Ford created the assembly line. As autos emerged from the line in growing numbers, the direction of the cost per auto trended down (in non-inflated or constant dollars, of course). The downward trend in cost per auto made possible a corresponding downward direction in the price per auto.

We refer to this often-cited example of the Ford mass product assembly line to underscore a basic relationship between costs and prices in a competitive market: the direction of prices flows from the direction of costs.

In this chapter we treat the exploration of the direction of costs as an entry-pricing question. Others may see it as an intermediate or final issue. We do not argue which should come first, the chicken or the egg. We posit cost directionality at the beginning only because from our viewpoint such seems to best accommodate the logic of a cost approach to pricing. Whether first or last, an effective pricing policy cannot be blind to the direction of costs. Pricing, both for the present and the future, must comport with the reality of costs. Current prices must support current operations at current costs. Future prices must support future operations at future costs.

Transition from the present to the future is an inevitable fact of life. The transition from present costs and present prices, to future costs and future prices, must be faced head-on by the rate maker. The changeover may be smooth or rocky, orderly or disruptive, depending upon the degree and quality of the preparation for it. Today's pricing policy should anticipate the pricing requirements of tomorrow so that price changes will follow in a rational sequence. The type of analysis which follows can contribute to a smooth, orderly transition.

But there is another reason for an analysis aimed at foreseeing the direction of costs, and hence the direction of prices.

In many regulatory jurisdictions, utility prices carry an extra burden not imposed upon prices in other sectors of the economy. Utility prices are called upon to present a proper "signal" to buyers as to whether future prices will be higher or lower. Massive speculation or informed judgment? Whichever, it is to be hoped that buyers will not be misled.[1]

It should be obvious that if a price signal is to be valid, it must have a valid foundation. Prices move in tandem with costs, so a forecast of the direction of costs is key to any price signal which reasonably can serve to suggest how prices are likely to trend in the future.

We now turn to how costs and their direction may be analyzed to establish, among other objectives, an insight into the direction of prices.

---

[1] The "signal" enigma introduces at least three uncertainties: what message is to be signaled? How should the message be couched in terms of present prices? And, will the message be recognized by the buyer, motivating the buyer to adjust buying habits to correspond to the signal?

2.2 Fixed and Variable Costs

The cost–price directional analysis segregates costs into two categories, fixed or overhead[2] and variable,[3] a classification referred to earlier in Chap. 1. *Fixed costs are those which remain constant (or relatively so) in total amount regardless of changes in the volume of business done.* Investment costs are fixed costs to the utility, because capital invested in plant and equipment does not change with sales fluctuations. Various other overhead costs are fixed also.

Fixed costs related to plant are also *sunk* costs. Once a capital investment has been made, the investment must be paid off regardless of whether the plant item is used or not, and regardless of the degree of utilization of the plant. The principal amount of the investment must be recovered, along with interest or equivalent on the unpaid balance. The alternatives, write-off of the unrecovered investment where the financial condition of the plant owner permits, or default on debt, where write-off is not feasible, are not viable considerations at the outset of instituting a capital investment.

Finally, fixed costs related to plant may be referred to as *embedded* costs, for the same reasons that they are sunk costs. They are embedded, i.e., included, in the utility's financial statements, and like other costs, are obligations which must be paid from revenues.

Variable costs are those which vary in total amount with increases or decreases in the volume of business. The cost of fuel (coal, oil, or natural gas) in a steam electric generating plant is a good example of a variable cost. As greater quantities of electricity are generated, more fuel is used, and fuel costs increase. Conversely, as generation drops off, fuel costs decrease. For natural gas companies buying gas for resale, the cost of purchasing gas at the wellhead is the principal variable cost.

It is important to understand the practical aspects of the relationship between fixed and variable costs. As production is increased with a given plant,[4] fixed costs,

---

[2] Fixed or overhead costs are called "constant" costs by some writers. Martin Glaeser, an outstanding utility authority of an earlier era, recommends that they be called "capacity" costs. This is a useful concept inasmuch as most fixed costs are associated with the provision of capacity. Glaeser calls variable costs "out-of-pocket" costs. Glaeser, M.G., *Outlines of Public Utility Economics*, The Macmillan Company, New York, NY, 1931, Ch. XXVIII, p. 623.

[3] There are other ways of classifying costs for this purpose, depending upon the degree of refinement desired. An example of a three-way classification (given by Thompson, D.W. and Smith, W.R., *Public Utility Economics*, McGraw-Hill Book Company, Inc., New York, NY, 1941, Ch. 5) is (1) capital costs; (2) fixed operating costs; and (3) variable operating costs.

[4] The term *plant* is used in this chapter in a very broad sense to mean all or any part of the physical facilities, including land, equipment, machines, tools, buildings and grounds, etc., which are necessary to provide the utility service. Major additions to plant might mean, in the electric industry, an additional generating station, an important transmission line, or a large substation; in the natural gas industry, looping a pipeline main, a new compressor station, an additional city gate, storage, etc. Such additions may be made in any phase of the utility's operations (production, transmission, or distribution) or may, for balanced development, encompass all phases. Often the latter will be the case.

remaining constant in total, are borne by a larger number of units of output, and the amount of the total fixed costs which each unit must support is decreased. Variable costs, however, while changing in total, remain approximately equal for each unit of output. Thus, to use our previous electrical example, investment costs *per kilowatt-hour* will decline as production increases, but fuel costs *per kilowatt-hour* will not change significantly.

The distinction between fixed and variable costs is seldom clear-cut. There are a number of different circumstances which may change the usual characteristics of costs. Investment costs, ordinarily fixed, will increase significantly if major additions to plant are made to expand production and sales, or will decline if major plant items are retired from service. This illustrates that there is a long-run relationship between fixed costs and business volume, and that costs generally considered fixed will react to large changes in output. Conversely, many costs which ordinarily are variable may remain constant for short periods. It may be desirable, for example, to keep trained workers on the rolls during temporary slack periods rather than lose them and later incur the expense of training new employees. Also, some types of costs have mixed characteristics. To illustrate, even a part of the fuel costs of the electric generating plant, which as before mentioned are predominantly variable, may be fixed. This is due to the frequent necessity to burn a minimum amount of fuel to keep the plant in a standby status during periods when the burning of fuel would not otherwise be required. *It is thus apparent that costs may be classified as fixed or variable only on the basis of defined ranges of output and given periods of time.*

2.2.1 The "Readiness to Serve" Concept

An important part of utility rate theory has been developed out of the fixed–variable classification of costs. In addition to investment costs which already have been mentioned, utility fixed costs include such items as property taxes, insurance, non-operating depreciation, basic maintenance, salaries of officials, and wages of the minimum staff of employees. If the utility is to be in a position to render service when needed by its customers, it must incur these fixed expenses.

The utility plant, whether it be electric, gas, or other, may be used to capacity only part of the time. Nevertheless, adequate capacity to take care of maximum service requirements "on demand" of customers must be provided. Once the plant capacity is provided, the investment expenses associated therewith are constant in the sense of being unavoidable.[5] Similarly, other expenses are unavoidable and constant if service is to be rendered as required. Together, they comprise the utility's fixed costs. These costs are all associated with the obligation of the utility to be in a

---

[5] Within the limits of ranges of output and periods of time previously mentioned. Also, accounting treatment of investment costs may cause annual booked costs to vary as depreciation changes the spread between gross and net plant; return requirements may change, as may property taxes, etc. *But investment costs must be met in any event.*

position to render service when needed. They must be incurred if electricity is to be available at the flip of a switch, telephone service at the lift of a receiver, or gas at the turning on of a jet. For this reason utility fixed costs are often called "readiness to serve" costs.

2.2.2 The "Use of Service (Product)" Concept

If the utility's fixed costs are incurred in order to put it in a position to render service whenever demanded by the customer, its variable costs arise as the result of the *amount* of service taken by the customer. Thus, these costs are classified as "use of service" costs.[6]

2.2.3 Relative Proportion of Fixed and Variable Costs

It is almost universally the case that in electric utilities the proportion of fixed to variable costs is high. This is true also for gas utilities, if the cost of gas at the wellhead is excluded. The proportions will vary not only between different types of utilities, but also between individual utilities of the same type.

2.3 Decreasing, Constant, and Increasing Costs Conditions

From a bird's-eye vantage point, cost conditions may be seen as falling characteristically into one of three types, each viewed in constant dollars.

Conditions of decreasing costs are those in which average costs per unit[7] decline as additional units are produced or sold. The usual utility combination of a high ratio of fixed to variable costs typically gives rise to decreasing costs conditions,[8]

---

[6]"Use of service" costs are often expressed in the specific terminology of the utility under consideration. In the electric industry, "use of service" costs are called "energy" costs and in the gas industry, "commodity" costs.

[7]Average costs are the result of dividing the number of units produced into total costs (fixed and variable). In the electric utility, the most common unit is the kilowatt-hour; in gas, either the cubic foot or the therm.

[8]Historically, utilities have been seen as characteristically operating under decreasing cost conditions. It has been generally true that utility firms experience decreasing average unit costs as their output increases. If so, often this is due to one or more of the following: first, a longer term circumstance, it may be due to the fact that most utility firms have not yet reached optimum size, i.e., the point where further increases in size would result in higher costs of operation; second, a short-term condition, it may be because utility firms have unused capacity so that output may be increased without a proportionate increase in fixed costs; or, third, an intermediate situation, utilities may be able to expand major plant units at costs comparable to existing units.

and will always do so where no substantial additions to existing plant are required for expansion of output.[9]

Plant expansion may alter the degree of the decline in unit costs, or even change the downward direction of the cost trend. For this reason it is necessary to explore costs within the ranges of output which can be supplied by existing plant separately from costs incurred where major new plant must be installed.

Conditions of constant costs are those in which average costs per unit will remain stable as *a whole* as additional units are produced or sold. This condition requires that substantial plant additions can be made at the same costs as existing plant. However, while costs as a whole may remain stable, decreasing costs will occur as the utilization of the new plant improves. New major plant additions almost always are sized to provide for future expansion, so at inception there will be space capacity. As this spare capacity is used, unit costs will decline.

Conditions of increasing costs are those under which average costs per unit increase as a whole as additional units are produced or sold. This condition results when the costs of significant plant additions are higher than for existing plant. However, as for constant costs, the decreasing cost phenomenon will take place as the new plant is brought from initial to full utilization.

Each of the three conditions is explored in the following pages.

2.4 Decreasing Costs

The condition of decreasing cost is illustrated from two perspectives, static and dynamic. The static assumption assumes rather unrealistically an unchanging, stable plant. The dynamic considers plant changes over time.

2.4.1 The Static Hypothesis

As a generalized—and over simplified—illustration of decreasing cost conditions, we examine the case of utility operations extending over a substantial period with no major additions to or retirements of plant capacity. To simplify the illustration, we treat only of an electric generating plant, without consideration of the transmission and distribution components of the electric system.

In lieu of a generating plant, other major electric or natural gas facilities could have been selected—an electric substation or transmission line, or a natural gas pressure booster station or pipeline. The only difference between these units and a generating plant is that the plant manufactures energy, while the other units only handle it, changing voltage or pressure or carrying it from one location to another.

---

[9]Theoreticians may treat conditions of decreasing costs as always being applicable only in the short run. The important reason for putting a time limit on such conditions is that over a longer period major additions to plant may be necessary, and since such additions are in the future their costs are unknown or at least speculative. This is a good point, but is an unnecessary refinement for our discussion.

2.4 Decreasing Costs

Table 2.1 Illustration of the operation of fixed and variable costs (Static Plant)

Annual output in billions of kwh	Annual cost ($ million)			Per kwh cost		
	Fixed cost	Variable cost	Total cost	Fixed cost	Variable cost	Total cost
4	600	40	640	15.0¢	1.0¢	16.0¢
6	600	60	660	10.0	1.0	11.0
8	600	80	680	7.5	1.0	8.5
10	600	100	700	6.0	1.0	7.0
12	600	120	720	5.0	1.0	6.0
14	600	140	740	4.3	1.0	5.3
16	600	160	760	3.7	1.0	4.7
18	600	180	780	3.3	1.0	4.3
20	600	200	800	3.0	1.0	4.0

System capacity: 20 billion kwh per year
Fixed costs: $600 million per year
Variable costs: 1¢ per kwh

Generating plant utilization is stated as *output*, while utilization of the others is stated as *throughput*. This difference does not detract from the applicability of the generating plant to exemplify decreasing cost conditions in general. We have merely adopted the plant as a proxy for any major utility facility or appropriate group of facilities. We add that the proxy applies equally to like facilities of other capital-intensive industries, such as a steel mill or an automobile assembly plant.

The input assumptions for the generating plant are stated at the bottom of Table 2.1. The plant capacity of 20 billion kWh annually represents dependable output as required by the load shape, at point of consumption (sales), after allowance for losses, necessary reserves, down time for maintenance, etc.

Table 2.1 illustrates that the fixed costs (in constant dollars) which must be borne by each kWh decline as additional units are produced. Fixed costs amount to 15 cents per kWh if only 4 billion kWh are sold. They decrease to 6 cents if 10 billion kWh are sold, further decreasing to 3 cents per kWh at capacity output of 20 billion kWh.

The trend of decreasing fixed costs per kWh as output expands is graphed in Fig. 2.1. Fixed costs, of course, are only a part of total costs. Variable costs of 1 cents per kWh are superimposed upon the curve of fixed costs in Fig. 2.2.[10]

---

[10] An example of an average variable cost of about 1 cent per kWh for a utility company with a mix of fuels is the 1993 experience of Kansas Gas and Electric Company. Its cost as reported in its 1993 Form 10-K was:

	Weighted average cost of fuel, per million BTU
Nuclear	$0.35
Coal	0.96
Gas	2.37
Oil	3.15

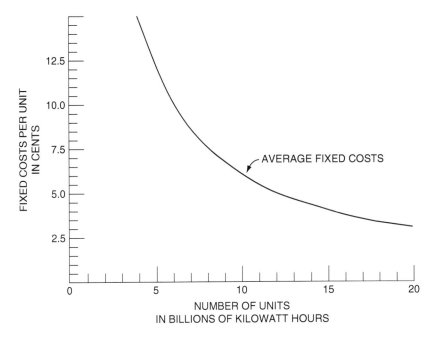

Fig. 2.1 Average fixed costs under decreasing cost conditions (static plant)

Figures 2.1 and 2.2 show the decline in fixed and total *per-unit* costs as output expands. Total fixed costs remain the same regardless of the stage of production, and variable costs increase. As indicated in Table 2.1, combined fixed and variable costs rise from $640 million at a low output to $800 million at full output.[11]

The foregoing illustrations are presented to hammer home the phenomenon of a decreasing per-unit cost situation which occurs as a major facility is brought from partial to full utilization. Essentially, a static situation is implied—a single very large plant progressing from minimal to full output. But utility operations are not static.

Cost per kWh generated: 0.93 cents.

Many utility operations are most efficient at or near capacity or name-plate output. For this reason, variable costs will change per unit as well as in total for different amounts of production, frequently being lowest near the point of capacity output. When this is true, it reinforces the trend toward decreasing unit costs. Variable unit cost changes, however, are minor as compared with changes in fixed costs per unit and are accordingly disregarded in this illustration.

[11] The reader is requested to note, and put in the back of his mind for later reference until marginal cost pricing is discussed, that the marginal cost per unit for any expansion of output along all of the ranges of output illustrated in Figure 2.1 and Table 2.1, except beyond the last increment reaching to 20 billion kWh, is 1 cent. For example, output can be increased from 10 billion kWh to 18 billion kWh at an additional cost per unit – marginal cost – of 1 cent.

2.4 Decreasing Costs

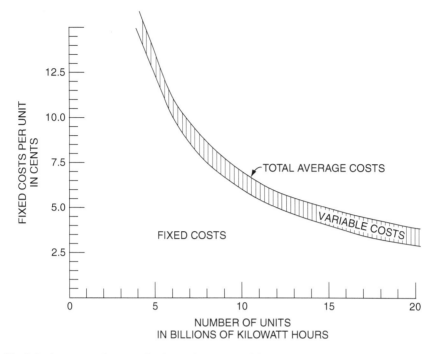

Fig. 2.2 Average total costs under decreasing cost conditions (static plant)

2.4.2 The Dynamic Hypothesis

We now drop the static plant scenario in favor of a more realistic growth-over-time paradigm, hoping that it will be sufficiently *de riqueur* in spite of some continued simplifications.

Our treatment of fixed costs incorporates an important simplification. We show total fixed costs remaining stable (levelized) for each plant throughout the following illustrations. Normal costing practice for regulated utilities would be to reduce the investment—and therefore fixed costs—each year by the depreciation for that year. This practice in itself would cause declining unit cost trends there shown. Stable costs over a period follow the "home mortgage" principle for repayment of investment with interest.

A second important simplification is the substitution of "stages of production" for time periods. Thus, we may refer to outputs ranging from 1, 2, 3, ..., 20, etc. as stages rather than as loads in any particular year. A stage may occur for less or more than a year. The stages do not forecast load growth. *The stages represent an annual output level with which is associated a given level of annual costs.* In this sense, a stage of production is equivalent to an annual output.

2.5 The Base System

As a foundation for exploring dynamic operations, past and future, we recast our prior illustration of fixed costs in a more realistic dimension. We substitute three plants for the single plant of Table 2.1, keeping output and investment costs (fixed costs) the same, as stated on Table 2.2:

Table 2.2 Base system plants

Plant	Annual output capability (billions of kWh)	Annual fixed costs ($ millions)
#1	4	140
#2	6	180
#3	10	280
Total	20	600

We refer to these three plants as the base system. Considering variable costs to be relatively constant per unit, we incorporate only fixed costs.

We assume that Plant #1 came online to supply the early, small magnitude loads, and remains online. Plant #2 was introduced when required to supply loads in excess of 4 billion kWh. It also remains online. Plant #3 became operative when the load exceeded 10 million.

Figure 2.3 diagrams sales volume in relation to additions to capacity. Neither the horizontal nor the vertical axis represents time periods. Load growth would not occur symmetrically. Figure 2.3 merely matches sales and capacity, regardless of the calendar.

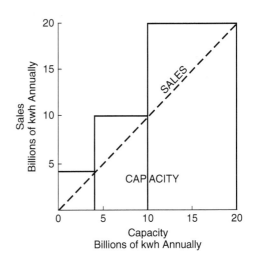

Fig. 2.3 Base system dependable capacity vs. output (sales)

2.5 The Base System

Table 2.3 Base three-plant generating system: fixed costs by plant

Annual plant output billions of kWh	Annual fixed costs — Total annual fixed costs ($ millions)	Costs per kWh (¢)	Dependable energy capacity factor (%)
Plant #1			
1	140	14.0	25
2	|	7.0	50
3	|	4.7	75
4	140	3.5	100
Plant #2			
1	180	18.0	17
2	|	9.0	33
3	|	6.0	50
4	|	4.5	67
5	|	3.6	83
6	180	3.0	100
Plant #3			
1	280	28.0	10
2	|	14.0	20
3	|	9.3	30
4	|	7.0	40
5	|	5.6	50
6	|	4.7	60
7	|	4.0	70
8	|	3.5	80
9	|	3.1	90
10	280	2.8	100

Table 2.3 tabulates fixed costs in total and per kWh individually for each plant of the base system. Unit fixed costs for the individual plants counterpart in miniature the declining costs shown in Fig. 2.1.

The right hand column in Table 2.3 introduces a new index to suit this and later illustrations, for which we have coined the term "dependable energy capacity factor." As we use it, the term means *the ratio of the output delivered to customers (sales), to the dependable energy-serving capacity of the plant or system*, over a calendar period or stage of production. Such capability is less than name plate capacity, which must be greater to accommodate peaking requirements, losses, reserves, etc.[12] We turn to sales as the numerator because we state per-unit costs in terms of the amounts which must be recovered by customer prices.

---

[12] Changes in load shapes from one stage of production to another are not integrated into this factor, which, as used here, assumes a generally consistent load shape but without specifying a given sales load factor or factors.

Table 2.4 Base three-plant generating system: fixed costs in total and per kWh

Sales (dependable output) (billion kWh)	Fixed costs ($ millions) Plant #1	Plant #2	Plant #3	System (combined)	System fixed costs per unit (¢)	Dependable energy capacity factor (%)
1	140			140	14.0	25
2					7.0	50
3					4.7	75
4	140			140	3.5	100
5	140	180		320	6.4	50
6					5.3	60
7					4.6	70
8					4.0	80
9					3.6	90
10	140	180		320	3.2	100
11	140	180	280	600	5.5	55
12					5.0	60
13					4.6	65
14					4.3	70
15					4.0	75
16					3.8	80
17					3.5	85
18					3.3	90
19					3.2	95
20	140	180	280	600	3.0	100

Now we can explain the fixed costs of the phased-in operation, with first one, then two, and finally all three plants online as stated in Table 2.4.

The dependable energy capacity factor is a consistent measure of the utilization of an integrated system. For example, Plant #1 reaches full utilization, a factor of 100%, at an output of 4 billion kWh. When Plant #2 is first added, the combined output is 5 billion kWh. The factor declines to 50%, since the 5 billion kWh output is only half of the new combined capability of 10 billion kWh.

Composited per-unit fixed costs for the base system are graphed in Fig. 2.4. Here we confront one of the more disagreeable facts of utility life—the *cost spikes* which are almost certain to occur when major new capacity comes in line. The fixed costs of Plant #1 have declined to 3.5 cents per kWh as it reached full operation. When Plant #2 is added, system average fixed costs jump to 6.4 cents per kWh (although they decline to 3.2 cents per kWh later as full production is reached). And when Plant #3 is added, they escalate from the prior average of 3.2 to 5.5 cents (but again declining with expanded production to 3.0 cents).

If the cost of spikes of the generating system of Fig. 2.4 were coincident in time of occurrence with cost spikes for other plant elements, a very difficult rate problem would be posed. If rates were to track costs precisely, they would be unacceptably erratic. However, such coincidence in time of occurrence seldom

2.6 Future Additions

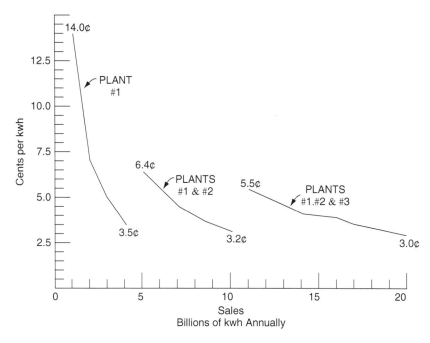

Fig. 2.4 Base system fixed costs per kilowatt-hour

happens. There tends to be the same diversity in the addition of facilities as there is in loads. Utility systems as a whole generally are so large that even the cost impact of a major facility addition is tempered if not absorbed in the overall body of costs.

Non-generating components of the electric system are a vast mix of diverse facilities which are at different stages of the cost curve. When intermingled in a company-wide cost of service, they tend to balance each other. Overall, the tendency in the entirety, in most cases, is declining unit costs in constant dollars.

2.6 Future Additions

The analyst seeking to determine the future magnitude and direction of costs as a guide to the future direction of prices will select some take-off point as being reasonably representative of the immediate past and current situation. For our purposes, we adopt as the beginning point the composite experience of the foregoing three-plant base system over the range of outputs from 11 to 20 billion kWh per year as indicated in Table 2.4.

To this base we add two new plants, Plants #4 and #5, under three different scenarios: a continuation of decreasing cost conditions; stable fixed costs, with the same per-unit investment for new plants as for the base system currently online (constant

Table 2.5 Millions of dollars of annual fixed costs per one million kWh of annual output (in constant dollars)

	The base system	
	Plant #1	$35
	Plant #2	$30
	Plant #3	$28

	The alternative scenarios		
	Decreasing cost	Constant cost	Increasing cost
Plant 4	$27	$30	$40
Plant 5	$26	$30	$45

cost conditions); or higher fixed costs, with a higher per-unit investment for new plants than for currently operational plants (increasing cost conditions).

The dollars of investment to be assigned to each of these three possible scenarios will unavoidably be judgmental. For the present illustrative purposes they need be no more than that. For a study which is made to be the basis for pricing policy decisions, however, the judgment should rest upon thorough engineering-economic analyses of the costs of alternative energy supplies. (Whether simple judgment or informed judgment, the costs adopted will be speculative to a degree since there is no certainty as to the future.)

We tabulate above the illustrative fixed cost values selected for Plants # and #5. (Table 2.5) in millions of dollars of annual fixed costs per 1 billion kWh of annual output (in constant dollars).

2.6.1 Decreasing Fixed-Cost Scenario

This case rests upon an optimistic outlook. We have not yet reached the limits of the economies of scale. Our engineers have not exhausted their ingenuity to introduce refinements in technology which will result in better, more efficient, and less costly designs. (The writer acknowledges a bias in favor of this assumption, being incurably influenced by the technological advances of the past. But this bias is beside the point, since the judgment as to which of the three possible scenarios to adopt is not his but that of the utility and its regulators.)

The optimism of the case is modest. Plant #4 costs 10% less than the base system, and Plant #5, 13% less, but these plants cost only 4 and 7% less, respectively, than Plant #3 of that system.

Results are summarized in Table 2.7. Per-unit fixed costs at selected utilizations of capacity given in Table 2.6:

2.6 Future Additions

Table 2.6 Comparative fixed costs at selected capacity factors: decreasing fixed costs

Dependable energy capacity factor (%)	Fixed costs per kWh (¢)		
	Base	Plants 1–4	Plants 1–5
80	3.8	3.6	3.5
90	3.3	3.2	3.1
100	3.0	2.9	2.8

Table 2.7 Decreasing fixed-cost scenario

Annual sales (dependable output) (billion kWh)	Annual fixed costs (millions of constant dollars)				Fixed costs per kWh (¢)	Dependable energy capacity factor (%)
	Base system	Plant #4	Plant #5	Dec. cost system		
11	600			600	5.5	55
12	|			|	5.0	60
13	|			|	4.6	65
14	|			|	4.3	70
15	|			|	4.0	75
16	|			|	3.8	80
17	|			|	3.5	85
18	|			|	3.3	90
19	|			|	3.2	95
20	600			600	3.0	100
21	600	270		870	4.1	70
22	|	|		|	4.0	73
23	|	|		|	3.8	77
24	|	|		|	3.6	80
25	|	|		|	3.5	83
26	|	|		|	3.3	87
27	|	|		|	3.2	90
28	|	|		|	3.1	93
29	|	|		|	3.0	97
30	600	270		870	2.9	100
31	600	270	260	1,130	3.6	78
32	|	|	|	|	3.5	80
33	|	|	|	|	3.4	83
34	|	|	|	|	3.3	85
35	|	|	|	|	3.2	88
36	|	|	|	|	3.1	90
37	|	|	|	|	3.1	93
38	|	|	|	|	3.0	95
39	|	|	|	|	2.9	98
40	600	270	260	1,130	2.8	100

2.6.2 Constant Fixed-Cost Scenario

Constant cost is a valid scenario, although to an extent it begs the issue. Essentially it assumes, for example, that the higher costs of electric generation imposed by environmental measures will precisely be offset by design improvements. Or, in the alternative, the case may be taken to represent conservation steps requiring invested dollars which are equivalent to the dollars required for one or the other of the two new plants. (The writer thinks it unlikely that even the most draconian conservation program could be a substitute for both of the new plants.)

The level of investment assumed in this constant cost case is $30 million per billion kWh of dependable output, the average for the base system.

Table 2.9 summarizes the results: per-unit fixed costs at the same selected capacity utilization factors given in Table 2.8:

2.6.3 Increasing Fixed-Cost Scenario

It is unfortunate that the future cannot be faced with undiluted optimism. Caution dictates that full consideration be given to a future in which increasing unit costs in constant dollars would materialize, a future which many see as likely.

For the electric industry, it certainly is possible that reliance may have to be placed on new nuclear generating units. It also is possible that these units will be more expensive because of environmental restraints, the still unresolved hazards of nuclear waste storage, the fear of locating such plants in proximity to population centers, etc. Conventional fuel plants also may be more expensive.

The costs of non-conventional electric generation are virtually unknown when considered as a primary reliable source for base-load power. Wind, solar, and cogeneration exist, but are still to be tested in the context of main-line electric system support. Will costs be high?

Conservation—i.e., reducing consumer demands—works, but only to dampen demand. When customer usage has been cut to the minimum as conservation runs its full course, new power supplies will be needed. Robust quantities of energy are essential to our economy as we know it, even assuming the maximum efficiency of use.

Table 2.8 Comparative fixed costs at selected capacity factors: constant fixed costs

Dependable energy capacity factor	Fixed costs per kWh		
	Base	Plants 1–4	Plants 1–5
80%	3.8¢	3.8¢	3.8¢
90%	3.3¢	3.3¢	3.3¢
100%	3.0¢	3.0¢	3.0¢

2.6 Future Additions

Table 2.9 Constant fixed-cost scenario

Annual sales (dependable output) (billion kWh)	Annual fixed costs (millions of constant dollars)				Fixed costs per kWh (¢)	Dependable energy capacity factor (%)
	Base system	Plant #4	Plant #5	Constant cost system		
11	600			600	5.5	55
12	|			|	5.0	60
13	|			|	4.6	65
14	|			|	4.3	70
15	|			|	4.0	75
16	|			|	3.8	80
17	|			|	3.5	85
18	|			|	3.3	90
19	|			|	3.2	95
20	600			600	3.0	100
21	600	300		900	4.3	70
22	|	|		|	4.1	73
23	|	|		|	3.9	77
24	|	|		|	3.8	80
25	|	|		|	3.6	83
26	|	|		|	3.5	87
27	|	|		|	3.3	90
28	|	|		|	3.2	93
29	|	|		|	3.1	97
30	600	300		900	3.0	100
31	600	300	300	1,200	3.9	78
32	|	|	|	|	3.8	80
33	|	|	|	|	3.6	83
34	|	|	|	|	3.5	85
35	|	|	|	|	3.4	88
36	|	|	|	|	3.3	90
37	|	|	|	|	3.2	93
38	|	|	|	|	3.2	95
39	|	|	|	|	3.1	98
40	600	300	300	1,200	3.0	100

Moving from electric generation to transmission, it is possible that public policy would dictate that electric distribution lines (both primary and secondary) be relocated from overhead to underground to avoid sight pollution; possibly transmission lines might have to be relocated because of electromagnetic fields. Or it might be that gas transmission lines would be limited to less than economic size or allowable pressures, or that fears of line breaks would force the relocation of high capacity long distance mains away from urban areas. Decreasing unit costs in these several areas could be reversed. The pessimist can go on and on.

As in our prior scenarios, to illustrate increasing fixed costs, we add two new plants to the base system. We assume that Plant #4 has fixed costs of $40 million annually for each 1 billion kWh of annual output. With the same dependable annual capacity of 10 billion kWh, yearly fixed costs are $400 million. These costs are 33 1/3% higher than the base system, and 43% higher than Plant#3 of that system.

For the second added plant, Plant #5, we assume even higher fixed costs, $45 million for each 1 billion kWh of dependable capacity, or, with a 10 billion kWh annual output, $450 million annually. The fixed costs of Plant #5 are 50% higher than the base system, and 61% higher than Plant #3.

This case is outlined on Table 2.11. At selected utilizations, per-unit fixed costs are given in Table 2.10:

Table 2.10 Comparative fixed costs at selected capacity factors: increasing fixed costs

Dependable energy capacity factor (%)	Fixed costs per kWh (¢)		
	Base	Plants 1–4	Plants 1–5
80	3.8	4.2	4.5
90	3.3	3.7	4.0
100	3.0	3.3	3.6

Decreasing costs prevail as output for each plant addition advances from minimum to maximum.

2.7 The Small Base-Load Plant

To this point, only larger-scale generating plants (as representative of any major facility, electric or gas, of comparable cost) have been incorporated into the possibilities to be considered for the future. Smaller-scale plants now are also under consideration. In electric terms, smaller generating plants may either be base-load generators, substituting for larger plants, or peaking or firming-up plants, where only peaking capability is deficient. The present scenario is directed to the former. In gas terms, a new smaller pipeline or distributor transmission main can be installed initially rather than a larger main, to be paralleled later in the same fashion as an additional small electric plant may be added to augment the capability of an earlier small plant.

The present scenario assumes that two smaller plants will be substituted for each of the larger plants. In other words, the smaller plants will have a dependable energy capability of one-half of that of the larger plants, or 5 billion kWh annually. But at what cost?

Not being Solomon, we resort to the pragmatic. Smaller new plants are not quite as efficient as larger plants, perhaps. And if larger new plants may be more expensive than earlier larger plants (our increasing cost scenario), then smaller new plants may be more expensive also, perhaps. We don't know. So, solely for illustration, we adopt the Plant #4 costs (under the increasing cost scenario) of $40 million per 1 billion kWh for the first two substitute plants, Plants #4-A and #4-B; and we adopt Plant #5

2.7 The Small Base-Load Plant

Table 2.11 Increasing fixed-cost scenario

Annual sales (dependable output) (billion kWh)	Annual fixed costs (millions of constant dollars)				Fixed costs per kWh (¢)	Dependable energy capacity factor (%)
	Base system	Plant #4	Plant #5	Inc. cost system		
11	600			600	5.5	55
12	|			|	5.0	60
13	|			|	4.6	65
14	|			|	4.3	70
15	|			|	4.0	75
16	|			|	3.8	80
17	|			|	3.5	85
18	|			|	3.3	90
19	|			|	3.2	95
20	600			600	3.0	100
21	600	400		1,000	4.8	70
22	|	|		|	4.5	73
23	|	|		|	4.3	77
24	|	|		|	4.2	80
25	|	|		|	4.0	83
26	|	|		|	3.8	87
27	|	|		|	3.7	90
28	|	|		|	3.6	93
29	|	|		|	3.4	97
30	600	400		1,000	3.3	100
31	600	400	450	1,450	4.7	78
32	|	|	|	|	4.5	80
33	|	|	|	|	4.4	83
34	|	|	|	|	4.3	85
35	|	|	|	|	4.1	88
36	|	|	|	|	4.0	90
37	|	|	|	|	3.9	93
38	|	|	|	|	3.8	95
39	|	|	|	|	3.7	98
40	600	400	450	1,450	3.6	100

costs of $45 million per 1 billion kWh for the second two substitute plants, Plants #5-A and #5-B. We suggest higher costs for the second two smaller plants for the same reason as we adopted higher cost for Plant #5 than for Plant #4, viz., that while the later plant might have the same or even better technology that the earlier plant, locational or other factors could be more difficult.

Costs for this configuration are calculated in Table 2.12. They may be compared with the costs for Table 2.11, since generation costs per billion kWh of output are the same on both tables. The cost spikes for the small plant system are much less drastic than for the large plant system, as would be expected. For example, as output progresses from 20 to 21 billion kWh, the spike for the small plant system is from 3.0 to 3.8 cents, a spread of .8 cents, while for the larger plant system it is from

Table 2.12 The small base-load plant (increasing fixed costs)

Annual sales (dependable output) (billion kWh)	Annual fixed costs (millions of constant dollars)				Fixed costs per kWh (¢)	Dependable energy capacity factor (%)
	Base system	Plant #4-A & #4-B	Plant #5-A & #5-B	Small plant system		
20	600			600	3.0	100
21		200		800	3.8	84
22					3.6	88
23					3.5	92
24					3.3	96
25		200		800	3.2	100
26		400		1,000	3.8	87
27					3.7	90
28					3.6	93
29					3.4	97
30				1,000	3.3	100
31			225	1,225	4.0	89
32					3.8	91
33					3.7	94
34					3.6	97
35			225	1,225	3.5	100
36			450	1,450	4.0	90
37					3.9	93
38					3.8	95
39					3.7	98
40	600	400	450	1,450	3.6	100

3.0 to 4.8 cents, a spread of 1.8 cents. Of course, there are twice as many spikes in Table 2.12 as in Table 2.11.

Table 2.13 compares the unit costs of the two systems. Unit costs are less for outputs from 21 to 25 billion kWh, and for outputs from 31 to 35 billion kWh, the outputs at which Plants #4-A and #5-A are substitutes for the initial stages of utilization of larger Plants 4 and 5.

Aggregate savings in costs are calculated from the unit cost savings. These also are shown in Table 2.13. (For example, at an output of 21 billion kWh, a unit cost saving of 1.0 cents per kWh results in a total saving of $210 million.) The total of these savings differs from the expected total due to rounding of the unit costs in Tables 2.11 and 2.12.

Expected savings are calculated from the differences in the fixed-cost burdens in the corresponding output stages as between Plants #4-A and #5-A, and Plants 4 and 5.

2.7 The Small Base-Load Plant

Table 2.13 Comparison of costs of large and small plant systems (Tables 2.11 and 2.12)

	Fixed costs per kWh (¢)		Reduction in costs due to smaller plants	
Annual output (billions of kWh)	Large plant system	Small plant system	Per kWh (¢)	Total ($ millions)
21	4.8	3.8	1.0	210
22	4.5	3.6	0.9	198
23	4.3	3.5	0.8	184
24	4.2	3.3	0.9	216
25	4.0	3.2	0.8	200
Subtotal				1,008[a]
26	3.8	3.8	–	–
27	3.7	3.7	–	–
28	3.6	3.6	–	–
29	3.4	3.4	–	–
30	3.3	3.3	–	–
31	4.7	4.0	0.7	217
32	4.5	3.8	0.7	224
33	4.4	3.7	0.7	231
34	4.3	3.6	0.7	238
35	4.1	3.5	0.6	210
Subtotal				1,120[b]
36	4.0	4.0	–	–
37	3.9	3.9	–	–
38	3.8	3.8	–	–
39	3.7	3.7	–	–
40	3.6	3.6	–	–
Total				$2,128[c]

[a]Differs from $1.0 billion due to rounding of per kWh costs.
[b]Differs from $1.125 billion due to rounding of per kWh costs.
[c]Differs from $2.125 billion for reasons stated above.

This calculation is given in Table 2.14:

With due regard to the heroic assumptions which have been the basis of this scenario, it would seem that there is little doubt that equivalent smaller plants will be cheaper than larger plants, provided that they can be constructed at about the same cost per unit of output. Of course, that is an essential and perhaps elusive proviso. Over many years of history, larger capacity plant elements, both electric and gas, have been cheaper than smaller capacity units.

Distributed generation: The "small" plants represented by this scenario are not really small except in relation to the large plants for which they are substitutes.

Table 2.14 Cost differences between large and small plants

| | Millions of dollars | | |
| | Fixed-cost burden | | Reduction in |
Outputs	Large plants	Small plants	burden
21	1,000	800	200
22	1,000	800	200
23	1,000	800	200
24	1,000	800	200
25	1,000	800	200
			1,000
31	1,450	1,225	225
32	1,450	1,225	225
33	1,450	1,225	225
34	1,450	1,225	225
35	1,450	1,225	225
			1,125
	Total reduction (savings)		2,125

Under the heading, "Thinking Small: Onsite Power Generation May Soon Be Big," Keith G. Davidson and Gerald W. Braun[13] suggest much smaller plants. They write (1993),

> Eventually, smaller and cleaner generation units located near major load centers could begin to supplement power from central plants.
>
> The technologies necessary to this transition are emerging in the form of "distributed generation." These technologies typically produce power on a relatively small scale (less than 50 MW per unit) and can be cited in congested urban areas as well as near remote customers. This allows utilities to meet new demand for electricity without building central generating stations or upgrading the power delivery system—in other words, at lower costs.[14]

2.8 The Peaking or Firming-Up Plant

Both electric and gas utilities may find that they have ample supplies of energy, but are deficient in peaking capability. In this situation it may be the best course to add a peaking resource rather than the usual balanced peak-energy resource. For the

---

[13] Davidson is director of power generation and transportation systems, Gas Research Institute, and Braun is director of advanced energy systems research, Pacific Gas and Electric Company. Davidson, K.G. and Braun, G.W., "Thinking Small: On site Power Generation May Soon Be Big," *Public Utilities Fortnightly*, July 1, 1993.

[14] In 1967, in a report prepared for the Bonneville Power Administration, the writer suggested the use of gas "in relatively small (20,000 kW to 50,000 kW each) gas turbine plants at the perimeters of electric transmission lines," for system reliability, peak shaving, supplementing hydro storage, or system reserve. Conkling, Inc., "The Potential for the Natural Gas Industry in the Pacific Northwest," US Dept. of the Interior, Bonneville Power Administration, 1967.

2.8 The Peaking or Firming-Up Plant

electric utility, this might mean adding a peaking generating plant; for the gas utility, it might mean adding storage capacity, doubling up on mains from its city gate to its distribution system, adding compression, or similar measures. (In the case of either utility it might mean the purchase of peaking from an outside source, an alternative we do not specifically consider in this scenario. Where that alternative exists, the utility will follow the least-cost route.)

A peaking deficiency also may arise because the utility is forced to sell energy on a non-firm basis since it does not have the capacity to guarantee delivery to customers during peak periods. Or, a version of the same, the utility may have the opportunity to buy non-firm energy which it could resell as firm energy if it had the capability to augment its non-firm energy when necessary.

For reasons such as the above, utilities may find it desirable to add special-purpose facilities. The construction of a model to fit such an uncertain array of circumstances is far from simple, and our attempt is far from perfect.

Continuing with electric operations as a base, we select for illustration a peaking generating plant to firm up an interruptible supply. To do this, we must put aside our assumption of prior scenarios that the capacity provided, while stated solely in energy terms, is capable of serving both the peak and energy requirements of the load as it exists. In other words, until this scenario we have assumed that the energy capability is delivered so as to fit the system load shape. This had the virtue of avoiding the complexity of distinguishing capacity as being firm or non-firm, or based upon assumptions as to sales load factors, diversity factors, etc. For the present case we must differentiate between firm and non-firm outputs, and hence at the relative values of firm and non-firm sales. We must again resort to heroically simplistic assumptions.

Referring back to Table 2.4 for the base system at outputs of from 11 to 20 billion kWh per year (the same beginning point as for our main case scenarios of Tables 2.7, 2.9, and 2.11), it will be recalled that the system was assumed to be able to produce up to 20 billion kWh annually so as to match the utility's load shape. With no change in the total market, we now assume that the system is able to produce only 15 billion kWh with sufficient peaking to serve maximum demands. The system can still generate the full 20 billion kWh (i.e., its energy capability has not been reduced), but it is short on peaking to be able to deliver the remaining 5 billion kWh as firm power. This results in the following output configuration given in Table 2.15.

Since interruptible energy can be sold only at a lower price than firm energy, we must assume a price for interruptible. For illustrative purposes, we assume 1.5 cents per kWh after covering variable costs.

The dilution of the output from all firm to part firm-part interruptible, means that the firm per kWh revenue requirement to satisfy fixed costs (which remain unchanged in total at $600 million per year), will be increased for outputs above 15 billion kWh. The relevant firm service revenue requirements, with and without dilution, are given in Table 2.16:

The dilution has raised the firm service revenue requirement, for 16 billion kWh annually, from 3.8 cents per kWh to 3.9 cents, an increase of 0.1 cents per firm kWh;

Table 2.15 Annual sales capability with and without interruptible

Total market	Firm	Interruptible
11	11	–
12	12	–
13	13	–
14	14	–
15	15	–
Total market	Firm	Interruptible
16	15	1
17	15	2
18	15	3
19	15	4
20	15	5

Table 2.16 Comparative results of firm and split outputs

Annual output (billion kWh)	Annual fixed costs ($ millions)	All firm (¢/kWh)[a]	Split output Int. rev. ($ millions)	Residual fixed costs	Firm rev. reg. (¢/kWh)
16	600	3.8	15	585	3.9
17	600	3.5	30	570	3.8
18	600	3.3	45	555	3.7
19	600	3.2	60	540	3.6
20	600	3.0	75	525	3.5

[a]Per Table 2.3.

at the 20 billion kWh stage of production, an increase of 0.5 cents per firm kWh, from 3.0 cents per kWh to 3.5 cents. Any steps which would reduce these increases to firm customers would be of benefit to these customers.

One route would be to purchase firming-up capacity (i.e., buying peaking without energy, probably through an energy exchange). If such capacity could be purchased so that the revenue requirement per firm kWh (the right hand column of the preceding table) would be reduced, the transaction would be advantageous to firm customers. An energy exchange would reduce the volumes available for interruptible customers. The reduction would depend upon the terms of the exchange, which might range from one-to-one to a multiple-to-one basis.

A more complicated route would be to add on-system peaking capacity. Since a generating plant cannot be operated without producing kilowatt-hours, such a plant would add energy as well as peaking. However, it would not be necessary that the on-system peaking plant be capable of producing the full energy output of the basic

2.8 The Peaking or Firming-Up Plant

Table 2.17 Output and costs with peaking plant

Output capability (billion kWh) Peaking			Sales (billion kWh)		Annual costs ($ millions)			Rev req. per kWh for firm (¢)
Base	Peaking	Total	Firm	Int.	Total	Int. Revenue	Balance for firm	
20	2.5	22.5	16	6.5	712.5	97.5	615.0	3.8
I	I	I	17	5.5	I	82.5	630.0	3.7
I	I	I	18	4.5	I	67.5	645.0	3.6
I	I	I	19	3.5	I	52.5	660.0	3.5
20	2.5	22.5	20	2.5	712.5	37.5	675.0	3.4

systems, since that system can produce the full energy requirement, being deficient only in peaking.

Since we have not specified any particular load shape for the basic system (and do not wish to add a further complexity by doing so at this juncture), we will assume that the peaking plant would generate one-half of the end-period volume to be firmed up, one-half of 5 billion kWh or 2½ billion, and that the fixed cost of such output is $45 million per billion kWh or $112.5 million per year. (This is the highest cost invoked in the preceding increasing cost scenario.) We now assume that the market is large enough to absorb the full capability of the combined plants (a change from the assumption that the market is limited to the 16–20 range).

With these assumptions, output, fixed costs, and the fixed-revenue requirement for firm sales are Table 2.17:

Given the assumptions (heroic, indeed) for each route, the results compare as in Table 2.18:

We do not specifically posit a case covering the opposite situation, namely where a utility has ample peaking capability but is energy deficient. In such a case the utility may attempt to exchange its surplus peaking for energy. Or it may advance the coming online of its next general purpose plant, which would provide the needed additional energy at least over the initial stages of production of that plant. In this event, it would have an early-on superabundance of peaking available for sale.

Table 2.18 Fixed cost revenue requirement for firm service with peaking

Split output without peaking (¢)	Purchase of peaking with energy exchange	Addition of on-system peaking
3.9	Less than 3.9¢	3.8¢
3.8	Less than 3.8¢	3.7¢
3.7	Less than 3.7¢	3.6¢
3.6	Less than 3.6¢	3.5¢
3.5	Less than 3.5¢	3.4¢

2.9 Power Purchases by Electric Utilities from Non-utility Sources, Bypass, and Discounts

Unless most prognosticators of the future of the electric industry are wrong, the tide is running strongly in favor of purchases by utilities of an appreciable part of their power requirements from non-utility sources.[15]

Part and parcel of this trend, and perhaps the casual factor, is the growing threat of "retail wheeling" or "open access," whereby an electric utility would be required to make available its transmission and distribution facilities to carry power from a non-utility generator to an end-user customer. This would enable larger industrial customers to bypass the utility's generation by buying their power supply directly from independent power producers (now EWGs, or exempt wholesale generators) or cogenerators (or marketers, brokers, or other sources) to obtain a cheaper price than the utility can offer. The California PUC formally proposed retail wheeling in an April 20, 1994 "Restructuring" order.[16]

This scenario may be of help in sorting out the fixed-cost elements which may be considered in making comparative evaluations of power purchases, on the one hand, and bypass, on the other hand. Table 2.7 is the foundation for each of these evaluations. Wheeling is assumed.

2.9.1 Purchase by a Utility

Table 2.7 covers a utility's base system plus Plants #4 and #5, the latter added under decreasing cost conditions.

At somewhere in the mid-range of outputs with Plant #4 online, the utility must consider the addition of Plant #5 or some other alternative to accommodate future load growth. As Plant #4 approaches full production, its fixed costs will decline to 2.9 cents per kWh. With Plant #5, the cost spike will escalate costs to 3.6 cents per kWh. Thereafter, unit costs decline over nine stages of production to a low of 2.8 cents.

Assumption: An Independent Power Producer (IPP) plans to construct a plant with a 5 billion kWh dependable energy capability. This plant can produce each billion kWh annually at a fixed cost of $260 million per billion kWh. (The same cost as assumed in Table 2.7 for Plant #5)

---

[15] In fact, the Division of Ratepayer Advocates of the California PUC, in its "Comments" of June 8, 1994 on the Commission's April 20, 1994 OIR and OII, R.94-04-031 and I.94-04-032, expresses a "preference that utilities ultimately be completely out of the generation business . . . . [when there is] a healthy wholesale generation market that can provide for all the utility's generation and reliability needs." California PUC, Division of Ratepayer Advocates, "Comments" on the Commission's April 20, 1994 Restructuring Order, June 8, 1994.

[16] "Wholesale wheeling" or "transmission access" is already required by the Energy Policy Act of 1992. FERC can require a utility to transmit power from an EWG to a purchasing utility (a wholesale customer of the EWG). But "retail wheeling," to an end-user customer, is still to be mandated. Public Utilities Commission of the State of California, Order of April 20, 1994, op. cit.

2.9 Power Purchases by Electric Utilities

The IPP sees this fixed-cost picture as in Table 2.19:

Table 2.19 Range of competitive costs

Annual output (billion kWh)	Annual cost ($ millions)	Fixed cost per kWh (¢)	
1	130	13.0	
2	I	6.5	(Non-competitive)
3	I	4.3	
3.5	I	3.7	(Possible)
4.0	I	3.3	(Competitive)
4.5	I	2.9	(Range)
5.0	130	2.6	

Clearly, the IPP cannot be competitive unless it can sell the bulk of its capability. After gauging the market by contacting prospective industrial buyers, the IPP concludes that it can sell 2.5 billion kWh annually to industry, and reach a total of 4.5 billion kWh annually if the utility will buy 2 billion kWh each year. The IPP offers a price which includes a fixed-cost component of 2.9 cents per kWh.[17] This is the same cost as that shown for the utility when Plant #4 reaches full utilization (output of 30 billion kWh), but less than the cost of 3.6 cents per kWh when Plant #5 first comes online.

Should the utility take the offer?

2.9.2 Construction by the Utility of Its Own Plant

Presumably the utility could build the same plant at the same cost as the IPP (we see no reason why it couldn't). If it did, the following would be substituted for the 31–32 billion kWh outputs of Table 2.7 (Table 2.20). (These are the initial outputs with large-scale Plant #5 online, reflected in Table 2.7.)

2.9.3 Purchase of IPP Power

If the utility accepted the IPP offer of 2 billion kWh annually at a price of 2.9 cents per kWh for fixed costs (with a requirement to take-or-pay) it could substitute a $58 million per year cost increment for a $130 million increment, with the results in Table 2.21.

Under the above assumptions, the savings in fixed costs of $72 million annually, a total of $144 million over 2 years with the power purchase, would seem clearly to outweigh the excess capability for exchange or other disposition available with the company-owned plant.

---

[17] It also offers system control and delivery arrangements satisfactory to the utility (deliveries to fit the utility's load shape, an appropriate share of reactive, scheduling, etc.).

Table 2.20 Utility-owned new plant

| Output[a] (billion kWh) | Annual fixed costs ($ millions) ||| Fixed costs per kWh[b] (¢) |
	Base plus Plant #4	New small plant	Total	
31	870	130	1,000	3.23
32	870	130	1,000	3.13

[a] In addition, under Table 2.4's assumption of the utility's total load, the utility would have excess capability, declining from 4 to 1 billion kWh annually during the first four stages of production, which could be used for exchange, etc. Its resources would be in balance with its load at the fifth stage, 35 billion kWh.
[b] To hundredths of a cent.

Table 2.21 Purchase of IPP power

| Output (billion kWh) | Annual fixed costs ($ millions) ||| Fixed costs per kWh[a] (¢) |
	Base plus Plant #4	Purchase (take-or-pay)	Total	
31[b]	870	58	928	2.99
32	870	58	928	2.90

[a] To hundredths of a cent.
[b] In addition, the utility would have 1 billion kWh available for exchange, etc., at this stage of production.

Table 2.22 Comparative costs of generation alternatives

| Output (billion kWh) | System average fixed costs per kWh (¢) |||
	With large Plant #5[a]	With utility—owned small plant	With purchase from IPP
31	3.65	3.23	2.99
32	3.53	3.13	2.90

[a] Per Table 2.4, to hundredths of a cent.

On a system-wide per kWh basis, unit costs would compare as in Table 2.22:

Decision: Other factors being equal, the utility would decide to postpone large-scale Plant #5, and would forego (or postpone) construction of its own small plant in favor of accepting the IPP offer of 2 billion kWh. It would foresee that additional capacity would be needed for the 33 billion kWh stage of production.

The utility would have no difficulty in accepting a long term take-or-pay contract with the IPP, since the fixed costs of that contract are lower-cost substitutes for the higher fixed costs which it would incur with the alternatives considered.

2.9 Power Purchases by Electric Utilities   53

Comment: The above scenario illustrates the magnitude of the fixed-cost savings which are possible if the output of a plant operating at full utilization can be substituted for the output of a plant of equivalent cost operating at only partial utilization. (Recall the prior related scenario dealing with the small base-load plant, where output utilization was dependent upon load growth.)

It is easy to overstate the significance of these results in terms of long-range public policy. The most cogent question is, why in the world would a generating plant (or other major electric or natural gas facility) be operated at a poor capacity factor? The answer is, because utility facilities are built to satisfy load growth. Larger capacity facilities generally are cheaper per unit of capacity than smaller ones. They can be sized larger with economic benefit. A parallel pragmatic reason is that it is not efficient to size today's capacity solely to serve only today's loads. Capacity for tomorrow should be built in. Beyond generating stations, with their associated issues of sitting and outgoing transformation and transmission, good examples of why allowance for growth should be built into utility capacity, rather than added incrementally, are: an electric transmission line crossing occupied or environmentally sacred terrain, or through a corridor restricted in size; a natural gas main running under public streets; or even the electric service drop or the gas service main supplying individual customers. The public convenience requires that disrupting construction activity be kept to a minimum.

It could be that super-accurate advance planning of electric requirements over a broad area, perhaps via a super-pool, could integrate requirements with supply so as to attain a full or near full plant utilization when new plants come online. To some extent this has occurred. But whether the process can be perfected, if tried, remains to be seen.

2.9.4 Bypass of the Utility

The situation just reviewed is one where an IPP offer is of advantage to a utility. This may be a unique situation. What is not unique is the threat of bypass of the utility; i.e., loss of load by the utility due to large customers switching from the utility to an IPP, because IPP offers a lower price.

The IPP's do not have the utility's obligation to have capacity ready to satisfy demands as they occur. They attempt to garner a market for the whole of their planned output. They can do this if they are allowed to capture large users previously served by the utility (or perhaps groups of smaller users buying collectively), as they would be under retail wheeling.

The prior illustration assumed that the IPP was able to attract industrial customers requiring an output of 2.5 billion kWh per year, selling another two billion to a utility. Here we look at a different utility, the one who previously had served some of the lost industrial customers. We assumed that this present utility loses 2 billion kWh of annual load just as it is beginning its 34 billion kWh stage of production, at which stage the fixed-cost component in its rates is 3.324 cents per kWh. The

Table 2.23 Results of bypass opportunities

Output (billion kWh)	Fixed costs Per kWh	Output (billion kWh)	Fixed costs Per kWh	Increase in fixed costs for remaining load Per kWh	Total
31	3.645¢	31	3.645¢	–	–
32	3.531	32	3.531	–	–
33	3.424	33	3.424	–	–
34	3.324	32	3.531	0.207¢	$66.2 million
35	3.229	33	3.424	0.195	$64.4 million
36	3.139	34	3.324	0.185	$62.9 million
//		//			
40	2.825	38	2.974	0.149	$56.6 million

IPP offers a fixed cost of 2.9 cents per kWh, a saving of 15% for the buyer. For the moment we assume that the utility is not permitted to match the IPP's lower fixed-cost component.

Before the loss of load, unit costs (to fractions of a cent) for the Plant #5 stages of production are as stated in the first two columns. Revised unit costs, reflecting the loss of load are stated in the next two columns (Table 2.23).

The boxed area highlights the immediate impact of the bypass. The increase in fixed costs (representing lost revenue) which would have been absorbed by sales to the bypasser(s), but which now must be picked-up by the remaining customers, are indicated in the two right hand columns. These total $131 million over the initial 2 years of the bypass. The impact per stage of production declines somewhat as system output approaches full system utilization due to the decline in fixed costs per-unit with increased outputs.

There is always, of course, a ray of sunshine even in a bad scenario. Here the sunshine is that the necessity for new generation capacity is delayed by the bypass for the time equivalent of two stages of production. Further, it seems reasonable to conclude that there is a limit to the utility loads which can be bypassed. When this limit is reached, plants (even smaller ones) will not be fully loaded at inception. Thus, the chain of high to low fixed costs per kWh over a range of outputs as we have reviewed in the earlier scenarios again comes into play.

The public policy issue: acknowledging that many economists contend to the contrary, nonetheless value judgments do enter into economics. The public policy issue here is, is the bargain gained by the large industrial bypasser(s) sufficient to override the resulting higher costs to the remaining body of the utility's customers? More narrowly, should bypass be encouraged (or even permitted) as an appropriate public policy, so as to lower rates to bulk users?

The essence of this public policy issue was raised early on by Frank Taussig, assistant commissioner of the Oregon PUC, in testimony before the Oregon Energy Facility Sitting Council (March 15, 1984).

2.9 Power Purchases by Electric Utilities

For sake of example, let us assume that some industry is contemplating a 100 mw cogeneration source. From the industry's point of view, the cost of cogenerated power may be 4¢/kWh after the value of steam is accounted for. (For instance, the full cost may be 6.5¢/kWh, but the value of the steam may be 2.5¢/kWh.) If the serving utility has a price of 4.5¢/kWh, the industry saves 0.5¢/kWh, which works out to a benefit to the industry of $3,504,000 per year (assuming an 80 percent capacity factor). This certainty looks attractive to the paper mill.

However, the serving utility has lost sales equal to the 100 mw generated by the paper mill. In the short run, since the utility has already put into place sufficient generating capacity to serve the paper mill, the utility has running costs (variable costs) of only 1.5¢/kWh to 2.0¢/kWh. Even at 2.0¢/kWh the utility would have made a margin of 2.5¢/kWh on those sales, and not making those sales therefore means that $17,520,000 of margin is lost. This lost margin, which represents primarily the fixed costs of generating capacity already installed by the utility, must be picked up by other customers of the utility.

Thus, although the paper mill comes out ahead by $3,504,000, the rest of Oregon will suffer to the tune of $17,520,000. This is a reflection of the fact that we currently have a surplus of generating capacity. So long as we have a surplus, it cannot be economically correct to add more capacity.

2.9.5 *An Alternative to Bypass: A Discounted Price*

Just above we examined the impact of a loss of load of 2 billion kWh annually due to bypass, under the assumption that the utility was not permitted to match (or did not choose to match) the fixed-cost component of 2.9 cents per kWh offered by the IPP. Now, we reverse this assumption. The utility meets the IPP's competitive offer by discounting its component from 3.324 cents per kWh to 2.9 cents.

Table 2.24 summarizes the results. Part A shows that at the reduced component, the sales which otherwise would have been lost, contribute to $58 million annually to fixed costs, bringing down the total fixed costs to be borne by core customers from $1.130 billion annually to $1.072 billion.

Part B shows that the $58 million revenue at the discounted price component reduces the $66.2–$56.6 million loss which a bypass would have engendered to no greater than an $8.5 million loss—and no less than a $1.4 million gain, over the seven 34–40 billion kWh stages of production. There is a net gain in the last two stages of production because the 2.9 cents per kWh fixed-cost component paid by the industrial customer(s) is higher than the component which otherwise would have been incorporated in the rates.

The public policy issue: If the foregoing exercise dealing with competitive pricing to avoid bypass even remotely mirrors reality there would seem to be little question that the utility should be permitted to offer a competitive price to a potential bypasser. But does a discounted (competitive) price, offered only to customers who are in a position to bypass, constitute unjust or unreasonable discrimination?

This is not an easy question. (The writer says this as one who for many years has wrestled with "discriminatory—yes?" or "discriminatory—no?" On one side is the catechism precept, "Everyone must be treated equally;" on the other side is the market dogma, "Prices must be competitive." Like east and west, the twain do not mesh readily.)

Table 2.24 A discounted price to industrial customer(s) to prevent bypass

Part A: Fixed costs borne by core customers with discounted price to retain sale

Output (billion kWh)			Fixed costs (millions of dollars)		
Total	Disc. sales	Core sales	Table 2.7 total ($)	Less: disc. sales	Balance for core ($)
34	2	32	1,130	58	1,072
35	2	33			
36	2	34			
37	2	35			
38	2	36			
39	2	37			
40	2	38	1,130	58	1,072

Part B: Loss/gain due to discounted price to retain sale

	Millions of dollars				
	2 billion kWh bypass rev. loss ($)		Discounted rev.	Net loss/gain with discounted rates	
Output	Per kWh (¢)		Gain ($)	Net loss ($)	Net gain ($)
34	3.324	66.2	58.0	8.2	
35	3.229	64.4		6.4	
36	3.139	62.9		4.9	
37	3.054	61.3		3.3	
38	2.974	59.4		1.4	
39	2.897	58.1			0.1
40	2.825	56.6	58.0		1.4

The issue of discrimination, however, rests upon the notion that the basic rates are "just and reasonable." Presumably they are so. But, as discussed in Chap. 3, rates are developed through a series of allocations of joint costs, none of which can be proved or disproved except judgmentally. Perhaps new allocations, oriented more toward the competitiveness of the final results, would dispose of the discrimination issue. (See Chap. 5, The Value Approach to Pricing.)

A secondary policy issue is whether lost revenue resulting from a discounted price should be made up through higher core rates, or shared by ratepayers and stockholders, or fall entirely upon stockholders.

2.9.6 Arrested or Contracted Output

The prior scenarios presuppose growth—in demand and hence of output—although the rate of growth is not specified. Current emphasis upon energy conservation dictates that the opposite condition be explored, namely, where output stops growing or even diminishes.[18]

The effect of this condition depends upon when it occurs.

If growth stops or is retarded when the existing plant is operating near the point of full utilization, new plant can be postponed. This delays the cost spike associated with a major new facility which at the outset will be only lightly loaded. If the new facility is more expensive than existing facilities, the higher costs of such facility also will be delayed.

On the other hand, if growth stops when the existing plant is operating well below full utilization, with plenty of spare capacity, the decreases in unit costs which otherwise would be achieved are sacrificed. Negative savings result.

In the first situation, the costs of demand-side management or other energy conservation measures will be offset in whole or in part by

a) The savings in capital costs resulting from the delay of the investment in the new plant which otherwise would be required earlier, or (the same in different terms)
b) The savings in per-unit costs resulting from the delay in the cost spike which otherwise would be experienced earlier.

In the latter case, there is no offset to the costs of energy conservation (except, perhaps, at some indefinite future time) and in addition to conservation costs, are costs equivalent to the per-unit cots savings which are foregone as a fuller utilization of the plant capacity is prevented or delayed. If the effect of conservation is so extreme as to cause a reduction in output below the prevailing level, the costs to be added to the costs of conservation will include not only the above-mentioned foregone savings in future lower per-unit costs, but also the increase to higher earlier levels of per-unit costs arising from the reduction in output.

There is no doubt that the reduction in output entails serious problems whatever the cause. The cause may be conservation, loss of load due to bypass, price elasticity, economic recession—it doesn't matter. Customers pay more for using less. They do not take kindly to such treatment from their energy supplier.[19]

Because there are so many variations in the timing and specific nature of the costs which must be dealt with in evaluating this no-growth scenario, we do not attempt to devise illustrations. A reexamination of the earlier tables, this time approaching them from the bottom-up rather than from the top-down, will give a bird's-eye view of the utility's internal dynamics.

2.9.7 Summary of Findings

The summary scenarios (Tables 2.7, 2.9, and 2.11).

---

[18] The writer is tempted to quote the question which appeared in a different context in bold type on the cover of the May 16, 1994 issue of *Business Week*: "Why are we so afraid of GROWTH?"

[19] This problem is discussed in relation to price elasticity in Chapter 5.

(1) Each shows decreasing per-unit fixed costs as the utilization of capacity improves. This is an axiomatic result.

Taking the full five plant systems as illustrative for each case, in index numbers with the unit cost at an 80% dependable energy capacity factor as 100, unit costs decline as shown in Table 2.25:

Table 2.25 Decline in fixed costs with improvement in utilization

Dependable energy capacity factor	Plants #1–#5 (80% DECF = 100)		
	Dec.	Constant	Inc.
80%	100	100	100
90	89	87	89
100	80	79	80

(2) The impact on per-unit fixed costs of the changing magnitude of the added costs for each output addition is felt for the decreasing and increasing cost scenarios, but the composite (rolled-in) unit cost change is less than the change in the new investment costs.

Decreasing costs: For this scenario, investment and other fixed costs per billion kWh of dependable output declined to $27 million for Plant #4 and to $26 million for Plant #5, as compared to $30 million for the base system. These declines are 10 and 13%, respectively.

Associated fixed costs per unit, at a 100% dependable energy capacity factor, declined to 2.9 cents per kWh with Plant #4 online, and to 2.8 cents per kWh with both Plants #4 and #5 online, as compared to 3.0 cents per kWh for the base system, declines of 3 and 7%, respectively. (Table 2.26)

Thus,

Table 2.26 Decline in costs with decline in investment

	Decline in new investment	Decline in composite per kWh cost
4 Plants	10%	3%
5 Plants	13%	7%

The impact of new investment at a lower cost will be dampened by compositing new with old higher-cost investment to reach a rolled-in per kWh cost.

Constant costs: By definition, the relationships remained unchanged.

Increasing costs: Here investment costs are increased to $40 million for Plant #4 and to $45 million for Plant #5, from the $30 million for the base system, increases of 33 1/3 and 50%, respectively.

With Plant #4 online, unit costs rose to 3.3 cents per kWh at 100% dependable energy capacity factor, and to 3.6 cents per kWh with both Plants #4 and #5 online, rising from 3.0 cents per kWh for the base system, increases of 10 and 20%, respectively. (Table 2.27)

2.10 Variable Costs   59

Thus,

Table 2.27 Increase in costs with increase in investment

	Increase in new investment	Increase in composite per kWh cost
4 Plants	33 1/3%	10%
5 Plants	50%	20%

The impact of new investment at a higher cost will be damped by compositing new with old lower-cost investment to reach a rolled-in per kWh cost.

Assuming the same overall fixed cost per unit of output (which assumption disregards the economies of scale), a series of small capacity additions will be less expensive in terms of fixed costs than equivalent larger additions. However, variable costs may be higher.

Power exchanges with other systems often may be the best route when a utility is deficient in either peaking or energy. However, a peaking plant is an alternative for a peaking deficiency provided its cost is viable and/or there is a robust interruptible market for surplus energy.

Purchases: If a utility needs additional energy, and if the price is right, power purchases from non-utility sources may be a least-cost alternative to utility-constructed new capacity.

Bypass: The impact of bypass is destructive, the degree of the harm being dependent upon the size of the revenue loss.

Discounted prices: If a utility is permitted to offer a discounted (competitive) price to a potential bypasser, the revenue loss is only partial, not full. Thus, the destructive impact of bypass is mitigated. However, the question of whether a discounted price offered on only a limited basis is discriminatory, must be faced.

When growth within the capacity of existing plant is arrested by conservation, the per-unit economies of fuller utilization are postponed.

When growth requiring new plant is arrested, the cost spike and the investment in new plant are postponed. Depending upon whether the new plant is more or less expensive, either higher or lower unit costs also are postponed.

The costs of conservation measures will either be a reduction in the advantages of postponement, or an addition to the disadvantages, depending upon the circumstances of occurrence.

2.10 Variable Costs

Oil, natural gas, and coal are the three most common fuels used for electric generation. The costs of purchasing these fuels comprise the most important variable costs of the electric utility.

Natural gas is the commodity transported and/or sold by gas pipelines and distributors. If the cost of buying this gas at the wellhead (i.e., the price paid to the producers) is commingled with the pipelines' and distributors' other costs, it becomes by far the most important element of their variable costs. On the other hand, if the gas itself is considered simply to be a commodity transported long distance by pipelines and distributed locally by distributors, as a railroad or other common carrier transports freight, it is not a part per se of the cost package of these utilities. From this viewpoint, it can be excluded from their variable costs, which for pipelines then would consist only of the ebb and flow with volume of relatively minor non-fixed expenditures for operations and maintenance. For distributors, a part of their pipeline bills would be fixed, with other parts being variable, together with most O&M expenses.

To this point, except for Table 2.1 and Fig. 2.2, variable costs have not been incorporated into the cost analysis. This has been done for different reasons in the two industries.

For the electric industry, while the costs of fuel for generation (and other variable costs) are significant, they seldom will be sufficiently large as to change the direction of average costs away from the direction indicated by fixed costs. This is generally true even though the prices of fuel tend to be highly erratic.

For natural gas, the earlier cost analyses parallel the pipeline and distributor segments of the industry. These segments are not subject to "the tail that wags the dog" vagaries of the market-set producer price. Like electric, absent the producer share, the economics of the operations of pipelines and distributors are driven by the surge of fixed costs. And, like electric, the direction of their average costs, the producer component excluded, will tend to be the same as their fixed costs.

It is the writer's opinion that the field price of natural gas is influenced by so many extraneous conditions as to be virtually unpredictable except relatively. The energy market, local, national, and world-wide, sets the producer price. The temptation to predict is near overpowering. It would be satisfying to be the guru of oil and natural gas prices. Many try, and these will vehemently disagree with the writer's opinion. There is one prediction, however, which the writer thinks is safe and which may be of help in evaluating the prices (and the direction of prices) which producers will charge. It is this: for gas supplied for core residential and commercial markets, and to some degree for industrial markets as well, the producer price, after allowance for the costs of gas transmission and distribution, will continue to permit these several markets to be supplied at a burner-tip price which is competitive with other energies.

Having said that, we conclude that variable costs are just that and not only by definition. They expand and contract in total with output. But also, both in total and per unit, they may change erratically with changes in the price per barrel of oil, per mcf of natural gas, or per ton of coal. Other variable costs also may change, but in all probability less erratically.

The volatility of oil and gas prices to either utility may rest in part upon the extent to which they rely upon spot market purchases. These short-term purchases tend to be unstable both as to price and availability. Longer-term purchases, guaranteed by contract, may substitute dependability but at a higher price. A given utility may rely upon a combination of both types of supply. Some may seek a degree of price stability by venturing into the futures market or other derivatives. In any event, contrary to our prior simplifying assumption, it is unlikely that variable costs will be constant

2.10 Variable Costs   61

per unit. They may differ from one generating plant to another or from one stage of production to another for a given plant. Gas supplies purchased by pipelines and distributors also will vary from one source of supply to another. The most likely pattern for these utilities is that the gas stream which they own or transport for other parties will arise from a mix of sources at a mix of prices. The constant variable costs per unit in Table 2.1 and Fig. 2.2 are illustrative, not representative.

2.10.1 The Dominance of Variable Costs

One point mentioned elsewhere needs clarification. It has been stated that to serve peak demands, the most efficient resource will be brought online first, the next efficient second, etc., until the last is the least efficient resource required to meet the peak. This is an operational rule which applies equally to generating plants owned by an electric utility, or to the purchase of energy by any utility from an outside source. "Efficient" means cheapest.

In applying this rule fixed costs do not count. They are sunk costs, which do not change with the degree of utilization. They must be met in any event. Variable costs determine the generating plant to be used. A plant having higher fixed costs will be placed online if it has lower variable costs (mainly fuel costs) than other plants. This rule applies not only to the multi-plant utility system, but also to many power pools. In a "tight" pool, all of the plants of the members are centrally dispatched as if under a single ownership. The plants in the pool are placed online in the sequence of their operating costs, from the cheapest to the most expensive.

Variable costs also determine from where and from whom energy supplies will be bought. The cost of the seller is unimportant in the short term. The seller's price is what counts. The utility, electric or gas, will buy from the seller offering the lowest price.[20]

2.10.2 The Uncertainty of Variable Costs

One of the most hazardous uncertainties facing the buyer of independent power production or cogeneration power is the variable cost of these generators over time. Despite the favorable world oil situation which prevails as this is being written, another oil crisis could occur. Such recurrence would inevitably boost natural gas prices as they tend to move in tandem with escalations in the price of oil. Also, unless the nation's evaluation of priorities to the use of energy are radically different in a future crisis than they have been in the past, fuel for electric generation will be low on the scale of energy priorities. The buyer of energy from non-utility sources will be advised to look ahead to future dependability of supply, and not focus too much on which supply appears to be cheapest at the moment.

---

[20]With due consideration, of course, to the terms and conditions of sale—volumes, duration of contract, minimum and maximum takes, dependability, etc.

2.10.3 High Capital/Low Operating Costs vs. Low Capital/High Operating Costs

Electric policy decisions increasingly focus on whether to employ new plants having high capital but low operating costs, the predominant pattern of the past, or new plants with low capital but higher operating costs, as in distributed generation which many foresee as the pattern of the future. Large gas-fueled combined-cycle projects are a good example of the latter. A key and unavoidable ingredient of these decisions is the project developer's prognostication as to future gas prices (an area of prediction in which the writer, like the angels of the proverb, refuses to tread).

Table 2.29 illustrates the choice. As a benchmark against which to compare a gas-fired combined-cycle plant we adopt a central station with the costs found frequently in earlier scenarios, viz. (Table 2.28)

Table 2.28 Typical central station costs

	Central station costs per kWh
Fixed costs	3.0¢
Variable costs	1.0¢
Total	4.0¢

The above variable costs do not attempt to distinguish between the types of fuels used at the central station, which may be a mix of fuels such as shown in footnote 10, supra, or a single fuel.

Two illustrative variations of combined-cycle fixed costs are given: at 50% of central station fixed costs, or 1.5 cents per kWh; and at 75% of the central station costs, or 2.25 cents per kWh. Variable costs are broken down into non-fuel, which is maintained at a constant 0.1 cents per kWh, with the residual representing fuel (gas) costs. Obviously, the higher the fixed costs per kWh, the greater is the competitive sensitivity of the end-result total cost to the price paid for the gas used as fuel.

To translate gas costs per kWh into the cost of gas per MMBtu we adopt a heat rate of 8,000 Btu per kWh, as proposed for this type of plant by Charles M. Studness, a contributing editor to the Fortnightly.[21] This heat rate is considerably lower (better) than the 10,000 Btu per kWh which often is used as a rough rule-of-thumb for central stations. A low heat rate is evidence of a high level of thermal efficiency of generating facilities.

The central station competitive benchmark, and combined-cycle plant costs which equate to this benchmark under the two alternative fixed-cost assumptions are enclosed in the three boxes of Table 2.29. With fixed costs at 50% of the benchmark, gas costs could be 2.4 cents per kWh or $3.00 per MMBtu for a total cost equal to the central station; with fixed costs at 75%, gas costs could be only 1.65 cents per kWh or $2.06 per MMBtu. The tolerance for upward fluctuations in the price of

---

[21] Studness, C.M., "The Pressures of Competition," *Public Utilities Fortnightly*, June 15, 1993.

2.11   Matters of Judgment   63

Table 2.29 Sensitivity of costs of combined-cycle generating plant to fluctuations in the price of gas

	Cost per kwh					Gas price per MMBtu[a]
	Fixed cost	Variable costs			Total cost	
		Non-fuel	Gas	Total		
Central station benchmark						
	3.0¢			1.0¢	4.0¢	
Combined-cycle fixed costs @ 50% of central station fixed costs						
	1.5¢	0.1¢	1.4¢	1.5¢	3.0¢	$1.75
	1.5	0.1	1.9	2.0	3.5	2.38
	1.5	0.1	2.4	2.5	4.0	3.00
	1.5	0.1	2.9	3.0	4.5	3.62
	1.5	0.1	3.4	3.5	5.0	4.25
Combined-cycle fixed costs @ 75% of central station fixed costs						
	2.25¢	0.1¢	0.65¢	0.75¢	3.0¢	$0.81
	2.25	0.1	1.15	1.25	3.5	1.44
	2.25	0.1	1.65	1.75	4.0	2.06
	2.25	0.1	2.15	2.25	4.5	2.69
	2.25	0.1	2.65	2.75	5.0	3.31

[a] At assumed heat rate, $\frac{\text{Gas Cost in cent /kwh}}{.8}$ = Gas Price in $/MMBu.

purchased gas diminishes inversely with the fixed-costs component of the total cost. In other words, an increase of 1 cents per kWh in the total cost (from 4 to 5 cents) could contain an increase in the price of purchased gas to $4.25 per MMBtu, with fixed costs at 50% of the benchmark. The same 1 cents increase in the total cost could contain an increase in the price of purchased gas to only $3.31 per MMBtu, with fixed costs at 75% of the benchmark.

2.11 Matters of Judgment

Ten main tables, four charts, and a goodly number of pages of explanation and shorter tables have been devoted to the arithmetic of utility fixed and variable costs. This is necessary, for the economics of operations, and the pricing, of utilities rest upon the principles derived from an economic environment dominated by the cost mixture presented. But we cannot leave this subject with the impression that the choices facing utility managements and their regulators are merely matters of arithmetic calculation. The reality is quite the contrary. The choices are judgmental.

(1) The first choice is whether the policy should be anchored to the long-run probability of decreasing, constant, or increasing costs. Whatever the depth of the

engineering studies which are brought to bear, the selection ultimately will reflect the predilections of those making the choice. The proper numbers—the pattern of Tables 2.7, 2.9, or 2.11–will not automatically evolve.

(2) Having opted for one of the long-run perspectives, specific implementing steps for both the immediate and more distant future must be set forth. These also will mirror the mindsets of those responsible.

Under a decreasing or constant cost scenario, pricing decisions would appear to be fairly clear-cut. Prices should encourage a full utilization of plant. Energy should be available for all types of consumption which are of benefit to the economy or the well being of citizens. Conservation should be limited to the elimination of wasteful energy uses. Cost spikes are the only real problem and these can be tempered by cost averaging.

The increasing cost scenario is difficult because it is intrinsically contradictory. New capacity is more expensive, but within the capacity of existing plant fixed costs per unit decline as the plant is brought to higher utilization. Neither factor can be ignored. Which should drive price policy?

It can be argued that greater weight should be given to the decreasing cost condition of online plants since that is always present, while new plant is added only intermittently. Or it can be argued that since the long-term direction of costs is up as new more expensive capacity becomes operative, this cost direction should be decisive.

If increasing costs are taken as the bellwether, conservation measures and the expenditures for them seem to fit into a rational pricing policy. These measures retard the advance toward greater usages, and thus delay a higher-cost plateau. Prices should discourage unnecessary and luxury energy use.

Pricing generalities such as those above for the opposing alternative scenarios can be stated almost casually for they hide the real issues which go to the specifics. It is in the specifics that judgment shows its hand. For example, should all classes of customers, residential, business, agricultural, or industrial, receive the same rate treatment, or should consumption by one class be encouraged or discouraged, as the case might be, while for another class prices remain neutral and for still another, the opposite? Should one type of energy be preferred? Are generous low-cost supplies of energy for industrial use necessary for the nation's economy?

Ideological differences also enter judgmentally into the framing of price policy. As this is being written, a classic confrontation seems to be brewing between two ideologies which formerly thought in tandem. Environmentalists and conservationists have both generally opposed electric industry growth, particularly nuclear generation. Environmentalists now are promoting the electric automobile in the push for cleaner air. But the use of electricity for vehicle propulsion on any widespread scale would necessitate huge additional electric capacity. This is hardly a step toward further electric energy conservation. When the implications are realized, the reaction of energy conservationists is anybody's guess. California may soon find out.

(3) It is likely that an analyses of the utility's cost will point in different directions for different functions or different parts of its service territory. It may be, for example, that major transmission lines are heavily loaded while generating plants (for electric) or city gates (for gas) are lightly loaded. One part of operations might show

2.11 Matters of Judgment

increasing costs, while another the opposite. If rates have been unbundled functionally or by area, there is no problem. Pricing for each separate bundle can follow its own cost trend. But if kept bundled, which of the opposing trends should be adopted for pricing? Again, a matter of judgment.

(4) There is a widely accepted view that today's prices should signal tomorrow's. Simple to say. But what is a correct price signal? The writer confesses to be perplexed by this question when applied to the rank and file of the utility's customers. (Big customers do not need a price signal embedded in their present rate to look forward to the future. They will be about as well informed as utility managers and regulators.) What price for current usage will advise the homeowner, small businessman, or small farmer that the price he will have to pay in the future will be higher or lower, and by how much?

Acceptance of the validity of the price signal concept is a requisite under present "political correctness" etiquette for utilities. Nonetheless, the question needs asking.

The unsophisticated customer receives a monthly bill, for a certain number of dollars. Say the bill is for $50. If interested, the customer may read the bill more carefully and find a summary of his rate on the bill.

This may say

> Customer charge: $3 per month
> Energy charge: 10¢ per kWh
>   (or 65¢ per therm)

What does that tell the customer about the amount of his future bills, or about the per-unit prices from which his future bills will be calculated? A common sense answer is, absolutely nothing.[22]

The beginning driver, to pass his driver's test, must know traffic signals. "Red" means stop. "Green" means go. "Orange" means the signal is about to change. These are clear and unambiguous. If utility customers should be informed that their bills would trend up or down, let's tell them. A brief statement on the bill would suffice. We should stop pretending that the customer has been in fact advised by a price signal which signals nothing. The writer confesses that this harangue states only his own personal view. It is a minority view.

Dropping our doubts, we return to the point, acceding arguendo that the price should present a proper signal to the customer. While we have admitted that we do not know how this can be achieved, we do say, safely, that the matter is one of pure subjective judgment.

---

[22] Time-of-day or "Real Time Pricing" rates, if spelled out on the customer's bill, are effective in advising the customer that it is cheaper or more expensive to use energy at one time period or another, and thus may influence the customer's usage pattern. But the signal they send is a *current* message. They tell nothing about the level of *future* rates. Even rates with inverted blocking do not signal the future.

2.12 A Note on Generating Plants

Operationally, there are two types of generating plants on the mature utility system, *baseload* and *peaking*. Baseload plants are built to operate continuously, in the load valleys throughout the night as well as during the daytime hours. They have heavy fixed costs, but these are low per unit because they are spread over a large volume of kilowatt-hours. Variable costs tend to be low also, except for large changes in output ("ramping" the level of output up or down). Peaking plants, as the name suggests are used intermittently to carry increases in load beyond the capability of baseload plants. Their fixed costs are lower than for baseload units, since they do not need as many built-in safeguards, but their variable costs tend to be higher.

"Distributed Generation" is a somewhat recent development. The term involves the use of small-scale electric generating technologies installed in, or in close proximity to, the end-users location. The facilities may be internal combustion engines, combustion turbines, wind turbines, photovoltaics, or fuel cells. They may be located at disbursed customer or utility premises. They may be stand-alone or system-integrated. They may range in capacity from a few kilowatts to over 100 MW, although they usually are only one-tenth the size of units recently thought to be most economic. Combined-cycle gas turbines may require as little as one-third of the capital investment required for a new coal-fired unit.

Distributed generation units are strategically placed to have localized benefits in the generation, transmission, and distribution systems. They may replace central stations as the primary source of incremental power. Robert L. Hirsch, a highly qualified expert, declared in 1996, "Gas-fired, combined-cycle power generation has developed into the least expensive, easiest, fastest to site, environmentally attractive choice for new central station electricity generation. Accordingly, a large portion of new electrical power generation is gas-fired combined cycle."

"Cogeneration" is a subset of distributed generation. It consists of the use of a heat engine, such as a combined-cycle turbine, to simultaneously generate both electricity and useful heat. The excess heat is used in the manufacture of the product produced by the operator. This heat is wasted in a conventional power plant.

2.13 A Note on the Level of Costs

The levels of the fixed and variable costs adopted earlier in this chapter for generating plants are necessarily arbitrary, due to the variety of circumstances which influence plant design, size, type, choice of fuel or fuels, and age. A further question is whether or not ancillary services, such as load following, reactive power support, and system protection, should be included in the cost. Individual utilities have special operational problems. For example, Pacific Gas and Electric Company operates specific generating units to provide critical voltage support, thermal relief, and stability to its transmission system, and has designated certain

2.13 A Note on the Level of Costs

plants as "must run" generation. These assignments influence both categories of costs.

Faced with these uncertainties, we have devised middle-of-the-road cost data for use in our examples, ignoring extremes on either side. We note, however, that these figures seem to fall within a wide range noted by Rebecca Smith, writer for *The Wall Street Journal*. She reported NRG Energy Inc., as a prospective buyer, had offered to pay the equivalent of $600–700 for each kilowatt of generating capacity it wanted to acquire from Calpine Corp., but its offer had been rejected because Calpine claimed that its replacement cost was $1,000–1,200 per kW.[23] However, another writer, at about the same time, gave a "notational" cost of $5 million per MW for a new 1,000 nuclear-powered plant. This translates to $5,000 per kW.[24]

---

[23] Smith, R., "NRG After Rejection, Ends Calpine Effort," *The Wall Street Journal*, June 1, 2008.
[24] Denning, L., "Energy Prey Can Find Partners," *The Wall Street Journal*, November 14, 2008.

Chapter 3
The Cost Approach to Pricing: Joint Cost Allocations

It is better to be roughly right than to be precisely wrong.
-Alan Greenspan quoting John Maynard Keynes

Abstract You are the manager of a large manufacturing plant located on the plains of Kansas, and you have just been informed that your company is being sued for selling one of its several products (product A) below cost in order to meet competition. All products manufactured at the plant use the same structure, the same machinery, and the same labor force. Your lawyer advises that your best defense is to prove that your price for product A meets or exceeds the cost of producing it. In other words, you must compute the cost of product A. What will you do? You might reread Chap. 3, leading you to divide total plant costs into those costs directly assignable to product A and those incurred jointly by product A and the other products. You might then functionalize the joint costs, to the greater-than-normal degree utilized by Southern California Edison Company, thus increasing the direct costs assignable to the individual products and decreasing the joint costs to be allocated among them. The remaining joint costs could then be allocated by the relative number of product units involved. Or, if you were an energy utility, you could follow Chap. 3 directly.

3.1 Direct and Joint/Common Costs

The need for this section stems from the confluence of interrelated requirements of economics and the law.

The law requires that utility prices be "just and reasonable," which requirement has been interpreted by the courts to necessitate that these prices be based on costs. Economics requires that there be a logical methodology for determining this link between the two. The cost justification—the link of cost to prices—must be reasonable and strong.

Some parts of this chapter are duplicative, so that it can "stand alone."

Unfortunately for the economist, a satisfactory link is hard to come by. This is because in our complex economy few costs can be directly associated with a single product or service. Most costs arise from the production by a given producer of multiple and/or differentiated products, or from the offering by a given originator of more than one service.

If, in automobile manufacturing by General Motors,[1] one assembly line in one of its plants fastened only Cadillac engines to their frames, the costs of that assembly could be directly charged to Cadillac, and to Cadillac only, as a direct cost. On the other hand, if the line mounted Buick and GMC engines as well as Cadillac, the costs of the line would have to be divided (i.e., apportioned, allocated, or spread) among the three different engines, on some logical basis, because these costs are joint (or common).

Although in this text we consider "joint" and "common" to be equivalent terms, technical economics distinguishes between the two. Joint costs are incurred only for joint products that can be produced only in fixed or unvarying proportions, such as beef and hides. Common costs arise from products that are produced in common in proportions that can be varied. They result when an entity produces several services using the same facilities or inputs. The Cadillac, Buick, and GMC vehicles were produced on the same assembly line, so the costs of the line are common costs and have to be divided among the three vehicles.

An entry point in a cost allocation process is a clear-cut understanding of the sought-for end-result. In the case of the above General Motors example, this would be a determination of the individual costs of the several brands of cars manufactured by the corporation. In the case of a utility, either natural gas or electric, this would be the costs per class of customer or per class of service, since rates (prices) are set by customer class or by service class (sometimes by a combination of the two).

---

[1] We digress at this juncture to point out that automobile manufacturing, like the utilities, is a capital-intensive industry. According to the press reports, in normal operations GM was making a profit on its larger SUV's and trucks, but taking a loss on its lighter, smaller vehicles. When the market crashed, sales of the larger types plummeted, erasing its profitable sales and creating spare, unused capacity. GM's plants were expensive to construct and operate. They needed volume production to be economical. When production fell, the cost per vehicle produced kept rising as fewer units were available to absorb fixed costs.

In Chap. 2, fixed costs were considered to be paid off in equal installments of the units produced. This was because they were incurred under price regulation, which deplores an excess or a deficit in cost recovery. However, in the absence of price control, the recovery of fixed costs in the price of the product may be construed to be quite different. To the extent that the price permits, the producer may consider that excesses of the price over the actual costs are cumulative, so that at some point in the productive process it can be said that all fixed costs have been recovered by the prices charged, and that all future prices represent gain. Thus, an automobile manufacturer might state that a break-even point would be reached at production of a given number of vehicles with additional vehicles built beyond this number representing profit. This type of thinking is quite common in the oil and natural gas producing industry, the well owners considering that they had to raise a certain number of barrels of oil or cubic feet of natural gas to cover their costs with profits starting only with subsequent production.

3.2 Cost Causation

In assigning a cost, a single principle must be observed. This is, that the assignment must be to the factor (i.e., the customer or service class) for whose benefit the cost was incurred.

3.2.1 The Classification of Customers

Because of the obvious impracticability of making a separate cost analysis and establishing a separate rate for each customer of a utility, all utility customers are divided into groups called "classes of customers" or "classes of service." Each customer class brings together customers having similar characteristics (as to facilities required to serve them, habits of use, etc.) and therefore similar costs of service. Within each customer class wide variations will be found, but nevertheless the customers are sufficiently homogeneous to justify grouping them together. The classification of customers as "residential," "commercial," or "industrial" is a very common basic breakdown. The classification may be further refined by sub-breakdowns, such as dividing the residential class into "urban," "rural," and "farm."

3.2.2 The Classifications of Services

Often, type-of-service classes are intermingled with, and in practice subordinate to, type-of-customer classes. Type-of-service classifications include categories whose nomenclature is suggestive of the use to which the service is to be put, such as irrigation power or street lighting. These classifications also include categories related to the quality of the service provided, such as firm and interruptible in both electric and natural gas.

3.2.3 The Classification of Costs

Cost analyses divide all costs into two types. First and simplest to work with are direct costs, which may clearly and definitely be assigned in whole to a given rate classification. The costs of meters at customer's residences, or installing, reading, and maintaining them, are easily identified and directly traceable to the residential class of customer. So also would be the cost of an electric distribution or telephone line, or gas main, which serves only residential customers. These are direct costs of residential service. More generally, the expenses of any equipment and facilities set up for the specific purpose of serving any one class of customer or service are direct costs of the customer or service class.[2] There is therefore no difficulty in assigning

---

[2] In case of doubt as to the classification of an expense, the decision must hinge on this question—is the equipment installed to serve a specific customer or customer group? If it is clear that except for

direct costs to the individual rate classifications as they are by definition associated only with these classifications.

Joint or common costs are the second type of costs.[3] These are costs incurred in the serving of more than one customer or service class and where common equipment or staff are jointly used for this purpose. Clear illustrations are an electric generating plant, or a natural gas city-gate interconnection between pipeline and distributor, from which all classes of customers and all classes of service are served. Similarly, electric substations found throughout a power system, pressure regulating, or pumping stations of the gas distributor, involve joint costs, as normally they will serve a number of rate classes. Wages for maintenance and repair as well as investment expenses of such facilities are a part of these joint costs. Inasmuch as joint costs are those associated with facilities or services jointly used by more than one rate class, they cannot be assigned in total to any single class, but must be allocated between the responsible classes. Thus, they are much more difficult to assess and assign fairly than are direct costs.

Simply stated, the rate problem arises because there are two groups of costs which must be ascertained and in some manner apportioned among the many users (grouped either as customer or service rate classes) of the services of a utility. Direct costs incurred solely in the process of rendering a specific type-of-service to a well-defined rate class, may be assigned with the knowledge that this procedure is most equitable to all customers, for if service had not been rendered to these customers the costs would not have been incurred. The amount of expense involved is definite and the responsibility for the incurrence of the cost is self-evident. Therefore, direct costs are assigned to the users responsible for their incurrence.

Clearly, the electric service line or gas main between the utility systems' distribution facilities running along the city street and the residence of the customer, is a facility associated directly with that customer and only that customer. Equally clear, the cost of that service line or main is directly and solely assignable to the urban residential customer class, assuming there to be such a classification. But does this mean that all such service connections are direct, not joint?

Not necessarily. Take the case of the electric service line (or drop) between the on-street cable and the customer's residence. Without question that drop is a facility directly assignable to the given customer and the urban residential customer class. Nonetheless, that drop is a joint facility and the costs thereof are joint, because, although only one class of customer is involved, three types or classes of service, not one, may be rendered over that same line: standard service, interruptible

---

the need of rendering the particular service to the particular users the equipment would not have been installed, the costs are direct and are solely the responsibility of these customers.

[3]For an interesting discussion of the definition and nature of joint costs, the reader may wish to refer to the Taussig-Pigou controversy which took place early in the last century. See Taussig, F.W., "Railway Rates and Joint Costs Once more," *Quarterly Journal of Economics*, Vol. XXVII, 1913, pp. 378–384; also pp. 536–538 and 692–694; and Pigou, A.C., "Railway Rates and Joint Costs," pp. 535–536 and 687–692, in the same volume of the Journal. See also, Sickler, B.J., "A theory of Telephone Rates," *Journal of Land and Public Utility Economics*, Vol. 4, 1928, pp. 175–188.

service, and a variety of "green" services. So, a cost may be direct insofar as a type-of-customer class is concerned, but joint in relation to a type-of-service class. Fortunately, this overlapping is not usually present for the residential electric and gas customer (although it may be).

For electric and natural gas, the primary classifications of service which give rise to joint/common costs because of jointly used facilities by the same class of customer are firm service vs. lower priority and interruptible service, because frequently the two are coupled for the same customer and rendered over the same facilities. To repeat, costs may be direct or joint not only in relation to classes of customers, but also in relation to classes of services. The result may be that most costs are joint.

After direct costs have been assigned, there remains the much more difficult problem of distributing joint/common costs in the most reasonable—the fairest?— possible manner. Inasmuch as jointly used facilities and services comprise the great bulk of all facilities and services, this problem is of greatest importance. Much original work has been done by the utilities in earlier years in devising rational (and salable) methods of solving this problem, and the general techniques which have been developed merit careful study by students of all types of industry, as well as by students of utilities.

3.3 Utility Cost Allocation Theory

The basic fact underlying utility cost allocation theory is found in the characteristics of the use of utility service. Customers of a public utility take service as different times of the day, week, month, and year. They take it in different amounts, varying as between customers and even with reference to the same customer at different times of the day or season. As a result, no single simple method of cost allocation will insure reasonably accurate results in all cases.

Two such simple methods may be noted, however. First, it would be possible to apportion the utility's costs equally among its customers. All customers, large or small, would pay the same amount for service each month. Quite clearly, this would be objectionable on many counts. It would subsidize the larger user, who would be paying less than his share of costs; it would penalize the small user, who would be paying more than his share; perhaps, even, the charge would be so prohibitive as to make it impossible for the small user to take service; and it would promote careless and wasteful use of service, in that it would offer no incentive for economy of use. Unmetered water service, still found in isolated instances, represents an application of this method.

As a second method, it would be possible to use a straight average unit charge, dividing the total number of units sold into total costs. Under this method, all customers would pay the same rate per kilowatt-hour of electric energy, per cubic foot of gas, per telephone call, etc. This would be slightly more equitable than the first method, bit it also has a number of disadvantages. It makes no differentiation between customers who make full use of the facilities provided to serve them and those who do not, thereby completely overlooking the cost situation of the utilities, and it furnishes no reward either for increased use or "off-peak" use. As a matter of fact, however, it must be noted that this type of rate is fairly common. Urban traction companies may use a single fare which applies whether a passenger rides several blocks or several miles.

What, then, are more equitable methods of cost allocation? As before mentioned we find no problem with direct costs. But many problems arise in the allocation of joint/common costs. Some of the best methods are those which have been devised by the electric utilities for the allocation of fixed (readiness-to-serve or investment) costs.[4]

3.4 The Functionalization of Costs

To insert order into the allocation process by reducing the number of costs to be considered at one time, costs are functionalized, i.e., grouped by the jobs they perform. The common series of groups for a utility are generation (for electric) or production (for natural gas); transmission; distribution; customer facilities; customer service; and administrative and general. The most appropriate method of allocation (or combination of methods) is selected for each function with the resulting cost applied to that function. Each function may be broken down into categories, such as demand-, energy-, or customer-related, the assignment depending upon the applicable type of cost.

3.5 Methods of Allocation

Although these methods were developed primarily in terms of joint investment costs of electric utilities, they are adaptable with modifications to the joint costs of other utilities.

3.5.1 The "Coincident Demand Peak-Responsibility" Method

First and oldest is the "peak-responsibility" method. This method, as summarized by L.R. Nash, "assumes that, as investment in power facilities is determined by the maximum or peak load which these facilities are called upon to handle, (the costs associated with) this investment should be allocated among the services (customer classes) in proportion to their participation in the peak load."[5] Since the size of the investment in facilities required by all types of utilities and many other industries as

---

[4]These methods are sometimes looked upon more narrowly as methods of allocating "demand" costs. However, their applicability is less limited if they are considered in relation to the broader category of joint costs.

[5]Nash, L.R., *Public Utility Rate Structures*, McGraw Hill Book Cp, Inc., New York, NY, 1933.

3.5 Methods of Allocation

well, is determined by the peak volume of their business, this method is obviously not limited to the electric industry.[6]

Under the peak-responsibility method, the composition of the load at the time of the peak is analyzed to determine the relative contributions to the peak of the several customer classes. Each customer class is then assumed to be responsible for the costs of joint facilities in proportion to its contribution. There are two different approaches to measuring peak responsibility. Both are shown in Table 3.1.

Table 3.1 Examples of peak-responsibility methods of joint cost allocations

	Coincident method			Non-coincident method		
	Time	Load (mw)	% of total	Time	Load (mw)	% of total
Residential, urban and rural	6 a.m.	17,000	33	6 a.m.	17,000	29
Small commercial and other	6 a.m.	12,500	25	2 p.m.	15,400	27
Large commercial and industrial	6 a.m.	21,700	42	8 a.m.	25,600	44
Total load served		51,200	100		58,000	100
Losses[a]		8,800			8,800	
Total generated		60,000			66,800	

[a] System losses are experienced by both electric and natural gas, by reason of the resistance encountered as the current or gas travels from one point to another, and as they pass through intermediate equipment, such as a substation for electric or a pressure station for gas.

The coincident demand method is illustrated on the left hand columns of the table. The peak (highest) load was experienced at about 6 p.m. At this time residential, urban and rural loads comprised 33% of the total peak of 51,200 MW. Small commercial loads comprised 25%; and large commercial and industrial loads 42%. Thus, if this method were to be followed, the joint investment costs—or any other type of joint costs being studied—would be allocated to the several classes of service in proportion to these percentages.

---

[6] It is a general characteristic of utilities that their product cannot be stored although, of course, water, both as a utility and for hydroelectric generation, and gas, can be stored to a limited degree. For all practical purposes, electricity must be generated simultaneously with customer requirements for it. Sufficient telephone circuits must be available to handle calls when subscribers wish to make them. As many busses must be provided as are needed to carry rush hour traffic. Water or gas mains must be large enough to keep water or gas flowing when required. These are commonly accepted minimum standards of utility service. It is obvious that the peak loads which must be handled determine the number and size of the facilities which the utility must provide.

In a hydro-electric system, water may be stored in storage reservoirs and, to a limited degree, as pondage in run-of-the-river plants. It also may be stored for short periods as part of a pumped-storage project. Natural gas can be stored in depleted oil or gas reservoirs, above ground in tanks as liquefied natural gas (LNG), or as line-pack in mains.

This is the coincident demand version of the peak-responsibility method, so-called by reason of the fact that demands of the several classes of customers are measured simultaneously, each demand occurring coincidentally in time with the others. A major objection to this method is that it assigns too much weight to the customer class whose peak occurs at the time of the system peak, and too little weight to the other classes whose peak occurs as other times. As an extreme example, interruptible loads, which may be completely curtailed at the time of the system peak, would bear no cost responsibility whatever.

3.5.2 The "Non-coincident Demand Peak-Responsibility" Method

A different version of peak responsibility is illustrated on the right hand columns of Table 3.1. This is the non-coincident demand approach. The table shows that the individual peaks of each of the three classes of service occurred at different times. The residential peak occurred at 6 p.m., the small commercial peak a 2 p.m., and the large commercial and industrial peak at 8 a.m. Only the peak of residential service occurred at the same time as the overall system peak. The cost responsibility has been shifted from that resulting in the coincident demand version. The residential burden has declined from 33 to 29%, while the burdens of the other two classes have risen: small commercial from 25 to 27%, and large industrial from 42 to 44%. These shifts in percentages appear small and insignificant, but a change of just 1% can amount to a reduction in cost to one class of customer of many millions of dollars, and an increase in cost of the same millions of dollars to a different class.

The non-coincident demand method of joint cost allocation assumes the size of the individual class peaks in relation to their total to be more important than the relationship of the class loads to each other at the time of the system peak. This is on the basis that each class of service should bear a share of joint costs proportioned to its maximum utilization of the facilities, regardless of how much of that utilization coincided with the time of the system peak. Also, it is considered to be more equitable since it takes into consideration the benefit derived by each class because of the existence of the others. Other classes mean more customers among whom the fixed charges may be borne, to the mutual advantage of all.

Under this method, the individual class peaks—17,000,000 kW for residential, 15,400,000 kW for small commercial, and 25,600,000 kW for large commercial and industrial—are added together to arrive at the system's non-coincident peak (so-called because the peaks comprising it do not occur at the same time). This total is 58,000,000 kW. Costs are then allocated on the basis of the relationship of each peak to the total.

The coincident and non-coincident allocation methods may be combined by giving partial weight to each. For example, one utility allocates 87.5% of its average transmission capacity cost to coincident demands and the remaining 12.5% to non-coincident demands.

3.5 Methods of Allocation

3.5.3 Other Peak-Responsibility Methods

Several other versions of the peak-responsibility method have been developed. Among these are as follows:

1. Summer and winter peak method, which measures either the highest coincident peak in each season or an average of the three highest;
2. Sum of 12 monthly coincident peaks method;
3. Multiple coincident peak method, measuring specified hours in the year;
4. All peak hours coincident peak method, which measures specified hours of the day and week throughout the year.

One electric utility contends that a single system-average transmission capacity cost does not accurately reflect how its system is planned and operated. Therefore, it divides its system into bulk transmission, for which a single capacity cost is appropriate, and many area systems of relatively independent capacity and very limited capability to share load with other systems. To these area systems, forecasted investment has been allocated based on their average annual load growth.

3.5.4 Various Other Methods

Other methods veer toward recognizing that energy loads, as well as peak loads, are a major determinant of production plant costs, and consequently use average demand together with peak demand as allocators; some are directed toward the view that on-peak generation is more expensive than off-peak generation, and allocate capital costs on the basis of the classes' proportions of on-peak energy use; still others adopt time-differentiated measures, such as costs during base load, peak hour and, possibly also, intermediate (or shoulder) hours. The variations are almost endless, depending upon the preferences of the rate maker and his objectives.

Two acronyms loom large, LOLP and POD. The first stands for "loss of load probability," which measures the expected value of the frequency with which a loss of load due to insufficient generating capacity will occur in each hour. The hours are grouped by their relative LOLPs into on-peak, off-peak, and shoulder hours. The second acronym means "probability of dispatch," the likelihood that given generator units will be used in serving the load. The per-hour cost of running the unit is assigned to each hour that the unit runs.

Another acronym, FAD, should be mentioned. This stands for "full availability dispatch." It allocates fixed costs to every hour in the year. The allocation of production costs to different customer classes changes depending upon the level of reserve margin currently on the utility's system. After determining its marginal generating capacity cost allocation by class coincident demands, one California utility adjusts cost using its value of service (VOS) method. The VOS method determines the amount of expected unserved energy (EUE) which would be avoided due to a one megawatt increase in generation capacity in a particular year, given the load and resource assumptions assumed for that year. The EUE is multiplied by customer outage cost estimates (costs customers would incur in the event of an outage, expressed in $/kWh unserved) derived from customer survey data. Dividing this total annual EUE cost by 1,000 yields the $/kW-year estimate of the marginal generation capacity cost.

3.5.5 The "Phantom Customer" Method

Perhaps a more equitable and certainly a more complex scheme is the "phantom customer" method. Because of its complexity it will not be described in detail, but the general theory merits notice.[7]

There are many hours during the day when electric facilities are not used to the full extent of the maximum demand because the load falls below the peak. These "valleys" represent idle capacity. If there were no valleys, i.e., if the facilities were used to the maximum demand at all times, the rate problem would be simpler. Fixed costs could be thought of as rental charges on capacity and could be assessed to the several classes of service directly on the basis of the proportion of their use (not peak or maximum demand) to the total use. Use could be measured by any convenient unit (kilowatt-hours for power, cubic feet for gas, etc.).

However, there are always valleys which represent unused capacity, and it is—according to this method—in the apportionment of the costs of such unused capacity that the real problem lies. If a customer or class of customers could be found who would use the otherwise idle capacity and fill up the valleys—and here is our "phantom customer"—it would be possible to use a capacity rental approach. Therefore, to provide a starting point the method assumes the existence of the phantom customer. Rental costs per unit of use are determined and are assessed directly to the responsible classes including the phantom customer. The costs assigned to the phantom customer are then charged as a further assessment to the classes of actual customers. This assessment is made by charging to each actual customer class taking service over the peak (probably all classes except those which are strictly off-peak) a share in the phantom's bill, which is proportioned to the excess of the class demand at the time of the peak over the average class demand.

3.5.6 The Nordin Proposal[8]

J. A. Nordin has criticized the above methods because in his opinion they do not fulfill the two objectives of a demand cost allocation, viz., to improve the system consumption pattern and to do justice among customers. He feels that the object

---

[7]For a complete discussion, see Nash, L.R., Ibid., Ch. XI, p. 234; Hills, H.W., "Demand Costs and their Allocation," *Electrical World*, January 22, 1927, pp. 198, ff; and Nordin, J.A., "Allocating Demand Costs," *The Journal of Land and Public Utility Economics*, May, 1946, p. 168.

[8]Nordin, J. A., Ibid, pp. 163—170.

of demand cost rates "is to move consumption from the peak hours to the trough hours; consequently it must be made relatively expensive to consume at the peak hours and relatively cheap to consume at the trough hours." Nordin contends that other methods may not only fail to accomplish this, but may also fail to discourage certain undesirable load shifts. Under other methods customers (or customer classes, presumably) might be able to shift more of their demand to the system peak without increasing their bills, or might be able to reduce their bills by making a change detrimental to the system. For example, under the phantom customer method, a customer whose demand at the station peak is less than his average demand might be able to shift some of his demand to the peak without increasing his bill.

To overcome these objections Nordin proposes hourly demand cost rates which vary directly with the amount of the hourly demand. Each hour would be charged "with the capacity cost for which it can reasonably be considered responsible" and such costs then would be divided among the customers taking service during the hour. The apparent difficulty with this method is its extreme complexity of computation and application. However, the concept of rates based on hourly charges (reflecting hourly cost allocations) is interesting and stimulating, and far ahead of its time.

3.5.7 Edison's Improvements[9]

Southern California Edison Company has introduced a superior method for the allocation of generation costs. This method encompasses two steps. First, it utilizes detailed accounting, including site "identifiers," to trace small increments of cost to their specific origins, thus enlarging the spectrum of costs that can be directly assigned, while reducing the extent of costs which otherwise would be allocated as joint/common. Second, it associates many of the remaining joint/common costs with independent cost-causation drivers, attributing to a specific end-result additional cost which otherwise would also be classified as joint/common. Together, the bottom line of these two steps is a much diminished group of costs to be allocated by formula—the broad general overhead classifications, such as administrative and general (A&G) or general plant.

Edison also establishes a middle ground cost classification to bridge the wide differences in cost assignment methodology between the two traditional classifications of costs, direct or joint/common. Edison substitutes three "pools" for the present two, adding an intermediate category called its "joint pool." This pool includes many costs which otherwise would be classified as joint/common, with the result that more costs can be directly attributed to end-uses than formerly. The three pools are the Direct pool, which includes traditional direct costs, but in addition includes costs which customarily would be allocated as overhead. An example of the latter is office equipment, which instead of being lumped in a company-wide account

---

[9]Conkling, R.L., "Generation Cost Unbundling: Untangling the Gordian Knot," *The Electricity Journal*, March 1997.

is identified by location "identifiers" at the site of generator units. The joint pool is the second category. This includes costs of the usual joint/common classification which are jointly consumed by multiple segments, attributed based upon a cause-and-effect relationship or a special study. An example is payroll taxes. These taxes correlate with labor costs, which are identifiable by segments as direct costs, and are assigned to each segment with the direct labor costs of that segment. The third pool is the common pool, which is a residual pool comprising the remaining joint/common costs not assigned to the joint pool. Examples of common pool costs are the cost of preparing and filing income tax returns, the salaries of general officers, and similar items. These must be allocated to the generating units. Edison adopts a "multi-factor" formula, which gives equal weighing to operation and maintenance expenses, labor costs, and capital expenditures.

3.6 Distribution

Distribution is the most complicated function, primarily because distribution costs may be demand-related, customer-related, or a combination of both.

Distribution plant is divided into primary and secondary segments, with the secondary segment further divided into facilities ending at the final line transformer and those extending from that transformer into the customer's premises.

Primary distribution costs are demand-related and can be allocated by any peak-responsibility method or combination of methods. One utility allocates 35.43% of the system-average primary distribution capacity cost to class coincident demands and 64.57% to class non-coincident demands. Secondary facilities ending at the final line transformer also are demand-related but may not have to be sized to serve the coincident demand of the customers supplied from it because the diversity of customer loads—many multiple residential and small light and power accounts—makes it highly unlikely that the maximum demands of these customers would occur at the same time.

The balance of the secondary distribution system is customer-related. This consists of the facilities and services associated with providing customers with access to the system: hooking up a customer, reading the meter, billing, and customer accounting and collection. Hookup equipment includes the meter, service drop, secondary voltage conductor, and final line transformer.

Generally, distribution substation costs are classified as demand-related, because substations are normally built to serve a particular load and their size is not affected by the number of customers to be served. On the other hand, the number of poles, conductors, transformers, services, and meters are directly related to the number of customers.

Either of two methods may be used to distinguish between the demand and customer categories of distribution facilities, the minimum-size and the minimum-intercept methods. Under the size method, a minimum size for each pole, conductor, transformer, and service is determined and costed, with the cost classified as customer-related. The difference between these costs and the total investment in the facilities is considered to be demand-related. Under the intercept method, installed costs are related to current carrying capacity or demand rating, to create a curve for various sizes of equipment, and extending the curve to a no-load intercept. The cost at the zero-intercept is the customer-related amount.

Administrative and General accounts also must be functionalized. Southern California Edison's approach, mentioned earlier, of adopting a formula which gives equal weighing to operation and maintenance expenses, labor costs, and capital expenditures, is one method of doing so.

3.7 Rate Schedule Divisions of Cost

The preceding sections outline how costs may be allocated among customer or service classes. The final step in rate-making is the actual formulation of rates. For this step it is necessary to consider yet another set of cost categories, those aimed at apportioning costs among the individual customers of each rate class. This step is concerned with collecting from the individual customers of each class their share of the costs which have been allocated to that class. The cost categories discussed below are used mainly in formulating the rate structure which is the basis for billing the customer.

3.7.1 Demand Costs

Fixed costs have been discussed earlier. These comprise a very considerable component of all costs, and they arise largely because of the necessity to provide capacity which, once provided, creates a fixed cost burden upon the utility. This burden must be carried whether or not the capacity is used and regardless of the extent to which it is used.

In rate formation, the fixed costs which are related to the capacity required to serve a particular rate class may be lumped together as demand or "readiness to serve" costs. These are frequently represented in the rate as a separate part of the utility price called a demand charge, and are apportioned on the basis of some measurement of the use of capacity. Demand charges are often shown as a separate element in rates. Whether or not they are set out separately in the rate, demand costs must, of course, be covered.

3.7.2 Customer Costs

Having allocated demand costs, the remaining costs must be considered. Certain of these are associated with the routine jobs of rendering service and are also relatively fixed. Costs of reading meters, preparing, issuing and collecting bills, and answering customer inquiries are examples of what are called *customer costs*. It is presumed that all costs of this nature are incurred because they are an incidental but necessary element in rendering service. Also, it is generally presumed that these tend to be about the same for all customers of a given class, and hence may be considered as a constant component in the rate. When this component is set out separately it is called a *customer charge*. Demand costs differ from customer costs in that the former vary with the amount of capacity provided, while the latter vary with the number of customers. Except in the three-part rate, customer and demand costs are lumped together.

3.7.3 Commodity Costs

A third type of cost includes all costs which are incurred because of the customer's volume of use (e.g., total kilowatts hours), as contrasted with his rate of use (e.g., maximum demand in kilowatts). These *commodity costs* are the variable or out-of-pocket costs incurred in the actual production and delivery of the product or service. In rates, these costs are ordinarily apportioned on the basis of actual consumption since they tend to vary with the amount of consumption. In electric rates, charges covering these costs are called *energy charges* and in gas rates, *commodity charges*.

3.7.4 The "Perfect" Rate

It is often considered that a theoretically perfect cost-based electric and natural gas rate would break down all costs into the three types above and charge separately for each type. To make the rate more "perfect," the demand charge could be varied from hour to hour (a "time-of-day" demand charge), from day to day (weekdays vs. weekends), or from season to season; and the energy/commodity charge could be blocked, either with declining unit prices or increasing (inverted) unit prices, as might be appropriate.

3.8 Suballocations

A thorough going job of joint cost allocation ordinarily will involve a number of subordinate allocations, the final allocation being a summation of several separate studies. To illustrate by a rather oversimplified example, an allocation of the joint costs of service for a residential electric customer would include at least the following: (1) an allocation of generating costs, i.e., of the capacity costs of the central or distributive stations. If there are a number of generating stations on the system, individual allocations might be required for each. The allocations would be expected to encompass all rate classes, system wide, which contribute to the need for peak generating capacity; (2) an allocation of transmission costs (the capacity costs of the high voltage network, including transformation). In this step, all transmission facilities would be grouped together if rates were set on a postage stamp basis. However, if rates differed as between load centers (such as major cities or other geographical areas), certain lines could be identified with a given load center, others with a different load center, etc.. Since transmission lines feed power to all rate classes, the allocation again would be expected to reach all rate classes which impacted on the need for the transmission capacity under consideration; and (3) an allocation of distribution facilities costs for (a) the secondary facilities ending at the final line transformer which are demanded-related and (b) the remaining secondary facilities which are customer-related. In addition would be the costs of residential meter reading, billing and collecting, plus an aliquot share of administrative and general expenses.

3.9 The Total Cost and Incremental Cost Methods

The total cost method is useful primarily as a means of allocating costs to existing, already developed types of service. These types of service are quite often considered as making up the utility's "Base Load," i.e., the customer requirements which the utility has an established obligation to serve. Such "base load" services represent relatively permanent responsibilities of the utility. They should therefore pay their full share—the total—of both direct and allocated joint costs. From the cost-of-service point of view, less than this might be unduly discriminatory and certainly might put the utility in an unsound financial position.

There are, however, always certain types of sales which cannot be developed, or if on line cannot be maintained, under rates which carry a full share of all costs. This is true of many new types and of existing types where competitive threats make likely the loss of sales if rates are held to the full cost-of-service. Although some sales cannot bear their full share of all costs, they nevertheless may be a desirable addition from the cost viewpoint. This will be so if the charge for the sale covers all direct (out-of-pocket or incremental) expenses incurred in rendering it and, in addition, makes some contribution to joint costs. The theory here is that any contribution to joint costs—which must otherwise be borne entirely by the "base load" services—is a financial help to the "base load" services. It reduces the amount of joint costs which they must pay. It has been argued that rates which essentially cover only direct costs are unduly discriminatory in that other types of service must cover the bulk of the costs of facilities jointly useful to both. However, most authorities agree that rates for some customers can best be based on incremental costs.

In theory, the determination of incremental costs for any customer or service class is not difficult. It is only necessary to assume first that the utility system being studied is operating without rendering service to that rate class and to determine total costs on that basis. Let us say these costs are "X" dollars. Then it is assumed that the rate class is being served. Under this assumption total costs are "Y" dollars. The increment or difference between the two costs, Y minus X, is the incremental cost of rendering the additional service. If rates are set so as to yield more than this difference, the excess decreases the costs which otherwise must be borne by other rate classes. Although the theory is simple, as a practical matter it may be quite difficult to estimate the "with-and-without" costs with accuracy, although such costs normally are the same as variable costs. Obviously, the equity of any rates based upon incremental costs is dependent upon how carefully this is done.

3.9.1 Marginal Costs

In passing, we may note that economists often speak of *marginal* costs rather than of incremental costs. For all practical purposes the meaning of the two terms *as used outside of economic jargon* is the same. However, there is a difference. "Marginal Cost in the New Economy" says, "strictly speaking, marginal cost is the extra (or incremental) cost of producing an extra unit (the marginal unit). ... in its opposite, it is the cost saved by producing one less unit, usually called the avoided cost ... it is the cost incurred, or the cost saved, in the production of the marginal unit of output." This definition implies that the unit will be relatively small. There is no size limit on our use of incremental. The *marginal unit* (in the present case, a unit of service supplied or to be supplied by the utility) is the unit for which some change is under consideration. The change may be either to add or subtract, i.e., to promote or discourage, the unit of service. The marginal cost is *the additional cost necessary to supply the marginal unit of service* (or the cost saved because the unit is not produced and sold). *Marginal revenue* is the additional revenue derived because of the sale of the marginal unit (or the amount of revenue lost due to withdrawal of the marginal unit).

3.9.2 Use of the Incremental Cost Method

Broadly speaking, incremental rather than total costs are used as a basis for rates under three circumstances. First, as already mentioned, they may be used for new kinds of service which as yet may not have received public acceptance and need a developmental period during which the market can be expanded to the point that the service can stand on its own feet. The justification for this lies in the expectation that ultimately the service will be a sufficiently valuable part of the utility's load to counterbalance temporary cost concessions. Second, incremental costs may be used for services in competitive fields, where no sales would be obtained at rates covering all costs. And third, they may be used where service is provided on an interruptible basis. By reserving the right to interrupt service, the utility is in effect utilizing only excess capacity in providing service, as it can curtail deliveries to an interruptible customer any time it needs the capacity for others. Thus, since no additional capacity is needed, it is reasonable that interruptible customers do not bear the burden of a full share of all costs.

It is important to note that interruptible service may be provided on-peak or off-peak. As long as it may be interrupted when necessary to serve other loads, the time of use is of no consequence. In fact, it is just a beneficial to utilize spare capacity at the time of the system peak as it is at any other time. However, rates sometimes are based on incremental costs solely because the service provided is off-peak. This is satisfactory only to the extent that such rates are actually applicable only when there is spare capacity—i.e., existing capacity not needed to serve base load peaks. Off-peak loads may grow to such a size as to themselves create new system peaks. If this happens the result no longer is to make better use of otherwise idle capacity. Rather, a need for new capacity has been created and the previously off-peak service then becomes responsible for a major part of capacity costs. Thus, it may be better not to consider a presently off-peak type-of-service as a service to be charged for on the basis of incremental cost unless it can be determined that this service is permanently off-peak—practically an impossibility—or unless the service is made interruptible.

3.10 The Separable Costs-Remaining Benefits Method of Cost Allocation in Federal Multi-purpose Projects

The separable costs-remaining benefits method for allocation of costs among the purposes of a multiple-purpose project was devised and recommended by the Federal Inter-Agency Subcommittee on Benefits and Costs in its May 1950 report on "Proposed Practices for Economic Analysis of River Basin Projects."[10]

The objectives of the separable costs-remaining benefits method of cost allocation are threefold.

First, to allocate to each purpose any costs which are made necessary because that purpose is included in the joint project. This is the minimum amount that should be allocated to each purpose.

Second, to allocate costs in such a way that no purpose is assigned more costs than the benefits that will result from such costs nor more than the cost of the most economical alternative way in which such benefits could be realized. This is the maximum amount that should be allocated to each purpose.

Third, between the foregoing minimum and maximum limits, the costs should be distributed among all purposes in such a way that each purpose shares equitably in any advantages of the "joint venture" as compared with alternative single-purpose plans.

The separable costs-remaining benefit method has the following steps:

> First, the "separable costs" of including each purpose or function in the project are computed. This means that if a project can be built to serve three purposes for $1 million but could be built to serve only two of those purposes for $800,000, it follows that a cost of $200,000 is made necessary solely because of the third purpose and is therefore definitely assignable to that purpose and is the minimum amount that should be allocated to that purpose. By estimating the costs of various combinations of purposes, the "separable costs" of each purpose can be determined. The separable costs are sometimes

---

[10] A draft of the above description of the method was provided to the author by Ed Woodruff, Regional Economist, North Pacific Division, Corps of Engineers, Department of the Army. Mr. Woodruff is credited with writing the cost allocation instructions for the payout of the Federal multiple-purpose projects of the Columbia River Power System, which includes numerous dams and power plants on the Columbia River and its tributaries, as well as flood control and irrigation projects.

referred to as "incremental costs" since they are the same as the increase in costs required to include the function in a multiple-purpose project.

Second, the "joint costs" of the project are determined by subtracting the sum of the "separable costs" from the total multiple-purpose project costs. These "joint costs" are the cost for which an equitable distribution procedure must be found.

Third, estimates are made of the most economical alternative way in which comparable results could be realized for each purpose. For example, in a case where flood controls benefits of a million dollars annually could be realized through construction of a multiple-purpose project, it may be possible to protect the same area and realize the same benefits by construction of levees for flood control only. If the estimated cost of such levees were only $700,000, it would be uneconomical to assign to flood control more than $700,000 of the total costs of the multiple-purpose project, even though it would be economically sound to incur up to $1,000,000 in costs for flood control if a less costly means of realizing the benefits were not available. Accordingly, for each purpose of a multiple-purpose project, the amount of benefits, or the cost of the most economical alternative means of realizing the benefits, whichever is less, is a limiting figure on the total amount that should be allocated to each purpose.

Fourth, the "separable costs" for each purpose is subtracted from the limiting figure for that purpose, as determined in the preceding step. These differences are called "remaining benefits."

Fifth, the "joint costs" are then distributed among the purposes in the same proportion that the "remaining benefits" for that purpose bear to the sum of all "remaining benefits."

Finally, the total allocation to each purpose is computed by adding the separable costs and the share of joint costs for each purpose.

An illustration of the foregoing procedure is given in Table 3.2.

Table 3.2 Illustrative analysis of allocation of project costs by separable costs-remaining benefits method

		Flood control	Power	Total
a.	Benefits	$320,000	$1,510,000	$1,830,000
b.	Alternate cost	$640,000	$1,470,000	–
c.	Benefits limited by alternate cost (lesser of a and b)	$320,000	$1,470,000	–
d.	Separable cost	$190,000	$1,020,000	$1,210,000
e.	Remaining benefits (c – d)	$130,000	$450,000	$580,000
f.	Allocation of joint cost	$100,000	$350,000	$450,000
g.	Total allocation of annual charges (d + f)	$290,000	$1,370,000	$1,660,000

3.11 Limits on the Ascertainment of Costs

For purposes of this illustration all project costs, including investment as well as operation and other costs, have been reduced to equivalent annual amounts. Costs, charges, and benefits for both the multiple-purpose and the alternative projects assumed for this analysis are given in Table 3.3:

Table 3.3 Comparison of costs of multiple purpose and single purpose projects

	Multiple-purpose project	Alternate single-purpose projects	
		Flood control	Power
First cost	$30,900,000	$15,800,000	$26,200,000
Interest during construction	$1,600,000	$600,000	$1,300,000
Investment	$32,500,000	$16,400,000	$27,500,000
Annual charges			$970,000
Interest and amortization of investment	$1,150,000	$580,000	$240,000
Operation and maintenance	$250,000	$60,000	$260,000
Taxes foregone	$260,000	–	–
Total	$1,660,000	$640,000	$1,470,000
Annual benefits			
Flood control	$320,000	$320,000	–
Power	$1,510,000	–	$1,510,000
Total	$1,830,000	$320,000	$1,510,000

Separable cost for flood control is total cost of multiple-purpose project minus cost of alternate power project (1,660,000 – 1,470,000 = 190,000).

Separable cost for power is total cost of multiple-purpose project minus cost of alternate flood control project (1,660,000 – 640,000 = 1,020,000).

Total joint cost is determined by subtracting from the cost of the multiple-purpose project the separable cost determined for flood control and power (1,660,000 – 190,000 – 1,020,000 = 450,000). The joint cost is then allocated in direct proportion to the remaining benefits determined in line "e" of Table 3.2.

3.11 Limits on the Ascertainment of Costs

The cost-of-service approach to rate-making appears to be precise in theory, and this theoretical precision tends to obscure an important limitation. The theory assumes that it is possible and practicable to accurately determine costs and to equitably apportion costs as necessary for the purpose to be served. Actually, with a few exceptions, it is rarely feasible to arrive at more than an approximation of costs.

As far as past costs are concerned, certain data are readily available. Overall costs of the utility as a whole are ordinarily kept with meticulous accuracy on the basis of accounting methods prescribed by the Federal Energy Regulatory

Commission (formerly the Federal Power Commission), Federal Communications Commission, Interstate Commerce Commission, or the state regulatory body, and may be observed at any time by an examination of the utility's books. However, the established cost categories are not sufficiently detailed, nor in most cases are they of the proper type, to serve the various rate-making purposes. The reason for this is a dollar-and-cents one. It would be far too expensive to maintain continuing records of the complexity and in the detail necessary to provide at a glance data containing all of the various types of costs discussed in this chapter. For this reason rates will commonly be based on special cost studies conducted intermittently as the occasion warrants. These must involve a number of assumptions, and the final results are no more accurate than the assumptions. Even the carefully recorded items in the expense accounts sometimes are based upon estimates, depreciation expense, for example. Further, as already pointed out, the allocation of the large body of joint costs to the various customer classes is itself necessarily arbitrary in that there is probably no one method which is both practicable and entirely equitable from all standpoints.

Past costs are not as important in rate-making as anticipated future costs, for future situations are the major concern of the rate maker. Here the element of uncertainty is even more marked. Past cost experience can and does provide a valuable index to cost levels which may be expected to prevail in the future. However, many factors can only be estimated. Cyclical fluctuations may raise or lower costs of labor, raw materials, even capital. Technological charges may shorten the useful life of facilities. And, perhaps most important of all, sales may vary from the expected, thus changing both the absolute and relative volume of production for the customer classes and consequently changing both the absolute and relative costs of service.

The problem is accentuated when a new type of use, such as the electric-fueled plug-in automobile, is being considered. What will be the costs of this service? To answer this question even approximately a host of other questions must be answered. What will be the size of the load of the typical customer? What saturation of this load can be expected? What diversity will there be between plug-in customers? Between plug-ins as a class and other classes? Can the load be restricted to the off-peak hours? Can a complementary load be developed to even out the usage? What affect will the load have on monthly and annual system load factors? Will plug-ins shift the peak thus establishing a new peak responsibility? Is the load controllable, by mechanical devices, customer education, etc.? Should the average or incremental cost method be used as a basis for cost allocation? These are illustrative of the unknowns that must be solved by analysis and tests before any cost answers are to be had.

However serious the difficulties encountered in determining utility costs may be, they do not alter the significance of the cost theory of rate-making. The cost approach is basic to the supply side of utility rates. It is a recognized part of the rate process. And at least a creditable degree of accuracy can be attained.

In any event, the involved details of the preceding discussion of selected methods of allocating joint costs should not be allowed to obscure the principle involved. The essential point is an appreciation of the fact that the existence of joint/common costs poses a problem in allocation to which there is no one answer, but for which, fortunately, there are patterns of analysis as guideposts. All allocations must of necessity be arbitrary. The objective is to do the job in what appears to be the fairest possible manner.

3.12 Definitions of Cost

Average costs: Cost per unit of output, where the costs of all inputs are included.

Avoidable costs: The average reduction in costs that would result from reducing output by a discrete amount. (Avoidable costs are analogous to incremental costs, but focus on a decline rather than an expansion of output.) For electric, AVOIDED COSTS in any time period are the costs the utility saves by not generating or acquiring energy during that time period. Professor Paul L. Joskow adds, "AVOIDABLE COSTS are future capital and operating costs that have not yet been incurred but which may be incurred in the future as a consequence of utility supply behavior."

Capital costs: Costs associated with investments, as plant and equipment.

Common costs: Costs associated with investments or processes that are linked to more than one function or provide more than one service, and which cannot be attributed to a single product or service. The term is considered to be synonymous with JOINT COSTS in this textbook, although joint costs arise only when the products or services can be produced only in fixed proportion. The term OVERHEAD COSTS is also used as an alternative to common cost. Common costs "occur" or "are found" in multi-product firms when a single asset can be used in producing more than one product, and this joint use creates cost savings.

Cost–benefit analysis: A conceptual framework for the evaluation of investment projects, particularly in government, which differs from a straightforward financial appraisal in that it considers all gains (benefits) and losses (costs) regardless of to whom they accrue.

Customer costs: A utility term, meaning customer-related costs as distinct from demand (or demand-related) costs and from energy (or energy-related) costs, often stated on a per-customer basis.

Demand costs: Also called "readiness-to-serve" costs. The investment costs of providing capacity in electric facilities (generating, transmission, or distribution) or in natural gas facilities (transmission or distribution) as necessary to serve load when needed by customers. Measured in kilowatts or therms/cubic feet.

Direct costs: Costs associated with only a single function, service, or sale, in contrast to joint or common costs which are associated with multiple functions.

Distribution costs: The investment or operating costs of transporting either electricity or natural gas from interconnections with high capacity transmission facilities to customers' premises, expressed in either capacity or volumetric units.

Embedded costs: Historic costs incurred to acquire resources, as shown in the accounting records of the company or as included in the company's cost-of-service study. May be synonymous with SUNK COSTS which, having been incurred, cannot be reversed. Are called STRANDED COST if their recovery is unlikely.

Energy costs: The costs of supplying volumes of electricity, measured in kilowatt-hours, or natural gas, measured in therms or cubic feet. Also, may be called COMMODITY COSTS.

Fixed costs: Costs associated with inputs that cannot be changed within the time period of the analysis, in contrast to VARIABLE COSTS which can be changed within the period. Fixed costs do not vary with output, while variable costs do. In contrast, AVERAGE COSTS include all inputs.

Generating costs: The costs, investment and operating, incurred in generating (producing) electricity, expressed in kilowatts if referring to units of capacity, or in kilowatt-hours if referring to volume.

Incremental costs: These are the average additional costs of supplying a discrete increase in output. They are nearly identical to MARGINAL COSTS and the terms are often used interchangeably.

Least-cost planning: Undertaken to assure an adequate and reliable supply of energy at the least cost (minimum cost) consistent with the long-run public interest. Essentially the same as COST MINIMIZATION, the choice of input combination which yields the smallest possible total cost for any given level of output.

Long-run: A time period long enough to adjust all inputs to their optimal levels, in contrast to SHORT-RUN, a period short enough that some inputs cannot be changed. In the short run, capital (plant size, amounts, and types of equipment) cannot be varied, but all other inputs can be varied.

LRIC and SRIC: abbreviations for long-run incremental cost and short-run incremental cost, respectively (or LRMC and SRMC, marginal cost rather than incremental). LRMC is the change in the cost of producing a product, or set of products, that results from a change in the production quantity of one or more of the products, where all factors of production can be varied. In SRMC, some factors remain constant. As an example of LRMC, assume an electric system having several large generating units. These units can be retired and replaced with distributed generation units. But with SRMC, the large units must remain in service, although their operations may change.

Marginal costs: Strictly, these are the increase in costs which result from supplying a single, additional unit, or the amount saved by not supplying that unit. However, in practice a small increase or decrease in the number of units is applicable rather than a single unit.

Opportunity costs: The opportunity cost of an action is the value or benefits of the foregone alternative action. Professor Dwight R. Lee adds, "because of scarcity, every time we do one thing we necessarily have to forego doing something else desirable. So there is an opportunity cost to everything we do, and that cost is expressed in terms of the most valuable alternative that is sacrificed."

Shortage costs: Costs that result from a deficiency in capacity, which may be reduced by adding additional capacity or additional operating and maintenance efforts.

Social costs: Also called EXTERNALITIES, because they affect parties *external* to the economic transaction that causes them, such as environmental damage which is not paid for by the originator of the damage. They encompass environmental, social, and political costs related to resource options, including air pollution, acid rain, global warming, wildlife preservation, and other options considered in conservation planning. An EXTERNALITY occurs when the action of one party affects the well-being of others, either positively or negatively, and these effects are ignored in the decision to take the action.

Sunk costs: These are costs which have been incurred by a decision to purchase which cannot be reversed, and which entail an obligation to pay. Professor Paul L. Joskow adds, "SUNK COSTS are capital investments and long-term contractual commitments that have been incurred in the past ... and whose magnitude is unaffected by future behavior."

Transmission costs: The costs of transporting electricity or natural gas from one point to another, by high capacity wire or main, expressed in either capacity terms (per kilowatt or per therm/cubic feet) or volume terms (per kilowatt-hour or per therm/cubic feet).

Chapter 4
The Cost Approach to Pricing: The Tenneco Pattern

Abstract Chapter 4 has two parts. The first discusses why and when fixed and variable costs should be assigned to the demand charges of multi-part rates. Each of the four famous methods is covered: the Atlantic Seaboard method, the United method, the modified fixed–variable method, and the straight fixed–variable method. Two other issues are included as well: the demand charge and zoning. The second part of the chapter covers the entirety of the accounting involved in a full rate case before the responsible US regulatory commission, starting with the aggregation of the pipeline's total costs of service stated pursuant to the commission's uniform system of accounts, and ending with the allocation of these total costs to the demand and commodity charges of the pipeline's individual rate schedules.

4.1 Tenneco Pattern

Elsewhere in this text, costs are explored from a variety of viewpoints, ranging from the elementary operating and ownership costs of the price-originating baker to the highly technical seasonal, daily, and hourly costs of modern utility operations. In most cases, these examinations have been largely discursive and theoretical. This chapter departs from the realm of broad description and ventures into the details of actual practice.

To this point, the peak-responsibility method of allocation has been emphasized, because it fits neatly into the traditional twofold breakdown of electric and gas prices into demand and commodity components, yielding the data necessary for the assignment of demand costs to the demand charges of rates.[1] In this respect, it should be kept in mind that the method, in a purist sense, is designed to allocate only the fixed joint/common investment costs of the concerned utility. These are the costs of the physical plant necessary to provide the capacity needed to supply the peak load. By common practice, however, in most cases the method has been extended to include O&M costs associated with this investment as well as other non-associated fixed costs, such as A&G.

---

[1] The methods first permit allocations to classes of service.

The objective of this chapter is to follow the several steps, and the reasoning governing each step, of the actual allocation and rate-making procedures from start to finish. Adopted as a pattern are the cost allocation methods and rate-making procedures of Tennessee Gas Pipeline Company (which we will refer to as "Tenneco"), as presented to the Federal Energy Regulatory Commission (FERC) on August 16, 1988 in Docket No. RP88-228. Tennessee Gas Pipeline Company (now Tenneco Gas, Inc.) is a subsidiary of Tenneco, Inc.

Tenneco is a long-distance interstate natural gas pipeline. It extends from supply areas in Texas, Louisiana, and the Gulf of Mexico to as far north as Connecticut, traversing 13 states in route. At the northern end of its system, Tenneco imports Canadian gas, interconnecting with the pipeline of TransCanada Pipelines Limited at the US–Canadian border near Niagara Falls, New York.

In addition to pipeline facilities, the system utilizes underground storage in Pennsylvania, New York, and Louisiana.

Tenneco's sales area is divided into zones for rate-making purposes.

4.2 The Issues

Chapter 4 does not review the entirety of Docket No. RP88-288. The first phase of a rate case is a determination of the total revenues the regulated entity will be allowed to collect through its rates. (These revenues are entitled the "revenue requirement," which is calculated based upon an overall company-wide cost of service.) This first phase is not reviewed here. The second phase covers the establishment of prices which will recover the allowed revenues. Chapter 4 covers this second phase.

Three main pricing issues, each of which involves allocations to one extent or another, have surfaced on the Tenneco system and are explored herein. These are as follows:

1. How should fixed and variable costs be assigned between the demand and commodity charges for rates? The philosophy of peak responsibility is examined in detail. The argument is not about the amount of the total fixed costs, which was not in question. The debate concerned the relative portion assigned to the commodity charge. The amount of the variable costs constituting the commodity charge, absent any addition of fixed costs, was also not in question.
2. Should the demand charge be a one-part or a two-part charge?
   The relationship in cost responsibility between peak use and annual use is debated.
3. Should rates of a long-distance pipeline be related only to distance or to zones plus distance?
   Alternative allocation methods are considered along with this question.

Commission rules on these issues usually will be part and parcel of every long-distance interstate natural gas pipeline rate determination. Of course, for some pipelines there will also be additional issues.

4.4 Assignment of Fixed and Variable Costs   95

This chapter examines four FPC or FERC determinations for Tenneco which have relevance to the three issues, as follows:

FPC Opinion No. 352, issued February 6, 1962;
FPC Opinion No. 769, issued July 9, 1976;
FERC Opinion No. 249, issued July 22, 1986; and
FERC Opinion No. 249-A, issued July 31, 1987.

Other FPC–FERC determinations also are cited, notably the two famous fixed–variable allocation cases, *Seaboard* (Atlantic Seaboard Corp., 11 FPC 43 (1952)) and *United* (United Gas Pipe Line Co., 50 FPC 1348 (1973) *reh'd denied,* 51 FPC 1014 (1974)), as well as generic Order No. 636 (1992).

4.3 The Regulatory Scheme in Brief

To keep in context the pricing procedures as they unroll in this chapter, below is quoted a summary of the regulatory measures followed by the Federal Energy Regulatory Commission (FERC), as described in Order No. 636 of April 16, 1992.

> Order No. 636: The commission engages in five tasks in fashioning a pipeline's rates for its jurisdictional customers. The first task is to determine the pipeline's overall cost of service.[2] The second task is to functionalize the pipeline's costs by determining to which of the pipeline's various operations or facilities the costs belong. This step is known as functionalizing and mainly turns on the particular characterization of the pipeline's facilities as production area, transmission, or storage facilities. The third task is to categorize the costs assigned to each function as fixed costs (which do not vary with the volume of gas transported) or variable costs, and to classify (i.e., assign) those costs to the reservation and usage charges of the pipeline's rates. This step is known as classification. The fourth task is to apportion the costs classified to the reservation and usage charges among the pipeline's various rate zones and among the pipeline's various classes of jurisdictional services. This step is known as allocation. The fifth task is to design each service's rates for billing purposes by computing unit rates for each service. This step is known as rate design. The entire process is known as rate making.

4.4 Assignment of Fixed and Variable Costs

> In setting rates the Commission is free, within the ambit of its statutory authority, to make the pragmatic adjustments which may be called for by particular circumstances.[3]

With steadfast confidence, FPC–FERC traditionally has asserted that its prescribed rates are based on cost. However, the commission sees cost differently at different times. This section examines FPC–FERC decrees for the assignment of fixed and

---

[2] The pipeline's cost of service is the total revenues needed to cover the pipeline's operations, including a just and reasonable return on its rate base.
[3] *Consolidated Gas Supply Corp. v. FPC*, 520 F.2d 1176, 1185 (D.C. Cir. 1975).

variable costs to the reservation (demand) and usage (commodity) charge of rates, as a required step toward "cost-based" rate structures. It traces a tortuous series of different fixed–variable cost assignment formulae extending over 40 years.

The examination reveals the commission's gradual (and perhaps reluctant) recognition of value considerations, i.e., the market, as a prime element in rate design. It also discloses the extent to which plausible justifications can be conjured up to support contradictory cost treatment.[4] We explore the transitions in some detail since the theories supporting each formula should be familiar ground for the ratemaker and regulator.

Where practicable, we focus our review on Tenneco's experience.

4.4.1 The Seaboard Formula[5]

The initial formal scheme was established by the Federal Power Commission in 1952, in the *Atlantic Seaboard* case.

In *Seaboard,* 50% of the fixed costs are assigned to the commodity component, with the end result that demand bears only one-half of fixed costs, while commodity carries all variable costs plus the other one-half of fixed costs. This "tilts" the two-part demand–commodity rate toward a much lighter demand change and a much heavier commodity change. The rationale is best explained in the commission's own words:

> The controversy generally engendered in rate proceedings as to the proper method for allocation of costs stems largely from the fact that the relative importance of the demand (capacity) and commodity (volume) functions cannot be measured with scientific accuracy In the final analysis the allocations of costs to these respective functions are and must be largely dictated by informed judgment.
>
> A natural-gas transmission facility performs both a capacity and a volumetric function. In this sense it is a joint facility, which thus presents the problem, always difficult, of allocating joint costs.
>
> ... A pipeline would not normally be built to supply peak service, that is to say, service on the peak days only...pipelines are built to supply service not only on the few peak days but on all days throughout the year ... Both capacity and annual use are important considerations in the conception of the project ... Both capacity and volume, therefore, are what are known as cost factors or incidences in respect to the capital outlay for a pipeline project. It follows that reasonably accurate results can be achieved only by allocating the fixed expenses flowing from the capital outlay to both operating functions, viz., capacity and volume.
>
> If fixed expenses are assigned wholly to the demand or capacity function, then gas service which is interrupted on peak days will not share in any of the fixed costs. Conceivably under such an allocation large quantities of natural gas could be sold to industrials 360 days of the year and interrupted on five or so peak days, and such gas would bear none of the

---

[4]Both the expert ratemaker and the experienced regulator become uniquely adept at such justification. It's part of the job.

[5]Re *Atlantic Seaboard Corporation and Virginia Gas Transmission Corporation,* 11 F.P.C 43 (1952).

4.4 Assignment of Fixed and Variable Costs

costs incurred in constructing the pipeline facility. In other words, under a strict application of this theory [the peak-responsibility method], the interruptible service would not bear any depreciation expense, return, income taxes, or any part of the other fixed expenses associated with the capital outlay. This would be so even though the capital outlay made the interruptible service possible by providing the means of transportation used extensively by such assumed interruptible service ...

This would result in free transportation for the interruptible gas.[6]

To reiterate-and emphasize – fixed costs or expenses are incurred for both peak use and annual use in respect to both demand and volumetric functions. They are important cost factors in respect to both services. To achieve a reasonably equitable result they must be apportioned to both services

...It is our opinion that these significant cost factors should be weighed equally, that is to say, 50% should be assigned to demand and 50% to commodity. In this manner all gas transported by the pipeline will share in all of the various kinds of expenses incurred to transport the gas which is associated with delivery on the peak day or group of peak days... That gas which is not associated with deliveries on the peak day or group of peak days will not share in 50% of the fixed costs. This solution recognizes the principle that costs associated with peak service are higher than those which are associated with interruptible or off-peak service...the equal weighting assigned to the two cost factors of demand and commodity for the purpose of allocating fixed costs or expenses is a judgment determination. It can never be otherwise for the allocation of joint costs is not and cannot be an exact science.

In its holding, as explained above, the commission expressly rejected "the theory that the capital outlay for a transmission facility varies with the size or the capacity of the facility; that the fixed expenses associated with this capital outlay do not vary with the volume of gas transported; and, therefore, such expenses should be assigned to the demand or capacity function." The commission declared, "We are unable ... to accept the premise that merely because certain costs do not vary with use they automatically become *in toto* demand or capacity costs."

With respect to the relationship between allocated costs and rates, the commission said,

While ... such an allocation of costs is not necessarily controlling in the fixing of the precise level of the demand and commodity components of the rates, they are, in the absence of other *mitigating circumstances,* a reasonably accurate guide as to the appropriated level for the demand charge and the commodity charge. [Emphasis added]

---

[6]In this paragraph, the commission unnecessarily overstates its case. It seems to postulate that neither quasi-firm (subject to limited curtailment) nor full interruptible rates can be designed with a demand charge component. While established commission practice had eliminated a demand charge for interruptible service, and no quasi-firm rates had been introduced, these precedents were not set in stone. And, as we will see, some 24 years later, a two-part demand charge was introduced, one related to peak use and the other to annual use, which would have tempered the commission's statement in this paragraph. (A specific purpose of this change was to provide cost relief to low load factor customers.) However, our point here is simply that the problem as stated did not necessarily require the shift for all rates, firm and interruptible, ordained in Seaboard.

Commissioner Connole, in a concurring opinion in a 1959 case, recapitulated the 50–50 formula dilemma[7]:

> ... it is not a simple thing to allocate costs between avoidable, out-of-pocket on the one hand and on the other, fixed or constant. Certainly, those costs which are functions of volume, are variable. Those which are functions of capacity are constant. The former are recovered through the commodity component in a two part rate; the latter through the demand component.
>
> But some capacity costs in addition should be borne by a sale that ties up no specific capacity year round (the interruptible). Clearly the very *existence* of the pipeline makes possible what otherwise would have been impossible- i.e., the interruptible sale. Hence, the interruptible ought to contribute toward the cost that is the function of the simple fact of existence of the line, i.e., the capacity costs
>
> How much should they contribute. In *Atlantic Seaboard* we said 50%. This was never more than an educated guess. Different conditions ... dictate a different proportion-but never lower than the out-of-pocket costs.

The mitigating circumstances foreseen in *Seaboard*, and the different conditions anticipated by Commissioner Connole, came to the forefront in a 1962 case. Application of the *Seaboard* formula produced high commodity charges, which would have resulted in the loss of sales by Natural Gas Pipeline Company of America.

The commission lowered the charges below the formula level so that the company's rates would remain competitive, thus introducing value of service directly into the cost allocation–rate formulation process.[8]

Value necessarily is injected into the costing–pricing process for at least two reasons: in certain areas, one pipeline may be in direct competition with another, in which situations the comparative commodity charges will dictate which pipeline will be awarded discretionary purchases by the buyer; and, in many areas, interruptible gas is in competition with oil or coal for high-volume industrial use.

A distributor buying from a pipeline cannot resell gas at a lower unit price than the unit price (the commodity charge) which it has paid for the gas, since such price is a direct out-of-pocket cost. It is the distributor's incremental per unit cost. If the unit price the distributor pays is higher than the unit price of the competitive fuel, the distributor therefore loses the sale because it will not be allowed to sell below incremental cost.

Since the commodity charge is a matter of arbitrary judgment under the *Seaboard* formula, rather than a representation of out-of-pocket variable costs, there is pressure to reduce it to a competitive level as long as out-of-pocket costs—plus some override—have been covered.

In 1964, the commission referred to its own formula in critical terms[9]:

> This record, as well as our previous experience, unmistakably reveals that use of *Seaboard* for rate design has serious infirmities. The primary infirmity results from its artificial

---

[7] Re *Midwestern Gas Transmission Company and Tennessee Gas Transmission Company* 21, F.P.C. 653 (1959).

[8] Re *Natural Gas Pipe Line Company of America* 28 F.P.C. 731 (1962).

[9] Re *United Fuel Gas Company and Atlantic Seaboard Corporation* 31 F.P.C. 1342 (1964).

4.4 Assignment of Fixed and Variable Costs

assignment of 50% of all fixed costs to the demand component of two-part rates. This assignment rarely reflects with accuracy utilization of the system by the various classes of service, and, inasmuch as mitigating circumstances of considerable variety appear in almost every case, it is generally necessary to adjust direct *Seaboard* rates to get workable results ...

It is short-sighted to assume that an allocation method...must forever remain immutable.

The commission adjusted the *Seaboard* formula in this case to tilt the cost incidence away from commodity, toward demand. It stated three reasons for doing so. First, the lowering of the commodity rate component was necessary to prevent loss of interruptible sales and to stimulate further growth of such sales. The commission found that interruptible sales enabled "more efficient use of facilities, thereby lowering unit gas costs." Second, an increase in the demand rate component was needed to encourage the purchasing distributor companies to provide storage facilities of their own and induce other types of peak shaving practices by their customers.

A low pipeline demand charge most likely will provide an inadequate incentive for the distributor and/or its customers to adopt peak shaving measures, since it probably is cheaper for the distributor to buy demand from the pipeline than to invest in expensive storage capacity or, in the case of the end-use customer, to upgrade his plant and operational practices so as to be able to reduce his peak requirement from the distributor.

Third, the revised rate tilt was needed to equalize the capacity costs borne by pipeline purchasers having disparate load factors, as was so in the situation being considered. The commission said, "... when 50% of fixed costs are included in the commodity component of a rate of a company selling gas at less than 100% load factor, the high load factor customer is assessed a disproportionate share of the cost of unused capacity created by the low load factor customer." A comment by the commission on the relationship between distributor storage and the distributor's load factor is worth quoting:

... low-load factor operations [of the distributor] make storage necessary, not possible It is because of low-load factor operations that companies undertake storage at very substantial costs. The operation of storage facilities reduces the costs below what they would be if additional pipeline capacity equivalent to peak requirements were constructed.

The influence of value upon cost allocations translated into rates was highlighted in a 1965 case.[10] Here, after the commission was about to approve a tilt away from commodity, certain "Coal Interests" urged higher pipeline commodity charges so that coal could be competitive in price with natural gas and thereby could displace gas for interruptible utility and industrial boiler-fuel sales in the Chicago area. The Coal Interests argued, in essence, that the commission should determine proper demand–commodity levels for pipeline rates without regard to the affect of such rates on pipeline sales (by reason of their resulting affect on distributor sales). The commission rejected this argument, thus affirming its prior positions on the validity of value considerations in cost allocation.

---

[10] Re *Midwestern Gas Transmission Company and Natural Gas Pipeline Company of America* 34 F.P.C. 973 (1965).

4.4.2 The United Formula

Tilts away from the Seaboard formula continued to be made whenever it was necessary to keep the gas price competitive. *Seaboard* was superceded in 1973 by the *United* formula, which assigns 25% of the fixed costs to demand and 75% to commodity. *United* was a reversal of prior rate lilts which favored a reduction in the commodity assessment in order to stimulate gas sales. The reversal reflected the gas shortage of the period and represented a policy objective to conserve gas for high-priority firm purposes by discouraging its use for low-priority purposes, such as interruptible boiler-fuel for industrial customers having alternative fuel-burning equipment.

The 1980s marked a dramatic change in the gas supply outlook, and the energy crisis was over. Once again, it appeared to be good public policy to make gas competitive in price so as to stimulate sales. Of course, the regulatory framework would be adjusted accordingly.

4.4.3 The Modified Fixed–Variable (MFV) Formula

Now we turn to the Tenneco system. In the Opinion No. 249 docket (1986), there was advocacy of the *Seaboard* and *United* formula,[11] as well as SFV. The commission rejected all three on the grounds that these approaches "would not permit Tennessee and its customers to meet their competition in the market place."

The commission elaborated on the market:

> The allocation issue is primarily concerned with the relative responsibilities for cost incurrence. However, that issue cannot be determined in isolation of other considerations.
>
> The record reflects a substantial concern for Tennessee and its customers to market gas. Thus, it is necessary to approve allocation and classification procedures that would enable the rate design adopted in this proceeding to meet the marketing concerns of Tennessee and its customers. The functions of rate design involve considerations in addition to revenue recovery based on customers' relative cost responsibility. Those additional functions should encourage maximum utilization of the system by both the pipeline and its customers, assure a stable revenue flow, provide correct signals to producers and the market place, assess similar rates for similar services, and give incentives to the pipeline to operate efficiently and to manage gas acquisition consistent with long-term system requirements and market constraints.
>
> In considering the above functions, we may take into account, among other things, load loss and the risk and costs of system underutilization.
>
> The record establishes that Tennessee and its customers are facing competition in the industrial market...
>
> The industrial market includes off-peak sales to industrial users of natural gas. The larger the market, the more each customer on the system benefits, since the system operates more efficiently because there is a higher load factor and, consequently, at a lower per unit cost for each customer. Thus the marketability of gas has a very important impact on the system and its customers.

---

[11] Re *United Gas Pipe Line Company* 3 PUR4th 491 (1973).

4.4 Assignment of Fixed and Variable Costs

The competition in the market place generally revolves around the cost of gas to the industrial user. That cost is generally determined in the industry by using the commodity charge plus the gas charge [where the two charges are stated separately] as the basic price to the purchasers. In other words, the system's customer establishes its charge to the industrial purchaser at the level of the commodity and gas costs to it as the minimum price for that sale. Accordingly, the marketability of the gas is substantially determined by the pipeline's commodity and gas rates to its customers. With all other things equal, the lower those rates, the higher the industrial sales.

[When a pipeline] and its customers face strong competition in industrial markets, that situation requires a methodology for cost allocation and rate design that will enable [the pipeline] and its customers to be competitive in the market place.

The commission explains its reasons for rejecting *Seaboard*, *United*, and SFV:

... we emphasize...that the cost allocation method selected should be closely related to the incurrence of cost on the pipeline's system. ...The rationale behind *United* is to accommodate a pipeline's inability to meet its peak day obligations. When that circumstance occurs, the annual obligations become more prevalent and the cost responsibilities and rates are properly shifted to more fully recognize annual usage of the system. To meet that situation, *United* places 75% of the transmission and storage fixed costs in the commodity component, and, generally, this is done both for cost allocation and rate design purposes.

United requires (as a basic element) an acknowledgment that current operational usage [as contrasted with peak usage] reflects the predominance of annual use. That acknowledgement was appropriate when a pipeline was in curtailment and was unable to serve its peak day requirements. The record in this case reflects that Tennessee is not in curtailment and has been able to meet its peak day obligations.

...a continuation of *United* would result in unjust and unreasonable rates for Tennessee. The peak use of the system has been fully served since 1980, while the annual use has diminished. Moreover, Tennessee is not in a curtailment position. Its system, however, is being underutilized on annual and peak day bases. Thus, the use of United for cost allocation and/or rate design on Tennessee's system is not warranted, and a change in methodology is required to meet today's conditions.

FERC staff, in the exceptions it took to the commission's rejection of the use of the *United* formula in Opinion No. 249, argued in support of *United* that "the 25/75% *United* methodology would both help to discourage industrial consumption of gas and also develop a commodity charge equal to the cost of replacement gas" (quotation from Opinion No. 249-A).

Clearly the staff was out of tune with the commission, which had as its pricing objective the encouragement, not discouragement, of sales by Tenneco. It seems fair to conclude that the staff was interested in continuing the conservation ethic of the shortage period, while the commission was not. The commission seems to have had in mind an additional consideration not apparent in the staff position, namely, that if Tenneco didn't sell the gas competitively, others would. The commission declared, "under the *United* methodology, Tennessee will be less able to meet competition in the marketplace."

We now continue with the commission's critique of prior formulae, per Opinion No. 249:

Seaboard has the same infirmities as *United*. It is not consistent with the present and expected future requirements of Tennessee's market. That market requires a rate design to produce rates that are more responsive to competitive forces. As such, we find that the use of *Seaboard* in today's market would result in unjust and unreasonable rates.

In the past, *Seaboard* was used when neither the annual nor the peak usage of a system predominated. This record, however, does not support the use of *Seaboard* for the Tennessee system. *Seaboard* does not provide the proper market signals, and marketing is the prime concern of Tennessee and its customers

The straight fixed-variable method (SFV), which recovers all fixed costs through the demand charge, would also result in unjust and unreasonable rates. While, as shown above, the peak day use of Tennessee's system has remained relatively stable, Tennessee must stand ready to serve the annual entitlements of its customers. Thus, the annual use of the system maintains a significant role that requires the annual users to pay their fair share of the fixed costs of Tennessee's system. The SFV procedure, if adopted, would place the fixed cost burden solely on the peak day users of the system. As a result, off-peak customers would not be assessed any of the fixed (capacity) costs although they use the capacity at times other than during the peak demand periods. In addition, the SFV method does not provide any incentive for Tennessee to perform in the competitive market place because it guarantees recovery of all fixed costs, including return on equity and related income taxes, regardless of whether any gas is sold. Consequently, the SFV method does not provide any incentive for Tennessee to minimize its purchased gas costs and otherwise maintain market-responsive charges and prices in order to maximize its service and sales.[12]

Having rejected earlier formulae, the commission in Opinion No. 249 adopted a new plan for Tenneco, the "modified fixed–variable" (MFV) formula, first introduced as a concept in 1985.[13] The significant departure of MFV was to divorce return on equity and associated taxes from the balance of fixed costs. The former were allocated 100% to commodity; the residual, to demand. As the commission saw it, the allocation of return and associated taxes to commodity meant that recovery of the cost of equity capital was entirely dependent upon maintaining throughput volume. In other words, the pipeline's viability was "at risk." It must sell, or else. It must meet price competition, or else. In the commission's own words,

...MFV creates an incentive for Tenneco to maintain market-responsive rates in order to sell more gas. This is accomplished by placing 100% of Tennessee's potential profit (equity return and related income taxes) into the commodity charge. Thus, Tennessee, to earn a profit, is required to sell gas. The more gas it sells, the more profit it realizes.

Apropos of the commission's finding, one intervener had challenged the commission on the grounds that "there is no assurance that the MFV method will facilitate marketing."

The commission responded in Opinion No. 249-A: "... the commodity charge under MFV will be at a lower level than the one established under *United* and the pipeline will thus be in a better position to meet competition in the market place. Greater sales (or improved marketability) can be anticipated from the lower commodity rate."

---

[12]Note the commission's recourse to cost as a partial justification for its position against SFV. It is ironic to contrast this disavowal of SFV with its later adaption of that method.

[13]*Texas Eastern Transmission Corp.*, 30 FERC 11 61, 144 (1985); *Transwestern Pipeline Co.*, 32 FERC 11 61,009 (1985).

4.4.4 The Straight Fixed–Variable (SFV) Formula

The SFV approach was formally adopted by FERC in Order No. 636 of April 8, 1992, to supersede MFV.[14] (The order was clarified by Order Nos. 636-A and 636-B. The three orders are discussed together below.)[15]

SFV requires that all of a pipeline's fixed transmission and storage costs be billed in the pipeline's reservation (demand) change for the purpose of billing firm transportation customers.

The definition of transportation is expanded to include storage. Storage is to be unbundled from transportation and separately charged, so that storage can be provided on an open-access non-discriminatory contract basis. Access to storage must be provided both on a firm and interruptible basis. The pipeline itself may not retain any downstream storage capacity (downstream meaning from the point where the pipeline has unbundled in providing its own sales service, which will be near the production area).

It was the intent of the commission that, from the originating point of receipt near the wellhead, all gas must move through the pipeline as transportation gas.

The commission left the door open a crack by allowing concerned parties to propose an agreed-upon alternative method, but warned that "any party (or parties) advocating something other than SFV carries a heavy burden of persuasion."

To minimize rate shock arising from the change to SFV from MFV (which was being followed by most pipelines at the time of the order), the commissioner authorized a phase-in of SFV over 4 years if the change would result in a 10% or greater rate increase for the concerned customer class. The 10% phase-in limit applies only to the class, not individual customers.

The commission categorized its decision as "part of [its] actions to improve the competitive structure of the natural gas industry." Among the specific purposes of SFV were to eliminate potential competitive distortions in pipeline rate structures; to further promote even competition among gas merchants; and to eliminate the distorting impact of pipeline fixed costs on wellhead competition.

In a dissent in part, Commissioner Elizabeth Anne Moler restated the purpose of adopting SFV:

> Order No. 636-A rests on the rationale that the current regulatory climate is unworkable and results in "anticompetitive consequences for *all* segments of the industry and consumers." Thus, the rule is necessary to create "a modern, viable natural gas industry specifically fashioned to the needs of *all* gas consumers and the Nation ..."

---

[14] The change from MFV to SFV was not a surprise, having been anticipated in a Notice of Proposed Rulemaking issued July 31, 1991, which was promptly dubbed the "Mega-NOPR."

[15] Order No. 636-A issued August 12, 1992, affirmed the final Order No. 636 of April 16, 1992. Order No. 636-B was issued November 27, 1992 in further clarification. These orders were the finalization of an order having the same designation (636) which had been issued October 18, 1985.

The Commissioner explained earlier shifts in the formulae:

> The Commission uses the cost classification aspect of the ratemaking process to achieve policy goals that are pertinent to current conditions. Because conditions change over time, the Commission's goals change and the weight given to various goals also changes. This balancing of goals is a matter of judgment and is not an exact science.
>
> Frequently, however, the Commission has emphasized one particular goal in its ratemaking. That goal is to design pipeline rates in light of competition. This has involved the shifting of costs from the commodity to the reservation charge to keep pipeline rates competitive.
>
> ... using cost classification to design rates to influence the consumption of gas is a traditional regulatory technique of the Commission. In a concurring opinion, Commissioner Branko Terzic added:
>
> The order recognizes that the Commission historically has found various rate designs that include different amounts of fixed coats in the commodity component of a rate to encourage or discourage the consumption of gas.

Referring back to the prior MFV formula, the commission commented that MFV had been adopted "in pursuit of the goal of competition by lowering pipeline sales commodity charges to enable gas to compete effectively with alternative fuels such as oil."

The commission ignored its parallel cost-based justifications for MFV.

In response to criticism that its rationale for SFV was based on predictions as to the effect of the method on the competitiveness of the gas market, the commission tartly responded:

> The Commission is not required to act only on the basis of hindsight. The Commission may make predictions about the markets it regulates.

4.4.5 Comparison of the Formulae

Table 4.1 compares the several methods of apportioning fixed and variable costs to the demand and commodity elements of rates.

We have now reached the end of the tedious saga of *Seaboard*, *United*, MFV, and SFV. To repeat our earlier comment, we have traced this evolving history in some detail because it is essential knowledge for the natural gas ratemaker or regulator, both of whom should know "why" and "how."

But we also have a larger reason. The saga is one of the better case histories to show the interplay of market (value) economics and public policy in a presumably cost-driven joint cost allocation process. It reveals that rarely, if ever, will an allocation be "pure" of non-cost considerations, however, carefully it may be guised to appear otherwise.

From the perspective of this larger reason, the evolution of FPC–FERC fixed–variable cost allocations merits consideration from economists and policy makers who will in the future be struggling to mesh the emerging realities of a competitive market for utilities within the constraints of a cost-conscious series of historical precedents.

4.5 The Demand Charge

Table 4.1 Comparison of fixed-variable allocation formulae

	Demand charge (%)	Commodity charge (%)
Straight fixed variable		
Fixed costs (including fixed production costs)	100	
Variable costs (including variable production costs)		100
Seaboard		
Production costs		100
Fixed costs		
Transmission	50	50
Storage	50	50
Variable costs		100
United		
Production costs		100
Fixed costs		
Transmission	25	75
Storage	25	75
Variable costs		100
Modified fixed variable		
Production costs (both fixed and variable)		100
Fixed costs		
(1) Transmission	100 except (3)	
(2) Storage	100 except (3)	
(3) Return on equity and associated taxes		100
Variable costs		100

Split 50-50 between demand 1 (D_1) and demand 2 (D_2), introducing a two-part demand charge

4.5 The Demand Charge

Until 1985 (the year preceding Opinion No. 249), the demand charge in pipeline rates had been a pure application of the peak-responsibility theory for spreading demand costs (although the costs themselves had been tempered by *Seaboard*, et seq.). While demand costs were allocated on the basis of the average of a 3-day peak period, they were recovered in pipeline rates by means of a single demand charge, geared to the customer's maximum daily use.[16] Opinion No. 249 coupled a major change in this demand charge practice with its change in the fixed–variable cost allocation. (As mentioned earlier, the two charges together are now often referred to jointly as the MFV method.)

In brief, Opinion No. 249 requires two separate demand charges in pipeline rates. One of the charges is billed under *peak*-responsibility criterion, namely, contract

---

[16] The customer's "maximum daily use" may be a measurement of actual usage, or a contract volume expressed as a contract demand or, the same, a maximum daily entitlement.

demand for customers served under CD schedules and highest daily take for other firm service customers, the D_1, charge. The other charge, D_2, is billed under *annual volume* responsibility criterion, namely, on the basis of each customer's annual volumetric limitations (AVLs).

We digress to explain the AVLs. The limitations originated in 1974, early in the energy crisis period, and were set at the level of each customer's then current annual requirements. "Thus," the commission explains, "customers purchasing at 100% load factor were not restricted by the AVLs. However, the lower load factor customers' AVLs were set at a level below their Maximum Daily Quantity (MDQ) times 365. As a result, even though these lower load factor customers could take their MDQ on any given day, their annual volumes were limited ...." The commission concluded that a single demand charge was unfair to the AVLs because it caused them to pay a demand charge for year-round capacity which they were unable to use, while the dual charge would "appropriately" take the limitation into account. We return now to the commission's reasoning in establishing D_1 and D_2, quoting from Opinion No. 249:

> [The objective is to maintain] the proper balance of *cost incurrence* criterion for establishing just and reasonable rates under the Natural Gas Act. [Emphasis added]
> One demand charge is based on peak usage. The other charge is based on annual entitlement. Thus, [the dual charge] properly reflects the cost incurrence of the system by requiring some of the fixed costs to be allocated on the basis of annual demands, while the remaining fixed demand costs are allocated to the peak users. Thus, the annual users of the system are required to pay their fair share of the system's costs.
> The record reflects that daily demands or entitlements are no more important [for Tenneco] than annual entitlements. Both limit a customer's entitlement to service, and, accordingly, that customer's relative responsibility for satisfying the revenue requirements of the system.

The commission laid down the following rule for the division of costs between D_1 and D_2:

> ... each demand charge should be computed separately with 50% of Tennessee's demand costs reflected in rates based on peak entitlement and the remaining 50 percent of such costs reflected in rates based on annual entitlement.[17]

Despite the foregoing justifications, FERC reversed itself in Order No. 636-A. Therein it found the two-part charge to be "inappropriate." The commission stated that "the D_2 charge was based on usage patterns [annual volumes] and is therefore not in harmony with the goal of SFV to minimize charges based on actual usage because usage charges can affect gas purchasing decisions."

4.6 Zoning

We turn back the clock to 1962 and Opinion No. 352, where the issue for Tenneco was zoning.

---

[17] Déjà vu, the 50–50 split of *Seaboard*.

4.6 Zoning

The commission disposed summarily of the threshold question of whether rates should be applicable system-wide (postage stamp) or differ by location (zoned).

4.6.1 A "Postage-Stamp" Approach

> ... differences in costs over a system as large as Tennessee's should [not] be completely ignored by adopting the "postage stamp" concept of rate-making... use of the average cost method without zone differentials would, in the circumstances of the present case, result in undue discrimination.

No such summary treatment was accorded to the method of zoning, where two different approaches were bitterly debated. We quote extensively from the opinion.

4.6.2 The Zoning Alternatives

> Two fundamentally different methods of allocation have been proposed for the Tennessee system, one based on rolled-in system-wide average costs and mileage, the other segregating and assigning to each of the six zones the costs associated with the particular facilities located within the zone. The controversy concerns the allocation of transmission costs, since all parties agree that gas supply and gathering costs should be rolled-in and allocated to volumes on a uniform average basis.
>
> Tennessee, the New England interveners, and the staff employ the *Mcf-mile method*: the volumes delivered at each point within a particular zone are multiplied by the number of miles from source of supply to such point to derive a total number of Mcf-miles for each zone; rolled-in system-wide transmission costs are allocated to each zone according to the ratio of the individual zone's Mcf-miles to the Mcf-miles of the system as a whole.
>
> The Columbia and Consolidated companies are the principal advocates of the *zone-by-zone method*: the transmission costs associated with the facilities physically located within each zone are assigned to the zone as if it were a separate operating entity which purchases gas from the next upstream zone and sells it to its own customers and to the next downstream zone; the transmission costs assigned to a particular zone (plus its cost of gas "purchased" from the next upstream zone) are allocated to all volumes sold in that zone or delivered to the next downstream zone on a uniform average basis.
>
> Both of these methods classify costs between the demand and commodity functions substantially in accordance with established *Seaboard* formula. (Opinion No. 225, II FPC 43)
>
> ... the ultimate determination to be made comes down to a choice between two basic philosophies or approaches:
>
> (1) The philosophy that the Tennessee system is a single, integrated pipeline system, operated as a single entity, with each part of the system contributing to every other part; that accordingly, although customers closer to the source of supply should pay less than customers located farther away from the source, all customers as customers of a single, integrated pipe-line system, should pay on the basis of average system-wide costs for each mile of transmission.
> (2) The conflicting philosophy that costs should be segregated by zones so that the customers in each zone would be treated as if they were customers of separate operating companies. This approach emphasizes the fact that the unit cost of transmission varies in different areas, and insists that an appropriate allocation method must give specific zone by zone effect to such differences in cost.

4.6.3 Which Alternative Is the Best?

At the outset it is important to recognize that there are "pluses" and "minuses" with respect to each of the varying and conflicting zone allocation methods proposed in this case, and that none of these methods are free from problems or difficulties. As realistically noted by Tennessee:

An argument can be made for a uniform rate for all customers ... An argument can also be made for different rates for each customer based on the "cost" incurred in serving each customer. An argument can be made, as Columbia and Consolidated do, for segregating "costs" within a geographical area. An argument can be made for rates based on mileage. An argument can be made for rates based on historical differentials. An argument can be made for rates based on a combination of mileage and historical factors Something can be said in favor of each of such methods of allocation or rate-making The difficulty lies in selecting the method. No one method can lay claim to being the "right" method ... the selection of the method of allocation to be used is bottomed on fairness and the exercise of judgment.[18]

4.6.4 The Legal Standards

The Supreme Court recognized this inherent (uncertainty) of cost allocation problems in *Colorado Interstate Gas CO, F.P.C*, 324 U.S. 581 (1945), as follows:

Allocation of costs is not a matter for the slide rule. It involves judgment on a myriad of facts. It has no claim to an exact science. But neither does the separation of properties which are not in fact separable because they function as an integrated whole. (324 U.S. at 589)

These circumstances illustrate that considerations of fairness, not mere mathematics, govern the allocation of costs. (324 U.S. at 591)

Similarly, the United States Court of Appeals for the Tenth Circuit in a subsequent case involving the same company, *Colorado Interstate Gas Co. v. F.P.C.*, 209 F. 2d 717, at 726 (1953), stated:

Mathematical exactness in the apportionment of cost is an impossibility. Because a method may have some infirmities does not of itself condemn it as a proper method. It is the duty of the Commission to select that method which in its considered judgment more nearly reaches a just and sound result.

4.6.5 The Commission's Appraisal Yardsticks

In approaching the problem of determining here which of the proposed allocation methods should be adopted for the Tennessee system, each of the alternative allocation methods has been measured against the following basic requirements:

---

[18] We particularly commend this paragraph to the reader as a succinct list of choices.

4.6 Zoning

(1) *The method selected should assign a fair share of the total system cost of service to each of the zones.*

(2) *The method selected should be a practical one. It should not be so complex as to require long, tedious studies involving speculations and assumptions, but rather should be a method, which can be expeditiously applied to facts quickly ascertainable.*

(3) *The results reached, through applying such method, should make sense.*

4.6.6 Commission Precedents

... In order to reflect the unity of operation and interdependence of service on an integrated pipeline of this type, it has long been Commission policy to use a system-wide average of mainline transmission costs as the foundation for any allocation of costs to zones or classes of customers. [Cited are cases as early as 1942.]

[The Commission cited with approval its prior findings in the *Northern* case (1955)]: ... it is a simple economic fact that the delivery cost of natural gas increases in close proportion to the length of the transmission line of any given size. Therefore, unless other circumstances are present which outweigh the importance of the length of transmission required to effect delivery, the distance factor is the prime determinant of the cost of rendering service. Since in our view of this record there are no such circumstances present to counterbalance the distance factor, we conclude that the distance of transmission required to effect deliveries at the various points of sale by Northern reflects with reasonable accuracy the relative cost of providing service to its customers.

4.6.7 The Commission's Findings and Orders

The Tennessee system is divided into six rate zones, namely, Southern (Zone 1), Central (Zone 2), Eastern (Zone 3), Northern (Zone 4), New York (Zone 5), and New England (Zone 6). The Commission has not previously determined a method by which Tennessee's cost of service should be allocated among its rate zones and classes of service.

Tennessee operates an integrated pipeline system, in which every portion of the system contributes in one way or another to the effectiveness of the entire system, whether directly or by displacement.

Both Columbia and Consolidated advocate a zone-gate (or zone-by-zone) allocation approach whereby each rate zone is treated as if it were a separate operating entity, and involving the segregation of physical property on the basis of zone boundaries. The zone-gate approach is inconsistent with the basic principles upon which Tennessee's integrated system was designed and is operated. In addition, it accentuates the impact upon cost allocation resulting merely from the historical location of the geographical zone boundaries on the Tennessee system. It is also unduly complex.

The Mcf-mile approach, which uses system-wide average costs, and allocates such costs on the basis of mileage, constitutes, in general, a fair and reasonable method for the allocation of costs between zones on the Tennessee system.

The Tennessee method for allocation of costs to Transportation Service, utilizing the mileage from the actual points of receipt of transportation gas to the points of delivery, is reasonable.

In allocating demand costs under the Mcf-mile method herein, demand volumes will be measured on the basis of the three-day sustained peak periods (adjusted for any obvious abnormalities), ... not on the basis of average billing demands [as some parties had advocated].

[As an exception to its foregoing orders, the Commission recognized that its new plan would entail a major change in rate levels for the New England Zone. To alleviate an immediate major rate increase for that zone, the Commission approved a transition arrangement.] ... we are of the opinion that revenue levels should be employed to apportion fifty percent of the demand and commodity transmission costs herein for the reason that it will provide a reasonable and practical means of insuring that the long-deferred transition to an Mcf-mile cost allocation will be accomplished in a gradual and orderly manner without unduly disrupting the marketing patterns which have been developed by Tennessee's customers. [The remaining fifty percent was to be allocated by the Mcf-mile method.]

4.7 A Resume

Moving forward 14 years, to 1976, it is instructive—and a good review—to quote Opinion No. 769. This puts in perspective all allocation steps, including those involving zoning. The Commission's description is

Tennessee's rate increase filing in this docket incorporated functionalization, cost classification and allocation, and rate design previously prescribed for the Tennessee system by the Commission [in Opinion No. 352]. Specifically, Tennessee's cost of service was functionalized by production, storage and transmission.

Transmission cost were then classified according to the *Atlantic Seaboard* methodology by which 50% of fixed costs are assigned to the demand charge and the other 50% of fixed costs, as well as all variable costs, are assigned to the commodity charge. Tennessee's cost allocation is directed to its six rate zones, there being no real jurisdictional/nonjurisdictional customer issue. These transmission costs were then allocated among the zones by use of the Mcf-mile method, transmission demand charges allocated by the three day peak Mcf-miles and transmission commodity charges by the average annual day Mcf-miles.

[Under the Mcf-mile method] the volumes delivered at each point within a particular zone are multiplied by the number of miles from the source of supply to such point to derive a total number of Mcf-miles for each zone; rolled-in system-wide transmission costs are allocated to each zone according to the ratio of the individual zone's Mcf-miles to the Mcf-miles of the system as a whole.

Production costs were also classified according to the *Atlantic Seaboard* method, and they were allocated to the zones on the basis of the average annual day sales.

Since Tennessee renders storage services for specific customers, as well as utilizing its storage facilities for system-wide operations, storage costs are allocated between these two. To begin with, storage costs are classified by assigning fixed costs to deliverability and space and variable costs to injection and withdrawal. Allocation between the specific storage services and system-wide storage is accomplished by use of the percent of storage units used for the storage service out of the total storage units available. Storage costs not allocated to the specific storage services are allocated among the system-wide operations. Storage demand costs (deliverability and space) are allocated by use of the average of the three-day peaks, and commodity costs (injection and withdrawal) are allocated by use of the average annual day.

Tennessee's rate design within each zone moreover utilized the *Atlantic Seaboard* methodology. Demand charges are determined by dividing the demand costs for each zone by the sum of the test period demand billing determinants. Commodity charges are determined by dividing the commodity costs for each zone by the total test period volumes.

The Administrative Law Judge accepted Tennessee's cost classification and allocation and its rate design, finding that the methodology found in Opinion No. 352 remains just and reasonable with no need for alteration.

4.8 The Minimum Bill

Entering into the Opinion No. 249 proceedings, Tenneco's contract demand rate schedule contained a minimum commodity bill, which required the payment of commodity and gas charges on a minimum monthly volume, whether taken or not. (Such minimum commodity bill incorporated only the fixed costs assigned to commodity, the variable costs having been excluded from minimum bills in 1984 by Order No. 380.) The minimum commodity bill was in addition to the demand charge, which operated as a minimum with respect to the fixed costs assigned to demand.

The minimum bill provision at issue was pegged at the lesser of (1) 66 2/3% of the monthly component of the AVLs or (2) 98% of the monthly component of the applicable curtailment period quantity entitlement (variable costs being excluded from recovery, as just mentioned).

The commission decided that a minimum commodity bill was at odds with MFV, and ordered it eliminated. Its reasoning was as follows:

> The minimum bill provision generates revenues by "encouraging" customers to purchase natural gas from a pipeline regardless of prices. On the other end of the pendulum, MFV ... for rate design "encourages" a pipeline to seek lower gas prices from its suppliers and otherwise maintain competitive prices to enable it to maximize sales. Those two elements (minimum bill and MFV), if permitted, generate conflicting responses. Therefore, if we permit Tennessee to retain its minimum bill, Tennessee will have a "disincentive" to maintain competitive rates. If both the minimum bill and MFV were operative, Tennessee would be assured compensation in excess of its non-equity related fixed costs (i.e., fixed costs other than equity return and taxes), since the MFV demand charges provide for recovery of 100 percent of the transmission and storage non-equity related fixed costs regardless of whether any sales are made. Therefore, in concert with the MFV methodology ..., the minimum bill must be eliminated in order to "encourage" the proper incentive reaction that is the basis of our determination to adopt MFV.

An interesting "mutuality of obligation" was considered in this respect. Tenneco argued that, absent a minimum bill, it must stand ready to meet the full requirements of its customers, yet these customers would not be required to purchase even a portion of their requirements from Tenneco. The obligation, said Tenneco, should be a two-way street (a persuasive argument, it would seem). However, the commission decided: "There is in fact no mutuality of obligation because Tennessee faces no penalty if it fails to meet a customer's requirement, yet the customer must pay Tennessee if its takes fall below the prescribed level."

4.9 Tenneco Allocations for Rate Design

Having explored principles, we now can move from the general to the specific, sketching in broad terms the several tables which translate a company-wide cost of service into rates. These steps are generic for pipelines. However, the mechanics of some steps will vary with the regulatory principles in vogue at the time.

The Tenneco allocation was made in accordance with Opinion No. 249 of 1986. It therefore incorporates the MFV formula and a two-part demand change. The MFV formula requires a division of fixed costs between demand and commodity, and a division of demand costs into two elements, D_1 and D_2. Neither of these would be required under an SFV approach made pursuant to Opinion No. 636 of 1992. We outline the MFV Tenneco allocation in preference to one geared to SFV because its greater complexity improves its value as an illustration. Tenneco's actual figures are used.

4.9.1 Step 1: The Company-Wide Cost of Service

In the instance chosen as illustrative, Table 4.2, the aggregation of the company's jurisdictional costs is $1,589,967,000, as stated in line 18. This total is $54,867 million (line 17) less than the total of all costs (line 16), reflecting a credit against

Table 4.2 STEP 1 The company-wide cost of service (take-off point for rate design)

Line		
		$000
1	Operating expenses	
2	Natural gas production and gathering exp	1,666
3	Exploration and development exp	83
4	Other gas supply exp. (gas purchases)	801,969
5	Underground storage expense	37,491
6	Transmission expense	238,215
7	Administrative and general exp	116,459
8	Total operating expenses	1,195,883
9	Depreciation, depletion, and amortization	142,350
10	Taxes	60,903
11	Federal income	9,041
12	State income	55,117
13	Other	125,061
14	Total taxes	
15	Return	181,540
16	Total cost of service	$1,644,834
17	Less: Revenues credited to cost of service	(54,867)
18	Net cost of service	$1,589,967

The above tabulation is couched in the terminology of FERC's "Uniform System of Accounts," which all pipelines must follow in their accounting. Many states have also adopted this system.

4.9 Tenneco Allocations for Rate Design

system costs for non-jurisdictional revenues. In Tenneco's case, non-jurisdictional sales (and therefore revenues) are minor, so for simplicity the revenue credit device is substituted for an allocation between jurisdictional and non-jurisdictional services. Where non-jurisdictional sales are more significant, a full allocation may be required. It is instructive to note the proportional division of the pipeline's total costs ($1,644,834,000 per line 16) by the broad classifications of the uniform system of accounts.

The tabulation in Table 4.2 is couched in the terminology of FERC's "uniform system of accounts," which all pipelines must follow in their accounting. Many states have also adopted this system.

Table 4.3 Recapitulation of expenses

	% of total	
Operating expenses	72.7	
Depreciation, etc.	8.7	
Taxes other than income	3.4	
Subtotal		84.8
Return	11.0	
Income taxes	4.2	
Subtotal		15.2
Total		100.0

Step 1 establishes the total dollars which rates may be designed to collect, viz., $1.59 billion (line 18).

4.9.2 Step 2: Functionalization of the Cost of Service

Next, the same costs are looked at from a different perspective: not whether they are incurred to operate and maintain the system, or to pay taxes, or to reimburse stockholders and bondholders for the use of capital, but *why* they arise. What is the reason for each cost? The reasons correspond to the types of different jobs the pipeline performs. The segregation of costs by the types of jobs which they cover (or the purpose which they serve) is the "functionalization" of costs, the second step in rate design.

Recall that the natural gas industry actually is a combination of three usually separate industries, production (the producer), transportation (the pipeline), and distribution (the local area distributor).

The traditional pipeline acquired gas by purchase from producers or other pipelines, or sometimes from its own wells, transported the gas from producing areas to consuming areas, selling the gas at the city gate to local distributors for delivery and resale to ultimate consumers. This would be a regulated or jurisdictional operation. Often, however, the pipeline might sell, en-route, directly to a large industrial customer for use by that customer (i.e., not for resale by that customer). Such direct sales would be non-regulated or non-jurisdictional. In Tenneco's case, as stated earlier, direct sales are minor, avoiding an allocation of costs between regulated and unregulated activities.

We digress at this point to make an important observation. In practice, the distinction between regulated and non-regulated sales is more fiction than fact. The end result, despite the fiction, is that both are regulated. This results inescapably because both sales are made from the same jointly used facilities: a separation of costs through allocation is required. Since the choice of allocation methods and the mechanics of the allocation process, whatever the method, rest with the regulatory authority, the commission can establish the cost burden assignable to the non-regulated sales. True, the pipeline can collect less from direct industrial customers than the costs assigned to them, but if it does so it must "eat" or absorb the deficiency, since the assigned costs in total, whether covered by direct sales rates or not, are deducted from the cost of service which can be recouped from regulated sales. Allocation is a mighty weapon!

As noted elsewhere, the traditional role of the pipeline is changing, from that of a "merchant" who almost exclusively *sells* gas which it has bought and transported to consuming areas, to that of (a) a combined merchant-transporter, both *selling* gas which it has bought and merely *hauling* gas of others from point to point, or (b) a pure transporter, like a railroad or other common carrier, which accepts a commodity owned by others and delivers it as directed by the owner. These changed roles do not, however, impact the substance of the allocation procedures now being described, since in any case most costs are joint and must be allocated.

As a merchant, Tenneco must acquire the gas it sells. The cost of this acquisition is functionalized under the head "Production" (line 7 of Table 4.4). Alternative headings might be "Gas Purchases" or "Cost of Gas."

As a merchant, or a transporter, or both, gas must be moved from point to point. The movement or transportation of gas is accomplished by means of transmission pipes or lines, so the hauling job is functionalized under the head "Transmission." Costs aggregated in this category include the investment costs of the pipeline facilities, the costs of operating and maintaining such facilities including compressor fuel and line losses (Operation and Maintenance expenses, or O&M), plus an aliquot portion of administrative and general expenses (A&G).

Tenneco subdivides its transmission function into main line, supply area, and New England laterals. These subdivisions are unique to Tenneco. Other pipelines would have different sub-classifications.

Storage is an important adjunct to a transmission system, since it reduces the pipeline capacity needed to meet peak day requirements and smoothes seasonal fluctuations.

The storage function includes "system" storage, which is utilized for overall load balancing purposes for the benefit of all customers, and "storage service" capacity, which may be purchased by individual customers under storage rate schedules.

For the allocation of storage costs, Tenneco subdivides the storage function into four sub-functions: deliverability, space, injection, and withdrawal. These sub-functional costs in turn are broken down between system and storage service

4.9 Tenneco Allocations for Rate Design

classifications. We do not itemize these subdivisions since our purpose is to illustrate a pipeline allocation procedure, rather than to follow every step.

As with transmission, storage costs include Tenneco's investment in faculties, 0 & M, and proportionate A&G.

Functionalized costs must, of course, aggregate to the net cost of service. Therefore, the total of $1,589,967,000 shown in line 8 of Table 4.4 is the same as appears in line 18 of Table 4.2.

Table 4.4 STEP 2 Functionalization of the cost of service

Line		$000
1	Transmission	
2	Main line	$394,898
3	Supply area	278,785
4	New England laterals	3,631
5	Total transmission	677,314
6	Storage	64,999
7	Production	847,654
8	Total net cost of service	$1,589,967

The functionalization of costs recognizes that different stimuli apply to the individual functions. Transmission stimuli, for example, are a combination of distance or length of haul, and size or capacity. But these stimuli do not apply to production. The cost of gas to the purchaser does not vary (at least directly) with distance to market. Storage stimuli are closer to those for transmission, but nonetheless differ, since they arise from the incentive to make better use of existing line capacity or to reduce the need for new capacity, whether such capacity is located on the system of the pipeline or the distributor.

For Tenneco's system, functionalized costs constitute the following proportions of total costs (Table 4.5):

Table 4.5 Relative size of functionalized physical components

	% of total
Transmission	42.6
Storage	4.1
Production	53.3
Total	100.0

A transportation-only pipeline company would have only the first two functions. The costs of a gas supply, production, would have been transferred to transporting customers.

4.9.3 Step 3: Classification of Functional Costs as Fixed or Variable

Most pipeline rates follow the two-part demand–commodity pattern, with demand charges reflecting fixed costs (to some degree) and commodity charges recovering variable costs plus any fixed costs not rolled-in to demand charges. So the next step is to classify the functional costs between fixed and variable, as in Table 4.6. This is done based on engineering analyses.

Tenneco's breakdown is as follows:

Table 4.6 STEP 3 Classification of functional costs as fixed or variable

		$000		
Line		Total (a)	Fixed (b)	Variable (c)
1	Transmission			
2	Main line	394,898	286,717	108,181
3	Supply area	278,785	271,501	7,284
4	New England laterals	3,631	3,450	181
5	Total transmission	677,314	561,668	115,646
6	Storage	64,999	62,137	2,862
7	Production	847,654	79,510	768,144
8	Total net cost of service	1,589,967	703,315	886,652

Table 4.7 Relative size of fixed and variable expenses

	% of total
Fixed	44.2
Variable	55.8
Total	100.0

4.9.3.1 Unadjusted Fixed and Variable Charges

We will assume a postage-stamp approach, i.e., that prices are not differentiated by locality. We also will assume only two rates, one for gas sales, the other for storage, without differentiation as to the quality of service, load factor, or size of takes.

As a starting point for comparison, no adjustments are made to fixed and variable charges. On this basis, the costs to be covered by the two rates are as shown in Table 4.8.

4.9.3.2 Straight Fixed Variable

Under an SFV allocation, the costs to be borne by the demand and commodity charges of the two rates would be as shown in Table 4.9.

4.9 Tenneco Allocations for Rate Design

Table 4.8 Unadjusted sales and storage rates

		Costs - $000	
		Fixed	Variable
The sales rate			
Transmission		$561,668	$115,646
Production		79,510	768,144
	Total, sales	641,178	883,790
The storage rate		62,137	2,862
	Total	$703,315	$886,652

Table 4.9 Adjusted comparative rates – straight fixed variable

	\$000				
	Demand charges		Commodity charges		
	$	% of total	$	% of total	Total charges
The sales rate					
Fixed (100%)	$641,178	42.0%			
Variable (100%)			$883,790	58.0%	
Total sales	$641,178	42.0%	$883,790	58.0%	$1,524,968
The storage rate					
Fixed (100%)	62,137	95.6%			
Variable (100%)			$2,862	4.4%	
Total sales	$62,137	95.6%	$2,862	4.4%	$64,999
					$1,589,967

4.9.3.3 Seaboard

Seaboard would produce the results as shown in Table 4.10.

4.9.3.4 United

Allocations under United are, of course, different as shown in Table 4.11.

4.9.3.5 Modified Fixed Variable

To test results under MFV, two additional calculations must be made. The first is to approximate return on equity and associated taxes. We estimate this to be about $130 million. The second is to approximate the division of the return on equity and associated taxes as between the sales and storage services. Storage plant constitutes about 1.3% of Tenneco's gas plant in service ($46 million out of $3.6 billion). Applying this percentage to the estimated equity return and taxes of $130 million,

Table 4.10 Adjusted comparative rates – seaboard

	Demand charges		Commodity charges		
	$	% of total	$	% of total	Total charges
The sales rate					
Production (100%)			$847,654		
Fixed trans (50%)	$280,834		280,834		
Variable (100%)			115,646		
Total sales	$280,834	18.4%	$1,244,134	81.6%	$1,524,968
The storage rate					
Fixed (50%)	31,068		31,069		
Variable (100%)			$2,862		
Total sales	$31,068	47.8%	$33,931	52.2%	$64,999
					$1,589,967

Table 4.11 Adjusted comparative rates – united

	Demand charges		Commodity charges		
	$	% of total	$	% of total	Total charges
The sales rate					
Production (100%)			$847,654		
Fixed trans (25–75%)	$140,417		421,251		
Variable (100%)			115,646		
Total sales	$140,417	9.2%	$1,384,551	90.8%	$1,524,968
The storage rate					
Fixed (25–75%)	15,534		46,603		
Variable (100%)			$2,862		
Total sales	$15,534	23.9%	$49,465	76.1%	$64,999
					$1,589,967

for the instant broad brush purposes, about $128,300,000 can be associated with sales service and $1,700,000 with storage service. Adopting these approximations, MFV produces the results as shown in Table 4.12.[19]

---

[19] These approximations are not stated in Docket No. RP88-228. They are derived by the writer as very rough estimates.

4.9 Tenneco Allocations for Rate Design

Table 4.12 Adjusted comparative rates – modified-fixed variable

	Demand charges		Commodity charges		Total charges
	$	% of total	$	% of total	
The sales rate					
Production (100%) Fixed trans (100%-ER +T)	$433,368		$847,654		
Variable (100%)			128,300 115,646		
Total sales	$433,368	28.4%	$1,091,600	71.6%	$1,524,968
The storage rate					
Fixed (100%-ER) +T	60,437				
Variable (100%)			1,700 $2,862		
Total sales	$60,437	93.0%	$4,562	76.1%	$64,999
					$1,589,967

4.9.3.6 Comparative Results

Like a sailing ship tacking in the shifting winds, the influence of value warps cost allocation along the course of changing policy! An easy way to compare the shifting winds is to reduce the end-result demand and commodity charges to index numbers.

This is done below for the sales service rate, Table 4.8, taking the straight fixed–variable formula as a base. Thus, SFV demand charges of $641,178,000 = 100 for demand, and commodity charges of $883,790,000 = 100 for commodity (Table 4.13).

Table 4.13 Comparative demand and commodity components of allocation methods

	Sales service rate index numbers SFV = 100	
	Demand	Commodity
Straight fixed–variable	100	100
Seaboard	44	141
United	22	157
Modified fixed–variable	68	124

The commodity charge is the bellwether of these shifts. This is so because the commodity charge of the pipeline rate is the distributor's out-of-pocket cost of gas. No theory of rate design permits a rate to cover less than out-of-pocket costs. Therefore, the absolute lower limit of the distributor rate is the pipeline's commodity charge. Since it is assumed that firm service customers purchase gas as a necessity (this is a generality, of course), a higher level of demand charges may not result in a pipeline's loss of sales. But the industrial market, particularly for interruptible service, is highly competitive. So a relatively high commodity charge, below which the distributor cannot venture, may result in loss of gas sales to oil, coal, or whatever, while a low commodity charge may retain these sales.

Straight fixed–variable, pegged to keep a low out-of-pocket gas price, fits competitive conditions. The commodity charge index is 100, the lowest of any method. On the other hand, *United* is designed for a conservation era, where non-necessary use is discouraged. Here the index is 157, the highest.

There would seem to be no leeway under SFV. The pipeline commodity charge is reduced to the commodity cost limit. We have said earlier that for practical rate-making, commodity (usage) prices should never sink to the absolute level of out-of-pocket costs. Some increment should be added for overhead costs, so that low-rate customers will contribute at least to a degree to the demand costs allocated to other customers. (When actual prices are set at precisely the out-of-pocket level, as the Order No. 636 translation of SFV costing into pricing directs, this principle is ignored.)

4.9.4 Step 4: Classification of Costs as Demand or Commodity

To this point, we have dealt with Tenneco's total net cost of service, $1,589,967,000 as given in Tables 4.2, 4.4, and 4.6. We now narrow our scope. As an illustration of the full procedure, we focus on just one selected sector, transmission assignable to market areas. This sector was allocated $516,876,000 (line 13, column (a) of Table 4.14) of the total transmission cost. Other sectors require similar allocations. These similar allocations are omitted, since it would be unduly unnerving to include in this chapter all the permeations and permutations of the full allocation. (It is enough that pipeline rate makers grow gray.)

The total for main line transmission of $394,898,000 in line 11, column (a) of Table 4.14 is the same figure as given in line 2 of Table 4.4 and line 2, column (a) of Table 4.6. Also, the division of this total between fixed and variable, $286,717,000 for fixed, line 6, column (a), and $108,181,000 for variable, line 10, column (a), Table 4.14, is the same as stated earlier in Table 4.6 (line 2, columns (b) and (c), respectively, of Table 4.6). Otherwise, the data in Table 4.14 are discontinuous from prior tables.

Columns (b) and (c) of Table 4.14 are necessary to carry out the commission's decision to invoke a two-part demand charge. The transfer in full of return on equity and income taxes, from demand to commodity, is to comply with the commission's MFV dictum. The division of commodity into gas and non-gas costs provides the basis for Tenneco's tariff structure which carries a similar differentiation. Account No. 858 covers the costs paid by Tenneco for the transmission and compression of gas carried for it by other pipelines.

4.9 Tenneco Allocations for Rate Design 121

Table 4.14 STEP 4 Classification of fixed and variable costs as demand or commodity with transfers for market area rate design -- Transmission sector --

$000

		Demand			Commodity	
Line		Total (a)	D_1 (b)	D_2 (c)	Total (d)	Non-Gas (e)	Gas (f)
1	Main line transmission						
2	Fixed						
3	Return on equity & income taxes	$62,184				$62,184	
4	Acct. 858	37,209	35,229	1,980	37,209		
5	Balance	187,324	93,662	93,662	187,324		
6		286,717					
7	Variable						
8	Acct. 858	59,696				59,696	
9	Balance	48,485				48,485	
10		108,181					
11	Total, main line transmission	394,898	128,891	95,642	224,533	170,365	170,365
12	Transfers from supply area, new England laterials, and associated acct. 858, to provide basis for market area rate design – net	121,978	56,287	80,724	137,011	(51,832)	36,799	(15,033)
13	Transmission assignable to market areas	$516,876	$185,178	$176,366	$361,544	$118,533	$36,799	$155,332

A logical question is why any gas costs should be applicable to the transmission function ($36,799,000, line 12, column (f) of Table 4.14) rather than the production function. The answer is, these costs represent gas used for compression or other transmission purposes, or lost in transmission, but not gas available for sale.

4.9.5 Step 5: Classification of Transmission Sector Costs

Table 4.15 picks up the totals of line 13 of Table 4.14, to pursue the further breakdown of the prior costs between those which vary with distance or length of haul (i.e., are "sensitive" to distance) and those which do not fluctuate with distance.

Table 4.15 STEP 5 Classification of transmission sector costs as distance sensitive and non-distance sensitive (Administrative and General)

Line		Total (a)	Demand D$_1$ (b)	D$_2$ (c)	Total (d)	Commodity Non-gas (e)	Gas (f)
1	Distance sensitive	$434,332	$143,906	$135,094	$279,000	$118,533	$36,799
2	Non-distance sensitive (Administrative and General)	82,544	41,272	41,272	82,544		
3	Total	$516,876	$185,178	$176,366	$361,544	$118,533	$36,799

Step 5 is a prerequisite for a zoned rate structure, which incorporates into prices the respective costs of the relative distances of haul over which gas must be carried by the pipeline to areas of consumption. (The division of A&G is 50–50 between D$_1$ and D$_2$. Distance-sensitive costs are divided 25% to mileag, and 75% to non-mileage.)

4.9.6 Step 6: Distance-Related Costs

Now we confront the question: how are distance-related costs to be apportioned among sales and transportation rate schedules? In accordance with Opinion No. 352, Tenneco must allocate these costs in a manner which gives due regard to the distances over which gas must be transported to reach delivery points.

Tenneco utilizes the "centroid" method. The principle of this method is to establish what is essentially a weighted average length of haul from sources of supply to market areas. Since the sources of supply are myriad, and may vary in volume from day to day or season to season, a central point is calculated as the approximate "center of gravity" of gas supply entry. This is the "centroid," the location at which a combined supply from numerous sources may be assumed to enter

4.9 Tenneco Allocations for Rate Design

the system. The centroid is the point of departure for the calculation of distance of haul.[20]

Tenneco sells, and transports, into six market areas, in each of which there are numerous customers. While absolute precision in pricing might imply that each customer be charged only for its own unique distance of haul to its own particular point (or points) of delivery, this would require an individual rate for each customer at each delivery point. Such precision is not required by Opinion No. 352, and for good reason. First, if the rate was to be absolutely precise, it would have to be variable throughout the year, fluctuating with delivery volumes. (An average annual weighted length of haul will likely be different in a cold winter than in a warm winter, for example.) Second, and more importantly, for maximum precision the rate would have to be calculated after the fact, remaining indefinite until actual experience was known, rather than being a definite fixed amount related to prior experience, before the fact. So pre-established rates would be impossible under an "absolute precision" approach to pricing. And pre-established uniform rates for each zone would be ruled out by definition, since uniform zone rates charge each customer within the zone the same, although the distance of haul may vary from customer to customer.

To achieve pre-established definite uniform rates within each zone, an average weighted length of haul into each zone is calculated. Rates for all customers within the zone are based upon this average. The haul is expressed in decatherm-mile units (Dth-miles).

One question remains: should the same method of allocation of distance-related costs be applied uniformly to both sales and transportation rate schedules?

Tenneco says yes. It explains:

> With regard to transportation our experience indicates that transportation in large measure is a replacement for sales because the transportation customers are serving the same major markets as the sales customers from the same major sources of supply. Indeed, in many instances Tennessee's transportation customers are also sales customers and switch back and forth between sales and transportation to meet their requirements...

---

[20] A single centroid, or several, may be appropriate depending upon circumstances. If appreciable volumes enter the system at widely separated locations, more than one centroid may approximate the distance of haul, on average, better than a single centroid. For example, the gas supply for the system may originate both from US production areas at the southern terminus of the transmission line and from deliveries from Canadian pipelines at the northern terminus. This would suggest a dual centroid, one southern, the other northern, with each given weight depending upon the volumes received at each as a proportion of the total volumes inputted into the pipeline. Or, appreciable volumes might enter the system from intermediate areas of supply, suggesting additional centroids, each to be given its proportionate weight. In its initial filing in Docket No. RP88-228, Tenneco proposed five centroids, a "pentacentroid" approach. This is the method reflected in the "allocation factors" stated in Step 7 and in later steps of this chapter. Later, Tenneco simplified its approach, adopting a single, or alternatively a dual, centroid. For all practicable purposes, the simplification does not impact upon the procedure's end-results, so Step 7 and later steps are stated in the original distance-of-haul units of "pentacentroid."

The use of the Tennessee system by the transportation customers now closely resembles the use by the sales customers. The transportation customers benefit from the integrated system, not just the segment between a certain receipt and delivery point, in obtaining reliable transportation service from Tennessee. Under these circumstances, it is appropriate to develop the transportation Dth-miles on the same basis as the sales Dth-miles. Assuring parity in treatment of sales and transportation services is also important because those services compete with one another. Inconsistent Dth-mile methods could result in a competitive advantage for one service over another and could distort price signals in the market and among producers selling gas from competing sources of supply ...

4.9.6.1 Distance-Sensitive Costs

There are four mileage-related allocations for each of Tenneco's six sales zones (Southern, Central, Eastern, Northern, New York, and New England). Two of the allocations are necessary for demand costs, and two for commodity costs. The Dth-mile method is used for all four allocations, but with different indices for each.

(1) D_1 demand costs are apportioned to sales zones on the basis of the ratio of (i) the sum of the distances of haul, measured in decatherm-miles (Dth-miles), for the volumes delivered over the peak period to each delivery point in the zone, to (ii) the total system distances of haul for peak period volumes. In simpler terms, the index is "peak period volumes times distance" for the zone as a proportion of a like total for the system.

(2) D_2 demand costs similarly are apportioned commensurate with relative zone-to-system distances of haul, but with the index being annual quantity limitation (AQL) volumes.

(3 and 4) The two gas commodity cost allocations to zones fall into the same pattern. Both adopt annual delivery volumes as an index (expressed as an "average day"), but the composition of the volumes included in the index differs. For the utilization of the system which includes both sales and transportation services, the index volumes include both. For system utilization for sales only, the index is comprised just of sales volumes. (As an aside, we mention another variation. For certain purposes, volumes may be differentiated as between "seasonal" and "total annual.")

In each case the Dth-miles for all the delivery points within a sales zone are totaled. The costs assigned to a sales zone are the same fraction of the total system costs as the ratio of the Dth-miles in the zone to the total system Dth-miles. To illustrate, if total system costs (whether D_1 demand costs, D_2 demand costs, or gas commodity costs) are $1 million, total system Dth-miles are 5 million, and the zone's Dth-miles are 1 million, the zone allocation would be

$$\$1,000,000 \times 1 \text{ million}/5 \text{ million} = \$200,000 \text{ or}$$

$$\text{Total system cost} \times \frac{\text{Zone Dth - miles}}{\text{Total system Dth - miles}} = \text{Zone cost}$$

As is apparent, calculations of the Dth-miles for each zone for each of the four indices are required for this formula, the total system Dth-miles being merely the

4.9 Tenneco Allocations for Rate Design   125

aggregate of the zonal miles. The zonal miles are themselves the aggregate of the miles from the centroid to each delivery point within the zone. In other words, for each of the four indices

1. Dth-miles from centroid to delivery point are calculated for each delivery point;
2. such delivery point miles are aggregated by sales zones; and
3. the zone miles are aggregated for the system total.

4.9.6.2 Non-distance-Sensitive Costs

As will be recalled from Table 4.15, non-distance-sensitive costs (administrative and general, or A&G) are an appreciable part of total costs. These also must be allocated to sales zones. By definition, these are not mileage-related, so Dth-miles of haul do not enter into the procedure. The D_1 and D_2 demand indices for non-distance-related costs (A&G) are the same as for the distance-related costs, namely, peak day volumes and AQL volumes, respectively, except that they are not weighted by distance of haul.

No non-distance-sensitive (A&G) costs are considered to be related to commodity.

4.9.7 Step 7: The New York Zone

Steps 4 and 5 indicated that transmission sector costs were $516,870,000, with this total broken down between distance-sensitive and non-distance-sensitive costs, each category being further classified as D_1 and D_2 demand, or non-gas or gas commodity. These data are the inputs for Step 7, which illustrates the procedure for allocating costs to sales zones via the indices discussed in Step 6. The New York sales zone is adopted as an example.

Costs to be allocated, which total to the before mentioned $516,876,000, are given in column (e) of Table 4.16. The several different percentages of these total costs applicable to the individual components of that total appear in column (d), arrived at as the ratio of New York data to total system data, i.e., as the ratio of column (c) to column (b). These percentages of the system demand and commodity costs produce the allocations to the New York zone given in columns (f) and (g). They add to a zone allocation of $73,334,000 (line 13, column (h)) of Step 4.

4.9.8 Step 8: Per-Unit Rate Elements

We have arrived at the final allocation step, which is to translate the two demand and the two commodity costs for the zone into per-unit charges to be incorporated into rates for the zone.

This translation is accomplished by prorating each cost on the basis of the appropriate "billing determinants." In simplest terms, a billing determinant represents the

Table 4.16 STEP 7 Allocation of costs to sales zones -- Allocation of transmission sector costs to New York zone --

Line		Index (a)	Allocation factors Total system (b)	New York sales zone (c)	New York as % of Total system (ratio c to b) (d)	Costs to be allocated ($000) (e)	Allocation t (d × e) ($0 Demand (f)	Commodity (g)
1	Distance sensitive costs		-- 100 Dth miles --					
2	Demand							
3	D$_1$	Peak day	34,502,425	5,356,247	0.15524	$ 143,906	$ 22,340	
4	D$_2$	AQLs	39,403,166	5,253,033	0.13331	135,094	18,010	
5	Commodity							
6	Non-gas		24,748,907	3,871,488	0.15643	118,533		18,542
7	Gas		11,392,190	2,429,117	0.21322	36,799		7,846
8	Non-distance sensitive costs (Administrative & General)		-- volumes --					
9	D$_1$ Costs	Peak day	4,580,478	408,120	0.0891	41,272	3,677	
10	D$_2$ Costs	AQLs	5,663,943	400,652	0.0707	41,272	2,919	
11	Total costs be be allocated					$ 516,876		
12	Total allocations to New York sales zone						$ 46,946	$ 26,388
13								$ 73,334

4.9 Tenneco Allocations for Rate Design

number of units which reasonably may be expected to be billed to customers over a year, so that the monthly per-unit charge for that unit will, over a year's time, recoup the cost. Thus, if a total of 4,932,641 per-dth demand units will be billed over a year, and the cost to be recovered is $22,340,000, each demand unit must be priced at $4.53. Obviously, if fewer units are sold, that per-unit demand charge will tail to recover costs.

Table 4.17 shows the derivation of the transmission sector component of the per-unit rates to be applicable to the New York.

Table 4.17 STEP 8 Assignment of costs to per-unit rate elements -- New York zone transmission sector costs --

Line		Cost to be assigned ($000) (a)	Billing determinant (b)	Per-unit rate (c)
1	Distance sensitive costs			
2	D_1 demand	$ 22,340	4,932,614	$ 4.53
3	D_2 demand	18,010	14,237,980	0.1232
4	Non-gas commodity	18,542	102,528,865	0.1808
5	Gas commodity	7,846	64,344,170	0.1220
6	Administrative and general costs (Non-distance sensitive)			
7	D_1 demand	3,677	4,932,614	0.75
8	D_2 demand	2,919	1,46,237,980	0.02
9	Total costs assigned	$ 73,334		
10	Recapitulation of per-unit rate elements:			
11	Combined D_1 demand charge	$ 5.28		
12	Combined D_2 demand charge	0.1432		
13	Non-gas commodity charge	0.1808		
14	Gas commodity charge	0.1220		

Re lines 4 and 5, and 13 and 14, note that the single commodity charge of past rate designs has been refined to distinguish between the cost of purchased gas and other variable costs, stating these two costs as separate note elements. Other pipelines, such as Transco, continued the use of the single commodity change.

The cost inputs to Table 4.17 column (a) are taken from Table 4.16. As shown there, the costs to be assigned to the zone's billing units total $73,334,000. Per-unit cost assignments of column (c) represent the division of the number of billing determinants, column (b), into the associated cost, column (a).

Obviously, the number of billing determinants for D_1 and D_2 demand costs are the same for both distance- and non-distance-sensitive costs (lines 2 and 7, and lines 3 and 8, of column (b)), since the costs will be combined and customers will be billed for the identical number of units.

Lines 11 through 14 recapitulate the end-result of the procedure. The following per-unit charges, representative of transmission sector costs, will be incorporated into final rates.

D_1, Demand charges per unit		
Distance sensitive	$4.53	
Non-distance sensitive	$0.75	
Total		$ 5.28
D_2, Demand charges per unit		
Distance sensitive	$0.1232	
Non-distance sensitive	$0.02	
Total		$0.1432
Non-gas commodity charge per unit		$0.1808
Gas commodity charge per unit		$0.1220

Since Steps 4 through 8 relate only to transmission sector costs, the foregoing per-unit charges do not represent final rates—storage and production function costs must be added so that rates will perform their purpose of recouping the system's costs in full.

4.9.9 Step 9: Total System Costs Revisited

Steps 1, 2, and 3 dealt with the costs of the entire system, $1,589,967,000. We return to this total now, to put into better perspective the transmission sector costs which were allocated in the later steps, and to present a more complete picture.

Since the relationships between the cost components are difficult to visualize using the actual figures as has been done to date (at least without a calculator in hand), the component data have been reduced to a form of index number with the total system cost of $1,589,967,000 = $1,000. Each resulting number can easily be converted in one's mind to the conventional index numbers of "Base = 100" by inserting a decimal point one figure to the left. Thus, $1,000 becomes 100.0, 100%, $441 becomes 44.1%, the percentages being in relation to the total system cost, of course. As restated in this fashion, the overall cost of service may be summarized as shown in Table 4.18.[21]

Table 4.18 gives considerable insight into the results of the modified fixed–variable allocation formula. Referring to the data in line 13, 44.1% of systems costs are fixed (column (a)). 31.1% of the system costs are recovered in demand charges (column (f)), 68.2% through commodity charges (column (j)), and 0.7% through special storage rates (column (k)).

MFV mandates that the fixed costs of transmission and storage, less return on equity and income taxes, be recovered through demand charges. Table 4.18 shows that the rate design allocations accomplish this. This conclusion can be confirmed from the data, with allowance for rounding, as given in Table 4.19:

---

[21] Because the actual numbers are so large, some inputs have been rounded. Therefore, the table should be taken as an approximation, not a precise calculation.

4.9 Tenneco Allocations for Rate Design

Table 4.18 STEP 9 The system as a whole (Base, Net system cost of service) ($1,589,967,000) = $1,000

Line Total		Cost allocation			Re-allocation for rate design									
					Demand			Commodity						
		Fixed (a)	Variable (b)	Total (c)	D_1 (d)	D_2 (e)	D_{1+2} (f)	Fixed (g)	Variable (h)	Eq. Ret. + Inc Taxes (i)	Total (j)	Other (k)	(l)
1	Production	$50	$483	$533	$5	$–	$5	$45	$483	$–	$528	$–	$533
2	Storage												
3	General storage	32	1	33									
4	Designated storage[a]	6	1	7									
5	Total storage	38	2	40	14	14	28	–	1	4	5	7[a]	40
6	Transmission												
7	Main system (exc. acct 858)	157	30	187	59	59	118	–	30	39	69	–	187
8	Account 828[b]	24	38	62	22	2	24	–	38	–	38	–	62
9	Subtotal	181	68	249	81	61	142	–	68	39	107	–	249
10	Supply area	170	5	175	67	67	134	–	5	36	41	–	175
11	New England laterals	2	1	3	1	1	2	–	0.3	0.7	1	–	3
12	Total trans.	353	74	427	149	129	278	–	73.3	75.7	149	–	427
13	Total system	$441	$559	$1,000	$168	$143	$311	$45	$557.3	$79.7	$682	$7	$1,000

[a] Costs assigned to SS-E/NE service, covered by specific rate. (General storage is used to reinforce the system as an integrated unit, and the costs therefore are rolled-in.)
[b] Costs for transmission and compression of gas by others.

Table 4.19 Confirmation of fixed costs to be borne by demand charges

	Index: Base = $1,000	Table source Line column
System fixed costs	$441	13 (a)
Less: designated storage (allocated separately)	(6)	4 (a)
		1 (a)
Less: fixed production costs	(45)	Less: 1 (g)
Fixed costs of transmission and general storage	390	
Less: return on equity and Associated taxes	(80)	13 (i)
Fixed costs to be borne by Demand charges	$310	13 (f)

4.9.10 Closing Reminders

One allocation has been outlined above in considerable, but not full, detail. It should provide some insight into the complexities of the process as a mathematical procedure. And, it should promote some understanding of the policy considerations entering into the process as an exercise in applied economics. At least, that is our hope.

We close by paraphrasing a quotation on prior pages from Opinion No. 352: "The allocation issue is primarily concerned with the relative responsibilities for cost incurrence." But, "that issue cannot be determined in isolation of other considerations," such as encouraging maximum utilization of physical facilities, both pipeline and distributor (and producer too?) thus avoiding load loss and system underutilization, assuring stable revenues, providing correct price signals to entities concerned as well as the market place as a whole (in other words, being in step with the market), and giving incentives for efficient operation and gas acquisition. So allocation is not just narrow-vision costing. As Tennessee noted, "No one method can lay claim to being the right method ... (the selection must be) bottomed on fairness ... and judgment."

Chapter 5
The Value Approach to Pricing: Demand Influence

Abstract In this chapter we reverse direction, turning away from cost-influenced supply to value-influenced demand. The market, which reflects consumer preferences, gauges demand. Demand for energy is both direct and derived. Natural gas, for example, is desired for its heating ability alone, a direct demand, and also for its use as a fuel in industrial processing, an indirect demand depending upon the market for the product being processed. Important to the forecasting of energy demand is price elasticity, the responsiveness of the market to changes in price. Ignoring the impact of price changes can have a disastrous affect upon the quantities of energy required. Price differences between products having the same or similar costs can encourage price differentiation, a permissible result, or monopoly pricing, prohibited under the anti-trust statues. The theory of class price establishes reasonable distinctions.

5.1 Preface

This chapter, like the preceding chapter, is couched toward the economics of the capital-intensive industries, with emphasis upon the regulated energy utilities.

Notwithstanding this emphasis, the downward trend of unit costs with increases in volume has huge influence on the pricing practices of industries other than utilities, who must overcome pervasive overheads with dependable sales volumes.

Utility experience provides a guide to operating and pricing policies suitable for adoption by businesses with high fixed costs and low variable costs. The economic necessities are the same for non-utilities as for utilities. Only the policy alternatives are different. Chapter 5 should be read with this similarity in mind.

5.2 Value of Service Defined

Value of service is the second approach to utility pricing. While the cost of service approach emphasizes the analysis of cost of production, i.e., *economic supply* factors, the value of service approach is primarily concerned with the factors influencing economic demand for the utility product or service.

As utility products or services are used for many varied economic purposes in the home, business, and industry—for lighting, cooking, water heating, space heating, air conditioning, appliances, irrigation, and industrial processes, to mention but a few—the analysis of the composite utility demand is necessarily an analysis of the individual demands for each of the different possible uses. Thus, the value of service approach may be defined as *the investigation, and implementation through pricing policy, of the economic demand factors affecting utility markets.*[1] It is *the accommodation of prices to demand.*[2]

5.3 Cost vs. Value in Juxtaposition

Prices, of course, are the sought for end-result of both the cost and the value approaches. In theory, prices resulting from a cost procedure could diverge radically from those resulting from value criteria. In practice, though, the differences may not be quite as drastic as theory might suggest. The reasons are that each approach operates as a constraint on the other and that both must result in a set of prices which in the aggregate come within the umbrella of the overall company-wide cost of service. As a very broad generalization, under cost-based pricing, rates will come closer to costs than to competitive market prices; while under value, rates will come closer to the market than to costs. Whichever approach is followed, rates will diverge from both cost and value, but to different degrees.

Although the cost and value approaches are different, and even contradictory in many respects, nevertheless, each includes important elements of the other. For example, a forward looking cost of service analysis must assume as a starting point an anticipated demand (or sales) schedule over some future time period. This is necessary to establish the level of production which will be required, and hence, the expected amount and utilization of necessary plant, personnel, and materials from

---

[1] The term "demand" has a general economic meaning, as in "supply and demand", and that is the sense in which it is used at this point. In utilities, the term is also used to indicate relative levels of use, e.g., a maximum level (a "peak" level) or an average level. It is commonly found as a term in utility rates, e.g., the "demand" charge (related to the customer's maximum rate of use) found in combination with the "energy" charge (related to the customer's total use).

[2] Emery Trozel presents the interesting thought, "In regulatory action the value of service is an ethical concept; it is what the commissions think the buyers should pay, not an objective or market-place measure of the customers' willingness to buy at various prices." *Economics of Public Utilities*, Rinehart & Co., Inc., New York, 1947, p. 544.

Some writers simply beg the definitional question. Marsha Gransee, a *Public Utilities Fortnightly* writer, quoting James C. Bonbright, *Principles of Public Utility Rates*, 1961 (not the updated edition) notes Bonbright's opinion that the value of service standard is "no easy question since the term has been used loosely, without benefit of any formal definition." She concludes, "The term seems to be used quite loosely by state pubic utility commissions. Perhaps the only way it can be defined is by contrast; under a cost-of-service standard, the price per unit of product is set at the cost per unit. 'Value of service' simply refers to the price which the consumer is willing to pay for a certain good or service." Gransee, M., "Natural Gas Pricing in a Competitive Market," *Public Utilities Fortnightly*, November 10, 1983.

which future costs may be estimated. Similarly, a value of service analysis cannot be made without some regard to costs and to the prices which would be required to cover these costs. The distinction, then, is one of emphasis.

In the cost of service approach, pricing policy is assumed to be influenced by demand objectives only as inherent cost considerations would dictate. For example, under cost, rates can be designed to encourage demand-shaping objectives, such as off-peak use, better load factors, etc., because these objectives result in cost savings. On the other hand, value or market oriented prices and price differentials may be consistent with the trend of costs even though they may be established quite independently of costs.[3]

The much publicized post-divesture price competition between AT&T and MCI for long distance services offers conspicuous examples of value-oriented prices which presumably were consistent with costs. A bit later, partial value orientation for prices was introduced for natural gas.[4]

5.4 The "Upper and Lower Limit of Rates" Concept

It is stated commonly as a truism that cost of service represents the lower limit of rates and value of service the upper limit. These statements are true as very broad generalities, but are valid in practice only with considerable qualification. Obviously no business can continue to operate for long if its costs are not covered by the prices of what it sells. No business can operate permanently at a loss. This is the basis for the cost as lower-limit rule. But one or more of the several individual rate schedules of a utility can return less than full costs without necessarily jeopardizing the utility's financial position. It is the composite result, in terms of total revenues, of the entire rate structure which counts. Thus, cost of service is a lower limit only for the utility's rates as a whole. It does not necessarily operate as a limit for an individual schedule. Furthermore, it will be recalled from the preceding chapters that the determination of the cost applicable to any given service is often arbitrary—it may not be possible to arrive at a conclusive cost figure. Under these circumstances the

---

[3] Professor Martin G. Glaeser in his *Outlines of Public Utility Economics* (The MacMillan Company, New York, 1931, Ch. XXVIII, pp. 637–639) cogently analyzes "some misconceptions of public utility rate theory". Professor Glaeser points out that neither the cost of service nor the value of service principle is a complete and independent explanation of the way in which utility rates should be fixed. The present writer hopes that this will be clear here also.

[4] In 1984 and 1985, the Federal Energy Regulatory Commission (FERC) was inaugurating new policies and pricing schemes for "unbundled" pipeline transportation of gas in a competitive environment. A 1985 directive of that commission introduced three descriptive terms for prices, which are strongly influenced by market conditions (or, as this chapter would call them, value prices). These terms are: market-sensitive rates, market-responsive rates, and market-based pricing. For all practical purposes, these three terms are synonymous. Federal Energy Regulatory Commission, "Notice Requesting Supplemental Comments," Docket No. RM85-1-000, issued October 9, 1985 (contemporaneously with the issuance of Order No. 436). The first two terms mentioned appear in mimeo, page 8; the third on mimeo, page 79.

generalized concept of cost as an inflexible limit for any particular utility price is not too useful.

Under regulation there has been, however, an inflexible cost-based lower limit for each and every individual rate schedule. This lower limit is current out-of-pocket or incremental cost.[5] While an isolated rate schedule may fail to recoup *average* costs in full, it must at least cover the additional costs which are brought about by customer usage under the schedule. If it fails to do so, the rate imposes a burden on other rate schedules. Consequently, the rule is that no rate schedule should be priced so low as to increase the costs which must be picked up by other schedules. The rule generally is expanded to provide that each schedule must cover not only its incremental costs, but also a bit more, so as to make at least a minimal contribution to the cost burden of the remaining schedules. It appears that this rule is being relaxed in a number of regulatory jurisdictions. The degree to which it will be enforced in the future is uncertain.

Value of service as the upper limit of rates similarly needs careful examination. In its theoretical sense, of course, value of service is always the upper limit, as no customer will pay more than the service is worth. But as a practical matter, how closely can value of service be determined? And even if determinable, is it always the upper rate limit, or may other factors be governing? Where a real substitute is readily available, as when electricity and natural gas compete in the same area for cooking, water heating, and space heating markets, the price of the substitute becomes an acceptable measure of the value of service. For either utility to increase its rates appreciably above those of the other for a comparable use would be to price itself out of the market. Thus, value of service is clear-cut and limiting. But just as frequently for utilities, there is no close substitute. When electricity is available for lighting, neither gaslights nor kerosene lamps offer any effective competition. Because of this lack of competition, it is probable that consumers would pay many times more than they actually pay in order to get electric service for lighting. As the real value in this case far exceeds the prevailing pricing, it is obvious that value has limited application as an upper limit.

Even where substitutions between electricity and natural gas are possible because of the ready availability of each, some customers may be constrained from exercising a price-directed choice. The most obvious example is the locked-in or captive residential customer, whose home is outfitted with appliances suited only for one or the other of the two alternative energy sources. Even a radical disparity in price

---

[5] The Department of Defense, for itself and all other federal executive agencies, in comments on new California telephone regulation, is emphatic. "Incremental cost is the only relevant standard for analyzing the price floors for services that face effective price competition or a highly elastic demand function ... Incremental cost identifies the minimum price that must be obtained from that service. A price above incremental cost yields a net financial improvement to the telephone company while one below incremental cost yields a net financial detriment." "Comments on the Scope of Cost Studies", submitted on behalf of the US Department of Defense and All Other Federal Executive Agencies, to California Public Utilities Commission in Investigation (I.) 87-11-033, Phase III (February 8, 1990).

5.4 The "Upper and Lower Limit of Rates" Concept

probably will not be sufficient to induce the locked-in homeowner to undertake the major investment needed to shift to the cheaper energy. Therefore, the customer continues to use currently installed appliances until they need replacement. In the case of the water heater, this may be 5 or 10 years into the future. For a heating system, the period usually will be much longer, from 20 years through the life of the home itself.

In passing, it should be noted that the ability to shift between fuels is much less constrained for the homeowner (or business) using oil or coal for space heating. The availability of gas conversion burners, which can be placed in an existing oil furnace, often makes a shift from oil to gas heat easy and economical. In fact, a significant part of the growth in gas demand has resulted from oil to gas heat conversions. Here relative convenience and other value factors, such as cleanliness, have played a role perhaps equally as important as relative price.

Returning to the natural gas/electric choice for the major home appliances (the water heater and furnace or other space heating method), the locked-in customer fact of life is an underlying reason for the intense competition between the two energies in the new home market. Whichever choice the customer makes when he plans his new home, the customer is likely to stay with the chosen energy for an extended period. The market gain is relatively permanent.

Value of service is sometimes termed "what the traffic will bear." One of the most straightforward examples is the situation of a dual-fuel industrial customer using fuel for process heating. The term "dual-fuel" means that the user has fuel burning equipment which can easily change over from one type of fuel to another, sometimes instantaneously, but more often in a few minutes or at most a few hours. Interruptible natural gas, i.e., gas whose delivery can be stopped entirely or diminished in volume by the gas utility when it needs the gas for higher priority purposes, and oil are the two fuels most often in juxtaposition. This is the classic case of competitive prices in action. Gas will not be burned unless its price, taking into consideration certain inherent advantages, is as cheap as oil, and vice versa.

The concept, "what the traffic will bear," also may be applicable in cases where the service which can be offered has some of the limiting characteristics of a by-product. To illustrate, the Pacific Northwest region is an area where hydro-generating plants on the Columbia River and its tributaries are the leading sources of electricity. The power supply situation varies with the seasons. In the spring and summer months of "wet" years, and often in other months as well, there is water available from stream flows in excess of the volumes available in other seasons, and over and above the volumes retained in storage for release to meet high winter demands. This excess seasonal water can be run through generators to produce power if there is a market for that power. (If there is no market, the water flows to the sea unused.) Therefore, in the "wet" years, the Bonneville Power Administration and other Northwest electric utilities can generate a supply of "secondary" energy which can be sold primarily only in the spring and summer and only in those "wet" years. Statistical analysis of the history of stream flows establishes the probabilities of occurrence, and thus lessens to an extent the speculative nature of availability. Nonetheless, because of its limited availability, such energy does not have a ready market at a price comparable to "firm" or dependable energy. "What the traffic will bear" may be the price standard. By-products such as secondary power can be sold only in a market which can accommodate uncertain delivery. The level of that market determines the rates which can be charged.

Computations of cost for by-product sales, if necessary at all, may concentrate on calculating only the incremental costs of service—the *additional* costs incurred in delivering that service—to determine the lower limit of price. As we have emphasized, when a utility is faced with a limited market, if it can sell in that market for a rate which covers incremental costs and in addition makes some contribution to other costs, the result is advantageous to all classes of customers.

5.5 Economic Demand

Economic demand generally is defined as a schedule of the amounts of a product which buyers will purchase at all practicable prices at any given time. This definition is too rigorous for our purposes. It is more useful to consider economic demand as an *estimate of the amounts of the utility product or service which can be sold for given purposes, under given rates (and given promotional efforts), during given time periods.* The estimate is usually that of the utility management, although on occasion the regulatory commission may substitute its own estimate. Note that, while demand is what purchasers will actually purchase under given conditions, it is the seller's estimate of demand that is the important factor in rate making since formulation must be prospective.

5.6 Direct and Derived Demand

Utility demand may be either direct or derived, or both. It is direct when the utility service or product is desired for itself, as an "end product." Thus, the demand for electricity for lighting is *direct*. When the utility product or service is used as part of a productive process, such as gas for heating in the manufacture of glass, the demand for these uses is dependent upon the demand for the manufactured product. If there is a good market for glass, the demand for the gas required in its production will be good, and vice versa. In such cases, the utility demand is *derived*. The importance of this concept is that it illustrates the complexity of thoroughgoing utility demand analysis. Any accurate estimate of utility demand must include, as a first step, estimates of the demand for all of the many different types of goods or uses for which the utility product is one of the productive agents, for only on this basis can the total utility demand be ascertained with any reliability.

5.7 Option Demand

An intriguing element of consumer demand is discussed by Berryhill and Reinking in relation to the choice of the telephone user between flat and measured service.

These writers suggest that a separate part of the appeal of flat rate service is the *option* to make as many calls as desired, for as long as desired, without the penalty of an additional charge, irrespective of whether the user has the habit of making a large number of calls. As evidence, the writers note that many subscribers continue to choose flat rate service even though measured service would be cheaper for them. In other words, the option to make the call has a value in itself, whether or not the call is made.[6]

Option demand is an elusive concept. The writer's personal experience tends to validate the general and somewhat broader proposition that the offering of a choice to the user may be a valuable concession.

To cite an example, in the days of full merchant service by natural gas pipelines and distributors, a distributor followed the practice of offering only "requirements" contracts to its large volume dual-fuel interruptible customers. This meant that customers could use oil only when gas was curtailed by the distributor—whenever gas was available it had to be used by the customer even though oil might be cheaper. These contracts were acceptable when gas, despite oil price fluctuations, was generally the least expensive fuel. But the outlook changed. The prognosis for gas prices appeared to be one of continuing upward escalation. To keep its dual-fuel customers online, the utility designed a special rate under which customers were given the option to switch to oil at their discretion, upon payment of an inversely blocked "option charge" (the customers referred to the charge as a penalty). When gas was taken, the distributor's regular rate applied. The inverse blocking of the option charge proved to be an attractive feature with customers. The charge was small when the customer shifted only a small part of its annual requirements to oil. It escalated in steps as the customer used higher proportions of oil. Thus, the customer had a limited amount of flexibility for negligible charge. The charge became significant only as the customer exercised the option to the full extent. Charge or penalty, the rate was successful, demonstrating that the option had a concrete value to the customer.

In the case of the small-use customer, it is probably than an option per se has a value, but only subjectively. A more definite value probably can be attached for the larger customer, who may be more inclined to weigh the cost of alternatives.

5.8 The Price Elasticity of Demand

Economists classify demand as being elastic or inelastic depending upon whether it is relatively responsive or unresponsive to a change in price. If a change in price results in a greater percent change in demand (for example, if a small price

---

[6]It remains to be demonstrated that the rank and file of residential customers are sufficiently cost conscious and knowledgeable of comparative rates, so as to compute comparative bills under the two rates, particularly if the price difference is viewed as being minor. Berryhill Estela B., Reinking, R.D., "Optimal Local Measured Telephone Service- Economic Efficiency with Consumer Choice", *Public Utilities Fortnightly*, January 5, 1984.

reduction will increase more than proportionally the amount demanded, or vice versa), demand is said to be *elastic*. If, however, the amount demanded changes less than proportionally with fluctuations in price, demand is said to be *inelastic*. This general economic concept is a highly useful tool, for it is hardly an oversimplification to state that the utility's problem in deciding whether to raise or lower a given rate, other considerations being equal, rests upon the decision as to whether or not demand under the rate is elastic or inelastic, and to what degree. The central question is: to what extent will a rate change impact demand, and accordingly raise or lower revenues?

It is helpful to measure the price elasticity of demand in mathematical terms, since this is a standardized method of presentation. The formula for price elasticity is as follows:

Elasticity = Percent change in quantity sold/Opposite percent change in price

If the result of applying the above formula (the elasticity coefficient) is less than one, demand is said to be inelastic; if greater than one, demand is said to be elastic.

Thus, if a price of 10% is accompanied by a decline in sales of 5%, elasticity is -0.5 and demand is inelastic. The formula is as follows:

$$E = -5\%/+10\% = -1.5$$

In the case of a price drop of 10%, if the quantity sold rises only 8%, demand is inelastic (0.8), while if quantity rises 12%, demand is elastic (1.2) as follows:

$$E = +8/-10 = +.8 \quad E = +12/-10 = +1.2$$

Generally speaking, demand for luxury uses tends to be elastic, and demand for necessities tends to be inelastic. A minimum amount of electricity for lighting, for example, will be used by the average consumer almost regardless of price, as a minimum amount of lighting is considered to be a necessity today. In like manner, the average consumer will use a minimum amount of gas or electricity for cooking, hot water, and space heating or cooling. However, above these minimums, usage will be more responsive to price. Lower rates will encourage less careful use of lights and hot water and lead to warmer home temperatures in the winter and greater use of air conditioning in the summer. Conversely, higher rates will discourage wasteful use. Any material change in rate levels will change usage, but the extent of the change in usage, either up or down, will tend to be inversely variable with the change in rates. However, price elasticity in practice is not a straight-line function.

Because a large portion of utility use is to supply necessary services, it is often stated that utility demand is less affected by changes in business conditions than is the demand for other products. This is a generalization to be accepted with caution. Insofar as the demand results from necessary uses, it is true. But the day is long past, for example, when the residential loads of the natural gas and electric utilities include only the small consumption per customer which represents the necessary typical minimum. Not only are most of the utilities supplying residential customers for uses, or in quantities, which could be curtailed in the event of economic recession, but they are also supplying increasing amounts for commercial and industrial uses, the demand for which is largely derived, and would be diminished as the nation's economy slowed.

The presence or absence of alternatives directly influences the elasticity of demand. It is important that this be kept in mind when analyzing the demand for commercial and industrial utility uses. If satisfactory alternatives are available, e.g., if oil or coal can be substituted for gas in an industrial process, the price of gas must be competitive with the prices of these alternative energies, or gas will lose its share of the market. Thus, the availability of substitutes tends to make demand highly elastic. Conversely, of course, the lack of substitutes tends to stabilize demand.

Another important concept is that of the *unitary elasticity* of demand. Demand for a product is said to have a unitary elasticity when the *total amount spent* for the product *remains the same* after a change in price.

There seems to be some early historical evidence that utility demand insofar as non-industrial uses are concerned may have tended toward unitary elasticity. In the last 1940s and 1950s rates of electric distributors supplied on a preferential basis by the Tennessee Valley Authority and the Bonneville Power Administration were declining. In almost all cases (and with the economy being stable), within a year or two after a rate reduction, total revenues of these distributors rebounded to the point where they were equal to or greater than they were before the reduction. This tendency of utility demand had theretofore been unrecognized. Earlier it had been almost axiomatic that "you can't reduce rates until you increase sales, and you can't increase sales until you reduce rates." This concept was referred to as the "vicious circle" of rate making. It led to elaborate devices such as the "objective" rate discussed elsewhere, designed to overcome this presumed difficulty.

5.9 The Crucial Importance of Price Elasticity

Let no reader make the error of assuming that the price elasticity of demand is just one more theoretical concept of little practical relevance. Precisely the reverse is true; for advance planning purposes, it is probable that no other single demand-side consideration is of equal importance, one writer has observed.[7]

The record of electric utility managements in forecasting electric demand has been an unenviable one ... The forecast failings of both the 1970s and 1980s appear to come from a single source, a seeming disregard for the price elasticity of electric demand. In both the 1970s and 1980s there have been substantial swings in the rate of change of real electric rates, first upward and then downward. In both cases managements effectively denied that these changes would materially alter the entrenched trend in growth of electric demand.

---

[7] Studness, C.M., "The Price Elasticity of Electric Demand and Utility Forecasts", *Public Utilities Fortnightly*, September 29, 1988.

Of more recent vintage, some share the view that responsibility for the nuclear generating plan fiasco that plagued the Pacific Northwest electric industry (WPPSS) can be traced to neglect of due consideration of the elasticity of demand with rising prices. The same neglect was a causal factor in the equally monumental take-or-pay dilemma of the natural gas industry, which took years to resolve. *Forbes* calls this elasticity the "lethal equation," noting, in connection with the US Postal Service, "every time postal rates go up, postal volume goes down".[8]

Throughout the remainder of this chapter we will occasionally be making reference to events such as those just mentioned. To help the reader keep these events in context, the more significant time frames which are involved are set forth in the following table:

Time frames

	1950's through 1972	The "Golden Age" of rate tranquility
Energy crisis	1973	Arab oil embargo: beginning of energy crisis
	1973–1979	Severe gas supply shortages
	1973–1982	Escalation of energy prices: conservation in, promotion out
	1978	Public utility regulatory policies act (PURPA) and natural gas policy act (NGPA) enacted
	1982	The energy bust: end of energy crisis
	1982–1987	Energy surpluses
	1988	Electric shortages foreseen
	1990	Gas bubble disappearing
	1996–present	Restructuring, including California electric crisis of 2000–2001

5.9.1 Electric—Washington Public Power Supply System (WPPSS)

Much of the blame for nuclear power plant debacles can be traced to a lack of correlation between the supply and demand forecasts; specifically, the demand forecasts did not take account of the market-depressing effects of higher costs which could only emerge as higher prices. Generally speaking, this flaw was aggravated

---

[8]Cook, J., "A Mailman's Lot is Not A Happy One", *Forbes*, April 27, 1992.

5.9 The Crucial Importance of Price Elasticity

on both the supply and demand sides; construction costs kept rising due to new regulatory requirements which imposed higher capital costs and led to expensive schedule delays. "Updated" cost estimates consistently were too low, while on the demand side, price elasticity was largely ignored or underplayed. The combination resulted in a deadly scenario.

The aggravating factors just mentioned were prominent in the default of $2.25 billion of bonds issued by the Washington Public Power Supply System which we cite as an example. The WPPSS default was described by the US Securities and Exchange Commission as "the largest non-payment default in municipal bond history."[9]

In a 1975 speech that has become legend in the Northwest energy community, the head of the Bonneville Power Administration had warned of an energy crisis of epic proportions and castigated the opponents of a plan to build a fleet of nuclear and coal-fired plants. "Homes will be cold and dark and factories will close."

The Securities and Exchange Commission report gave this analysis.

> The original estimate of the total cost ... was $2.25 billion. The estimate after the last bond sale was almost $12 billion.
>
> The projects were undertaken based on the projected need for the power that was to be produced by the projects ..... During the period of the sales ... of the bonds, each successive forecast showed a smaller increase in power demand. Moreover, the actual demand for power during the sale of bonds was less than even the reduced forecasts ... [Information was not disclosed which] would have indicated that the forecasts might be overstated and could continue to decline.

There were wide variances in the forecasting techniques that the utilities used. *Some utilities did not consider price elasticity of demand in their calculation* ... Utilities did not necessarily update their forecasts annually ... The absence of a region-wide review led to duplicative forecasts.

While ignoring price elasticity as an essential ingredient for forecasts was a causal factor in the WPPSS electrical demand forecasting errors, other sectors of the electric industry recognized elasticity, but persuaded themselves that it had no relevance to electricity "under the prevailing circumstances."

The decision to undertake the latter two of the WPPSS projects had been reached in June 1973. The date is significant, 1973 being the year of the Arab oil embargo and natural gas supply shortages. The under estimation of price elasticity was not confined to electric. In 1983, looking back at the energy crisis, *Business Week* advanced this retrospective analysis[10]

> During the decade of skyrocketing petroleum prices, U.S. consumers surprised economists by resolutely cutting their consumption of oil products as prices rose. In economic parlance, "demand-price elasticity" turned out to be high rather than low. Forecasters had believed that consumers depended so heavily on energy supplies that they would pay virtually any price for them rather than cut consumption. The forecasters were wrong.

---

[9]"Staff Report on the Investigation in the Matter of Transactions in Washington Public Power System Securities", Division of Enforcement, US Securities and Exchange Commission, September, 1988.

[10]"Energy-Guzzling: Most Consumers are Cured," *Business Week*, April 4, 1983, p. 16.

5.9.2 Gas—Producer-Pipeline Take-or-Pay Contracts

Gas has had its full quota of problems arising from a lack of sensitivity to price elasticity. The gas take-or-pay problem is a second illustration of the impact of "price elasticity ignored."

The "energy crisis" of the 1970s began with the oil embargo of 1973. Oil shortages inflated demands for natural gas. A serious gas shortage developed, falling most heavily on the interstate market. The gas shortage, coupled with the crisis atmosphere, led to fears on the part of interstate supplied distributors that they might fail to have sufficient gas to serve their forecasted future market in full. Growth might be stopped, even reversed. The pessimistically inclined envisioned the possibility of having to deny service to new customers (some state commissions considered a blanket prohibition on the acquisition of additional customers by gas distributors); and the even more pessimistic entertained the prospect of being forced to ration deliveries to firm customers already on-line. It was commonly taken as a given that "the days of cheap energy are over."

In this near panic atmosphere, distributor company managements were inclined to feel that price was the least of their worriers. What they wanted was an assured supply. Distributor concerns were passed on to pipelines, who saw their own supply positions as tenuous.

Producer inventories of gas available for sale were low, primarily because artificially low prices for interstate gas imposed on producers by Federal regulation had discouraged exploration and development. It was a seller's market. The inevitable happened. Pipelines clamored to buy gas in volumes sufficient to meet the burner-tip demands forecasted by distributors as well as the demands of their own direct-service industrial customers. The shortage had led to the Natural Gas Policy Act (NGPA) of 1978 which, to stimulate exploration and development, permitted producers to charge higher prices. So producers, in a good bargaining position, held out for the best terms and conditions permissible under NGPA.

The result was that both wellhead prices and take-or-pay provisions in new gas supply contracts escalated. Take-or-pay provisions require the pipeline to purchase the contract volume in full, even if that volume cannot be taken. In utility terminology, such a provision would be called a minimum charge. Under the strenuous bidding-up by pipelines for the then still limited producer inventory of reserves, the take-or-pay percentage was raised from a general level of 60–70%, to as high as 90% or even more. The market flexibility of the pipeline buyer thus was narrowed to the point of being negligible.

Shortage changed to surplus overnight sometime around 1982. Gas was suddenly in drastic oversupply—a gas "bubble" existed.[11] Marketers would not absorb the volumes available at anywhere near recent-vintage wellhead prices. Take-or-pay provisions, relatively unimportant earlier, became decisive.

---

[11] The drilling boom of 1979–1982 following the passage of NGPA was a parallel factor contributing to the oversupply. Other factors, including an adverse change in economic conditions, also played a part.

Estimates vary as to the extent of take-or-pay amounts, but they seem to have reached about $16 billion.[12]

As was the case in WPPSS, factors other than price elasticity contributed to the growth of take-or-pay liabilities to multi-billion dollar proportions. But, also as in WPPSS, elasticity had a notable role.

We conclude that it seems inescapable that demand forecasts which disregard or downplay the depressive impact of price increases are almost certain to be in serious error.

5.10 The Revenue Effects of Elasticity

For system planning purposes, elasticity effects must be stated in actual units—kilowatt-hours or therms for the energy utilities. And for budgeting and financial planning, the volumetric demand analysis must be carried forward to pinpoint the corresponding revenue changes. Tables 5.1 and 5.2 present volumetric and revenue data on an illustrative basis for a variety of elasticities involving both upward and downward rate changes. The two tables are similar in format and are largely self-explanatory. A single base case is followed for all examples which are patterned in electric terms. This base case assumes that the take-off data are as follows:

Volume: 2 million kWh
Unit Price: 5 cents per kWh
Revenues: $100,000

Table 5.1 deals with price increases, Table 5.2 with price decreases. Each presents the same range of elastic and inelastic demand coefficients. Generalized conclusions with respect to revenue impact are stated on the right hand columns. For clarification, we have added "+" or "−" signs to indicate the direction of movement of price and demand.

It will be noted that the generalized conclusions are mirror images of each other. They assume ceteris paribus, other things being equal. Restating the conclusions in a different fashion

1. Revenue will be *decreased* by a price increase with elastic demand
   Or
   A price decrease with inelastic demand.
2. Revenue may be *either increased or decreased* by a price increase with inelastic demand
   Or
   A price decrease with elastic demand, depending on the difference between the percentage changes in demand and price.

---

[12]Doane, Hollye C., "Take or Pay: FERC's Regulatory Dilemma", *American Bar Association, Natural Resources and Environment*, Spring, 1987. Ms. Doane is legal advisor to a FERC Commissioner.

Table 5.1 Price increases with elastic and inelastic demands

			Quantity			Unit price			Revenue			
	Line	Elasticity coefficient	Base	Change	After change	Base	Change	After change	Base	After change	Change	
Elastic demand												
Price	1	−10.1/+10.0 = 1.01	2,000,000	(202,000)	1,789,000	5.0¢	+0.5¢	5.5¢	$100,000	$98,890	($1,110)	A price increase, with elastic demand, will decrease revenue
Change	2	−10.5/+10.0 = 1.05		(210,000)	1,790,000					98,450	(1,550)	
	3	−11.0/+10.0 = 1.1		(220,000)	1,780,000					97,900	(2,100)	
Constant	4	−15.0/+10.0 = 1.5		(300,000)	1,700,000		+0.5¢	5.5¢		93,500	(6,500)	
Demand	5	−10.0/+9.9 = 1.01		(200,000)	1,800,000		+0.495	5.495		98,910	(1,090)	
Change	6	−10.0/+9.5 = 1.05					0.475	5.475		98,550	(1,450)	
	7	−10.0/+9.1 = 1.1					0.455	5.455		98,190	(1,810)	
Constant	8	−10.0/+6.7 = 1.5	2,00,000	(200,000)	1,800,000	5.0	0.335¢	5.335¢	$100,000	$96,030	($3,970)	
Inelastic demand												
Price	9	−9.9/+10.0 = 0.99	2,000,000	(198,000)	1,802,000	5.0¢	+0.5¢	5.5¢	$100,000	$99,110	($890)	A price increase, with inelastic demand, may or may not decrease revenue depending upon the difference between the percentage changes in demand and price
Change	10	−9.5/+10.0 = 0.95		(190,000)	1,810,000					99,550	(450)	
	11	−9.0/+10.0 = 0.9		(180,000)	1,820,000					100,100	100	
Constant	12	−5.0/+10.0 = 0.5		(100,000)	1,900,000		+0.5¢	5.5¢		104,500	4,500	
Demand	13	−10.0/+10.1 = 0.99		(200,000)	1,800,000		0.505	5.505		99,090	($910)	
Change	14	−10.0/+10.5 = 0.95					0.525	5.525		99,450	(550)	
	15	−10.0/+11.1 = 0.9					0.555	5.555		99,990	(10)	
Constant	16	−10.0/+20.0 = 0.5	2,000,000	(200,000)	1,800,000	5.0¢	1.000¢	6.000¢	$100,000	$108,000	$8,000	

5.10 The Revenue Effects of Elasticity

Table 5.2 Price decreases with elastic and inelastic demands

	Line	Elasticity coefficient	Quantity Base	Change	After change	Unit price Base	Change	After change	Revenue Base	After change	Change	
Elastic demand												
Price Change Constant	1	+10.1/−10.0 = 1.01	2,000,000	202,000	2,202,000	5.0¢	(0.5¢)	4.5¢	$100,000	$99,090	($910)	A price decrease, with elastic demand, may or may not decrease revenue, depending upon the difference between the percentage changes in demand and price
	2	+10.5/−10.0 = 1.05		210,000	2,210,000					99,450	(550)	
	3	+11.0/−10.0 = 1.1		220,000	2,220,000					99,900	(100)	
	4	+15.0/−10.0 = 1.5		300,000	2,300,000		(0.5¢)	4.5¢		103,500	3,500	
Demand Change Constant	5	+10.0/−9.9 = 1.01		200,000	2,200,000		(0.495)	4.505		99,110	(890)	
	6	+10.0/−9.5 = 1.05					(0.475)	4.525		99,550	(450)	
	7	+10.0/−9.1 = 1.1					(0.455)	4.545		99,990	(10)	
	8	+10.0/−6.7 = 1.5	2,000,000	200,000	2,200,000	5.0¢	(0.335¢)	4.665¢	$100,000	$102,630	$2,630	
Inelastic demand												
Price Change Constant	9	+9.9/−10.0 = 0.99	2,000,000	198,000	2,198,000	5.0¢	(0.5¢)	4.5¢	$100,000	$98,910	($1,090)	A price decrease, with inelastic demand, will decrease revenue
	10	+9.5/−10.0 = 0.95		190,000	2,190,000					98,550	(1,450)	
	11	+9.0/−10.0 = 0.9		180,000	2,180,000					98,100	(1,900)	
	12	+5.0/−10.0 = 0.5		100,000	2,100,000		(0.5¢)	4.5¢		94,500	(5,500)	
Demand Change Constant	13	+10.0/−10.1 = 0.99		200,000	2,200,000		(0.505)	4.495		98,890	($1,110)	
	14	+10.0/−10.5 = 0.95					(0.525)	4.475		98,450	(1,550)	
	15	+10.0/−11.1 = 0.9					(0.555)	4.445		97,790	(2,210)	
	16	+10.0/−20.0 = 0.5	2,000,000	200,000	2,200,000	5.0¢	(1.000¢)	4.000¢	$100,000	$88,000	($12,000)	

These conclusions are generalities. They are not to be accepted as rules or even guides. Each effect should be worked out using the utility's own data.

The revenue changes indicated above refer to *gross* revenue, not *net* revenue. Changes in volumes sold will affect costs. Increased costs may be incurred with greater sales, or costs may decline with a drop in sales. So, *net* revenue may respond to elasticity quite differently than the generalized conclusions suggest. An elasticity study is acceptable as a policy guide only as cost changes are factored in.

Tables 5.1 and 5.2 should not be taken to illustrate a homogeneous total utility demand—a most unlikely occurrence. Rather, they are intended to represent whatever *segment* of the utility's demand might be considered homogenous, such as the residential customer class or a part of it. Each segment requires separate analysis. The segments then must be combined to show the total effect upon the utility's operations and finances.

5.11 Immediate, Short-Run and Long-Run Price Elasticities of Demand

When does elasticity take hold? That is, when there is a price change, how soon will demand react to that change? The answer to that timing question can never be known precisely before that fact, as indeed, neither can the precise degree of elasticity. Tables 5.1 and 5.2 shed no light on either. The tables may represent the forecaster's estimate *before* the fact—in which event the coefficients must be regarded as speculative—or the tables may show the forecaster's reconstruction *after* the fact—in which case the coefficients approach certainty as a statement of past experience, but remain only a guide to the future, since the future may not be replicative of the past.

Generally speaking, it is safe to conclude that demand response to a price change will not be immediate. There will be a lag. The exception to the lag is in the case of the ready substitutability for the utility's service of a like service from a different source. Our oft-quoted example of the energy user having dual-fuel capacity illustrates the exception. A gas price increase may lose the load to oil with no appreciable delay; a gas price decrease may result in a quick restoration of the load to gas. But in the absence of ready substitutability, some delay will ensue.

In addition to the immediate impact of a price change, if any, it is necessary to distinguish between short- and long-run effects.

The presence of "captive" customers, who are wedded to their present appliances or other energy-using equipment, gives stability to the short-run demand of the electric and gas industries. Captive customers can lower their use of electricity or natural gas in response to a price increase, but cannot substitute one energy source for the other without replacing equipment. Similarly, they may increase their use if the price drops, but only to the extent that further energy expenditure actually yields a reward in greater comfort or productivity, unless they invest in additional energy-using devices.

5.12 Repression and Stimulation 147

In the longer-run, however, the customer is not bound. He may install a gas water heater when his electric appliance wears out. The industrial user may upgrade the fuel efficiency of his plant.

5.12 Repression and Stimulation

Two descriptive terms are often used to short-cut the somewhat obtuse formal elasticity verbiage: "repression," indicating the drop in demand which follows a price increase; and "stimulation," the improvement in demand associated with a reduction in price.

Earlier in this chapter we have alluded to the energy crisis which began in 1973. The several years following were not happy ones for the gas consumer. Nor were they happy for the gas distribution utility company. During these years, the writer was in the unenviable position of an executive of such a utility with responsibility for establishing rates and the much more difficult task of justifying higher rates to the regulatory commissions and the public. Responding to higher rates and a general feeling that it was unpatriotic to waste energy (the conservation ethic), consumers reduced their usage. However, the drop in consumption did not result in equally lower monthly bills. The company's fixed costs still had to be recovered (and with lower usage, the increment of fixed cost per-unit sold had to be spread over a lesser number of units, resulting in a higher increment per-unit). At the same time, the variable cost per-unit sold was rising rapidly as the energy shortage induced higher producer-to-pipeline commodity prices and in sequence higher pipeline-to-distributor prices. Pipeline prices not only reflected the higher field prices paid to producers, but also the same expanded increment of fixed cost per-unit sold due to reduced volume, as just mentioned, for distributors. So, what did the consumer see? Often a higher bill for less usage. Explain that, if you will, to an unreceptive customer!

But these personal reflections are an aside. In 1973 my company's average price per therm sold to residential customers was 16.6 cents. Residential customer usage per degree day was 0.196 therms.[13] By 1980, the average price had risen to 53.2 cents per therm, and the average consumption had dropped to 0.120 per degree day. Elasticity in action! The price-consumption movements over the 1973–1980 period are charted in Fig. 5.1. (The chart, incidentally, is exactly as presented to the Oregon PUC in 1981.)

---

[13] Because much of the total usage of the residential gas customer arises from the volume of gas needed to heat his home, total heating usage varies with temperature. In warm weather, little gas is needed. In cold weather, a great deal more is used. To measure changes in volumes purchased from year to year on a consistent basis, usage over different weather conditions must be reduced to a common denominator. That measure is usage per degree day—fewer degree days in warm weather, many more in cold weather.

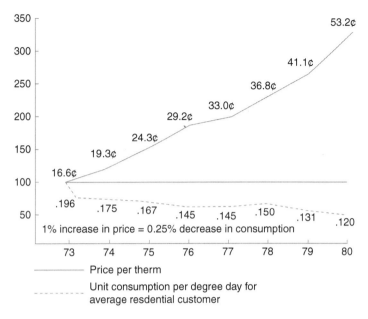

Fig. 5.1 Residential price vs. consumption

5.13 The Principle of Diminishing Utility

The elasticity of demand cannot be fully understood without bearing in mind the basic economic principle of diminishing utility. Simply stated, it is that in any given period a person's desire for additional units of any commodity or service diminishes with each successive unit he purchases. The first home television set and the first stereo (and the electricity to operate them) may be greatly desired. The second is less desirable, etc. Accordingly, quantity discounts are common in almost every phase of merchandising. A single can of peaches may cost 90 cents, but two cans might be purchased for just $1.75.

As alluded to earlier, this principle is recognized very frequently in utility rates. Declining block rates grant a decreasing price for additional units purchased. An important relationship may be emphasized here. Decreasing cost conditions indicate the desirability from the cost standpoint of providing an incentive in the form of lower prices for increased use, since unit costs are lower as more units are sold. The supply situation of decreasing costs thus operates toward the same end as the demand principle of diminishing utility. This consistency is, of course, fortunate for the rate maker. The duality, however, illustrates one of the many practical difficulties which are found in attempting to distinguish whether cost of service or value of service principles have actually been controlling for any given rate.

5.14 Economics of Pricing on a Value of Service Basis

When the value of service approach is reflected in rates, this is sometimes construed to be an application of what economists call monopoly or monopolistic pricing. It is, of course, usually true that utilities enjoy at least a partial monopoly, but, since utilities are regulated by government authority, that does not mean that they are free to set their prices in the same fashion as the monopolist is presumed to set his. Therefore, our present concern is not so much with the actual presence or absence of monopolistic conditions in the utilities, as with the contrast between utility pricing and monopoly pricing.

5.15 Monopoly Pricing

Essentially, monopoly pricing differs from pricing in a purely competitive industry in that the monopolist has a great deal of latitude in fixing his price,[14] while in a perfectly competitive market, price is determined by the interaction of supply and demand. Under perfect competition no individual producer can influence price.

Since the monopolist has the freedom to set his price at any point he sees fit, it is assumed that he will set price (and therefore production) at a point which will yield him the greatest net profit.[15] The social significance of this is that the stage of production which will yield the most profit to the monopolist may not be, and probably is not, the stage of production which will be most desirable for society. It may be to the monopolists' benefit profit-wise to restrict production. An illustration will make this clear.

Assume an electric company's system annual capacity to be 20 billion kWh, its fixed costs $600 million, and its variable costs 1 cent per kWh, a decreasing unit cost situation. Fixed costs represent a high proportion of total costs, so that expansion of output lowers unit costs. To explain what the theoretical monopolists might do, it is necessary to introduce the constraints which price places upon demand. In Table 5.3 of this chapter the demands stated are assumed to be associated with prices as shown. Cost data remain constant.

Referring to the top segment of Table 5.3, at the upper and lower ranges of demand, 8 billion kWh at a price of 8.5 cents per kWh, and 15 billion kWh at 5.0 cents, costs (including full return) are just met, with no excess profit. In between,

---

[14] For purposes of simplification, the various degrees of monopoly are disregarded in this discussion. Obviously a total monopoly has greater latitude than a "duopoly", which in turn can be more arbitrary than a business merely operating under "conditions of monopolistic (or imperfect) competition".

[15] This assumption of general economic theory presupposes that the monopolist is guided only by a profit motive, which, of course, may or may not be true. General theory also contemplates the possibility that the monopolist may withhold supply in order to drive up the price, the profits arising from which are called *monopoly rents*.

Table 5.3 Monopoly pricing

| Price per kWh | Application of Revenue ($ millions) ||||
	Demand/output (in billions of kWh)	Total revenue (in millions)	Fixed costs	Variable costs	Excess (monopoly profit)
8.5¢	8	680	600	80	0
8.0¢	9	720	600	90	30
7.5¢	10	750	600	100	50
7.0¢	11	770	600	110	60
6.5¢	12	780	600	120	60
6.0¢	13	780	600	130	50
5.5¢	14	770	600	140	30
5.0¢	15	750	600	150	0
7.0¢	11	770	600	110	60
6.75¢	11.5	776	600	115	61
6.5¢	12	780	600	120	60

excess profits are realized. Such profits are maximized at $60 million at either a price of 7 cents for a demand of 11 billion kWh or of 6.5 cents for a demand of 12 billion kWh.

Our theoretical monopolist is not one to leave 1/2 cent in price up to the flip of a coin. Presumably he would test the intermediate point. This is done on the bottom segment of Table 5.3, where the intermediate price of 6.75 cents is assumed to induce an intermediate demand of 11.5 billion kWh. This intermediate step yields the highest excess in revenue, $61 million. QED, the monopoly price is 6.75 cents, with an output far below plant capacity of 20 billion kWh.

For the reader, the most valuable lesson of the above discussion is simply to clarify what is meant in the literature by references to monopoly or monopolistic pricing. Monopoly pricing itself, particularly in the context of limiting production to maximize profits, has little relevance to actual utility pricing. The reasons may be summarized very briefly at this point; in situations where the utility has de facto monopoly, regulation will prevent, or at a minimum tend to narrow to an inconsequential degree, a profit maximization scenario.[16]

---

[16] Some writers may contest this view by pointing to earlier experiences of the electric and telephone utilities. In the 1940's and early 1950's, many rural areas were without electricity. Some observers saw the reluctance of electric utilities to develop rural markets as occasioned by an unwillingness to accept the lower profits thought to be associated with rural service. At the time utility policy was described as "skimming the cream," letting the "thin milk" areas take care of themselves. Whatever its motivation, utility company inaction led to the widespread formation of local publicly owned REA cooperatives and public utility districts to bring electricity to unserved farms. The very large number of telephone cooperatives has been alleged to represent the result of the same policy on the part of major telephone companies. The writer does not believe that these experiences are being replicated today.

The practical functioning of the regulatory process, in fact, tends to encourage management initiatives to expand sales, not restrict them. This is so because management sees opportunity in growth, not contraction. As sales grow, regulatory lags may ease a bit—temporarily—the continuing limitations on equity earnings. Also, underutilization of plant is likely to be penalized, not rewarded. Unused plant capacity may be judged to be not "used and useful" in the public service, a possibility now fully constitutional under some circumstances if authorized by state law.

Where the utility falls short of a monopoly position, competition in various degrees supplements the regulatory process in repressing the profit maximization-output restriction tendency attributed by theoretical economics to the monopolist. For energy utilities, in the residential and commercial markets the competition between natural gas and electricity for water and space heating loads is a case in point. Neither utility readily yields to the other. Both energy utilities now fight the highly competitive threat of bypass.

As a final comment on the matter of restrictions of output, we note that American business psychology stresses "growth." Growth (rightly or wrongly, as the reader chooses to see it) is envisioned as the key to success. Utility managers are no exceptions. To voluntarily relinquish market development goes against the grain. Utility managers are predisposed to develop markets in a decreasing unit cost environment in order to be able to lower costs and prices. They are not inclined to a "public be damned" attitude. Too much rides on the public's conception of their performance.

5.16 The Theory of Class Price

Textbook examples of monopoly pricing, as illustrated in Table 5.3, implicitly assume that the monopolist sells his entire output at some single price. More often the monopolist will attempt to increase his profits by setting a different price for different income groups. This can be done in several ways; mainly, however, by minor modification of the product, into higher priced "luxury" and lower priced "utility" models, or by selling the identical product at different prices in different grades of stores or in different localities. The principle underlying this practice, of course, is to exploit the market to the fullest extent by establishing class prices, whatever the basis of the classes may be. Whenever essentially the same product is sold at different prices, *price discrimination* is involved.

Monopoly class pricing is more relevant to the utility industries than is restricted-output monopoly pricing. Class rates are established as part of the cost of service approach to rate making. Various customer classes are defined so as to group together customers having similar characteristics of use, location, size, etc., and consequently cost. Restating the same from a different perspective, the class definitions are designed to separate customers having dissimilar characteristics. The fundamental criterion is cost. But class rates are also inherent in monopoly pricing. Wherein lies the difference?

5.16.1 Price Differentiation

Price differences which reflect differences in costs cannot be considered to be discriminatory. No one would seriously propose that a business must sell a product which is in fact more expensive than another at the same price as that of the cheaper product. A hand tailored suit of high quality material is expected to sell for more than a factory produced suit of mediocre quality, although both are suits. Price differences based on costs may be called, for convenience, *price differentiation*. Price differences which do not reflect differences in cost are a different matter. These differences properly may be considered to discriminate cost-wise, against or for the customers paying the higher or lower price as the case may be. This is not to say, however, that such discrimination necessarily is unreasonable.

5.16.2 Reasonable Price Differences

A number of circumstances may make discriminatory class rates socially desirable and, hence, reasonable.

(1) A new class rate which offers a lower price not based on present cost considerations may be necessary to develop a new market which would ultimately improve the utility's utilization of its plant. The present discrimination is reasonable because of its future benefits to all users.[17] The astute reader may question whether this case is not actually one determined by cost considerations, albeit the cost benefits are in the future. The answer is moot. But it is important to note the difficulty in distinguishing whether cost or value considerations apply. This difficulty illustrates a real problem in evaluating any existing rate. In any given instance, has a cost of service or a value of service approach been followed? With few exceptions, a clear-cut answer is not possible. The basic reason is simple. Every rate represents, in effect, a market price. And two forces come into play in every market—supply and demand. Demand considerations never can be considered entirely apart from supply considerations, and vice versa.

(2) Rates which will return to the utility less than total (average unit) costs—and these probably comprise the bulk of value of service rates—are considered to be justified if they are necessary to secure or retain a market and will yield all incremental costs as well as some contribution to overhead costs. This contribution reduces the

---

[17]Irston R. Barnes explains the emergence of utility class rates solely on this basis. He states, "Historically, many utility companies began by serving only a single class of customer at a uniform rate. As they found that they had idle capacity, companies naturally sought to develop a market for the capacity through offering price concessions. Experimentation with such price adjustments soon developed that it would be possible for the utility to supply a quite diversified market if it would adjust services and prices to the conditions of that market. It was this attempt to develop new markets, in order to achieve full utilization of productive capacities, that led utility companies along the road to the complex rate structures which now quite generally prevail." *The Economics of Public Utility Regulation*, F.S. Crofts & Co., New York, 1942, Ch. X, p. 319.

overhead which other classes of service otherwise would have to bear and therefore results in a cost benefit to all. Thus, the cost rationale is apparent even in a value of service rate which is relatively lower than the main body of rates. Interruptible service rates are a good example of this value-based departure from full average cost.

(3) Value of service rates which discriminate in the other direction, i.e., yield more than total costs, by definition are of benefit to other classes. If the higher rate pertains to a luxury class of service, the support given by this luxury class to other classes may be deemed to be socially desirable.

The justification for this case clearly depends on the effectiveness of regulation. It differs from the comparable case in an unregulated monopoly, in that the excessive profit gained at the expense of luxury users is not pocketed by the producer, but is passed on in the form of lower rates to other classes of users. Obviously, if this passing on is not insured by effective regulation, unreasonable discrimination may exist.

As we examine this case, questions immediately arise. What is a luxurious use, in contrast to a necessary use, and who decides? Is a higher rate for the luxury class tantamount to a tax authorized by the regulatory authority, which body has no statutory taxing power? The difficulty of determining a proper value-based definition of luxury vs. necessity parallels the difficulty of choosing a proper cost-based method of cost allocation. The end-result must be judgmental. Is energy to heat a swimming pool a luxury and, therefore, to be subject to a higher price than other heating? Are gas lamps for street lighting or other decorative purposes a luxury? The reader's imagination will expand this list indefinitely.

A variation of this case on a massive scale is found in the lifeline rates mandated by the California legislature. A minimum amount of energy is set as being necessary for the residential customer. This minimum is granted a lower per-unit price. Use by the customer in excess of this minimum is charged a higher per-unit price. The higher rates for excess consumption are presumed to tend to compensate for the lower rates for the minimum level of use. ("Lifeline" rates, and other inverted rates, are discussed more fully in the chapter on the Public Policy-Social Engineering Approach. They are mentioned here also because they fall within the parameters of this instant case.)

(4) A fourth case is where a low rate is offered for a new type of use, in most cases an industry, in order to induce the new use to locate in the service area. It is assumed that the impact of the new industry upon the economy of the area in terms of increased employment opportunities, purchases of materials in local markets, expansion of commercial establishments and similar factors, will be of sufficient general benefit to warrant rate concessions. The discrimination involved under these circumstances would be considered reasonable. Tax concessions often are offered to new industries with the same justifications.

This case assumes that the utility has ample resources to accommodate the new user as well as present users. Otherwise, the impact of the new user might be the detriment of a shortage of supply rather than the benefit of area development.

(5) A final case, though rather hard to distinguish, may also be noted. This is the case where political factors dictate discrimination in favor of one class. The majority of utilities probably offer residential consumers (as a class) rates which are lower than the associated costs of service would indicate. Other customer classes (mainly the commercial class where the value of service is very high due to the unavailability of feasible alternatives) must, of course, bear this difference. It does not matter whether one chooses to explain this on the basis that residential consumers have more votes than any other class; or in terms of the social desirability of making the utility service available to homes at the lowest possible rate because of the importance of the welfare of the family; or as recognition for the fact that the utility product in a commercial establishment is used to produce profits, and should, therefore, be sold at a higher price than for nonprofit uses. The results are the same regardless of the rationalization. In the "Golden Age" of declining utility costs, the majority of rate reductions approved by the regulatory commissions benefited residential customers primarily. Such discrimination, to the extent it was acknowledged, was construed to be reasonable.

Perhaps the classic example of case (5) was the unbalanced relationship between long-distance and local telephone rates which prevailed in the days before long-distance service became competitive. Pursuing a dual public policy objective of universal service and low local rates, long-distance prices were kept high so as to subsidize the local rates.

A rather novel criterion of reasonableness may which be mentioned in passing is "the reasonableness of the rates *to the person charged.*" Stated in a Canadian decision by the Privy Council, the criterion was summed up as, "... the principle must be, when reasonableness comes in question, not what profit it may be reasonable for a company to make, but what it is reasonable to charge the person who is charged. That is the only thing he is concerned with."[18] It is questionable whether this standard as stated, would be upheld in the United States.

Professor Martin Glaeser has noted the possible effects of discriminatory pricing upon businesses which use the utility product as part of their productive processes. His words merit serious consideration from the social point of view. "Since a public utility sells most of its product to consumers who use the service for further production under conditions of competition, it becomes a utility's duty to hold the balance even between competitors. Utilities thus have the important social function of making the competitive organization of industry workable".[19]

The question that counts is not whether discrimination as measured by cost exists, but whether the discrimination is reasonable.[20] However, because of the unfortunate

---

[18] *Canada Southern Railway Company*, V. *International Bridge Company*, Law Reports, Appeal Cases, Vol. 8, p. 723.

[19] Glaeser, M.G., *Outlines of Public Utility Economics*, The MacMillan Company, New York, NY, 1931, p. 625.

[20] In theory it is possible to go even further. To illustrate, Albert L. Meyers states; "As a matter of pure theory, it may interest the reader to know that Professor A.C. Pigou (Economics of Welfare, p. 287 ff. The Macmillan Co., New York, 1933) one of the most socially minded economists,

5.16.3 Determination of Rate Classifications Under Value and Combined Cost-Value Approaches

connotations associated with the term, it is probably preferable to confine its use to value of service situations, substituting the term "price differentiation" for cost of service rate differentials. This is, of course, merely a matter of semantics.

The foregoing discussion illustrates the fact that almost every rate represents an integration of elements of both the value of service and the cost of service approaches. Which approach predominates in any given rate is largely a matter of degree.

5.16.3 Determination of Rate Classifications Under Value and Combined Cost-Value Approaches

The general rule for determining rate classes under the cost of service approach is to define each class so that customers having similar characteristics of usage, geographical location, etc., and hence of cost, are grouped together. From this it follows that a separate or new class would be established only when the cost characteristics of the proposed rate class are essentially different from those of established classes.

The criteria under the value of service approach are the same, except that demand rather than cost is the important element. *Value of service rate classes will group together customers having approximately the same desires for the utility product or service. In some cases, the groupings will combine customers with analogous bargaining strengths and abilities to pay.* Thus, residential customers have a common desire for energy for lighting, and water and space heating, plus, in many localities, for air conditioning. Churches as a group may have political bargaining power, as may irrigating farmers. Industrial plants of one type or another which are large users of energy may argue that their ability to pay for energy is circumscribed by their necessity to meet competition from other localities.

There is, however, a practical limit upon the establishment of rate classes on value bases, which is not operative to the same extent in establishing rate classes based on cost. Cost differences, and the rationale of adjusting prices to reflect them, can ordinarily be explained satisfactorily, thereby gaining a good deal of customer acceptance. People are accustomed to paying for what they get. It has, therefore, been possible (though never easy) to establish higher rates for the farm home than for the urban residence. The effect upon cost of service of customer density, distance from main sources of supply, etc., can be made understandable and acceptable. But to attempt to establish per se separate customer classes for the rich, the middle class, and the poor groups of residential consumers would obviously be foolhardy,

---

believes that under certain circumstances perfect discrimination may be a fairer method of pricing than perfect competition. He points out that perfect discrimination charges each buyer exactly the full amount that the product is worth to him individually. Thus prices are charged in accord with the 'ability to pay' rather than imposing a single price on all, regardless of difference in income or in desire for the product." From *Modern Economics – Elements and Problems*, Prentice-Hall, Inc., New York, 1946, p. 316. We note that these early references bring to mind current marginal cost-Ramsey pricing theories.

though this would be quite consistent with value pricing theory and is a common (though veiled) practice. The establishment of value of service classes in utilities must be more subtle and price differences must be founded on, or at least explainable on, socially acceptable grounds. (The rather recent lifeline rates may illustrate the hybrid type of justification to which we allude, since the price differentials of these rates are partially oriented to ability to pay, but with other factors also influential.)

With the notable exception of telephone, value of service considerations have historically been more influential in industrial rate making than for other classes. It is easy to appreciate the necessity of offering a competitive rate to industry. Industrial firms have relatively larger resources than individual customers of other classes, and, therefore, greater opportunity to utilize alternatives, including bypass. Value of service rate classes for industry need not necessarily be camouflaged, which is not to say, however, that they are not frequently subject to attack. The next question to consider is to what extent value of service considerations enter into the establishment of non-industrial customer classes. In many cases we can only speculate on this score. Therefore, we turn to examples.

5.16.4 Combined Value and Cost Bases

Historically, several local rates were usually available for residential telephone users. One could choose between single party, two party, and four party service in most localities. In fact, in rare instances ten party service can still be found in some rural areas. There is no question but that there are differences in the costs of these several types of service. Of course, quality of service also varies. Whether cost or value considerations were uppermost in the minds of telephone rate makers in establishing these service classes, and of regulators in approving them, is unimportant. The result was to reach a greater market in total, and to take advantage of those segments of the market which were willing to pay a higher price. A single class residential telephone service, presumably an intermediate grade of service at an intermediate price, would have had the effect of charging consumers at the top of the demand scale much less than they would be willing to pay and losing entirely the sales to subscribers at the lower end of the demand scale who were not willing or able to pay the intermediate price. Keep in mind that until recently (the breakup of the AT&T system in 1982 is good, although imprecise, dividing point) local service as a broad classification was subsidized by long-distance service. Within long-distance service itself were numerous value-based sub-classifications; direct dialed vs. operator-assisted calls, and off-peak evening and weekend rates vs. peak-period daytime Monday–Friday rates, for example. Each of these differentiations is supportable on a generalized cost basis, although the writer knows of no cost studies regarding these differentiations which could be construed to be definitive. The differentiations resulted from value judgments.

These telephone rate examples illustrate quite well what is probably the typical rate making situation in practice—rates represent an intermingling of cost and value elements, with the cost differences at least sufficiently apparent to rationalize any market exploitation.

It is helpful to examine additional historical examples. Let us turn to the electric industry. As we know, the residential market for electricity is a composite market, representing requirements for electricity for lighting, appliances, water heating, cooking, space heating, etc. Lighting combined with the operation of small appliances was the first of these markets to develop. Next came water heating. This presented the rate maker with a problem made difficult by two main circumstances: (1) the lighting market was, for all practical purposes, non-competitive, while the water-heating market was extremely competitive—gas having attained a strong foothold with most consumers; yet (2) the lighting customer was the same individual as the water-heating customer. The problem was how to differentiate rate-wise. It was solved initially (as many new rate problems are) in a rather complex fashion. A special water-heating rate was developed that was much lower than the rate for lighting, and was competitive in level with gas. Partly to justify the price difference between the lighting and water-heating rate, and partly as a hedge against future costs being out of line with the rate, the rate was made available only for off-peak use. Expensive timing devices and double metering were established for electric cooking with the same results. Later, as lighting rates were lowered and more knowledge accumulated about the extent of costs of water heating and cooking, a single rate was substituted for the separate rates. Price differentials were established effectively through *blocking*. In many localities, electric space heating (and later, air conditioning) followed a similar pattern; first, a separate rate (often with a demand as well as an energy charge) that was later combined back into a single rate. The most recent step has been the promotion-geared "all electric" blocked rate, under which residential customers using electricity for all three main uses—lighting, water heating, and space heating—are served under a single schedule which is substantially lower (but with a higher minimum charge) than the schedule available to other residential customers. The lower blocks of the all-electric rates are priced to meet gas competition.

5.17 Bases of Rate Classes

Establishment of customer classes is mandatory under both the value and cost approaches. No two customers are the same either with regard to the costs of serving them or their desire for utility service. Accordingly, a complete development of either the cost or value approach would call for an individual rate for each customer. This is neither practical nor possible under either approach, due to the large number of customers served by the usual utility. Let us, then, examine some of the bases for establishing rate classes, differentiating to the extent possible between the two approaches.

1. Classifications based upon *conventional economic groupings*: Perhaps the most common classifications of customers in utilities today is by the customary divisions of the community's economic groups, namely residential, commercial,

and industrial. Utilities may further subdivide the residential class into "urban" and "rural" (as discussed under item (6) below) and the commercial and industrial classes into "large" and "small" (as discussed under item (5) below). These groupings are as relevant in non-utility usage as they are in utility usage, and for this reason have a high degree of customer acceptance. This method of classification has the further advantage of fitting fairly well into both the cost and value approaches. For the normal service area with a balanced stage of economic development, it is probable that these classifications (by bringing together into the same group customers with fairly similar use characteristics) make it possible, through suitable rate schedules, to apportion cost appropriately *among the individual customers in each class*.

On the contrary, the demand (as well as some of the cost) characteristics of each group are different. The most conspicuous example of the value element overriding cost is the frequent instance of a commercial rate being higher than the residential rate, although it is doubtful that the cost of serving the former is demonstratively higher than for the latter. The rationale for the higher commercial rate is that the utility service is just one of a number of essential inputs for doing business, and its cost is passed along to customers as are the costs of other inputs. Therefore, it is no particular burden. Further, like all business costs, the utility bill is a tax deduction to the business, an advantage not available to the residential user. These are entirely value of service considerations. Thus, the composite price levels of the several class rates can be adjusted so as to reflect value of service considerations, while price levels within the class can be more closely oriented to cost differences. This method seems to represent a reasonably effective compromise between the two approaches, which no doubt accounts for part of its popularity.

2. Classifications based on *type of users*: This method is essentially the same as item (1) above, except that the classes do not parallel orthodox economic groupings. Special rate classes for churches, charitable institutions, and municipalities illustrate the use of this method. Quite obviously, rate classes of this type represent almost unadulterated value of service pricing. It is interesting to note that when such classes as churches and municipalities are established they are often given a very low rate. This is probably done on social and public relations grounds. The result in these cases, of course, is the converse of "what the traffic will bear." Probably due to the apparent discrimination involved, few modern rate systems utilize this method to any extent. Unreasonable discrimination may not in fact exist, however. Broader social goals may outweigh discrimination considerations.

3. Classifications by *purpose of use*: Numerous finely tuned rate classifications based upon purpose of use are rare in modern rates, but when used, as for irrigation or agriculture generally, they can be helpful because their application is, by definition, limited to the specified purpose. The market is circumscribed and thus subject to a measure of control not possible for a broader classification.

It is this limitation to usage for a specified circumscribed market (or purpose of use) which distinguishes this classification from the prior one. Under (2), for example, a city under a "municipal" schedule could utilize energy for any purpose, street lighting, lighting, or heating of its office buildings or whatever. But under (3)

5.17   Bases of Rate Classes   159

a "street lighting" schedule could not be extended to service to a city-owned office building, or any purpose other than street lighting.

Usually, purpose of use rate classifications are readily explained on both the cost and value bases, and actual rate levels may reflect the results of either. The cost of providing utility service for specific existing uses can be determined with considerable accuracy, as the probable load factor, time of peak and other characteristics of a special type of load are easily found and individual customers can be expected to vary only slightly from the average. (Note that the irrigation classification is narrower, and thus more finely tuned, than the broader agricultural classification.) These certainties are lacking, of course, for future new uses. It is significant to observe that even a finely subdivided classification system (such as this method provides) cannot accord full recognition of all cost of service elements, even for existing uses. For although load characteristics can be taken into account insofar as known, location differences, for example, are not, unless the classifications are further subdivided by location, as discussed under item (6) below.

A parallel case may be made to demonstrate that this method fits quite well into the value of service approach. Each purpose has fairly well-defined economic demand characteristics which can be distinguished from the demand characteristics of other purposes. A variety of classes could make it possible to take full advantage of high value uses while being as competitive as necessary for low value uses. In theory, probably no other method permits as complete an exploitation of the individual utility markets.

This method, although much in vogue at one time, is not popular today. For one thing, it is difficult to justify to the public. The average person cannot easily understand why a cubic foot of gas or a kilowatt-hour of electricity should cost more when used for one purpose than another. The method is also complicated and expensive to administer, requiring a large number of rate schedules and, in many cases, multiple metering installations carried to extremes. A single commercial electric customer, for example, might take service under separate rates for lighting and other base use, winter space heating, and summer air conditioning. The customer would have to provide separate circuits feeding into separate meters for each use, and his monthly bill would be the aggregate of these components. Imagine the problems of resolving a billing complaint under these circumstances!

4. Classifications based on *grade of service*: This method may represent anything from an almost "pure" application of the cost of service approach to an equally perfect application of value considerations. Utilities will usually establish an "interruptible" as distinct from a "firm" class of service. The interruptible service is subject to curtailment in favor of firm service at any time that the utility's capacity is insufficient to provide both.[21] As only spare capacity is utilized, interruptible

───────────────

[21] Reflecting the fact that in the natural gas industry, the gas originates with producers (a nonutility segment separate from the utility pipeline and distributor segments, except, of course, where a pipeline or distributor may have production of its own, which is the exceptional circumstance), the gas supply function may be thought of as distinct from the transportation and distribution

service can therefore be provided by the utility with only minor, if any, increases in capacity costs. A low interruptible rate is justified by the cost situation; and such a low rate is completely consistent with the inferior grade of service provided. It may be equally consistent with other market factors.

We have previously mentioned that single party as compared with multiple party local telephone service rate classes illustrate classifications for different grades of service involving elements of both cost and value approaches. In this same context, we have mentioned long-distance telephone tolls. The customer may choose between high-priced person-to-person service and lower-priced station-to-station service. For this particular example, value considerations probably predominate, although some differences in cost are also involved. The choice between these alternatives usually involves a mild gamble—whether to place a cheaper station-to-station call and assume the risk of the right party not being available, or to incur a greater expense and let the telephone company bear the risk by placing a person-to-person call.

That this risk is not always negligible is illustrated by the following news item from *Life* which the writer found in some early notes: quoting verbatim[22]

> "Long distance" gets its man.
> When R.J. Bedgood left Savannah, Ga. 15 months ago, he owned a lot of people a lot of money. The police grew discouraged in their search for him, but Hazel Gardner, manager of a Savannah finance agency, kept trying. When she got a feeble tip that Bedgood was working for a construction company somewhere in the U.S., she spent six weeks making 500 long distance phone calls to 500 construction companies and finally caught her man in La Porte, Texas. Miss Gardener's thorough detective work cost nothing but the goodwill of the phone company, for she made every call to Bedgood himself—person-to-person.

5. Classifications based on *characteristics of use*: This method is basically a cost method. It is perhaps the most theoretically accurate of all cost methods for it presumes to take directly into account the most significant of the factors influencing cost. Value considerations are not ignored, of course, but these follow from, rather than dictate, the conclusions reached from cost analyses.

Among the more important elements of this method are the *time* of use and the *magnitude* or *duration* of use. The prime example of the former is the off-peak rate class. The magnitude of use element embraces consideration of the cost advantages and disadvantages of supplying a number of ranges of customer requirements, varying in size from the high load factor industrial plant taking tremendous quantities of the utility product, to the small, low load factor summer cottage. All of the elements entering into the relative economics of large-scale production and delivery as contrasted with small retail sales have a bearing upon the establishment of such customer classes and the rates applicable to them. Separate rate classes for large and

---

functions. FERC so considers it. In its Order No. 436 the Commission distinguishes between capacity-induced curtailments and supply-induced curtailments. The latter refers to curtailments caused by an insufficiency of gas supplies (i.e., inadequate volumes) to satisfy all demands. Federal Energy Regulatory Commission, Order No. 436, issued October 9, 1985, mimeo. p. IV. A. 58.

[22] *Life*, Vol. 34, No. 17, April 27, 1953, p. 47.

small commercial, and large and small industrial customers illustrate the end products of this method. Note that this illustration represents the common occurrence of a combination of two classification methods.

Rate schedules having more than one billing component (two part or multiple part schedules) are an application of this category within a customer class. Separate demand charge and energy components of an electric or gas schedule permit the schedule to differentiate between the high load factor customer, who ordinarily will be charged a lower average price, and the low load factor customer, whose average price will be higher.

6. Classifications based on *location*: This method is usually found in combination with other methods. It is almost always based on cost. In electric and gas rates it gives recognition to variations in distance from sources of supply, as well as relative customer densities. The breakdown of the residential customer class into urban and rural is the most frequent example of this method.

7. Classifications based on *facilities provided*: Closely related to both grade of service and location classifications are classifications which reflect differences in the service facilities provided by the utilities. Electric utilities, for example, may establish one rate for customers taking service at high (transmission) voltage and a more expensive level for customers served at lower (distribution) voltages. In the latter case, the utility must provide voltage step-down transformation equipment which is not needed for high voltage deliveries, as well as absorb the energy losses occurring through the high voltage substation and the lines to the low voltage delivery point. Since the telephone divestiture of 1984, a large portion of telephone company tariffs is devoted to "access services," where the customer utilizes a part but not all of the utility's facilities to provide the complete telecommunications link which the customer needs, the customer itself providing the remainder of the required facilities. These are strictly cost-based methods of classification.

8. *Single-customer tailored rates*: Although rare up to the present time, it sometimes is necessary to develop a special negotiated contract for service to a large individual customer; the necessity may arise from a variety of factors. The most common reason in the past has been the unsuitability to the customer of any of the multiple-customer schedules in the tariff. An example from the writer's experience will illustrate. An Oregon ammonia plant, a large user of natural gas, was in direct competition with Alaskan ammonia plants. The Alaska gas price dropped precipitously. The Oregon plant could not market its product at a price competitive with the Alaskan product. It could remain in business only if it could buy gas at a low-tariffed price. Since the Oregon plant was significant to the local economy, a special contract was designed for this single customer and duly approved by the Oregon PUC. The gas price was, of course, sufficient to cover all incremental costs of service plus a small contribution toward fixed costs.

It may be that ongoing industry changes dictated by rapidly emerging technology and movements in the country's institutional structure will lead to more frequent special contracts. The "unbundling" of telecommunications and energy services makes practicable a degree of tailoring of service terms and conditions, including price, to individual large customers, which has been virtually impossible under the traditional "bundled" tariff structure. The threat of bypass may force unique adaptations of service arrangements to keep individual customers online. The problem here, faced by both the utility and regulatory commission, is to insure "a level playing field" for all customers so that economic weight alone will not cause the big customer to receive concessions not justified by the economics of the situation. To insure equity, pre-approval of contracts may be required.

5.18 The Cost and Value Approaches Compared

Many of the advantages and limitations of the cost and value approaches have been mentioned previously. But it may still be worthwhile to recapitulate the more important "pros and cons."

The main advantage of the cost of service approach is that of equity, or at least the appearance of equity. Its objective is to charge each customer a fair share of the utility's costs. Because of its plausibility, cost-type rates can be explained in down-to-earth terms and justified in such terms to the public and to regulatory commissions. On the other hand, there are six principal objections to the cost approach. *First*, it is ordinarily impossible, except by arbitrary cost allocations, to determine the costs of serving any particular customer or customer group. Therefore, the accuracy of any cost-type rate is at best approximate, and the appearance of accuracy may be misleading. *Second*, technological progress makes shifts in costs inevitable and sometimes frequent. A serious attempt to follow cost principles without deviation could, therefore, result in frequent rate changes of an irregular and unpredictable character. *Third*, when many types of service are being rendered, each use has its own distinct value and hence, if the price charged were to be based solely on cost considerations, the number and extent of the uses to which the utility service would be put might be seriously limited. *Fourth*, a strict application of the cost approach might operate to restrict the utility from enlarging its plant to optimum size by reaching out for a new market which could be developed only by rate concessions based on value. *Fifth*, under adverse market conditions, untempered cost of service rates might be so high as to be prohibitive to a class or classes of customers. And *sixth*, rigidly applied cost of service principles might have socially undesirable results. It might, for example, result in higher rates for necessary services to offset a reduction in rates for luxury uses. This final disadvantage may or may not be present, of course, depending upon the existing rate schedule levels of the individual utility.

The foregoing disadvantages of the cost of service approach indicate by implicating some important reasons why value considerations must enter into rate development. These may be summed up as: First, the value approach may lead to a fuller utilization and expansion of the utility plant. Accordingly, assuming proper administration, it may be expected to lead to lower costs and lower prices through the benefits of large-scale production. Second, the approach recognizes market conditions and is therefore more realistic in terms of our American economy than a strict cost approach. Third, a value-tempered application of cost avoids unreasonably high rates for necessary uses. Five dollars for a single local telephone call might

5.18 The Cost and Value Approaches Compared

well be in line with cost for a customer making only one call per month (and might not be too high a price to pay if a doctor were needed in an emergency), but such a price might fail miserably to gain public acceptance. The opposite side of the coin is that in the absence of proper regulation the value approach could lead not to better plant utilization and efficient production as stated above, but to the practice of limiting output and the worst type of monopoly pricing. However, this should be precluded under good regulation. Also, it is possible that value of service rates, if set too low, may promote the uneconomic overdevelopment of certain types of uses or industries.

Perhaps the main overall objection to the use of the value approach is that in the absence of effective competition value-based prices may not necessarily be justifiable on the yardstick of equity and fairness. In a non-competitive environment, cost considerations must operate as a check at least upon the use of the value of service basis as a rate-making device.[23] As competition becomes workable, increasing reliance can be placed upon value.

It is regrettable that a simple formula cannot be proposed which would bring together the two approaches, or show how to choose between them. The complexity and continually varying nature of the problem precludes this easy solution. As previously pointed out, even the oft-quoted rule that cost of service marks the lower limit, and value of service the upper limit, of prices for an individual rate schedule, is not too helpful. The commonly accepted criterion that "no value price should be so low as to fail to cover incremental costs plus some contribution to the fixed costs" is useful and valid, but its application is subject to many uncertainties which vary from situation to situation. Much must be left to the judgment of the rate maker, and the social consciousness of the utility management and regulatory commission which, in their turn, approve or reject the rate. Each utility faces different cost and market conditions and different degrees of competition. Rate schedules must reflect their unique environment.

It may be that the often blurred distinction between cost of service and value of service, as alternative approaches to rate making, arises because the focus of these terms is directed toward the price-originating utility and its regulatory commission, not the customer. Michael Messenger hints that utility demand may be seen as comprised of two types of users: "price sensitive" and "value sensitive" customers.[24] Taking the liberty of carrying Messenger's customer distinction far beyond his own analysis, we suggest that if such a distinction between customers is correct, value of service pricing would go forward in two different directions at the same time. The price sensitive market sector would be approached with the aim of maintaining the

---

[23] Customers who have no viable alternative to the utility's service often are categorized as "core" customers. Order No. 87-402 of the Oregon PUC, issued March 31, 1987, explains, "Utility regulation is designed to protect those 'core' customers by restricting the utility's discretion with regard to both service and pricing." Petition of Pacific Bell (U 1001 C) for Modification of General Order 96-A, Application 85-01-034, et al., February 23, 1990.

[24] Messenger, Michael T., "How to Cut Costs and Maintain Market Share: The Dilemma of Electric Utilities", *Public Utilities Fortnightly*, December 10, 1987.

price as low as necessary to meet competition from alternatives, including bypass, subject only to incremental (minimum allowable) cost recovery. This sector would be offered service without frills. On the other hand, the value sensitive sector would be offered improved or expanded customer accommodations to enhance the value being received as seen through the customer's eyes. As examples, Messenger lists "new rate schedules that offer unique packages of bill stability (fixed rates or fixed bills for periods of one, two, or three years based on levelized utility costs), energy management services, and hedges against an uncertain future." For residential customers, he includes, "more convenient ways to control their home temperatures or pay their utility bills."

While Messenger's attention is directed to electric utilities, the benefit of isolating the "value sensitive" customer for analysis may be greater in telecommunications. The using of a particular carrier for perceived values offered and received, plus customer inertia, may impinge upon price elasticity to a much greater degree than is though. Perhaps, even in the tumultuous arena of telecommunications competition, value sensitivity matches (or at least, could match) price sensitivity.

5.19 Unreasonable Discrimination

Discrimination has always been a nasty word, meaning as it does to act toward someone or something with partiality or prejudice. These days it has more specific unfavorable connotations. As a society we agree that discrimination is obnoxious and illegal when applied in matters regarding race, sex, and age, so use of the term makes it necessary to distinguish carefully between socially desirable and legal utility pricing practices, and those which affront social norms and the law.[25] Unfortunately, this is easier said than done.

As the previous pages have pointed out, in utility parlance price differentiation is not discrimination. And when price discrimination is defined as price which is not directly consistent with cost, we have noted a broad range of conditions under which price discrimination so defined is both economically desirable and socially acceptable. Pricing within this range we designate as *reasonable* discrimination. Such pricing is clear-cut in the circumstances cited, and has been affirmed as reasonable by years of utility practice, with the approval of regulatory commissions at both state and local levels of government, and with sanction by both state and federal courts.

---

[25] Alan R. Schriber, a member of the Ohio Public Utilities Commission, also noted the negative connotation of the term. He says "If ever a word was in need of a synonym it would be 'discrimination'. In its most familiar context its meaning is clearly insidious. When referring to a scheme by which prices are set, however, it simply pertains to the charging of different rates to different customers for the same service depending upon the latter's demand characteristics." Schriber, A.R., "Price Discrimination: Creatively Coping with Competition", *Public Utilities Fortnightly*, September 1, 1988.

But beyond these obvious cases and traditional pricing patterns, the boundaries between the reasonable and the unreasonable become fuzzy and more subjective.

5.19.1 The FERC Lists

Comparative shopping lists of reasonable and unreasonable discriminatory practices relating to a common core of the same type of service are hard to come by. It is possible, however, to abstract comparative lists from the Federal Energy Regulatory Commission's bellwether Order No. 436, which proposed rules for opening up gas pipeline transportation to all who might desire that service.

The core theme upon which the lists are based is that any practice which would *restrict access* to transportation is considered discriminatory and preferential.[26] Examples of "undue or preferential" discrimination are denial of access to exclude a particular competitor from a given market or to disadvantage a shipper engaged in a manufacturing business in competition with a pipeline affiliate; refusals to transport for exiting sales or non-fuel switchable customers, including refusal by the pipeline to transport gas in competition with its own sales service (i.e., to avoid displacing its own sales); preferences or favoritism for affiliates; arrangements which tie or "bundle" gathering, production, storage, or other service not required by shippers to transportation services; the withholding of available or underutilized capacity. Not unduly discriminatory or preferential are reasonable operating and load management conditions imposed on shippers if imposed on all similarly situated shippers and if stated in filed transportation tariffs.

Also, rates below an established maximum are permitted down to a minimum floor ("rate discounting") to allow pipelines "to respond flexibly to market conditions" provided they are not unduly discriminatory and are filed, but the pipeline is at risk for any under-recovery of costs. The Commission's explanation of its approval of discounting is relevant to value pricing in general. The Commission observes, "... competition in the natural gas industry today is proliferating. In theses circumstances, it makes little sense to withhold from pipelines the basic weapon other businesses have to wage the competitive battle: the ability to lower prices to beat the competition."[27] And, "... a discount offered because of competitive conditions is not unduly discriminatory."

5.19.2 Statutory Prohibitions

Unfortunately, statutory language is of little help in distinguishing between reasonable and unreasonable discrimination—the statutes merely mandate the former and preclude the latter, leaving it up to enforcement forums to interpret given cases.

---

[26] Federal Energy Regulatory Commission, Order No. 436, op. cit., mimeo., IV.
[27] Ibid., mimeo, p. IV, A, 145–146.

Some examples will illustrate. We will first look to our two case-history states. California declares[28]

> All charges demanded or received by any public utility, or by any two or more public utilities, for any product or commodity furnished or to be furnished or any service rendered or to be rendered shall be just. Every unjust or unreasonable charge demanded or received for such product or commodity or service is unlawful. (451)
> No public utility shall, as to rates, charges, service, facilities, or in any other respect, make or grant any preference or advantage to any corporation or person or subject any corporation or person to any prejudice or disadvantage. (435a)
> No public utility shall establish or maintain any unreasonable difference as to rates, charges, service, facilities, or in any other respect, either as between localities or as between classes of service. (435c)

Texas, whose statues are of recent vintage, states[29]

> ... The regulatory authority is empowered to fix and regulate rates of public utilities (electric and telephone), including rules and regulations for determining the classification of customers and services and for determining the applicability of rates ... (Sec. 37)
> It shall be the duty of the regulatory authority to insure that every rate made, demanded, or received by any public utility, or by any two or more public utilities jointly, shall be just and reasonable. Rates shall not be unreasonably preferential, prejudicial, or discriminatory, but shall be sufficient, equitable, and consistent in application to each class of consumers ... (Sec. 38)

In the writer's home territory, Oregon statutes relative to "utility regulation generally," under the heading "Illegal Practice" state, at Section 737310, that "a utility must collect the same charges ... for a like and contemporaneous service under substantially similar circumstances" and that the absence of such is "unjust discrimination." The revised Code of Washington at 80.28.020 prohibits rates which are "unjust, unreasonable, unjustly discriminatory or unduly preferential." It is safe to say as a generality that state utility regulatory statutes prohibit "unreasonable" or "unjust" discrimination in utility rates.

On a federal basis, with particular respect to the regulation of power entering into interstate or foreign commerce, the United States Code at 16 Section 813 states, "the rates charged and the service rendered shall be reasonable, nondiscriminatory and just to the customer, and all unreasonable, discriminatory and unjust rates or services are prohibited and declared to be unlawful."

Section 4(b) of the Natural Gas Act, 15 U.S.C. 717c (b), provides that

> No natural gas company shall, with respect to any transportation or sale of natural gas ... (1) make or grant any *undue preference or advantage* ... or subject any person to any *undue prejudice or disadvantage,* or (2) maintain any unreasonable difference in rates, charges, service, facilities, or in any other respect, either as between localities or as between classes of service (emphasis added).

---

[28] State of California, Public Utilities Code, article XII. Division I, Chapter 3, Article I, Rates.
[29] State of Texas, Public Utility Regulatory Act, Article VI.

5.19 Unreasonable Discrimination

FERC throws some light on the meaning of this typical statutory requirement of the Natural Gas Act (NGA) in a 1985 order.[30] The Commission says, "There is no per se rule under the NGA for determining whether a preference or advantage is "undue" or when a difference in rates in "unreasonable." The general rule is that discrimination is "undue" when there is a difference in rates or service among similarly situated customers that is not justified, whether by differences in the costs of providing the service or by some other legitimate factors. "... in virtually all cases [where discrimination was adjudicated under NGA] the finding of undue discrimination was predicated on actual or potential harm to the non-qualifying customer ... the advantage conferred on the favored party came at the expense of some other customer".

In essence the utility price discrimination statues prohibit per se price favoritism for the benefit of a particular buyer(s), or price bias to the detriment of a particular buyer(s), except where such are judged to result in some benefit to buyers at large, i.e., to be in the public interest. It may or may not be necessary that any harm of a significant nature flow from the unreasonable discrimination. But if the public benefit is absent, the price difference is suspect.

Speaking as a regulator, Commissioner Schriber gives an insight, in a contemporary time frame, into reasonable vs. unreasonable discrimination.[31]

> Most states, like Ohio for example, forbid "unreasonable" discrimination. To be more precise, it is necessary to distinguish "good" discrimination from that which is "bad." Where there is competition for a utility's load, setting prices in order to meet the competition is surely reasonable. There is good precedent for this conclusion: the federal antitrust statutes expressly grant exemptions from the prohibitions against price discrimination where the thrust of the action is to "meet the competition." Further, there is sufficient case law to suggest that "meeting the competition" takes place when one attempts to protect one's market share from rivals. It is also clear that discrimination to increase one's market share is illegal. The law is somewhat vague as to whether discrimination is appropriate for the purpose of vying for new markets.
>
> It is important to note that, in many cases, the competition for a share of the regulated utility's business comes from those in the unregulated segments of the business. Natural gas, for example, must compete with propane and fuel oil while telephone companies must wrestle with unregulated providers of PBXs and billing-and-collection services. In these instances, the utilities must be enabled to compete on the same basis as their unregulated rivals since there is no authority to bring the latter in line with the former. In some instances, utilities that are regulated by different jurisdictions compete with one another, interstate pipelines with local distribution companies (LDC), for example. In states such as Ohio, where LDCs are not accorded exclusive territorial franchises, companies occasionally compete with one another for new load.
>
> To further distinguish "good" discrimination from "bad" it is necessary to determine whether or not the practice actually harms anyone, because traditionally "harm" has been a necessary condition for finding of illegal discrimination.

---

[30] Federal Energy Regulation Commission, Order No. 436, *op.cit.* mimeo, pp. IV, A. 136–137.
[31] Shriber, op. cit.

5.20 Predatory Pricing

General price discrimination statues are narrower in scope, but add a further dimension. Most of these non-utility statues are designed to protect competition in the economy. Thus, they focus on competitive impact—will the price discrimination result in a weakening or elimination of competition?

Many states prohibit price discrimination in trade and commerce generally if the end-result is to undermine the competitive thrust which safeguards the consumer in the free markets of our economic system. An example is the anti-price discrimination law of Oregon which reads in part[32]

> It is unlawful ... to discriminate in price between different purchasers of commodities, or services or output of a service trade, of like grade and quality, or to discriminate in price between different sections, communities, or cities or portions thereof, or portions thereof in this state, *where the effect of such discrimination may be to substantially lessen competition.* [Emphasis added]

The nationally applicable federal anti-trust laws against pricing which weakens competition are best known and most rigorously enforced. The Clayton Act declares,[33] "It shall be unlawful for any person ... to discriminate in price between different purchasers of commodities of like grade and quality, ... where the effect of such discrimination may be substantially to lessen competition or tend to create a monopoly."

At this point we can formulate a working definition of predatory pricing. It is a form of discriminatory pricing which drives prices down to unprofitable levels for a time, resulting in the possibility of weakening or eliminating existing competitors. A seller desiring to introduce a predator price would have to possess a significant degree of market power (i.e., the ability to influence the price of the product or service in which it is trading).[34] It would also need the financial ability to offset the loss on the unprofitable product by profits from other products or, in the alternative, the financial strength to absorb the loss temporarily until it could be recouped after rivals had been weakened or eliminated and new entries discouraged.[35]

---

[32] Oregon Revised Statutes, 646.010.

[33] Section 2 of the Clayton Act, as amended by the Robinson-Patman Act, 49 stat. 1526, 15 USS Section 13.

[34] A definition of "seller market power" from a different point of view is: the ability of a seller to impose artificial restrictions on the availability to the customer of a desired service in order to effect an increase in the price for that service.

[35] "Dumping" is another term with which the reader should be familiar. The normal meaning is "the practice of selling goods in a foreign country at a price below their domestic selling price, with due allowance for transportation, tariffs, etc." The practice could have relevance within the United States, however, as when a surplus in one region is "dumped" into a different (foreign) region. Damage is seen if economic injury is inflicted upon the receiving area.

5.21 Is There a Problem?

Allegations of unreasonable utility price discrimination have been rare in the past, at least as seen in the literature and the writer's own experience. Suspicions of predatory pricing have been rarer still. The future could be different.

The unbundling of rates for both electric and natural gas utilities—a separate price for each unbundled segment—multiplies the classes of service but narrows each. With each narrowing the ascertainment of a proper cost benchmark becomes more tenuous. And, with each narrowing, the number of customers within the class shrinks, which can be expected to accentuate the importance of value considerations vis-à-vis cost considerations in the selection of the utility's price. As value-dominant situations rise in a greater-than-proportional relation to cost-dominant situations, the evaluation of the reasonableness of price discrimination could become perplexing and time consuming. New ground rules might be called for.

An example of such a "new" ground rule is contained in one of the Federal Energy Regulatory Commission's rules for open-access gas pipeline transportation. These rules provide for an unbundling of the transportation function of the pipeline from its customary total market service function (i.e., from transportation plus gas supply as a single package to transportation and gas supply as separate packages).[36] The rule prescribes ceiling and floor transportation rates between which discounting may be allowable. The Commission explains, "... the only purpose of allowing maximum and minimum rates is to allow flexibility in pricing to meet competition." It adds, however, "charging the floor rate may not necessarily constitute a defense to a predatory pricing charge under the antitrust laws."

By prescribing discount rates, FERC clearly sees value as the dominant factor for pricing when competitive forces are at play in the marketplace. But discounting of gas pipeline transportation rates is just one illustration of a much broader transition in utility pricing which is taking place. The unbundling movement itself, the genesis of the discount just discussed, arose from the same competitive market. FERC took the initiative in proposing a solution to its own most pressing problem which met the discrimination issue head on. It remains to be seen whether other regulatory bodies will see fit to bite the bullet within their own jurisdiction.

In more and more cases, the cost of the service the utility offered is not decisive as to price, the price of the competitor is. This shifts price leadership away from the traditional utility toward the non-regulated, or at least less regulated, competitor. Prior regulatory straitjackets may be outmoded.[37]

Overshadowing this, however, is the emergence of competition for utilities on a drastic unprecedented scale. Unbundling is a result of competition. The already

---

[36] Federal Energy Regulatory Commission, Order No. 436, *op.cit.* The quotation first following is at mimeo. p. IV. A. 141; the second quotation at mimeo. p. IV. A. 138.

[37] The fact that aggregate price structures may be subject to price caps and limitations on overall earnings does not dilute the influence of value upon prices for *individual services*.

experienced competitive impacts may prove to be only tangential to larger movements in the ways prices will be conceived and regulated, or not regulated, in the future.

Intra-energy competition is not new. Electricity, gas, and oil (and sometimes coal) have long been in competition. But it was competition in a mode following a well-traveled path—electric utility vs. gas utility vs. conventional oil.

The new competition is different. The energy utilities no longer can compete just with themselves and with oil. They now must also compete with non-utilities, many of which have strong market power.

Regulators are struggling to update their thinking and their regulatory frameworks on all fronts. At this time it is impossible to know what direction the new guidelines will follow. It is not even possible to assert with any assurance that the current trend toward deregulation will continue at the current pace, although that seems probable, but "Past is Prologue." The standards of the past may appear in a different guise, but the principles will live on. However, it does seem certain that the principles will be more difficult to apply. The greater the degree of competition, the greater the tendency—and the necessity in most cases—to shave prices in the competitive market. And, savage competition may give rise to the temptation to engage in cut-throat competition or even predatory pricing. The rate practitioner will be well-served to have in mind the standards of the past as he or she ventures into still uncharted territory.

5.22 Concluding Observations on Cost vs. Value

Many regulatory jurisdictions insisted for years that pricing, from the overall cost of service down to the individual rate schedule, should be directly related to cost (however indefinite and convoluted the costing process might be). The Federal Energy Regulation Commission (notably during its previous existence as the Federal Power Commission) has been an exception.[38] The Commission has consistently recognized that cost must be tempered by value in the final setting of the pipeline price. Thus, the Commission will adhere to rather precise costing procedures in establishing demand and commodity costs for the pipeline, but will depart from costs in establishing demand and commodity charges to be set in the pipeline's rates. Such departures are made to the extent necessary to satisfy the exigencies of the pipeline's market and/or policy objectives. The departure may be supported by a *Seaboard* cost allocation in one case, or a *United* allocation in another, or further allocation mixes in still other cases, but the result is the same—arriving at a composite demand-commodity rate which is oriented to the energy values prevailing in the pipeline's market at the time. (Since we discuss pipeline allocations in detail elsewhere, we need not elaborate further here).

---

[38] We speak here of FPC regulation of pipeline rates. The commission's unfortunate excursions into cost-based regulation of producer prices following the *Phillips* decision of 1954 are another matter.

5.22 Concluding Observations on Cost vs. Value

Having in mind FERC's rather straightforward history of admitting value to be an essential ingredient in price determination, we think it is revealing to examine a December 1985 FERC order in this respect.

The order, No. 436-A[39], includes a response by the Commission to a distorted concept of value of service rate making which had been advanced by one of the parties, namely, that under a value standard for interruptible service, "all fixed" costs will be charged to on-peak customers, thus giving off-peak customers a "free ride" rather than meeting the issue of cost vs. value rate making on its merits as this chapter attempts to do. Addressing the exaggeration in the quoted concept, the Commission retreated to a defensive posture. It simply reiterated its general proposition that rates, "must be cost-based and must be designed so that the pipeline has a reasonable opportunity to recover its costs," disavowing any "concern that [it] will permit pipelines to abandon cost-based rate making in favor of value-of-service ratemaking."

Here we may be observing an exercise in semantics. Clearly, no rates should, or will, be divorced from costs. So cost-based rate making will not be abandoned. But value-based rates simply mean rates where strictly cost considerations are tempered by market realities. The series of FERC orders dealing with natural gas transportation and sales under NGPA (Orders No. 436, 436-A, and 500) reiterate time and again that the objective of that Act is to recognize competition and the market (namely, to recognize value). For example, in Order No. 436-A, the Commission states

> The NGPA is predicated on the proposition that the price and allocation of natural gas can and should be determined to a greater extent by market forces rather than by means of the strict utility-type regulation previously employed under the NGA.

FERC's "Policy Statement Providing Guidance with Respect to the Designing of Rates," issued May 30, 1989, states,[40]

> The Commission's (ratemaking) task is to weigh all relevant considerations by 'integrating cost factors with *non-cost factors and policy considerations'* to fashion rates for each customer which are within the zone of reasonableness. (Emphasis added)

The Policy Statement quotes a 1987 circuit court opinion: "Pipeline transportation service is marked by a degree of natural monopoly ... In such an industry, *"value of service" ratemaking* (i.e., rates varying on the basis of differing demand characteristics) *has an established place, through not an uncontested one* ..."[41]

Commissioned Trabandt, in a separate concurring statement, interrelates value and cost considerations at several points. He fears rates which could be "largely

---

[39] Federal Energy Regulatory Commission, Order No. 436-A, issued December 12, 1985.

[40] Federal Energy Regulatory Commission, "Policy Statement Providing Guidance with Respect to the Designing of Rates," issued May 30, 1989, mimeo., p. 5.

[41] Federal Energy Regulatory Commission, "Policy Statement Providing Guidance with Respect to the Designing of Rates," issued May 30, 1989, mimeo., p. 5.

unrelated to the value and true cost of the rendered service." He endorses "the allocation of costs which will reflect better the costs associated with (the) service and the value of the service to customers."

Perhaps it is appropriate at this point to speculate as to why regulatory commissions—not just FERC—are so reluctant, if not downright skittish, to admit value as a full-fledged partner with cost in rate design. One reason may be that in prior periods most pricing objectives could be reached through cost justifications. Thus, for pipelines, costs supported both the *Seaboard* and *United* sought for end-results, although *United* costs put the lie to the prior *Seaboard* costs, and later combinations of fixed and variable costs put the lie to both *Seaboard* costs and *United* costs.

A second reason for the skittishness which seems to obstruct any forthright admission of the limitation of cost in pricing is that cost has become an almost sacred basis for rates in many commission and court decisions. Legal precedents in large part are grounded on costs. The dividing line between total costs as a basis for a company-wide cost of service, and allocated costs as a basis for an individual rate is, as a legal matter, fuzzy.

Another reason may be the linkage between cost and discrimination, particularly when the latter is defined solely as a departure from costs. Relatively speaking, it is easy to defend a particular costing procedure as resulting in a non-discriminatory rate. It is hard to defend as "reasonable" a departure from cost made to satisfy a particular market price requirement. The costing procedure has the appearance of objectivity—the resulting rate need not meet the test of reasonable discrimination since, by definition, being cost-based it is not discriminatory. On the other hand, the market-based rate is discriminatory by definition, and the discrimination must be proved to be reasonable. Value judgments entering into the marketplace are seemingly subjective, and being subjective are prima facie suspect.

The writer's observations suggest a final reason for down playing the role of value in price determination. Regulatory commissions and their staffs shy away from acknowledging the uncertainties of carrying cost down to the level of the individual rate, because if cost is uncertain so is the position of those who rely upon the generic cost rationale to support the end-result they advocate. Regulated entities can be just as oblique. They may wish to avoid undermining any of their own cost-justified rate proposals by admitting that costing has weaknesses. Why rock the boat?

Whatever the reasons, more often than not cost is accorded at least lip service as the favored ratemaking standard. Value is not the preferred term to enlist. However, notwithstanding built-in lethargies, the pricing climate is changing, if only gradually. As recent competition intrudes upon the earlier tranquility of the utility industries and their regulators, the marketplace is replacing historical costing procedures as the essential guide to prices.

5.23 Marketing and Advertising

Marketing and advertising are components contributing to the demand for the utility's product or service. The contribution is highly variable and difficult to measure. We make no attempt here either to generalize, or to measure results. We simply consider these activities in their usual contexts: (1) the enhancement of the utility's stature in the community and/or the stimulation of demand for its services or (2) the education of the public so that consumers can be knowledgeable in making decisions.

5.23.1 Civic Participation

Some might object that we include community-related activities under "marketing and advertising." Fine. We will not quibble. But in a broader sense, this chapter treats of demand; demand originates from people, and people, other things being equal of course, prefer to buy from those they like. So, whether it is "public relations" or "marketing," the community's opinion does impact demand.

Most utilities vigorously participate in civic affairs. Although policies and practices vary greatly, a few may be mentioned: sponsorship of civic activities either by corporation donations or participation of employees or both, such as charitable campaigns; memberships for employees in community-booster organizations and clubs; active leadership in local and state business/industrial economic development efforts; and encouragement of company personnel to run for political office.

Utility companies work hard to be good citizens of the communities they serve, often going beyond the bounds of what might be expected of them. Utility executives take prominent roles in broad-based national and international movements, such as environmental improvement. For example, Richard Clarke made the cover of Fortune's February 12, 1990 issue as an activist environmentalist. No small feat for the chairman and CEO of Pacific Gas and Electric Company, a major utility which had been at odds with environmentalists for years.

5.23.2 Marketing

There are many more books on marketing than there are on utilities, so we do not need to belabor the subject, but we can sketch utility practices very briefly.

Most utilities maintain a marketing or sales staff whose job it is to bring new customers to the company, to keep existing customers, and, often, to encourage greater usage per customer. On the other hand, "demand management" programs may supersede staff efforts for stimulation of demand. Demand management encourages customers to use less or to use capacity more efficiently and is particularly appropriate if the company is in the position of needing additional capacity.

The intensity of marketing activities can vary greatly, depending upon the amount of excess capacity on the system and the stress imposed by management. The tone of such activities also can vary, ranging from the bland and good-natured to vitriolic cutthroat competition.

Residential energy marketers will be concerned with establishing favorable relations with subdivision developers and other home-builders. They will assist at home shows and fairs, subdivision openings, and like events. The thrust of their work in energy companies will be to sell the "all gas" or the "all electric" home. They will be experts in comparative gas, electric, and oil prices, and can quote relative appliance efficiencies and usages given the slightest opportunity. They will check building permits for leads, and follow-up on "prospects" submitted by other organizational units of the company. Normally they perform a valuable service, for on the whole the information they convey will be accurate so that they can maintain credibility.

Commercial salespeople function in a somewhat larger arena, dealing with the developers of shopping centers, office buildings, and apartments as well as institutions such as hospitals and schools, and architects, heating engineers, and other professional groups.

Both residential and commercial marketing staffs are concerned with existing users as well as prospective new users.

Industrial marketing is the most sophisticated of all. Since the industrial salesperson deals directly with experienced personnel of present or prospective high-volume users, he or she must be equally knowledgeable. Often the industrial marketing staffs will be composed of experts in each of the several types of industries most prevalent in the service area of the company.[42]

5.23.3 Giveaways

One marketing practice which occurs from time to time is "buying business" by "giveaways." Unlike the marketing functions just discussed, buying business is difficult to condone. Methods which have been observed include: payments to

---

[42] Jahn and Berndt see post-1982 marketing practices of electric utilities as falling into three classifications: (1) Programs offering rate options designed to promote "efficient use," i.e., to promote an "optimal" load shape. These practices might discourage growth in both demand and energy usage if, for example, a capacity shortage was coupled with high-cost oil-fired energy. (2) Programs to increase energy sales, but not demand and thus to improve system load factor. (3) Programs to increase both demand and energy usage, as where sizeable excess capacity is online. Conservation programs would seem to fit into either group (1) or group (2) above, or both. All three groups are fundamentally cost-based in their rationale. Nevertheless, each is a marketing program designed to influence demand, and as such falls within the broad umbrella of value of service. Jahn, L.R. and Bernd, M.S., "A Cost-of-Service Basis for Utility Marketing Programs", *Public Utilities Fortnightly*, September 19, 1985.

5.23 Marketing and Advertising

developers to elect its service over that of competitors, free appliances to customers either for initial installation or replacement, and footing the bill for developer promotions.

Electric and gas companies, having long been in competition with each other as well as with oil dealers, are the traditional examples of utility giveaway practices.

Buying business, even if allowed or ignored by the regulatory authority, usually can be counted upon to be counterproductive. A giveaway by one company is met by the competitor, who may even "up" the ante. A vicious cycle is started, and seldom results in any long-term gain to the originating company.

5.23.4 Advertising

All readers are familiar with media advertising in TV, newspapers, magazines, billboards, and now the web. For the purpose of helping the reader to more easily study utility advertising, the individual ad may fall into one or more of the following classifications:

1. Institutional, designed to familiarize the public with a new company or to enhance the stature of a well-known company;
2. Service promotion, to introduce a new service or further "sell" an existing service;
3. Competitive, where the advertiser favorably compares its type, quality, and/or price of service with that of a specific competitor or competitors;
4. Informational, where the purpose is primarily to present a set of facts to the public.

Chapter 6
The Value Approach to Pricing: Planning for Demand

Abstract This chapter instructs on how to prepare a load forecast for both the short-run and long-range. The latter involves conforming the forecast to a strategic plan and accommodating it to the limits of available supply. Often the difficult issue of market share must be faced. Procedural issues are encountered: should the forecast indicate a single trend or include a range of trends? Availability of the product, the reliability of supply, and the anticipated impact of public-awareness programs, such as conservation, must each be considered. The higher importance of forecasts involving public-policy issues is emphasized.

6.1 Units of Measurement

Energy utility operations require that both short- and long-range forecasts be cast in a dual framework, the "peak" requirement and the volumetric requirement.

The peak measures the capability which the system must have to cover the aggregate of all customer demands which may occur simultaneously. The *electric unit* is the kilowatt; the peak period adopted may be instantaneous, quarter-hour, half-hour, or hour depending on the practice of the individual company. The short duration of the peak period reflects the fact that electricity cannot be stored.[1] Generating capacity to supply the full extent of the maximum demand must be available on call. The *gas unit* may be either the cubic foot (a volumetric measure) or therm (a measure of heat or energy content). Whichever it may be, the peak period usually is 1 day.[2] This longer period is appropriate since a limited amount of gas storage normally is present in a gas system due to "line pack" and other measures which can increase throughput temporarily.

The volumetric requirement is self-explanatory. What is the total amount of energy which will be used in a specified period? The electric unit is the

---

[1] There is an exception to this rule, viz., reservoir storage for a hydro system. But for almost all systems electricity cannot be generated and held for later delivery.

[2] The 1-day peak used for system planning as mentioned here is not to be confused with the 3-day peak often adopted for pipeline cost allocation purposes.

kilowatt-hour; the gas volumetric unit is the same as the peak unit, the cubic foot or therm, or their multiples, the Mcf (one thousand cubic feet) or the decatherm (ten therms). When the Btu content of gas is one thousand Btu per cubic foot, an Mcf equals a decatherm. Both equate to 1 million Btu.

For the reader who is not oriented toward utility operations, the difference between the peak requirement and the volume requirement can be visualized by assuming that the utility supplies energy to a bakery for two ovens. If both are being used simultaneously, the peak requirement equates to the energy needed by the two together. But, if the ovens are used at different times, the peak requirement equates only to the energy needed by one oven. The volume of energy required to heat both ovens, however, is the same regardless of whether they are in use simultaneously or at different times.

The automobile provides a somewhat more complicated analogy. The vehicle may be capable of reaching a top speed of 100 miles per hour. That is its peak capability. Its tank may have capacity for 300 miles of travel without refill. That is its volume capacity. In this context, peak measurements indicate the maximum *rate* of use, while volume measurements gauge the total *extent* of use.

6.2 Procedure

Energy utilities are weather sensitive, i.e., both their peak and volumetric loads may vary considerably with weather conditions. Very hot summer weather causes air conditioning loads to rise spectacularly. Very cold winter weather boosts space-heating demands in similar degree. As a common denominator, the primary energy forecast is likely to be related to "normal" or "average" weather conditions. The normal condition is most often used for budgeting and financial planning. However, subsidiary forecasts are developed for the extremes on either side of the normal weather prediction. System engineering must be based on the maximum loads the system will be called upon to carry. Cash flow requirements must take into account minimum sales probabilities.

One further introductory point, energy utilities must have greater capabilities owned or purchased, than the sum of their customers' demands, because each experiences "losses" in the transmission and distribution of the energy, and, for electric utilities, at the generating plant as well. Losses must be factored into the determination of the supply requirement. Also, reserve capacity usually is factored in as a safeguard against equipment failure and to allow down time for maintenance.

6.3 Planning: Short-Run Demand Forecasts

Natural gas and electric utilities normally prepare forecasts each day for the following day's operations. Why?

6.3.1 Natural Gas

With a keen eye toward the weather forecast, the gas distributor must inform its pipeline supplier as to what its requirements from that supplier will be, probably in detail by delivery point. Abnormal hourly variations will be pointed out. The pipeline must inform a large number of producers and processing plants, perhaps in many scattered locations, of its probable "takes," including volumes received and transported for others; it likewise must inform other pipeline companies, if they also are sources of supply. Supplying producers may need to alert field operators, particularly if the expected demands are much less or more than might usually be expected. New unbundled transportation arrangements increase the complexity of the pipeline scheduling job multifold.

6.3.2 Electric

Electric utilities also use the weather forecast as an input to the forecast of electric needs for the following day. Fortunately, if electric needs turn out to be different than predicted the day prior, the electric utility has considerable flexibility to meet these load fluctuations. Additional plants can be brought on line, particularly if the utility operates as a part of a power pool rather than as a completely independent system. The rule is that the least expensive plants are added first with the most expensive being the last in line. Operational differences between the gas and electric industry occur because while gas can be stored or packed in the line to meet additional demands, electricity must be used as it is produced. If electric resources are not sufficient to simultaneously match demand, service quality deteriorates.

Because of the instantaneous relationship between demands and production, most electric utilities today operate as part of a power pool. The power pool is the utility's first source for additional power if the utility cannot meet an unforecasted change in load or has an unplanned outage. Beyond the pool, do non-pool but inter-connected utilities have power to sell that may be cheaper?

Operational generation scheduling for a hydro-system must take into account additional factors which constitute a science of their own. When should water be stored in a given reservoir, rather than being released? Assuming a series of storage and run-of-the-river hydro plants on the same stream, what is the optimal time to release water through the generators of an upstream plant for the power production at that plant, so that, after travel time, the released water will reach plants lower on the river at the most effective time? Are water releases for power production consistent with rules (minimums and maximums) for the protection of fish runs, navigation, flood control, irrigation, and recreation?

6.3.3 Common Issues

In months of "tight" or restricted supply, both gas and electric utilities have an additional common problem. Both may serve customers on an interruptible basis, i.e., where deliveries to these customers may be cut back or "curtailed," either partially or entirely, if the available energy will fall short of meeting their needs in addition to the needs of higher priority firm customers. Interruptible customers may be entitled to advance notice, often a contractual obligation, of anticipated curtailment. Therefore, the short-run process may include customer notification procedures.

Orderly operation also dictates intermediate term planning. A year-to-year forecast is made on a somewhat broader basis. In the case of a hydro-electric system which incorporates cyclical storage, operational planning will extend over an even longer period—the refill cycle of the cyclical reservoir or reservoirs.

For the forecasting sectors of distributors of both energies, the demand forecast will be broken down between firm and interruptible requirements and, in periods of tight supply, perhaps between priorities within these broad classes also.

For the pipeline acting as a merchant, it will incorporate such considerations as take-or-pay obligations, relative field rules for maximum or minimum "takes," and the relative prices of gas from different fields and different producers. As a transporter, the pipeline will have no direct control over short-run planning for the use of its system except to reflect the maximum obligations to transport in its transportation contracts and to utilize its own system storage for balancing. Within contractual customer usage limitations, the pipeline is expected to be able to accept volumes offered at receipt points and to deliver these volumes elsewhere on its system pursuant to instructions from customers.

For the electric generating department, or the power pool, it will encompass "rule curves" for reservoir operation and the scheduling of out-of-service maintenance periods for generating plants. For gas producers, they must try to balance projected requirements with MERs (maximum efficiency rates) of take, proration levels, and similar restriction derived from state authority or contract.

We do not attempt to discuss the criteria upon which the above multiple choices may be based because these choices are largely non-policy, resting upon the considerable expertise of the scheduler-dispatcher and the short-term forecaster. Policy becomes significant, and perhaps decisive, in the longer-range forecasts which will be covered shortly.

6.4 Planning: Long-Range Demand Forecasts

It is extremely difficult to make accurate predictions, especially about the future.

Economic forecasting is the occupation that makes astrology respectable[3].

Energy demand forecasting is not a precise science. It lies somewhere in the intriguing borderland between a pure hunch and a low grade skill.

...M.B. Katz[4]

---

[3] Among our favorite quotes, sources lost in our files.
[4] Katz, Myron B., Chairman, Public Utilities Commission of Oregon, letter of May 25, 1990 to the writer.

6.4 Planning: Long-Range Demand Forecasts

Forecasts ... have a way of coming back to haunt the forecaster.
...Fern Shen[5]

It takes more than numbers from the past to plan ahead. It also takes judgment.
...Robert J. Beck[6]

Statistics are no substitute for judgment.
...Henry Clay

It is beyond the scope of this text to incorporate a manual explaining the many details of the techniques of preparation of the long-range demand forecast. To attempt to do so with any precision would require a volume at least as large as the present work, since there are probably as many techniques as there are forecasters. Rather, our purpose is to sketch out what might be considered to be a checklist for the utility executive or regulator; a rough basis for setting forth the ground rules which the forecaster should follow and, upon completion, some thoughts which may throw light on the probable validly—or weakness—of the end result. Perhaps the single major suggestion is as follows: warn the forecaster in advance that he or she will be required to explain in rational down-to-earth terms the "why" of the results. When the forecast is complete, the management should demand such explanations.

This becomes even more important as the use of involved econometric forecasting models proliferates.[7] A complex formula is not endowed with ever greater accuracy simply because its convolutions become more intricate and more intertwined with other equally complex formulae. The reverse may be true.

A Harvard Business School project report makes some illuminating observations on econometric models which are appropriate to our comment.[8] Because of the prevalence of these models, and the credibility accorded them, we quote selectively from the report.

> Econometricians build and operate models which consist of mathematical equations based upon relationships derived from economic theory and estimates based on historical statistical relationships. The use of such models is often characterized as "looking forward through a rear view mirror."...
>
> The major studies since 1973 have given us predictions about the U.S. energy situations that have consistently been more optimistic than the reality has proved to be, especially in regard to energy supplies. ... It seems abundantly clear that some of the optimistic forecasts issued did influence and mislead both the energy policy makers and the informed public about the causes and possible solutions for the energy problem.
>
> What went wrong with the models? ... the modeling enterprise needs to be demystified ... *all too often overlooked is the critical importance of the various assumptions made by the*

---

[5] Shen, F., "Northwest Power Surplus Seen Continuing," *The Oregonian*, June 23, 1985.

[6] Beck, R.J., "Forecast Requires Data, Assumptions," *Oil and Gas Journal*, January 29, 1990.

[7] The economist frequently credited with laying the scientific groundwork for large-scale economic model building is Trygve Haavelmo of Oslo University. Professor Haavelmo belatedly received a Nobel Prize for his early forecasting work of the 1940's in October 1989. Mandel, M.J., "At Long Last, Laurels: An Economics Pioneer Wins the Nobel Prize for Early Forecasting," *Business Week*, October 23, 1989.

[8] Stobaugh, R and Yergin, D (eds.), *Future Energy – Report of the Energy Project at the Harvard Business School*, Random House, New York, NY, 1979. See "Appendix; Limits to Models."

modelers, for these assumptions, in effect, determine the results of the models ... [emphasis added]

The use of formal models to provide insight can be very useful. The dilemma of formal models, however, is ... the scientific aura surrounding them ...

... models must be used with great care. When present conditions are far different from the historical expertise, it is possible that the models can do more harm than good.

... a model is not reality.

Neither our cautions nor those of the Harvard Business School are to be construed as an indictment of econometric demand forecasting. They constitute no more than a statement that utility managements and regulator alike should ask "why" when the market is projected to rise or fall. The answer that an influential Paris designer is known to be coming out with new fall fashions which will lengthen or shorten women's skirts should not be enough—nor should reams of computer printout.

6.4.1 The Purpose of the Forecast

The fundamental purpose of the long-range demand forecast is to present a realistic view of the utility's future market, including the several component submarkets which together constitute the market as a whole. In utility parlance, such a market appraisal is called variously a load estimate, a load forecast, an economic forecast, the sales outlook, a market survey, or simply a demand study.

The demand forecast provides the basis for: (1) system facilities planning; (2) financial planning, including budgets and financial forecasts; and (3) support for regulatory presentations.

The forecast may be static, in the sense that it is overhauled and completely redone only every several years, with some patching up in the interval to take account of massive changes. Or, it may be fluid, kept current by a zero-based new forecast each year. The latter is preferred, if staffing permits.

6.4.2 The Strategic Plan

Many businesses today have adopted the approach that the overall direction of company policy and movement should be in accordance with a broad "strategic plan." The scope, intricacy, and time span of the strategic plan will vary with the architect, and the variations are myriad.[9] It is not our intent here to explore strategic planning.

---

[9] An adjunct to the strategic plan which has been adopted by some companies is called "scenario planning." Under this variation an initial step is to develop several alternative scenarios as to how the future might unfold, with particular attention to identifying "critical uncertainties" in matters which would have a crucial impact upon the company, which distinguish one scenario from the others. The strategic plan would then be formulated so as to be best suited, in general, to whichever sets of conditions envisioned by the scenarios might actually occur. The several scenarios assist in building flexibility into the strategic plan.

It is merely enough to point out that a strategic plan may be the first step in the planning process. If it is, policy direction for the future will be laid out for the forecaster to follow.

Whether or not a strategic plan is involved, executive policy has an influence. The forecaster should approach the job with a clear vision. What is seen, however, will be impacted by the managerial direction of the firm. If the firm is growth-minded, and hence likely to follow a market expansion program, prospects for utility markets may be viewed by the forecaster through rose-colored glasses. If the firm views diversification as more attractive than utility expansion, and hence may be expected to wish to divert its dollars to non-utility enterprises, the lenses of the forecaster may be tinted gray. The hope is for neither rose nor gray; but in actual practice that is easier said than done. A "kill the messenger" attitude of management can rob the forecast of any validity.

6.4.3 The Supply Forecast

It may seem contradictory to mention a forecast of supply in a section dealing specifically with the forecast of demand. Yet, it is required, since a demand outlook cannot be realistic unless there will be supply (demand-serving capability) to satisfy the demand. (By the same token, of course, supply will not be provided unless a demand for it is foreseen.)

The interlocking mechanism between the demand and supply forecasts is the cost–price relationship; the cost of providing the needed supply, on the one hand, and the price which the market will support, on the other hand. The two dovetail.[10] The supply forecast has been discussed in a preceding chapter. This is just a reminder of the supply–demand relationship.

6.4.4 Matching Supply and Demand

It is only after the market parameters have been drawn, consistent with the broadly estimated costs of a matching supply, that the physical system which will be needed for future service can be designed and specifically costed. This is not quite a "chicken and the egg" proposition. The market must first be visualized; then, and only then, how it can best be served may be laid out. It may be redundant to add

---

[10] John C. Sawhill observes that "the key characteristic of today's utility industry is...increasing competition on both the demand and the supply sides." Referring to electric, he notes: "On the demand side, customers can choose from an expanding array of options," such as on site generation in lieu of utility supply, or for wholesale customers, a switch of utility suppliers. "On the supply side, the utility monopoly on generating capacity is disappearing with the emergence new entrants – principally co generators and independent power producers – who have lower cost structures." Sawhill, J.C., "Planning to Win in the New Utility Environment," *Public Utilities Fortnightly*, October 12, 1989.

that revision of the supply forecast undoubtedly will be required to match it with the final demand data.

The most popular current version on an extended span match between supply and demand is dubbed a "least cost plan." Such a plan devises different supply routes, each with different costs, for meeting the foreseen demand. These routes often include conservation measures to reduce demand as an alternative to adding capacity. A number of state regulatory commissions require utilities to prepare and submit such plans.

6.4.5 The Input Assumptions

Demand forecasting is not a simple matter of extending into the future a trend line connecting two or more historical points. Predicting the future is always a precarious act. To predict in a haphazard fashion increases the exposure.

We have just mentioned one of the most important input assumptions, the cost of supply. But that factor does not stand alone.

It is easy to overlook, or at least to minimize, the significance of carefully defining the broad economic and political assumptions, or "ground rules," upon which the forecast will rest. The assumption as to future overall business conditions is an obvious example. This writer commented on that point in one of his own forecasts as follows: "A market forecast is an attempt to look forward to a future market, and if that forecast is to have any meaning it must be placed in context with the economy as a whole. It is clear that an entirely different market would be foreseen on the basis of an assumption of general conditions of business recession, than on the assumption of general conditions of business prosperity. So the first step in a market forecast is the establishment of the ground rules or assumptions on which that forecast will be based."[11] Another writer put it this way: "Economic [forecasting] models are like prescription medicines; they are created for a purpose and directions for use should always accompany them."[12]

Linked to the assumptions of general business conditions are related national economy assumptions concerning the degree of employment or unemployment, the growth rate of the gross national product, and other economic indices considered to have a bearing. A choice must be made as to whether to present the forecast in actual dollars, in which event a rate of inflation must be decided upon, or in constant dollars. There are pros and cons for each. Since utilities are integral to the national economy, and are depended upon to support any emergencies which may arise, the broad ground rules should specify the adopted assumption as to the world political situation—peace, cold war or war, disarmament or heavy defense spending, or

---

[11] Conkling, Inc, "The Potential for the Petroleum Industry in the Pacific Northwest," a report prepared for the Bonneville Power Administration, US Department of the Interior, 1966.

[12] Federal Energy Regulatory Commission, "Notice Requesting Supplemental Comments," Docket No. RM 85-1-000, issued October 9, 1985, Exhibit S, "An Economic Analysis of Supply Adequacy in the Natural Gas Industry," p. 1.

6.4 Planning: Long-Range Demand Forecasts

some variation of such conditions. The final result of a forecast cannot be interpreted accurately unless these entry points are known. Perhaps just as important, the forecaster will be plagued with inconsistencies, omissions, or duplications, unless that unhappy individual has these general parameters firmly in mind.

Broad economic assumptions are also vital on the local level (i.e., specific as to the geographic area covered by the forecast, be it a metropolitan area, a portion of a state, a whole state, or a group of states). These local assumptions include projections of population, employment, personal income, and households, as well as the market outlook for the larger users of the utility's service (the derived demands). The number and variety of input assumptions calls for expertise in divergent economics fields, compounding the difficulty of meshing the interrelated components of the forecast so that it will be internally consistent.

Both of the energy utilities have a common problem: what will be their share of the total market for the services they provide? Electricity and natural gas share the utility market for energy. Oil, a non-utility, also shares this market, as do to a lesser extent, coal, wood, solar, and wind as well as bio fuels.

Many econometric forecasting models for energy require, as inputs, estimates in precise dollar-and-cents terms of future electric, natural gas, and oil prices (on a constant dollar basis usually, unless some rate of inflation is applied uniformly). To accommodate such models, price forecasts for the three energies must be—and unfortunately are—made.

It may or may not be possible for an electric utility to project accurately its own specific costs and, therefore, its own prices at the generating plant. On this subject, in 1982, the writer stated,[13]

"While [the cost elements of electric supply] forecasts are speculative to some extent, one normally would expect the degree of uncertainty to be nominal..."

"A few years ago [prior to 1982], I would have suggested ... that if an electric generating plant of a given design was to be constructed, one could be quite sure that from that plant a given number of dependable kilowatts of capacity and a given number of dependable kilowatt hours of output, could be expected almost beyond any reasonable doubt. Furthermore, I would have said that when the design had been completed and the specifications had been prepared, a reliable estimate of costs could be made. In other words, output is certain; costs are predictable within a narrow margin of error."

"That was before restructuring. We have now been taught to be extremely wary of forecasts of electric production costs."

---

[13] Conkling, Roger L., Rebuttal testimony on behalf of the Association of Washington Gas Utilities, et al., in the matter of the 1982 Proposed Wholesale Power Rate Adjustment, US Department of Energy, Bonneville Power Administration, June 17, 1982.

6.4.6 Other Market Share Considerations

An appraisal of the market share issue goes beyond the question of the relative prices of competing services. Also to be considered in relation to the price of the utility service itself is whether the utility price will increase faster than inflation. If it will, this means that the utility bill will be taking a greater share of the consumer's dollar, with the possible, if not probable, result that price elasticity will set into motion a downward trend in utility usage.

At least four other factors in addition to relative price have a bearing on market share. *One is the substitutability of a different source of service for the utility's service.* Is gas available at given locations as a competitor to electricity? If so, the two will be in direct and continuing competition for heating loads, although utility-supplied electricity will preserve its monopoly on the new lighting, small appliance, and small motor loads. There is a possibility, however, that gas might invade these historically impregnable electric markets if gas-fueled electric home generators become practicable. Self-generation and cogeneration by industrial users may make inroads upon utility-supplied electricity utilized in industrial processes, and may establish a market for gas if the generation is gas-fueled. Both gas and electricity face competition in the heating sector from oil and, in some localities, coal, wood, solar, and wind. Convenience, cleanliness, and environmental considerations may influence the customer's energy choice.

Both energy utilities will experience growth from increased population, the increase in the number of households, industrial expansion, and local economic development. But a household can find use for only a limited number of ranges, television sets, water heaters, and computers, and there is a limit to the amount of energy needed for space heating and air conditioning. Industrial usage is highly competitive and oil cannot be written off for a share in the expansion of industrial energy consumption. At this point in time, other than the probability of widespread use of natural gas or electricity for automotive fuel, no significant new markets for energy are on the horizon.

The dilemma of substitutability includes a core issue which the energy utilities have in common—bypass. We treat bypass elsewhere. Suffice to say at this point that *bypass appears to be a market share consideration of major importance.*

A related factor is the effectiveness of *any current or proposed marketing program* of the company itself (whether acting alone, or through a trade association or equipment manufacturer), including demand-management programs. An independent appraisal by the forecaster of marketing effectiveness is not a happy task, for it may require a dampening by one part of the organization (the forecasters) of the announced expectations of another part (the marketers).

6.4.7 Availability and Reliability

Both electricity and natural gas have gone through periods when availability was limited: electric brownouts and gas shortages. Both have faced prolonged serious questions as to the availability of future supply; will the nation permit the construction of new generating plants to support increasing demands for electricity? Will these plants be nuclear, or non-conventional at the present time? Are reserves of natural gas, present and potential, sufficient to supply growth in demand? And in what locations will exploration for new reserves be permitted or denied?

Reliability, in the sense of service outages due to equipment failures, seems good for both energy sources. When outages happen, it seems that the causes most often are beyond the utility's control. (This conclusion is based upon the writer's observations, not any special study.)

It should be noted that public perceptions of availability and reliability may be just as significant to an accurate market appraisal as the facts.

6.4.8 Finally, the Factor of Governmental Policy

Of all considerations, governmental policy is the most elusive and the most difficult to foresee. Governmental action may influence each consideration bearing upon market share (in fact, it may influence other facets of the demand forecast as well). Conservation and the environment are cases in point for the energy utilities. The impact of government is pervasive.

No forecaster can be expected to resolve the uncertainties of future governmental policy, whether at the local, state, federal, or foreign level. Neither, however, can the subject be ignored. The forecaster must make assumptions, in the alternative if that seems best. These assumptions should be delineated as part of the forecast so that results can be interpreted clearly, and, even more important, so that results will not be misinterpreted.

Finally, we quote a word of advice offered by *Fortune* (March 26, 1990) in its introduction to the 1990s,

> "TossOut Your Old Assumptions": *Public Policy on Conservation vs. Development*: A single public policy issue towers above a myriad of others: conservation vs. development. That issue cannot be avoided by the energy forecaster, who must pose and attempt to answer the question:
> In what magnitudes can energy demand be controlled (that is, kept within utility company or governmentally established limits) by price elasticity and demand management policies aimed at reducing or modifying energy consumption?

6.5 Final Results

Unfortunately, almost a quarter century after this question was posed; there still is sparse empirical evidence of a decisive nature on this question upon which the forecaster can rely—although estimates proffered by experts are lacking neither in quantity nor in diversity of opinion.

The extremes are clear. It is the mid-point which is missing. As one boundary, it would appear to be beyond dispute that price elasticity and demand management programs are effective in dampening demand. But how far can they be stretched? On the opposite boundary, also beyond dispute, certain quantities of energy are necessities, not luxuries, in our economy as we know it. What is the minimum the public and the industrial base will tolerate?

The forecaster is handicapped in arriving at a reasonable middle ground because he must steer a neutral course between two polarized, diametrically opposed camps—those who contend that conservation can essentially eliminate the need for any new energy resources and those who argue that we should continue to add to our energy base to avoid stifling the economy and our quality of life. Each side tends to be inflexible and intransigent, and obstructive of the serious formulation of an unbiased position.

The forecaster can expect to be overwhelmed with advice—if not directives—as to the course to be taken. Our suggestion is only this; let the forecaster call the shots as he or she sees them. You can't please everybody, so one camp or the other, or perhaps both, will disagree. If the forecaster presents reasoned conclusions which the forecaster actually believes, they will stand the test of time and apologies with excuses will not have to be offered in a year, or two or ten, when the political climate changes as assuredly it will.

6.5.1 The Single Forecast vs. a Range

Forecasts may be developed to produce a single end figure—demand at year X, will be Y units—or a range—demand at year X may be as high as Y plus a, as low as Y minus a, or in between. Other forecasts refine the range even further. Bonneville Power Administration has actually presented five different forecasts: high, medium-high, medium, medium-low, and low. Loads between the medium-high and medium-low are considered to be most likely. BPA calculates that there is a 50% chance that the actual load will fall within that range. BPA supports its power demand forecasts by detailed and sophisticated economic studies.

The range has the advantage that it quantifies, or helps to quantify, the magnitude of uncertainty. (Although such magnitude may be as much in error as the single forecast.) For the forecaster the range provides an "out," for the chances that actual results will fall within the range are much greater than that actual results will coincide closely to the single forecast.

The disadvantage of the range is that it solves very little. Assume a new facility or any other addition to existing capacity is needed under the high estimate, but not under the medium and, of course, not under the low estimate. The dilemma is unavoidable. The answer, one suspects, lies in an evaluation of the respective input assumptions, which is a reason why it is so essential that these assumptions be fully and carefully delineated. If the high estimate assumes that electricity will recapture all market share lost to natural gas, that is one thing; if it assumes that natural gas will continue a modest gain in market share, that is another.

The single forecast has the advantage that it tells the forecaster, "Put up or shut up. We want your best estimate of what you think is likely to materialize, given your assumptions, without hedging." This does not relieve management of the grave burden of assessing the validity of the end results, including the reasonableness of the input assumptions, but it does bring the end results into sharper focus. If management moves ahead to provide new capacity, or doesn't, the basis is clear, "Our best forecast told us we should do as we did." The disadvantage of the single forecast is that it narrows the flexibility of management—management must either accept or reject the forecast rather than maneuver within a range.

6.5.2 The Components of the Forecast

However the forecast may be developed, which will depend upon the preferences of the forecaster, the end results should permit "zero-based" analysis. By this we mean that the building blocks upon which the forecast rests should be identified and quantified, often called an "end use" model. An example will illustrate this. A forecast for residential demands for electricity should reveal the total number of residential customers; the KWh use of these customers for basic lighting and small appliances; the number of residential water heaters and the KWh use of each; the number of electrically heated homes, with the per home energy use—perhaps the electrically heated homes should be broken down into homes with preconservation insulation standards and those with post-conservation improved insulation techniques, with a per-home KWh usage for each; and the same for home air conditioning. The total of these components of demand would equate to the overall residential demand. Without component detail, the overall demand is nearly impossible to evaluate.

Similarly, the building blocks should be identified and quantified for other sectors of the utility's demand.

The derived demands may be the most difficult to quantify, but they are equally necessary for the forecast. Aluminum, paper, lumber, steel, ship building, auto manufacture, fabrication of all kinds, you name it, for the energy industries.

Even with all the refinements and detail just enumerated, there will be much room for error.

There is one element of risk which is inherent in every utility-originated forecast. This element is structural; it arises because forecasts are made by individual utility companies, who seek only to foresee demands to be supplied by their own system. Such narrow focus can result in a "tunnel-vision" forecast. Likewise, competing suppliers only look at their own respective demands. Unless company forecasters suddenly develop a pessimistic view of the futures of their own companies, it is more than likely that the sum of the forecasts of competing utilities will considerably exceed any rational appraisal of the size of the total markets they jointly serve.

6.5.3 Testing the Forecast

This risk need not go unchecked. Managements can check by requiring that an estimate of the total market accompany the forecast of the utility's own market. The total market estimate should be broken down into the portions presumed to be served by each supplier competing for a share.[14]

These data (if they have not already sent our forecaster back to the drawing boards) permit the examination by management of at least two probing questions. First, is the growth (or decline) of the total market reasonable, from the viewpoints of annual growth rates, usage per capita, per household, per business customer, per type of industry, etc.? Second, are the market shares assigned to competitors unreasonably small and to ones own company, unreasonably large?

The second question is not a duplication of our prior suggestion that input assumptions should include a pre-forecast market share outlook. Rather, it is a check on whether the market share envisaged by the assumptions, and presumably incorporated in the forecast, actually turns out to be reasonable when the total market is examined.

Another area for management scrutiny concerns whether company policy biases, or departmental preferences, may have crept into the forecast. Is the forecast skewed upward to justify facility additions which executives desire? Or downward, to save new construction funds for other purposes? Have marketing or engineering personnel unduly influenced the forecast for their own purposes?

As an aspect of the American economy, the ups and downs of the business cycle have not yet been repealed. We experience good and bad economic years. Assuming that the basic forecast is predicted upon "average" economic conditions, it may behoove management to ask for a "worst case" scenario when any particular year's forecast is being examined. This may be of particular relevance in financial planning.

Finally, management would be well served to consider related observations about forecasts of *The Wall Street Journal* and *Fortune*.[15] The *Journal's* comment was made some years ago as the turn-about of the earlier energy crisis was first being seen clearly:

> Because soothsayers share the same statistical techniques, economic theory and data, they also tend to share the same ignorance, so they're either going to be all right as a group or all wrong as a group.

---

[14]The writer's personal experience confirms the desirability of checking an individual utility's forecast against the total market. One example stands out. Energy policy concerning both electricity and natural gas for a region was at issue before a governmental body. The electric entities presented a forecast (derived from an econometric model as it happened) which appeared excessive to gas interests. Examination showed that the electric forecast could be accurate *only* if gas did not capture *any* of the space and water heating loads of new households. No oil would be used for heating either. *All* new construction would opt for electricity for every purpose. The same was imbedded in the forecast for the replacement of existing gas and oil installations—gas and oil would be replaced by electric when old equipment wore out in *all* instances. These were patently unreasonable assumptions, but the error did not become apparent until the total energy market was taken into consideration.

[15]Getschow, G., "More or Less Oil Will Go Up or Down or May It Won't," *The Wall Street Journal,* May 5, 1982; and Fisher, A.B., "Is Long-Range Planning Worth It?" *Fortune,* April 23, 1990.

... When the energy market's going up, they think it's going up forever; when it's going down, they think it's going down forever.

Fortune's caution is expressed in an article on long-range planning as it "looked ahead" in early 1990:

Corporate deep thinkers looking toward the next millennium are well aware of a phenomenon that the late Herman Kahn, the dean of American futurists dubbed "educated incapacity." Kahn observed that experts so often turn out to be mistaken because they are experts. They know the past and present in such detail, and have formed such iron clad assumptions, that their knowledge prevents them from anticipating surprises.

These tendencies of soothsayers and experts can be hedged by heeding the down-to-earth advice of John F. Smith, a former business associate of the writer, who admonishes; "Listen to the man in the field. He is closer to the market."[16]

A different, unrelated Smith approaches the problem by mandating deliberate understatement. Upon ascending to the position of president and chief operating officer of General Motors Corporation in April 1992, as a result of a directors' coup, John F. Smith, Jr. laid down the rule "draw up financial plans using the most pessimistic sales forecasts, and don't use price increases to turn a red forecast into black."[17]

6.5.4 Reliance on Forecasts

Our concluding comments on demand forecasting are directed toward emphasizing a single theme: However carefully prepared and reviewed, the forecast will be off the mark to some degree. To adopt a heading from *The Wall Street Journal*: there are always "Clouds in the Crystal Ball."[18] The unforgivable error which management can make is to adopt any forecast as gospel. This does not imply that forecasts are not useful: in fact they are indispensable. What it does suggest is that no forecast should be followed without a clearly set forth scheme of hedges—alternative sets of actions which can be brought into play if significant deviations from the forecast materialize.

Elsewhere we mention two examples of grossly erroneous demand forecasts—the inflated demand calculations that played such an important role in leading to bond defaults for WPPSS's nuclear generating projects, and the same overstatement of demand forecasts which led to mammoth take-or-pay liabilities for the gas industry. In both cases, meshing supply forecasts continually understated costs, each update being a masterpiece of cost downplay. In take-or-pay, the price elasticity of natural gas supply in response to higher producer prices was overlooked.

---

[16]Smith, John F., retired Director, Regional Energy Policy, Northwest Natural Gas Company, Portland, Oregon in conversation with the writer, 1992.
[17]White, J.B., "GM's President Exemplifies a New Breed," *The Wall Street Journal,* April 8, 1992.
[18]"Energy Switch," *The Wall Street Journal,* January 27, 1982.

Other facts, however, contribute to forecasting error. These may be summed up as the universal limitation of the human being—we are not clairvoyant. To drive home the point that no forecast should be taken as the last and final work on the future, we note a favorite quote, vintage the energy crisis of the 1970s, "In the complex field of energy forecasting, there seems to be only one certainty: whatever number is chosen will be wrong."[19] In generalized explanation, "There are so many factors involved in decision making by both buyers and sellers that yesterday's logical conclusions may be invalid today."[20]

6.6 Public Policy Forecasts

Public projects are pervasive, ranging from the smallest such as filling a pothole on a city street, to the largest, like constructing a new bridge across a major river. In retrospect, it often seems that the planning for both large and small projects has been defective, the completed job being delayed and/or over budget. Construction costs have been forecasted too low, a cost issue, or some part of the design has been overlooked, a value defect, or both. Experience points to the need for more careful forecasting as well.

There are two areas of forecasting for public projects which are of such pressing importance that they need special mention. The first of these is in the planning of significant changes in public policy, where errors or omissions can result in grave disadvantage; the second is where changes in existing practices impacting on the public welfare are adopted without appropriate notice and planning. Each of these can have disastrous results if overlooked.

6.6.1 Errors in Public Policy

Chapter 12 covers a policy error, which had adverse consequences affecting electric services to the entire state of California, and adjoining states as well. The policy called for the divorce from government regulation of power generating facilities and management, with the established electric companies to be responsible in the future only for power transmission and distribution under continued regulation. In short, the generation function of the electric industry was to be deregulated, but its two other remaining functions were not. The combining of deregulated and regulated functions proved to be a major policy error. Generating companies were free to charge the utility companies high-unregulated prices for wholesale power, but the utility companies were forced to sell to the general public at prices far below what they had to pay to generators. This led to the bankruptcy of the largest electric company in California and to near-bankruptcy of others. None of this had been

---

[19]McDonough, S., "Energy Growth Forecasts Vary Widely," *The Oregonian,* March 21, 1982.
[20]"Let's Talk Prices," *Butane-Propane News,* May 1972.

anticipated although the policy had been under intensive review for months before its adoption.

6.6.2 Omissions in Public Policy

Neglect in recognizing the need to establish a new policy may be fully as harmful to the public as an error in an adopted policy. This point is also illustrated in Chap. 12, which explores the 2008–2009 recession.

The recession, claimed to be the worst since the Great Depression, undoubtedly had many causes. Among the most recognized of these causes was the widespread proliferation among the larger investment houses and banks of an exotic financial device called a CDO or "collateralized debt obligation." The CDO is a derivative backed by pools of risky subprime mortgages to create a "Toxic Asset." Financial houses and banks held billions of dollars of these overvalued bonds to create the credit crunch, which was at the heart of recession.

Many experienced people—heads of banks and financial institutions, economists, and investment advisors—knew of the spread of CDOs, yet none rang the alarm. No one called for an analysis: no one demanded a forecast of what the proliferation would lead to and how it would end.

6.7 Concluding Comments

Gene T. Kinney, editor of the *Oil & Gas Journal*, reports a forecast of 100 years ago which was cited by a speaker at the 1989 World Energy Conference.[21] "Future transport needs of the city of London were predicted accurately but were thought to be impossible to meet. The daily pollution from the horses would have reached 3 m deep." The flaw—underestimation of new technology. Kinney observes, "While inherently impossible to predict, surprises from science are still a certain part of the future. Only the degree of impact is in question."

London pollution aside, Chap. 12 emphasizes the disastrous consequences of errors or omissions in planning which have not been seriously challenged. The purpose of this emphasis has been to drive home one vital point: no long-range forecast can be taken as representing a fully accurate picture of the future, and the reliance to be placed upon it is in direct ratio to the depth of the critical examination to which it has been subjected. Having made this point, it is equally essential to point out that long-range forecasts can be accurate within the limits of the assumptions upon which they are based, and often are. They are an indispensable planning tool. It is because they are so important, and because we cannot do without them, that the writer has gone to such lengths to urge that the closest, the most critical, and, yes, even the most skeptical, scrutiny be given to any forecast which is intended to be

---

[21] "Review and Outlook," *The Wall Street Journal*, September 4, 1977; and "How Shale-Oil Fever Burned Colorado," *Business Week*, April 9, 1990.

the basis for either a company policy decision or, an even higher goal, to set the direction of regional or national policy.

6.7.1 Conflicting Forecasts

In the real world of the regulated public utility, regulation increasingly is looking foreword rather than back. This trend means that decisions based on the predicted future are having ever-greater consequences. The greater the consequence which may flow from the forecast, the more is the likelihood that there will be substantial differences in the forecasts made by regulators and the regulated, not to mention the prognostications advanced by other "interested parties." Most of these differences will reflect honest differences of opinion. A few, unfortunately, will arise because the forecast seeks to advance some policy goal, either pro or con– a sought for result, rather than a true vision of the future.

There is no simple magic formula which will lead to an accurate evaluation as to which of conflicting forecasts may be the most reliable, even assuming that no conscious policy bias has been introduced into any. Only guidelines for review may be suggested.

6.7.2 Guidelines

The first and broadest guideline has already been alluded to, namely, a review of the logic and workmanship of each forecast as a whole. While inferior preparation may not necessarily lead to an unreliable end result, the burden of proof rests more heavily upon the advocates of the poorly prepared forecast than upon the supporters of the competing forecast which shows superior preparation.

The second guideline is a side-by-side comparison of the input assumptions. Here the analysis becomes subjective. Two questions may be relevant: (1) Are the stated sets of assumptions complete? If not, assumptions as to which areas are missing? What were these missing assumptions, and were they simply not stated or were they overlooked or ignored? (2) Are the assumptions (stated or not) logical? Are there differences in the forecasts due to differences in the assumptions, and, if so, which assumptions seem most realistic?

The third guideline goes to the reasonableness of the end results. Earlier in this chapter we have mentioned some approaches for testing the validity of forecast conclusions. But perhaps the most important test of all is would the forecast, if accepted, lead to exaggerated inferences (huge construction programs or none at all; exclusive reliance on conservation as a total panacea for energy supply, or ignoring conservation possibilities)?

A final guideline is offered as much in a spirit of hope as of confidence. This is that the review be disassociated from preconceived end results and policy biases. Much may depend upon which alternative forecast is accepted. The consequences may be millions of dollars of increased or decreased revenues to the utility, and commensurate rate increases or decreases to the customer; allowing or prohibiting competition on the provision of service; encountering environmental risks or avoiding environmental issues; benefit to one class of customer or competitor to the disadvantage of another—the list is endless. The temptation is to support the forecast which best suits one's own position, but this is a deadly temptation unless the public interest is to be made subservient to ulterior motivations. What more can be said? So as one final guideline, we suggest that forecast analysis by all participants can and should be approached as an attempt to look foreword objectively. The analysis should not be approached as a means to skew the consequences toward a desired policy goal.

6.7.3 A Personal Note

The writer is aware that he may be considered to be incredibly naïve in suggesting that opposing parties may be persuaded to examine conflicting forecasts from the single lens of forecasting objectivity, divorced from policy bias. But the seemingly impossible may be possible. One early experience of the writer bolsters this view. One of his first major assignments on joining the staff of a federal power agency was to analyze that agency's power forecasts, which consistently were getting the agency into trouble with Congress. It was found that the agency actually produced three different demand forecasts. One forecast, always high, was prepared for "power resources" purposes, the objective being that power-generating capability would be high enough to meet all conceivable demands. Another forecast, always low, was used for finance and payout studies, and was conservative so that realized revenues from the indicated demands would be sufficiently low as not to be in danger of falling short of financial payout requirements. A third forecast, normally intermediate, governed the installation of new system transmission and substation facilities. The latter was oriented to providing delivery capacity, with normal allowance for reserve, as actually might be expected to be needed at delivery points throughout the system. Presented with three different forecasts offered simultaneously, Congress understandably was confused and irritated. The adopted solution was to substitute a single forecast which would be used for all purposes, and which could be presented as representing the agency's best vision of the future. Internally, the struggle was bitter. Dire results were foreseen by all concerned. "Our power resources will fall short," "our revenues will be overstated," etc. But with a single forecast Congress began to have confidence in the agency's predictions, a confidence entirely lacking earlier.

6.7.4 Alternative Forecasts

While the foregoing guidelines, and the writer's note, aim toward a single unified forecast which best approximates a realistic forward look, there may be circumstances under which a single forecast is neither possible nor desirable. Perhaps the best example is the case where basic governmental policy is at a cross roads, with entirely different impacts depending upon which path the government authority decides to follow. At the crossroads, the authority must ask: What will be the results if we follow path A? If we follow path B?

6.7.5 Resolving Forecasting Conflicts

Differences between forecasts will not be resolved by a miracle from on high. Experience suggests that the poorest method of resolution is the traditional formal adversary hearing. Minutia may cover hundreds of pages of transcript, obscuring the real questions—not clarifying them. The writer believes that the best approach may be the "workshop" used successfully for a variety of issues by the California PUC among others. In a workshop atmosphere, the concerned parties can meet with a degree of informality and a spirit of give and take. Even if a full resolution of all differences cannot be reached, the number of conflicting issues can be substantially lessened and the scope of the remaining issues narrowed. Thus, the final decision can be confined to substantative matters.

Nota bene: To the forecasters, Good Luck!

Chapter 7
The Public Policy/Social Engineering Approach to Pricing

Abstract The five preceding chapters are normative, addressing pricing in an orderly fashion. Chap. 7 departs from this course, covering a diverse array of subjects alike only in that they result from public policies or social engineering or both. Six different subjects are explored: California's lifeline/baseline rate, designed to provide cheaper energy for the minimum essential amount of energy used; price consciousness, with the public wanting detail about the functions financed by their energy payments; timed pricing, with prices varying with the time of use in accord with the changing costs of the service provider; the color GREEN, with pricing adjusted for conservation measures, on the one hand, and non-conventional methods of energy production, on the other hand; a venture by an important regulatory commission into marginal cost as a basis for regulation; and, finally, how wind power is accommodated by a large-integrated electric grid.

Chapter 7 explains a few of the notions of public-policy protagonists, and some of the visions of social engineers, which were originated since the later part of the past century to influence, and perhaps improve, the practices and institutions of our society. We do not judge any of these ideas. We merely report.

> Hamlet: "What piece of work is man!
> how noble in reason!
> how infinite in faculties!"
> *or*
> Puck: "Lord what fools these mortals be!"
> *Midsummer Night's Dream, 111.3.116*[1]
> We report. You decide. *{Fox News}*

7.1 California's Lifeline/Baseline Rate

The earliest venture into public policy described in this chapter regards a determination by the California legislature that each residential user of electricity and natural gas should receive a minimal supply of that energy at a discounted price, while

---

[1] Borrowed from John Conlisk, "Why Bounded Rationality?" *Journal of Economic Literature*, June, 1996.

paying a higher price for energy taken in excess of that minimum. The legislature coupled this policy with a conservation objective.

The philosophy reflected in this action had been vigorously debated both in New York and California in the early 1970s. It was rejected in New York but adopted in California.

7.1.1 The California Lifeline Philosophy

The lifeline program originated from the Miller-Warren Energy Lifeline Act of 1975. As described by the California Public Utilities Commission (CPUC), "the legislature sought to ensure that energy utilities would provide a basic necessary amount of gas and electricity to residential customers at a fair cost but one which would also encourage consumer conservation of scarce and expensive energy resources."[2]

The lifeline program was revised by the 1982 Baseline Act, which set the baseline rate at 15–25% less than the system average rate. This rule was later amended. The inverted rate relationship of the two prices, combining welfare and conservation objectives, results from the same legislative mandates.

The Miller-Warren Act required the CPUC to designate "a lifeline quantity of electricity which is necessary to supply the minimum energy needs of the average residential user for ... space and water heating, lighting, cooking and food refrigeration ... [taking into account] differentials in energy needs caused by geographic differences, by differences in severity of climate, and by season." Reflecting this mandate, current lifeline/baseline volumes vary with location (climate zone), season, and whether the customer has basic or all-electric service.

Miller-Warren was signed by the governor on September 20, 1975. The CPUC anticipated this legislative mandate by a week, in a decision for PG&E. Lifeline rates went into effect in California on January 1, 1976.

7.1.2 The Lifeline/Baseline Rate Schedule

Whatever its variations in detail may be, the fundamental characteristic of the lifeline/baseline rate design is that the customer will be charged a minimum-level price per kWh (the *tier-one price*) for an initial limited amount of consumption (the *baseline* or *tier-one allowance*), plus a substantially higher price per kWh (the *tier-two price*) for consumption in excess of the tier-one allowance. Thus, pricing involves two interrelated issues: the price itself and the volume of usage to which it will apply. The determination of each requires a sequence of procedural steps. For a

---

[2]California Public Utilities Commission, *PUC News*.

7.1 California's Lifeline/Baseline Rate

description of these steps, quotations are taken from a CPUC decision relating to Southern California Edison Company (SCE).[3]

The decision describes SCE's residential rates.

Approximately 86% of Edison's customers take service under Edison's domestic (residential) rate schedules. Domestic customers account for 30% of Edison's kWh sales and 38% of Edison's revenues.

Most of Edison's domestic customers take service on Schedule D [the lifeline/baseline rate], which provides for an inverted, two-tiered energy rate that does not vary by season or time of day. The two-tiered rate consists of a first-tier baseline rate, and a higher, nonbaseline second-tier rate.

7.1.2.1 Baseline Allowances

Baseline allowances are designed to provide residential customers with a minimum necessary quantity of electricity at the lower rate, taking into account differentials in energy use by climate zone and season. (PU Code Sec 739 (a).) Accordingly, baseline allowances vary between climatic zones, seasons, and customer type (basic or all-electric).

Per PU Code Sec 739(d) (1), the number of kWhs applicable at baseline rates is based on 50–60% of average residential consumption of electricity except that, for all-electric customers, the winter baseline allowance is based on 60–70% of average consumption. These percentage parameters are established based on average aggregate consumption, rather than simple average usage.

> ... simple average usage is not utilized since many customers do not have usage which exceed their baseline allocations and thus would result in less than the guideline kWh billed at baseline rates. Average aggregate consumption is the monthly kWh consumption of residential customers which occurs at or below a given number of kWh. This consumption is derived from a bill frequency distribution which shows the kWh usage block at which the percentage of aggregate consumption is equal to the baseline allowance percentage.

Edison's basic customers currently receive baseline allowances set at 55% of average use in both the summer and winter seasons. For all-electric customers, baseline allowances are currently determined at 70% of average use in the winter and 60% in the summer. [Zone 15 is an exception, due to extreme weather conditions.]

A 4-month summer and 8-month winter season were adopted for all zones.

Rate treatments for second homes and continuation of employee discounts also were considered.

---

[3] California Public Utilities Commission, Decision 96-04-050, "In the Matters of the Application of Southern California Edison Company, A. 93-12-025...and Order Instituting Investigation {SCE} I. 94-02-002," issued April 10, 1996...

7.1.3 Pricing Procedure

Next is the important issue of the prices to be attached to the volume allowances. The California legislature has followed an up-and-down-the-ladder approach. The decision first gives a brief legislature history, and then describes the procedure.

7.1.3.1 Tier Differentials

> ... the Legislature has spoken to the issue of the residential tier differential on several occasions. In particular, in 1988, the Senate passed Senate Bill (SB) 987 in response to high winter bill complaints. SB 987 mandated a reduction in nonbaseline residential rates and a narrowed tier differential. It removed a former requirement that baseline rates be established at 15% to 25% below the system average rate. It amended PU Code Sec. 739.7 by providing that we establish "an appropriate gradual differential" between the rates for the baseline and nonbaseline tiers. It also added Sec. 739.7, providing among other things that "the commission shall reduce high nonbaseline residential rates as rapidly as possible."

Since SB 987 was enacted in June 1988, residential tier ratios have been reduced considerably. PG&E's mid-1988 ratio of 1.74:1 for electric service has been reduced to 1.15:1. SDG&E's electric tier differential has been reduced from over 1.40:1 to 1.265:1. Edison's tier ratio has similarly been reduced to the current level of 1.15:1.

A second piece of legislation, AB 1432, became effective on January 1, 1993. AB 1432 modified Sec 739 and repealed and reenacted Sec 739.7. Where Sec 739.7 once required a rapid reduction in high nonbaseline rates, it now provides that the commission "shall retain an appropriate inverted rate structure." The legislature found and declared as follows:

> "(1) In response to high residential winter gas bills in southern California in the winter of 1987–1988, the Legislature by enactment of Senate Bill 987 of the 1987–1988 Regular Session (Chapter 212 of the Statues of 1988) directed the Public Utilities Commission to reduce high nonbaseline residential rates as rapidly as possible and granted the commission greater flexibility in establishing rates for baseline service in order to achieve that objective."
>
> "(2) It was never the intention of the Legislature that the commission eliminates inverted residential rates. Inverted residential rates provide conservation incentives for residential consumers and also provide reasonable rates for the domestic consumption of gas and electricity."
>
> "(3) It is therefore the intent of the Legislature in enacting this act to require the retention of an inverted rate structure for the residential use of gas and electricity, as specified."

In this SCE decision, the CPUC decided,

7.1 California's Lifeline/Baseline Rate

... we will adopt a 1.15:1 composite tier ratio for both summer and winter seasons at this time. The average nonbaseline energy rate for each season will need to be derived from an initial calculation of the average baseline rate. This can be done by (1) dividing the revenue requirement allocated to the season by the sum of baseline sales plus 1.15 to yield an average nonbaseline energy rate. The baseline revenue requirement is then calculated by subtracting nonbaseline energy revenues (using the energy rate derived above) and basic charge revenues from the total revenue requirement allocated to the season. Dividing the result by baseline sales yields the baseline energy rate.

Table 7.1 Simplified illustration of calculation of baseline and nonbaseline rates for season

---

Assumed simplified data

Baseline seasonal volumes	1,000 kWh
Nonbaseline seasonal volumes	1,000 kWh
Total seasonal volumes	2,000 kWh
Revenue requirement at 12.320 ¢/kWh (2,000 kWh × 12.320¢)	$246.40

Derivation of energy rates

Baseline rate

$$\frac{\text{Rev. req.}}{\text{Baseline vol.} + (1.15 \times \text{Nonebaseline vol.})} = \frac{\$246.40}{1000 + (1.15 \times 1000)\text{kWh}} = 11.46 \text{ ¢/kWh}$$

Nonbaseline rate

$$11.46 \text{ ¢/kWh} \times 1.15 = 13.18 \text{ ¢ kWh}$$

NOTE: The baseline and nonbaseline volumes assumed above bear a 50–50 relationship to each other.

The arithmetic of the foregoing procedure is simple. It is illustrated by Table 7.1. Volumes for baseline and excess usage are assumed to be the same. The revenue requirement per kWh is the average of the Tier 1 and 2 rates, calculated for the purpose of Table 7.1. As of a May 12, 2009 bill from Pacific Gas and Electric Company for service in Hollister, CA,[4] these rates were per kWh:

Tier 1, applicable to baseline usage	$0.11531
Tier 2, for usage above baseline	$0.13109

The average of these two rates is $0.12320, which is applied in Table 7.1.

The two natural gas rates differed by date, before and after May 1, 2009. They were, per term:

	Before May 1	After May 1
Tier 1, applicable to baseline Usage	$0.90567	$0.81736
Tier 2, above baseline	$1.15138	$1.06307

---

[4]Pacific Gas and Electric Company, Account 6359902078-9, statement dated 05/12/2009, rendered to John Wilton, Hollister, CA., for gas and electric service from 04/14/2009 to 05/11/2009.

7.2 Cost Components of Rates

The disarray in electric rates which accompanied the deregulation of electric generation from the previously totally regulated functions of the electric utility, aroused a great deal of interest in the cost to consumers of the new unregulated power. This in turn created an interest in the electric bill as a whole. The result is the current trend of the electric utilities toward showing the several cost components of their operations on their bills to customers. As an example, below is shown the bill given by Pacific Gas and Electric Company under "California's Lifeline/Baseline Rate."[5]

The bill is divided into two periods, 04/14/2009–04/30/2009, during which 216.14 kWh were taken, and 05/01/2009 to 05/11/2009, wherein the consumption was 139.86 kWh, for a total of 356 kWh. Component costs for these two periods as shown on the bill are itemized in Table 7.2:

Table 7.2 Example of lifeline/baseline rate

	4/14–30	5/01–11
Generation	$10.55	$6.87
Transmission	2.17	1.40
Distribution	7.56	4.93
Public-purpose programs (1)	1.27	0.82
Nuclear decommissioning	0.06	0.04
DWR bond charge (2)	1.06	0.68
Ongoing CTC (3)	1.80	1.17
Energy cost recovery (4)	0.49	0.33
Net charges	$24.96	$16.24
Energy commission tax	0.05	0.03
Total charges		$41.28

(1) For low-income customers and energy-efficiency programs
(2) For bonds financing historic cost of power purchased by DWR
(3) For early purchased power agreements and restructuring implementation
(4) For energy recovery bonds

Only data shown in the bill are listed above. Not shown is the average bill per kWh, 11.6 cents. Also, not shown is the total amount retained by PG&E for its current transmission and distribution operations, $16.06, as compared to $17.42 for generation and $7.80 for non-utility costs.

Since the bill covers gas as well as electric service, it also includes data on its cost of purchased natural gas, $0.49616 per therm in the first period and $0.40785 per therm in the second period.

---

[5] Ibid.,

7.3 Timed Pricing

Timed Pricing (i.e., pricing which varies with the time of the day, the day of the week, or the season of the year) is not new. It dates from the earliest years of the electric industry, as soon as it was recognized that there was cost-saving benefit in encouraging customers to minimize their electric use during peak-load periods. What is new is a greatly increased emphasis on "Demand Management," encouraging an ever widening use of pricing techniques to control peak consumption, while at the same time utilizing the most economical type of generation capacity.

Demand management is not simple to accomplish. Customers vary widely in their habits, their size, and their needs. One residential customer may be a large young family, another an older husband and wife living alone; one retail store may be open for business from 8 am to 5 pm on weekdays only, another continuously, 24 h per day, 7 days per week; one factory may operate on a single shift, another two shifts, another three; one may be a larger user of electric energy, another needing energy only for lighting and small motors; one may have a huge, but short-lived burst of demand for start up, say—but modest usage otherwise, while next door electricity is used quite evenly over the operational period. Agricultural usage varies just as much from farm to farm and between the types of crops under cultivation. This wide diversity in customer usage is a valuable asset in that it reduces the magnitude of the demands for capacity which occur at the same time, but it creates a difficult problem in controlling differences in customer habits.

7.3.1 Prior to 2000

Before the California energy crisis, demand management in that state had made significant progress. In place were seasonal summer and winter price differentials, refined by *daily* time-of-use differentials between weekdays (except holidays) and weekends (plus holidays), and by *hourly* differentials where specified hours were classified as being peak, partial-peak, or off-peak. The pricing of most schedules was set to provide a strong incentive for peak shaving. Different combinations of demand and energy charges were being tried.

There were several patterns of summer (peak period) time-of-use differentials. The *base* pattern of one company divided the day into three periods, a peak, a partial-peak, and an off-peak period. Weekdays were treated differently than weekends and holidays. On weekdays, a 6 hour peak period extended from noon to 6 pm. On either side of the peak period were 3 hour spans, from 8:30 am to noon before the peak, and from 6 pm to 9:30 pm after the peak, which were partial-peak periods. Such periods often were considered to be the "shoulder" hours, leading up to and tapering down from the peak. All other weekday hours, i.e., from 9:30 pm to 8:30 am, were classified as off-peak. All weekend hours, plus weekday holiday hours, were off-peak.

The summer-base pattern, therefore, placed on the peak, 30 hours of the 168 hours of the week (6 hours per day for 5 week days); on partial-peak, 35 hours

(7 hours per day for 5 week days); and on off-peak, 103 hours (11 hours per day for 5 week days, plus 24 hours per day for 2 weekend days).

In winter-base patterns, no peak period was specified. A partial-peak period extended from 8:30 am to 9:30 pm of weekdays (the same hours as covered by the combined peak and partial-peak periods in summer). Other weekday hours, and all weekend and holiday hours, were off-peak. In winter, 65 hour of the week were partial-peak, the remaining 103 hour off-peak.

There were variations from the base patterns: the split week, substituting a 3-day peak period for a 5-day period, and dividing the customers into two groups for the shorter period, and the short peak, shortening the peak from 6 hour per weekday to 4 hour, as well as other alternatives.

7.3.2 Real-Time Pricing (RTP)

The concept is that the customer can take advantage of lower-cost generated power. The customer is informed, usually a day in advance, of what the energy prices will be on the following day, hour by hour, and can then shape his load to take advantage of lower cost periods if desired. Customers with the ability to shift load are most interested. Some favor this rate form over standard curtailable/interruptible rates because the customer retains control. With this rate, the customer can continue operations during high-peak periods if he decides to do so.

The history of timed pricing as of 1996 has been summarized as follows[6]:

> Time of use (TOU) rates have been mandatory for roughly 15 years for essentially all customers with demands exceeding 500 kW, optional TOU rates have existed for most customers for a number of years, and in some cases a number of customers are served on optional TOU rates
>
> (For example over 100,000 PG&E residential customers are served on TOU rates) Real Time Pricing (Rl P) rates have also existed for several years, with dozens of large customers being served on them, and encouragement for developing RTP rates for additional customer classes being stated in Commission decisions ...

7.3.3 Now

The years since 2000 have seen the spread of timed rates to the residential class. An example is the time-of-use rate of Portland General Electric Company.[7] The rate is divided into two seasons, the summer months beginning May 1 of each year, and the winter months beginning November 1 of each year. Each season is further divided into three daily periods, on-peak, mid-peak, and off-peak. The on-peak period extends from 3:00 pm to 8:00 pm Monday through Friday in the summer, and from 6:00 am to 10:00 am and from 5 pm to 8:00 pm Monday through Friday in the winter. Other hours apply to the other periods.

---

[6]California Public Utilities Commission, "Comments of the Division of Ratepayer Advocates on Draft Implementation Roadmap Decision," R.94-04-031 and. 94-04-032, dated February 20, 1996.
[7]Portland General Electric, "Your Guide to Time of Use" and "Time of Use Puts you in control."

PG&E's pamphlet specifies prices for the three periods as follows:

On-peak	7.751 cents per kWh
Mid-peak	4.641 cents per kWh
Off-peak	2.843 cents per kWh

(Prices quoted above are only to show relationships between the periods.) The pamphlet says, "The time-of-use option could result in a lower electricity bill, but only if you are able to significantly shift the number of kilowatt hours you use during on-peak time periods to mid- or off-peak periods. Otherwise, you could end up paying more. Time-of-use pricing will work best for customers who use electricity late at night or on the weekends."

A special meter is needed to participate in the program. $2.00 per month is added to the customer's monthly bill for a single-phase meter.

If the customer's energy charge billings under time-of-use exceed the basic service energy charge by more than 10%, the excess over 10% will be refunded.

PG&E's basic service rate[8] consists of a basic charge ($10.00), an energy use charge (with inverted two-step pricing), a transmission charge, and a distribution charge, each on a per-kWh basis, plus the usual miscellaneous charges, taxes, and fees. The inverted-energy use charges are 5.124 cents per kWh, and 6.699 cents per kWh. The total bill for 500 kWh averaged 11.12 cents per kWh.

A bill of the same vintage for natural gas[9] states only a monthly service charge ($6.00) and a gas usage charge per therm ($1.39384), plus the usual small adjustment charges.

7.4 The Color GREEN

At the turn of the century, the color GREEN swept the country, ranging from organic foods to hybrid automobiles. For the electric industry, the trend centered about encouraging the development and use of what were loosely termed "renewable resources" in the generation of power. Renewables include wind, biomass, solar, geothermal, and other energy sources. These renewables would replace oil and natural gas as fuels for electric power production. However, by-and-large they are considerably more expensive to use than conventional oil and gas, and less reliable.

The green umbrella covers many diversified groups and causes. Environmentalists, conservationists, global-warming evangelists, clean-energy converts, renewable-energy advocates, eco-friends – the list goes on and on. Each claims some part of the color green. Clearly, a movement so diversified and broad cannot be explained in a sub-chapter. So this discussion is confined to a few highlights.

---

[8] Portland General Electric, bill for service from 05/05/09 to 06/05/09, Schedule 07, rendered to Roger L. Conkling, Portland, Oregon.

[9] NW Natural, bill for service from 05/05/09 to 06/05/09, Schedule 02R, rendered to Roger L. Conkling, Portland, Oregon.

7.4.1 Comparisons

Some statistics as published in *The Wall Street Journal* of February 2, 2009, provide background. Total per-capita energy consumption in the United States in 2005 (the latest year available) was 7,886 in kilograms of oil equivalent per person, as compared to Canada's of 8.473. Total energy consumption, in thousand tons of oil equivalent, in that same year, was 2,341.883; the next highest was China, with 1,717,153.

The United States had the most nuclear power generation in 2007, with 807 billion kilowatt-hours. France was second, with 420 billion.

In 2008, Germany had the most solar power capacity installed, with 5,781 MW. The United States was fourth, with 1,407 MW.

Installed wind capacity varied by state, in megawatts: Texas, 4,446; California, 2,439; Minnesota, 1,299; Iowa, 1,271; Washington, 1.163; Colorado, 1,067; Oregon, 885; Illinois, 699; Oklahoma, 689; and New Mexico, 496.

Portland General Electric

PGE customers can choose from two different renewable options – each is 100% renewable energy generated from sources in the Northwest.[1] Plus, they all provide an easy way to support wind farms in the Northwest while encouraging the development of new renewable sources of energy.

Green Source℠ is based on matching 100% of your actual energy use with renewable power, and with Clean Wind℠, you purchase small units of renewable energy at a fixed price. With both of these options, your energy usage is billed at your Basic Service or Time of Use rate and you pay an additional charge for the renewable option you choose.

A new feature of PGE's renewable program allows you to supplement any renewable plan with Habitat Support, which goes directly to the Nature Conservancy for salmon habitat restoration projects in Oregon.

No matter which option is selected, you will continue to receive the same reliable PGE electricity service. The table below explains the features and benefits of each option.

Renewable Option	Renewable Power Sources Used	How This Option Works	Renewable Costs
Green Source℠	100% renewable energy from new wind and new biomass sources	100% of your monthly usage is offset with renewable resources	Your regular PGE energy rate plus an additional $0.008 per kWh About $7 more per month[2]
Clean Wind℠	100% renewable power from new wind	Available in 200 kWh units (each represents about 20% of your monthly usage)	An additional $3.50 per 200 kWh unit – You can purchase as many units as you wish.
Habitat Support Supplement to one of the options above	(not applicable)	A monthly fee goes directly to the Nature Conservancy to support stream habitat for salmon and other fish	$2.50 per month (added to one of the plans you select)

[1] You will not have electricity from a specific generation facility delivered directly to your home. Your purchase of a renewable power option ensures that the amount of energy purchased by you is generated from the renewable sources indicated for the option you select. To verify this renewable energy generation, we retire renewable energy certificates on your behalf.
[2] Additional amount based on PGE's Basic Service rate as of January 1, 2008 for a typical PGE customer using 910 kWh per month. Your actual cost will vary based on your actual usage.

Fig. 7.1 "Make the choice for renewable power today"

7.4.2 Electric Utilities: Clean-Energy Programs

Electric utilities have had to struggle to participate in the green movement, largely because electricity at its point of use is non-identifiable as to its source and no utility can rely upon renewables for its total supply. Therefore, all any utility can do is to claim that renewables are a new part of its energy mix, and provide some means for its customers to participate in its increased costs.

An effective means of doing both at the same time is to offer customers an option to pay an additional amount on their bill to finance the costs of greener power sources.

Electricity is supplied in Portland, Oregon by two companies, Pacific Power and Portland General Electric. Each offers a slightly different clean-energy plan. Pacific Power offers three options in addition to its basic service, which applies if the customer does not elect one of the options. The first of the options is called fixed renewable, and allows the customer to upgrade to wind power in 100 kWh increments, at an added cost of $2.95 per increment. The second, renewable usage, provides for 100% renewable energy at a price $0.0078 per kWh higher than basic service. This gives support for clean energy which varies with usage rather than the fixed monthly amount of the fixed option. The third option, habitat, is the same as renewable usage, but adds an additional $2.50 monthly which is donated to the Pacific Salmon Watershed Fund. Portland General Electric's plan differs only in a few details. Its plan, as circulated to its customers, is reproduced on an earlier page.

7.4.3 From the Printed Media

The meager measures taken by the utilities fail to do justice to the public's deep interest in Green activities. To better reflect this interest, bits and pieces from published articles, mostly from *The Wall Street Journal* (WSJ), are extracted below. These excerpts cover the 2-year interval ending in mid-2009, and are intended to be illustrative of news content, only a sampling, not complete. They merely show how major media have responded to a national trend.

First are items covering renewable energy in general and then alternative energy sources: wind, solar, biofuels, tidal and wave, each of which is renewable and aptly classified as "clean" energy. Following are landfills (methane), oil sands, and LNG, which border on present sources. Next are conventional coal and nuclear, representing more extensive use of currently used fuels, with excerpts relating Green influences on broader subjects, transmission (the grid), meters, light bulbs, vehicles, and buildings and homes. Finally, are interrelated topics, the environment, conservation, clean energy, and politics and regulation.

7.4.3.1 Renewable Energy – Clean Energy

Although wind and solar are cheaper now than in earlier years, subsidies are needed for them to be competitive with conventional energy sources.

Wind and solar need backup from conventional sources.

Small combustible pellets from fast growing trees are being sold for electric generation.

Attempts by California utilities to match the state's requirement to generate 33% of their power from alternative sources by 2020 could result in power shortages.

Low natural gas prices diminish the appeal of alternative energy sources.

Colorado governor says state's future depends upon renewable energy.

A series of state laws passed recently require utilities to generate specified portions of their power from renewable resources. Standards vary.

7.4.3.2 Wind

A project fifteen miles off the Scottish Coast tests the first offshore deep water wind farm. The project has 200 turbines and can produce enough power for a million people, but is very expensive. Also, some commercial fisheries are planning for a wind farm off the New Jersey coast.

Many of the solar and wind power sources are located far from consumer centers.

Experts estimate wind power prices to be $70–$90 per MWh.

PG&E has bought wind and geothermal energy from Oregon.

BPA has more than 2,000 MW of wind power connected to its grid (see Item 7.6 below).

7.4.3.3 Solar

The world's largest solar plan, in the Central Valley of California, consists of rows of mirrors that follow the sun, arranged in a one-square mile grid. The mirrors capture the sun's heat and transfer it into water-filled pipes, creating steam that turns a turbine in a nearby generating plant. No greenhouse gas is produced.

Another type of solar power uses mirrors to heat salt to more than 1050F. This is pumped by heat-resistant pumps to turbines that can generate 500 MW of peak power to run continuously at 50 MW.

A rooftop solar system (a photovoltaic or PV system) costs about $8.25 per W installed, or $8,250 for a 1 kW system to more than $40,000 for a 5 kW system. These costs are expected to decline.

A solar land rush is underway in the desert southwest, from California through Arizona, Nevada and New Mexico.

"Concentrated photovoltaics" technology was the basis for a $103 million 10 MW generating plant in southern Spain. The process uses smaller solar panels made from low-cost glass and aluminum rather than more expensive silicon.

Arizona requires 4.5% of its electricity to come from solar by 2025, and New Mexico requires 4% by 2020. There are currently 500 MW of solar generating capacity in the United States, which is expected to have 900 MW by 2014.

Oregon State University is developing new technologies to make hydrogen fuel from the sun.

7.4 The Color GREEN

7.4.3.4 Biofuels

Biofuels are used to power vehicles. Vehicles may use ethanol or biodiesel mixed with petroleum-based fuels, or with corn and vegetable oil as feedstock. New processes are testing variants of plant feed stocks—switch grass, miscanthus, wood from poplar and willow trees—to produce fuel from cellulose and lower costs. Carbon-neutral fuel is also important to utilities because it removes the threat of a tax on greenhouse emissions.

Ethanol refined from corn is dominant, but biodiesel may also be refined from leftover cooking grease, agricultural waste, or garbage. About 9 billion gallons of biofuels were produced in a recent year, but the recession and environmental concerns have raised questions about the wisdom of their use. Some recently constructed plants have gone bankrupt. Two-thirds of US biodiesel production capacity is now unused.

7.4.3.5 Tidal and Wave Power

There are several types of power production which can be developed from the ocean. These are: tidal stream, the deployment of underwater turbines in the sea; tidal barrage, the installation of turbines across a river or estuary to function like a hydro-electric dam; and wave power, the conversion of the ocean's up-and-down movement. Up to three million tons of water per second flow through Pentland Firth twice a day at speeds up to 12 knots.

Tidal power costs about 10–22 cents per kWh, wave power, even more.

7.4.3.6 Landfills (Methane)

Methane is a greenhouse gas. About 50% of the gas emitted from landfills is methane. Most incinerators feed garbage into a chamber where it is set on fire by the methane. The heat creates steam which turns a turbine to produce electricity. The burned trash shrinks in volume to a tenth of its original size, leaving only ash.

7.4.3.7 Oil Sands

Canada has oil sands in a forest area larger than Florida. These sands contain bitumen, which can be converted to synthetic oil, but are very expensive to convert. High-pressure steam must be injected to separate the bitumen from the sand and clay surrounding it, and natural gas must be burned to produce the steam, Canada has 174 billion barrels of recoverable bitumen. Only Saudi Arabia has more.

7.4.3.8 LNG

LNG, or liquefied natural gas, is gas cooled from a gaseous to a liquid form, shipped as a liquid in specially designed tankers to ports of entry into the United States, where it is heated to return to a gas to be transported to consumers by pipeline.

Sempra Energy is constructing a $2 billion LNG terminal on the West Coast, and a second in Louisiana.

7.4.3.9 Coal

Although half of the electricity in the United States is generated from coal, the government frowns upon further coal plants. It encourages the development of "clean" coal, which refers to safely disposing of the CO_2 produced by its burning either by pumping the CO_2 underground for permanent storage or by scrubbing the CO_2 as it is released. But clean coal will not be cheap.

Also, new coal-fired generating plants require large amounts of water, while solar and wind require none.

Although there is more than ample coal in the ground in the United States, relatively little of it can be extracted profitably and recent findings of new natural gas supplies have diminished its prospects.

7.4.3.10 Nuclear

Nuclear power has reappeared on the US energy horizon as the nation seeks new environmentally acceptable energy sources. A main reason is that nukes emit no carbon dioxide. However, they may be expensive, they are susceptible to a terrorist attack, and they present the challenge of disposing of the nuclear waste which they leave after use.

A storage site for nuclear waste is 10 years overdue in the opinion of some experts.

Rising concerns about global warming have set the stage for a comeback of nuclear energy.

Many utilities, including Duke, are considering new nuclear generating plants.

7.4.3.11 Transmission/The Grind

Utilities are building, or planning, new transmission lines to improve interconnections between regions which will boost the amount of renewable power available across the country, as needed to transport renewable wind power from producing to consuming states and to handle fluctuations in its availability. New transmission would cost about $100 billion, and wind turbines about $720 billion.

7.4.3.12 Meters

Present conventional utility energy meters record only the total amount of energy used over a billing period. The three big utilities of California plan to replace these present meters with new high-tech "time of use" meters which will give up-to-the-minute data about how and when homes and small businesses use energy during the billing period, thus providing information which enables consumers to shift their use from expensive to cheaper hours if they wish. The utility benefits in controlling outages and from the ability to terminate or restore service remotely. About 15 million conventional meters will be replaced in California with a cost of approximately $3.6 billion.

Meters are expensive, ranging in cost from $250–$500 each installed. But benefits to customers are hard to sell. "You don't need a meter to tell you how to save energy. Just turn off the lights." By the first quarter of 2009, PG&E had installed

7.4 The Color GREEN

557,000 meters, but only 12,000 customers had taken advantage of their new ability to obtain cheaper rates.

7.4.3.13 Light Bulbs

The incandescent light bulb is highly inefficient, generating 90% heat and 10% light. A 25 watt compact fluorescent bulb produces as much light as a 100 watt conventional bulb but uses only one-quarter as much electricity. But Americans have been so unwilling to buy the new bulbs that the federal government has been threatening to ban incandescent bulbs by 2014.

To slash energy use, PG&E and other California utilities have spent millions of dollars subsidizing CFL bulbs, with the result that bulbs which cost $5–$10 in 1999 can now be bought for 25–50 cents in California. PG&E subsidized the sale of 7.6 million compact florescent bulbs in 2007, and expected to raise that number to 29 million. When questioned about the emphasis that the company placed on light bulbs—in contrast to increasing the energy-efficiency of equipment in industrial plants and commercial buildings, and selling more air-conditioning—PG&E stated that they did not know of any other single measure that provided a faster and cheaper result. Retail chains have adopted selling CFLs to cement their own green credentials.

7.4.3.14 Vehicles

Hybrid and battery-powered vehicles themselves generate low or no emissions, but they need electricity generated by power plans which typically do.

AT&T is spending up to $565 million over 10 years in alternative-fuel vehicles.

The federal government sets a standard of 25 mpg for new vehicles to apply in 2016.

There are two types of hybrids (full and mild) and two types of power train configurations (series and parallel).

> Full hybrid: can go short distances on electric motor; after the charge is used or the vehicle reaches a certain speed, gas engine turns on, driving wheels and recharging.
> Mild hybrid: electric motor supplements gas engine, acting as a stop–start system.
> Series hybrid: propulsion entirely from electric motor; outboard gas engine generates electricity directly for motor and batteries.
> Parallel hybrid: uses both gas and electricity for propulsion.

White House established grants of $2.4 billion to jump-start the auto industry.

7.4.3.15 Buildings and Homes

"The Green House of the Future" will have the following:

> Integrated solar tiles to produce electricity and heat water
> Ground source heat pumps to heat, cool and provide hot water

Photovoltaic awning
Wind turbines
Rooftop evaporative reservoir
Hydroponic panel storage

Germany's parliament building is set up to run solely on green energy.

7.4.3.16 Clean Energy

Clean energy projects are being cancelled or delayed because financing of new power plants appears risky, whether they be nuclear, wind, or solar. This is a change in attitude, brought on by the financial crisis of the recession.

7.4.3.17 Green Power Purchase Plans

More than 750 utilities offer customers the opportunity to pay an extra amount on their electric bills to pay higher costs of green power. However, it seems that little of these extra payments go for additional renewable energy. (See also Section 7.4.2 above.)

7.4.3.18 Politics and Regulation

Twenty-two states have widely different requirements for utilities to use "cleaner" resources in the production of their power. California requires that 20% of utility power be from renewable sources by 2010; 27% by 2015; and 33% by 2020. Under its plan, utilities are awarded 12% of the costs they avoid if they meet their targets. In essence, regulators give utilities a chance to earn as much profit by reducing sales as by increasing them.

Whether green policies create jobs is debatable, since energy from alternative sources displaces equal amounts from conventional sources, with no necessary change in the long-term employment rate. The conversion to corn-based ethanol may be an exception depending upon the nature of the conventional source.

7.5 Venture into Marginal Cost Regulation[10]

This survey explores the erratic first steps taken by the California Public Utilities Commission (CPUC) in its venture of introducing marginal costs into its regulation of utility prices. It covers the initial several moves of the Commission, revealing the

---

[10]Roger L. Conkling "Marginal Cost Pricing for Utilities: A Digest of the California Experience," *Contemporary Economic Policy*, January, 1999. Also, unpublished manuscripts: "Marginal Cost Utility Pricing vs. Microeconomic Theory-the California Experience," and "History of Marginal Cost Pricing in California."

uncertainty which seemed to characterize its efforts to translate electric operations into marginal cost terms.

7.5.1 Marginal Cost Defined

In accordance with neoclassical micro-economic price theory which it had adopted, the California Commission defines marginal cost as "the cost to society of producing the *last unit* of a good or service." Restating this definition in industrial terms, marginal cost is the cost to produce one additional unit of a commodity or the savings from producing one unit less. Theory contends, "economic efficiency requires that the price for each good or service be set at that cost. When this occurs, consumers face prices that reflect the cost of their choosing to buy that additional unit. In theory, consumers will then allocate their spending among goods and services until the 'value' they receive from the last unit purchased, as reflected in the price they pay for it, equals the cost of producing it. When this happens, across all sectors of the economy, the economy is operating as efficiently as possible." The commission explains, "When prices do not reflect the marginal cost to society of producing a good or service, then consumers allocate their spending based upon incorrect price signals ... Society is allocating its resources inefficiently." Consumers are either buying "too little" of a product because the price they are paying is higher than its marginal cost, or they are buying "too much" of it because the price is lower than its marginal cost.

7.5.2 The Steppingstone

The seeds for the CPUC's venture into marginal cost pricing were planted by a 1974 directive of the California Assembly ordering the CPUC to investigate marginal costs as one of six alternatives to existing rate structures. The Commission's response came some 18 months later in its Decision No. 85559 of March 16, 1976. The decision concluded, "efficient resource allocation requires that all prices be set equal to their 'incremental' costs" (using "incremental" as being synonymous with "marginal."), and adopted a policy "to make conservation in the sense of efficient allocation of electricity the keystone of the rate structure." That was where the matter stood until December 19, 1979, when the Commission issued its Decision No. 91107, which stated the types of marginal costs associated with electric utility operations: capacity costs (unit: $ per kW), energy costs (unit: cents per kilowatt-hour), and customer costs (unit: dollars per customer). Capacity costs were to be segregated by function into generation, transmission, or distribution functions. In the following pages we trace the cost which proved to be the most troublesome—the capacity cost of generation. Unable to define the dimensions of the last unit of generating capacity in terms of generators actually producing electricity, the Commission substituted an elusive proxy with ever-changing modifications. The Commission struggled with these over the entire term of this survey.

7.5.3 The Proxy, a Combustion Turbine

Decision 93887 of December 30, 1981, adopted a combustion turbine as a proxy for generation costs. A turbine was selected because it has low-capital costs, but high-energy costs, and therefore is considered to be well-suited to provide peaking capacity which would be operated only during short-duration peak-load periods. The turbine costs are equated to "shortage costs," which were defined as "what a customer would have to pay to avoid a shortage," the least cost being that of the least capital-intensive addition to capacity. Stated in another way, the shortage cost is the value of additional capacity, or conversely demand reduction, to the utility system.

The Commission adopted a 24-year useful life for the turbine, with a 9.1‰ carrying cost, totaling $76.56 per kW per year at transmission voltage in 1982 dollars, comprising a "levelization factor."

For the test year, the approved revenue requirement totaled $2.0 billion. Short-run marginal costs were $3.7 billion, $1.7 billion higher than the allowed revenue, requiring a massive scaling down. This scaling down was done pursuant to the "equal percentage of the difference" (EPD) method.

7.5.4 Levelization Out, RECC In

A year later, December 13, 1982, in Decision 82-12-055, the Commission retained the combustion turbine as a proxy, but substituted a "real economic carrying charge" (RECC) for the previously used "levelization factor." The factor would have resulted in a turbine cost of $128 per kW per year. The adopted RECC was $58 per kW per year. The reduction in cost was explained by the circumstance that the actual reserve margin was higher than target levels.

Although the choice between short-run and long-run marginal cost was debated, the Commission affirmed its prior position in favor of the short-run for setting retail rates, as relying "more on the value of customer responsiveness to current conditions."

The Commission opted to stay with the equal percentage of the difference (EPD) method for balancing the revenue requirement and marginal costs.

7.5.5 EPMC Adopted, EDP Dropped

In the ensuing year, as reflected in its Decision 83-12-065 of December 20, 1983, the Commission dropped the EPD method for the allocation of revenues authorized to be collected from the several customer classes because it "does not move toward marginal cost-based allocations {of the revenue requirement} when total system marginal cost revenue is less than total system present revenue." In substitution the

7.5 Venture into Marginal Cost Regulation

Commission adopted the "Equal Percentage of Marginal Cost" (EPMC) method for this revenue allocation. EPMC distributes the burden of each customer class to contribute revenues in proportion to the ratio of total marginal costs to the total revenue requirement. This ration, the fraction, *total allowed revenue/total marginal costs* is a multiplier applied to the actual class revenue to set the allowed revenue for the class. If the multiplier is more than one that means that marginal costs are deficient and that the test year class revenues must be increased; if the multiplier is less than one, marginal costs are excessive and must be reduced. In the case before the Commission in Decision No. 83-12-065, the calculation was

$$\frac{\text{Total allowed revenue}}{\text{Total marginal costs}} = \frac{\$1,200,668,000}{\$972,085,000} = 1.235147.$$

Test year customer class revenues were multiplied by 1.235147 to arrive at the allowed revenues for the class.

The EPMC methodology remained unchanged over the period of this survey.

7.5.6 Energy Reliability Index (ERI) Established

In its earlier Decision 93887 of December 30, 1981, the Commission had adopted the annual cost of a combustion turbine as representing a *shortage cost* (the value of additional capacity to the utility system). In Decision 83-12-068, enacted 2 years later on December 22, 1983, the Commission decided to adjust this cost, either up or down, by a multiplier called the energy reliability index, the ERI.

The ERI represents the amount of the kilowatt-hour energy requirement that could remain unserved with the system operating at design reliability. With surplus capacity, there would be only a remote probability of unserved energy, so the ERI would be less than one. When capacity is short, it should be adjusted upward. The Commission decided on an ERI limit of two (i.e., a multiplier of two) which should apply for the first 5 years, with a limit of one after that.

For revenue allocation purposes, the Commission chose an ERI of 1.335.

Interestingly, the Commission did not adopt, except in part, the EPMC method it had endorsed only 2 days earlier. It selected a 95% SAPC—5% EPMC combination, to avoid a disproportionate increase in residential class rates. SAPC, system average percentage change, moves the revenue for a given class by the percent change in total system revenues.

7.5.7 Excess Generating Capacity and the ERI

Although the ERI had been adopted in earlier cases, whether it should be applied when there was excess generating capacity remained an open question. In Decision 89-12-057 of December 20, 1989, the Commission decided that it was appropriate to apply an ERI adjustment to dampen the effect of utilizing the full-annualized cost of a combustion turbine for revenue allocation and rate design under the current situation of excess generating capacity. It chose a 6-year average ERI of 0.418, which, when applied to the generation capacity cost of $56.17 per kW per year, reduced the cost to $23.48 per kW per year.

7.5.8 The Resource Plan and the ERI

In Decision 91-12-076 of December 20, 1991, the Commission reviewed resource plans under study in a general rate case, to decide whether they should be "bare-bones" or "fully built." It decided on a "fully built" plan for the case under consideration, while reserving judgment on its propriety, and adopted a 6-year average ERI of 0.63.

7.5.9 Long-Run vs. Short-Run and the ERI

Resolving a dispute over whether the ERI should give weight to the long- or short-run, in Decision 92-06-020 of June 3, 1992, the Commission determined that a 6-year average ERI calculation results in a reasonable balance of long- and short-term marginal cost measurements. An ERI of 0.78 was adopted.

7.5.10 The Capacity Response Ratio (CRR)

Also, in Decision 92-06-020, the Commission reaffirmed its CRR of 1.12, which provides a reserve margin of 15%.

7.5.11 VOS In, ERI Out

With the goal of improving its methodology, the Commission in its Decision 92-12-057 of December 16, 1992, substituted a value of service (VOS) approach for the ERI-adjusted combustion turbine proxy it had used previously in determining marginal generation capacity costs. Costs of $5.24 per kW per year for the year 1993 and $8.81 per kW per year as a 6-year average were adopted.

7.5.12 The Abrupt Halt

On September 23, 1996, the California Legislature's Assembly Bill No. 1890, restructuring the state's elective industry, was signed into law. A key provision of this new law mandated that electric rates for all customers of regulated electric utilities be *frozen* at their June 10, 1996 levels, except for a rate reduction of no less than 20% for residential and small commercial customers. This put a temporary end to rate reviews, including those enumerated above.

7.6 Wind Rates on an Integrated Electric System[11]

The Bonneville Power Administration (BPA), whose current wind rate is discussed here, is the Federal agency which markets the power produced from Federal dams in the northwest and constructs, maintains, and operates the Federal high voltage electric transmission system in the region. Collectively, these dams are part of the hydro-electric projects on the Columbia River and its tributaries which are referred to as the Federal Columbia River Power System (FCRPS).

BPA reports that it has the highest concentration of wind power on its system of any US balancing authority, now approximately 20%, and expects this to double to 40% over the next 2 years. Figure 7.2 shows the expansion of BPA's wind-generation capacity from 1998 to the present. However, nearly 80% of the wind on the BPA system is exported to other balancing authority areas.

7.6.1 A Primer on Wind and the Electric Grid

An electric grid, such as BPA's, takes power generated at a central station and delivers the same amount of power, less losses in transmission and distribution, to load centers. A load center is usually a substation to which power is delivered at a higher voltage and transformed to a lower voltage for distribution to customers.

A central requirement of a functioning grid is that generation and load be in balance, i.e., that they be equal. If at any time, load is greater than generation, or generation is greater than load, the reliability of the grid is compromised and reliable service is threatened. The frequency will no longer be stable. This can damage electronic equipment, cause generators to trip offline, necessitate suspension of some loads, or lead to cascading blackouts.

Loads rise and fall as customer demands fluctuate, and the generation on line must rise and fall to match the changing loads. To maintain balance between the two, the grid must have reserve generating capability, i.e., generators that are standing by ready to increase or decrease their output when called on. This is generally

---

[11] The writer is grateful to Daniel Fisher and Gerard Bolden of BPA's Rate Staff for their guidance, and for the following documents:
2010 Wholesale Power and Transmission Rate Adjustment Proceeding (BPA-10) "Administrator's Final Record of Decision," July 2009
2010 BPA Rate Case, Wholesale Power Rate Final Proposal, "Generation Inputs Study," July 2009
2010 BPA Rate Case, Wholesale Transmission Rate Final Proposal, "2010 Ancillary Service and Control Area Services Study and Study Documentation," July 2009
2010 Wholesale Power and Transmission Rate Adjustment Proceeding (BPA-10), "Administrator's Final Record of Decision, Appendix C, 2010 Transmission, Ancillary Service and Control Area Service Rate Schedules (FY2010-2011)" July 2009
2010 BPA Rate Case, Wholesale Power Rate Initial Proposal, "Direct Testimony" February 2009
2010 BPA Rate Case, Wholesale Power Rate Initial Proposal, "Direct and Rebuttal Testimony and Statements of Witness Qualifications" April 2009
Quotations from the documents may not be enclosed in quotation marks.

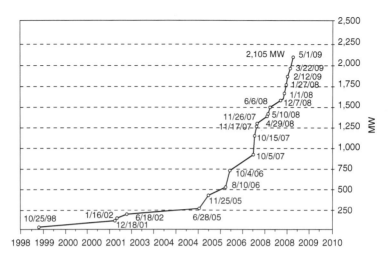

Fig. 7.2 BPA's Wind Generation Capacity

not difficult for an extensive hydro-system such as BPA's, for water flows to the generators are easily changed, and it is also relatively easy for a thermal system where online generators have been designed for flexibility. However, wind generation is unique. Output fluctuates as the wind blows, without consistency or outside direction. Reserve generating capability must match these fluctuations. To accomplish this match, generating capacity is set aside, or reserved, so that it will be available when needed.

To plan for the varying needs of customers, grid operators require major users to submit on a day-ahead basis hourly schedules of their planned use of the system. This is referred to as a pre-arranged schedule. It is updated shortly before the start of each hour. At this time the schedules must be balanced, i.e., the power put on the system must equal the power taken off.

Time-windows for this balance range from seconds up to 10 min. The generating reserves required are classified as "within-hour balancing reserves." These may be either incremental *(inc)* or decremental *(dec)*. *Inc* reserves are provided from generators that can increase generation when loads increase or other generation decreases. *Dec* reserves are provided from generators that can reduce generation when loads decrease or other generators increase. *Inc* reserves are either spinning or supplemental reserves. Spinning reserves are unloaded generating capacity that is synchronized to the power system and can be increased on very short notice. Supplemental reserves are generating capacity that is not spinning, but that can be brought on line, synchronized, and be capable of serving load on a sustained basis within 10 min. *Dec* reserves are spinning reserves, because generation can be reduced only at units that are already producing energy.

BPA uses three types of within-hour balancing reserves:

> *regulating reserve*, which compensate for moment-to-moment variances in generation and load;

7.6 Wind Rates on an Integrated Electric System   219

or, the amount of reserve needed to balance the changes in load or wind generation on a minute-by-minute basis

following reserve, which compensate for larger variations that occur over longer periods during the hour;

or, the amount of reserve needed to balance the changes in average load and average wind generation every 10 min over the course of an hour, and

imbalance reserve, which compensate for differences between the load's or generator's schedule and the actual load or generation during an hour.

or, the additional amount of following reserve caused by a difference between the actual hourly average load or wind generation and the hourly amount estimated (scheduled) for the load or wind generation.

These components are added together to determine the total reserve requirement.

The above division of reserve types is important for each is separately charged for in the wind rate schedule, and, as a basis for the charges, each is separately costed.

7.6.2 Amount of Wind Generation

As of the end of calendar year 2008, there were about 1,800 MW of wind generation operating in the BPA area, which was expected to increase to 3,155 by the end of 2009. By the end of 2011, there will be 4,500 MW. At this time, BPA will have one of the highest ratios of installed wind in North America (4500 MW to peak load of 10,500 MW).

Substantially more than 50% of Pacific northwest wind generation is being located in the BPA area. Currently BPA has pending requests for 90 wind projects, representing 14,000 MW, seeking interconnection by 2013.

7.6.3 Wind and Planning

BPA notes that wind generation has led to increases in the amount of reserves which must be carried. It says, "The magnitude of wind generation has led to increasing commitments of the operational flexibility of the Federal system to address uncertainty associated with wind-generation variability and scheduling accuracy." BPA further notes that the output of wind generation is subject to the variable and uncertain nature of wind speed, giving rise to difficulties in forecasting accurately. "Wind speed can change greatly within minutes ... BPA can experience swings in generation of hundreds of megawatts within a single hour .... To manage these tremendous swings in wind generation and to maintain load and resource balance, BPA must carry an increasing amount of reserve generation."

7.6.4 Planning: Wind Generators

With respect to planning regarding the behavior of wind generators, BPA says,

"When BPA is planning the operation of the hydro-system, BPA plans both to meet an expected operation and to hold sufficient flexibility to respond to a number of uncertainties, including the output and scheduling behavior of wind generators. BPA assumes that wind generators will attempt to schedule each hour of generation accurately. BPA also assumes that the uncertainties associated with wind-generation output and forecasting will result in generation that does not conform to the schedule. BPA plans system operations to allow for *inc* and *dec* capability to absorb the differences between scheduled and actual generation."

7.6.5 Planning: Persistence Models

Persistence models are a BPA protocol tool which bases the forecast of a future event on the level of an observed value from a current or previous time period. An example is a forecast of wind-generator output for the next hour based upon the level of the current hour.

Under a 2-hour persistence forecast, generation schedules submitted by wind generators are consistent with the output of the generators 2 hours prior to the scheduling hour.

BPA develops reserve forecasts using 30-, 45-, and 60-min persistence forecasts as well as the 2-hour forecast.

Initially, the wind fleet on BPA's system operated at about a 2-hour persistence scheduling accuracy. Later pricing estimates were based on 45-min persistence scheduling. Presently, this has been reduced to 30-min scheduling. BPA points out that this entails a quality of service vs. a rate trade-off, since higher reserves with higher costs mean fewer curtailments, and vice versa. Some participants were worried about this relationship. The consensus preferred a lower rate and was prepared to accept a lower quality of service.

Although it is difficult to forecast the diversity of wind ramps for a fleet that continues to expand rapidly, for the near term BPA accepts that most of the wind on its system will be located just east of the Columbia Gorge, suggesting little diversity of ramp rates between projects.

BPA recognizes that wind operators have difficulty in predicting wind output from hour to hour, but feels that it must adopt a persistent deviation penalty charge, the absence of which would encourage a lack of effort on the part of wind operators to schedule as accurately as possible. The imposed penalty for deviations is a charge equal to 125% of BPA's highest incremental cost that occurs during the day. This penalty applies after 4 hours of schedule deviations that exceed 15% of the schedule for the hour and 20 MW, and the deviation must be in the same direction. New generation reserves that are undergoing testing before commercial operation during reasonable test periods for up to 90 days are exempt from the penalty.

Persistent deviations may occur in either generation imbalance service or energy imbalance service. Deviations may be either negative or positive. Negative deviation occurs when actual generation is greater than scheduled, or energy taken is less than scheduled. Positive deviation is the reverse, when generation is less than scheduled, or energy taken is greater than energy scheduled.

7.6.6 The Generation Reserves

The automatic system control system adjusts the differences hourly between scheduled and actual as *inc* or *dec:* if load increases or generation decreases, the system increases *(inc)* generation; if load decreases or generation increases, the system decreases *(dec)* generation. The cumulative *"inc"* and *"dec"* required to maintain load-resource balance within the hour forms the basis of the reserves required to provide balancing services.

As stated earlier, the reserve requirement consists of regulating reserve, which is that needed to provide continuous balancing of resources with load, following reserve, the spinning and non-spinning capacity to meet within-hour shifts of average energy due to variations of actual load and generation from forecasts, and imbalance reserve, which measures the impact on the following reserve due to the difference (imbalance) between the average scheduled energy over the hour and the actual. Imbalance does not affect the regulating reserve.

Each of these reserves must be estimated and compared with the load and wind forecasts. The amount of wind generation comes from existing and future projects which are expected to be on line during the rate period, FY 2010–2011. This amount is an average of 3,053 MW. Wind generation is estimated on a minute-by-minute basis.

BPA has just finished the installation of 14 anemometers or wind meters which will add crucial surface measurements to data from the National Weather Service. BPA explains, "They'll act as sentinels for moving fronts to give our dispatchers and wind project operators a better idea of what the wind generation plants will produce over the next minutes to hours. Dispatchers have always had moment-to-moment information on how each dam in the hydro system is performing. Now they'll also have a real-time picture of what each wind project is doing, as well as local wind speeds and forecasts and any unexpected variations in wind power production." The new meters are mounted atop towers in strategic locations around the region.

BPA, along with other western utilities, is also moving toward a common dynamic scheduling system, which would allow a balancing authority to control a load or generation in another balancing authority's geographic area. A balancing authority is the geographic area in which one transmission provider maintains the constant balance between generation and loads needed to keep the lights on. Currently, BPA supplies reserves exclusively from the federal hydro-system to balance the variations in wind power. Improved dynamic scheduling with other utilities could provide access to more reserves at lower cost.

Table 7.3 summarizes BPA's conclusions relative to the reserve generation it will need, ending at September, 2011.

The term "load net wind" refers to the load less wind generation, either actual or forecasted.

Table 7.3 BPA's forecast of reserve requirements

	October 2009	September 2011	
Average installed wind capacity	2,655 MW	4,530 MW	
Total reserve (load net wind)			
Inc	1,446 MW	2,011 MW	1,777 MW
Dec	−1,882	−2,613	−2,340
Wind reserve			
Inc	683	1,312	1,042
Dec	−979	−1,785	−1,480
Load reserve			
Inc	764	699	735
Dec	−902	−828	−860

7.6.7 Costs

Costs to be recovered by the wind rate consist of allocated embedded and variable costs. Embedded costs are a portion of the per-unit costs of the Big 10 hydro projects of the FCRPS, determined as their total costs divided by their average annual capacity. The Big 10 projects are on automatic generation control, which allows immediate response to provide sufficient regulating margin.

Capacity is computed as the average annual 120-hour peaking capability of 14 major hydro projects available to serve load, including certain independent hydro resources, under average water conditions.[12]

The annual average net revenue requirement allocation is $768,028,000, capacity is 134,201,520 kW. The result is the embedded unit cost portion of regulating and wind balancing calculated to be $5.72 per kW per month ($768,028,000/134,201,520 per month = $5.72 per kW per month).

The embedded cost revenue from wind balancing is $40,154,400 per year ($5.72 per kW per month × 585 MW × 1000 kW per MW × 12 months).

Variable costs are incurred to ensure that sufficient machine capability is ready and capable of responding to and delivering the required regulating reserve, following reserve, and imbalance reserve. The need to be ready and capable of automatically increasing generation is referred to as an incremental *(inc)* reserve; the need for automatically decreasing generation, as a decremental *(dec)* reserve.

---

[12]The 120-hour period is the highest 6 hour of generation for each of 5 weekdays of a 4-week period for each of the 12 periods (120 hour for all months except for the split months of April and August, each of which uses two 60-hour periods representing the highest 6 hour of generation for each of the 5 weekdays of each 2-week period). These 120 hour are averaged for each month, and this average is considered to be the amount of reliable monthly sustained capacity that would be available for operational planning purposes.

7.6 Wind Rates on an Integrated Electric System

Variable costs may be "stand ready" (those associated with making a project capable of providing reserves) or "deployment costs" (which are incurred when the system uses its capability to actually deliver). Costs also may be categorized into spinning and non-spinning. Further refinement divides stand ready costs into energy shift, efficiency loss, and base cycling losses. Deployment costs are further divided into responses losses, incremental cycling losses, incremental spill, and incremental efficiency losses.

By massaging the monumental amounts of data through two computer models, matching variable costs for wind balancing are found to be $7, 255, 487, bringing the wind balancing reserve total to $47, 409, 887. This is the revenue requirement. Service covering this requirement is $1.29 per kW per month.

These figures are based upon a 30-min persistence scheduling assumption. However, BPA can increase the rate under certain conditions (if asked to do so by participants in the northwest industry in order to increase the amount of balancing reserves, or if BPA is prevented from following an existing dispatch procedure). If BPA does so, the rate shall not exceed a rate based upon a 45-min persistence schedule, $1.58 per kW-month. This would be an increase from $1.29 per kW-month.

7.6.8 Balancing Measures

Wind balancing service is provided by raising or lowering the output of committed on line generation (predominantly through the use of automatic generation control equipment) as necessary to follow the moment-by-moment changes in wind generation. The wind generator must either purchase this service from BPA or make comparable arrangements. This service is necessary to support the within-hour movement of wind generation from the hourly generation schedule (Table 7.4). (Small generators—20 MW or less—have a one-time exemption extending through September 30, 2010.)

Table 7.4 Illustration of balancing transaction

	Scheduled	Actual-#1	Actual-#2	Deviation
1st hour	2 MWh	2 MWh	0 MWh	2 MWh
2nd hour	2 MWh	2 MWh	2 MWh	0 MWh
3rd hour	2 MWh	2 MWh	1 MWh	1 MWh
4th hour	2 kW	2 kW	2 kW	0 MWh
	8 MWh	8 MWh	5 MWh	3 MWh

The left hand column above indicates scheduled generation for a 4-hour period. The next column, "Actual-#1," shows the actual generation which occurred, assuming it corresponded with the schedule. The two columns are in balance.

The column "Actual-#2" assumes that the actual generation which occurred deviates from the schedule, creating an imbalance. In comparison with the scheduled total of 8 MWh to be delivered, only 5 MWh were actually generated, with a deficiency imbalance of 3 MWh.

The generator may makeup the deficiency by (i) buying the requisite power from another supplier, or (ii) by increasing its generation at a later date beyond the amount normally scheduled for that date. It is assumed that the scheduling system has in fact supplied the deficiency as it occurred, so it is for that system that the wind generator supplies the extra power, to be accepted when it can be used for load or storage.

7.6.9 Points of Contention

For a system as large and complex as the FCRPS, it is unreasonable not to expect a wide diversity of opinion and some bitter disputes as to policy, particularly when a new service is being inaugurated. This certainly was the case for the wind rate. Space does not permit a discussion of each matter of contention, so we mention below just two examples to illustrate the variety of issues.

Whether 120-hour peaking capacity is an appropriate measure for system capacity and allocating embedded costs: decision, yes it is.

Whether the embedded cost pricing methodology should use average or critical water as an input: decision, BPA will use average water to establish the 120-hour peaking capability used in the generation inputs embedded cost pricing methodology.

7.6.10 Services Offered

Six ancillary services are offered with transmission service to maintain reliability within and among the areas affected by the transmission service. Also, five control area services are offered to meet the reliability obligations of generation or loads in the balancing control area. These include wind balancing service, the wind rate described herein.

Wind balancing service is provided to wind generators in support of within-hour movement of wind generation and to maintain the balance between loads and resources. BPA must utilize balancing reserves to maintain compliance with reliability standards. The rate (WI-10) establishes charges for each of the three components of the service: regulating, following, and imbalance reserves.

7.6.11 Rate Design

Officially, the designation of the rate is, "2010 Transmission, Ancillary Service and Control Area Service Rate Schedules (FY2010–2011), July 200), SECTION III, CONTROL AREA SERVICE RATES, E. WIND BALANCING SERVICE." In shorthand, it is "Section III.E. of the ACS-10." The rate is short, and is reproduced in Fig. 7.3.

E. WIND BALANCING SERVICE

The rate below applies to all wind plants in the BPA Control Area except as provided in sections III.E.3 and III.E.4. Wind Balancing Service is comprised of three components: regulating reserves (which compensate for moment-to-moment differences between generation and load), following reserves (which compensate for larger differences occurring over longer periods of time during the hour), and imbalance reserves (which compensate for differences between the generator's schedule and the actual generation during an hour). Wind Balancing Service is required to help maintain the power system frequency at 60 Hz and to conform to NERC and WECC reliability standards.

1. RATE

Except as provided in section III.E.4.ii, the total rate shall not exceed $1.29 per kilowatt per month. Each component of the rate shall not exceed the following:

(i)	Regulating Reserves	$0.05 per kilowatt per month
(ii)	Following Reserves	$0.26 per kilowatt per month
(iii)	Imbalance Reserves	$0.98 per kilowatt per month

2. BILLING FACTOR

The Billing Factor is as follows:

(i) For each wind plant, or phase of a wind plant, that has completed installation of all units no later than the 15th of the month prior to the billing month the billing factor will be the nameplate of the plant in kW. A unit has completed installation when it has generated and delivered power to the BPA system.

(ii) For each wind plant, or phase of a wind plant, for which some but not all units have been installed by the 15th day of the month prior to the billing month, the billing factor will be the maximum measured hourly output of the plant through the 15th day of the prior month in kW.

3. EXCEPTIONS

(i) This rate will not apply to a wind plant, or portion of a wind plant, that, in BPA's determination, has put in place, tested, and successfully implemented no later than the 15th day of the month prior to the billing month, the dynamic transfer of plant output out of BPA's Balancing Authority Area to another Balancing Authority Area.

Fig. 7.3 BPA Wind Rates

(ii) Any component of this rate will not apply to a wind plant, or portion of a wind plant, that, in BPA's determination, has put in place, tested, and successfully implemented in conformance to criteria specified in BPA-TS business practices, no later than the 15th day of the month prior to the billing month, self-supply of that component of balancing, including by contractual arrangements for third-party supply.

(iii) Through September 30, 2010, this rate will not apply to any wind plant with a nameplate capacity of 20,000 kW or less.

4. RATE ADJUSTMENT

(i) On 30 days' written notice posted on BPA-TS's OASIS, BPA may increase the rate as set forth in section III.E.4.ii, with a commensurate increase in the amount of balancing reserves set aside for Wind Balancing Service, if

　　a. one or more participants in the Pacific Northwest utility industry, including regional organizations, asks the Administrator to increase the amount of balancing reserves set aside for Wind Balancing Service in order to reduce the frequency or magnitude of BPA's implementation of Dispatcher Standing Order (DSO) 216; or

　　b. because of a legal challenge to DSO 216, BPA is prevented from implementing DSO 216 or is required to amend it materially.

(ii) The new total rate shall not exceed $1.58 per kilowatt per month. Each component of the rate shall not exceed the following:

　　a. Regulating Reserves　　$0.05 per kilowatt per month
　　b. Following Reserves　　$0.27 per kilowatt per month
　　c. Imbalance Reserves　　$1.26 per kilowatt per month

Fig. 7.3 (continued)

The rate schedule includes a three-component capacity charge to be applied to the wind generator's installed wind-generating capacity, which cannot exceed a total of $1.29 per month (unless adjusted upward to a new total of $1.58). The three components are separate to allow for their self-serve by the generator.

In commenting on the $1.29 per kW per month rate, BPA head Steve Wright noted that it was dramatically lower than the initial proposal of $2.72 per kW per month. He said that the reduction was due primarily to actions taken by wind generators to reduce their use of BPA generation for reliability when wind power ramps up or down unexpectedly. He explained, "The explosion of wind power on the BPA system, especially since 2005, has led to operational challenges including risks to reliability and substantial costs. The new rate, reduced due to collaboration with the wind power industry, will help address those issues and put us in a position to bring more wind on board."

7.6.12 *Physical Specifications*

While there are many variations, a typical wind-generating installation will include a tower rising about 300 ft, on top of which is a generating assembly comprised of a three-bladed propeller and a generator. The assembly weighs about 670,000 pounds (300 metric tons). The blades of the propeller extend about 150 ft from nub to tip. The nameplate rating of the generator is 2,000 kW. The propeller will rotate at a top speed of 16 rpm, with the wind blowing at 8–50 miles per hour. The total cost of a completed installation ranges from $20 to $300 millions. Installations can be no closer than 450 ft from each other.

7.6.13 *What's Left Out*

The new BPA rate does what it is called upon to do: it provides "wind balancing" for wind-generation plants in BPA's control area. In doing so, it reserves sufficient generating capacity from BPA's own facilities to compensate for the uncertainties of a fluctuating wind supply, and it accomplishes this capacity reservation at its own low-cost level. So the rate promises to be a success. Mission accomplished!

But the rate fails in one important respect. It does not solve the location problem. Winds are sufficiently strong and prevalent to support a plant only at locations which are distant from load centers, where their output is used. Transmission links—high voltage electric transmission lines—are needed to carry the power away from the wind plant to homes, businesses, and manufacturing sites where it will be consumed. The new rate applies only to the generating function of the wind plant. The operators of the plant must purchase transmission capacity to carry its output to points of use (such as by PTP-10, the point-to-point rate for transmission).

The new rate may also fall short in another respect, although this may or may not occur. If BPA finds it necessary to supply makeup power from its own sources to compensate for wind-generation imbalances in excess of those covered by the new rate, the wind operator must purchase this makeup power from BPA at an additional cost. BPA's generation imbalance service might be one way of doing this.

Chapter 8
Introduction to Rates

Abstract Chapter 8 introduces the environment surrounding utility prices (or rates, in utility jargon) by outlining the viewpoints brought to bear on the subject by customers, utility managements, and the public. The chapter also includes some pertinent definitions.

8.1 The Unregulated Marketplace

The unregulated marketplaces are everywhere. They can't be ignored. They are the ads tempting buyers with great values at negligible prices. From the morning newspapers to the last television show in the evening, the bombardment is continuous. Featured prices share the message with vivid descriptions of the product being promoted.

Prices range from the simple to the complicated. The simplest appear in grocery store ads: price per item, per pound or dozen. "Buy one can for 50 cents; buy three cans for $1." Or, "25 cents with one coupon." Or, "A discount of 10% for all purchases of $50 or over." Or, "Buy one, get one free." Or a mail rebate may be offered.

A national outlet for men's clothing conducted a series of ads promoting its sale prices. The merchandise differed for each sale. One would highlight suits, another coats, others shirts and ties, and still others, some combinations of the above. Pricing was varied, including "10% off" to "Half Price." Most interesting was "Buy one item at regular price. Get another at half price. And buy a third at one-quarter price." The first combination gives a 25% discount on each of the two items; the second, a 42% discount on each of the three items.

Furniture and other large appliance sellers often offer payment concessions, such as "Buy NOW in 2011. No interest. No pay until 2013."

Each of these variations offers a different version of the description of price. In rate terminology, such differences are called variations in the FORM of the rate. The form is different from the statement of the price, which normally will be in terms of dollars and cents or a percentage. The price itself is referred to as the LEVEL of the rate. In the same fashion as the price maker in the unregulated market has to weigh and decide on the form and level of the price of his merchandise, the rate maker has to weigh and decide on the form and level of his proposed rate.

8.2 The Marketplace Under Regulation

In making his evaluations and selections, the rate maker must realize that he is subject to the rules of a regulated market, and should keep in mind the objectives of that market. In brief, the objectives of regulated rate making are as follows: (1) to provide adequate revenues; (2) to distribute the burden of providing these revenues equitably among the customers of the utility; and (3) to encourage the maximum economic use of the utility's service, or, in some cases, to discourage uneconomic use.

In reaching these objectives, the rate maker must consider three viewpoints, those of the customer, the utility management, and the public, the latter including the regulatory commissions and the courts. Naturally, the three points of view represented by these three different groups do not always coincide. This presents an ever-present problem to the rate maker, whose reward is nothing but trouble unless he succeeds in developing a rate which is acceptable to all three. For this reason it is not an exaggeration to say that every rate is a compromise between conflicting views and objectives. Feeling and intuition often are as important as facts in rate design.

8.3 The Customer Viewpoint

Beyond a doubt, the customer's main interest in his bill is the price he has to pay. When this price is low—or more important, when the customer *thinks* it is low—the chances are that he will have no further interest. But if the customer considers his bill to be too high, then the form of the rate becomes important.

Any interest on the part of the consumer to look beyond the amount of his bill triggers consideration of the virtue of simplicity. The rate form should be such as to be easily explained by the utility and easily understood by the consumer.[1] The more closely the rate form approaches conventional pricing methods, the better from this point of view. Thus, a single-part rate, which to the ordinary consumer represents the single-price schedule to which he is accustomed, is more acceptable than a multi-part rate.

The prices themselves should be as clear-cut as possible. The writer's personal view is that it is far better to state a price as an even number (say 25 cents per unit), than as an odd figure (say $24.95 or $25.05 per unit) even though the odd amounts might be more "accurate." Unfortunately, however, this preference, which once was virtually unchallenged, is no longer fashionable. One easily can find residential class prices which are carried out to two or more tenths of a cent. The writer recognizes that changes in technology may be one of the factors which

---

[1] The idea of simplicity seems to come and go in rate making. Originally rates were fairly simple. In the late 1920s and 1930s, the trend was toward more "scientific"—and consequently more complicated—rate structures. This trend was then reversed for some years and simplicity was the keynote. The current trend to emphasize "cost-based" rates represents another reversal toward complexity; for example, the "unbundling" of costs into separate billing elements.

have lessened the onus of complex prices. Now, cheap hand-help calculators make computations easy which previously would have necessitated tedious long-hand arithmetic.

Simplicity is a many-faceted problem. A simple rate seldom can be made as equitable as a more complex rate, due to the involved nature of utility costing. So simplicity often clashes head-on with refined cost-based pricing theories. Also, simplicity as an objective can be carried too far. It is a great virtue in rates applicable to smaller-use customers, such as the residential, and to a lesser degree the commercial, classes. But the importance of simplicity diminishes where large-use customers are concerned. For large wholesale sales the proper allocations of costs to different customers to reflect their usage characteristics is much more important than simplicity. Also, with large users, lack of simplicity causes no particular problem. They ordinarily will employ trained technicians who can understand even the most complex rate. Finally, sometimes an appearance of simplicity is deceptive. Bonneville Power Administration's early "kilowatt-year" electric rate was simple in form but the application of that rate to the different customers served under it probably was as complicated as any rate application found anywhere. Simplicity is not merely a matter of rate form, but also one of ease of application.

The consumer is also concerned about being treated equitably, without discrimination. Since class rates generally prevail in utilities and since class rates necessarily involve some discrimination, the rate maker is faced with a dilemma. The most practical solution is to establish only those rate classes which can be readily differentiated by the average individual.

Finally, consumers value stability and predictability in the bills they receive from their utility company: stability, so that the utility's call upon their income will not yo–yo beyond their control from period to period; predictability, permitting them to fashion their future budgets with some assurance that their increment for utility services will not be widely off the mark. Stability and predictability are important considerations to be kept in mind whenever a restructuring of the tariff is being implemented. Rate shock is not a sought for result.

8.4 The Management Viewpoint

The major concern of utility management, of course, is that all costs, including profit, will be returned by its rates. But this is at best a superficial statement of managerial interest. The many varied considerations of cost and value ratemaking are all pointed toward the coverage of costs, but nevertheless differ from each other materially. A further cost objective is imposed on the rate maker by utility management, however. That is that the rate structure be sufficiently elastic to meet changing needs and conditions without drastic alteration, a result most difficult of attainment. Most past periods have been notable for a relative rigidity of utility prices stemming in part from the difficulty of adjusting rates. Unless originating from the action of the regulatory body, a rate change, involving the substitution of one rate for another, is almost always a lengthy process, particularly when the change is accompanied by an increase in the rate level which will result in a higher customer's bill. Perhaps the most practical means of achieving some elasticity in revenue without a formal rate-level change is the escalator or adjustment clause, which permits the rate level to be raised or lowered as some predetermined base, such as the price of fuel, changes. This method is discussed more fully later.

Utility management often may impose other special objectives on the rate maker.[2] It may be desirable, for example, to promote, discourage or otherwise control a certain type of use (demand management), and the rate maker is called upon to devise a pricing schedule which will accomplish these ends. Or management may desire to confront a competitive situation by new price differentials between its prices and those of competitors. There are almost an infinite variety of special considerations which management may impose on the rate maker.

Perhaps herein lies part of the explanation for the large number of rates which many electric and gas utilities have accumulated. It is a great temptation for management to visualize a new special-purpose rate as the solution of some pressing problem. So another schedule is added and the tariff grows like Topsey. The addition of each new schedule adds to the confusion as to which rate applies in any given case, and eventually there is likely to be serious overlapping and duplication among schedules. Sooner or later this leads to the need for simplifying the tariff, with all the administrative and public relations problems attendant upon shifting customers from one schedule to another.

8.5 The Public Viewpoint

Finally, the rate maker must attempt to please that indefinable body, the general public. This may be said to include regulatory commissions and the courts, as legal

---

[2] Although special rate-making objectives can be stated simply, this does not indicate that the problem involved is simple. As an illustration, we may note some aspects of developing promotional rates as discussed a half-century ago by G.C. Delaville of the California Electric Power Company.

"In establishing rates which will encourage the greater use of the electricity, the rate engineer must keep his eye on increases in net income rather than increases in gross revenue. It is easy to design a rate which will increase gross revenue by increasing use, but this increase in use may force a utility to make such large increases in facilities that the increase in revenue is completely offset by the charges, fixed and other, on the increased facilities."

"These remarks are especially applicable to any rate which encourages the use of air heating in areas with relatively warm winters subject to occasional cold spells of short duration. These same remarks may become applicable to domestic rates as a whole, if the present tendency toward low incremental rates in this sales classification continues. Thus, taking the record for the nation as a whole, we find that, from 1926 through 1950 annual domestic sales were increased 117 kWh per customer at an increment rate of 2.46 cents per kWh, but from September, 1945, through September 1946, annual domestic sales were increased 104 kWh per customer at an increment rate of only 1.2 cents per kWh. How long will the industry be able to increase sales at such low incremental rates, considering that these sales require additional capital expenditure and that all operating costs are increasing?" See Delaville, G.C., "What Does the Rate Engineer Do?" *Public Utilities Fortnightly*, Vol. XXXIX, No. 13, June 19, 1947, pp. 820–821.

representatives of the public. Most members of the public are also customers of the utility, but as customers they are interested only in a small segment of the rate maker's work, the rates under which they themselves take service. As members of the public, they are interested, at least indirectly, in all rates.

Commissions and courts, when reviewing a rate case, have a more specific interest, of course. The basic criterion to be met is that the rates be fair and equitable, a criterion for which, as we have seen, judgment plays the predominant part. It is always possible to argue that a rate and the assumptions upon which it is based are fair and equitable, but this is rarely possible to *prove* in the strict sense: logical arguments in favor almost always can be countered by equally logical arguments against. Therefore, fairness and equity are elusive standards, although it is to these standards that the courts ordinarily confine their attention. Commissions have tended to be a bit more practical in their approach. If the utility's tariff is accepted without much objection by consumers and the public, if friendly relations seem to exist between the utility and its customers, the commission may be satisfied.[3] For this reason it seemed to be characteristic during the Golden Age and before that commissions concerned themselves much more with the overall rate levels (total allowed revenues) than they did with the design of individual rates.

The "Golden Age," 1950–1972, is a term coined by the California Commission to describe the period of rate tranquility for electric and natural gas companies which preceded the energy crisis and high inflation of the mid-1970s.

Since the Golden Age, the primary attention of regulatory commissions has shifted away from overall revenue control to rate design and restructuring. In many jurisdictions, the latter has tended at least in part to replace the traditional cost of service and value of service criteria, and new objectives, theories, and techniques have been introduced. These changes have been multiplied, by geometric ratio, the number and complexity of the considerations entering into rate making.

8.5.1 *The California PUC*

Few state commissions have set forth succinctly the requisites for rate structure. One that has is California. It has said,[4]

An ideal electric rate structure should:

Reflect the different costs of serving different customers at different times;
Promote system and overall economic efficiency by including understandable "price signals" which (1) inform customers of the costs they impose on the utility by their

---

[3] However, commissions may not necessarily be satisfied. The California PUC has declared: "[The company and the commission] should not be indifferent to a rate structure merely because it collects its revenue requirements and the customers who benefit from that rate structure are satisfied."

[4] California PUC, *"The 1988 Workplan" Glossary*; Ratemaking Goals.

consumption practices and (2) customers can actually respond to through changes in their consumption practices;

Promote efficiency by discouraging uneconomic bypass by customers who have alternatives to taking service on the utility system;

Remain reasonably stable over time so that customers who make investments in facilities, equipment, and practices that affect consumption in response to price signals are not unduly harmed as cost measurements and pricing signals change;
Be accepted by customers as fair and reasonable;

Collect no more and no less than the utility's adopted revenue requirement while providing a stable revenue flow; and

Promote and implement goals and programs such as energy conservation and assistance to low-income customers.

The Commission added this comment:

It is our goal in electric utility ratemaking to establish a rate structure with these attributes, but reaching that goal can be difficult for a variety of reasons. These include the fact that precise measurement of costs cannot always be attained and the fact that the above attributes sometimes conflict with each other.

8.5.2 The Federal Energy Regulatory Commission

From a different perspective, FERC summarized its views concerning gas pipeline *sales* rates. Under the heading "The Economic Criteria for Just and Reasonable Rates," FERC said,[5]

The Commission believes that there are four necessary conditions to a just and reasonable [pipeline] rate for natural gas ...

First, a rate is just and reasonable that brings about efficiency in both production and consumption of natural gas .... An efficient price is one that relates current costs with current values [that is, reflecting current, not past, circumstances].

Second, the rates so established must permit "fair" competition ....

Third, the rate should not lead to the wasteful depletion of scarce, non-renewable resources.

Finally, [the rate should be] appropriate to changing conditions in the natural gas industry, and should not inhibit the growth of competition envisioned by the NGPA [Natural Gas Policy Act].

Note that the above-FERC criteria apply to pipeline *sales* rates. National policy has moved toward changing the role of pipeline companies from that of a merchant (i.e., a seller of gas) to that of a transporter who carries gas bought by or for users (who formerly were, in most cases, buyers of gas from the pipeline). Thus, pipeline *sales* rates would be superseded in importance by *transportation* rates. As a kick-off for the transportation mode, FERC offered its prescription for the transportation

---

[5]Federal Energy Regulatory Commission, Notice Requesting Supplemental Comments, Docket No. RM85-1-000, issued October 9, 1985.

8.5 The Public Viewpoint

components of new sales rates (i.e., excluding the gas cost components) by listing four goals and three rate objectives. These later were declared to be equally applicable to open-access transportation-only rates.[6]

> First, ratemaking policies should lead to prices that communicate clear market signals to all participants ...
>
> Second, the pricing system should embody strong incentives to minimize costs in order to provide services at the lowest reasonable costs consistent with reliable long term service.
>
> Third, customers should be given maximum flexibility in making choices among services and among suppliers of these services.
>
> Finally, the Commission must also be concerned with the development and maintenance of a regulatory framework that will be appropriate to all conditions of gas supply and pipeline investment [not geared to shortage or surplus conditions, etc.]. [The framework] should apply equally well to different market conditions.
>
> More particularly, rates for transportation [components of sales rates] should be designed to achieve three objectives concurrently:
>
> —Peak rates should ration capacity;
>
> —Off-peak rates should maximize through-put; and
>
> —The pipelines revenue responsibility allocated to transportation should be attained through transporting the expected peak and off-peak volumes at the maximum rates [as contrasted to discounted rates].
>
> .... The Commission recognizes that the goals at times pull in conflicting directions and that good ratemaking reflects large amounts of fairly subjective judgments.

We quote the above at this juncture to suggest the soul-searching which goes into the launching of a dramatic shift in regulated pricing, as must accompany a revolutionary government-mandated change in the role of a regulated company.

If change is on the horizon, why explore the past? The writer believes that while the stage changes, the actors change, and even the plot changes, new themes will largely be variations of yesterday. "Past is Prologue." Principles still apply, although their applications will be different. (Or, to adopt a heading on the front page of *The Wall Street Journal* of April 4, 1994, "Updating ... means Respecting History Without Repeating It.")

---

[6]Federal Energy Regulatory Commission, Order No. 436, issued October 9, 1985. Later, FERC followed up by a lengthy "Policy Statement Providing Guidance with Respect to the Designing of Rates," issued May 30, 1989, geared to open-access transportation-only rates, finding that the same goals and policies set forth for the transportation components of sales rates were equally applicable to both types of rates.

8.6 Related Objectives

Other criteria of a general nature may be mentioned in passing to complete this review of the considerations to be borne in mind by the rate maker. *First*, the rate structure should be such as to discourage waste. While ideas as to what constitutes waste vary greatly (is a high horsepower motor car wasteful when a smaller car would serve the same purpose? Is a home dishwasher, which uses a great deal of hot water, wasteful?) The prevention of waste is a broad economic objective of importance. Largely because they are conductive to waste, "flat" rates, discussed later, are often avoided (although local telephone rates were a conspicuous example of the contrary not too long ago). *Second*, the rate structure should prevent or at least discourage fraud. Nothing is more conductive to friction between the utility and its customers than a rate which tempts the customer to cheat. Early electric rates which used the number of "occupied" rooms as a basis for demand charges were of this character. If a customer insisted that a room in his residence was closed off and not occupied, it was very difficult for the utility to argue the point even though all the evidence pointed to the contrary. And *third*, the rate structure should be such as to permit the utility to operate efficiently. It should induce customers to take service in such a manner as to reduce their peak demands, improve their load factor, etc. This objective also calls for rate treatments which are economical to administer.

8.7 Some Expert Opinions

Early writers in the field summed up the rate design problem succinctly. What they said remains applicable today, and more recent commentators do no better. J. Maurice Clark, a noted economist of Columbia University, has said, "The chief purpose of a rate system should be to earn a reasonable total return, to develop the utmost use of the facilities as long as every service pays at least its differential cost, and to distribute residual costs fairly according to the responsibility of different users for the amount of these costs."[7]

G. C. Delaville, vice president, California Electric Power Company, said, "In actual practice the main problem that confronts the rate engineer is to obtain the total amount of money necessary to operate the utility at a reasonable profit with the least complaints from any one class of customers and the greatest opportunity to increase sales and profits. Naturally, such increased sales and profits are of benefit not only to the utility, but also to the customer, since such increases make possible further rate reductions."[8]

---

[7] Clark, J.M., *Studies in the Economics of Overhead Costs*, University of Chicago Press, Chicago, IL, 1923, Ch. XVI, p. 322.
[8] Delaville, G.C., op. cit. p. 819.

A third point of view, asserted by L. R. Lefferson, manager, Rate Department, Ebasco Services Inc., directed toward rate classifications, is, "Public utility rate structures should be such that a customer can ask for, and be permitted to take, any kind of standard service he wants, provided his operations do not interfere with the good service to others and, provided further, that he pays any extraordinary costs of supplying the service."[9]

Helene C. Bateman, exchange rate engineer, American Telephone and Telegraph Company, writing from extensive experience in the development of Bell System telephone rates, answered the question, "What is a good schedule of telephone rates designed to accomplish?" as follows: ".... telephone rates are designed to bring in enough money to run the business, enough so that the company can furnish good service, pay fair wages, and earn a fair return ...." The rate schedule which will best serve the public "obtains the necessary revenues with the lowest practicable rates and in ways which will keep revenues as stable as possible, thus minimizing the need for future rate increases. It encourages more people to have telephones and to use them more. It meets the needs of groups of customers whose requirements are different from the average. It promotes a high quality of telephone service and at the same time helps to keep down the costs of furnishing it. And the distribution of charges among customers is fair and reasonable."[10] Note the difference in emphasis as well as the similarities in these four statements.

8.8 Definitions

In common parlance, "rate" simply means "price." We speak of one rate being higher than another—the price is higher. We speak of a rate change—the price is increased or decreased, or otherwise altered. In most cases in this book, the term is used in this non-technical, layman's language sense.

It is helpful to note the technical distinctions between the terms "rate" and "rate schedule." Technically, "rate" refers to *the unit prices and the quantities to which they apply as specified in the rate schedule;* while "rate schedule" means *the statement of the rate and the terms and conditions governing its application.*[11]

---

[9] Lefferson, L.R., "Residual Rates for Tomorrow's Loads," *Edison Electric Institute Bulletin*, Vol. 17, No. 7, July 1949, p. 250.

[10] Bateman, Helene C., "Design for a Good Rate Schedule," *Bell Telephone Magazine* for winter 1952-53, p. 230. In this article it is also stated that the Bell System objective, which the System's Rate Engineers seek to implement, is "the most telephone service and the best at the least cost to the public consistent with financial safety." See p. 231.

[11] "Glossary of Important Power and Rate Terms, Abbreviations, and Units of Measurement." 1949 (by Subcommittee on Glossary of Federal Inter-Agency River Basin Committee, under supervision of Federal Power Commission), U.S. Government Printing Office, p. 6.

This distinction is seldom drawn, however, and in practice the terms are used interchangeably.

The term "rate design" covers the complete rate, embracing both the rate level and the rate form. As such, it refers to a process as well as an end result.

The process consists of the conceptual planning whereby the objectives being sought are integrated into an appropriately tailored price pattern, as much as an architect "designs" a building which will perform the function for which it is intended (the type of rate), and which at the same time will blend harmoniously into its surroundings (the position of the rate's price level in the array of the prices of other rates). Design then progresses from the general to the specific—from the plans to actual construction—culminating in a specific rate form to which is fitted a specific price or series of prices. As with the building, which may be remodeled frequently, an original rate may be changed again and again.

Since this text sees rate design as referring to any given rate (or rate schedule) as a complete whole, including both the form and the level of the rate, these elements for a simple two-part gas rate (explained later) might be distinguished as follows:

Form	Level
Demand charge	$3.50 per month
Energy charge	$0.64 per therm

In practice, a routine change in the rate level only, would not be viewed as a change in the rate design. An example of such a routine rate-level change would be a passing on by the gas company of an increase or decrease in its cost of purchased gas (as a result of a purchased-gas cost adjustment clause). Even a change resulting from a general rate increase, provided that the new higher-price levels did not distort the prior balance between the prices of the several schedules, might be construed to be simply routine. Any change in form is a change in rate design.

Definitions and usage vary for almost all of the common rate terms. The California Public Utilities Commission defines rate design as "the allocation of revenue requirement among various services and customer classes" with the elaboration that the process also includes, "determining the component rates and charges (such as energy, demand, and customer) and the dollar values for these rates and charges for each schedule."[12]

The Oregon PUC simply says, "rate design indicates the way in which the revenues allocated to a customer class are collected within that class."[13] Other jurisdictions and authorities use the term in still other fashions, so it is essential to observe the context within which the term appears.

"Rate structure" is an overlapping term being generally synonymous with rate design. A convenient distinction, if a distinction is desired, is to use "rate structure"

---

[12] California PUC, op. cit.
[13] Oregon PUC, Order No. 78-521, issued July 20, 1978.

8.8 Definitions

to describe a static or existing rate or set of rates, and to reserve "rate design" to suggest the dynamic process of devising new rates. However, such distinctions may be ignored for most often the terms are used interchangeably.

The Oregon PUC sees it this way.[14]

> Rate structure includes both rate spread and rate design. Rate spread refers to the allocation of the revenue requirement among the several customer classes. Rate design indicates the way in which the revenues allocated to a customer class are collected within that class.

California's definition is, "Rate Structure– The various rates charged by a utility for its services."[15] More often, however, the term is used with reference to a single rate. Relative to this meaning, the American Gas Association's Rate Structure Committee a number of years ago commented,[16]

> The structure of a rate corresponds to the steel skeleton of a building. This is made up of many members varying in strength and position according to the stresses on the various parts of the building, but calculated to adequately support the building as a whole.
> The correct price for any service or commodity must be supported by a structure designed with a full knowledge of the weight and significance of all the factors entering into values.

This statement points out the often overlooked fact that a rate is more than just a schedule of prices—it is basically a price schedule, of course, but just as essential to the purpose of the rate are the terms and provisions which define precisely how, when, and with what qualifications the rate may be used. The "fine print" of the rate, like the "fine print" of an insurance policy, often may be more important than the more conspicuous elements.

As pointed out by the California definition above, rate structure is also used with reference not to a single rate, but to all of the rates of the utility in effect at any given time. In this sense a utility's rate structure may be spoken of, for example, as being compromised of a large number and variety of rates, ranging from the simple to the intricate, in which event the rate structure might be described as complex. Or the structure might be composed of a relatively small number of rates of a less complicated nature, in which case it might be considered to be simple. It is preferable, because of the possible confusion, to avoid the use of the term in the plural sense. The terms "Tariff" or "Book of Rates" make good substitutes.

---

[14] Oregon PUC, Order No. 78-521, Ibid.

[15] California PUC, op. cit.

[16] American Gas Association, Proceedings, 8th Annual Convention (Rate Structure Committee Report) 1926, p. 101.

Chapter 9
Elements of Rate Design

Abstract Chapter 9 introduces the non-price clauses which frequently are inserted into the rate to modify its price statements. Minimum charges are an example. The chapter also introduces the non-price features of the basic rate design. These design features include, for example, whether the prices are blocked or not (i.e., whether or not different prices are applicable as the volumes taken change) and whether the prices are applicable throughout the system (a "postage stamp" pattern) or vary in different locations in the system (a zone pattern). Finally, the chapter mentions the generalized "fine print" provisions which ordinarily are included in the package of rates as a routine matter.

9.1 Frequent Features

Before turning to the specific types or forms of rate structure as we do later, it is helpful to examine features which often are incorporated into rates regardless of their particular form. The genesis of any feature may be cost, value, or public policy, or a combination of these three criteria.

9.1.1 Minimums

Minimum charges are frequently found as a separate element in utility rates. Minimum charges range from the simple to the complex. The simplest form would merely require that the customer's total *monthly* bill could not be less than a stated dollar amount; a minimum *annual* bill expressed in dollars would be consistent with that same pattern. At the other end of the range are separate minimums for the demand and commodity charges of a multi-part rate, either or both of which are likely to be stated in units of energy demand and/or usage (i.e., specifying that billing shall be based upon a higher prior level of usage, or a percentage of such usage, if the current level of usage is lower, or in units of a contractual level of demand and/or energy delivery to which the utility is committed, or a percentage of such contractual level, if actual usage is less).

A minimum charge can be stated in the rate schedule in either of two ways (or both ways, for that matter): (1) it may be explicitly identified, as "the minimum monthly bill for service taken under this rate schedule shall be $____," or (2) it may be incorporated into the first step of a blocked rate, as "first 10 units $____," the same dollar amount being billed whether zero or ten units are used by the customer.

There is no accepted measure of what *types* of costs should be covered by the minimum charge, nor as to the extent of coverage. Therefore, it is possible only to regard the minimum charge as an attempt to make certain the recovery of some indefinite portion of the costs of the utility. The major application of the minimum charge is to customers whose use is small, although often the minimum is an important part of wholesale-type rates.

The minimum charge is an imperfect cost-recovery device, since the net contribution which it induces is uncertain. If the customer does not use any service during the month (in the case of a monthly minimum), or during the season or year (in the case of minimums applicable to longer periods), the utility will have experienced no variable out-of-pocket costs by reason of the customer's usage. The full minimum charge, then, will represent an offset to the utility's fixed and other non-usage variable costs. On the other hand, if the customer's usage is such as to equal or exceed the minimum, the minimum has no effect and provides no cost offset beyond that built into the applicable rate.

A restaurant's minimum charge is a clear analogy. If the customer merely sits, without drinking or eating, the restaurant collects the minimum fee clear of any costs for food and drink. However, to the extent that the customer does eat or drink, the restaurant incurs costs for the customer's consumption, earning only its normal profit on the meal. In the no-drink, no-eat example, the minimum represents the price assigned to the restaurants' implicit readiness-to-serve offer.[1] Changes in regulatory thinking about natural gas pipeline minimums (i.e., minimums applicable to large-scale or wholesale rates) show how conceptions of a minimum can evolve from acceptance to rejection. Many earlier pipeline rates included a demand charge which operated as a minimum with respect to the fixed costs assigned to demand, and in addition specified a minimum monthly volume for which full commodity charges were assessed. Variable costs, essentially the actual costs of purchased gas, were excluded from minimum commodity bills by FERC in 1984 by Order No. 380. Thereafter, only the fixed costs assigned to commodity could be recovered in the commodity minimum. By orders No. 249 and 249-A of 1986 and 1987 (Tennessee Gas Pipeline Company) the Commission disallowed a commodity minimum of any kind. The reason was that it encouraged customers to purchase gas regardless of the pipeline's prices.

On the whole, there has been a similar evolution away from the minimum in small usage rates.

---

[1] It also can be said that a restaurant minimum assumes that the customer's occupancy of a table may preempt other customers from being served at that table. Preemption could be a consideration for a utility also, but this would be rare.

The restaurant minimum serves as a powerful incentive to the customer to order food or drink at least up to the amount of the minimum. Why not? Why pay for something you don't receive?

The minimum charge of a utility rate is precisely parallel. While the minimum may serve a cost recovery purpose, its collateral result is value-based (i.e., promotional). The minimum acts as an incentive to the customer to use the utility's service, while at the same time setting a floor on the revenue the utility will receive from the customer. Most current objections to the minimum arise from the promotional characteristic. Any promotion of energy use is seen to fly in the face of conservation or demand side management.

A minimum charge is not to be confused with a cover charge. The latter includes no allowance for customer usage. The cover charge is an addition in full to the customer's bill, without offset for the food or drink which the customer may order. The parallel in utility rates is a "Customer" or "Service" charge which is separate from usage charges.

9.1.2 Ratchets

Another pricing device is the *ratchet*. The ratchet operates as a variable minimum charge, the amount of the minimum being dependent upon previous usage. The gauge of previous usage may be (1) earlier customer bills, or (2) earlier demand charges.

A ratchet provision of the first type would provide that billing for any given month cannot be less than monthly billing (or some percentage thereof) for some immediately prior period. For example, the minimum bill provision might state that the customer's bill in any month shall not be less than the highest monthly bill rendered to the customer in the preceding 11 months. This perpetuates for a year the revenue stream associated with a high usage month. The obvious objections to this type (conducive to waste of energy, unacceptable to the customer, etc.) preclude its use except for narrow specialized purposes such as standby (service taken only when the main energy source fails), warehouse heating to prevent freezing (taken only when the temperature drops below 0°C), and the like. Its use may be justifiable when the revenue prospect is erratic, and unlikely to be sufficient to support the utility's investment if confined to billing for actual usage over a short span. A specific minimum tailored to the investment related to the service, and applicable every month, probably is preferable.

The second method, however, is common. Here the ratchet is applied only to the demand charge of a multi-part rate, rather than to the total bill. In that event, the rate may provide, for example, that "the demand charge for any month shall be 75 cents per kilowatt of the maximum demand established during the year ending on the last day of the current month." This is a 12 months' ratchet, for it establishes demand charges based not on the highest demand established during the month but on the highest demand occurring in the entire year. The *period* of the ratchet may vary greatly. Some extend only over a season: others may extend over more than a year.

The *extent* of the ratchet also may vary. The examples cited illustrate a 100% ratchet. In the latter example the demand charge was computed on the basis of the full amount of the highest demand during the year. An alternative applying a lesser ratchet would be to provide that "the demand charge for any month shall be 75 cents per kilowatt of the maximum demand established during the month, but not less than 80 percent of the highest demand established during the preceding eleven months." This, of course, is an 80% ratchet. In practice, ratchets ordinarily will vary from 50 to 100%.

A more complicated version is a ratchet provision which includes more than one period and more than one percentage. For example, "the demand charge for any month shall be the higher of (a) 75 cents per kilowatt of the maximum demand established during the year ending on the last day of the current month (which is a twelve month, 100 percent ratchet); or (b) 80 percent of the highest demand charge billed during the five-year period ending on the last day of the current month" (which is a 60-month, 80% ratchet). Another complicated version might apply the ratchet only to peak season months.

Essentially, the ratchet is a means of assuring that the utility will receive a minimum amount of revenue over some predetermined period based on the highest demand or use (or a given fraction of that demand or use) which occurs during the period.[2] Because of its complexity the ratchet is found normally only in wholesale rates, particularly industrial, but to a lesser extent commercial, rates. The ratchet is probably a more equitable and realistic method of accessing demand costs than when the demand charge is based only on the current month's maximum use, for it recognizes that the provision of capacity represents a long-term investment. It is also a workable method by which the utility may hedge against large fluctuations in use, or reduction of load due to a business recession.[3] It is not possible to set forth any generally applicable principles as to the period or extent of the ratchet—these will vary with each case. The determination of the ratchet is a problem of balancing the ratchet against the rate level. The same total revenue which the utility should receive under the rate schedule can be obtained, of course, by establishing a higher rate for current usage coupled with a lower ratchet, or vise versa. This decision is one of the more difficult problems in rate making.

9.1.3 Adjustment Clauses

Sometimes included in the rate structure are so-called *clauses* or *riders* which operate under certain circumstances to modify or change the prices prescribed in the rate. Most common is the "fuel" clause, an escalator-type provision which causes

---

[2]For an interesting analyses, see Randazzo, Samuel C., "Ratchets and Electric Rates," *Public Utilities Fortnightly*, April 26, 1984.

[3]One writer observes that the ratchet also provides a "price signal" to consumers. Ferguson, John S., "A Function of the Ratchet Provision in Electric Rates," *Public Utilities Fortnightly*, July 5, 1984.

the established prices to vary with the changes in the price of fuel to the electric utility or the price of purchased gas to the gas utility. This serves to protect the utility against rising fuel costs and, on the other hand, to insure a reduction of rates if fuel or purchased gas prices decline. Less frequently, rates may be tied to some standard cost index, with provision for variation in rates as the index fluctuates. Obviously in such cases the index made applicable must be chosen with great care. Special-purpose clauses, adding or subtracting a specified increment to the basic charges, are also found, as are clauses and riders of a variety of other types. The use of adjustment clauses proliferated in the energy crisis years.

9.1.4 Penalties and Discounts

Occasionally, *penalties* and *discounts* of various sorts are also found in utility rates. The penalties most common in prior years are those for late payment of bills (which are essentially the same as discounts for prompt payment)[4] or for some characteristic of use which is particularly onerous to the utility. An example of the latter is the "power factor" penalty (or discount) in some wholesale electric rates which calls for an added charge if the customer's power factor falls below certain standards (or a reduction in the bill if the standard is exceeded). In addition to prompt payment discounts, discounts may be given on occasion for quantity use but this would be rare in a modern rate. Such a discount might call for a 10% reduction in the customer's bill for use in excess of some set amount, for example. This type of discount is to be distinguished from the implicit quantity discount which is a usual result of the blocking principle discussed below.

Promotional-type discounts also may be given for commercial and industrial electric service. Examples are load factor and primary service discounts, both of which are cost related. The load factor discount may provide, for example, "for monthly use in excess of 540 times the measured demand,[5] a discount of __ percent from the energy charge otherwise applicable will be given." The discounted price applicable to the excess usage could approach the incremental cost-of-service.

Primary service discounts are given when customers take service at primary or high voltage. The customer furnishes the step-down transformer if needed. With a provision of this type a separate rate schedule for primary service is not needed. Both types of discount are promotional, for they provide a rationale for low average prices to larger customers. Although the example of load factor and primary service discounts cited above refer to the electric utility, their application to gas can be easily visualized.

---

[4]The trend has been toward discontinuance of penalties for delinquent payment of bills. Current emphasis upon cost-based pricing could resurrect the practice.

[5]Since there are 720 hour in a 30-day month, 540 hour of use of the demand would represent a 75% monthly load factor.

9.1.5 "Frozen" Rates

A convenient way to make a transition away from an obsolete schedule without the discomfort of transferring existing customers to a new schedule which might be disadvantageous to them, its to maintain the old rate in the tariff but to limit its availability to only those customers currently being served. The old rate is "frozen." Existing customers are grandfathered in, but no new customers can elect to be served under it. Thus, existing customers need not be transferred to their detriment, yet the obsolete schedule will be phased-out over time as existing customers are terminated or transferred to a new schedule with their permission.

9.1.6 Caps and Floors

Tariff restructuring—as, for example, when a change from average cost pricing to marginal cost pricing in mandated by regulatory authority—may lead to drastic increases in price for some classes of customers or for individual customers. (The dreaded Rate Shock.) To minimize the sudden impact, rate increases may be "capped" at some predetermined percentage amount. (A "cap" may also be described as a "rate limiter.")

In moving to marginal cost rate-making, the California PUC stated[6]

> .... The Commission has found it necessary to balance its goal of achieving marginal cost ratemaking against the potentially negative impact on certain customer groups that can occur with restructuring of revenue responsibilities. The use of caps which limit the amount by which the class average rate can increase is the standard technique for mitigating harsh bill impacts on customers. Caps are typically defined as the total of the system average percentage change (SAPC) plus a given percentage.

> We affirm our policy that the use of caps to mitigate rate increases can be appropriate in [marginal cost] revenue allocations.

> .... The selection of a cap requires a balancing of competing objectives, and the choice is ultimately one of judgment as to what is the maximum reasonable increase that can be imposed on a customer group. Thus, for example, while achievement of a full ... allocation ... is a reasonable target, we do not consider it an inflexible goal that must be achieved regardless of present or future circumstances. Doing so could require that we suspend judgment on reasonableness in favor of a formulaic approach.

In the proceeding from which the above quotations are taken, the respondent company, Southern California Edison Company, proposed that there be a "floor" to price decreases to match the cap on price increases. The Commission rejected the Edison floor proposal, saying

> Edison proposes that ... decreases for any class be made subject to a floor of 5%. Edison proposes a floor in order to avoid large changes in annual customer bills and to prevent the possibility of widely fluctuating allocations from one proceeding to the next. Edison believes that application of a floor in this proceeding will reduce the likelihood that a large

---

[6]California PUC, Decision 92-06-020, June 3, 1992; Caps and Floors.

increase will be required in the future for any floored group. Edison further believes that floors are equitable because customers protected from increases by caps should be limited in the decreases they receive.

.... A strong likelihood of large future increases for groups receiving large decreases now might justify a floor, but no such likelihood has been shown to exist at this time ... we will not adopt a floor.

9.2 The "Blocking" Principle

Electric and gas rates commonly are "blocked," i.e., charges are established which vary as the quantity of service taken increases. When the pricing is downward, as in the example below, the rate is promotional and suited to conditions of decreasing costs; when the pricing is upward (inverted),[7] the rate effect is to discourage higher usage by customers, accommodating an increasing cost situation. A block-type rate form typically might be as follows:

> First 40 units used during the month @ 10¢ per unit
> Next 60 units used during the month @ 8¢ per unit
> Next 100 units used during the month @ 6¢ per unit
> Over 200 units used during the month @ 5¢ per unit

IF the rate designer wished to incorporate a minimum of $4.00 into the blocking, the initial step of the above example could be stated as, "first 40 units, or less, used during the month, $4.00." This produces the same 10 cents per unit if all 40 units are taken, but yields $4.00 regardless of a smaller usage. If the designer was an extremely cautious individual, and worried about customer misunderstanding, the rate schedule might in addition include the statement: "Minimum monthly bill, $4.00."

The downward sloping blocking form has a number of significant advantages. (1) It allows a quantity discount, and is therefore consistent with the economic principle of diminishing utility as well as ordinary commercial practice. Because of this consistency it has a high degree of customer acceptance. (2) The form permits the establishment of a series of prices which fit the typical decreasing cost conditions of the electric and gas utility industries. For example, the higher price associated with the first block can be set so as to cover a major portion or all of customer costs, and a part at least of demand costs, plus the commodity costs associated with the number of units in the block. As usage of the customer increases into the next block or two, customer costs will have been completely covered and a higher proportion of demand costs as well. The remaining demand costs should be recovered in the next blocks,

---

[7]When the term "blocking" is used without a qualifier, it is used to indicate descending prices; "inverted blocking" means ascending prices.

until the price set for the final block can be as low as need be to cover only commodity costs plus a modest overage. It is, of course, true that the usage of a given customer may not be sufficient to reach the point where all customer and demand costs are covered. Conversely, the usage of a different customer may be more than enough. The two customers balance out. If a minimum charge is combined with the use of a block rate, the cost-coverage protection is increased. (3) The form permits a high degree of flexibility, as the size of blocks (i.e., the number of units at each price) can be tailored to suit closely the several requirements and objectives of cost recovery.

The concept described above of tailoring the steps of a blocked rate so as to recover customer and demand costs in a systematic step-by-step fashion (plus commodity costs in all steps, of course) is highly theoretical. It is doubtful that the several types of costs can be ascertained and embedded in the steps with the precision which the concept implies. It is also doubtful that the rate levels (prices) of the early steps can be set high enough to recover all customer and essentially all demand costs in these steps—the prices are likely to appear too high in the regulatory and public eye—while the price in the final step may seem to be too low.

The concept that the blocked rate is strictly cost-based is highly theoretical (even misleading) for a more important reason, particularly for residential rates. For example, in a residential electric rate the blocking may be designed with specific types of household use in mind rather than cost steps. Assuming that lighting and minor appliances require about 100 kWh per month, the number of units in the first block may be set at 100. The next block may vary in size from 100 to 200 kWh to cover consumption for a range and refrigerator; and perhaps a further block of 300 to 500 kWh may be added to encompass water heater consumption, a dish washer, clothes washer, drier, etc. To this point, we have assumed that all household uses except space heating have been rolled into the blocking. The seasonal space heating load presents a problem of entirely different magnitude than the superimposition, one upon the other, of the prior household uses. This load increases substantially the amount of capacity which *must be* provided by the utility and consequently its demand costs, while at the same time dampening load factor. If space heating is to be permitted under the rate, either higher demand costs must be inserted into the prices of the prior blocks, forcing all customers to share the space heating burden imposed by a few, or the downward array of prices must be reversed. Assuming the latter, the final block price can be set higher than the prices of the preceding blocks, so as to be sufficient to cover incremental demand costs as well as commodity costs (a "fish-hook" or inverted block). Combination conventional and inverted blocking of this type serves in a single rate the same purpose as separate rates for lighting and minor appliances, refrigerators and ranges, water heaters with related appliances, plus space heating, and recognizes value elements about as well as do separate rates. Thus, the blocking form is suitable for an "all purpose" residential single-part rate.

"Fish-hook" blocking was proposed with a different rationale in 1972. Robert Smith[8] predicted, ".... Additional use of utility service, whether made possible by

---

[8]Smith, Robert, "Rates and Rate Structures in a Changing World," *Public Utilities Fortnightly*, Nov. 23, 1972.

9.2 The "Blocking" Principle

purchase of energy or additional generating plants for electric supply, is going to be at a unit cost which is greater than the means of supplying the old demand." To fit such a situation of increasing supply costs, he proposed that the final, high use block be priced substantially higher than the earlier blocks.

> ".... This type of rate structure," he argued, "has the merit of permitting growth at a rate which is controlled by the desire of consumers to purchase additional utility service at its reasonable true cost and it removes the false growth incentive, and resultant wastage, which results from present sales of increasing quantities at reducing unit prices."

Smith submitted the following rate prototype (Table 9.1):

Table 9.1 Illustration of fish-hook blocking

KWh used *per month*	Price per kWh	
0–50	$4.50 (minimum bill)	(Basically to cover fixed costs)
Next 50	8¢	
Next 100	5¢	
Next 100	2¢	(Basically to cover variable costs)
Next 500	1¢	
Over 800	6¢	(To cover long-run incremental costs of additional facilities)

Inverted blocking may be adopted to reflect specific governmental objectives. The modern lifeline or baseline rate form, for example, combines a welfare objective of making energy available at the cheapest price for essential purposes, with the conservation objective of penalizing usage in excess of the essential by progressively higher prices. Luxury or extravagant consumption must pay more per unit.

With specific respect to electric conservation, as far back as 1952, a British writer, commenting on the desirability of penalizing the use of electricity for space heating and reserving "electricity for the purposes it serves incomparably well – lighting and certain forms of industrial power" states, "One suggestion – put forward as a shock treatment for the consumer – would be to turn the BEA (British Electricity Authority) 'variable block' tariff upside down. The domestic consumer would receive enough electricity to cover lighting and other essential uses at a moderate rate; further units would become progressively more expensive."[9] Was the writer clairvoyant? Did he foresee the electric auto?

Other writers have opposed any trend toward inverted blocking. For example, R.W. Carpenter in 1973[10] observed that the price inversion idea "... .will not die gracefully because it has caught the fancy of .... the environmentalists, the economists, and the sociologists ...." Environmentalists assume that "big is bad;" economists, that higher pricing will stifle demand which is in part elastic; and sociologists, that there is "a social obligation to overcharge the large user, enabling the smallest users to be further subsidized." He adds that sociologists "ask the industry

---

[9]"The Price of Electricity – II: Promoting the Peak?" *The Economist*, June 21, 1952, p. 837.

[10]Carpenter, R.W., "Rate Regulation and Pricing of Utility Service," *Public Utilities Fortnightly*, March 15, 1973.

to play Robin Hood so that a part of the true cost of social welfare will appear in the large user's [utility] bill rather than in his tax bill."

All three groups, he says, disparage blocked rates as "quantity discounts," "volume discounts," or "promotional discounts," disregarding the fact that the blocked price differentials "are simply recognition" of costs.

The block form may be, and is, also used for one or both of the separate elements of a two-part rate. It is not uncommon to have both demand and commodity charges blocked in a two-part rate. This practice represents a modified application of the theories described above.

9.3 "Postage Stamp" vs. Zone Rates

The "applicability" and "availability" of a rate involve two questions. The first, what types of customers or uses may take service under the rate, is a function of the classification of customers and services (the rate classes). The second relates to the *area* within which service may be taken under the rate. This presents the issue as to whether postage-stamp or zone rates will be established by the utility.

The term "postage stamp" rate is taken from the postage-stamp principle of the postal service under which a letter may be mailed anywhere in the United States for the same price, i.e., service at the same price regardless of distance. In utility rates this means an identical rate over a prescribe area, usually the entire area served by the utility, regardless of the section of the territory in which the customer is located.

Zone rates contrast sharply with postage-stamp rates. Under zone rates the area served by the utility is broken down into different zones and different rate levels prevail in the different zones. Zoning generally is justified on a cost basis. The general theory, for example, is that cities may merit a lower rate because the more concentrated urban load is more economical to serve, while a more sparsely settled area where costs are higher warrants a higher rate. But zoning in precise theory involves much more than the differences in customer density in urban and rural areas. *Zoning is an application of differential pricing based on differences in costs of service to the same type of customer or use due to differences in location.*

In addition to variations in customer density, there are variances in distances of the customer from sources of supply in the electric and gas utilities (particularly the gas pipeline), in the distance between the calling and called parties in the telephone industry, and the length of the passenger ride in urban traction. A strict application of the zoning principle would establish different rates applicable to each distinguishable segment of the above-mentioned situations. Zoning also may be approached from the value viewpoint, in which case zones would reflect value differences. However, courts have rejected zoning if it is not based on the primary cost factor of distance from the starting point.[11] Many times both cost and value considerations point in the same direction. This is generally true of telephone zoning.

---

[11] Public Service Company of North Carolina vs. Federal Energy Regulatory Commission, 852 F. 2d 1548 (5th Cir. 1988).

9.3 "Postage Stamp" vs. Zone Rates

The choice between postage-stamp and zone rates involves public policy as well as cost and value considerations. At the local level, is it socially desirable to give the farmer utility service at the same rate as the city dweller, even though the cost of serving the farmer is higher? Perennial controversies have raged on this point. It is often argued, for example, that a city benefits from the trade brought to it by the farmers in surrounding areas, and, consequently, that urban users should bear a part of the added cost of farm utility service.

At the regional and interregional level, such as for gas pipelines and electric grids, the issue devolves into the settling of zone boundaries—a highly judgmental matter since so many elements must be balanced: political boundaries, terrain differences, population centers, lengths of haul, to name just a few.

The postage-stamp vs. zone question is as significant in the case of federally owned power systems as it is for investor-owned utilities, due to the social aims inherent in the legislation authorizing such systems. As an illustration, the act establishing the Bonneville Power Administration stipulates that the Administration's rate schedules "may provide for uniform rates or rates uniform throughout prescribed transmission areas *in order to extend the benefits of an integrated transmission system* and encourage the equitable distribution of the electric energy developed at the Bonneville project" (emphasis supplied).[12] The act also provides that the Bonneville Power Administration should encourage use over the widest possible area and at the lowest possible price. The Administration holds that its postage-stamp rates accomplished these purposes better than would zone rates[13] and this conclusion seems sound.

Obviously, the distinction between postage-stamp and zone rates is a matter of degree. Even under the zone principle a fairly large area—a whole state or region, perhaps—may be served under a uniform rate. It is impracticable to have zones which are too small.

One theoretical disadvantage of zone systems is the requirement that the zones must be changed fairly frequently if they are accurately to reflect cost differences, as customer densities and distance factors are often in flux even on a relative basis. Another disadvantage is the multiplicity of rates which occurs when the zone principle is carried too far. Any increase in the complexity of a utility's overall rate structure means added billing and public relations problems to the utility.

A number of utilities have had in effect for many years a workable middle ground between postage-stamp and zone rates. This is to establish a uniform blocking

---

[12] Bonneville Project Act (Act approved August 20, 1937, Ch. 720, 50 stat. 731) as amended, Sect. 6.

[13] It is also held that the postage stamp rates of the Administration encouraged the early decentralization of industry in the Pacific Northwest—an important national defense consideration—as they made electric energy available to new industry in the World War II era (particularly aluminum) at the same price regardless of where the new plant might be located. Thus, it was not necessary for new industry to locate close to generation or in a heavily populated area in order to secure low rates.

schedule having system wide applicability, but to vary the prices for the several blocks in accordance with a zoning classification. This is illustrated in Table 9.2.

Table 9.2 Domestic rates of pacific gas and electric company, vintage 1950

Zone:	1	2	3	4	5	6
Service charge ($)	0.40	0.50	0.50	0.50	0.50	0.50
First 40 KWh	2.9	2.9	3.2	3.5	3.7	4.4
Next 60 KWh	2.1	2.2	2.3	2.4	2.5	3.0
Next 100 KWh	1.7	1.8	1.9	2.0	2.0	2.3
Excess KWh	1.0	1.0	1.0	1.0	1.0	(1.1)(0.9)

Source: Reproduced from *Land Economics,* Vol. XXVI, No. 4, November 1950, p. 333.

In 1950, the Pacific Gas and Electric Company had established six zones for residential service, as the table shows. Zones 1, 2, 3, and 4 applied to incorporated areas having different populations, while zones 5 and 6 applied to surrounding unincorporated areas. This geographical method of zoning may be somewhat arbitrary from an economic standpoint, as one writer has pointed out, for if an unincorporated area is annexed to the city, customers formerly charged under rates for zone 5 or 6 automatically are shifted over to rates for zones 1, 2, 3, or 4 although the costs of serving them remain as before.[14] However, though admittedly political boundaries may be somewhat less than perfect from a theoretical standpoint, they nevertheless represent what is probably the best practical solution. In closing, note that the classifications illustrated by the Pacific Gas and Electric Company example achieved uniformity in rate *form* but not in rate *level*. PG&E's rates now incorporate new concepts and designs, but the zoning technique is still followed.

9.4 All-Purpose vs. Special-Purpose Rates: Unbundling

The next basic decision to be made in rate development has to do with whether to establish all-purpose or special-purpose rates as a general pattern.

To illustrate the alternatives involved in this decision it is convenient to couch the matter in terms of an example. Residential electric or gas rates provide such an example. In both cases, service may be rendered to the electric or gas residential customer under a single rate if the utility so elects, or under a number of different rates, perhaps one for general use, with separate rates for air conditioning or space heating, etc. The advantages of a single rate, as previously mentioned, are simplicity and the likelihood of customer acceptance, while different rates permit a higher degree of differential pricing from both the cost and value viewpoints. Different

---

[14]Kennedy, Wm. F., "Territorial Aspects of Electric Rate Making by the Public Utilities Commission of California," *Land Economics*, vol. XXVI, No. 4, Nov. 1950, p. 331.

9.4 All-Purpose vs. Special-Purpose Rates: Unbundling

rates for the same customer, however, require more equipment (such as meters, etc.) and more time for meter reading and bill computations, and thus increase costs.

The problem is more than an aspect of the larger problem of determining rate classes; it is a fundamental issue involved in rate classifications. Of course, no completely consistent decision covering the utility's entire rate structure is to be expected. Rather, the several rate classifications of the utility will *tend* one way or the other. Recent practice seems to favor all-purpose rates.

The foregoing three paragraphs could have been written 50 years ago. The issue there discussed is not new, and is the same today as then for energy distributors. But now the issue has much larger dimensions.

The past two decades has seen the emergence of a new rate issue, "unbundling" and a new revenue-loss danger, "bypass."

Unbundling means the breaking down of formerly combined functions which had been offered at a combined price, into separate functions, each with a separate price. The purpose is to permit buyers to select the individual function or mix of functions which they prefer, so that they need not purchase a complete packaged service or none. In the future, hopefully the unbundling trend may lead to new imaginative offerings beyond the mundane division of the present functions—production, transmission, distribution.

Bypass is the utility's loss of patronage from existing or prospective customers, as these customers elect to substitute a competing entity, or to provide their own facilities, in lieu of using the utility's service.

Telecommunications led the way. As competition in long-distance telephone became possible,[15] the bell system's monopoly was lost. In the initial instances, large companies having extensive communication requirements between cities—the Chicago to St. Louis route was the first instance—could bypass the Bell transmission network by shifting their intercity traffic to a competing transmission entity at a lower price, using pre-existing local facilities only from the telephone of entry or completion of the call to the transmission switch at either end. So Bell was forced to offer a separate rate just for transmission, divorced from its traditional complete phone-to-phone service. The separate transmission rate was "unbundled" from the prior "bundled" through rate. The unbundling has now progressed to cover almost every distinguishable phase of both long-distance and local carrier operations, except for local service for small subscribers.

For different reasons, pipelines followed telecommunications down the same rate design path. Starting with FERC Order No.436 of 1985 and culminating with Order No.636 of 1992, the role of the pipeline was changed from that of a "merchant" who delivered gas to the city gate of the distributor at a bundled price which rolled-in the functions of purchasing gas, maintaining a gas inventory, storage, and transmission,

---

[15] The real beginning may be the inauguration by MCI of competitive long distance service between St. Louis and Chicago in 1969. However, it is convenient to accept the date of the Bell System breakup in 1984 as the climactic dividing line.

to that of a long-distance hauler only, at an unbundled transmission-only price.[16] Pipelines also may offer storage service, but must do so under a separate rate.

The electric industry is headed in a similar direction, due to restructuring with regulatory encouragement of independent power producers (IPP's) and the treat of bypass.

The rate maker in both of the energy sectors now must mull the question of into what separate segments should formerly combined services be divided? Requiring greater ingenuity, can entirely new services be crafted out of the available physical facilities?

9.5 Seasonal vs. Year-Round Rates

Since utility loads fluctuate seasonally, the rate maker has the choice between a year-round rate which reflects an annual average cost-of-service, or one in which the price level and perhaps the rate form changes with the season. Peak season prices would reflect the higher demand cost of peak operation, while off-peak season prices would be lower. The rate form could be the same, with only the level changing, but the form also could be different. For example, a two- or three-part rate with no blocking (or even inverse blocking) might be appropriate for the peak season, while a single-part blocked rate could be selected to promote usage in "valley" months and to be consistent with the lower demand cost of these months. In this example, the two rate designs would have to be carefully matched to minimize rate shock as the transition was made from the cheap off-peak to the more expensive on-peak rates. (Of course, rate variations could be made quarterly or even daily rather than annually, following the same approach.)

Seasonally differentiated rates are a precursor of modern time-of-day (or real-time pricing) rates. These modern rates are nothing more than an extreme refinement of the older (but still popular) seasonal rates.

9.6 Rolled-in vs. Incremental Pricing/Old Customer vs. New Customer Rates

We link the above two issues because the considerations impacting them are essentially the same. The issues arise because energy supplies and system capacities must be increased to meet growing demands (plus, in the case of gas, to replace depleted fields and, for electricity, to substitute new generating capacity for retired or ageing plants). In many cases, the required additions cost more per unit than those of the existing system.

---

[16]Pipelines are permitted to purchase gas for transportation customers if the customer so chooses, but such purchases must be handled under a rate separate from the transportation rate.

9.6 Rolled-in vs. Incremental Pricing/Old Customer vs. New Customer Rates 255

Should existing costs be kept isolated as the basis for a lower-rate plateau, with the higher cost of new supply or capacity additions being supported by a higher-price plateau, thus treating the new additions incrementally; *or* should both existing and new costs be combined as the function for a single system-wide intermediate rate level, rolling-in the new cost with the old? That is the question. Stating the same question in a different way, should all customers pay rates based upon a single company-wide cost-of-service combining old and new costs *or* should customers be grouped into two (or more) categories paying at different rate levels depending upon the apportionment of the total system costs into two (or more) components, old and new?

When we speak of rate levels being the same (reflecting rolled-in costs) or different (reflecting segregated old and new incremental costs), we assume continuation in place of the several schedules of the existing tariff. The price relationships (including customer and use classifications, zoning, and any other pricing niceties) would remain: only average price levels would be affected.

An example helps. In 1974 the writer's company, a gas distributor, was considering the importation of LNG from Kenai in Alaska. The liquefied gas would be delivered by ship into the company's system in Newport, Oregon, a coastal port. The LNG would be much more expensive than the company's current supply from its pipeline wholesaler, but a shortage from that source was foreseen.

Incremental pricing of the LNG would keep a lower rate level for gas purchased from the pipeline, but a higher-rate level would be necessary for the LNG. Rolled-in pricing would raise the rate level to some intermediate point, with all customers served from the same tariff.

The writer testified as follows in the Kenai Proceeding

> Alternate means are available for the pricing of the Kenai LNG gas. One is to consider the LNG supply to be separate and apart from other inputs of gas into the system, establishing a separate set of price schedules for it, a method which often is referred to as "incremental" pricing. The other method integrates the LNG supply with the Company's other gas sources so that the entirety of the Company's gas stream is composited and sold under a single set of price schedules, in the same fashion as is currently done. This method is referred to as "rolled-in" pricing.
>
> The Company strongly recommends against separate or incremental pricing for a number of reasons. First, this kind of pricing would present in practice an administrative monstrosity of nightmarish proportions. Second, it would be difficult if not impossible equitably to determine separate rates for the LNG on the one hand and for the remainder of the Company's supply on the other. Finally, if priced separately, the LNG might be noncompetitive under certain conditions... If the LNG supply is to be sold separately from the Company's other supply, how is the separation to be made? ... The assumption could be made that this gas would be earmarked to serve demands closest to the point of entry, fanning outward until the volumes available equaled the volumes needed by customers .... The remainder of the Company's system would be assumed to be supplied from other gas sources and charged accordingly. On this basis, there would be marked disparity in rates between the "Kenai gas service area" and other parts of the system, for all classes of customers, creating a second class ratepayer group around the port of entry. Even assuming the first and second class ratepayer groupings created by this segregation-by –geography to be o.k.—a very dubious assumption,—how are the two areas to be defined? For example, if the hypothetical LNG area actually was intended to encompass with precision those customers whose demands

equated to the LNG volumes, the area would be constantly expanding and contracting like a bellows as the seasons came and went, because individual customer requirements ebb and flow with the seasons. With a marketed difference in rates at stake, who is to make the decision as to where the boundary would lie?

A different approach to incremental pricing would disregard segregation-by-geography and substitute instead segregation-by-type-of-customer. *Customers could be segregated by vintage, such as old and new*; by size range, such as large or small; or by conventional classifications, such as residential, commercial, industrial and interruptible. Whatever the method, the problems remain: how are the segregation guidelines to be drawn? and when drawn, how are they to be administered? This is the nightmare of segregation-by-type-of-customer-

The difficulty of establishing equitable rates under separate pricing is even more formidable then the difficulty of determining how to make the segregation between geographical areas or types of customers. This difficulty of determining a proper price arises fundamentally from the changing character of the use to which the LNG actually will be put, from day-to-day and from season-to-season. On a peak winter day, 56.7% of the Company's supply is taken by residential customers, another 21.3% by small commercial customers, and the remaining 22% by other firm customers. No interruptible customers are served. Based upon this situation and applying commonly accepted allocation principles, all fixed or non-variable costs of LNG would be apportioned among the customer classes being served in relation to the percentages cited. The per unit assessment of variable or commodity costs might be higher on the peak also, following the same allocation principles.

An entirely different situation prevails in July. On an average day in that month, residential customers comprise only 6.2% of the Company's demand, and small commercial customers, only 8.1%. While in a peak day these two classes pre-empted 78% of the supply, in mid-summer their share drops to 14.3%. The share of other firm customers rises to 34.5% and interruptible sales take more that half of the Company's total throughput, 51.2%. There are intermediate situations also. Which of the situations should be accepted as representative and adopted for the allocation of joint costs, or if no single one, how should the variations be combined? There are innumerable formulas for the allocation of joint costs, but all necessarily are arbitrary. When allocations are unavoidable, they must be used. But in the instant case they are avoidable, for they are not necessary under rolled-in pricing. Allocations are needed only under incremental pricing.

The final major objection to incremental pricing is the possibility that under depressed price conditions for oil, an incremental LNG price might be noncompetitive. It is easy to lose sight of this very real possibility at this time [1974], when the nation is still stunned by the astronomical upward spiraling of oil prices which took place during the last few months. Oil prices may not stay on their present high plateau. It must be recognized that they could go down rather than up in the future.

Over the long haul, the fuels market is highly price sensitive. Gas competes with oil on a price basis. Even small differences in price often are important. This is particularly true with respect to large industrial users who are consistently sensitive to inter-fuel price differences.

Arguments against the vintaging of customers, old vs. new, the second issue under this heading, are similar.[17] How are the two groups to be differentiated over an extended period?[18]

---

[17]See also, Hanke, Steve H. and Wenders, John T., "Costing and Pricing for Old and New Customers," *Public Utilities Fortnightly*, April 29, 1982.

[18]For further arguments in favor, see Davis, N. Knowels, "A Case for Rolled-in Pricing" *Public Utilities Fortnightly*, May 24, 1973.

The argument in favor of incremental pricing (and for the vintaging of customers) seems to rest on the desirability of sending an unmistakable "price signal" that it will be costly to meet growing energy demands by increasing utility capacity. The highest legal price is the price of the new supply. From this it follows that incremental pricing should be adopted and conservation measures pushed. Such measures, it is argued, are cheaper than new conventional capacity and delay the time when additional conventional capacity must be provided. Conservationist and others in favor of incremental pricing feel that rolled-in pricing will dampen the impact of the "price signal".

9.7 Rate-Level Changes Across-the-Board

When a utility company receives regulatory approval to institute a change in rate level, either upward or downward, with the caveat that it be put into effect "across-the-board," i.e., applied equally to all rates, there is a choice of methods. The change can be achieved either by increasing (or decreasing) all prices by an equal amount per unit (per therm or kWh) or by an equal percentage. However, the two may not be equal in their impact.

Assume that additional revenue of ½ cent per unit, or 8% is to be gained. Take a residential customer and an existing rate (the rate given earlier as our first example of blocking), as given in Table 9.3.

Table 9.3 Base blocked rate-light consumption

Present rate	
First 40 units @	10¢ per unit
Next 60 units @	8¢ per unit
Next 100 units @	6¢ per unit
Over 200 units @	5¢ per unit

Let us further assume that the average monthly use under the rate is 400 units. The customer's bill at present prices is $24.80. On either basis, each block price being increased by ½ cent or by 8%, that bill would rise to about $26.80. Except for rounding, the two methods produce exactly the same results. The new rates which yield these results are given in Table 9.4:

Table 9.4 Base rate increased by alternative methods–light consumption

Price per unit	Equal *per-unit* increase	Equal *percentage* increase
First 40 units	10.5¢	10.8¢
Next 60 units	8.5¢	8.6¢
Next 100 units	6.5¢	6.5¢
Over 200 units	5.5¢	5.4¢

The rate is balanced at the average monthly use of 400 units.

At one-half of the volume, 200 units, the monthly bills are $15.80 on the per-unit approach basis and $15.98 on the percentage approach—not exactly the same but close enough.

At double the volume, 800 units, the bills are $48.80, per-unit basis, and $48.38, percentage basis—still close enough.

From the above, it might seem that the choice is moot. It is, for the residential schedule adopted for illustration. But . . . .

Let us now continue the same comparison of a ½ cent per unit vs. an 8% increase, but shift to a wholesale rate for a large dual-fuel industrial plant using 100,000 units per month. Duel-fuel means that the customer has the alternative of shifting away from the utility to another fuel. Given in Table 9.5 are a large volume industrial base rate and increased rates on the two bases.

Table 9.5 Industrial rate increased by alternative methods–high consumption

Price per unit	Base	Equal per-unit *increase*	Equal percentage *increase*
First 10,000 units	5¢	5.50¢	5.4¢
Next 10,000 units	4¢	4.50¢	4.32¢
Excess	3¢	3.50¢	3.24¢
Total monthly bill	$3,300	$3,800	$3,564
Increase in percent		15%	8%

With cheap competitive energy available, an 8% increase per the percentage increase method might still be tolerable, but a 15% increase—almost double—brought about by the per-unit method might likely be the straw that broke the camel's back. The customer might be lost.

On the other hand, if utility energy such as gas is priced at the time at a substantial discount relative to oil, the chance to adjust rates upward on an across-the-board per-unit basis might be a godsend to the utility. Industrials find it difficult to launch a hue-and-cry in protest when they are being treated exactly as everyone else.

Another difference in results between the two methods is easy to overlook. The percentage method preserves the current price relationships between schedules and customer classes. The per-unit method will alter these relationships.

To test this in a cursory fashion, we can compare the relationship of average prices under the residential and large volume base rates with the relationship of average prices under the increased rates per the two alternative methods, at the same volumes of 400 and 100,000, respectively (Table 9.6).

Table 9.6 Relationship of class rates before and after rate increase

	Average prices per unit		Ratio: Industrial *to residential*
	Residential	*Industrial*	
Base rates	6.2¢	3.3¢	53%
% increase	6.7¢	3.56¢	53%
Cent/therm increase	6.7¢	3.8¢	57%

The base rate relationship is that the industrial price is 53% of the residential price. When rates are increased by the uniform percentage approach, the relationship remains the same. The equal cents per unit changes it to 57%—industrial moves a bit closer to residential. Continued use of the per unit method over several rate increases will result in prices which are far out of line with the original. This may be good or bad in any specific instance. The above is only to say that the choice of method is not an indifferent one although both methods can be taken to apply the rate change across-the-board. The impact of each method on all classes of customers must be considered before a decision is made, particularly with respect to those customer classes which are vulnerable to loss. Although our examples represent rate increases, these cautionary words apply equally to rate decreases.

It should be mentioned that sometimes the across-the-board concept is diluted, although still being guised as "across-the-board." For example, a per-unit approach may be adopted for residential and commercial customers, but a percentage approach applied to industrial.

9.8 The "Fine-Print" Provisions

A number of highly important terms and conditions, as well as certain more or less routine matters, are found in the non-price provisions which are an integral part of the rate schedule. The most common of these are mentioned below.

The *designation* of the rate: Ordinarily utility rates for convenience in reference will be given some short form designator, such as a letter of the alphabet, a numeral, or a combination of both.

The *effective date*: A formal part of most rate schedules is the date on which the schedule will be or has become effective.

The *availability* of the rate: One of the more important rate provisions is that which defines the geographical area or areas in which the rate is made available. Such area(s) may be a single town, a group of towns, designated rural territories, etc., or the utilities entire system.

The *applicability* of the rate: The applicability provision sets forth in precise detail the class of customer or use to which the rate applies. The applicability provisions ordinarily are the only formal definitions published by the utility of its rate classifications. Clear and unambiguous wording of these provisions is thus highly important, both to the utility and its customers.

Character of service: Many rates contain a provision which specifies the standards and characteristics of service provided. Thus, heat (Btu) content per cubic foot might be specified in a gas rate, type of current (AC or DC), voltage, or phase in an electric rate. If the service is interruptible, or of a priority lower than that of another service, this also should be specified.

Period of contract: Schedules which require a more than usual investment on the part of the utility, such as those for large commercial and industrial users, often specify a minimum period over which the customer must agree by contract to take service. This period may be 1 year or more. A specified minimum period assures the utility of at least some reasonable use of the facilities provided to serve the customer.

In addition to the above, the rate schedule will specify any special charges, discounts, or adjustment clauses which are included in the rate. General provisions which apply to more than one rate schedule—such as meter accuracy standards, deposit requirements, bill payment regulations, etc.,—to avoid repetition in each rate schedule are often separately published in *"general rate schedule provisions."*

9.9 Nota Bene

The careful (and skeptical) reader would have noticed that this and the preceding chapter contain quotations and other references which go back many years. This is intentional. When the writer had the choice between two equally appropriate sources, one old vs. one recent, he chooses the old. The reason is to make the point that many of the "new, emerging" issues of today are retreads in another guise of the old issues of yesterday.

Utility history is far from empty of costly mistakes. The writer is old enough to have a personal memory of the endless pages of transcript devoted to the fruitless argument as to whether "reproduction cost" should be a basis for a utility's cost-of-service. One wonders if the more recent quagmire of calculating marginal costs in the name of economic efficiency has been of the same genre. The writer also recalls joining in the prediction that nuclear power would be too cheap to meter. One wonders today if conservation and demand side management will suffice to satisfy the nation's future need for power in bulk quantities.

Utility history also has its victories. Many principles and practices have withstood the test of time—so far. This book attempts to recapitulate the principles of costing and pricing which have survived, but in the context of evolving public policy and new technology. We do not ignore the fact that "change is in the air." We do, however, resist the temptation to dismiss the lessons of the past as irrelevant to the future. We hope to persuade the reader to do likewise.

Chapter 10
Traditional Types of Rate Forms

Abstract Chapter 10 covers the types of rate forms for the energy industries which have been developed and tested throughout the past century and which are widely used today. Distinctions are made as to whether the rate incorporates only a single price (a single-part rate), or two or more prices, which in combination comprise the total charge (a two- or three-part rate). The single-part rate is the most common for a large customer group with relatively small usages per customer, such as the residential customer class. The two-part rate is almost universally applicable to customers with greater usages, where their takes can be divided, and priced separately, for total volumes taken (the commodity or energy charge) and for the highest amount required at any one time (the demand charge). By far the most popular rate form for larger electric customers is the two-part Hopkinson rate, which combines a commodity charge per kilowatt-hour for total volumes taken, with a demand charge per kilowatt for the greatest amount taken at any one time. All rate forms are discussed in Chap. 10.

10.1 Introduction

The preceding chapter touched upon some elemental considerations of the rate maker: should rates be applicable to the entire system or zoned? Should rates be designed for a narrow or broad spectrum of energy uses or functions? Should minimum charges, ratchets, adjustment clauses, or penalties or discounts be incorporated?

This chapter turns from that potpourri of choices to the most difficult single choice, the packaging of the price; the decision as to the rate form (or pattern) of pricing.

The rate forms in this chapter are traditional, in the sense that they were adopted by electric and gas utilities almost from the inception of these industries and were used almost exclusively until the early 1970s when a series of emerging events set in motion an overhaul of old tariffs. The revamping is still continuing today. While many new rate forms are now in vogue, the traditional patterns remain the foundation of modern rate designs. Without this foundation no complete understanding of current utility pricing—and the direction it may take in the future—is possible.

10.2 Rate Elements Defined Again

In our chapter on the cost approach to rates, it was brought out that the costs of the energy utilities fall into three categories, customer, demand, and energy. Rates may be stated so as to charge separately for two or three of these cost elements, rather than lumping all three together as a single element. When the elements are charged for separately, the terms used are as follows:

> *Customer charge*—a fixed amount which does not fluctuate with demand or energy consumption, designed to cover the costs of meter reading, billing, collecting (and in some cases the service drop), which do not change with variations in usage and which collectively are called customer costs. An alternative term is *service charge*. This term may be used when the costs include more than direct customer-related costs, such as, in addition, some small portion of demand costs.
> *Demand charge*—an amount which varies with the customers measured demand, in theory designed to cover the demand costs incurred in serving the customer. In practice it may cover less than full demand costs.
> *Energy/commodity charge*—an amount which varies with the customer's measured take of energy, in theory designed to cover the costs incurred in providing energy. This charge may also cover any demand costs not recouped through the demand charge. It is called an energy charge in electric rates and a commodity charge in gas rates (the latter being common when reference is made to both energies).

While the three types of charges are defined above as oriented to costs, it is important to keep in mind that as a practical matter value considerations may heavily influence the assignment of the price levels. Simply because a price is entitled "demand" or "energy" charge is no assurance that the amount is actually cost-based.

Below we will see how these separate charges may be incorporated into the form of multi-part rates.

10.3 Single-Part Rate Forms

The simplest rate form is that which is based upon only one, rather than a combination of pricing elements. In general, there are three types of single-part rates: (1) "flat" or unmetered rates, (2) metered "commodity" rates, and (3) metered "demand" rates.

10.3.1 Flat Rates

All rates which establish a set charge which does not vary with the quantity of use are called flat or unmetered rates. They are the oldest and simplest of all rate forms.

10.3 Single-Part Rate Forms

The flat rate consists of a set charge per customer per month, regardless of the kind or extent of use made of the service; an example, "$15.00 per month." A refinement might be interjected to vary the charge according to the kind of use made, with a certain flat charge levied for one purpose, such as lighting and small appliances, and a higher charge for these purposes plus water heating. A further refinement is the so-called flat demand rate. Some convenient measure of the customer's relative call upon the utility's demand is adopted as a measure for the price. The monthly rate is the appropriate multiple of the price. Found to any extent only in early electric rates, typical examples might be

$1.00 per socket (electric outlet) per month
or
$4.00 per room per month

The flat rate has been widely criticized by rate experts in the electric and gas industries, even though this rate type is still widely used in the telephone and transit industries. It is inequitable, the argument runs, being unfair to the small consumer who pays the same amount as the customer who takes large quantities of energy. It exacts no penalty for wastefulness and is therefore conductive to waste. Since the level of the flat rate of necessity must be high enough on average to cover the costs of servicing the large as well as small user, it is likely to prove excessive for the small buyer and to discourage the adoption of the service. Essentially, flat rates are condemned as being by their very nature discriminatory.

This argument is well taken in relation to a utility operation where significant differences in energy (and possibly, demand) costs exist as between users of varying quantities of the service within the applicable rate class. Stated in another way, the wasteful consumer in all cases increases the utility's commodity costs, and in some cases may increase its demand costs as well, without any change in his bill.

In contrast we note that while it is a certainty that variations in usage for every rate class trigger changes in electric and gas utility costs, variations in small user local usage may have negligible or even zero impact upon telephone utility costs. Assuming readiness-to-serve engineering of its trunk and switching capacity, one call more or less does not trigger a cost change. Even the notorious illustration of the teenager making innumerable calls of interminable length, may not increase telephone costs. Certainly, teenager habits may give rise to subscriber irritation, as "busy signals" proliferate and parents chafe, but tempers and costs are not necessarily in tandem.

The flat rate is not without some rather substantial advantages. It is simple to understand. It is inexpensive to administer. Meter installations and meter reading can be eliminated. Bill computations are cut to a minimum. These combine to represent a very considerable savings in costs. For this reason even rate experts who normally would avoid the flat rate recognize that there are some situations, as in the case of isolated resort cottages, where even an electric or gas utility properly may employ a flat rate (geared to an estimated consumption level), because it is cheaper to do so than to incur the expense of installing and reading meters.

The flat rate is promotional in the sense that once a customers decides to receive service, he is encouraged to use it as fully as he wishes. Thus, the flat rate in the telephone industry undoubtedly has done much to promote the "telephone habit," which in turn has increased the value of telephone or wireless service to the typical subscriber.

Flat rates were the earliest rate forms adopted by the electric, gas, and water industries. The added costs of meters, meter reading, and billing tended to delay the adoption of an improved rate form. At the present time, however, the bulk of these three utility services are provided under measurement or metered rates.

10.3.2 Metered Commodity Rates (Also Called Straight-Line Commodity Rates)

These are rates in which the charge varies with the amount of energy used. The earliest and crudest rate of this type is the *straight-line meter rate*, which consists of a fixed price per unit of service used per month, regardless of the number of units taken. A rate of this character might be stated as:

5 cents per kWh
or
65 cents per therm

Obviously such a rate form, though it recognizes differences in amount of use among customers, falls short of the yardstick of cost-based pricing. The most important practical objection is that the price does not take into account differences in the characteristics of use among customers. Some would view it as suitable only as a special purpose rate, such as for off-peak water heating where differences in use patterns are unimportant. The rate form neither promotes nor discourages usage; it is completely neutral in these respects. But neutrality can be carried too far.

The rate form does not distinguish between large and small users, or between users with good and poor load factors, and therefore does not recognize the important differences which are most certain to be present in the costs of service to the different user types. For this reason, the pricing associated with this form should apply only to a single customer class where usage patterns do not vary over a wide range. That is a cost conclusion. Value considerations may point otherwise, and regulators may deem neutrality to be a virtue rather than a vice.

The most usual form of the metered commodity rate is the blocked meter rate, which utilizes the "blocking" principle, discussed in the preceding chapter.[1] This

---

[1] A now outmoded rate form is the *step meter* rate, which assesses the charges for a customer's *entire* consumption in one of several steps, with the price graduated downward as the use range in each step increases. An example of this rate form is as follows:

<blockquote>
5 cents per unit used per month for consumptions of from 0 to 10 units
4 cents per unit used per month for consumptions of from 11 to 50 units
3 cents per unit used per month for consumptions in excess of 50 units
</blockquote>

10.3 Single-Part Rate Forms

is, of course, a much better rate from most viewpoints. The main objection to an energy-only block rate is that it does not expressly recognize the factor of demand. Therefore, unless any given rate of this type is applied only to a group of customers having very similar demand characteristics, the relative prices charged to the customers served under the rate will not correspond to the relative costs of serving them.

Recalling that "blocked" means progressively lower prices, while "inversely blocked" means upward pricing, the direction of the prices will determine whether the rate promotes usage or deters it. Since per-unit utility costs decline with volume in most cases, the blocked rate form comports with the trend of costs, while inverse blocking usually runs counter to costs. Inverse blocking, however, may be chosen to promote conservation or demand-side management objectives.

10.3.3 Metered Demand Rates

These are rates in which the charge varies with the customer's maximum demand. Where demand is seen to be a more important element in the utility's costs than is the quantity taken, such as in a hydro-system where energy costs are minimal, metered demand rates may permit more accurate cost of service pricing than do commodity-based rates. However, demand is more difficult to measure – or to estimate – than is consumption, and is a harder concept for the customer to grasp. For these reasons, demand-only rates ordinarily are not used for smaller consumers, particularly for consumers of the residential class.

Perhaps the most dramatic examples of the single-part metered demand rate were Bonneville Power Administration's early "kilowatt year" power rates, "A" and "C," which remained in effect until 1966. These were the same in form, but different in level. The "A" rate, which applied only for use within 15 miles of a Federal dam site, established a charge of $14.50 per kW per year; the "C" rate applied anywhere on the Administration's system, and provided for a charge of $17.50 per kW per year.

This type of rate emphasizes demand in what is probably an extreme degree. It is suited only for consumers who can take service at a very high load factor,[2] as otherwise the consumer must pay for a large number of energy units which he does not receive. To illustrate this point on the basis of the Bonneville "C" rate, a customer with a maximum annual demand of 1,000 kW would pay $17,500 for a

---

Under this rate, a buyer who consumed 50 units per month would pay $2.00 (at $0.04 per unit, because his total usage falls in the second bracket or step), while another buyer who used 51 units would be charged only $1.53, thus obtaining more units for a smaller total bill. This clearly discriminatory (and wasteful) result cannot occur, of course, under a block-type rate form.

[2] Or at least a relatively high-load factor. It is possible to adjust the level of the rate to the load factor characteristics of any given class of consumer or type of use. Nevertheless, consumers having less than the average load factor for their class would pay a markedly higher average price per unit taken than other customers.

year's service. If the customer's load factor is 100%, he would take 8,760,000 kWh, at an average price per kilowatt-hour of two mills. But if the customer's load factor is 50%, he would receive only half as many kilowatt-hours yet pay the same total bill, for an average cost per kilowatt-hour of four mills.[3]

Generally speaking, an all-demand type rate is suitable only in circumstances where it is to the utility's advantage to promote high load factor use on a widespread scale and where there are customers (such as aluminum plants) who can usefully consume the volume of energy paid for. Seldom will this be the case. Nonetheless, the rate form may fit well into certain special circumstances, such as for wholesale rates of a nuclear generating plant with extremely low variable costs and brief down time. Here demand costs would represent the great bulk of total costs.

All-demand type rates may be stated on a monthly, seasonal or yearly basis, and conceivably could include some form of blocking.

10.3.4 Single-Part Rate Forms and Rate Theory

With the possible exception of flat rates, single-part rate forms are not necessarily either more or less "scientific" than the more complex rate types to be discussed below. Even the flat rate, if tailored to meet a single specific service situation such as electric street lighting, can recover allocated costs with precision. In the instance of street lighting, for example, the size and number of lights and the hours of use can be calculated accurately prior to the setting of the rate; and the rate remains good until these factors change. How equitably single-part commodity or

---

[3] The theory underlying this rate is interesting. It was originally developed for the Bonneville Power Administration's system, now more accurately referred to as the "Federal Columbia River Power System," on the basis of the circumstances then existing. The system at the time had only one source of power, Bonneville Dam, at which only two generators with a total rating of 90,000 kW were installed. Stream flows were adequate to run these two generators 100% of the time, year after year, with water to spare. In other words, power could be generated at 100% annual load factor. The kilowatt-year rate was the proper rate under those circumstances. If the energy sold was not used at 100% load factor no saving to the supplier resulted, as the water merely was spilled over the dam rather than being used for power production

The same situation was true at Grand Coulee Dam, the second plant to come into operation, during the period when only the first 7 or 8 generators were installed at that plant. During this period, additional generator installations were completed at Bonneville. The amount of water was then sufficient to run the generators at Coulee continuously; and although Bonneville generators could not be operated continuously, they could be operated at a very high annual load factor, so the kilowatt year rate was still well adapted to the supply situation.

Now with additional generators installed at Grand Coulee, and many other run-of-the-river and storage projects completed, the situation has changed. In a critically dry water year all generators on the system cannot be operated continuously. Load factor may fall to 60%. As load factor goes down, the original reasons for the kilowatt-year rate tend to disappear. However, although the early situation changed radically, Bonneville Power Administration retained the kilowatt-year rate until 1966. Instead of changing the form of the rate the Administration adopted various devices which gave a reasonable result in the application of the rate, and also established alternative rates suitable for lower load factor use.

10.3 Single-Part Rate Forms

demand type rates will recover costs depends largely upon the relative homogeneity of the customers served under the rate and how closely the use characteristics of most of those customers resemble the norm or average about which the rate was designed. *(1) Any rate form, including single-part rates, can be made to produce equitable results if the rate classification to which it applies is tailored with sufficient rigidity (2) Most objections to single-part rates implicitly assume that the rate classifications are broad. The broader the classification the more difficult it is to achieve an acceptable cost allocation and, hence, the more important is the rate form (3) With single-part rates, even with narrow classes, it is more difficult to adapt pricing which is appropriate for the whole class than with multi-part rates.*

Non-blocked metered commodity rates deserve special attention from the theorist because they have been widely adopted for the residential customer class (either with or without a separate customer charge—in the latter case, of course, being classifiable as two-part rates, but this difference in definition is ignored for our present discussion).

It seems that the unblocked form has been chosen by most authorities because of value, not cost, considerations. Since a blocked rate with its declining unit prices is promotional, energy conservation thinking opposes it. While applying a conservation view would point to inverted blocking, no blocking, neither up nor down in unit pricing, has appeal as a middle ground. Such a middle ground becomes somewhat more plausible as more tilted to cost, if a separate customer charge is added.

Costing for the unblocked commodity rate is simple. Total demand and energy costs for the rate class are added together and apportioned pro-rata among the energy units taken by the class. Thus, each unit incorporates an equal share of demand and energy cost. That is the only way in which class revenues will match class costs. Assuming that all the customers in the class were homogenous, or nearly so, the resulting unblocked rate would distribute costs equitably.

This is so because *non-blocking distributes costs (and therefore cost responsibility) strictly in proportion to the customer's annual volumes*, which is valid if the peak use of all customers in the class is essentially the same—homogeneity—so that the element of peak use can be disregarded in pricing within the class.

The question then is: are the customers in the class sufficiently alike in their volumetric usage as a function of their use patterns (load factors) as to be deemed homogenous? More importantly for evaluation of the unblocked commodity rate in its major current application, are residential customers homogenous? This can only be answered on a case-by-case basis, and look-alikes are a matter of degree, but it is incontestable that the residential class embraces homes that are large and small, families that are large and small; homes that use electricity for space and water heating, and homes that do not; homes that use gas for cooking and water heating as well as space heating and those that do not. The class is a mixed bag.

When the importance of peak use may be disregarded, single-part blocked rates (or blocked rates with a separate customer charge) may be adopted.

10.3.4.1 Unblocked vs. Blocked Single-Part Rates: (Residential)

As a comparative example of the unblocked and blocked, we hypothesize a residential customer class with a total annual consumption of 1,200,000 kWh and 100 customers. Our "bill distribution" report tells us that 25 of these customers have an average monthly usage of 500 kWh (6,000 kWh annually, for a total of 150,000 kWh); 50 have an average monthly usage of 1,000 kWh (12,000 kWh annually, for a total of 600,000 kWh); and 25 have an average monthly use of 1,500 kWh (18,000 annually, for a total of 450,000 kWh).

The costs assignable to the class are given in Table 10.1:

Table 10.1 Costs by rate elements

	Total	Per kWh
Demand (including customer costs)	$48,000	4 ¢
Energy	12,000	1 ¢
Total	$60,000	5 ¢

Therefore, our *base unblocked rate* is
5 cents per kWh

With this rate, each kWh collects 4 cents to cover demand costs and 1 cent for energy costs. The total revenue at 5 cents per kWh equals the total costs of $60,000.

To develop a blocked rate which assigns demand costs unequally to reflect differences in assumed characteristics of use, to produce the same annual revenue, takes a little longer.

Energy costs are no problem since we continue our prior assumption of an earlier chapter in relation to decreasing/increasing costs that such costs are a constant 1 cent per kWh, or $12,000 for the class in the present hypothetical.

For demand costs, we note as a point of reference from the same earlier chapter, that these were 5.5 cents per kWh at a low dependable capacity factor; 4.0 cents at an intermediate factor; and 3.0 cents at full utilization. We emphasize that we consider these only as a guide, a take-off point for demand cost assignment in our rate design calculations.

Choosing the blocking is an initial step. The following blocking was selected.

First block:	500 kWh
Second block:	500 kWh
Third block:	over 1,000 kWh

This seems reasonable in view of the usage profile for the class: 25% of the customers averaging 500 kWh per month; 50% averaging 1,000 kWh per month, and the final 25% averaging 1,500 kWh per month. The chosen blocking puts the entire take of the small use customer in the first block; half of the take of the intermediate customer in the first block, with the remainder in the second block; and a third of the take of the large customer in each of the three blocks (Table 10.2).

Assigning fixed costs to the blocks may entail a little trial and error. In this instance, the final assignment was as given in Table 10.3:

10.3 Single-Part Rate Forms

Table 10.2 Energy consumption by rate blocks

	Small customers	Intermediate customers	Large customers	Total
First block	150,000	300,000	150,000	600,000
Second block		300,000	150,000	450,000
Third block	–	–	150,000	150,000
	150,000	600,000	450,000	1,200,000

Table 10.3 Cost/Price assignment to rate blocks

	Fixed costs *set on* kWh
First block	4.8 ¢
Second block	3.5 ¢
Third block	2.3 ¢

Table 10.4 shows that this assignment produces the required annual total of fixed costs, $48,000.

Table 10.4 Annual contributions to demand costs by rate blocks (in $)

First block				
At the rate of 4.8¢/kWh	7,200	14,400	7,200	28,800
Second block				
At the rate of 3.5¢/kWh		10,500	5,250	15,750
Third block				
At the rate of 2.3¢/kWh			3,450	3,450
	$7,200	$24,900	$15,900	$48,000

Adding 1 cent per kWh for energy costs to the demand costs previously selected gives the following *base block rate*:

First 500 kWh taken per month at 5.8¢ per kWh
Next 500 kWh taken per month at 4.5¢ per kWh
Over 1,000 kWh taken per month at 3.3¢ per kWh

Monthly billings for the three customer usages compare as given in Table 10.5:

Table 10.5 Blocked and unblocked customer bills

	Base unblocked rate	Base blocked rate
Small (500 kWh)	$25.00	$29.00
Intermediate (1,000 kWh)	$50.00	$51.50
Large (1,500 kWh)	$75.00	$68.00

All meticulous rate engineers check their figures. If they don't, they become ex-rate engineers. It remains to check these bills against the required annual revenue of $60,000 (Table 10.6).

Total monthly revenue would be as follows:

Table 10.6 Revenues from blocked and unblocked customer bills

	Monthly revenue	
	Base unblocked rate	Base blocked rate
Small-25 customers	$625	$725
Intermediate-50 customers	$2,500	$2,575
Large-25 customers	$1,875	$1,700
Monthly total	$5,000	$5,000
Annual revenue (monthly × 12)	$60,000	$60,000

If it is assumed that smaller usages entail higher *per-unit* costs than larger usages, the blocked rate form approximates cost better than the unblocked form.

10.3.4.2 Adding a Separate Customer Charge

In many cases, it might be desired to alter the foregoing single-part rates to two-part rates having separate customer and energy charges so as to come closer to approximating costs. To illustrate this, we assume customer costs to be $36 annually per customer, or $3 per month. These costs, previously included as fixed costs, are to be recouped by a $3 monthly customer charge. Annual revenue will then be comprised of

Customer charges	$3,600
Energy charges	$56,400
Total revenue	$60,000

Looking first at the base unblocked rate of 5 cents per kWh across the board, the new customer charge makes it possible to reduce the straight-line energy charge to 4.7 cents per kWh.

The revised unblocked rate is as follows:
Customer charge $3.00 per month
Energy charge 4.7¢ per kWh

Average bills are different than before, being somewhat more tilted toward costs since the portion of the fixed costs now included in the customer charge have a greater relative impact on the smaller-use customer than for the base rate, and vice versa for the larger-use customer.

Monthly bills under the base unblocked rate and the revised unblocked rate compare as indicated in Table 10.7.

The revised unblocked rate has moved closer to the base blocked rate (the small customer bill being higher than before, and the large customer bill being lower).

10.3 Single-Part Rate Forms

Table 10.7 The customer charge–monthly bills with unblocked rates

	Base rate	Revised rate
Small (500 kWh)		
Customer charge		$3.00
Energy charge	$25.00	$23.50
Total	$25.00	$26.50
Intermediate (1,000 kWh)		
Customer charge		$3.00
Energy charge	$50.00	$47.00
Total	$50.00	$50.00
Large (1,500 kWh)		
Customer charge		$3.00
Energy charge	$75.00	$70.50
Total	$75.00	$73.50

Turning to the base blocked rate, a separate customer charge can be inserted without in any way changing billings. The only change in the rate is that the charge for the first block is reduced from 5.8 to 5.2 cents per kWh. The *revised blocked rate* with a separate customer charge is as follows:

>   Customer charge $3 per month
>
>   First 500 kWh taken per month at 5.2¢ per kWh
>
>   Next 500 kWh taken per month at 4.5¢ per kWh
>
>   Over 1,000 kWh taken per month at 3.3¢ per kWh

In Table 10.8 we compare billings under the revised unblocked and blocked rates.

Table 10.8 The customer charge–monthly bills with blocked and unblocked rates

	Monthly bills under revised rates	
	Revised unblocked	Revised blocked
Small (500 kWh)		
Customer charge	$3.00	$3.00
Energy charge	$23.50	$26.00
Total	$26.50	$29.00
Intermediate (1,000 kWh)		
Customer charge	$3.00	$3.00
Energy charge	$47.00	$48.50
Total	$50.00	$51.50
Large (1,000 kWh)		
Customer charge	$3.00	$3.00
Energy charge	$70.50	$65.00
Total	$73.50	$68.00

While the addition of a customer charge to the unblocked rate changes the bills for the small and large customers, the addition can be made to the blocked rate without any change for any customer. This is so because customer costs represented by the customer charge were imbedded in the per-kWh charge for the first block. Their separation from the per-kWh charge of this block has no effect.

Single-part demand rates are suitable mainly for customer classes where the load factors of all customers in the class are about the same, otherwise the form produces inequitable results. This limits its applicability. Also, the demand form is not suited for utilities whose commodity costs are high relative to demand costs, such as for gas utilities where the cost of purchased gas dominates total costs. These comments have been pointed to cost of service rate principles. It is impossible to generalize at all concerning the appropriateness to value of service theory of the several rate forms, except to repeat again the statement made previously that from the value viewpoint the end result, the customer's total bill, may be more important than the rate form.

10.4 Two-Part Rate Forms

The fundamental proposition underlying the conventional two-part rate is that, since utility costs are of two different kinds, commodity and demand, a more equitable cost-based result can be attained by separately charging for each.

10.4.1 The Hopkinson Rate

Two quite different methods have been developed in accordance with this proposition, both with reference to electric rates but quite applicable as well to the gas rates. The first is the Hopkinson two-part rate, originated in England in 1892.

This rate form establishes two separate metered charges—one for demand and the other for commodity—which together determine the customer's total bill. Either or both of these charges may be blocked. In most cases the commodity charge is blocked. The demand charge is blocked less often. An illustration of the Hopkinson rate form adapted to the electric industry with both demand and commodity charges blocked (the *Base Hopkinson Blocked Rate*) is as follows:

> *Demand charge*
> $2.00 per kW per month for the first 20 kW of the monthly maximum demand
> $1.40 per kW per month for all kilowatts in excess of the first 20
> *Energy charge*
> 2 cents per kWh for the first 800 kWh used per month
> 1 cent per kWh for the next 1,200 kWh used per month
> ½ cent per kWh for all kWh used in excess of the above

An example of billing under this rate is as follows:

10.4 Two-Part Rate Forms

Assume a customer has a maximum demand during a 30 day month of 35 kW and a consumption of 12,600 kWh (note that this represents a 50% load factor).

1. Demand charge-		
20 kW at	$2.00 each	$40.00
15 kW at	$1.40 each	$21.00
		$61.00
2. Energy charge-		
800 kWh at	2 cents each	$16.00
1,200 kWh at	1 cent each	$12.00
10,600 kWh at	½ cent each -	$53.00
		$81.00
3. Total Bill		$142.00

This results in an average price per kilowatt hour of 1.1 cents, and an average price per kilowatt of demand of $4.06.

Very commonly, commercial and some residential electric rates follow the Hopkinson-type form, but with the demand charge applicable only to demands in excess of some specific amount, usually in the neighborhood of 10 kW. The usual practice in this case is to install a demand meter only where it is expected that the customer's use will exceed the specific amount, in order to eliminate the expense of demand meters for the larger number of smaller customers.

A special application of the Hopkinson rate is the "all-electric" or "all-gas" residential rate, designed for customers who use all of the major appliances, each of which must be either electric or gas, as the case may be. The rate is promotional in two respects: (1) the level of commodity prices is low and (2) customers can earn these low prices (i.e., become eligible for service under the rate) only by using the specific large-use appliances. It is particularly promotional where there is competition between electricity and gas, and the commodity prices are set with that competition in mind.

An example of this rate form is as follows.[4]

Demand charge
>First 10 kW of demand per month—No demand charge
>Excess above 10 kW of demand per month—$1.20 per kW.

Energy charge
>First 300 kWh or less used per month, $4.85
>Next 700 kWh used per month at 0.7 cents per kWh
>Over 1,000 kWh used per month at 1.0 cents per kWh.

Note that this schedule (1) does not impose a demand charge for demands under 10 kW; (2) incorporates a rather high minimum embedded in the first step of the

---

[4] Schedule 9, All-Electric Residential and Farm Service, of the Portland General Electric Company of Portland, Oregon, an early version of the all-electric rate.

blocked energy charge; and (3) contains inverted blocking, the last step being at a higher price than the previous step, a "fish hook" feature designed to level off the unit commodity charge.

The Hopkinson rate form with no demand charge for the initial increments of demand has an inherent drawback. If the customer expands his establishment or if his average use increases beyond the free base increments for any other reason, the utility may (and should) install a test meter to determine if the actual demand is running above the base. If it is, a permanent demand meter is then installed. Thereafter, the customer undoubtedly will find that his bill is markedly higher due to the new demand charge, an unwelcome change.

The impact of the Hopkinson rate is different depending on (1) whether its constituent charges are blocked or not and (2) the tilt of the relative levels of the demand and energy charges. Because of the widespread utilization of this rate, we examine each of these separately.

10.4.1.1 Blocked vs. Unblocked Hopkinson Rates: Per-kWh Price Changes

The foregoing Base Hopkinson Blocked Rate illustrated blocking of both the demand and energy charges. At a 50% load factor, the total bill amounted to $142, of which total $61 or 43% was demand and $81 or 57% was energy. The average price per kWh was 1.1 cent.

Under this same rate, but substituting a 100% load factor for the prior 50% load factor, consumption rises to 25,200 kWh. The total bill now is $205, for an average price of 0.8 cent per kWh.

Substituting a 25% load factor, consumption is 6,300 kWh, for a total bill of $110.50, resulting in an average price of 1.75 cents per kWh. Comparatively, these trials are shown in Table 10.9.

Table 10.9 Base Hopkinson blocked rate–demand and commodity components in total and percent

Load factor	Avg. price per kWh	Charges Demand	Charges Commodity	Charges Total	Percent Demand	Percent Commmodity
25%	1.75¢	$61.00	$49.50	$110.50	55%	45%
50%	1.1¢	$61.00	$81.00	$142.00	43%	57%
100%	0.8¢	$61.00	$144.00	$205.00	30%	70%

The per kWh price declines as load factor improves.

A Hopkinson unblocked rate (the *Base Hopkinson Unblocked Rate*), giving the same per kWh price of 1.1 cents, and the same demand charge to commodity charge relationship, at 50% load factor, might be as follows:

$$\text{Demand charge, per kW } \$1.75$$
$$\text{Energy charge, per kWh } 0.64 \text{ ¢}$$

10.4 Two-Part Rate Forms

Assuming the same volumes (35 kW and 12,600 kWh) the total monthly bill is $141.89. The difference from the blocked rate is due to rounding. Applying 25 and 100% load factor trials to this unblocked rate gives the results as given in Table 10.10.

Table 10.10 Base Hopkinson unblocked rate–demand and commodity components in total and percent (equivalent at 50% Load factor to blocked rate)

Load factor	Avg. price per kWh	Charges Demand	Commodity	Total	Percent Demand	Commmodity
25%	1.6¢	$61.25	$40.32	$101.57	60.7	40
50%	1.1¢	$61.25	$80.64	$141.89	43	57
100%	0.9¢	$61.25	$161.28	$222.53	28	72

The per kWh price declines with the load factor but to a lesser degree, due to the removal of blocking. (The range with blocking is from 1.75 to 0.8 cents, a spread of 0.95 cent; without blocking, the range is from 1.6 to 0.9 cents, a spread of 0.7 cent.)

10.4.1.2 Blocked vs. Unblocked Hopkinson Rates: The Impact of Size

To complete this set of trials, we explore the effect of size on per-unit prices. We use the same base rates, but double the volumes (Table 10.11).

Table 10.11 Hopkinson rate–doubled volumes

Load factor (%)	Prior volumes Demand kW	Energy kWh	Doubled volumes Demand kW	Energy kWh
25	35	6,300	70	12,600
50	35	12,600	70	25,200
100	35	25,200	70	50,400

First we test the impact of size on the blocked rate (Table 10.12).

Table 10.12 Base Hopkinson blocked rate–the impact of size components in total and percent

Load factor (%)	Avg. price per kWh	Charges Demand	Commodity	Total	Percent Demand	Commmodity
25	1.5¢	$110.00	$81.00	$191.00	58	42
50	1.0¢	$110.00	$144.00	$254.00	43	57
100	0.75¢	$110.00	$270.00	$380.00	29	71

Doubling the size of the load reduces the average price per kWh at lower load factors when the charges are blocked. Size is rewarded.

We turn next to a load of the same doubled size with the unblocked rate (Table 10.13).

Table 10.13 Base Hopkinson unblocked rate–the impact of size components in total and percent

Load factor (%)	Avg. price per kWh	Charges			Percent	
		Demand	Commodity	Total	Demand	Commmodity
25	1.6¢	$122.50	$80.64	$203.14	60	40
50	1.1¢	$122.50	$161.28	$283.78	43	57
100	0.9¢	$122.50	$322.56	$445.06	28	72

Doubling the size of the load when the charges are not blocked increases the average per kWh price, but still gives a discount for size.

Assuming a consistent demand charge to commodity charge relationship, and other rate elements being equal, conclusions are as follows:

(1) The blocked Hopkinson rate gives a substantial quantity discount for better load factors.
(2) The unblocked Hopkinson rate also gives a substantial, but somewhat dampened, quantity discount for better load factors.
Either form, blocked or unblocked, will be favored by high load factor customers; both forms result in a per-unit price disadvantage and lower-load factor customers.
(3) The blocked rate (because of the blocking) reduces unit prices as size of take increases, at all load factors.

10.4.1.3 The Hopkinson Demand/Commodity Tilt: Increasing the Demand Component

Now we move to the demand/energy charge tilt. The Base Hopkinson Blocked Rate and the foregoing rate design exercises, swing about a 43% demand change and a 47% commodity charge relationship at 50% load factor. We change this relationships in the next set of trials, this time substituting the Base Hopkinson Unblocked Rate as the reference fulcrum.

Increasing the demand component, we design two rates, each resulting in a total price of 1.1 cents per kWh at 50% load factor per the base rate: in the first, the demand charge is increased by 43% to round out at $2.50 per kW, in the second it is doubled to $3.50 per kW, each with a corresponding decrease in the commodity price. The base rate and the two new rates areas are given in Table 10.14.

The tests continue earlier volumes, which we restate in Table 10.15 for the reader's convenience.

Results are as given in Table 10.16.

We digress from our trials at this point to explain why the doubled demand charge rate, with such an extremely low commodity charge as 0.153 cents per kWh, might be chosen by a buyer. First, take the case of an electric utility purchasing power

10.4 Two-Part Rate Forms

Table 10.14 The Hopkinson rate–increased demand component

	Demand charge		
	Base	Increased by 43%	Doubled
Demand charge, per kW	$1.75	$2.50	$3.50
Energy charge, per kWh	0.64¢	0.43¢	0.153¢

Table 10.15 The Hopkinson rate–restated volumes

Demand	35 kW
Energy	
25% load factor	6,300 kWh
50% load factor	12,600 kWh
100% load factor	25,200 kWh

Table 10.16 The Hopkinson rate–the impact of size–per kWh charges in total and percent with increased demand costs

Load factor	Base rate			Demand charge: +43%			Demand charge: doubled		
	Ave. price per kWh	Bill in percent		Ave. price per kWh	Bill in percent		Ave. price per kWh	Bill in percent	
		Demand	Commodity		Demand	Commodity		Demand	Commodity
25%	1.6¢	60	40	1.8¢	76	24	2.1¢	93	7
50%	1.1¢	43	57	1.1¢	62	38	1.1¢	86	14
100%	0.9¢	28	72	0.8¢	45	55	0.6¢	76	24

from an Independent Power Producer (or, the same example for gas, the case of a distributor buying from a pipeline or other gas supplier). The buyer will resell the energy in part at least to industrial customers who have other alternative suppliers. Under all known regulatory principles, the floor price for resale is the incremental cost to the seller of its energy. A floor price of 0.153 cents is more competitive – allowing greater freedom to compete – than is a higher price. A second case is that of an industrial user who from time to time may wish to add a second or third shift to its plant operations. Additional shifts will not change its demand, but will increase its energy consumption. So additional shifts can be accommodated with minimal additional cost for energy with a low energy charge.

10.4.1.4 The Hopkinson Demand/Commodity Tilt: Decreasing the Demand Component

Decreasing the demand component to tilt the charges more heavily toward commodity, we again design two rates, also working form the base rate's total price of 1.1 cents per kWh at 50% load factor: in the first, the demand charge is reduced by

Table 10.17 The Hopkinson rate–decreased demand component

	Demand charge		
	Base	Reduced to ½	Reduced to 1/4
Demand charge, per kW	$1.75	90 ¢	45 ¢
Energy charge, per kWh	0.64 ¢	0.88 ¢	1 ¢

about half to an even 90 cents per kW, in the second it is reduced again by half to 45 cents per kW, each with corresponding increases in the commodity price. The base rate and the two new rates are given in Table 10.17.

Retaining the same 35 kW demand, results are as given in Table 10.18.

Table 10.18 The Hopkinson rate–the impact of size: per kWh charges in total and percent with decreased demand charges

Load factor	Base rate			Demand charge: 1/2			Demand charge: 1/4		
	Ave. price Per kWh	% of bill		Ave. price Per kWh	% of bill		Ave. price Per kWh	% of bill	
		Demand	Commodity		Demand	Commodity		Demand	Commodity
25%	1.6¢	60	40	1.4¢	36	64	1.3¢	20	80
50%	1.1¢	43	57	1.1¢	22	78	1.1¢	11	89
100%	0.9¢	28	72	1.0¢	12	88	1.06¢	6	94

Conclusions are: with the unblocked Hopkinson rate as a base, changing the demand charge to commodity charge relationship, other rate elements being equal, will have these results:

(1) Increasing the tilt toward a heavier demand charge gives a larger discount for better load factors and a greater disadvantage for lower load factors.
(2) Reducing the emphasis of the demand charge and tilting the relationship toward a heavier commodity charge, minimizes the quantity discount, giving relatively minor reward for better load factors.

Higher load factor customers will opt for a tilt toward a higher demand charge, and lower load factor customers the reverse.

There are almost unlimited variations in possible blocking alternatives which might illustrate changes in the tilt of the demand–commodity charges. These are best explored on a case-by-case basis. However, the general conclusions given above relative to the unblocked Hopkinson rate form may serve as a guide to probable results.

10.4.2 The Wright Rate[5]

The second two-part rate form is the *Wright demand rate*, developed by Arthur Wright of Brighton, England, in 1886. This was probably the first really "scientific" utility rate. It preceded the Hopkinson rate by 6 years, but is discussed after the Hopkinson rate because of its greater complexity.

The Wright demand rate is a measured blocked commodity rate with the size of the blocks varying with the number of hours of use by the customer of his maximum demand. Therefore, it is a single-part rate in superficial appearance, but a two-part rate in reality, since the price fluctuates both with demand and use. For example, the first 30 kWh used for each kilowatt of the customer's demand might be at a certain price, the next block (also 30 kWh times the customer's same kilowatt demand) at a lower price, etc. Blocks may run in multiples of 30 (an hour's use of the maximum demand each day of the month) for no particular reason except convenience and custom. The Wright rate form as applied to an electric rate (the *Base Wright Rate*) is illustrated below:

First 30 h' use of maximum demand per month at 4 cents per kilowatt-hour
Next 30 h' use of maximum demand per month at 2 cents per kilowatt-hour
Over 60 h' use of maximum demand per month at 3/4 cents per kilowatt-hour

The following illustrates the application of the rate cited:
Suppose again a customer with a monthly maximum demand of 35 kW and a consumption of 12,600 kWh.

Thirty hours use during the month of a maximum demand of 35 kW (30 × 35) is 1,050. This is the number of kilowatt-hours in the first and second blocks. The computation of charges proceeds as follows:

1,050 kWh at 4¢ each –	$42.00	
1,050 kWh at 2¢ each –	$21.00	
10,500 kWh at 3/4¢ each –	*$78.75*	
Total bill...........................		$141.75

This results, as did our illustrations of the two base Hopkinson rates, in an average price per kilowatt-hour of 1.1 cents.

The rate form illustrated above can be utilized only where a demand as well as an energy meter have been installed (unless some formula for estimating demand is established, which usually is quite unsatisfactory). For this reason the form is

---

[5] Some authorities might prefer to classify this rate as a single-part rate. The classification is immaterial. It is discussed in this book as a two-part rate because it recognizes demand and commodity cost elements separately.

unsuited for smaller consumers, such as the residential class. It is easily modified to fit the cases where demand metering is impractical, however. This is done by adopting some other measure, such as the number of rooms served or connected load, or pump size for a small irrigator, as an index of demand. It is only by such modification that the Wright rate form is useful for small user gas rates. Demand meters are not practicable for small gas consumptions. The following illustrates the Wright demand rate set up on a room count basis:

First 7 kWh per room per month at 6.8 cents
Next 5 kWh per room per month at 5.0 cents
Next 5 kWh per room per month at 3.0 cents
Over 17 kWh per room per month at 2.0 cents

A major difficulty inherent in any rate form such as the above, which substitutes some more or less arbitrary index for an actual measurement of demand, is the unreliability of most practicable indices. The number of rooms in a residence, for example, may be quite unrelated to the customer's demand. While superficially it may seem that the larger house would require more electricity for lighting, a moment's reflection will show that it is the user—his habits, the number of persons in the family, his use of appliances, etc.—more than the number of rooms in the house he occupies, which determines demand.[6] A further difficulty present in the room count index, as well as many others, is the inducement to deceit which is offered the customer ("we don't use this room," for example).[7] Still another objection is the difficulty in maintaining the index up to date.

Connected load is an index which is particularly hard to maintain accurately. If the customer adds to his equipment and the utility is slow to discover this, the customer receives an unmerited rate reduction. But in spite of these shortcomings, the modified Wright rate is useful in certain circumstances.

Connected load is a billing element which can be linked to any type of rate form. We discuss it further here only because of its historical association with the Wright rate. One example of linking it is as an additional element to an otherwise applicable rate schedule. This is found in a "Standby" rate of Southern California Edison Company authorized by California PUC Decision 87-12-066 of Dec. 22, 1987. The following charge is added to the charges of the regular applicable schedule for service to a qualified cogeneration facility or for standby or breakdown service:

---

[6] It is possible, in fact, to speculate that the small house actually may have a larger demand than the larger house. The larger house may not have—or utilize—as many pieces of electrical equipment as the smaller house. Perhaps in the larger house the occupants send their laundry out, for example, while those living in the small house may make extensive use of clothes washing machines, etc.

[7] Because of these shortcomings, New York on July 1, 1937 prohibited the use of residential rates based on room count and area charges.

10.4 Two-Part Rate Forms

Standby Charge

Table 10.19 Standby wright rate

	Service Voltage	Per meter Per month
All kW of Standby demand, per kW	Below 2 kV	$2.70
All kW of Standby demand, per kW	2–50 kV	$2.00
All kW of Standby demand, per kW	Above 50 kV	$ 0.25

The standby demand (Table 10.19) is the lower of (a) the nameplate capacity of the customer's generating facility; or (b) the company's estimate of the customers' peak demand.

The company has the right to install, at the customer's expense, a demand meter. The highest recorded demand is then used to determine the customer's standby demand.

10.4.3 Comparison of Hopkinson and Wright Rate Forms

As previously explained, the effect of the blocked Hopkinson rate is to give a lower-average rate to larger customers, because larger customers with high demands will use in excess of the initial high-cost commodity and/or demand blocks relatively more quickly than smaller customers and therefore will get a greater proportion of their use at the lower priced blocks. Rate theorists who advocate the blocked Hopkinson rate based their argument upon the economies of size—the greater the use of the customer, they say, the smaller average price he should have to pay. The Wright rate, on the other hand, puts customers of all different sizes on the same basis, whether they may use one unit of demand or 1,000 units, provided their load factors are the same. The rate is such that (1) all customers having the same load factor pay the same average price per unit of commodity regardless of their size, and (2) the average price per unit of commodity fluctuates directly with the load factor, declining as the load factor improves, rising as it declines. Thus, under the Wright rate customers having high (good) load factors pay a lesser average rate (per commodity unit) than do customers with lower (poor) load factors. This is also the case under the unblocked Hopkinson rate, as pointed out in earlier pages. However, most comparisons between the two rate forms align the blocked Hopkinson (not the unblocked) against the Wright. On the basis that the blocked Hopkinson rate rewards size, it is rejected by Wright rate advocates who contend that the load factor, rather than size, is the more meaningful index of utility costs.

We resort again to examples to illustrate results. As a take-off point to measure the impact of size, we adopt the 50% load factor base load which was used previously and quadruple its size:

We test each of these loads using the base Wright rate (page 279) and the two Hopkinson base rates, the blocked (page 272) and the unblocked (page 274), with the following results:

Table 10.20 Wright and Hopkinson rates–restated volumes

	Base	Quadrupled
Demand	35 kW	140 kW
Energy	12,600 kWh	50,400 kWh

Table 10.21 Wright and Hopkinson rates–comparative charges

	Base load			Quadrupled load		
		Hopkinson's			Hopkinson's	
	Wright	unblocked	blocked	Wright	unblocked	blocked
Total bill	$141.75	$141.89	$142.00	$567.00	$567.56	$478.00
Ave. price per kWh	1.1¢	1.1¢	1.1¢	1.1¢	1.1¢	0.95¢
Ave. price per kW	$4.05	$4.05	$4.06	$4.05	$4.05	$3.41

The blocked Hopkinson rate tends to favor the large user, even when the large and small users have the same load factor. In contrast, size is not a factor for the unblocked Hopkinson or the Wright rates (Table 10.20). Only load factor counts.

It is futile to take sides on the issue of whether or not larger loads should be granted a price reduction. There is much to be said for either point of view. Realistically, the issue is best resolved from a value rather than an academic-cost perspective. Which end price best fits into the utility's competitive position?

It is also futile to argue in favor of either the unblocked Hopkinson or the Wright rate. The advantage of the former is its relative adaptability. The latter incorporates (on its face) only a single set of prices.[8]

It is well to mention at this point that hybrid combinations of the two forms sometimes have been used. For example, it is possible to set up a two-part rate on the Hopkinson pattern with a single-step demand charge or with the demand charges blocked in the usual manner, complete with the commodity charges blocked on the Wright basis.

10.4.4 Two-Part Rate Forms and Rate Theory

Since two-part rates on their face appear to give greater recognition to the cost characteristics of the utility industry than do single-part rates, usually they are considered to be the more accurate in terms of cost recoupment. *Certainly it is true that the two-part form permits a broader grouping of customers into a single class with less chance of inequity within the class between customers of differing characteristics. But the theoretically proper relationships between costs and charges are not*

---

[8]The writer cautions that all conclusions stated with respect to both the Hopkinson and Wright rates are generalizations. They do not substitute for case-by-case analyses of specific alternative rate schedules of whatever form and/or level.

10.4 Two-Part Rate Forms

guaranteed by the rate form. For example, it is seldom in practice that the demand charge of the Hopkinson rate recovers full demand costs, or that the commodity charge approximates only commodity costs. In fact, until fairly recently rate makers seem to have made little effort to be precise on this score. Generally, as mentioned earlier, demand charges which actually covered demand costs would be too high to win customer acceptance. (This would be particularly true for the hydro-electric system.) This, of course, is a matter of rate level, not form, but is interjected here as a note of caution.

Assuming for the moment, however, that the demand and commodity charges of the two-part rate accurately correspond to the utility's demand and commodity costs, it must be noted that nevertheless the appearance of precise pricing is somewhat misleading. For, although both demand and commodity uses are measured accurately, the *time* of use has not traditionally been a billing factor in most schedules.[9] Yet, the time of use, i.e., whether use coincides with the system peak or occurs at other periods, is a critical factor is assessing demand costs. Thus, to follow costs meticulously, demand charges would vary depending upon whether the demand occurred in the winter or summer, the midnight hours of the day or peak hours, etc. Under a rate schedule which does not recognize these differences, the price theoretically is too cheap for service sold during the peak and too expensive for service sold off the peak.

To be weighted against the greater precision in pricing possible with two-part rate forms, is the loss in simplicity, as compared with single-part forms, which results. As one writer has said, "the rate schedule which the customer reads is actually a price tag."[10] We have referred to it as "the packaging of the price." Understandability of the price plays a significant role in any kind of selling. A price tag which the customer cannot readily understand violates the principles of good merchandising, and certainly a two-part rate is more difficult for the average customer to understand than a single-part rate.

The same factors which cause a lack of simplicity result in greater administrative expense. Demand meters are costly, as is the job of separately reading and billing for demand as a separate component. These increased expenses, however, are not prohibitive, particularly in this age of computers, nor is it impossible to educate customers and win their acceptance. Under conditions of an energy shortage or concerted conservation efforts the extra expense can be afforded and the public can be educated, provided that the utility and regulators make adequate efforts in this direction.

10.4.4.1 The Demand Charge

The real question, then, in both theory and practice, is whether the demand charge with its accompanying difficulties, is justified for the smaller-use customer. Few argue against its application to larger customers.

---

[9] Electronic demand meters show, of course, the time of use. But in the past these have been installed only for the largest customers.

[10] Keslip, Malcolm, "Electric Rate Patterns for Residential Service," *Public Utilities Fortnightly,* Vol. XLII, No. 10, Nov. 4, 1948, p. 655.

The major practical advantage of the demand charge, which is completely independent of the more theoretical reasons for its use, is that it serves to make customers aware of the significance of demand costs in utility operations and to give them a monetary incentive to hold down their maximum use. No other rate device, aside of course from the all-demand rate, achieves this objective so successfully. Needless to say this is a consideration of high importance.

On the other hand, a demand charge will result in lower customer peaks only if customers conveniently can reduce their maximum demands. To the extent that customers may use the service wastefully and easily can elect to conserve, or simply can change their use habits so as to be able to buy more economically, a price incentive may be effective. But there is considerable evidence to the effect that most customer use patterns will be substantially the same regardless of whether or not a demand charge is imposed. Doubt as to the real effectiveness of the demand charge, together with the loss of simplicity which results from it, has led many early authorities to argue against it.[11]

There is some popular misconception concerning the theoretical and practical aspects of demand charges. This is that only customers served under demand-type rates contribute to demand costs.[12] Back in 1950, one writer, for example, cited an electric utility which supplied 80% of its energy sales during its peak month under blocked commodity and flat rate schedules, and 20% under demand schedules. From this he concluded, "the burden of meeting [the whole of the utility's fixed costs] is reserved for approximately only 20% of the consumption."[13] Nothing could be more fallacious yet this belief keeps cropping up. The demand charge is a theoretically sound way (subject to the qualifications previously mentioned) of recovering demand costs. It is not the only way. Since demand charges do not ordinarily approximate full demand costs except in abstract theory, commodity charges even in two-part rates may bear demand cost increments. Blocked commodity and flat rate schedules, if properly designed, will recover all types of costs associated with the service. Two-part rates are not essential for this result. Also, demand costs may be taken into account specifically in a number of ways other than the demand charge of the two-part rate. A ratchet which reflects the capacity utilized, can accomplish the same purpose when combined with the single-part block rate form. Similarly, for large customers, the return of demand costs may be assured by special contract provisions or other measures.

Perhaps the clearest illustrations of the component of demand costs which is included in demand charges are revealed in the rate design practices prescribed for natural gas pipelines by the Federal Energy Regulatory Commission (formerly the Federal Power Commission). The increment of demand costs borne by

---

[11] Representative arguments *for* a demand charge are made in the following articles: Lefferson, L.R., "Residential Rates for Tomorrow's Loads," *Edison Electric Institute Bulletin*. Vol. 17, No. 7, July 1949, pp. 250–252. Hills, Henry W., "Why a Demand Charge?" *Public Utilities Fortnightly*, Vol. XLVI, No. 4, pp. 349–356.

[12] See Roberts, Alfred V., "Is the Demand Charge Justified?" *Public Utilities Fortnightly*, Vol. XLVI, No. 1, July 6, 1950.

[13] Ibid., p. 26.

10.4 Two-Part Rate Forms

demand charges has varied depending upon the policy objectives sought by the Commission.[14]

To cite three examples—

	Portion of demand costs Borne *by demand* charges
Seaboard formula	50%
United formula	25%
Straight fixed–variable Formula	100%

One cannot be sure of what components of costs are covered by demand charges without knowledge of how demand costs have been apportioned.

Certain conclusions can, however, be drawn as to rate design. These are as follows: (1) The higher the demand charges vis-à-vis the commodity charges, the greater will be the incentive of customers to purchase more energy, since additional energy purchases may be made at a low price. The price tilt favors the commodity charge and the rate is to that extent promotional.

To illustrate this very important aspect of rate design, we return to our prior example of the base-blocked Hopkinson rate and reconfigure it to double the assignment of costs to demand charges, with a reduction of commodity charges, so as to produce the same total bill (at the same load factor). This we will call the tilted rate. For ease of comparison, we assume the quadrupled customer takes of a few pages ago, 140 kW demand and 50,400 kWh consumption.

The two rates and billings are as given in Table 10.22.

Table 10.22 Base Hopkinson Rate with Tilt toward Demand

	Base rate	Tilted rate
Demand		
First 20 kW	$2.00	$4.00
Excess per kW	$1.40	$2.80
Energy		
First 800 kWh	2¢	1¢
Next 1,200 kWh	1¢	0.5¢
Excess kWh	0.5¢	0.1¢
	Billings	
Demand		
First 20 kW	$40.00	$80.00
Excess (120 kW)	$168.00	$336.00
Energy		
First 800 kWh	$16.00	$8.00
Next 1,200 kWh	$12.00	$6.00
Excess (48,400 kWh)	*$242.00*	*$48.40*
Total	$478.00	$478.40

---

[14] We do not here discuss theories leading to the allocation of costs to demand, which are explored at a different point.

The above example is exaggerated, since the tilted rate with its extremely low energy charge represents the arithmetic carry-forward of a small-usage rate to a large-usage rate, but it does show the principle clearly. Certainly there is a greater opportunity to expand usage at 1/10 cents per kWh than at five times that price.

The next conclusion is: (2) a relatively high-demand charge instills an incentive (a) for all customers, to adopt peak shaving, demand management, and other demand-related conservation measures, which may result in bill reductions and (b) for the gas distributor, to install its own storage capacity, so as to temper its demand costs (from the pipeline if a pipeline is the distributor's energy supplier, or to be able to purchase gas in the field at a better load factor, if the distributor buys directly from producers.)

(3) Buyers having a high-load factor will be advantaged by a high-demand charge—and likely will argue for it—while buyers with low-load factors will be opposed.

The rate maker does not live in a vacuum; neither do regulators. The selection of a rate design usually is not just a simple matter of translating costs and prices, even though the procedure may be camouflaged as such. (The writer contends that value considerations are fully as important in rate design as are cost considerations. But this is a rebuttable view.) Often, however, social-engineering/public-policy motivations are openly stated, as in lifeline rates and these take precedence over both cost and value if sanctioned by law or regulatory direction.

10.4.4.2 Energy and Demand Costs/Charges in the Fuel and Hydro-electric System

For the steam or other fuel-fired electric generating plant, fuel costs are a principal component of energy costs. Therefore, it may be said generally that for the thermal system the demand charge of the two-part rate is related to investment while the energy charge is related largely to fuel. For a hydro-system the approach is more complicated. Insofar as non-storage or "run-of-the-river" hydro-generating plants are concerned, practically all costs are related directly to the capacity of the plant, which is a function of demand. Once generators are installed, it makes little cost difference whether they are in operation or not. Energy costs are practically non-existent. But the hydro-storage plant presents a different situation in theory. Stored water in effect fulfills the same purpose as coal, natural gas, or oil in a steam plant. Annual-fill reservoirs are provided to store water accumulated annually during abundant stream flow periods for use in the low stream flow season. Cyclical-fill reservoirs (i.e., reservoirs which if emptied in any year take more than the following year to refill) store water over 2 years or more for release only in a year where that year's stream flows are at a critical or below critical level.[15] For either type of reservoir, the annual costs on the reservoir investment may be said to correspond

---

[15] The use of the cyclical reservoir to serve firm loads is a gamble. The bet is that two critical water years will not occur back-to-back. If they should occur, the reservoir will not be refilled to meet next year's firm loads.

to fuel costs. Demand costs in this case are principally the investment costs of the generating plant, while energy costs may cover the investment costs of the storage reservoir. Once incurred, of course, both types are fixed. (Reservoir costs are variable only in the sense that the size of the reservoir may be a matter of wider discretion than the size of the plant.) For a number of years, the Bonneville Power Administration followed this theory in establishing its rates. BPA's Hungry Horse reservoir is a cyclical reservoir, while Grand Coulee is an annual reservoir.

10.5 Three-Part Rate Forms

These rate forms are rare and, when used, are most frequently assigned for special purposes.

10.5.1 The Doherty Three-Part Rate

In 1900 an American, H.L. Doherty, proposed a more elaborate rate form than that of either Wright or Hopkinson. Doherty's proposal follows cost-of-service rate theory more closely, perhaps, than any other traditional rate form. Briefly, it provides for three separate charges, a customer, a demand, and a commodity charge. The customer charge is a fixed amount for all customers in the rate class, on the twin assumptions that (1) customer costs do not vary with usage of either demand or energy and (2) there are no appreciable differences in the costs of reading meters, preparing bills, and collecting amounts owed, among individual customers within a class. A strict application of Doherty's rate theory would require that the demand charge be blocked in every case where the utility operates under conditions of decreasing costs (with inverse blocking under increasing costs), while the commodity charge would incorporate only variable costs and ordinarily would be the same per unit regardless of the number of units consumed.[16] Ordinarily, however, the Doherty rate is taken to specify merely a rate with separate customer, demand, and commodity charges, with no restrictions as to how the latter two charges are set up. Like the Wright and Hopkinson rates, the Doherty rate was devised as an electric rate, but it too is equally applicable to gas utilities.

Perhaps the main reason why this rate form was seldom used until recently is that separate billing for customer costs is of real importance only where these costs are a significant part of total costs. This is the case usually only for smaller customers, residential and small commercial class customers in general. In the case of larger customers, customer costs are an insignificant part of total costs. Yet, smaller customers to whom the form is most applicable may find the Doherty rate hard to

---

[16] Commodity costs may vary with consumption in some cases, for example, when a gas utility has to draft storage to carry peaks, or an electric utility has to put on line expensive generating capacity or purchase expensive outside power, for the same peak carrying purpose. However, as the writer understands Doherty and other contemporary observers, this refinement of the energy charge was not contemplated at the time. Recent time-of-day rates consider the extra costs of peaking.

understand and tend to resent it. The theoretical advantages gained have not proved enough to induce utilities voluntarily to use the form in the face of customer resistance. Use of the three-part rate to comply with regulatory commission directives is another matter.

But Doherty's idea of a separate customer charge has recently become popular for smaller customers, although as a component of a two-part—not a three-part—rate. (See earlier discussion.) When adopted, it may be called a "service charge," and may be calculated to cover an increment of demand costs as well as customer costs.

10.5.2 The Lester Special-Investment Three-Part Rate

In 1946 Claude R. Lester of the Bonneville Power Administration's rate staff developed a three-part rate form which provides a very flexible method of taking into account differences in the amount of the investment required to extend service to new outlying customers. Although the idea of recovering unusual investment costs from benefited customers was not new in utilities, Lester was the first, to the best of this writer's knowledge, to incorporate such a method into the rate form.[17] Lester's rate was designed to promote electric irrigation pumping service. For this reason he was anxious to hold down to the extent possible the demand and energy charges prescribed, in order to encourage use; yet, he was at the same time cognizant of the need to protect the utility against the very high costs of the special facilities which might be needed. Differences among customers in the amount of special investment required due to differences in location and demand also had to be taken into account. It is not practicable to attempt to establish an average charge in these circumstances. Therefore, Lester proposed a fixed charge which varied with the special investment required, coupled with the normal demand and energy charges. Lester's rate is as follows:

Fixed charge	-10% of special investment each season
Demand charge	-$1.25 per kW per month
Energy charge	-First 200 kWh per kW per month at 3.5 mills
	-Excess kilowatt-hours at 2.0 mills

Lester calculated the 10% figure as follows: 3% for operations and maintenance; 2% for replacements; 4% for interest and amortization (35 years); and 1% for insurance and miscellaneous costs.

This rate form, of course, is applicable to gas utilities also. Its great virtue is that it permits the establishment of uniform demand and commodity charges applicable to the appropriate customer class even in situations requiring widely varying extensions of facilities.

---

[17] Claude Lester was a co-worker with the writer at BPA at the time.

10.5 Three-Part Rate Forms

Variations of the Lester ideas have been proposed. In 1974 Charles E. Olsen suggested an initial connection charge which would cover the cost of connecting the customer's premises to the distribution network.[18]

10.5.3 The Zanoff Three-Part Gas Pipeline Rate

The type of three-part rate proposed by Louis Zanoff in 1972[19] introduced two new concepts. First, the traditional demand charge would be broken down into two separate charges, a demand charge and a capacity charge. Second, such charges, as well as the commodity charges, would be inversely blocked in two steps, base use and excess use.

Zanoff presents his hypothetical example as given in Table 10.23.

Table 10.23 The Zanoff rate

	Per MCF
Demand	
Base use	$2.04
Excess use	$2.25
Capacity	
Base use	7 $\frac{1}{2}$¢
Excess use	9¢
Commodity	
Base use	35¢
Excess use	42¢

To implement this rate, the year must be divided into summer months and winter months. The base use block of all three charges applies to the summer, the excess use block applies to the volumes taken in the winter over and above summer takes (of course, the inverted blocking presupposes a winter season peak. But the rate form could be adapted to a summer peak—say, electric air conditioning—merely by switching the seasons).

Demand charges: The customer nominates a peak-day demand quantity (a maximum daily entitlement) for each month of the year. This is in contrast to a single peak day (or an average of the three highest peak days) for an entire year, charges for which must be paid year-round. The average value of the summer period demand quantities constitutes the base demand to which the base demand prices apply. The overage of nominations for each of the winter months above this averaged summer-base demand constitutes the excess demand which is subject to the excess use demand prices.

Capacity charges: The customer nominates a monthly volume for each month called the capacity quantity for that month. The average of these volumes for the

---

[18]Olsen, Charles E., "Reforming Electricity Rate Structures in the United States." *Public Utilities Fortnightly,* Feb. 14, 1974.

[19]Zanoff, Louis, "A Positive Rate and Service Concept for Natural Gas Pipelines," *Public Utilities Fortnightly*, January 20, 1972.

summer months establishes the base capacity quantity, and the excess over the base in the winter is the excess quantity to which the respective capacity charges are applied.

In passing we note that the FERC philosophy adopted much later in 1985 of dividing pipeline demand charges into D_1 and D_2 components seems to be, at least in underlying theory, an adaptation of Zanoff's demand–capacity differentiation.[20]

Commodity charges: For the winter months the base commodity rate is applied to the base capacity quantity and the excess commodity rate is applied to the difference between the volume actually taken during the month and the base capacity quantity.

The minimum monthly bill consists of the sum of the demand charge and the capacity charge.

Zanoff does not specify how demand costs should be allocated between demand and capacity. He states, however, that the two charges together should equal the revenues collected by conventional demand charges.

10.6 Modifications of Rate Forms and Special Applications

10.6.1 Promotional, Incentive-Type Rates

During the depression of the 1930's, utilities—the electric and gas companies in particular—were faced with declining sales and adopted numerous expedients designed to counteract the trend. It is interesting to review these chiefly because the experience gained in this period serves to indicate whether similar steps might be fruitful in comparable future situations.

One type of promotional rate which became popular provided that a customer might use all the electricity which he desired in any 1-month period without paying more than the amount of his largest monthly bill in the preceding year. Sometimes one month of the year was designed as a norm, and if the user's consumption was higher during any later month than it had been in this specific month, he was charged only the amount of his bill for the norm month. The regular rate applied, of course, if his usage fell below that of the norm month. In connection with this scheme, the utility ordinarily conducted an intensive campaign to sell new appliances, encouraging the customer to buy the equipment on the grounds that his monthly bill would not be higher than previously. The "preceding year" was on a rolling basis, so that the loss of revenue would only be temporary. Because they are complicated, it is doubtful whether plans such as this are really effective.

10.6.2 The Objective Rate

Another very similar type of developmental pricing plan which was widely discussed during the depression of the 1930 s was the objective rate, first employed on a large scale by the Alabama Power Company in 1933. The basic principle involved

---

[20] The D_1 component assesses half of the demand cost based upon *peak* responsibility; the D_2 charge assesses the remaining half to reflect *annual volume* responsibility.

in the objective rate is that the user is given an opportunity to "earn" a cheaper rate by increasing his use. Although the application of the plan varies in minor details, ordinarily the customer's consumption of the previous year is used as a base. For all months in which his use is less than that of the corresponding month of the previous year, the customer is billed at the regular rate; for all months in which the customer's use exceeds that of the base, he is billed at a lower "objective" rate. The form derives its name from the fact that the customer is given an objective toward which to strive.[21]

The objective rate plan proved cumbersome and relatively ineffective. It is doubtful whether such a complex plan can be practicable when applied to a widespread customer class.[22] However, the plan received so much attention at the time that a word or two more concerning its advantages and disadvantages is in order.

Among the advantages claimed for the objective rate are that it stimulates the sales of load-building appliances and thereby acts to improve the load factor of both customer and plant; that it may be used in conjunction with efforts of the utility to achieve better rate uniformity and simplicity; and that it gives the utility an opportunity to explain to the public the constituent elements and purposes of rate schedules. The last factor is important if true, inasmuch as inadequate consumer understanding of pricing policies has created major difficulties for utilities—then and now. It is said that the objective form is also a solution to the "vicious-circle" problem of rates which arises because "utilities often cannot afford to lower rates until usage is increased, while buyers in turn are unable to increase their consumption until prices are reduced." The most obvious criticism which has been leveled at the objective rate is that it is discriminatory, in that customers whose use is comparable may be placed under different price schedules because an arbitrary line of demarcation has been drawn.[23]

10.6.3 Additions to Standard Rate Forms

An earlier chapter mentioned that minimum charges, ratchets, adjustment clauses, etc., were devices frequently used in utility pricing. Practically all electric and

---

[21] "The principal factor motivating the introduction of Objective type rates was a realization that the primary problem of the electric utility industry today [1933] is a sales problem, that is, the stimulation of increased consumption by existing customers, particularly those in the lower brackets of consumption. Other factors, such as competition, decreased use of electric energy during the depression, pressure for rate reductions, rising costs and taxes, and excess capacity, have, of course been advanced and they are important aspects of the matter. They are secondary, however, in the sense that each is a separate demonstration that the primary problem is one of merchandising kilowatt-hours ..." The Committee on Public Utility Rates, 48th Annual Proceedings of the National Association of Railroad and Utility Commissioners, 1936, p. 216.

[22] In the same general time frame, i.e., the post-1929 depression period, utilities offered, in additional to the rates discussed here, "Bargain Rates," "Inducement Rates," "Promotional Rates," "Low Cost Plans," "Free Electricity," "Half-Off Plans," "Share-the-Profits Plans," "Service-at-Cost Plans," "Centennial Rates," "Sliding Scales," and a host of other incentives to increase use. See "Commonwealth and Southern Objective Rate Plan," *Journal of Land and Public Utility Economics*, XI (May, 1935), pp. 117–122.

[23] Is "incentive Regulation" of today merely a different version of an old idea?

gas rate schedules incorporate one or more of these devices. They continue to be valuable adjuncts to the standard rate forms just discussed, further increasing the flexibility possible in the design of rates and providing the means for handling many special problems.

10.7 Miscellany

10.7.1 A 1946–1950 Case History with Overtones for Today[24]

We tend to think that today's rate problems are overwhelming in contrast to the past. They are new problems, assuredly, but not necessarily more numerous nor more difficult.

The quandaries of selecting the correct rate form—and what can happen if a poor choice is made—is illustrated with great clarity by the post-World War II experience of the Wisconsin Southern Gas Company. We summarize,

In 1946 the company had converted from manufactured to natural gas. The management felt that the company's position was somewhat unique as it served a summer resort area and its peak load came in the summer. If they promoted winter gas heating, management reasoned, the result would be a high-load factor operation; the winter load valley would be eliminated in part. Since the company purchased its natural gas under a two-part wholesale rate, this would give them a very low wholesale price of gas. Accordingly, the company established the blocked commodity type rate shown below, with the intention that gas for space heating would be sold at the highly competitive rate of 7 cents per hundred cubic feet.

Service charge: 60¢ net per meter per month,
Commodity charge:

First ... 800 cubic feet at 27¢ per hundred cubic feet
Next ... 1,700 cubic feet at 16¢ per hundred cubic feet
Next ... 500 cubic feet at 8¢ per hundred cubic feet
Excess ... cubic feet at 7¢ per hundred cubic feet

The rate accomplished the promotional job with extraordinary success. Before long the company used up its natural gas allocation and had to impose restrictions on the sale of gas for house heating. But as to the other results, company president Knoblock reported, "While our gross revenues were increased by leaps and bounds, we found to our dismay that our expenses were following closely behind, and instead of a high-load factor, we had a 'common garden variety' low one that resulted in higher wholesale gas costs than we had anticipated. Our former 'high' summer peak

---

[24] The case history is presented by Kenneth D., Knoblock, President, Wisconsin Southern Gas Company, in his article "New Tools for Gas Service," *Public Utilities Fortnightly*, Vol. XLVI No. 8, Oct. 12, 1950, pp. 501–505. All quotations under this title are taken from the article.

became our low period of the year because of the high increase in our heating load. Not only did our purchased gas cost rise, but we were also compelled to increase the capacity of our transmission and distribution systems, and, as a natural sequence, we outgrew our original operating organization. As a matter of fact, our service department had to be quadrupled in size. We realized then and there that something had to be done." The company's analysis of its operations led to the conclusions that the space-heating load had, in Mr. Knoblock's words,

"(a) Made it necessary for us to enlarge our distribution system and greatly increase our capital investment."
"(b) Made it necessary for us to expand our operating organization."
"(c) Increased our peak daily load, lowered our load factor, and increased the unit cost of gas purchased."
"(d) Actually reduced our net income."

It was clear that the heating customers, who had caused the company's higher costs, were being subsidized by range and water-heater users.

The company therefore decided to:

"(1) Increase the heating rate so as to economically limit the market to one that we were financially and physically able to serve."
"(2) Adopt a form of heating rate that would, in effect, require the heating customer to pay a demand charge. Our reason was that the collective demands of our space-heating customers caused the demand that was the basis of the demand charge we had to pay the pipe-line company, so they in turn should pay that demand charge."
"(3) Offer a real incentive to heating customers who would stay off the peak-load periods. These would be seasonal heating customers or fall-spring users, and users of the dual-fuel type of gas-oil burners."

The company substituted a two-part schedule for the rate in effect previously, adding a demand charge and reducing the commodity charges. The service charge was not changed. The company concluded that the two-part heating rate had solved its problem. Some important lessons were learned as the new schedule was put in effect. First, it was found necessary to very fully explain that although a demand charge was being added, the commodity charges were being reduced, to avoid the implication that the price to the customer was being increased excessively. Second, considerable customer friction was engendered since the bills rendered under the new rate set out the demand charge as a separate item; this friction was mitigated when only the total bill was discussed. Third, the rate proved highly effective in the promotion of the dual-fuel burner, a "peak-shaving" device.

10.7.2 Rate Forms and Rate Comparisons

It perhaps needs to be pointed out that for valid comparisons between schedules having different prices a very careful analysis of the entire rate is essential. To cite an example from the writer's own experience, Bonneville Power Administration at one time proposed to establish a schedule (S-1) under which secondary energy would be sold at 1 mill per kilowatt-hour.[25] Secondary energy under this schedule was guaranteed by BPA to be available to the purchaser 80% of the time. Concurrently the administration was selling essentially the same type of energy (but without the guarantee to deliver) under its H-3 dump energy schedule at 2.5 mills per kilowatt-hour. The schedules were applicable to different classes of customers. Both were straight-line energy rates. The customers served under the H-3 rate argued that they were being discriminated against inasmuch as they were forced to pay 2.5 mills per kilowatt-hour while another group of customers would pay only 1 mill.

Superficially this was true. However, the secondary schedule required that the customer pay for at least 90% of the energy made available. Therefore, the customer would pay at an annual minimum rate of $6.31 per kW (8,760 h × 80% = 7,008 h × 1 mill = $7.01 × 90% = $6.31). If utilized at less than 90% load factor, the per kilowatt-hour cost to the customer would, of course, increase rapidly. At 45% load factor the cost would be 2 mills per kilowatt-hour.

In contrast, the dump schedule imposed upon the customer no requirement to purchase any quantities whatsoever, either large or small. In fact, the customers supplied under this schedule actually took delivery at an average load factor of only 16% or less. At this load factor secondary energy under the S-1 schedule (because of the 90% purchase guarantee) would cost about 4.5 mills per kilowatt-hour as compared with 2.5 mills. It is obvious that a comparison which takes into account all of the provisions of the schedules yields an entirely different conclusion than the comparison which looks only at the prices prescribed. This again emphasizes the related point that the "fine print" provisions may be the most important parts of the schedule.

Inter-utility rate level comparisons are even more treacherous. Not only must respective rate forms be taken into consideration, but also the full range of cost and value factors, if comparisons between companies are to be valid. Alexander J. Zakem (1986) suggests that without normalizing the data, abstract differences in the prices of one company in comparison with another are misleading.[26] Zakem would apparently agree with the writer. But there is debate on this point.

---

[25]This was considered in 1946. Shortly thereafter, due to the rapid post-war increase in loads, the Administration found that it had a market for practically all of its secondary power under its existing schedules and withdrew the proposed S-1 rate Before it was withdrawn the writer had the job of justifying it to the FPC.

[26]Zakem, Alexander J., "Comparing Utility Rates," *Public Utilities Fortnightly,* Nov. 13, 1986.

10.7 Miscellany

Charles M. Studness (1993) seemingly would disagree, at least insofar as comparisons are between adjacent companies. He contends, "the absurd disparity in [electric] rates between neighboring utilities stems from a basic inefficiency rooted in the absence of competition."[27] He makes no effort to reduce the relative prices to a common denominator.

10.7.3 A 1971 Gas Distributor and Pipeline Tariff

Under this chapter's discussion of traditional rate forms, which were in full bloom until the early 1970's, it is revealing to examine an actual tariff or two of the end of the period. For this purpose, we move from electric and select the tariff of a gas distributor and a gas pipeline. The distributor is Northwest Natural Gas Company,[28] which serves about 2.5 million residents in northwest Oregon and southwest Washington. Some important features of its tariff as of January 1971 are noted on Table 10.24.

The company offered 17 rate schedules, but almost 98% of both its sales volume and its revenue came from 9. These are classified as major schedules, each accounting for more than 1% of the volume. Almost an equal number of schedules—eight —accounted for only 2%, each yielding less than 1% of the volume. In terms of rate form, all but two of the schedules were single-part metered commodity rates. One of the exceptions was a two-part Hopkinson rate (Schedule 27). The demand charge was $40,000 per month for takes of up to 100,000 therms, constituting a minimum monthly demand charge. Above this volume, a per-therm demand charge of 40 cents per therm came into play. The four commodity blocks, in therms, were 600,000, 800,000, 2,600,000, and excess. The schedule included an annual minimum charge per therm of contract demand.

The other exception to the predominant rate form was an extremely simple rate for gas lights (Schedule 19). The charge was $1.50 for one mantle, with additional mantles at $1.00 each. The therm usage was unmetered, the charge being based on an estimate of the therms used per mantle. (Such estimation is common for electric street lighting.)

The table suggests relative differences in prices among schedules, even though no prices are stated. For example, the residential rate (Schedule 2) contributed almost 30% of total revenue, but only about 15% of the volume. The price per therm is relatively high, indicating a higher per-unit cost for serving residential customers. On the other hand, the main interruptible rate (Schedule 23) was responsible for close to half of the volume but only one-quarter of the revenue. The per-therm price is relatively low, suggesting a lower per-unit cost for high volume sales with an inferior grade of service, and the influence of value—competitive considerations— on the pricing of the schedule.

---

[27] Studness, Charles M., "The Geography of Electric Rates," *Public Utilities Fortnightly*, Oct. 1, 1993.
[28] The writer's alma mater.

Table 10.24 Characteristics of tariff of Northwest Natural Gas Company, January 1971

Schedule. #	Use type	Type of rate form	Description	Volume (%)	Revenue (%)
Major rates					
2	Residential	Single-part, metered commodity	Three blocks, minimum in first	14.73	29.82
3	Comm. and Ind.	Single-part, metered commodity	Six blocks, minimum in first	6.51	13.83
4	Large firm	Single-part, metered commodity	Three blocks, separate minimum	2.22	2.60
5	High-load factor, large firm	Single-part, metered commodity	Uniform charge, annual and monthly minimums	5.45	3.75
21	High-load factor, firm	Single-part, metered commodity	Six blocks, separate minimum, surcharge above base period use	12.87	11.39
23	Interruptible	Single-part, metered commodity	Six blocks, separate minimum surcharge above the base period use	47.10	25.25
24	Residential, all gas	Single-part, metered commodity	Three blocks, minimum in first	4.65	8.11
27	Firm, large volume	Two-part, Hopkinson	Demand charge: fixed amount to 100,000 therms; excess on per therm basis. Four blocks, minimum annual bill per therm of contract demand	2.98	2.04
40	Modified firm	Single-part, metered commodity	Five blocks, minimum in first	1.27	0.84
Subtotal, major rates				97.78	97.63
Minor rates					
1	General (firm)	Single-part, metered commodity	Five blocks, minimum in first	0.01	0.09
10	Seasonal swing and off-peak firm	Single-part, metered commodity	Three blocks, April through October; three larger blocks, March and November; 3 blocks, December, January, February. Separate minimum, July, August, September	0.58	0.56

10.7 Miscellany

Table 10.24 (continued)

Schedule. #	Use type	Type of rate form	Description	Volume (%)	Revenue (%)
11	Building construction, temporary	Single-part, metered commodity	Uniform charge, no minimum	0.35	0.49
13	Interruptible	Single-part, metered commodity	Two blocks, separate minimum	0.13	0.09
17	Air conditioning	Single-part, metered commodity	Six blocks, May through September; Seven blocks, October through April, minimum in first	0.04	0.06
19	Gas light	Single-part, unmetered mantle	Two per-mantle blocks, no minimum	0.09	0.11
22	Dual fuel	Single-part, metered commodity	Four blocks; minimum in first	0.87	0.76
26	Residential air conditioning	Single-part, metered commodity	Three blocks, minimum in first	0.15	0.21
Subtotal, minor rates				2.22	2.37
Total, all rates				100.00	100.00

Cust. class as % of total system

It is reasonable to wonder why it was considered necessary or desirable to include the eight minor rates in the tariff, since they represented only about 2% of both volume and revenue. The reason lies in one or more of these considerations: (1) existing customers on a minor schedule find that it is of advantage to them, vis-à-vis other schedules, and they do not want to lose this advantage. The utility has no reason to arouse the resentment of these customers. (One expedient available to the rate maker is to "freeze" the schedule, making it unavailable to new customers but grandfathering in existing customers.) (2) A minor schedule may serve a unique customer requirement. The seasonal swing and off-peak firm rate (Schedule 10) is a good illustration. Ocean fishing is an important business in the northwest, with canneries and other fish processing plants located in coastal ports (particularly Astoria). These plants run full bore during the fishing season, and shut down at other times of the year. To accommodate this cycle, a favorable price is offered for April through October (minimum bill for July, August, September only), with a somewhat higher but still favorable price in the shoulder months of March and November. These are off-peak months for the distributor. The schedule also may be used in the peak months of December, January, and February, but at much higher prices, if the customer finds it necessary to keep his plants in operation during these winter months. (3) The utility may wish to encourage a special type of use, such as general air conditioning (Schedule 17) and residential air conditioning (Schedule 26). There is little gas air conditioning and this is an advantageous off-peak load to a utility with a winter space heating peak. (4) Last but not least, regulatory authorities and/or state public policy may urge, if not require, a given rate.

The characteristics noted on the table are only a cursory list of the data examined by the rate maker. Bear in mind that three sequential cost allocations are needed for rate-level determination: to the customer or usage class, to each schedule within the class, and to the components within the schedule (customer, demand, energy, plus each step of a blocked rate or each unit—therms in the instant case—of an unblocked rate).

Among the statistics analyzed are the schedule to schedule revenue and volume relationships (shown on the table); usage patterns under each schedule, indicating minimum, average, and maximum per customer usage, plus, perhaps, lower quartile, median, and upper quartile per customer use, and load factor. For a distributor purchasing its gas supply from a pipeline, an essential guideline is the margin by which each assigned unit price exceeds the unit cost of gas bought from the pipeline.

Northwest Natural purchased its entire supply from Northwest Pipeline Corporation (then the Northwest Division of El Paso Natural Gas Company). The two companies are not affiliated. The distributor obtained its firm gas supply under the pipeline's large distributor schedule (ODL-1), a two-part Hopkinson rate having no blocking in either the demand or commodity charge. The demand charge was geared to the contract demand, and, since it did not vary with usage, constituted a minimum charge. The rate as of January 1971 was as follows:

Demand, per therm of contract demand 31.921¢
Energy, per therm taken 2.1¢

10.7 Miscellany

Minimum annual bill: $4.98 per therm of the average monthly demand.

This rate is titled heavily to emphasize demand, penalizing less than a high load factor. At 100% load factor the demand component is 1.0495 cents per therm.[29] When this is added to the energy component of 2.1 cents, the total charge is 3.1495 cents. At 90% load factor, the demand component rises to 1.1661 per therm, an 11% increase, bringing the total price to 3.2661 cents per therm, a 4% increase. High load factor customers, of which Northwest Natural was one, were in favor of a high demand charge and a low commodity charge. Lower load factor customers of the pipeline favored a lower demand and higher commodity tilt.

Comparative per-therm prices for other illustrative load factors are as given in Table 10.25:

Table 10.25 Pipeline prices to distributors

Load factor	Demand charge	Energy charge	Total price	Price increase over 100% LF
80%	1.3318¢	2.1¢	3.4118¢	8%
70%	1.4992¢	2.1¢	3.5992¢	14%
60%	1.7491¢	2.2740¢	4.0231¢	28%
50%	2.0989¢	2.7288¢	4.8277¢	53%

The minimum annual bill triggers at 60% load factor. This is why the commodity charge increases from $2.1 as per the schedule to $2.2740[30]. The rate, therefore, imposed a minimum charge on both demand (per unit of contract demand) and energy (which sets a 60% annual load factor energy use as a floor for pricing).

We labor this point to expand our prior comments on the Hopkinson and Wright rate forms. The ODL-1 schedule points out that the Hopkinson form can reward high-load factor usage, and penalize a low-load factor, if the demand–commodity charge relationship is tilted toward demand. The schedule also illustrates two different techniques of minimum billing; in this case both were used in combination.

The distributor also purchased from the pipeline on three other schedules. Two of these were single-part unblocked metered commodity rates, and the third a two-part Hopkinson rate unblocked. These schedules provided for the purchase of peaking gas from underground storage, and high priority interruptible and standard interruptible supplies.

10.7.4 Some Concluding Observations

1. It will be apparent from the foregoing review of traditional rate forms that there is no one rate form which can be singled out as better in all respects that the others. Each has certain advantages which make it more suitable than other forms

---

[29]The arithmetic is [31.921¢ × 12 months (or $3.8305 per year)]/365 = 1.0495¢.
[30]The arithmetic is 365 × 0.6 = 219, the number of annual therms taken per unit of demand at 60% LF. 219/$4.98 − 2.2740¢, the per-therm commodity charge resulting from the annual minimum.

for some purposes, and each has certain disadvantages as compared with other forms. But seldom are these advantages and disadvantages sufficiently clear-cut as to indicate only one logical choice in any particular case. For this reason the selection of the rate form to be used often will depend upon the personal preferences of the rate engineer or the regulatory commission. More often, however, the rate form cannot be freely chosen by either, for most rate work involves the revision of existing schedules rather than establishing entirely new rate classes or entirely new schedules. Existing rate structures have established pricing patterns which may be disturbed only for the most serious reasons. (Exceptions may be changes brought about by "social engineering" mandates of the regulatory commission.) In practice it is most difficult to make meaningful changes in rate form without materially changing the incidence of the price burden. Thus, to avoid rate shock, changes in rate form usually are made gradually.
2. It also will be apparent that all kinds of rate form combinations are possible by utilizing different patterns of blocking, and by combinations of the Wright, Hopkinson, Doherty, Lester, or Zanoff rates. Further variety is possible by incorporating "minimums" and "ratchets" of various sorts. The available rate devices are such that *the rate can be tailor-made to fulfill the pricing policy which has been determined.* It is important to emphasize that the rate follows the policy rather than the reverse. Any desired objective can be attained by correct selection of the rate form and level, provided value limitations are not violated.

At one time it was popular to criticize electric and gas rates for their variety and lack of uniformity. Criticism may have been warranted but not on this score. Uniformly is not sacred. The best pricing practice is the practice which accomplishes the result sought after. The real measure of the effectiveness of a rate can be taken only in terms of the results attained. The essential point is that rates are an instrument of policy and cannot be judged apart from the policy.
3. The rate *form* is important, but is only one part of the problem. The other part is the rate *level.* Both must be considered hand-in-hand.
4. Rate making based on the cost of service approach represents an attempt to apportion costs precisely (1) to the rate classes and (2) in the rate form, to the increments of use, with distinction between demand and commodity cost increments in many cases. But the actual rates, past and present, often, if not usually, fall short of accurately representing the costs associated with each of the several rate classes or of the billing units within each class. This is so because of the unavoidable fact that cost allocation is inherently subjective, the influence of value of service considerations which in most cases are as important as cost considerations, and the hazards of disturbing established pricing patterns which make for rate stability and militate against rapid adjustment of relative rates to new cost conditions.

Chapter 11
Tools of the Trade

Abstract Chapter 11 is aptly termed "Tools of the Trade." It opens the door to measures that are essential for an understanding of the economics of all industries, particularly capital-intensive industries as are the energy utilities. The factors of measurement are fully explained for the beginner, and their implications are developed for the practitioner. Load factor gauges whether facilities are heavily or lightly loaded, and gives insight into the impact of these conditions upon the economics of operations of the concerned firm. Diversity factor, the second most important measure, assesses the variety of uses to which a facility can be put simultaneously, the greater the number, the greater the efficiency. Other factors—capacity factor, utilization factor, demand factor, and for the electric technician, power factor—are also covered in Chap. 11.

11.1 Introduction

In this chapter, the more important means for measuring and illustrating the factors which influence and guide the managements of the electric and natural gas utility industries are defined and described.

These definitions and descriptions are presented in utility terms, reflecting the focus of this book on the pricing of these two energy purveyors. And, since they are subject to the same economic influences, the closely related independent wholesale electricity producers who sell to the electric utilities are included in that focus, as are large energy-consuming industries who purchase their requirements from non-utility suppliers.

But the potential usefulness of these definitions and descriptions is not confined to that small group. Utilities are capital-intensive industries. Most heavy manufacturing is also, including auto, airplane, steel, and the like. Utilities engage in continuous operations which fluctuate wildly, with hourly, daily, and seasonal swings. So do transportation providers, airlines, trains, buses, and trucking and shipping. The similarities in planning and operational characteristics between utilities and these other industries are striking. However, the measures included herein have not been widely adopted. Perhaps this chapter will be a step toward their acceptance in non-utility operations.

We are deeply indebted to Pacific Gas and Electric Company for permission to extract figures and other data from their superb training manual *Resource, An Encyclopedia of Utility Industry Terms*, second edition, 1992.

11.2 Knowing the Market: Load Curves

Graphics are an easy means of visualizing the utility market. These graphics generally are called "load curves" or "demand curves." They show the ebb and flow of the utility load over a given time span, a day, week, season, year, or any other period ripe for scrutiny.

"Load" is a term very loosely used. Depending on the context, it may refer either to the energy requirement of the total market or only to component sectors of the market (e.g., individual customer classes). In either case, load may be stated in terms of the volume of energy generated or otherwise inputted into the system, a gross amount, or a lower volume, the energy delivered to the customer, a net amount. The difference arises because there are losses in transferring energy from one point to another. A generating plant must produce enough electric energy to satisfy customer requirements plus losses in transmission, transformation, and distribution. Gas well flows must be greater than usage at the burner tip to accommodate the same types of losses, as well as gas used for compression and any volume reductions due to liquid extraction or purification.

Stated summarily, load is the amount of energy being supplied (gross) or being used (net) over a given interval of time.

11.2.1 Load/Demand Curve

The context will indicate whether the reference is historical (a prior load), current, or future (a forecasted load), or, as Fig. 11.1 below, simply an illustration.

Figure 11.1 is a sample system-wide *daily* load curve, illustrating the fluctuations in load typically experienced by an electric utility system throughout the day. As shown, PG&E's load reaches its highest levels between 4 and 8 p.m., and its lowest around midnight. That company experiences an *evening* peak, heavily influenced by lighting. A different utility might have a *morning* peak, if space heating was dominant in the winter or air conditioning in the summer.

Figure 11.1 also introduces the concept of dividing the daily load into segments, base, intermediate, and peak, relative to the length of time over which the load level extends, as a general index to the types of generation which will be on line.

Base load is that load which must be supplied continuously (or almost so), at all hours of the day (or any other period being studied). It remains essentially constant over the applicable period. The generation having the least variable costs will be used to supply the base, as will must-run/must-take capacity. Examples of *must-run* capacity are units required for spinning reserve, and hydro from run-of-the-river

11.2 Knowing the Market: Load Curves

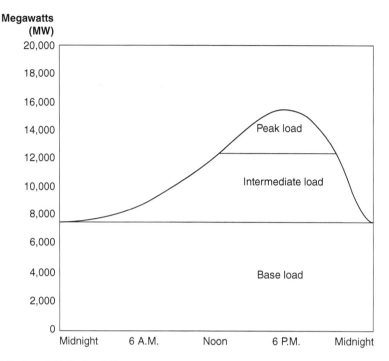

Fig. 11.1 Sample Daily Load Curves

plants where stream flows otherwise would be wasted. *Must-take* capacity includes power purchases where the energy must be taken or paid for, such as QF power.

Time periods differ as among utilities for all load segments. Generally, the peak load will be supplied by peaking sources having high variable costs but easily switched on and off.

Obviously, the intermediate period comes between the base and the peak[1].

In some instances the divisions of the day into different periods are used as a basis for costing, each period having a different cost level. Such costing periods may be further broken down for time-of-use rates.

11.2.2 Season Usage Patterns

PG&E's system peak comes in the summer. The differences in its seasonal peak-day load shapes is illustrated in Fig. 11.2.

---

[1] For base-load PG&E utilizes its nuclear and geothermal capacity, conventional thermal units at minimum operating levels, energy from QF's and other scheduled purchases, and hydro. For peaking, PG&E can call upon pumped storage and other hydro, purchases, and combustion turbines. The turbines can go from a cold start to full load in 10 min or less. Intermediate loads are met by various mixes of resources.

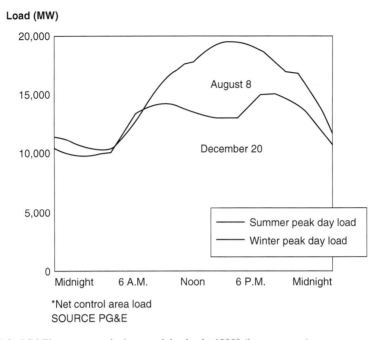

Fig. 11.2 PG&E's summer and winter peakday loads, 1990* (in megawatts)

While the peak (summer) load profile of Fig. 11.2 is similar to that on Fig. 11.1, the figures differ in that Fig. 11.1 incorporates only PG&E's own loads while Fig. 11.2 reflects loads in its expanded "control area." "Control area," an electric utility term not used in gas, is an area over which the utility (or perhaps a group of utilities) has responsibility to maintain generation system frequency[2] and scheduled interchanges with other control areas.

The important element for the non-utility observer to note from Fig. 11.2 is the difference between the seasonal summer and winter peak-day load shapes. It is perhaps redundant to add that load shapes change from day-to-day as well as from season-to-season, although day-to-day changes normally will be gradual absent a drastic weather change.

System-wide (area) load/demand curves show the total generation capacity and/or power purchasing rights which the electric utility needs to have available when the aggregate demands of its customers reach their highest point.[3] The curve

---

[2]For most of us, system frequency is notable because it guides the accuracy of our clocks: if frequency sags, our clocks run slow; if it gains, our clocks run fast. The objective is to maintain frequency at an even level, correcting for slow or fast. Unexpected heavy loads may cause a sag; unexpected light loads, a gain. The trick is in the balancing. The generation dispatcher must be on the alert.

[3]Bear in mind that the load-serving requirement may be either gross (total energy input into the system) or net (a lesser amount, total energy delivered to customers). Illustrative charts do not require this distinction.

11.2 Knowing the Market: Load Curves

also shows when a reduced call for energy occurs. In the off-peak period, less efficient generating plants may be placed on stand-by or shut down, or more expensive power purchases reduced.

An hourly area load curve for a gas utility does not have quiet the same significance with respect to total hourly energy input into the system, since gas, unlike electricity, can be stored from hour to hour due to line packing ability or, perhaps, hourly peaks can be supplied in part from on-system storage. Pipeline deliveries to gas distributors usually will be scheduled on a total day basis.

The forgoing formats also may be used to picture the market supplied by a given component of an electric or gas system, such as an electric transmission line, substation, or distribution feeder; also, with less emphasis on hour to hour changes, by a gas pipeline for a given city gate, or by a gas distributor for some major facility or other part of its system.

11.2.3 Duration Curve

Figure 11.3 changes the time span from a day to a year, and adopts a different form of graphics called a "duration curve."

Figures 11.1 and 11.2 present a picture of the market configuration as it unfolds, from hour to hour in sequence, as the classical artists' portrait of a face will place each feature from the throat to the forehead in its natural order. Figure 11.3 is akin

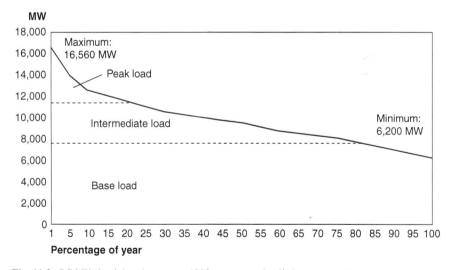

Fig. 11.3 PG&E's load duration curve, 1990 net system load* (in megawatts)

*PG&E's maximum area load in 1990 was approximately 19,400 MW, but this demand level included PG&E's system load and other loads within the entire control area. Net system load represents gross system load less deliveries within and outside of PG&E's service territory, including energy used to operate the Helms Pumped Storage Facility.

SOURCE: PG&E

to an impressionistic Picasso where the features are disconnected. Like the Picasso painting, it presents a coherent although not simple message.

Figure 11.3 arranges the daily loads of the year in descending order of magnitude, regardless of the date of occurrence. In this example, the net system loads range from a high (peak) of 16,560 megawatts (MW) to a low of 6,200 MW, a ratio of about 2.7:1. The highest single day peak, 16,560 MW, occurs only once,[4] but some peaking capacity may be needed intermittently, in varying amounts, up to 20% of the year. Capacity for intermediate loads may be needed, off and on, over this same 20% and beyond to 85% of the year. Base load capacity must run full-bore (although not necessarily the same generation units or the same purchases) over a span of 85% of the year. During this 85% time span, loads may exceed the base to varying degrees requiring intermediate and peaking resources as well. Base loads drop below a continuous base level in the remaining 15% of the year.[5]

11.2.4 Planning

Descriptive types of figures are valuable planning tools, but the Fig. 11.3 format is perhaps the most widely used for *resource* planning. It shows concisely the load-carrying characteristics of the energy sources which are most suited at given times. For the electric base load, for example, the generating plants on line should couple a low-operating cost with a limited down-time requirement. It is much less important that the operating costs of a peaking plant be low, or that such plant be capable of enduring extended continuous operation. To the extent that power purchases are relied upon rather than self generation, they also can be tailored to the realities of the duration curve. Similarly, the gas purchases of a gas distributor from its array of suppliers, its arrangements with the pipeline for transportation, and its utilization of storage, can be tailored to fit the duration curve.

For both electric and gas, the operating rule is the same, and, while alluded to earlier, bears repeating. Energy sources having the least expensive variable costs,[6] and a high reliability, will be on line for the base load. Progressively, more expensive sources will be introduced as the load approaches the upper segments of the

---

[4]Peaks sometimes are described as either "needle" or "broad-based" peaks. If sharp, infrequent, and of short duration, they will be of needle type, while if they extend over a longer time span and are more consistent one to another, they will be described as broad-based.

[5]The utilizations shown in Fig. 11.3 are not rules-of-thumb. They will differ from year to year for the same company, and will be different for different companies as well as for different service areas or regions. Also, forecasts will differ from actual experience.

[6]Sunk or embedded costs are irrelevant, since these costs must be met whether or not the capacity is operated.
Any fixed operating costs which do not fluctuate with the utilization under consideration also are irrelevant, since these also will be incurred even if the plant is not put on line. The "least expensive" criteria refers to short-run incremental or marginal costs. In most cases these will be only the additional cost of fuel, plus some minor increment for possible increased maintenance and staffing. For a hydro plant, incremental costs may approach zero.

11.2 Knowing the Market: Load Curves

curve. For most utilities, the higher peaks offer an option. In lieu of very expensive energy inputs, the utility may have arrangements with industrial customers whereby deliveries to the customer may temporarily be cut back in whole or part (interruptible service), thus reducing the peak. Demand-side management schemes satisfy this same peak-reducing objective.

The operating rule just stated would appear to be so obvious as to deny the need for emphasis. And indeed it is, being simply a matter of common sense. But planning to accommodate a future duration curve is tricky. Take energy purchases, either gas or electric, as an example. Except for spot market purchases, which might not be available at the time in the quantity needed, longer-term purchases may be indicated. These may involve a choice between a lower-unit price, but with a high-take requirement, or a higher-unit price with greater flexibility of take. Which to select? The utility gambles on the accuracy of its conception of its future market—the load shapes of Figs. 11.1 and 11.2, as summarized supply-wise on Fig. 11.3.

Weather is an ominous unknown. Will it be normal, warmer than normal, or colder than normal, wet or dry, influencing demands for air conditioning, space heating, and agriculture? No one wants to gamble on the weather, but the utility supply planner cannot avoid it. Electric utilities may be forced to buy power they don't need from QF's or at prices higher than the cheapest sources. Or they may be discouraged from buying power they think they will need. It may be a no-win situation. For the hydro system, snow pack, stream flows, and reservoir levels vary from year to year over a wide range. The list of uncertainties goes on and on. Often, planners will prepare three future duration curves for management, low load, normal or expected load, and high-load scenarios.

The duration curve is readily adapted to including more information than given on Fig. 11.3. The load groups may be broken down into sources of energy, such as thermal and nuclear generation, hydro generation, wind, solar, geothermal or other less conventional types of generation, and power purchases and interchanges, for electric; or gas purchases by supplier, spot market or long-term purchases, company owned production, or inputs/outputs of owned and purchased storage, for gas.

Returning to the duration curve in general, it is seldom used for short periods, such as only a day or a week, although the portrayal is completely consistent with a single day or week. Rather it is mainly used for longer periods, a season (such as the heating or air conditioning season), a year as incorporated in Fig. 11.3, or even a span of years.

Load curves comparing monthly consumptions are a useful aid to the visualization of annual peak and valley usages. For a gas distributor, the valleys dramatize the huge amount of capacity which lays idle during off-peak periods and is therefore available for sale. Figure 11.4 shows the consumption by months of customers on an all-gas residential schedule of Northwest Natural Gas Company. Each bar represents the percent of the total years consumption which is taken in the indicated month. In January, for example, about 16% of the total annual use is taken, while in August only 3%. The figure shows the responsiveness of residential gas demands to the space heating requirements of residential customers. Demands are high in the colder months, very much lower in the warmer months. A glance is sufficient to show the immensity of the summer and fringe-month valley. The seasonally unused

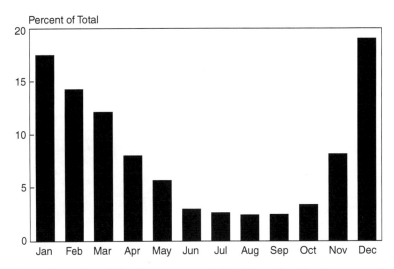

Fig. 11.4 Northwest Natural Gas Company rate schedule 24 - residential - all gas seasonal usage pattern - 1993

capacity in these months should be put to work if at all possible. Commercial and firm industrial loads help some, but for most distributors interruptible customers are a godsend.[7]

Figure 11.5 depicts deliveries to interruptible customers. The pattern there is the converse of Fig. 11.4 (The interruptible pattern is not a perfect converse. The "real world" of the market docs not mirror the planners' aspirations.)

Figure 11.5 reflects the usefulness of an interruptible load which will fill in the summer valleys created by the highly seasonal characteristic of the firm load. Interruptible service is curtailed in part or cut off entirely during peak periods when capacity or gas supply is needed for firm service.[8]

11.3 Gauging the Market: Analysis Factors

Figures 11.1 through 11.3 give the total system composite electric load shapes of Pacific Gas and Electric Company. They show the combined demands of all electric

---

[7] This point is true whether the distributor is selling its own gas, or transporting for the customer. While some distributor mains supply only residential and other firm customers, many facilities are joint to the service of all customers, including interruptible.

[8] Historically, many gas companies have required that interruptible customers for whom they are "merchants" maintain a dual-fuel capability, so that the customer can shift to oil when gas deliveries are curtailed, thus not having to shut down their plants and avoiding a resulting loss of production and worker lay offs. It appears that the trend toward "transmission service" in lieu of merchant service for industries may result in the elimination of duel-fuel requirements.
Our explanation of pipeline formulae for cost allocation shows that the costing and pricing of interruptible gas is a ticklish business.

11.3 Gauging the Market: Analysis Factors

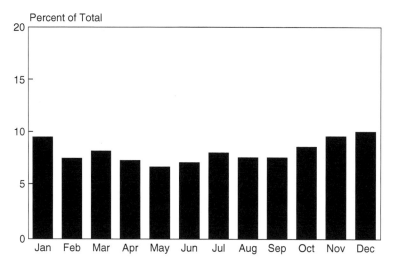

Fig. 11.5 Northwest Natural Gas Company rate schedule 23 - interruptible seasonal usage pattern - 1993

users served by that utility, aggregating the demands of diverse classes of users. They do not reveal patterns of any class.

In contrast, Figs. 11.4 and 11.5 portray comparative usages by months of two gas customer classes. The divergence in load shapes of different customer classes gives rise to the need for common denominators as means for evaluation of load level and timing differences on a uniform basis.

11.3.1 Diversity and Diversity Factor

One such common denominator is *diversity factor* which measures the variations and divergences of the usage characteristics of the utility's customers.

We only need to look to the family unit to understand diversity. No two families are identical in their habits: the call upon the utility for service will vary from home to home in both time of occurrence and quantity of energy taken. Families arise in the morning at different times, take showers at different times, cook breakfast at different times, etc., throughout the activities of the day and evening.

A simplistic illustration may demonstrate why we labor this elementary fact. Taking only one home activity, the use of a clothes washer and dryer, assume that the use of these appliances requires one unit of energy demand. If both homes A and B wash and dry their clothes at 10 a.m., the utility must provide 2 units of capacity to serve them. But if home A washes and dries at 10 a.m. while home B does so at 2 p.m. only one unit of capacity is preempted by the two homes.

In the same fashion that residential use varies from home to home, commercial customer use will vary among the businesses of the class, and the same is true for the

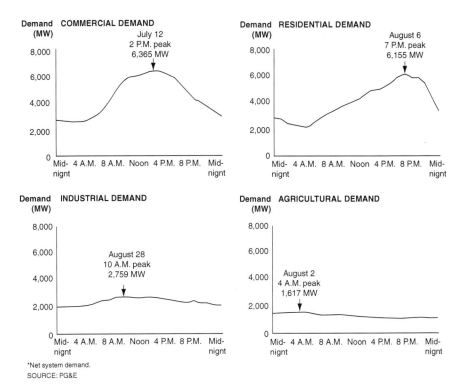

Fig. 11.6 Diversity of energy demand in PG&E's electric power system, 1990* (in megawatts)

industrial and other categories of use (such as agriculture). Even more important, the typical (or consolidated) usage patterns of each class will diverge from each other, giving rise to *class diversity*.

Reasonably enough, the fact that the demands of all customers do not occur to the same degree and at the same time is called *diversity*. The utility must provide sufficient capacity to handle all demands which occur simultaneously. Because all demands are not made at the same time, i.e., diversity, the capacity requirement is reduced.

Once again, PG&E data are most helpful. The four quadrants of Fig. 11.6 give its daily system-peak load curves for four of its customer classes, residential, commercial, industrial, and agricultural. Note the divergence in timing (Table 11.1):

Table 11.1 Timing of peak loads

	Peak hours	Peak day
Residential peak	7 p.m.	August 6
Commercial peak	2 p.m.	July 12
Industrial peak	10 a.m.	August 28
Agricultural peak	4 a.m.	August 2

11.3 Gauging the Market: Analysis Factors   311

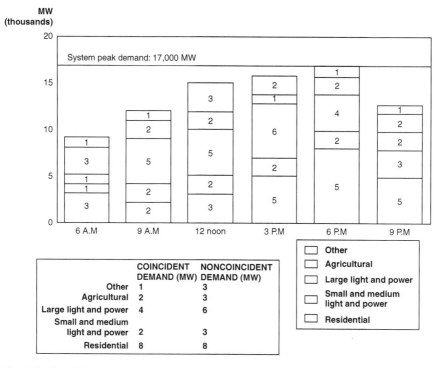

Fig. 11.7 Coincident (Peak) demand (in thousands of megawatts)

Figure 11.7 gives a more specific picture of diversity, showing coincident (simultaneous) system demands by customer classes for six different hours on the day of the system peak, including the peak hour of 6 p.m. All classes are shown. Figure 11.7 combines the commercial and industrial classes of Fig. 11.5 into two size groups, "large" and "small-medium" light and power, and adds a miscellaneous group, "other." The latter combines smaller-size classes, such as street lighting.

Diversity factor, the common denominator for evaluating the degree of diversity, measures the extent of the variations in the timing of the peak demands of a utility's customers or classes of customers in relation to the peak demand experienced by the utility when these customers or customer classes are combined. The individual peaks are termed "non-coincident" since they may not occur at the same time. The peak which occurs when they are combined is termed "coincident."[9]

---

[9] Other types of diversity are *inter-system* diversity, which may exist between two or more utility systems because of differences in the predominant types of load they serve, which makes peak and energy exchanges between such systems of value; for hydroelectric systems, *watershed* diversity between two or more hydroelectric plants located on rivers or streams of different flow characteristics; and *interregional* diversity, the difference between load patterns of adjoining regions.

Obviously, there also is diversity within each customer class. A residential customer who uses electricity for house heating will have a different use pattern than one who heats with gas. An

Technically, diversity factor is defined as *the ratio of the sum of the individual maximum demands of the various subdivisions of a system, or part of a system, to the maximum demand of the whole system, or part under consideration.*

The formula is,

$$\text{Diversity factor} = \frac{\text{Sum of the maximum non-coincident demands}}{\text{Maximum coincident demand}}.$$

The diversity factor will vary depending upon the customer classes and the time periods being considered. Results will differ depending upon the selections. Figures 11.6 and 11.7 may be contrasted to illustrate this.

Figure 11.6 shows a residential peak of 6,155 MW on August 6; a commercial peak of 6.365 MW on July 2; an industrial peak of 2.759 MW on August 28; and an agricultural peak of 1,617 MW on August 2. These four non-coincident class peaks total 16,896 MW.

Other data (not shown) indicate that the annual system-peak load was reached on August 8. At this time the combined loads of the four classes totaled 15,569 MW. The diversity factor for these classes then, was as follows:

$$\frac{16,896 \text{ MW}}{15,569 \text{ MW}} = 1.09.$$

This result represents annual class peaks which are non-coincident both as to the hour and the day of their occurrences. They are related to a system annual peak for the four combined classes which occurred on a different day.

Figure 11.7 illustrates a different version. Here non-coincident peaks for all classes as they occurred on the day of the system peak are related to the system peak.

Turning to the data of Fig. 11.7 (in thousands of megawatts), the diversity factor on this basis is,

$$\frac{3+3+6+3+8}{17} = \frac{23}{17} = 1.35.$$

It would equal one only if all customers maximized their demands at the same time, in which case there would be no diversity.

For completeness, the term *coincidence factor* should be defined. This factor, which is infrequently used, is simply the reciprocal of the diversity factor,

$$\frac{\text{Maximum coincident demand}}{\text{Sum of maximum non-coincident demand}}.$$

---

industrial customer using electricity in processing (such as a 24 h, 7 days a week electro-process aluminum smelter) will not have the same usage characteristics as an industrial customer needing power only for motors and lighting.

Diversity *of whatever nature* when incorporated into system planning or rate designs is a gamble on likelihoods, some high risk, some low. Future diversity is a shifting target. Of course, this statement is true of all planning.

11.3 Gauging the Market: Analysis Factors

Using the same Fig. 11.7 data, it is,

$$\frac{17}{3+3+6+3+8} = 74\%.$$

As might be useful for any given purpose, diversity factors may be derived on other than a peak hour basis (or for gas utilities, on a peak-day basis), provided the numerator and denominator are apples-to-apples equivalents. For example, *volumetric* diversity might be calculated as follows:

$$\frac{\text{Hi-month residential volume + hi-month commercial volume + hi-month firm industrial volume}}{\text{Hi-month total system firm volume}}.$$

11.3.1.1 Applications

As will have been apparent from the foregoing, diversity permits a greater number of customers to be served with the same facilities, or the same number of customers to be served with lesser facilities: it enables the utility to serve its customers with a smaller investment in plant and equipment than would be required were the maximum demands of all customers to come at the same time. As a result demand costs, which form a large part of total cost's, are reduced and the cost of providing utility service is less.

The advantage of diversity is easy to state and easy to prove. But tinkering with diversity to improve it is quite a different matter.

Diversity would be enhanced by shifting loads away from the system peak. But how? Peak and off-peak rate differentials, favoring off-peak usage, may help. So would time-of-use rates, which also would favor off-peak usage. However, these differentials motivate mainly larger customers having the capability of adjusting their takes and for whom the expense of installing and reading a recording demand meter is worthwhile. Smaller customers are likely to be uninfluenced to any great extent. Getting to work on schedule, or opening the store on time, will not be subordinated to any utility rate concession even if the energy companies are able to design an inexpensive and practical means of load surveillance. (Perhaps the information superhighway looming ahead will include a solution. Current improvements in metering and remote meter reading indicate that this is more than likely.)

Pacific Gas and Electric Company's electric operations invoked a novel approach to peak shifting. For agriculture, where water-pumping loads are controllable, the company offered price incentives for the division of customers into groups, each group to receive energy only on alternate days. Other approaches of similar nature are possible, but only for a limited type of customer.

Inhibiting system-peak load growth, by definition, would improve diversity. Should customer classes who contribute substantially to the system peak be discouraged or even penalized by higher average prices or inverted rates? Air conditioning consumption for a utility with a summer peak could be dampened by an on-peak surcharge. While stores and offices doubtless would deem it necessary for business reasons to continue air cooling even with higher prices, residential and other types of customers less sensitive to the lure of hot weather comfort might see fit to forego the luxury of uninhibited cooling or at least settle for somewhat warmer indoor temperatures.

Stimulating new uses which can be expected to fall off-peak is another possibility. The most promising is the electric automobile. Visionaries contend that batteries for the most part would be recharged overnight, in daily off-peak hours. Whether recharging could be confined to these hours is still conjectural, of course.

Only the brave will promote another possibility, fuel switching. Natural gas, electricity, and oil are viable alternatives for many energy uses. Should demand be directed toward one energy source, and away from another, by regulatory encouragement or direction?

Finally, the possibilities need not necessarily be limited to energy suppliers. Public policy, stirred by a whole complex of motivations, might suggest more draconian measures. Suppose working hours over the whole economy of a state (or a region, for that matter) were to be staggered. This would reduce traffic congestion and lessen peak-hour overloading of highways and public transit—non-utility results —as well as smoothing out the peaks and valleys of utility usage. (The trend toward office-work-at-home promises to induce the same results.)

The possibilities mentioned above are merely facets of "Demand-Side Management." We touch upon them here to establish the link between diversity as merely a unit of measurement, and diversity as an objective for implementing the social engineering/public policy approach to utility pricing. We have not included usage reduction per se in our menu of possibilities because conservation, if reaching all classes of use about equally, might not change the diversity factor.

11.3.1.2 Calculating Diversity

In the present stage of the art of metering, which lack universal recording demand meters, past diversity can only be calculated by a sampling of class load configurations. Resulting estimates probably are sufficiently accurate for all practicable purposes.

Estimating a future diversity is a different matter. Demand-side management and/or conservation measures and new pricing schemes such as time-of-use rates, introduce unknown dimensions.

But probably the greatest unknowns will result from restructuring. To what extent will non-utility generation cancel the utilization of utility generating capacity? To what extent will pooled operations, whether mandatory or voluntary, change generation scheduling? To what extent will bypass impinge upon the historical utilization of utility transmission and distribution facilities? The broader question is: how will the introduction of competition change the magnitude of utility loads and customer load shapes? Such unknowns are not new. What is new is the sheer magnitude of their possible impact.[10]

---

[10]From the standpoint of the non-utility operator, the uncertainties promise to loom very large indeed. Except as all deliveries it makes are guaranteed by contract as mandatory customer takes,

11.3 Gauging the Market: Analysis Factors   315

Going back in history, one can see similarities to the presently looming unknown dimensions. Take the oft-cited example of electric-space heating when it was being introduced as a new load. Would the maximum demand for space heating occur at the same time as the system peak, viz., in the early evening hours? If so, the service would be very expensive to provide and rates must be high. Or, would space heating fill up the load valleys relatively more than it increased the system peak? If so, it might be a good load to encourage. But if encouraged, would space-heating usage grow to such proportions as to create a new system peak at a different time? It did! The introduction of electric air conditioning raised similar questions and with similar results. For many companies, air conditioning shifted the peak from winter to summer, and from an evening to a morning hour.

The careful rate maker will not shrug-off the lessons of history. Just a few paragraphs earlier the writer ventured the possibility that electric auto battery charging could, if it materialized, be an off-peak night-time load. It is easy to imagine chargers humming around midnight and through the wee hours of the morning. But might not they be turned on sometime soon after 5 p.m. when the car is garaged after a day's use? For a utility with a 6 p.m. peak this would hardly be a cheap off-peak load.

The rate makers diversity dilemma extends to each and every usage modification which might be experienced and incorporated into the tariff —and there are many. No matter the difficulty, diversity questions must be answered before decisions as to rate levels can be reached.

11.3.2 Load Factor

Undoubtedly the most frequently used, and probably the most important, of the analytical tools which have been developed for utility cost and operational analysis is *load factor*. In concept, load factor is an index of the efficiency of the usage pattern of a system, a customer class, or an individual customer, depending upon to whichever it may relate. As a measure of efficiency, a good-load factor suggests lower costs and therefore lower rates, and a poor-load factor, the reverse.

The measure accepts the relationship between average loads and maximum loads as the most useful gauge for approximating the quality of a usage pattern, and hence of efficiency.

Load factor is defined as the *ratio of the average to the maximum (peak) load*. It may be found for a 24 hour period, a week, a month, or a year. It may be applied to a single customer, a group of customers, or an entire system.

Starting at home, the writer's Portland, Oregon residence is heated with gas, has gas water heating and clothes drying, a gas barbecue, and a gas log lighter.

---

it must rely upon (informed?) speculation as to the degree of diversity upon which it can depend. This may not be too important for large-volume industrial sales, but it may be critical for aggregated smaller-customer sales.

It uses electricity for lighting and the usual small appliances, plus an electric clothes washer.

Gas and electric monthly consumptions over the most recent year prior to writing this chapter are given in Table 11.2:

Table 11.2 Monthly home consumptions of electricity and natural gas

	Natural gas (therms)	Electricity (kWh)
July	32.5	540
August	42.3	540
September	88.1	600
October	175.9	620
November	328.7	540
December	583.9	660
January	763.8	620
February	554.4	660
March	384.0	580
April	331.7	620
May	197.1	520
June	105.2	580
Average monthly use	299.0	590
Maximum monthly use	763.8	660
Annual load factor	39.1%	89.4%

The gas usage pattern reflects the very large fluctuations in use which accompany space heating even in a moderate climate. The load factor, taking total consumption in the highest month as the peak (rather than the highest day in the month) is a miserable 39.1%. The electric usage pattern, influenced neither by space heating nor air conditioning, is an excellent 89.4% on the same total peak month basis.

11.3.2.1 Limitations

It is now time to examine what the above illustration tells and *does not tell* about efficiency. An incomplete or overblown understanding of load factor as a measure is counterproductive. Its use in fixing rates is too pervasive: its deficiencies as well as its virtues should be clear.

Generally speaking, the following may be said, in terms of the individual customer such as the writer in the above illustration, load factor measures how closely his average use matches his maximum use, indicating efficiency of use. A high-load factor means good efficiency, extensive use of maximum demand, while a low-load factor means that the customer is an inefficient user of his maximum demand, and may buy little or no energy at *certain* times, though the utility must be ready to serve him at all times up to the extent of his maximum demand.

That is "generally speaking." More precisely, while the average monthly consumption does accurately depict the *average* load (the numerator of the ratio), the peak monthly load (the denominator of the ratio) understates the *maximum* load.

11.3 Gauging the Market: Analysis Factors

It is not the maximum month that counts for an efficiency standard, but the maximum day for gas or the maximum hour for electric. So the monthly load factors cited merely *suggest* relative efficiency. They do not pinpoint it. Nevertheless, this is the best that can be done for a residential customer (or other small use customer) since present-metering practices do not incorporate daily gas or hourly electric measurements for this customer class.[11]

Peak-hour and peak-day measurements are, of course, available for electric and gas systems. For example, in terms of a system, if the maximum or peak load of the system is 1,000,000 kW and the average load 600,000 kW, the load factor—the ratio of the two—is 60%. This is an accurate ratio. However, it still falls short in one respect of measuring system efficiency. The peak load of one million kilowatts does not represent the capacity provided—the load may well fall considerably below actual capacity even with due allowance for prudent reserve leeway. To the extent that the peak load is below capacity, load factors will overstate efficiency. (Capacity factor, *infra*, is more accurate on this point.) The reason why the somewhat simplified maximum load is used is due to the difficulty of measuring capacity. The difficulty arises primarily because of the numerous individual physical components of utility operations, in electric the generating plant, transmission lines, distribution lines, substations and switching stations, local transformers, and service drops. It is difficult enough to get engineers to agree on the usable capacity of any one facility, let alone an entire system. On the other hand, if a load actually has been served, there must have been adequate capacity to do so. So a theoretical, disputable capacity figure is bypassed in favor of a concrete measured maximum demand figure. In the pure efficiency sense, load factor is a proxy for capacity factor.

Another deficiency is that load factor does not pinpoint the time of occurrence of either the peak load or the average load. If the peak load for any class does not come at the same time as the system peak, this is more efficient than if it occurs on-peak (diversity). And if the load *on average* comes during off-peak periods, this is more efficient than if it occurs mainly during peak periods (again, a version of diversity).

Having said that load factor is not a perfect gauge to efficiency, what can be concluded? It safely can be said that a system with a low-load factor must provide a large amount of equipment to meet its peak which it does not use for its average load; that is, a smaller number of energy units are sold than could be sold with the facilities provided, and therefore the smaller number of units sold must cover the costs of more extensive facilities than would be required if the average use more nearly approached the peak use. Conversely, the system with a high-load factor is advantageously situated. In other words, the high-load factor system is more

---

[11] If daily/hourly consumption records were available, it would be necessary to restate the average monthly consumptions (the numerator) to a daily/hourly basis so as to match the maximum peak day or hour (the denominator). For gas, the total years consumption would be divided by 365, the number of days in the year; for electric, the total years consumption would be divided by 8,760, the number of hours in the year.

To Town / Return	Factory Workers	Office Workers	Students	Shoppers	Others	Total Riders
6 a.m. / 6:30 a.m.	5 /	/	/	/	/ 1	5 / 1
7 / 7:30	27 /	10 /	/	/	/ 5	37 / 5
8 / 8:30	4 /	33 /	1 /	/	/ 9	38 / 9
9 / 9:30	3 /	8 /	13 /	8 /	/ 1	32 / 1
10 / 11	/	/	4 /	7 /	/	11 /
12 noon / 1 p.m.	/	/	/	5 /	/	5 / -
2 / 2:30	/	/	/	2 /	/ 1	2 / 1
3 / 3:30	/ 7	/	/ 8	/ 14	1 /	1 / 29
4 / 4:30	/ 15	/ 16	/ 1	/ 5	1 /	1 / 37
5 / 5:30	/ 16	/ 17	/ 6	/ 1	10 /	10 / 40
6 / 6:30	/ 1	/ 16	/ 2	/ 1	2 /	2 / 20
7 / 7:30	/	/ 2	/ 1	/ 1	3 /	3 / 4
To Town Total	39	51	18	22	17	147
Return Total	39	51	18	22	17	147

Fig. 11.8 Daily ridership of the One-bus One-route Transit Line, Lake Woebegon, MN. - permanent schedule

efficient than the low-load factor system. By logical extension, a high-load factor system is less costly to operate than a low-load factor system (other things being equal, of course). The same logic applies when groups of customers or individual customers are compared.

As a locale for a final look at load factor, we settled on Garrison Keillor's home town of Lake Wobegon, Minnesota. From the flourishing utilities there we selected its bus line, The One-bus One-route Transit Line. The manager of One–One (as it is affectionately called) gave us the ridership for a typical day, as shown on Fig. 11.8.

The "others" class of riders is comprised mainly of domestics and yard workers who ride into the residential areas in the morning and back to town in the afternoon, the opposite of the travel of the other classes.

We are informed that the bus has seats for 41. It can accommodate ten standees in addition, the maximum permitted by state law. However, the runs are frequent enough so that typically there are seats for all.

11.3 Gauging the Market: Analysis Factors

To Town	Return	Factory Workers	Office Workers	Students	Shoppers	Others	Total Riders
7 a.m.		36	9				45
	7:30 a.m.					6	6
8			34	14			51
	8:30	3				11	11
9			8	4	22		34
	4:30 p.m.	21	16	xx	14		
5 p.m.						2	2
	5:30	17	17	xx	6		40
6						15	15
	6:30	1	18	18	2		39
*students prohibited on these runs							
To Town Total		39	51	18	22	17	147
	Return Total	39	51	18	22	17	147

Fig. 11.9 Daily ridership of the One-bus One-route Transit Line, Lake Woebegon, MN. - condensed schedule

Overall relationships are as follows:

Trips	24
Total riders	294
Average riders	12.25
Maximum riders	40

$$\text{Load Factor} = \text{Average Riders/Maximum Riders} = 30.6\%$$

$$\text{Diversity Factor} = \frac{27 + 33 + 13 + 14 + 10}{40} = \frac{97}{4} = 2.42$$

The diversity factor is a class diversity. The maximum number of factory workers riding on any bus is 27, etc. The maximum total riders on any bus is 40.

One—One's manager (who also manages the water bureau and is head of the volunteer fire department) says that a few months ago he tried to drop trips having few riders.

His experiment reduced the number of trips to ten but he was forced to prohibit students on the crowded 4:30 and 5:30 p.m. return trips. The condensed schedule results arc tabulated in Fig. 11.9.

Overall relationships changed under the condensed schedule, as follows:

Trips	10
Total riders	294
Average riders	29.4
Maximum riders	51

$$\text{Load factor} = \frac{\text{Average riders}}{\text{Maximum riders}} = 57.6\%,$$

$$\text{Diversity factor} = \frac{36 + 34 + 18 + 22 + 15}{51} = \frac{125}{51} = 2.45.$$

From a technical point of view, the experiment was a success. Load factor improved from 30.6 to 57.6%, with diversity essentially unchanged. But urban transit in Lake Wobegon does not run on technical efficiency alone. The experiment lasted exactly 2 weeks and 1 day. The dropped trips were reinstated. With this we bid adieu to Lake Wobegon.

11.3.2.2 Applications

As pointed out, load factor is a general index to relative efficiency. It is important, though, that the relative efficiencies compare apples-to-apples, not bananas to oranges. A comparison between an electric and a gas utility will generally be meaningless. However, a comparison of one customer class to another of the same utility generally will be meaningful, as will a prior-load factor with a later-load factor for the same utility, for the same class of customer, or the same customer. Load factors *without* a given type of load, and *with* that load, can usefully be compared.

Beyond general comparisons, load factor is an omnipresent element in rate design. A rate schedule for high-load factor use might well offer a lower per-unit price than a schedule for low-load factor use. A given rate schedule might be designed to reward (and therefore encourage) higher-load factor use. Another given rate schedule might be structured so as to put in place a price floor relative to a given minimum load factor, so that the bill would never be less than that which would have resulted from takes at the specified load factor.[12] These are just a few examples. Few changes in rate design are made without regard to their effect on load factor.

On occasion, the level of one rate schedule will be pegged in relation to another via load factor. The Federal Energy Regulatory Commission, for example, frequently has required that the level of an interruptible schedule be set at the equivalent of the 100% (or some other percentage) load factor price of a firm schedule.

Demand-side management and similar steps which may be taken to improve diversity factor also are appropriate for the improvement of load factor.

11.3.2.3 Relationship of Load and Diversity Factors

The common objectives of improving load factors and diversity factors in rate making (and demand-side management) usually move in tandem. Utilities often offer price concessions (such as off-peak rates) to fill up load valleys. These are efforts to improve and increase load factor. But these same price concessions also serve to improve diversity, provided only that the system peak is not raised in the new load shape.

---

[12] That is even though the customer's actual usage was at a lower-load factor, the billing would not be less than the equivalent of the higher-specified load factor.

11.4 Capacity Factor

However, a 100% system-wide load factor could be attained only if the diversity among loads was in perfect balance. As a practical matter, diversity can arise only when customers (as among themselves) and customer classes (as among other classes) have less than a 100% load factor.

Efforts to improve load factor and diversity factor may be undertaken simultaneously by a utility with good reason. With rare exceptions, such as certain electro-process industries, load factors of most types of customers will necessarily fall considerably below 100%. Any improvement is to the good. Since a 100% system load factor is thus unattainable for all practical purposes, diversity should be promoted. Experience has taught that improvement of load factor does not necessarily reduce diversity—in fact, such is the nature of the business, it may actually increase. (Recall Lake Wobegon.) Conversely, improvement of diversity factor—such as by shifting the timing of loads—may actually increase load factor.

Other standard measures, or factors, of less importance in rate making are defined next.

11.4 Capacity Factor

Capacity factor, sometimes known as plant factor, is basically an electric term. It is defined as *the ratio of the average load to the rated capacity of the generating unit,* or

$$\frac{\text{Plant-average load}}{\text{Plant-rated capacity}}.$$

Annual capacity factor for the system as a whole can be defined as annual kilowatt-hour sales divided by the product of the total hours in a year and the rated generating capacity of the system in kilowatts, or

$$\frac{\text{kWh sales per year}}{8{,}760\,\text{h} \times \text{rated generating capacity in kW}}.$$

The term is also used on occasion for gas pipelines, as the ratio of actual volume throughput to the flow that the pipeline can carry considering its size, compression, etc.

No electric utility ever plans to operate at full capacity under normal conditions and the amount of excess capacity over peak demand (the reserve margin) is largely a matter of management's discretion. The significance of capacity factor is twofold: first, it indicates the degree to which the plant capacity is being utilized on the average; second, it is an indication of the reserve capacity which the system has at hand to meet emergencies, such as load surges due to extreme weather conditions or the failure of facilities.

By the same token no gas utility will rely for firm loads on continuous flows at the full volume of which the pipeline is capable.

It is regrettable that the interwoven nature of the physical components of a utility system makes it difficult to arrive at a composite system (or even a sub-system) capacity figure. Cost-based rate-making might be more precise if an appropriate capacity figure could be used in lieu of maximum demand as the denominator of the load factor ratio. Then, the actual degree of utilization of the provided capacity (i.e., of the investment) could be known. As it is, it is quite possible that a high-load factor can be indicated even though the use of the relevant capacity is low. This will be the case whenever the maximum demand falls short of the available capacity by more than the necessary reserve increment.

11.5 Utilization Factor

Capacity factor, just defined, relates the *average* load to the rated capacity. Utilization factor relates the *maximum* load to the rated capacity, as,

$$\frac{\text{Maximum demand}}{\text{Rated capacity}}.$$

The factor can be applied to a whole system or a part thereof, provided that capacity data are available. As with capacity factor, however, the lack of such data for system units other than an electric generating plant or a pipeline city gate, usually limits the factor to these units.

11.6 Demand Factor

Demand factor is defined as *the ratio of the maximum demand of a system to the total connected load of the system*, or, in terms of a customer rather than a utility system, it is *the ratio of the customer's maximum demand to his connected load.*[13] If a customer has a connected load of 100 kW but never uses more than 50 kW at any one time, his demand factor is 50%.

A demand factor of less than 100% makes it possible for the utility company to serve a customer adequately without being required to install facilities sufficient to serve the customer's total connected load. If there is any diversity among the various customers, the amount of facilities necessary is reduced still more. This saving of facilities, which means a saving of capital costs, makes it possible for the ultimate user to secure the utility service cheaper than would otherwise be possible. Thus, the smaller the demand factor, and the larger the diversity factor, the greater is the amount of potential demand that can adequately be supplied per unit of facilities.

Demand factor, in practice, is mainly an intuitive measure rather than a precise calculation, except for heavy energy using processes. Electric rules of thumb will suggest that a distribution transformer of a given size will suffice for "x" number of modest-size homes which have gas space and water heating; a larger transformer would be needed for the same number of similar homes using electricity for these purposes, or for bigger homes. No count of electric outlets and no accumulation

---

[13]Connected load is seldom calculated in today's practices, except for large industrial customers. Nonetheless, connected load is a fact for all customers and all customer classes. The circumstance that an individual customer's demand (or a class demand) will fall below its connected load is the result of customer's timing—diversity—in the use of energy appliances.

of appliance nameplate ratings is made. The same is true for the sizing of gas distribution mains, meters, and regulators.

In terms of revenue allocation and subsequent rate design, load factor is the most useful of the factors, with diversity factor in a second place. Capacity, utilization, and demand factors are of lesser significance. All, however, are gauges of relative degrees of use of the facilities installed by the utility to provide service to customers, and may be applied as appropriate in fashioning rates.

11.7 Power Factor

Power factor is an electrical engineering concept which often is recognized directly in electric rate schedules and which always must be taken into consideration in the design of electric rates. Technically, *power factor is the ratio of kilowatts to kilovolt-amperes*. Since this definition imparts little to those who are not electrical engineers, power factor is better understood in terms of its practical effects. The following analogy, written many years ago by Edwin Vennard, then vice president, Middle West Service Company, describes these effects.

> ... Assume a horse pulling a railway car on a straight track. The car is held to the track by the flanges on its wheels and can move only in the direction of the track.

If the horse pulls straight ahead on the track, he moves the car and all of his power is effective in producing motion. In this case, he may be said to be working at 100%, or unity power factor.

If the horse now turns and pulls at right angles to the track he may pull just as hard, but his effort serves no useful purpose because he only pulls against the rails and cannot move the car. There is no component of his pull in the direction of the track. His pull is all useless and the power factor is zero.

Now suppose the horse turns halfway back and pulls at an angle of 45° to the track. Part of his pull is now in the direction of the track and useful in producing motion, while the other part is at an angle to the track and useless in producing motion. In this case, the power factor would be determined by dividing the component of the pull in the direction of the track by the total pull in the direction the horse is pulling.[14]

Most electric wholesale or large-power rates include a power factor adjustment provision. Like load factor, power factor is an index of the efficiency of the use of the electrical facilities. Low power factor conditions put an added burden on the electrical system, requiring additional capacity. Therefore, customers taking power at low power factor are more expensive to serve, and it is appropriate that the added costs be recognized in the rate schedule.

Ordinarily, power factor adjustment provisions call for an additional charge if the customer's power factor is less than a specified percent, with a reduction in the customer's bill if his power factor is above that percent.

---

[14] From pamphlet "Electric Terms." September, 1947, by Mr. Vennard.

PG&E's adjustment, for example, increases the demand charge and the base rate part of the energy charge by 0.1% for each 1% that the power factor falls below 85%, with a commensurate decrease in the charges for power factors above 85%.

Poor power factors can be corrected by the installation of capacitors. There is some difference of opinion as to the proper amount for a low power factor charge. Some utilities believe that the charge should constitute a penalty to make it economically unwise for the customer to fail to install corrective equipment. Under such a theory the power factor penalty will considerably exceed the cost to the customer of installing corrective equipment. The utility's objective in this case is to induce the customer to correct the condition, rather than to gain revenue. Other utilities hold that if customers wish to purchase at a low-power factor they should be permitted to do so and that the power factor adjustment should cover only the added cost to the utility. It sometimes has been suggested on this score that the utility sell—and separately bill for—kilovar-hours (to compensate for low-power factor) as well as kilowatt-hours (energy useful for work).

A few electric utilities, such as Houston Lighting and Power Company, bill larger customers on a direct kva (kilovar-hour) basis, thus incorporating a built-in power factor adjustment.

11.8 A Note to the Rate maker

The purpose of load/demand and duration curves, as discussed at the beginning of this chapter, is to accurately portray the market. The purpose of the several factors of measurement, also explored earlier, is to provide an accurate guide for operations planning and rate design. It is important, therefore, that each be labeled clearly and unambiguously. To avoid misinterpretation, each figure or factor (or its description) should specify:

1) The geographic or operational area to which it applies—city or state, urban or rural, system-wide or some part or parts of the system.
2) The time period encompassed—day, week, season, or year, historical or forecasted.
3) The title and nature of the load—
   Title: residential, commercial, industrial, all classes, etc.
   Type of service: firm, modified firm, interruptible, etc.
   Unique characteristics: average (such as average day), peak (such as peak day), weather (such as normal, cold, warm), and losses (included or excluded).

Chapter 12
Matters of Judgment

Abstract Preceding sections introduce the process of pricing energy delivered by the electric and natural gas utilities. Guidelines and opinions are directed toward executive decisions governing internal operations. Decisions governing external relationships are for the most part left unexplored, leaving a gap between internal utility decision-making and external decisions applicable to other sectors of the economy. But even the most meticulous internal operations fall short if a company's external relationships are deficient. There is a gap between internal and external in the earlier chapters. To narrow this gap, Chap. 12 addresses an often overlooked phase of management's responsibilities: its decisions on outside issues. Chapter 12 is not intended for technical readers only. It is written to be read by a wider audience, by those who are affected by business or governmental micro-economic decisions, which means all of us. Chapter 12 has three distinct parts. The first addresses those who, directly or indirectly, contribute to the preparation of the company's published business reports, particularly those of a financial nature. It points to frequent loose or inaccurate statements often found in these reports which are misleading and should be avoided. These are basic guidelines, intended to be instructive for those who originate the reports as well as for those who read them. The second part goes beyond basics. It aims at the top executives of businesses of all sizes who fashion the policies of their companies. Here good judgment in decision-making is of vital importance to the operations they control. As a prime example of a failed policy in the utility sector, this part cites the California energy crisis, where ill-fated decisions by executives of two major utilities led to the disastrous bankruptcy of one of the companies and the near-bankruptcy of the other. The third part is directed toward upper-level government executives who are responsible for the nation's macro- and micro-economic policies. It reviews the 2008–2009 recession, and highlights the short-sighted decisions of the nation's financial heads whose leadership (or lack thereof) permitted the recession to develop. The message for all three addressees is the same: be judicious in your decision-making, for its results may be greater and more far reaching than you realize.

12.1 Part 1: Dubious Accounting

The financial reports of your company should not be marred by distortions of the facts, whatever they may be. Almost as bad as conscious omissions are statements which conceal the real nature of the data under consideration or point the observer toward a false conclusion. Each of these is an example of "dubious accounting" which is the subject of this first section of Chap. 12. All of these practices should be avoided, so that a clean and accurate statement of the facts will be presented by your report.

12.2 Earlier Accounting Results

Early in the 1990s, in an unpublished article, we described various accounting measures used to distort factual results under the umbrella term "aggressive accounting." We said then, "The literature indicates that public attention has repeatedly been called to dubious accounting."

In 1984, *Forbes* coupled the captions "cute accounting" and "indecent disclosure," referring to "controversial methods of sweeping losses and mistakes under the rug."[1] A month later, *Business Week* called attention to "cooked books"—combining "either puffed-up corporate earnings or exaggerated net worth," "the stretching and bending, rather than out-and-out breaking, of accounting rules," and cited to "an SEC drive against reckless accounting."[2]

Also in 1984, *Fortune* printed an interesting explanation of why a $7 hammer could cost the Pentagon $436, a question which mystified many taxpayers. The answer is found in "legally permissible, but questionable, accounting practices," which allowed defense contractors "to allocate the cost of overhead evenly among all the items in a defense contract," overhead including engineering costs of other items such as printed circuit boards and electronic instruments. (Overhead is now required to be allocated more realistically.) The article also explains why a 12-cent wrench could be priced at $5,205 (the price including not only overhead, but also a $1,287 profit per wrench that being the company's allocation of the total profit allowed under the contract). The Air Force rejected the price,[3] but headlines were made nevertheless.

In 1985, *Forbes* enlisted pungent language to explain how thrifts were "getting out from under their old, low-yielding mortgages without taking a big loss." The title of the article was "Banking by Mirrors." The text speaks of "razzle-dazzle accounting," "a complicated shell game," and "creative accounting."[4]

---

[1] Andresky, Jill, "An SEC crackdown on "cute accounting" is making lots of people nervous," *Forbes,* August 13, 1984.

[2] "The SEC Turns Up the Heat on 'Cooked Books,'" *Business Week,* September 3, 1984. See also Berton, Lee, "Accounting Rule ... Raises Questions," *The Wall Street Journal,* November 16, 1984.

[3] "Politics & Policy," *Fortune,* October 29, 1984.

[4] Clifford, Mark, "Banking by Mirrors," *Forbes* August 26, 1985.

At about the same time, *The Wall Street Journal* headed an article "Double-Entry Doubletalk," referring to how an S and L considered a debt to be an asset rather than a liability.[5]

Two articles in early 1986 noticed the profusion and huge size of write-offs then being made. *The Wall Street Journal* described these as "big bath" write-offs, adding that the activity was causing concern to accountants.[6] *Forbes* was less charitable in its terminology, reporting under the head "Rumpelstiltskin accounting," with the introductory note "rumpelstiltskin spun straw into gold. Last quarter dozens of leading businessmen spun past sins into current virtue."[7] The past sins, of course, were improvident acquisitions and the like, for which management received credit by taking a write-off when times were propitious, raising the question: were earnings overstated prior to the write-off?

We turn to 1989, for some priceless tidbits from *Fortune's* report on "Cute Tricks on the Bottom Line."[8]

> ... profits, like sausages and laws, are esteemed most by those who know least about what goes into them.
>
> To most companies today, managing earnings is almost irresistible. The proof is in this year's annual reports, which are laden with obfuscations, special items and accounting gimmickry.
>
> Many managements view GAAP (generally accepted accounting principles) not as a standard to be met, but as an obstacle to overcome.

12.3 Current Accounting Results

We have recently updated our research to determine whether accounting for public consumption has improved. Unfortunately, we conclude that it has not.

The abuses of the 2008–2009 recession should not have been a surprise!

Since investors rely heavily on published data, from annual reports or news articles, we list below some of the most common of accounting abuses. We do not imply that these reported practices are illegal, or even violate FASB regulations. They may or may not be exceptionally out of line, depending upon the circumstances in each case. But each distorts the facts, and the investor should be wary of relying on the accuracy of any statements which are based upon them. Equally important, these abuses should be anathema to the accountant.

Most of the items are shown generically, without unnecessary identification either as to source or the name of the company reported on.

The objective of most instances of aggressive accounting is to improve earnings and thus enhance the company's stock price. The impetus for the action may arise at the top management level, with the company's overall well-being in mind, or

---

[5] Berton, Lee, *The Wall Street Journal,* September 17, 1985.

[6] Berton, Lee, and Miller, Gay Sands, "Accountants Debate Tightening Rules for 'Big Bath' Write Offs by Companies," *The Wall Street Journal,* February 11, 1986.

[7] Weberman, Ben, "Rumpelstiltskin accounting," *Forbes,* February 24, 1986.

[8] Hector, Gary, "Cute Tricks on the Bottom Line," *Fortune,* April 24, 1989.

at a lower level, reporting to top management and desirous of achieving favorable operating results. Higher earnings may be induced either by greater revenues (sales), on the one hand, or by lesser expenses (cost savings), on the other hand. Both point in the same direction.

12.3.1 Overstatements

Overstatement of assets: A movie company, to disguise mounting losses, revalued assets, going from a negative net worth of $45 million to a positive net worth of $21 million. Also, it valued a $175 million advance against future revenue, which should have been treated as deferred earnings, as cash received in part ($50 million).

Overreporting of revenue: Examples are: including installment purchases in revenues before sales are final; booking revenue from equipment leases as if they were outright sales, rather than spreading them over the life of the lease; classifying contingent sales as final; booking revenue when products are shipped to dealers who can return them; booking revenues from long-term leases immediately, although actually dollars will flow in only over the life of the product.

A manufacturer reported locomotive sales which had not yet occurred to boost revenues by $370 million.

A supercomputer maker allowed shipments to universities that didn't have funding, shipments to distributors that didn't have customers, and shipments where payment was contingent on the customer getting upgraded machines in the future.

A company reported bogus revenue totaling $300 million over 3 years, from claiming revenue in the short term that should have been reported late; reserves set aside for one purpose, merger costs, but used for another; and credit card rejections that were recorded late.

In 1991, *Business Week* described as "funny money" a practice followed by some software makers of booking sales as soon as customers promised to buy, thus adding to "accounts receivable" in advance of the time of delivery to the customer. SEC guidelines now prohibit such advance booking, although many have tried since.

Hoarding reserves: Some banks squirrel away reserves in a good year, to be used when earnings are down by cutting back on reserve provisions for that current year.

Hoarding earnings: To have smooth earnings instead of wild swings, some companies "bank" earnings by understating them in very good years and using the banked profits to polish results in bad years. Generally, artificially depressed current earnings assure a big gain in later years.

Overhead: To slash its bloated overhead, a leading company wrote off $2.1 billion in buildings and equipment.

12.3.2 Understatements

Understatement of expenses: A trash company deferred recognition of certain "indirect" landfill-development expenses, writing them off over the life of the landfill. These included executive salaries and travel, and legal and public relations costs.

12.3 Current Accounting Results

A company understated its expenses by pushing into the future its costs of investments and retirement plans, and understating their costs.

Underfunded pensions: A major oil company had underfunded pensions—the gulf between promised benefits and the money set aside to pay for them—which widened by nearly a third in 1992, to $38.05 billion.

Inadequate reserves: An insurance company, having disregarded high claims in prior years, increased its reserves by $1.2 billion. The article describing this action made this comment:

> When the auditor's certificate appears in the company's Annual Report, it will say that the company's statements "present fairly" its financial position.
> The auditor said the same thing about last year's financial statements, the ones that the company now says contained a $1.2 billion flaw.
> Until improvements are made, do not expect the financial statements to "present fairly" the facts.

Questions: Re-inventory—How much is obsolete? Re-pending litigation: how much will it cost to settle? Re-accounts receivable: how much will be uncollectible?

12.3.3 Special Issues

Mark-to-market asset valuation: This rule (MTM) requires banks and insurers to value their debt instruments at current market value, or what the asset would be worth if it were sold in an orderly fashion to a willing buyer. This is in contrast to valuing at acquisition cost.

In 1992, a change to MTM was advocated by those who wanted to avoid a new S and L mess, before the issue arose dramatically in the 2008–2009 recession. There was argument pro and con. "Fairy tale accounting" is how the SEC's Richard Breedon described existing rules that focus on past values. Fed chairman Alan Greenspan countered that forcing banks to carry bonds and loans on their balance sheets at market value "would undermine investors' and depositors' confidence ... jettisoning established accounting conventions for new, untested rules depending upon highly subjective estimates of market values would undermine confidence ... Marking loans to their market value could make many banks appear insolvent."[9]

During the 1980 s, many thrifts engaged in wild and disastrous speculation. They could do so and still have black balance sheets because S and L's were then allowed to book a debt security at its purchase price, masking how much it may have dropped in value. This drop in value led to the sentiment in favor of MTW. However, some bankers still objected to MTM, saying, "MTM forced them to price securities well below their real valuation, making it difficult to purge toxic assets from their books at anything but fire-sale prices."[10]

---

[9] Fred S. Worthy, "The Battle of the Bean Counters," *Fortune*, June 1, 1992.

[10] James S. Chanos, "We Need Honest Accounting," *The Wall Street Journal*, March 24, 2009.

The Wall Street Journal posed the current MTM question on June 3, 2009, "Are hardest-to-sell securities worth no more than the market is willing to pay, or did the market grow too dysfunctional to properly set values?"

Restructuring: Basically, a restructuring charge is a company's estimate of the future costs of some drastic change, such as closing a division. Restructuring cost write-offs can be used to make future earnings seem unrealistically rosy. Also, a restructuring charge can improve the look of subsequent periods by reducing the company's reported expenses. Further, instead of being a response to a unique situation, such as selling a line of business, companies may use these charges to pay for normal costs of operation.

Available-for-sale investments: Declines in the value of these investments can be taken as "unrealized losses" that get assessed on the balance sheet but don't affect earnings—all banks have to do is to say they don't intend to sell. If they do, only "credit losses" would have to be recognized in earnings.

Goodwill: When one company buys another, it creates goodwill if it pays more than the appraised value of the physical assets. Goodwill is the difference between the price paid for a franchise and its book value. Or, goodwill is the difference between the fair value of the company's net assets and the price of acquiring the company.

A company acquired another for $5.8 billion, of which $2.8 billion was goodwill.

Pro forma reporting: Reporting on a pro forma basis enables a company to employ almost every trick to pump earnings and fool investors.

12.3.4 Potpourri

A trash company realized it couldn't keep growing, and resorted to "cooking the books" to preserve its stock price. Instead of lowering expectations, it continued to promise turbocharged earnings—then failed to deliver. It began booking ordinary losses as one-time "special charges." It kept the company's fleet of garbage trucks and steel trash containers on the streets longer, forcing it to spend millions to keep broken-down trucks on the road. It would tow a truck across three states so it could be salvaged for spare parts. The company began stretching depreciation schedules, and claiming a fictitious value for the trucks. In some cases, the company kept two sets of books. The accounting maneuvers inflated pretax profits by $176 million. The company claimed that expansions of its landfills were likely, and recycling facilities, hazardous waste plants, engineering operations—all were massively overvalued, artificially brightening the balance sheet.

Another company, a medical lens maker, under hard pressure for profits from its CEO, played fast and loose with accounting principles and ethics. These included booking big sales, but not shipping the goods; instead sending the goods to an outside warehouse from which sales managers would try to persuade distributors to buy the excess; giving customers extraordinarily long payment terms in exchange for big orders; constantly rolling over unpaid bills so that customers wouldn't return unwanted goods for credit; and diverting goods into the gray market.

12.3 Current Accounting Results   331

A company lengthened depreciation periods for machinery and equipment, taking the benefits of investment tax credits into accounting profits in the year they arose instead of spreading them over time.

To enhance current income, a company sold its headquarters building and realized a big gain, although it might have been better in the long run to keep it. "Letting the accounting tail wag the economic dog."

A change in accounting for spare parts by a major company increased its net income by $585 million.

A company adopted these sales gimmicks—free upgrades, stretched-out payment plans, a "try and buy" plan with no initial payment, and "price protection" refunds if prices later drop.

A company opted for quick amortization, by writing off a large chunk of a deal with another company—2/3 or $56.8 million—as an unusual one-time charge 2 months after the deal was made, instead of amortizing it over its 2-year term.

A growth-seeking company booked too much revenue up front and deferred expenses to future periods, thereby easing the sting to earnings, practices described as "Vaunted Plans for Growth Get Dicey."

A company employed these techniques: changing accounting methods, fiddling with managers' cost estimates, and shifting the period when expenses and revenues are included in results.

A machinery company, in the midst of an economic downturn when other suppliers were cutting back on production, kept up shipping, booking strong sales of $5.4 billion. Its dealers were swamped with inventory. The company had to unload its machinery at fire-sale prices, taking a loss of $247 million.

12.3.5 Three Tidbits over 10 Years

> *Business Week*, August 17, 2009. "Old Banks, New Tricks" Lenders haven't sworn off risky financial products—they've just come up with different ones . . . Regulators, lawmakers, and consumer advocates see another round of risky loans . . . banks again are making dangerous loans to borrowers who can't repay them and selling toxic investments to investors who don't understand the risks (by Jessica Silver-Greenberg, Theo Francis, and Ben Levisohn).
>
> *Business Week*, October 4, 2004. "Fuzzy Numbers" Despite the reforms, corporate profits can be as distorted and confusing as ever. . . corporate financial statements are often incomplete, inconsistent, or just plain unclear, making it a nightmare to sort out fact from fancy—the financial reporting system is completely broken . . . Estimates—of pension-fund profits, unpaid receivables, old inventory—are easy to manipulate . . . The big question is whether increased scrutiny is yielding more realistic estimates or just more estimates documented by reams of assumptions and rationalizations . . . Even among execs who wouldn't dream of committing fraud, there are plenty who are ready to tweak their numbers in an effort to please investors (by David Henry).
>
> *Business Week*, May 14, 2001. "The Numbers Game" Companies use every trick to pump earnings and fool investors . . . The pricking of the Wall Street bubble has stepped up pressure on desperate CEOs to shore up earnings ravaged by the sudden economic slowdown . . . The latest abuse: "Pro forma" reporting. Way too often, pro forma results can be used to distract investors from the actual results (by David Henry). The *Editorial* adds, Anything-goes accounting must end. It is becoming impossible to compare price-earnings

ratios because companies define their earnings in so many different ways. Stock indexes are increasingly suspect. Investors are at sea. Companies still must publish true figures according to GAAP, but they are usually hidden somewhere in quarterly reports, often in obscure footnotes.

12.3.6 Debt Concealment

In the middle of 2010, a newly discovered strategy to improve a firm's balance sheet made the financial news. Reported under the head "debt masking" is an alleged practice to avoid the risks of debt showing up on accounting statements by erroneously classifying short-term purchase agreements ("repros") as sales rather than as borrowings. The Securities and Exchange Commission is considering new rules which would prohibit the practice. Bank of America and Citigroup have been accused of hiding billions of dollars of debt from investors. Lehman Brothers Holdings also did so to obscure its level of risk before it folded.

12.3.7 At the Borderline

Ford S. Worthy, writing for *Fortune*, points out a qualification which the reader should keep in mind when scanning these pages. He admonishes against drawing too extreme conclusions as to the degree of blame to be associated with any cited accounting practice. He says, "Executives rarely have to violate the law to put a gloss on dreary earnings. Accepted accounting principles leave ample room for those who want to fudge the numbers." He elaborates, "there are several strikingly different ways to account for a single set of facts. Sometimes managers have leeway because situations call for highly subjective estimates."[11]

Jerry Adler, in *Newsweek*, strikes a more quizzical note. He suggests, "This gives rise to the suspicion that many statistics come from sources less interested in precisely measuring a given problem than in showing that it's even worse than anyone thought." But he ends a bit more seriously, "... even our best statistics are based on a long chain of 'assumptions,' the scientific term for 'faith.'"[12]

The recession of 2008–2009, with its exposure of the existence and risks of toxic securities, seemingly caught the financial world by surprise. However, this should not have happened. There had been ample warnings. To cite one authority whose voice should have been heard, but was ignored, Kelly Holland, *Business Week's* Money and Banking Editor, issued calls for disclosure in 1993 and again in 1994. In 1993, Holland wrote, "banks should come clean about their derivative operations before big troubles start. Maybe more disclosure would stop problems from

---

[11] Ford S. Worthy, "Manipulating Profits: How Its Done," *Fortune*. June 25, 1984.

[12] Jerry Adler, "The Numbers Game," *Newsweek*. June 25, 1994.

developing in the first place."[13] A few months later, he renewed his warning, "A spate of big losses from derivatives sparks a call for disclosure."[14]

12.4 An Appraisal

Does the foregoing array of illustrative aggressive accounting procedures suggest that most, if not all, financial statements are inclusive of intentional misinformation? Or that auditors are sleeping at the switch? Or, to ask the same question in Herb Greenberg's more pungent words, "Are the reports of independent auditors worth the paper they've written on? Is the current system *really* protecting investors from accounting chicanery?"[15]

We do not answer these questions directly. Our purpose has been different: it is to alert the investor of the possibility of error in financial reports, for which possible error he or she should be watchful. Regulatory authorities are active in preventing aggressive accounting by the utilities. This surveillance does not extend beyond these heavily regulated entities.

Nonetheless, having pointed to a number of misleading accounting procedures, it behooves us to clear the air as to our opinion. We believe that by far the overwhelming number of financial reports, composed by management and affirmed by outside auditors, are accurate as stated. Our comments are directed to the exceptions, and should be read as such.

An example of the exceptions which falls into the never–never land between innocence and fraud was the $50 million settlement of the suit brought against General Electric Company by the Securities and Exchange Commission, as reported on August 5, 2009. The company paid this fine without admitting or denying any of the SEC's allegations that it had used improper accounting methods to boost earnings and avoid disappointing investors.[16]

12.5 Difference: Utility and General Corporate Accounting

There is one major difference between a utility's estimate of financial requirements, which is used as a basis for determining the rates the utility will be allowed to charge, and the usual corporate financial statements. This is that the financial requirements of the utility must include an appropriate recompense for the owner's

---

[13] Kelley Holland, "Once Again, Banks Are Leaving Investors in the Dark," *Business Week*, November 4, 1993.

[14] Kelley Holland, with William Glasgall, Maria Mallory, Rick Melcher and Grey Burns, "A Black Hole in the Balance Sheet," *Business Week*, May 16, 1994.

[15] Hank Greenberg, "The Auditors Are Always Last to Know," *Fortune*, August 17, 1998.

[16] Paul Glader and Kara Scanell, "GE Settles Civil-Fraud Charges . . . Fine of $50 Million Resolves SEC Probe Into Firm's Accounting Practices," *The Wall Street Journal*, August 5, 2009.

capital (i.e., a return on equity) as a part of the total cost of doing business. Else the financial requirements fall short.

Corporate accounting does not attempt to approximate the total cost of doing business, inclusive of a return on equity. Rather, the income statement itemizes all costs (including the non-cash cost of depreciation) other than equity return, to arrive at residual revenues which are identified as "net income."[17] This residual represents revenues left over, after covering prior costs, for equity owners (holders of preferred and other preference stock, and common stock). It is in this sense that the corporate income statement fails to delineate a "cost" of doing business, specifying an actual overage or shortfall: the statement may show revenues which are higher that sufficient to equate to "cost" as an economist might see that term, or revenues which are deficient, the income statement does not say which.[18] The point is that income statements reveal only what they purport to reveal, solely the results of operations for a given period. They do not purport to represent a "profit" over cost, or a "loss" in relation to the cost.

While we do not wish to be guilty of introducing a further complication into an already complicated picture, we suggest that management might add its evaluation of the real return on its equity which the firm has achieved over the past accounting period, plus its estimate of the return which will be realized in the future. The latter might be a meaningful measure on which to gauge management's performance.

12.5.1 Lack of Uniformity

Gas often is found in the same pool as oil. In any event, the two energy sources usually are the twin products of the oil and gas producer. The lack of uniformity is illustrated by producer accounting.

---

[17]"Net income" and "profit" are often used in business as interchangeable terms. In this sense, profit represents a total return on equity, from which a realized rate of return on equity can be calculated. This rate of return, though, does not necessarily represent the cost of equity capital in the economic context. In the economic context, the cost of equity capital is that rate of return which is required to induce, and maintain, the capital necessary for the operation of the particular business under consideration, with due regard to the peculiar circumstances of the specific business and to its peculiar risks. This, indeed, is a tough, if not impossible, yardstick to apply precisely. Consequently, there is validity to the conception of "cost plus profit" per the income statement as a general summation of what business revenues should cover provided it is understood that the required amount of profit is left unspecified.

[18]Costs, both hard and soft, are stated (whether overstated, understated, or correctly stated, as may be the case) in the income statement for a given period, and the realized profit is given. The results shown by the income statement are incorporated into the balance sheet which includes that period. There is backup for all entries except for the bottom line, which is simply a residual. Are the profits reported on the bottom line of the income statement good, bad, or indifferent? High, low, or just right? in relation to meeting the total cost of the business. Competitive finance solves these questions, as capital ebbs and flows from one business (or type of business) to another. The market for capital decides. But if one is anxious to know what the cost of equity capital is, that element of cost is illusive and indeterminate. The only thing we can be sure of is, it is a cost.

12.5 Difference: Utility and General Corporate Accounting

An oil and gas producer expends "x" dollars in explorations for new oil and gas reserves. That is, the producer drills wells which he hopes will result in discovering and trapping new, hereto undiscovered gas or oil (new discoveries, or new "reserves" in industry parlance). Some proportion—say two-thirds—of these "x" dollars result only in "dry holes" (i.e., wells which do not yield oil or gas.)

How are these expenditures to be accounted for in financial statements? One producer would consider the costs of the dry wells as a current expense, to be absorbed (expensed) in the current year's financial statements, namely $x. 2/3, since the dry wells did not yield any reserves. These wells were not assets, having no future value. That producer would consider as assets, only the costs of the successful wells, $x. 1/3. Only these would be capitalized and amortized as the reserves they had unlocked were produced. This treatment is known as the "successful efforts" approach.

Another producer reasons differently. He feels that the entirety of the exploration effort is incurred to find new reserves: dry holes are an inseparable part of exploration. Therefore, he contends, the entirety of "x" should be charged against the new reserves actually found, not just 1/3 of "x." This alternative treatment is referred to as the "full costing" approach.

The percentages will vary, but let us pursue for illustration the 1/3 vs. 3/3 option.

Assuming $1 billion of revenues for the concerned producer, and exploration to be 3/10 of its total expenditures (before taxes, etc.), each company will have expended $300 million in exploration for new reserves. Two hundred million of the explorations expenditure has resulted in dry holes, the remaining $100 million in successful wells. The first company reasons that since $200 million has been expended with no fruitful results—dry holes do not unearth additional reserves—that amount should be written off as a current expense. In other words, it should be a deduction from before-tax operating income for the year. Only the remaining $100 million which has resulted in successful wells—and therefore the acquisition of reserves—should be capitalized and amortized[19] (the rough equivalent of depreciation) as the resources are sold over future periods.

The second company sees the expenditure differently. It reasons that the entire $300 million was expended to find reserves, and therefore that the entire amount should be capitalized.

Both approaches are recognized as valid under "generally accepted accounting principles," although numerous authorities have questioned the validity of inconsistent approaches. In any event, the financial statements of both companies are presented as valid pictures of operations.

---

[19] Usually on a unit-of-production basis.

In the financial statements, the results compare in pertinent part as in Table 12.1:

Table 12.1 Producer accounting: alternative approaches to dry hole costs

	Income statement	
	Company A	Company B
Revenues	$1 billion	$1 billion
Less: exploration expense	$200 million	$0
Balance	$800 million	$1 billion
	Balance sheet	
Addition to capital (assets)	$100 million	$300 million

In relation to cost, do A's financial statements properly reflect cost? Or do B's? What is cost?

12.5.2 The Question of Prudence

For the regulated utilities, cost has been made subject to the question of "prudence:" was the cost incurred prudently, or, for a variety of reasons, imprudently? Note that there is no doubt that the expenditure has been made—that is agreed; and there is no doubt that the expenditure was free from fraud or other abuse of like character—that is also agreed, since fraud is a matter quite aside from prudence. The only question—from hindsight, which is also at least implicitly agreed in most cases—is whether it was smart (or prudent) to undertake the expenditure.

Thus, prior conceptions of cost encounter a new, and incredibly massive, degree of uncertainty. No longer is it sufficient to examine cost within the relatively narrow confines of questions such as, what is a reasonable rate of depreciation, or a reasonable rate of return on stockholders' equity. Now, cost must be examined, both before and after its incurrence, as having been reasonably or unreasonably incurred. And beyond a clear-cut yes or no both before and after, a cost incurrence may be adjudged to having been perfectly reasonable at the time it was being evaluated, i.e., from foresight, yet turn out to have been unwise due to unforeseeable events, i.e., from hindsight. Solomon might be great enough to adjudicate such opposing views. Such wisdom is not claimed for this text.

The prudence issue itself is simple. Should the costs of questioned plant be rolled-in to the utility's other costs and be passed on to customers through higher rates, recognizing that the plant was conceived in good faith and legitimately built? If so, cost would have the meaning we have attributed to that term at the beginning of this section, and cost would be translated into price in conformity with traditional utility practice. Or, should all or a part of the costs be disallowed as "imprudent" for rate purposes, to be absorbed by the utility's stockholders, even, perhaps, to the brink of bankruptcy for the utility? In this event, cost becomes practically meaningless, passing from the "uncertain-and-speculative to a degree" to pure conjecture.

12.5.3 AFUDC

These initials stand for allowances for funds used during construction. Under historical principles of regulation, utilities are proscribed from including in the "rate base" (i.e., the amount of investment upon which they are entitled to a return at the allowed rate of return), any expenditures which represent "construction work in progress." The expenditures cannot be included in rate base until the construction is completed and the plant becomes "used and useful." While construction is underway, the utility is expected to be able to defer payment of the principal component of its investment until the project is completed (as a home owner, building his own home, will not begin to pay-off the principal until the home is ready for occupancy). The utility cannot, however, defer payment of current costs of capital on the money financing its construction-in-progress. The longer-construction periods stretch out, and the greater the interim investment is, the more significant are the interim costs. These are costs, by whatever definition one may invoke; and all costs, whatever the scheme of recoupment may be, must be recovered in either present or future prices if the business entity is to remain financially viable. Under regulation, an eternal question is, when the recoupment shall be permitted, now or later, when the plant finally becomes operative.

AFUDC is something of a middle ground, blending the several considerations. The allowance is treated as a soft non-cash item. The cost of the monies tied up in construction work appears as a *reduction* to normal interest charges (which is equivalent to an increase in revenue of like amount) and an *addition* to rate base. Adding AFUDC to the rate base entitles the item to future cash recoupment starting with the completion of the project and extending over its useful life. Thus, no current cash is realized.

Note that the reduction of AFUDC from current interest charges is pure bookkeeping. Such charges are hard-cash costs which must be paid currently. The offset is anticipated future revenue. This is a trade-off of a hard current cost for a soft later recoupment. This trade-off is not apparent from the bottom line (although it would have been clearly identified in preceding entries of the income statement).

The virtue for utility finance lies in this divorcement of AFUDC from the bottom line. When huge construction programs are underway, such as for a new large-generating plant, revenues are likely to fall far short of covering AFUDC plus other charges. Without the AFUDC deduction, the utility might be required to report a very low, or even negative, net income.

The vice of AFUDC in relation to "cost" is that it tends to conceal the degree of softness of the future recoupment of costs which have in fact been met by a hard-cash payment. If all goes well, there should be no bar to future cash recovery. But much can go wrong. Prudency can be questioned. Construction quality can be in doubt, as can operational safety. Licenses may be withheld. Or it can be alleged that the plant is unneeded when it is ready to go on line.

Related to AFUDC's role in the income statement is its role on the *balance sheet*. At this juncture our discussion broadens. When a new plant is completed, it can be considered to be an asset, and the utility's investment in that plant, together with related AFUDC, can be recorded on the balance sheet. The expectation is that rates will be set so as to be sufficient to permit recovery of the cost of the asset over its useful life. *Forbes* asks the question, "... what if regulators don't set rates high enough? Or what if the plant is abandoned? What, then, to do with the phantom AFUDC income, and the bloated balance sheet entries?"

Nuclear generating plants, pose a further issue, *the cost of eventual decommissioning*. Most nuclear utilities have established and carry on their books a fund to defray such future costs. These costs, while unknown now, of course, are expected to be large, perhaps amounting to a major percentage of the initial cost of construction. The adequacy of the fund is a significant issue in itself. Bypassing that issue, another question is, in what manner should the fund be deployed? One approach would allow the utility to spend the money now for current operations (as are funds arising from depreciation charges), raising funds through other means when the time for decommissioning arrives. An opposite approach would require the segregation of the decommissioning monies into a separate fund, not to be usable in-house for customers' current benefit. In both cases, the decommissioning fund would be shown as a separate item on the utility's books, but in the former case the actual cash will have been spent, in the latter, the cash will be available as a fund. States differ in their view of this matter.[20] What is cost?

12.5.4 Deferred Income Taxes

For utility companies, the amount of income taxes paid as shown on their books, if they elect to do so, may differ from the amount of taxes actually paid, the amount paid lagging behind the booked amounts. The difference arises from the premise that the booked amounts should incorporate the taxes which would be payable on a normalized basis, so that current ratepayers pay full current tax rates without acceleration benefits. The differences amount to postponements or deferments, not forgiveness, of the tax. When the deferred taxes become payable in the future, the utility is expected to absorb the difference, since ratepayers have already recompensed the utility for the full tax amount.

Recurring arguments have arisen over this tax option. Opponents allege that the difference between the booked tax amount and the tax actually paid represents an "interest free loan" for the benefit of the utility, and moreover, a loan which may never have to be paid (as long as the utility's growth continues). Proponents assert that the option is granted under the law with a specific purpose, namely, to make the utility stronger financially.

Along which avenue does cost tread?

---

[20]For a good contrast in the two view, see Richards, Bill, "Retirement of Commercial Reactors is Stirring Debate," *The Wall Street Journal,* March, 18, 1987.

12.6 Part 2: The California Energy Crisis

The "California Energy Crisis," the second part of Chap. 12, identifies a period during which wholesale electricity prices escalated to unprecedented levels, massively exceeding then-prevailing retail electric rates. This occurred principally from May/June 2000 to June 2001.

The genesis of the crisis was a California law of September 1996, AB 1890, which restructured the electric industry of the state. Although the law was well-intentioned, it produced disastrous results.

Previously, the electric industry had been integrated, with the local utility providing generating, transmission, and distribution services, with a single bill to customers for the combined services. The new law contemplated the divorce of the generation function from the menu of the local utility, based upon the premise that electric generation was no longer a monopoly to be price regulated: that there were numerous generators who could supply power at wholesale and that competition between them in an unregulated market would reduce generation costs. The lure of AB 1890 was the unqualified expectation that electric bills would go down due to a decline in generating costs.

The law was sponsored by the California Public Utilities Commission (CPUC), the major investor-owned utility companies in the state (IOUs), and large electricity consumers.

It seemed to offer attractive alternatives to the IOUs. To them it gave a chance to switch from being a regulated electricity generator selling at regulated prices, to a non-regulated generator that could sell at unregulated market-driven prices. Also, the removal of the burden of continuing to be a regulated provider of wholesale energy seemed to offer unlimited opportunities to reorient their regulated investments into more profitable avenues, including acquisition of non-regulated generation capacity in other areas or into new ventures such as energy trading. The law offered a further carrot to the IOUs. They were given the opportunity to recover sunk past costs, which recovery had seemed doubtful before.

The law was also attractive to large electricity consumers, major industrial plants in particular. They had been vocal in claiming that California's industrial rates were too high, and were certain that market-based competitive rates would be lower.

The public at large was relatively uninvolved in the debates on AB 1890. Being promised that their electric bills would decline, and with the option to choose alternative suppliers, their voices were muffled.

This section summarizes AB 1890. Then it recounts the reactions of the IOUs in 1996 after its passage as "Optimism Reigns, No Doubts." The interval from 1997 to 1999 is next explored as "The Lull before the Storm." During these years, the IOUs were busy selling their California generating capacity and acquiring capacity in other regions. "The Storm Hits," 2000 and 2001, reveals the depth of the crisis and its aftermath.

These topics are covered first from primary sources, the annual reports for the years 1996 through 2001 of the affected utilities: PG&E Corporation, parent of Pacific Gas and Electric Company (PG&E); Edison International, parent of Southern California Edison Company (SCE); and Sempra Energy, formerly Enova Corporation, parent of San Diego Gas and Electric Company (SDG&E). These sources are supplemented by reports of actions taken by the state of California, the California Public Utilities Commission (CPUC), the Federal Energy Regulatory Commission (FERC), the California Department of Water Resources (DWR), plus events noticed by the media. The sequence of events is roughly chronological.

12.7 1996: Assembly Bill 1890

AB 1890, restructuring California's electric utility industry, was signed into law on September 23, 1996.

AB 1890 gives electric consumers the choice of continuing to purchase their electricity as a package from their local utility, or to contract with other energy service providers for the generation component of their service (direct access), or to buy the generation component from the power exchange (PX, see below). With the latter two options, the local utility would still transmit and deliver the power.

The law establishes a power exchange (PX) and an independent system operator (ISO). The PX serves as a wholesale power pool allowing all energy producers to participate competitively. IOUs are obligated to sell their power supply, including owned generation and purchased-power contracts, to the PX and also are obligated to purchase from the PX the power that they distribute. The PX purchases power at auction on a day-ahead and a real-time basis to establish market-clearing prices. The ISO provides operational control over most of the state's transmission facilities and provides comparable open access for electric transmission services. It schedules power transactions and ensures system reliability. The PX and ISO began operations in April 1998.

The law mandates a rate freeze at 1996 levels for all IOU customers, with a 10% reduction in these 1996 rates for residential and small commercial customers. The freeze begins in January 1998 and extends to March 31, 2002, unless the utility's CTC costs (see below) are collected earlier. The law provides for the issuance of rate reduction bonds by an agency of the state to enable the IOUs to finance the rate reduction. These bonds are to be repaid over 10 years by residential and small commercial customers via a non-bypassable charge on their electricity bills.

AB 1890 allows the IOUs, within certain limits, the opportunity to recover their stranded costs incurred for certain above-market CPUC-approved facilities, contracts, and obligations, through a competition transition charge (CTC). Most transition costs must be recovered by March 2002.

The law encourages the divestiture by IOUs of their utility-owned generation facilities. In 1995, the CPUC set a target for divestiture of at least 50% of the utility's fossil-fueled power plants.

12.8 Optimism Reigns: No Doubts (1996)

Below are reported the initial reactions to AB 1890 of the three major California utilities. Each company was optimistic, even enthusiastic. No doubts were expressed. As PG&E said, the restructuring promised "a new beginning."

PG&E Corporation is the parent of Pacific Gas and Electric Company. Its 1996 Annual Report to Stockholders is entitled "A New Beginning." The report includes these comments:

> Over the next five years, a significant portion of our business will be transformed from a monopoly to a competitive enterprise... Some components, such as distribution, will remain regulated. Others, such as electric generation, will be largely deregulated and fully competitive ...
>
> In 1996, California enacted Assembly Bill 1890. This law provides a clear legislative road map for achieving electric restructuring in California. It also reduces the financial uncertainties surrounding the restructuring by providing legislative assurance that the state's utilities will have a fair opportunity to recover significant costs associated with the transition to a competitive electric marketplace ...
>
> The legislation establishes the operating framework for the competitive generation market in California. This framework will consist of a power exchange (PX) and an independent system operator (ISO). The PX, open to all electricity providers, will conduct a competitive auction to establish the price of electricity. The ISO will ensure system reliability and provide all electricity generators with open and comparable access to transmission and distribution services.

The 1996 Annual Report of Edison International, parent corporation of Southern California Edison, says,

> The unanimous passage of restructuring legislation, which Edison advocated, placed California in the forefront of a national movement offering customer choice among electricity suppliers ...
>
> The new law substantially deregulates the generation of electricity and opens retail markets to competition. Under California's new law, Edison has the opportunity to recover about $5 billion of its past, prudent utility investment. This otherwise could have been confiscated through industry restructuring. About $2 billion of this total will be received by year-end 1997, contingent upon the issuance of innovative rate-reduction bonds made possible by the legislation. These bonds not only pay off an obligation owed to us, they also allow a 10 percent rate reduction for our residential and small business customers next January 1. With the exception of this reduction, rates in effect when the bill was signed will remain frozen through the end of 2001. The remaining approximately $3 billion owed to us will have to be collected from the gap between total revenues under the freeze and our aggregate costs. To recover fully the prior investment, SCE will have to achieve high levels of productivity while maintaining excellent service. We are resolved to achieve that end.
>
> In order to facilitate a smooth and timely transition to a competitive electricity-supply market, we decided in 1996 to divest all 12 of our natural gas-fired power plants.

Enova Corporation was formed on January 1, 1996 as parent of San Diego Gas and Electric Company. On October 14, 1996, Enova merged with Pacific Enterprises, bringing its subsidiary, Southern California Gas Company, along. Therefore, Enova (now Sempra Energy) controls both San Diego G and E and Southern California Gas.

Enova's 1996 Annual Report had this to say, recapping some of the more important features of AB 1890:

> The most important milestone in 1996 for California's electric industry was the landmark signing of Assembly Bill 1890. Enova Corporation believes this sweeping legislation, which sets in law most of the proposals issued in a December 1995 ruling by the California Public Utilities Commission, represents a balanced approach to restructuring the electric utility industry—customers will have more choices and reduced rates while the interests of Enova Corporation shareholders and employees are protected.
>
> *Recovery of Stranded Assets.* Of great importance to Enova Corporation and its shareholders, Assembly Bill 1980 allows each electric utility the opportunity to recover the cost of its stranded assets, estimated at more than $26 billion total for the three major investor-owned utilities. Our portion of these costs, approximately $2 billion, represents the past capital investments and contractual obligations we made to serve customers. These stranded costs will be recovered through a Competition Transition Charge that all customers will pay.
>
> *Customer Choice, Direct Access and the Power Exchange.* Beginning January 1, 1998, customers can continue to purchase their electricity from their utility, which will buy from the Power Exchange. The Power Exchange will function like a stock exchange for electrons, where buyers and sellers of electricity can complete transactions based on market supply and demand. SDG&E will deliver all the power it generates, or has contractual rights to, into the Power Exchange. Customers also can opt for "direct access," buying their power directly from a retailer outside the Power Exchange. Responsibility for controlling, coordinating and maintaining the integrity of the state's power grid—the transmission system—will be in the hands of an impartial Independent System Operator.
>
> *Lower Costs and Protections for Consumers.* Assembly Bill 1890 ensures that approximately 1 million residential and 100,000 small commercial SDG&E customers will receive a 10 percent rate decrease, beginning January 1, 1998. These customers also will benefit from a rate cap that could last until April 1, 2002, when an additional 10 percent rate decrease is anticipated. The rate cap provides that SDG&E's system average electric rates cannot exceed 9.985 cents per kilowatt hour. The bill also requires utilities to create an education and consumer protection program to help inform customers about the new choices they will face.
>
> *Competition and Industry' Consolidation.* As competition increases, natural gas and electric companies are moving toward becoming "one-stop" energy-service providers, with the ability to offer multiple forms of energy and other products, as well as related management services. In the past year, more than 50 mergers or acquisitions have been announced in the natural gas and electric utility industries. The proposed merger between Enova Corporation and Pacific Enterprises anticipates this new environment. As the natural gas and electricity businesses face further competition, the ability to offer a variety of energy solutions is considered critical to the future success of companies in the industry.

12.9 The Lull Before the Storm (1997–1999)

The years 1997 through 1999 were tranquil in comparison to the energy crisis that followed, but they were far from tranquil in terms of the industry's operations. The utilities were busy in divesting the generation plants which they owned in California, while at the same time were acquiring generation plants in other parts of the country. In effect, they were exchanging generation capacity with other regions. In addition, they were busy in switching their investments to utility operations outside of the

12.9 The Lull Before the Storm (1997–1999)   343

United States as well as to other non-regulated activities such as energy trading (following the lure of Enron's then-successful precedent).

These activities are outlined under five topics below: sales of California-owned generation capacity; acquisitions of "merchant" generation capacity outside of California; other thoughts as mentioned by the majors; the California PX as seen early on; and rate reduction bonds.

A note on FERC's early approval in 1997 of the PX and ISO precedes these topics.

12.9.1 FERC's Approval

In October 1997, FERC-approved key elements of the California restructuring plan of AB 1890, including transfer by the IOUs of the operational control of their transmission facilities to the ISO (which is under FERC jurisdiction) and the establishment of the PX to operate as an independent power pool.

12.9.2 Sales of California Generation Capacity

In 1997, PG&E agreed to sell three of four utility-owned fossil-fueled power plants to Duke Energy for $501 million. These plants had a book value of $346 million and a combined capacity of 2,645 MW. (This sale was completed in 1998.)

PG&E's report stated the purpose of the sale, "we are divesting power plant assets currently owned by our California utility where our returns would be unacceptably low under state regulation, and we are investing in power plant assets ... in regions with attractive markets where we can create shareholder value as an unregulated plant owner and operator."

In 1998, PG&E agreed to sell three other fossil-fueled generation plants and its complex of geothermal generation facilities for $1,014 million. These had a book value of $523 million and a combined capacity of 4,289 MW. (The sale was completed in 1999.) In 1998, the company notified the CPUC, "it does not plan to retain its hydroelectric generation assets as part of the utility." The utility's net investment in hydro assets was $1.4 billion at year end.

In 1997, Edison International reached agreements to sell 11 natural gas-fueled power plants, having a book value of $531 million, for $1.1 billion. Combined generating capacity sold was 8,062 MW. Its reasons for the sale were explained, "The company sold the plants to facilitate the transition to a competitive electricity supply market in California. The divested plants were bought by established energy companies."

In 1998, it closed the sale of its 12 gas-fueled generation plants in California for $1.2 billion, over $500 million more than book value. It stated its management goals as follows:

Our strategy for several years has been to restructure our basic utility business, with a focus on transmission, distribution and customer service, and to expand significantly into non-utility businesses, particularly independent power generation and infrastructure finance.

In 1997, Enova Corporation (later Sempra Energy) presented this outline of its plans for the future:

In November 1997, we announced plans to auction SDG&E's generating assets and use the proceeds to pay down competitive transition costs—so that shareholders' past investments in generating assets will be recovered more quickly.

We will be auctioning off our two fossil fuel power plants—the South Bay plant in Chula Vista and the Encina plant in Carlsbad—as well as our 20 percent stake in the San Onofre Nuclear Generating Station and long-term power contracts. We expect the auction process for the fossil fuel plants and power contracts to be completed by the end of 1998 ...

In this new competitive environment, there is little profit for SDG&E and the other California investor-owned utilities in actually generating electricity.

In 1998, Sempra Energy brought these plans up to date. It said,

On December 11, 1998, contracts were executed for the sale of SDG&E's South Bay Power Plant, Encina Power Plant and 17 combustion-turbine generators, having a net book value of $100 million. The South Bay Power Plant is being sold to the San Diego Unified Port District for $110 million. The Encina Power Plant and the combustion-turbine generators are being sold to a special-purpose entity owned equally by Dynegy Power Corp. and NRG Energy, Inc. for $356 million.

12.9.3 The California PX

In July 1999, the California Power Exchange (Cal PX or PX) issued its "1998–1999 Market Year Report to Californians." It stated that the purpose of the PX is "to provide an efficient, competitive marketplace for trading electricity in the state of California ... From its inception, the purpose of Cal PX has been to provide participants an exchange where they can easily sell power at the price that best reflects truly competitive market conditions ... Cal PX performs a valuable price discovery function, which informs the public and all interested parties of the market price of electricity at all times."

Looking ahead, the report said, "By facilitating fair and open competition, the Cal PX will be a major factor in reducing electric rates in the long term."

From April 1998 through March 1999, "the average Day-Ahead hourly price was $24.44/mwh or 2.4 cents per kilowatt-hour ... (but) peak demand on September 3, 1998 set a record price of $190.94/mwh in the 4 P.M. to 5 p.m. hour."

The report cites the following dates (among others):

September 1996: California enacts Assembly Bill AB 1890 to restructure the state's electric utility industry.

March 31, 1998: Cal PX opens the Day-Ahead market to begin competitive electricity trading throughout the state.

April 1, 1998: California Independent System Operator (Cal ISO) begins operation of the states electrical transmission system.

12.9 The Lull Before the Storm (1997–1999)

July 30, 1998: Cal PX opens the Hour-Ahead market to facilitate trading nearer the delivery hour.

November 1998: Moody's Investor Service grants Cal PX a short-term issuer rating of Prime-1 and Standard & Poor's grants Cal PX a first-time A-1 issuer credit rating.

12.9.4 Acquisitions of Generating Capacity Beyond California

In tandem with their divestitures of their owned generation capacity within California, the utilities were busy with investing in non-regulated activities. These included investments in non-regulated or "merchant" electric capacity beyond the jurisdiction of CPUC, which are outlined below. The utilities also invested in non-utility activities, such as energy trading and finance, and their natural gas divisions in gas operations, which are not discussed herein.

In its 1998 Annual Report, PG&E Corporation capsulized the policy that sets the stage for this outline of acquisitions of electric capacity outside of California by itself and others. It said, "Deregulation created clear incentives for moving the ownership of power plants away from utility companies."

Quotations from its annual reports summarize the actions of PG&E:

> In 1998, PG&E Corporation completed the $1.59 billion acquisition of 18 hydroelectric and fossil-fueled generating plants from New England Electric System. The sale was one of the largest utility asset acquisitions in US. history, transferring three fossil-fueled generating plants, 15 hydroelectric stations, and 23 multi-year power purchase agreements, which in total added approximately 4,800 megawatts of capacity to PG&E Corporation's power generating subsidiary, U.S. Generating Company (USGen).
>
> In 1999, we established the PG&E National Energy Group to integrate our national competitive business units. In 1999, this unit both grew and positioned itself for further growth.
>
> The National Energy Group operates an electric generation portfolio of more than 7,000 megawatts. In 1999, construction continued on the Millennium Power project, a 360-megawatt natural gas-fueled plant in Charlton, Massachusetts, scheduled for operation in the fourth quarter of 2000, and we started construction of the Lake Road Generating Plant, a 792-megawatt natural gas-fueled plant in Killingly, Connecticut, scheduled for operation in 2001. Shortly after the new year, we began construction of the 1,048 megawatt natural gas-fueled La Paloma Generating Plant near Bakersfield, California. Also in 1999, we announced development of a 12-megawatt wind generating project, to be located in New York, one of the first competitive wind power generating facilities in the eastern United States. This project is scheduled to begin construction in May 2000 and to begin operation in September 2000.
>
> Our development portfolio includes an additional 7,500 megawatts of new generating projects with planned operating dates between 2002 and 2004.

Quotations from the reports of Edison International summarize its actions for the years 1996 through 1999:

> *1996:* Marking its tenth anniversary, Edison Mission Energy had a record year in 1996, reinforcing its position as one of the world's leading independent power producers.
>
> The acquisition of First Hydro Ltd. in the United Kingdom by EME in December 1995 paid immediate and substantial dividends in 1996 when the U.K. experienced one of its coldest winters on record. First Hydro's pumped-storage system has more than 2,000

megawatts of capacity, providing both energy and system stability for the competitive market in Great Britain. It will be a long-term mainstay of EME's operations. Elsewhere in Europe, EME closed financing and started construction on the 512-megawatt IS AB energy project in Italy. At ISAB, high-sulfur refinery waste will be processed to remove pollutants and produce clean-burning synthetic gas to fuel electricity generation.

On the other side of the globe, more than 9,000 construction workers passed the 40 percent completion mark on EME's 1,230-megawatt Paiton project in Indonesia. In Australia, EME achieved commercial operation at two generating facilities—the 500-megawatt second unit of the Loy Yang B power plant near Melbourne and the 166-megawatt Kwinana cogeneration plant at Perth. In the U.S., the 286-megawatt Brooklyn Navy Yard gas-fired power plant began selling electricity and steam in November under a long-term power-purchase agreement.

1997: Edison Mission Energy reached agreements for new power generation projects in Thailand and the Philippines with a combined capacity of 1,038 megawatts. EME also purchased the remaining 49 percent of a 1,000-megawatt, coal-fired power plant in Australia.

1998: Homer City—In the third quarter of 1998, Edison Mission Energy entered into agreements to acquire the 1,884-megawatt Homer City Generating Station in western Pennsylvania for approximately $1.8 billion . . . . Edison Mission Energy will operate Homer City as a merchant plant, meaning that its output will be sold in a competitive market rather than under a fixed contract.

EcoElectrica—In 1998, Edison Mission Energy acquired a 50 percent interest in EcoElectrica, a 540-megawatt liquefied natural gas (LNG), combined-cycle cogeneration project currently under construction in Penuelas, Puerto Rico.

Progress on major projects

Indonesia—Construction on the $2.5 billion, 1,230-megawatt Paiton project is nearing completion.

Italy—Construction on the 512-megawatt ISAB gasification project in Sicily is now more than 98 percent complete. The plant will convert high-sulfur oil refinery waste to low-sulfur "syngas" for power production, recycling the recovered sulfur for sale to the agriculture and chemical industries.

Turkey—Construction on the 180-megawatt Doga Enerji cogeneration project near Istanbul reached the 97 percent completion mark in 1998.

Thailand—In July, Edison Mission Energy and its partners, Texaco Global Gas and Power and Banpu Public Company Limited, closed $400 million of financing for the 700-megawatt Tri Energy project.

Construction on the Tri Energy project was 79 percent complete at the end of 1998.

Edison Mission Energy (EME) has more than $5 billion in assets and owns interest in fifty-five projects totaling more than 11,500 megawatts.

1999: Commonwealth Edison Power Plants—In December, we acquired the entire non-nuclear generation portfolio of Commonwealth Edison of Chicago for $4.96 billion. In one transaction, we became one of the largest electricity generators in the Midwest.

Contact Energy—In the second quarter, we acquired a 40 percent stake in Contact Energy, New Zealand's first privatized electricity company for $635 million.

Fiddler's Ferry and Ferrybridge—The acquisition of 4,000 megawatts (MW) of capacity at Fiddler's Ferry and Ferrybridge for about $2 billion gives us a balanced portfolio of generation plants in England and Wales markets. In 1995, we acquired more than 2,000 MW of pumped hydro storage peaking capacity in Wales.

Storm Lake/—Edison Capital invested almost $100 million in the largest wind generation project in the United States, located in western Iowa. All output of the project will be sold under a twenty-year, fixed-price contract.

12.9 The Lull Before the Storm (1997–1999)

In 1997, Enova Corporation (now Sempra Energy) reported: In December 1997, Enova Power Corporation, a subsidiary of Enova, and Houston Industries Power Generation formed El Dorado Energy, a joint venture to build, own and operate a natural gas power plant in Boulder City, Nevada. Enova invested $2.3 million in El Dorado Energy in 1997 and expects to invest an additional $37 million in 1998 and $17 million in 1999.

The above figures were restated by Sempra Energy in 1998.

Sempra Energy Resources invested $19.7 million and $2.3 million in El Dorado Energy in 1998 and 1997, respectively. Total cost of the project is projected to be $263 million.

In 1999, Sempra Energy reported that in June 1999, the company and PSEG Global (PSEG) jointly acquired 90% of Chilquinta Energia SA (Energia). In January 2000, the company and PSEG purchased an additional 9.75% of Chilquinta Energia SA, increasing their total holdings to 99.98%, at a total cost of $840 million. In September 1999, the company and PSEG completed their acquisition of 47.5% of Luz Del Sur SA, a Peruvian electric company, for $108 million. This acquisition, combined with the 37% already owned through Energia, increased the companies' total joint ownership to 84.5% of Luz del Sur SA.

12.9.5 Other Notes of the Majors

Below are selective comments of the major utilities, chosen because they shed light on their thinking as the "Lull Before the Storm" progressed.

First, are some comments of PG&E made in 1998.

> To create a competitive generation market, a Power Exchange (PX) and an Independent System Operator (ISO) began operating in 1998. The Utility is required to sell to the PX all of the electricity generated by its power plants and electricity acquired under contract with unregulated generators. Also, the Utility is required to buy from the PX all electricity needed to provide service to retail customers that continue to choose the Utility as their electricity supplier. The ISO schedules delivery of electricity for all market participants to the transmission system. The Utility continues to own and maintain a portion of the transmission system, but the ISO controls the operation of the system...
>
> During 1998, the average price paid per kilowatt-hour (kWh) under the Utility's long-term contracts for electric power was 7.4 cents per kWh. The average cost of electric energy for energy purchased at market rates from the PX for the period from April 1, 1998, to December 31, 1998, was 3.2 cents per kWh.

Edison International had this to say in 1998.

> In the first nine months of the new marketplace, approximately 11 percent of the electrical load of California's three investor-owned utilities shifted from the utilities to electric service providers (ESPs). In 1998, SCE facilitated the successful introduction of competitive electric service in California by helping more than eighty ESPs enter the marketplace.

Sempra Energy commented in 1998 and 1999:

1998: AB 1890 includes a rate freeze for all electric customers. Until the earlier of March 31, 2002, or when transition-cost recovery is complete, SDG&E's system-average rate will be frozen at the June 10, 1996, levels of 9.64 cents per kwh, except for the impact of fuel-cost changes and the 10-percent rate reduction described above. Beginning in 1998, system-average rates were fixed at 9.43 cents per kwh, which includes the maximum permitted increase related to fuel-cost increases and the mandatory rate reduction.

1999: AB 1890 allows utilities, within certain limits, the opportunity to recover their stranded costs incurred for certain above-market CPUC-approved facilities, contracts and obligations through the establishment of the CTC.

In June 1999, SDG&E completed the recovery of a majority of its stranded costs. The recovery was affected by, among other things, the sale of SDG&E's fossil power plants and combustion turbines during the quarter ended June 30, 1999. Costs related to the above-market portion of qualifying facilities and other purchased-power contracts that were in effect at December 31, 1995, and the San Onofre Nuclear Generating Station (SONGS) will continue to be recovered in rates.

12.9.6 Rate Reduction Bonds

To finance the mandated 10% decrease in the rates of residential and small commercial customers called for in AB 1890, the utilities issued rate reduction bonds. These had a 10 year repayment period, with repayment to be made by a non-bypassable charge on the electric bills of residential and small commercial customers. These bonds were issued as in Table 12.2.

Table 12.2 Rate reduction bonds of utility companies

PG&E	$2.9 billion	Interest rates, 6.01–6.49%
Edison International	$2.5 billion	Interest rates, 5.98–6.46%
SDG&E	$658 million	Average interest rate, 6.26

12.10 The Storm Hits: The Energy Crisis (2000–2001)

The height of the storm came in the 13 months between May/June 2000 and June 2001. During this period incredibly high wholesale power prices were exacted in a market dominated by energy traders. These prices were far in excess of the frozen retail rates, which the utilities could collect, leading to overwhelming deficiencies in their revenues. The imbalance between the prices they paid for power and the rates at which they sold it brought one of the principal utilities to bankruptcy and another to the brink. There were frequent blackouts, endangering the public welfare. Remedial measures were hurriedly considered, some discarded, some adopted. It was a period of emergency.

The events of the storm, and its still-continuing aftermath, are now unrolled.

12.10.1 PG&E Corporation and Edison International

In the terse language of a formal legal document, PG&E Corporation's 2000 Annual Report (which extends through April 9, 2001) declared, "The state of California is in the midst of an energy crisis. The cost of wholesale power has risen to almost ten times greater than in 1999.

Rolling blackouts have occurred as a result of a broken deregulated energy market. Because of this crisis, PG&E Corporation and the utility (Pacific Gas and Electric Company) have experienced a significant deterioration of their liquidity and consolidated financial position. The utility's credit rating has deteriorated to below investment grade level." The report explains

> ... Beginning in June 2000, the wholesale price of electric power in California steadily increased to an average cost of 18.16 cents per kilowatt-hour (kWh) for the seven month period of June 2000 through December 2000, as compared to an average cost of 4.23 cents per kWh for the same period in 1999. Under California Assembly Bill 1890 (AB 1890), the Utility's electric rates were frozen at levels that allowed approximately 5.4 cents per kWh to be charged to the Utility's customers as reimbursement for power costs incurred by the Utility on behalf of its retail customers. The excess of wholesale electricity costs above the generation-related cost component available in frozen rates resulted in an undercollection at December 31, 2000, of approximately $6.6 billion, and rose to approximately $8.9 billion by February 28, 2001.
>
> The difference between the actual costs incurred to purchase power and the amount recovered from customers was funded through a series of borrowings ... At December 31, 2000, the Utility had borrowed $614 million against its 5-year revolving credit agreement, had issued $1,225 million of commercial paper, and had issued $1,240 million of floating rate notes ...
>
> On January 10, 2001, the Board of Directors of the Utility suspended the payment of its fourth quarter 2000 common stock dividend in an aggregate amount of $110 million payable on January 15, 2001 ... In addition, the Utility's Board of Directors decided not to declare the regular preferred stock dividends for the three-month period ending January 31, 2001, normally payable on February 15, 2001. Dividends on all Utility preferred stock are cumulative. Until cumulative dividends on preferred stock are paid, the Utility may not pay any dividends on its common stock, nor may the Utility repurchase any of its common stock.
>
> On January 16 and 17, 2001, the outstanding bonds of the Utility were downgraded to below investment grade status.

In equally laconic language, the 2000 Annual Report of Edison International (dated April 16, 2001) states,

> ... this has been a very difficult year for our company. Overshadowing everything we have accomplished over the last several years, the California power crisis has pushed Southern California Edison (SCE) to the edge of bankruptcy.
>
> Early last summer, the cost of unregulated wholesale power in California rose sharply, moving above the revenues allowed in regulated rates to make such purchases ...
>
> Beginning last May, SCE had to borrow heavily to raise cash for wholesale power purchases necessary to keep electricity flowing to our customers. Through the fall, the California Public Utilities Commission (CPUC) took no action on our requests for a rate increase until January 4 of this year, and when it finally acted, the commission granted only a small increase—far below what was necessary to keep us creditworthy.

With that, lenders lost faith in California regulation and both Pacific Gas and Electric Company, our utility neighbor to the north, and Southern California Edison were unable to borrow further. By mid-January, SCE had to stop making payments to procure new power and to stop paying existing creditors. From that point forward, the major challenge of providing reliable power under tight supply conditions spiraled into a full-fledged crisis. Power generators sought to avoid sales in California, large risk premiums were added to wholesale prices, and the State of California went into the procurement business at massive cost to the state treasury. Compounding the problem, natural gas prices soared throughout the winter—greatly increasing fuel costs for power generation, and precipitation was below normal in both the Pacific Northwest and California, promising reduced availability of hydropower.

... in December and again last month, we were forced to suspend Edison International common stock dividends and defer SCE preferred dividends, as cash preservation measures. The California power crisis marks the first time in more than 100 years as a business that we have had to take this drastic action, and we deeply regret it.

At this juncture, the two largest California utilities were in roughly comparable positions. But they selected opposite remedies. PG&E Corporation chose bankruptcy for its utility unit. Edison International chose a negotiated settlement.

The 2000 PG&E Annual Report stated,

Our utility unit, Pacific Gas and Electric Company, on April 6, 2001, filed for reorganization under Chapter 11 of the U.S. Bankruptcy Code in San Francisco Bankruptcy Court. We took this action because of the following: (1) our unreimbursed wholesale electricity costs were increasing at an estimated $300 million per month, or more; (2) continuing CPUC decisions, some of which we believe are illegal, were economically disadvantaging the utility; and (3) negotiations with California's governor and his staff were no longer making progress.

Neither PG&E Corporation nor any of its other subsidiaries, including the National Energy Group, have filed for Chapter 11 reorganization.

We chose to file for Chapter 11 reorganization affirmatively because we expect the court will provide the venue needed to reach a solution, which thus far the state and the state's regulators have been unable to achieve.

Our objective is to proceed through the Chapter 11 process as quickly as possible, without disruption to our operations or inconvenience to our customers, and to emerge and rebuild value for our shareholders.

The 2000 Edison International Annual Report stated its alternative course,

... On April 9, 2001, after two months of intense negotiations, we finally reached a detailed Memorandum of Understanding with California Governor Gray Davis, charting a path to financial health for SCE. Under the terms of the agreement, SCE will play a substantial role in helping restore stability and reliability to the California electric system.

The Memorandum of Understanding with the governor and the California Department of Water Resources provides for SCE to generate cash to pay off past power procurement undercollections through the sale of bonds, which would be serviced by less than one half cent per kilowatt hour in customer rates and through a gain on the sale of SCE's transmission system to the State of California. SCE would commit to capital investment of at least $3 billion over the next five years in its utility infrastructure to assure a reliable power grid for transportation of power to customers, and to maintain and enhance SCE's remaining power generation fleet.

The Memorandum of Understanding (MOU) of April 9, entered into between Edison International and its subsidiary, Southern California Edison Company (SCE) and the California Department of Water Resources (CDWR), has the following principal provisions (abstracted, not quoted). These provisions are designed to "set forth a comprehensive

12.10 The Storm Hits: The Energy Crisis (2000–2001)

plan calling for legislation, regulatory action and definitive agreements to resolve important aspects of the energy crisis."

The MOU contained the following principal provisions:

1. Sale by Southern California Edison to CDWR of its transmission system at 2.3 times its book value, or about $2.78 billion.
2. Establishment of a "dedicated rate component" to permit SCE to recover its under collected power procurement costs through January 31, 2001, about $3.5 billion.
3. Continued ownership by SCE of its own generation through 2010, and collection by SCE of its generation costs, and costs of power purchased under existing contracts, from January 1, 2001.
4. Assumption by CDWR of the "entire responsibility" for procuring the power needed by SCE in excess of SCE's own generation and contracted purchases, through December 31, 2002. After this date, the procurement responsibility returns to SCE.
5. To permit SCE to "achieve and maintain an investment-grade credit rating" under the above provisions, the California Public Utilities Commission (CPUC) will adopt cost-recovery mechanisms consistent with this objective, including maintaining SCE's current authorized return on equity at 11.6%, and its current capital structure, through December 31, 2010.
6. Commitment by Edison International and SCE to make at least $3 billion of capital investments in SCE's regulated business through 2006.
7. Edison Mission Energy, a subsidiary of Edison International, agrees to " sell the output of a new natural gas-fired power project in Kern County, California (the Sunrise Project) to the state under a cost-based 10-year contract."

As previously mentioned, the MOU was designed for, and did, require action by the legislature and the CPUC. Neither of these actions came easily.

As a second step in its bankruptcy plan, Pacific Gas and Electric Company, and its parent, PG&E Corporation, on September 20, 2001, jointly filed a "Plan of Reorganization" in the US Bankruptcy Court. (The plan was amended on December 19, 2001 and February 4, 2002.) As described in PG&E Corporation's 2001 Annual Report, "The plan reorganizes Pacific Gas and Electric Company and PG&E Corporation into two separate stand-alone companies no longer affiliated with one another." One of these would be a retail-focused gas and electric distribution company, having 70% of the book value of the utility's assets and about 16,000 employees, and remain under the jurisdiction of the CPUC. The other, a wholesale business, would consist of electric transmission (ETrans), interstate gas transmission (GTrans), and generation (Gen). These would be federally regulated as to price, terms, and conditions, by FERC and the NRC, and would continue to be wholly owned subsidiaries of PG&E Corporation.

In addition, Gen would provide to the retail unit firm capacity and energy at an average rate of about $5.00 per MWh, under a 12-year bilateral contract.

PG&E Corporation reports that the plan has been endorsed by the Official Committee of Unsecured Creditors. However, the CPUC has objected, and on February 13, 2002, filed an alternative plan of reorganization which "provides for the continued regulation by the CPUC of all of the utility's current operations," rejecting the realignment of the utility's business. The CPUC proposes that, after hearings, its alternative plan become effective on or before January 31, 2003.

PG&E's 2001 Annual Report states, "PG&E Corporation and the utility do not believe the CPUC's plan is credible."

12.10.2 Other Activities of PG&E Corporation and Edison International

The energy crisis did not entirely preempt the attention of utility managements in 2000 and 2001. They continued to aggressively expand into non-regulated activities, including electric generation.

PG&E's 2000 Annual Report lists the following electric acquisitions made by its National Energy Group in 2000.

- The signing of contracts for 50 turbines to support the developement of new power plants capable of generating approximately 16,000 MW of electric power.
- An agreement to acquire Duke Energy North America's 500-MW Attala power plant in Mississippi.
- The initiation of construction of the 1,048-MW La Paloma power plant near Bakersfield, California. The plant is expected to enter service in summer 2002.
- Completion of an 810-MW long-term tolling agreement with Southaven Power, LLC, that provides the NEG with marketing control of the power from a third-party-owned generation asset in the Southern US market.
- Completion of a 10-year 160-MW tolling agreement with DTE Energy Services that provides the NEG with control of its first generating asset in the midwest market.
- The filling for permits to build the 550-MW Umatilla Power Plant in Oregon, which will be adjacent to the National Energy Group's existing 474-MW Hermiston facility. The plant is expected to begin operation in 2003.

In addition, in December 2000 and in January and February 2001, the National Energy Group was restructured in a "ringfencing" transaction. "Ringfencing is intended to reduce the likelihood that the assets of the ringfenced companies would be substantially consolidated in a bankruptcy proceeding involving such companies' ultimate parent, and to thereby preserve the value of the 'protected' entities as a whole."

PG&E's 2001 Annual Report adds the following projects of the National Energy Group for that year:

12.10 The Storm Hits: The Energy Crisis (2000–2001)

- Commencing commercial operations in June at the 526-MW Attala power plant in Mississippi, and in Galion, Ohio, beginning operations at the final unit of the 144-MW multi-unit, multi-site peaker project.
- Starting construction on the 1,092-MW Harquahala plant in Arizona, the 1,080-MW Athens plant in New York, and the 111-MW Plains End facility in Colorado.
- Breaking ground on the 1,170-MW Covert generating project in southwest Michigan.
- Announcing an agreement between the PG&E NEG and the city of Denton, Texas, under which the company acquired a 178-MW generating facility and agreed to a power sales contract with the city.
- Taking ownership of the 66-MW Mountain View wind-generating facility in southern California, which sells its power to the California Department of Water Resources under a 10-year contract.

At year's end, the group's portfolio of megawatts owned and controlled totaled 7,100 MW in operation and 7,740 MW in construction.

Edison Mission Energy (EME), the unregulated power acquisition unit of Edison International, was also active. The holding company's 2000 Annual Report lists the following acquisitions by EME in that year

> In March 2000, EME completed its acquisition of Edison Mission Wind Power Italy B.V., formerly known as Italian Vento Power Corp. Energy 5 B.V. Edison Mission Wind owns a 50 percent interest in a series of wind-generated power projects in operation or under development in Italy. When all of the projects under development are completed, currently scheduled for 2002, the total capacity of these projects will be 283 MW ...
>
> In November 2002, EME completed a transaction with Texaco Inc. to purchase a proposed 560-MW gas-fired combined cycle project (Sunrise project) in central California.... As part of this transaction, EME also acquired an option to purchase two gas turbines that it plans to utilize in the project..... Phase I is scheduled for completion in August 2001 and Phase II is scheduled for completion in June 2003 .... One of the elements of the MOU is the commitment of the entire output of the Sunrise project being developed by EME, at cost-based rates for ten years ....
>
> In February 2001, EME completed the acquisition of a 50 percent interest in CBK Power Co. Ltd. CBK Power has entered into a twenty-five-year build-rehabilitate-transfer-and-operate agreement with National Power Corporation related to the 726-MW Caliraya-Botocan-Kalayaan (CBK) hydroelectric project located in the Philippines. Financing for this $460 million project has been completed ...

For the following year, Edison International's 2001 Annual Report comments as follows:

> Among all our subsidiaries, only EME retained its investment-grade credit rating. That was achieved through divesting power projects, adopting governance protections for EME creditors, and forgoing new growth initiatives. The most important of those steps was the sale of the Fiddler's Ferry and Ferrybridge (FFF) power plants in the United Kingdom, which we purchased in 1999. The lost was large, but the sale was essential ...
>
> During the summer of 2000, when it became apparent that California desperately needed additional power supply, I (John E. Bryson, Chairman, President, and CEO) challenged our people to find a way to help fill that need. EME scoured the state, located a partially permitted but abandoned project, negotiated to buy both the project rights and turbines for it, and set out to meet a near-impossible deadline. In the end, EME beat the deadline by forty-five

days, bringing online in June of last summer California's first new generating station in thirteen years. This was an extraordinary achievement. The 320-MW Sunrise Plant, located in central California, moved from groundbreaking to ribbon cutting in a record six months, and EME committed Sunrise's electrical output to serve Californians under cost-based pricing for the next ten years (See MOU).

In Asia, after persevering through the backdrop of a severe five-year economic slump in Indonesia, the EME Asia team, along with our project partners, secured a binding agreement on terms for a renewed long-term power sales contract between our Paiton generating station and the Indonesian national utility. This important step was achieved with the support of the Indonesian government. Detailed agreements remain to be worked out during 2002.

In Illinois, the more than 100 represented employees who operate seven power plants owned by EME's Midwest Generation subsidiary went on strike on June 28, 2001. Throughout the summer, our management team ran the plants ... In October, a collective bargaining agreement ... was finally reached. The strike came at the worst possible time for our customers in Illinois and for our company but the management team handled it with true excellence.

Above, in brief, is the status of PG&E and Edison as of the date of their 2001 Annual Reports. As of this date, the plans of both had substantial hurdles to overcome, ranging from different interpretations of the MOU for Edison, to widely divergent opinions as to its plan of reorganization for PG&E.

12.10.3 The Special Case of Sempra Energy, Parent of San Diego Gas and Electric Company

The 2000 Annual Report of Sempra Energy was triumphant in tone. It begins on this note: "Simply stated, in 2000 we met or exceeded every goal we set." Although affected by the energy crisis, Sempra's San Diego Gas and Electric Company did not incur billions of dollars of debt due to undercollections of electric energy purchase costs, as had its two companion California utilities, and did not see its securities downgraded, as they did.

The basic reason is simple. SDG&E was relieved of the frozen retail rate level to which the other two were subjected, in June 1999, because it had recovered its stranded costs by that time. Therefore, it had freedom to adjust its retail rates. But the details are not quite that simple.

Sempra's 2000 Annual Report fills in the missing details.

In 1996, California enacted legislation restructuring California's investor-owned electric utility industry. The legislation and related decisions of the CPUC were intended to stimulate competition and reduce electric rates. During the transition period, utilities were allowed to charge frozen rates that were designed to be above current costs by amounts assumed to provide a reasonable opportunity to recover the above-market "stranded" costs of investments in electric generating assets. The rate freeze was to end for each utility when it completed recovery of its stranded costs, but no later than March 31, 2002. SDG&E completed recovery of the stranded costs in June 1999 and, with its rates no longer frozen, SDG&E's overall rates were initially lower, but became subject to fluctuation with the actual cost of electricity purchases.

12.10 The Storm Hits: The Energy Crisis (2000–2001) 355

> A number of factors, including supply/demand imbalances, resulted in abnormally high electric-commodity costs beginning in mid-2000 and continuing into 2001. During the second half of 2000, the average electric-commodity cost was 15.51 cents, kWh (compared to 4.15 cents, kWh in the second half of 1999). In December 2000, the average was 17.91 cents/kWh (compared to 3.73 cents/kWh in December 1999). These higher prices were initially passed through to SDE&E's customers and resulted in customer bills that were double or triple those from the prior year. In response, legislation enacted in September 2000 imposed a ceiling of 6.5 cents/kWh on the cost of electricity that SDG&E may pass on to its small-usage customers on a current basis. Customers covered under the commodity rate ceiling generally include residential, small-commercial and lighting customers. The ceiling, which was retroactive to June 1, 2000 extends through December 31, 2002 (December 31, 2003) was deemed by the CPUC to be in the public interest. As a result of the ceiling, SDG&E is not able to pass through to its small-usage customers on a current basis the full purchase cost of electricity that it provides. The legislation provides for the future recovery of undercollections in a manner (not specified in the decision) intended to make SDG&E whole for the reasonable and prudent costs of procuring electricity.
>
> In the meantime, the amount paid for electricity in excess of the ceiling (the undercollected costs) is accumulated in an interest-bearing balancing account. The undercollection ... was $447 million at December 31, 2000, and $605 million at January 31, 2001, and is expected to increase to $700 million in March 2001, and remain constant thereafter, except for interest, if the DWR continues to purchase SDG&E's power requirements.... The rate ceiling has materially and adversely affected SDG&E's revenue collections and its related cash flows and liquidity. SDG&E has fully drawn upon substantially all of its short-term credit facilities. Its ability to access the capital markets and obtain additional financing has been substantially impaired by the financial distress being experienced by other California investor-owned utilities....

Sempra's 2000 Annual Report also notes the continuing ventures of its subsidiary, Sempra Energy Resources (SER), into merchant power plants.

> El Dorado Energy (El Dorado), of which SER is a 50 percent partner, began commercial operations in May 2000 at its 500-megawatt power plant near Las Vegas, Nevada, generating energy to serve 350,000 households as discussed in "Other Operations" above. Its proximity to existing natural gas pipelines and electric transmission lines allows El Dorado to actively compete in the deregulated electric-generation market.
>
> In December 2000, SER obtained approvals from the appropriate state agencies to construct the Elk Hills Power Project and the Mesquite Power Plant. The Elk Hills Power Project is a 500-megawatt power plant project near Bakersfield, California, in which SER will have a 50 percent interest. It is scheduled to begin construction in the second quarter of 2001 and to be operating in 2002. The plant is expected to generate energy to serve 350,000 households. The Mesquite Power Plant is a 1,200-megawart project located near Phoenix, Arizona, which is scheduled to begin construction in the second quarter of 2001 and to be operating in 2003. The plant is expected to generate energy to serve 700,000 households.
>
> Construction of the *Termoelectrica de Mexicali* power plant is expected to begin in mid-2001, with completion anticipated by mid-2003. The 600-megawatt power plant will be located near Mexicali, Mexico.

Sempra's 2001 Annual Report echoes the same triumphant tone of its predecessor, but with one discordant note. This relates to a June 2001 memorandum of understanding (MOU) with California "to resolve a multi-million-dollar undercollection of wholesale power costs incurred by its customers during the energy crisis. This undercollection represents the difference between what SDG&E paid for wholesale power purchases and what it has been allowed to collect from its customers under the provisions of a 2000 state law, AB 265." This law is described in Sempra's 2000 Annual Report as "imposing a ceiling of 6.5 cents/kwh in the cost of the electric commodity rate that SDG&E may pass on to its small-usage customers on a current basis." In early 2002, "a key component of this agreement was denied by the CPUC. SDG&E is proceeding with litigation on this matter."

While the foregoing summaries attempt to describe the principal actions of the three major California utilities as revealed in their annual reports, it is important to be aware that many intricate points of theory and application have not been mentioned. These may sway the final solutions.

12.11 Chronology: The Crisis and Its Aftermath (to Early 2002)

The preceding topic has been confined to the reactions to the energy crisis of the three main California utilities. Pacific Gas and Electric Company, Southern California Edison Company, and San Diego Gas and Electric Company, as portrayed in the annual reports of their parents (PG&E Corporation, Edison International, and Sempra Energy/Enova Corporation).

This prior review presents only an incomplete picture of the crisis. This picture is expanded and more fully explained in the chronology that follows.

The chronology covers many topics, including legislation considered or enacted by the state of California, and the actions of other bodies which played a role: the Federal Energy Regulatory Commission (FERC), the California Public Utilities Commission (CPUC), the California Department of Water Resources (DWR), and the new players in the state's restructuring game, the independent system operator (ISO) and the power exchange (PX). The participation of California governor Gray Davis is also included.

This chronology could have been presented separately under each of the several subjects covered, such as legislation, blackouts, financial interplay involved in the bond issue matter, and so forth. Or it could have been presented in terms of the main participants, such as FERC and DWR.

The problem with each of these options is that the interactions among the subjects and/or the participants becomes blurred and their relative timing fuzzy.

To avoid these difficulties, the chronology is couched in straight timing terms, by date. It unrolls events as they occurred: as they would have been observed by a reader following the news. To fully capture the events as they would have been seen by a reader, extensive use is made of the headlines and text appearing in articles published by the *Wall Street Journal* (WSJ) and by the *Oregonian*. The *Oregonian* carries many reports originated by the wire services, including, among others, the Associated Press, the LATimes-Washington Post service, and Bloomberg News.

The texts that are quoted often add a rich background to the headlines under which they appear, usually giving the context for the reported action itself, plus its relationship to other associated current events. These background comments are

12.11 Chronology: The Crisis and Its Aftermath (to Early 2002)   357

sometimes duplicative, but they remind the reader of the situation as it was seen to be at that particular time.

Headlines and texts are not enclosed in quotation marks. If a headline is given, it is understood that the text that follows is a direct quote. Items listed only under month and year come from various sources.

12.11.1 November 1999

FERC issued Order 2000, concerning the formation of regional transmission organizations (RTOs). It requires all public utilities that own, operate or control interstate transmission to file by October 15, 2000 a proposal for an RTO, except that utilities who are members of an existing FERC-approved regional entity must file by January 15, 2001. RTOs are to be operational by December 15, 2001.

12.11.2 August 2000

CPUC approves bilateral contracts for power purchases by IOUs.

September 2000

AB 205 sets retail rate caps for small-use electric customers of SDG&E, retroactive to June 1, 2000, of 6.5 cents per kWh (one-third or less than the actual price paid). The ceiling extends through December 31, 2002 (or December 31, 2003 at option of CPUC).

October 2000

PG&E and SCE petition FERC to have FERC find the California market to be non-competitive and to impose a price cap.

November 2000

FERC reported its findings from its formal investigation of the electric rates and structure of the ISO/PX, including the finding that high short-term energy rates during the summer of 2000 were excessive.

Cap Urged for California Power Rates (*Oregonian, November 23, 2000*)

Energy Secretary Bill Richardson proposed tighter price controls Wednesday on the California electricity market to help fight skyrocketing rates that have plagued the San Diego area since summer.

He urged the Federal Energy Regulatory Commission to cap wholesale prices at the cost to generators for the next two years.

That would go beyond the commission's proposal to create a "soft cap: for auctions on electricity of $150 a megawatt hour, Richardson said ... Under the agency's proposal, companies bidding more than the $150 rate would have to file paperwork with the commission defending the higher price.

Currently, open bidding fluctuates under a state-ordered cap of $250 a megawatt hour.

Governor Gray Davis has said the Federal Energy Regulatory Commission proposal does not go far enough. Davis said retail power prices in California have quadrupled in the past year to $ 150 a megawatt hour as of September 2.

Wholesale prices have soared throughout the West Coast . . .

Richardson's comments come in response to a commission ruling November 1 that prices were "unjust and unreasonable," setting the stage for a federal order to help remedy the problems.

Richardson called for a broader investigation of pricing during recent months to determine whether utilities cheated customers during the summer . . .

The state Public Utilities Commission on Tuesday said Federal Energy Regulatory Commission has failed to intervene decisively in California's electricity market. The PUC estimated an excess of $4 billion in wholesale electricity was charged through the summer.

Generators testified to the Federal Energy Regulatory Commission that the inadequate power supply in Southern California helped lead to the higher prices and that any limits on rates would discourage construction of new generation the state needs . . .

The commission also offered the prospect of refunds if it determines power costs to consumers were exorbitant between October 2000 and December 31, 2002 . . .

The state PUC and the utilities said power generators and traders had manipulated the market to raise electricity prices . . .

December 2000

ISO announced that generators of electricity were refusing to sell into the California market due to concerns about the financial stability of PG&E and SCE. On December 14, 2000, the secretary of Energy ordered power companies to generate and deliver power to the ISO, after the ISO had certified its inability to acquire adequate energy in the market. This order expired on December 6, 2001.

FERC issued order regarding its investigation, allowing California IOUs to buy and sell power outside the PX, replacing the PX/ISO boards with independent boards, and requiring market buyers to schedule 95% of their transactions in the day-ahead markets. It also ordered the PX to modify the single price auction so that bids above $150 per MWh cannot set the prices for all bidders: higher bidders to be paid as bid.

Gas Shortage Is Likely to Force California to Slash Electricity Output Temporarily (*WSJ December 2000)*

California is learning there is no "offseason" for the electric industry as an unexpected electrical emergency struck the state despite generally moderate temperatures. The underlying cause of the problem: tight supplies of both electricity and natural gas.

Yesterday, a top official at the agency that operates the state electricity grid said there is a "high probability" that electrical-generating plants in California could be forced to reduce their output within the next few days because of insufficient supplies of natural gas to fuel the plants. Such an event almost certainly would trigger rolling blackouts. It would be ironic if a gas curtailment were the force that finally pushed the state into blackouts—threatened but averted all summer—since the California Independent System Operator had assumed that it was past the worst danger as temperatures cooled ...

Amid all the uncertainty, prices on California's competitive electricity auction market bumped up against a price cap of $250 per megawatt hour, no longer dropping at night. But even that price—eight times the level of a year earlier—has been inadequate to attract enough supply. The ISO put out a special plea early yesterday for extra power. It then found it had to compete with utilities and generators in the Pacific Northwest that were willing to pay as much as $1,200 per megawatt hour.

There are several reasons why electricity supplies are tight. In California, nearly one-third of the state's generating capacity is shut down for repairs after operating at full capacity throughout the summer ...

The high price of natural gas, needed to fuel most plants, also complicated the picture, hitting near-record levels of $22 to $27 per million British thermal units, both in California and on the border between Washington state and British Columbia, ten to twelve times the price gas sold at a year ago.

California Energy Officials Discontinue Price-Cap System, in a Surprise Move *(WSJ, December 11, 2000)*

California grid officials unexpectedly abandoned their main tool for managing prices after it proved incapable of reining in runaway energy costs. Instead of capping bids at $250 per megawatt hour, they will now accept electricity at any price so long as suppliers can prove it is justified by production costs.

The unilateral move by the California Independent System Operator, or ISO, came at the end of a chaotic week in which energy prices spiraled out of control and the world's seventh largest economy was threatened by blackouts. Originally meant to have a small role in the state's deregulated market, the ISO, which guarantees electricity reliability, has lately found itself buying as much as one-third of the power consumed daily. In order to do so, the ISO has paid ever-higher prices for last-minute power purchases. On Monday, it spent $5 million. By Friday, the figure had climbed to $81 million.

Generators, which already had 30 percent of the state's power plants down for repairs after running them hard all summer, offered progressively less power to a computerized day-ahead market run by a state-sanctioned auction. They held back thousands of megawatts, offering the juice to the ISO only if prices got high enough. That put the ISO in the position of having to beg and haggle for power despite the fact that actual demand wasn't anything extraordinary.

"My people were making phone deals—10 to 15 an hour—when I needed them running the grid," said Terry Winter, ISO chief executive. "We had a gun to our head."

In the end, the ISO took the rogue action of abandoning its "hard price cap" of $250. It did so without advance approval of its governing board, Governor Gray Davis or even the Federal Energy Regulatory Commission to which the ISO reports ...

Governor Davis, who has come under fire from consumer groups for the sharply rising energy costs, immediately lambasted the ISO for what he called an "outrageous assault" on consumers. Governor Davis, who favors a $100 price cap—a level that generators say is below their operating costs—threatened to "dismantle" the ISO in retaliation.

Generators and traders, on the other hand, said that by freeing up prices, the ISO is actually doing what is necessary to make sure the market works. They argue a better match of supply and demand should eventually bring down prices. "Price caps distort the market," says Kenneth Lay, chairman of Enron Corp., the nation's largest energy trader ...

The ISO action, though, should give the organization some breathing room. By promising generators they can offer energy at more than $250 per megawatt hour and not have their bids rejected outright, the ISO saw the amount of juice offered on Friday jump from nearly zero to 3,000 megawatts, giving it the biggest cushion it had all week. Some of the offers came in below $250.

By yesterday, more trading had shifted back into the day-ahead market run by a sister organization, the California Power Exchange. But that pushed up its average price for power to be delivered today to a record $611.80 per megawatt hour, nearly one and a half times the prior daily high.

That price run-up may reflect the fact that the ISO, in its emergency market, now is forcing suppliers to provide "appropriate cost information" to the energy commission and state officials when they offer power at prices above $250 per megawatt hour. The daily auction has no such requirement. When emergencies are declared, the ISO also is asserting the right to fine generators who refuse to provide power.

Regulators Step in to Ease Price Shocks in California's Deregulated Power Market (*WSJ, December 18, 2000*)

Federal regulators took long-awaited steps to fix California's broken deregulated electricity market. But their actions didn't quite soothe lenders worried about the solvency of the state's utilities or satisfy politicians concerned that soaring power prices will stifle the state's continued prosperity.

The basic thrust of the action Friday by the Federal Energy Regulatory Commission is to push the state's big utilities out of a daily spot market, where they currently buy nearly all their power, and into less-volatile, long-term contracts ...

The commission suggested a benchmark price, for five-year contracts, at $74 per megawatt hour ...

The commission also capped prices for bulk power at $150 per megawatt hour, on an interim basis, but said it will permit suppliers to charge a price above that amount if they can demonstrate higher production costs. High prices in the wholesale-power market have been dragging the state's utilities steadily toward bankruptcy because they have been allowed to pass on to customers only a fraction of the cost under the state's four-year-old experiment in deregulation. So far this year, they have spent $8 billion more for power than they have been allowed to bill.

Friday's action by regulators effectively settles the question of how the federal government, having encouraged states to deregulate their electricity markets, would react when those markets go haywire. The commission has allowed states to experiment with different market models and acknowledged it wasn't certain of the best approach, but vowed to make sure deregulated rates would remain "just and reasonable" ...

California Governor Gray Davis accused commission members of being "armchair Washington bureaucrats, fixated on economic ideology," who have abdicated their duty to protect consumers. He said the FERC's action falls short of what is needed and will permit "unconscionable profits for the pirate generators and power brokers who are gouging California consumers." ...

Friday's order also effectively "defederalizes" some 12,700 megawatts of generating plants still owned by the state's three big investor-owned utilities: Pacific Gas & Electric Co., a subsidiary of *PG&E Corp.,* San Francisco; Southern California Edison, a unit of *Edison International,* Rosemead, California, and San Diego Gas & Electric Co., a unit of *Sempra Energy,* San Diego. Since deregulation, the utilities have been selling power from those facilities into an energy auction run under the FERC's oversight. If California's Public Utilities Commission agrees, from now on the utilities will be allowed to retain the power for use by their own customers, thus reducing their exposure to open-market prices ...

Although the FERC order reduced the importance of the increasingly rough-and tumble spot market, it didn't do what state politicians and consumer advocates wanted most: set region wide price caps and pare down profit of power traders and generators. Prices in the daily market in California have reached as high as $1,400 per megawatt hour this month compared with an average price of about $30 per megawatt hour a year ago. A combination of short supply, strong demand, surging fuel costs and flawed market rules are blamed for the skyrocketing rate.

It appears unlikely the commission will order the generators to give refunds because its four members are deadlocked on the issue. Furthermore, in Friday's order the commissioners said they would only reserve the right to challenge prices above $150 per megawatt hour for sixty days after each trading day. Previously, there was no statute of limitations and it was felt that the prospect of far-reaching audits might help restrain prices.

The push for long-term contracting goes against warnings from several economists who say it is unwise to force utilities to sign such contracts just now, when prices are highest. Utilities run the risk of obligating consumers to pay these prices over the long term, just when the field of suppliers is the most limited and when natural-gas prices, fuel for nearly all the divested plants, is at an all-time high.
Power Shortage Called Critical *(Oregonian, December 20, 2000)*

12.11.3 January 2001

FERC prohibits sales to the PX.

AB IX prohibits utilities from divesting retained generating plants before January 1, 2006.

CPUC allows an "interim energy procurement surcharge" of 1 cent per kWh, to remain in effect for 90 days.

PX announces that it will permanently cease operations by April 2001.

DWR begins making emergency purchases of power, pursuant to an emergency order.

Back to the Future in California *(WSJ, editorial, January 17, 2001)*
Sooner or later, the state can expect to be stuck holding the bag for high-priced power. The whole cycle that launched deregulation in the first place will start again ...

There was always an easier, more honest solution to this problem, such as admitting that the state screwed up deregulation and using government money to reorganize the utilities debts. Had Gov. Davis acted when the trouble became glaring last summer, the cost would have been negligible and it probably could have been done without any rate increase at all.

Power Crisis in California Hits High Mark *(WSJ, January 12, 2001)*
On January 11, 2001, the DWR bought electricity in the Pacific Northwest, providing an extra 1,200 MWH.

Blackouts Roll in California *(Oregonian, January 18, 2001)*
Hundreds of thousands of people are hit, as Governor Gray Davis signs an emergency order that allows the state DWR to buy power for the grid .... A power shortage pushes the two largest utilities close to bankruptcy.

California Is Hit with Series of Blackouts *(WSJ, January 18, 2001)*
After bouncing off the guard rail for eight months, California's electricity market finally crashed for the first time. Rolling blackouts were ordered in Northern California by the state's grid operator shortly before noon and still threatened other parts of the state late in the evening. Blackouts could be even more widespread today ....

The critical power shortages come on the heels of a continuing financial crisis at the state's two largest utilities, Southern California Edison, a unit of *Edison International,* and Pacific Gas & Electric Co., a unit of *PG&E* Corp. PG&E failed to pay off $76 million worth of commercial paper that came due yesterday in part because it was cut off from its existing bank credit lines. Southern California Edison said earlier this week that it wouldn't pay nearly $600 million in power bills and bond payments. Both utilities have said they may soon be forced into US. bankruptcy court.

Some energy experts have suggested that power suppliers are deliberately withholding energy from California's market because of fears that they won't be paid by the utilities ....

California Power Crisis: Blackouts and Lawsuits and No End in Sight—Blame and Brinkmanship Dog Efforts to Resolve Threat to the State's Economy *(WSJ, January 19, 2001)*
California has weathered earthquakes, wildfires, floods and droughts. But now a man-made disaster is threatening to short-circuit the world's sixth largest economy.

12.11 Chronology: The Crisis and Its Aftermath (to Early 2002) 363

For a second day, rolling blackouts shut down businesses, dimmed households and even threatened California's citrus crop. People were trapped in elevators and traffic was snarled. Supermarkets were crowded with customers buying flashlights and firewood. California Steel Industries Inc. in Fontana shut down its steel-rolling lines yesterday, losing about $2.4 million worth of production. And the crisis set off new legal fireworks as the city of San Francisco, hit by blackouts, sued power traders and generators, accusing them of conspiring to restrict supplies.

The California Independent System Operator, which runs the state's electrical grid and ensures reliability, declared its highest level of power emergency for the fifth time this year. Engineers at the ISO's control room in Folsom, California, were pressed into service phoning suppliers to coax a few more megawatts into the system . . . .

The crisis has blown up into a dangerous game of brinkmanship by the state's two biggest utilities, power-generating companies, and politicians—with the California economy in the balance. Many of these players helped design a complex electricity deregulation plan that became dysfunctional when it ran into a tight energy market.

Governor Gray Davis signed an emergency order Wednesday empowering the state's Department of Water Resources to temporarily become a power buyer. But with only limited buying authority and a mere $400 million to spend—less than two weeks' worth of electricity at current prices—the DWR isn't expected to offer much relief. That's especially true because the DWR wasn't authorized to help fund the ISO's critical last-minute power purchases.

The state's unwillingness to commit large sums for buying power is a key sticking point in the two-month-long standoff over how to restructure this market . . . .

The state's problems are chilling enthusiasm for deregulation in several other states, such as Nevada, which has postponed opening its retail power market to competition. It has also highlighted what economists say is a lesson repeatedly learned but just as often ignored: that deregulating only part of a highly regulated market is a prescription for trouble. Under California's plan, the rates charged to consumers were frozen while wholesale electric costs were allowed to fluctuate. When those wholesale prices soared last year, the state's utilities were hit by a financial tidal wave.

Bush Extends Power Order *(Oregonian, January 24, 2001)*
President Bush ordered a two-week extension Tuesday of federal directives requiring power and natural gas companies to keep supplying California's cash-strapped utilities . . . .

The extension came as California eked sufficient power out of tight West Coast electricity supplies to avoid blackouts. The federal directive, first issued by the Clinton administration [in December] was set to expire at midnight . . . .

Suppliers have threatened to cut off the state's two big investor-owned California utilities—PG&E and Southern California Edison—because of fear their mounting $12 billion debt might drive them into bankruptcy and prevent future payments.

State officials reported Tuesday they have spent more than a quarter of a $400 million emergency fund established for the state to buy power from wholesalers on behalf of the state's two largest and struggling utilities.

Tight supply, high demand, high wholesale prices and the utilities' financial shakiness have pushed California into its hour-by-hour search for electricity and resulted in two days of rolling blackouts last week ....

Governor Gray Davis's administration began accepting sealed bids Tuesday from electricity suppliers as lawmakers debated measures that could put the state in the power business for years to come.

California is asking power producers for contracts lasting from six months to ten years. Negotiators acknowledged the contracts would keep the state in the power business for a long time ....

California power grid managers told the energy commission that the state's utilities paid $30 billion for power last year, more than four times the wholesale power costs in 1999.

Blackouts Cast Pall over Economy *(Oregonian, January 25, 2001)*

For Power Suppliers, the California Market Loses Its Golden Glow *(WSJ, January 25, 2001)*

States, Sobered by California Crisis, Delay Deregulation *(WSJ, January 25, 2001)*

Lawmakers Mull Bonds to Aid Utilities—to Cover the Multibillion Debts, the State Would Issue Bonds That Customers Would Repay over a Decade *(Oregonian, January 26, 2001)*

The debt for PG&E and SCE is $12 billion. The state is buying power on their behalf because their credit is practically worthless.

California Wants Stake in Utilities *(Oregonian, January 27, 2001)*

The plan for the state to take options *or* warrants for PG&E and Edison *resembles the* US bailout of automaker Chrysler.

Governors Are Divided on Power Price Caps *(Oregonian, January 31, 2001)*

Western governors head into this week's summit on the California energy crisis with no consensus about one of the fastest ways to curb escalating power costs: slapping price controls on wholesale electricity ....

Billed as an "Energy Policy Roundtable," the gathering comes in the wake of California's rolling power blackouts and mounting fears that high energy prices could prove devastating to the region's ratepayers and economy ....

The debate about price caps has been a subplot since wholesale prices started to rise last summer in California.

Davis has been the most urgent advocate, asking the Clinton administration last year for a federally imposed "hard" cap that would set a regional ceiling for wholesale power until energy markets could stabilize.

In mid-December, however, the energy commission rejected a hard cap and instead opted for a system requiring sellers to report when prices exceeded $150 per megawatt hour. Critics said the move had no real teeth, and prices continued to spike, reaching as much as $1,000 per megawatt hour on the spot market ....

Energy suppliers oppose price caps, saying that they take away financial incentives to build new power plants needed to meet rising consumer demand and that they can hamper conservation by keeping prices artificially low.

February 2001

AB 1 Gives California's Department of Water Resources (DWR) authority to buy power under long-term contracts of up to 10 years on behalf of PG&E, Southern California Edison and SDG&E. This authority ends on December 31, 2002.

AB IX extends preliminary authority of DWR to purchase power for IOUs. DRW initially purchased power on the spot market until it was able to enter into contracts for the supply of electricity, and still continues to buy some power on the spot market at prevailing prices.

It authorizes funds from the state's general fund for immediate power purchases and authorizes DWR to issue up to $10 billion in revenue bonds to purchase power.

There is dispute with respect to the interpretation of AB IX. Does it mean that DWR will assume full responsibility for purchasing all power needed by the IOUs in excess of the output of their generating plants and obtained under existing contracts, or does it mean that DWR will only purchase power it considers to be reasonably priced, leaving it to the ISO to buy the excess needed in the short-term market?

California's Governor Signs Law to Let State Buy Long Term Power Contracts *(WSJ, February 2, 2001)*

With California's electricity system straining from intense supply and financial pressures, Governor Gray Davis yesterday took what could be the first step toward easing the crisis, signing a new law that allows the state to purchase billions of dollars of power under long-term contracts.

The law, which allows the state Department of Water Resources to sell the power to consumers through utilities, also authorizes the state to sell an estimated $ 10 billion in revenue bonds to raise funds to pay for the power. The law calls for the bonds to be paid off through the existing electric rates charged to consumers, presumably over ten years.

Observers say the passage of the bill is an important step in efforts to ensure the reliability of the state's electricity supply, which has been extremely tight and last month produced forced blackouts. But the state is still negotiating the contracts with power suppliers, and it is still unclear how much power will be offered up and at what price. That, in turn, leaves open the question of the eventual impact on consumers' pocketbooks ....

Some Republican lawmakers were also concerned about a section of the bill signed yesterday that would authorize the state Public Utilities Commission to increase residential electric rates only on usage that exceeds 130 percent of baseline consumption—a standard monthly measure of usage by households that varies across fifteen regions and is calculated according to climatic conditions and other factors. That guideline for rate increases, which would expire after the bonds are paid off, would have the effect of transferring the burden of rate increases to large commercial and industrial customers . . ..

The governor said he has given his team of negotiators until February 5 to sign the first round of contracts with generators and traders, hoping to lock up power purchases for as long as five and ten years at an average of 5.5 cents to seven cents a kilowatt hour. Current rates are 35 cents to 40 cents. As such, said the governor, "every day we miss is a real tragedy." Indeed, the state has burned through $535 million in funds over the past two weeks buying electricity on the spot market and still faces $40 million to $50 million in daily spending in order to avoid forced blackouts.

Worries on Payments May Be Slowing California Talks on Electricity Contracts *(WSJ, February 16, 2001)*

Some power generators say negotiations on crucial electricity-supply contracts for California are being slowed by concerns over the state's willingness and ability to pay for the power.

A state agency, the California Department of Water Resources, was empowered to purchase electricity on the wholesale market, because two of the state's biggest utilities were so drained by the costs of procuring power that they have been pushed to the verge of insolvency. The two companies, *Edison International's* Southern California Edison Co. and *PG&E* Corp.'s Pacific Gas & Electric Co., have already defaulted on hundreds of millions of dollars of debts.

The idea of California's governor, Gray Davis, and the state Legislature was to stabilize a shaky market by exercising the vast buying power of the state.

But so far, things haven't worked out quite as planned. The state only has signed one supplier . . . several generators are worried that the state agency doesn't have enough money, currently, to back multibillion-dollar contracts lasting as long as ten years . . ..

Generators themselves have been heavily criticized for their role in the crisis. Many observers say that suppliers have deliberately pushed up prices for wholesale electricity. Fueling this suspicion is the fact that unusually large numbers of power plants have been out of service for maintenance in recent months, thus reducing the amount of supply and putting upward pressure on electricity prices. Generators have denied any wrongdoing.

Wholesale electric costs have been astronomical, complicating the contract negotiations. California energy costs average $305 per megawatt hour in January, nearly ten times the price of a year earlier. For the month, the total bill was $5.34 billion, the second-costliest month since California deregulated its energy market in March 1998, trailing only December's record $6.15 billion tab.

Measured against those high costs is Mr. Davis's oft-repeated intent that the state sign long-term supply contracts at about one-quarter the going rate today. Mr. Davis has said the state is making progress toward its goal of securing long-term, affordable supplies.

What is more, the water-resources agency has said it doesn't feel compelled to pick up all of the tab for the ISO's power-procurement costs . . ..

12.11 Chronology: The Crisis and Its Aftermath (to Early 2002) 367

Uncertainty about which bills the water-resources agency will pay may be poisoning the atmosphere for extended supply contracts. Generators say they thought the state would be buying all necessary power that the utilities couldn't supply ....

March 2001

PX files for bankruptcy protection on March 9.

CPUC, on March 27, 2001, authorized an additional 3 cents per kWh surcharge for IOU rates, and made permanent the earlier surcharge of 1 cent per kWh.

FERC, on March 9, directed 13 wholesalers to refund $69 million or to justify their prices above $273 per MWh during ISO Stage 3 emergencies in January 2001. On March 16, directed six wholesalers to refund an additional $55 million or to justify prices above $430 per MWh in February 2001. A Stage 3 emergency refers to 1.5% or less in reserve power, which could trigger rolling blackouts.

California Bond Issues May Exceed $10 Billion *(WSJ, March 9, 2001)*
California Treasurer Philip Angelides said the state may have to issue more than the $10 billion in bonds it previously proposed before it can bring soaring power costs under control and restore two big utilities to a state of financial health.

> ... Mr. Angelides said that even staying within the $10 billion target would require the state to get wholesale power for an average price of $150 per megawatt hour or less in 2001 and to slash the cost of buying electricity from renewable and cogeneration facilities by half. Both of those conditions appear very optimistic, given today's energy situation.

Although California hasn't divulged the amount of money it is spending for power, it has said it is paying for the bulk of expensive last-minute power purchases by the state's grid operator. During the three weeks ending March 5, those costs exceeded $700 million and were equivalent to $374 per megawatt hour. Only a minuscule amount of power was made available at prices less than $150 a megawatt hour in that period.

Mr. Angelides said the state's ability to issue $10 billion in bonds, which would be the biggest municipal bond issuance in history, now depends on the state Public Utilities Commission. Later this month, the PUC will consider proposals to reimburse the state for costs incurred since Governor Gray Davis authorized it to buy power in mid-January ....

The state has actually been buying power on behalf of nearly bankrupt utilities *Pacific Gas & Electric* Co. and *Southern California Edison* Co. since December. Thus far, it hasn't been reimbursed for its costs and has dipped into the state general fund for $3.2 billion that it is using to buy power. Under a state law signed on February 1, the state can sell bonds and use the money to reimburse the general fund and subsidize power costs on an interim basis.

But there's a rub. The law says the state only can issue bonds valued at no more than four times the estimated revenue available to repay them. In this case, that would require a revenue stream of $2.5 billion a year. But the law also says utilities get to pay their own generation-related costs before funneling money to the state. By various utility estimates, the money left over for the state will fall far short of that $2.5 billion. That means rates would have to rise to meet utilities' and the state's funding needs. Mr. Davis repeatedly has said he believes he can solve the state's electricity crisis "within the existing rate structure."...

The treasurer said he still would like to do a $10 billion issuance, somehow, and is proceeding to make the necessary arrangements. First, he hired JP Morgan Securities Inc. to spearhead the bond issue and to lead the way on putting together $4 billion to $5 billion in bridge financing by the end of March. That money would be used to repay the state for its costs so far. The first bonds, he said, would be issued in June and be used to repay lenders and fund continuing electricity costs.

Mr. Angelides said he is considering twelve-year bonds that would carry a 5.45 percent interest rate. Servicing the debt would require revenue of $1.3 billion a year.

DWR (*WSJ, March 12, 2001*)

California's DWR is now the nation's largest purchaser of energy. As of the week ending March 18, 2001, the state has dipped into its general fund for $3.7 billion to cover power procurement costs, meaning that in less than three months it has tapped the equivalent of 64 percent of the state's expected 2001 fiscal budget surplus of $5.8 billion.

Electricity Suppliers Ordered by Regulators to Refund $55 Million (*WSJ, March 19, 2001*)

Excessive pricing was based on a determination that prices as much as $430 per megawatt-hour—about 10 times as high as prices in the East—were to be regarded as "just and reasonable" for regulatory purposes.... Suppliers were allowed to charge far more in February than in January, for instance, when prices of more than $273 per megawatt-hour triggered the refund mechanism.

California Blackouts Viewed As an Omen—Monday's Rolling Blackouts Are Seen As a Problem Which Could Quickly Stretch Beyond Borders and Sap the U.S. Economy (*Oregonian, March 20, 2001*)

Rolling Blackouts Hit Almost All Parts of California (*WSJ, March 20, 2001*)

Blackouts Darken California's Day (*Oregonian, March 21, 2001*)

California Regulators Approve Electric-Rate Rise (*WSJ, March 28. 2001*)

California regulators approved a $5 billion-a-year increase in retail electric rates yesterday that will fall hardest on businesses. But even that hefty increase—which could cause electric bills to rise by more than 50 percent for many companies—may not be enough to fully cover the state's out-of-control wholesale power costs....

The state has estimated it will need to buy sixty million megawatt hours of power this year to keep customers of the two utilities supplied with electricity. So far this year, the cost of such purchases often has exceeded $300 a megawatt hour. Even if prices don't go higher this summer, when demand is at its peak, the state will need to come up with at least $14 billion this year to pay power suppliers....

The commission also ordered utilities to resume paying independent generators. These so-called qualifying facilities—often renewable suppliers or cogeneration facilities—haven't been paid since October. Southern California Edison, alone, owes them nearly $900 million.

Although the action yesterday will increase the amount of money available to the state to fund its continuing purchases, the commission did nothing to defray the cost of power already purchased by the utilities. Since last May, when prices on the deregulated market exploded, the two utilities have spent $10 billion more for power—that is $6.7 billion for PG&E and $3.7 billion for Edison—than they were permitted to collect from their customers through rates . . . .

Standard & Poor's kept California on its CreditWatch list with "negative implications" following the commission action. Although the rate increase will help the state's cash flow, "there are still lots of uncertainties" about the financial impact on the state, says David Hitchcock, a director in S&P's state and local government group.

The state treasurer has said he intends to issue $10 billion or more in revenue bonds and use the proceeds to pay for energy costs. But Mr. Hitchcock said it is still not clear that there is enough money in rates to cover the bond-repayment costs and provide adequate protections to investors.

For one thing, there has to be a dedicated revenue stream to pay the bonds—which can't be interrupted if one or both of the utilities file for bankruptcy-law protection. In order to give the bonds an investment-grade rating, S&P has to be confident that "the state would clearly have first claim" on the revenue produced by the electric rates, said Mr. Hitchcock.

Calpine Plugs Into a Winning Electric-Power Strategy—Key Factor is Company's Ability to Build Plants That Burn Much Less Fuel (*WSJ, March 30, 2001*)

Calpine Corp. is the rare power generator nowadays admired not only by investors, but by regulators and environmentalists as well.

The San Jose, California, independent power producer has become a juggernaut, propelled by opportunities created by rising U.S. demand for electricity and its ability to construct plants that burn 30 percent to 40 percent less fuel than those of rivals—but get paid the same. As the mismatch between the nation's power needs and its aging generating plant base becomes more acute, Calpine has increased the amount of new megawatts it intends to put on line within the next five years from 27,000 to a stunning 70,000 . . . .

Calpine finds itself in the right place at the right time. The company has two big power plants cranking up this summer to fill part of California's acute shortage. Even with the additions, the state is expected to be 6,000 megawatts short of meeting its needs. Another Calpine plant will begin running this summer in Arizona, capable of sending power throughout the West, and a fourth is expected to begin producing electricity during the summer of 2002. Plants Calpine is building in California represent more than half the capacity now under construction in the Golden State and a significant portion of their output already has been sold to the state government under ten-year contracts . . . .

A key part of Calpine's strategy is to pick markets where natural-gas-fired plants set the market price for power. Since older-generation natural-gas plants are much less efficient than the new ones that Calpine builds, it is able to make each kilowatt hour of electricity much less expensively than its competitors. But in the nation's newly deregulated markets, the market price is set by the last generating plant called into service. That's invariably an older non-Calpine plant that must command a higher price in order to run. That runs up the profit for Calpine.

Even so, the company rarely is accused of making an untoward profit because it's doing what merchant generators are supposed to do: building new supply that is less costly to operate and produces less pollution. Over time, so the economic theory goes, its plants should displace the less-efficient units and give the nation better sources of electricity.

April 2001

PG&E filed for voluntary bankruptcy protection under Chapter 11 on April 6, 2001. This filing did not include PG&E Corporation or other subsidiaries of the corporation.

Southern California Edison (and Edison International) executed memorandum of understanding (MOU) with the state on April 9, 2001.

Bills Proposed in Congress to Cap Electricity Rates—Administration Opposes Price Caps (*Oregonian, April 5, 2001*)

A handful of bills are proposed in Congress to cap electricity rates:

- *Senate Bill 26:* By Senators Dianne Feinstein and Barbara Boxer, both D-California. Authorizes the secretary of energy to impose a temporary cap on wholesale power prices if high rates threaten the health or economy of a state or region. Introduced in the House by Rep. Duncan Hunter, R-California.
- *Senate Bill 287:* By Feinstein and Boxer. Directs the Federal Energy Regulatory Commission to impose rates for wholesale electricity in the West based on cost-of-service plus a reasonable profit.
- *House Resolution 264:* By Rep. Peter DeFazio, D-Oregon. Requires FERC to return to a system of cost-based regulation of wholesale electricity, reversing the shift to a deregulated electricity market nationwide.
- *HR268:* By Rep. Bob Filner, D-Califomia, and other Democrats. Requires FERC to order refunds of unjust electricity rates and set cost-based rates for wholesale power in the West if it determines that prices are unjust. Also introduced in the Senate by Boxer.
- *HR443:* By Filner. Enacts a "windfall profit" tax on energy producers when profits exceed the cost of production and a reasonable return on investment.
- *Pending:* By Senator Gordon Smith, R-Oregon, and Feinstein. Directs FERC to impose caps on wholesale power based on cost-of-service and a reasonable return. Applies only in states that don't cap retail electricity costs. Lets states decide how to pass on wholesale costs. Encourages the Bonneville Power Administration to reduce price spikes in economically distressed areas.
- *Pending:* By Rep. Jay Inslee, D-Washington, and Western Democrats. Declares a power emergency in eleven Western states. Requires FERC to set cost-based rates and order refunds of overcharges. Allows states to sue energy companies in federal court to recover unjust rates or other relief.

California's Davis to Support Raising Electricity Rates *(WSJ, April 6, 2001)*

After months of fighting "tooth and nail" against raising electric rates, Governor Gray Davis announced in a TV and radio broadcast last night that a rate increase is necessary "to keep our lights on and our economy strong."

The governor's proposal comes just a week after the state Public Utilities Commission approved the biggest rate increase in state history, increasing the amount consumers pay two utilities for electricity by about $4.8 billion a year. Mr. Davis had previously insisted that the state could solve its power woes without a rate increase, although wholesale power costs have outstripped retail rates in California, by billions of dollars since last May.

Now, Mr. Davis, who has no direct authority over power rates, is in essence asking the PUC to dump that plan in favor of his proposal. The governor's advisers estimate that his proposal would cost customers of *PG&E* Corp.'s Pacific Gas & Electric Co. and *Edison International's* Southern California Edison an additional $3.5 billion over the next nine months, compared with the PUC plan's $4 billion cost over the same period.

In his speech, Mr. Davis said that, under his plan—which is aimed at Pacific Gas & Electric, Southern California Edison and *San Diego Gas & Electric* Co.— more than half of residential customers "won't pay a penny more." For the rest of residential customers, the average increase will be 26.5 percent. The heaviest residential and commercial customers will see their rates rise an average of 34.5 percent. "That includes business paying" its share, the governor said. These rate increases, the governor acknowledged, would be in addition to the 7 percent to 15 percent surcharge that Californians have been paying since January.

Mr. Davis linked his rate increase to three demands on the state's investor-owned utilities: They must "provide low-cost regulated power to the state for 10 years"; they must agree to sell the state their transmission systems; and the utilities must dismiss lawsuits they have filed against the state . . . .

For months, the governor had rejected arguments and pleas from Wall Street and elsewhere that rate increases had to be part of the answer to stabilizing California's imbalance of supply and demand, and to righting the state's utilities that were tottering on the brink of bankruptcy.

"If I wanted to raise rates, I could have solved this problem in 20 minutes," the governor had grown fond of saying.

S&P Lowers Bond Rating for California *(WSJ, April 25, 2001)*

The California electricity crisis produced another casualty, as Standard & Poor's lowered its rating on about $25.7 billion of state bonds . . . .

The S&P downgrade is the most tangible sign to date that concerns are growing over whether California's state budget is being sucked into a financial quagmire. "The downgrade reflects the mounting and uncertain cost to the state of the current electrical-power crisis, as well as its likely long-term detrimental effect on the state's economy," S&P said . . . .

So far, the state has spent about $5 billion from its general fund to purchase electricity and continues to spend more than $70 million a day. The general fund is supposed to be reimbursed from the planned loans and bond sales. FERC, on April

26, 2001, issued order prescribing price mitigation for hours of an ISO-declared emergency, and requiring that all generators in California offer available generation to the ISOs real-time energy market in all hours.

States Try to Deter Power Price Gauging—California, New York Weigh Penalties on Generators That Charge High Prices (*WSJ, April 30, 2001*)

California Blackouts Are Rolling Once Again (*Oregonian, May 8, 2001* and *WSJ, May 8, 2001*)

California Electricity Bills Will Balloon—The State's New Rate Plan is Retroactive, and It Gives Breaks to Agricultural and Industrial Power Users (*Oregonian,* **May 16, 2001**)

California's residential ratepayers will pay up to 47 percent more for electricity under a plan approved 3-2 Tuesday by the state's utility board.

The California Public Utilities Commission had approved the overall amount of the rate increase earlier, but not how it would be allocated. The allocation was worked out by PUC President Loretta Lynch after heavy lobbying by groups representing industrial, commercial, agricultural and residential ratepayers.

The increases will begin appearing on June bills and will be retroactive to March 27—the day the record rate increases were approved.

Lynch's recommendations, which will affect about 9 million customers of the state's two largest utilities, Pacific Gas and Electric and Southern California Edison, were revisions of a plan she released last week. That plan would have spared many residential users and placed more of the burden on businesses and farms.

Lynch's new proposal lowers a cap on rate increases for agricultural customers from 30 percent to a maximum of 20 percent, and it suggests a new rate cap for industrial customers ...

Unseasonably hot weather last week forced the state's utilities to impose blackouts on two consecutive days, darkening as many as 295,000 homes and businesses and causing traffic snarls statewide as signals went dark.

June 2001

FERC orders prospective price mitigation for wholesale spot markets throughout both California and the Western Systems Coordinating Council. It also establishes a maximum market-clearing price for spot market sales in all hours. These caps are set to expire September 30, 2002.

DWR and SDG&E executed a memorandum of understanding on June 18, 2001 that provided for the sale of SDG&E's transmission to the state for about $1 billion; settlement for recovery of about $750 million of undercollections; and dedication to retail customers of the output of generation resources owned by SDG&E or in which it has an interest.

Power Crisis in California Threatens to Trigger Credit-Ratings Downgrades Affecting Borrowing (*WSF, June 25, 2001*)

California's power crisis threatens to trigger credit-ratings downgrades that would make it more expensive for businesses and local governments to borrow in the credit markets.

So far, most downgrades have affected utilities and power projects. Additional debt-market issuers could be affected if the power crisis persists, said analysts.

"Ultimately, the solution they come up with in California is going to have to include higher electricity rates," said Thomas Watters, an S&P analyst. "That added cost is going to have an unfavorable impact on companies in California, and it's going to have an impact on credit quality."...

Analysts said high-tech and chemical companies are particularly sensitive to power interruptions, although the impact of blackouts can be widespread.

States Encourage Electric Utilities to Build Plants *(WSJ, June 27, 2001)*

Determined to avoid a California-like debacle, more states are making it easier for energy companies to build new power plants....

With these moves, states are applying a lesson that California has learned the hard way: It doesn't make sense to deregulate local electric markets if there aren't enough suppliers competing at the wholesale level to both provide enough juice and keep prices low....

The rush to build has critics. Some suggest that states are overreacting and may end up with a glut of plants that they will be stuck with for decades. But the main complaints are from environmentalists, who worry that the new laws attack a short-term problem by inflicting long-term environmental damage.

Regulators Order Formation of Big Grids to Ease Bottlenecks in U.S. Energy Supply *(WSJ, July 12, 2001)*

In a bid to break bottlenecks in the U.S. energy grid, the Federal Energy Regulatory Commission ordered the formation of four big electric-transmission organizations to optimize the flow of juice in the Northeast, the Southeast, the Midwest, and the West....

The federal orders are intended to jump-start development of electric-transmission organizations that the FERC permitted in a landmark decision called Order 2000, issued in December 1999.

In that order, the FERC urged utilities to voluntarily surrender control of their transmission systems to grid organizations that would run daily markets for power and manage the flow of electricity across broad regions. The agency said the nation would benefit from larger, more efficient wholesale-electricity markets, in which transmission owners no longer would be able to favor their own power sales over those of competitors.

In addition, the FERC expressed a desire in the 1999 order to see regional transmission organizations, called RTOs, formed. Those organizations would boost transmission investments and introduce "postage-stamp pricing" for transmission services, so suppliers could move power across long distances for a single charge instead of incurring "pancaked" costs as power flowed across separately owned and operated transmission lines....

The FERC actions also indicate the commission is becoming more confident about the market structure it wants, especially in view of California's troubles. When it began pushing energy deregulation in the early 1990s, the agency conceded it didn't know which market structure would work best and encouraged experimentation.

Now the commissioners are clearly worried that too much local autonomy can backfire. In California, the governor's office effectively has taken control of the governance of the California ISO, installing his own advisers on its board. In two weeks, the commission may issue an order overturning the California ISO board on the grounds that it isn't independent, a condition of Order 2000.

Taking Charge—Hurt by Deregulation of Utilities, California Gives Itself a Lead Role—State Becomes Major Buyer of Electricity and Faces Little Oversight of Deals *(WSJ, July 17, 2001)*

With the acquiescence of other state leaders, Governor Davis has put California on the road to creating what amounts to a mammoth state-owned electric utility, answerable largely to the governor. Moreover, though designed to solve a short-term emergency, the governor's policies are loading consumers with obligations that could affect the economy of the most-populous state for fifteen to twenty years.

His actions in some ways hark back to the system of central control that preceded the disastrous 1996 foray into utility deregulation. But they aren't simply a return to the days of monopoly utilities strictly regulated by the state's Public Utilities Commission. What is emerging now is a California power colossus that operates in important ways beyond the reach of regulators or the public.

Mr. Davis says his actions will ensure that Californians have a secure supply of reasonably priced electricity. "This is not a power grab," the Democratic governor says in an interview. "I had no desire to intervene. I would get out tomorrow if you would let me out. This is my least-favorite thing to do."

'Colossal Failure'

Yet in the past six months, pushed by what he calls the "colossal failure" of a deregulation plan hatched under his Republican predecessor, the governor has put the state deep into the power business. In January, Mr. Davis ordered the state Department of Water Resources to begin buying power in place of California's cash-strapped utilities. Since then, the state has purchased or committed to purchase $45 billion to $50 billion of electricity, with some contracts as long as twenty years.

The governor has in effect seized control of the state's electricity-grid operator, the California Independent System Operator, installing his hand-picked team as board members. As its name implies, the ISO was supposed to manage the grid without favoring any one participant.

Mr. Davis also is pushing to have the state buy huge chunks of the transmission system that are owned by the financially beleaguered utilities. He recently signed into law a bill that creates a state power authority, whose director will be appointed by the governor. This agency, which so far exists just on paper, could be used to build power plants and help run a state-owned transmission system. Mr. Davis says that the authority is part of what he sees as a "hybrid" system where public power plays an important role augmenting private enterprise in the electricity business.

Reviving the Utilities

Having healthy utilities is extremely important, says the governor. He adds that he has been working hard to revive the state's two biggest utilities, the Pacific Gas & Electric Co. unit of PG&E Corp. and the Southern California Edison Co. subsidiary of Edison International. But as the state's role in the electricity business has grown, the utilities don't seem as essential as they once did . . . .

The state's utility-deregulation law, which was enacted in 1996, worked fairly well until May of last year. Under the deregulation plan, the state's investor-owned utilities sold off many of their power plants to other companies and repurchased that electricity through a state-sponsored auction. Consumer rates were frozen and customers were given the option to buy electricity from nonutility retail suppliers.

But tight electricity supplies and a flawed auction system led to a sharp rise in wholesale power costs. With retail rates frozen, Pacific Gas and Edison racked up multibillion-dollar deficits. In January, Mr. Davis declared an emergency and put the state into the power-buying business.

Since then, he hasn't been bashful about exercising his emergency powers. When Mr. Davis couldn't get legislative permission to borrow money short-term for power purchases, he signed an executive order authorizing the state to borrow up to $5 billion from commercial lenders. That borrowing is supposed to be repaid from a roughly $13 billion municipal-bond issue, the biggest in U.S. history, scheduled for later this year . . .

Mr. Davis says his actions have been essential and are working. He credits the long-term power contracts with helping to cool the spot market for electricity, where prices in recent weeks have dropped sharply. In June, the state paid an average price of $167 a megawatt hour for electricity. That was down from $243 in May, though still far about the $25-to-$27 range of two years ago...

'Crisis of Governance'

The electricity mess has produced "the most extraordinary crisis of governance we've had in California in the postwar period," says Bruce Cain, director of the Institute of Governmental Studies at the University of California at Berkeley. Mr. Cain says more power has been placed in the governor's hands and, as a result, the state has "gotten away from the separation of powers and the checks and balances that we expect in American government."

California's Next Test in Electricity Crisis: Selling Power Bonds—The $12.5 Billion Offering, Crucial to State Finances, Faces Skeptical Investors *(WSJ, July 31, 2001)*

For the past seven months, Governor Gray Davis has begged, cajoled and even threatened legislators and regulators, to lay the groundwork for a $12.5 billion bond issue California needs to cover the cost of keeping its lights on.

Now comes the tough part: persuading investors that the bond is an attractive investment. On that score, Mr. Davis's team, whose credibility has been battered by California's months-long electricity crisis, is hoping to bounce back from a rocky start . . .

Doubts arise because this giant bond issue won't be backed by the full faith and credit of the state or by tax dollars—the types of guarantees public-debt investors often prefer. Instead, the bonds, which will have maturities of as long as fifteen years, are to be paid off by the state's electricity ratepayers from their monthly bills, which some view as a riskier source of cash flow Moreover, there is still a question as to whether the issue's proceeds will be adequate to repay the bonds, restore the state's financially troubled private utilities to health and finance future electricity purchases.

Electrical Switch: Now, Cheaper Power is Causing Hefty Losses for California *(WSJ, July 31, 2001)*

Mild weather means that California is escaping blackouts, but it also means that the state is amassing power-trading losses that are adding to the cost of an energy mess now in its fifteenth month.

> ... The California Department of Water Resources got into the power-purchasing business in a big way in January, when the state's biggest investor-owned utilities quit buying power because they were no longer creditworthy. Since then, the state has signed $43 billion worth of contracts, one for as much as twenty years, in a bid to tamp down high spot-market prices. Critics now say it was a mistake to lock in so much power at such a high cost ...

Internal numbers from the DWR, which the agency has confirmed, show that on average the state paid, from July 1 to Thursday, $123 per megawatt hour for some 1.8 million megawatts of power purchased under long-term contracts, and $148 per megawatt hour for some 2.2 million megawatt hours of power purchased under short-term contracts. In the same period, the records show it sold excess power amounting to 320,000 megawatt hours at an average price of $27 per megawatt hour, less than what it costs to fuel many plants. At times, the DWR sold the juice for as little as $2 per megawatt hour ....

Since January the state has spent $9.5 billion buying power at an average cost of $237 per megawatt hour, according to internal DWR documents. That is more than double the price of wholesale electricity last year, when prices averaged $114. The state's cash-strapped utilities have reimbursed the agency $1.53 billion of the $9.5 billion it has spent so far. As a result of the huge shortfall, the state has tapped California's general fund and now is pursuing a plan to sell $12.5 billion worth of revenue bonds to replenish its coffers.

The state signed dozens of long-term power contracts after January, pushed by federal energy regulators to protect itself against spot-market volatility. So far this year, it has spent $851 million under long-term contracts, $2.36 billion under short-term arrangements, and $5.54 billion on spot-market purchases, according to the DWR documents.

But the state's "long" position in July, in which it had too much power, has at times given power-trading companies an arbitrage opportunity. Last Wednesday, for example, the states sold electricity for as little as $2 per megawatt hour on the same day that it was paying $22 to $75 on the spot market, presumably because its advance purchases did not exactly match the actual shape of demand ....

California Now Faces Expensive Electricity Glut—The State May End Up Urging Consumers to Use More Power to Avoid Selling Surplus at a Loss *(Oregonian, August 3, 2001)*

California may be facing a persistent, escalating glut of electricity as a result of its buying too much power through long-term contracts, according to energy experts and a Los Angeles Times analysis.

... Just last month, the state racked up $46 million in losses after selling surplus power for one-fifth the price it paid. If that rate is sustained, the deficit could reach as much as $500 million next year alone.

And if the surplus grows, the state could even find itself in the paradoxical position of encouraging Californians to use more electricity to help the state avoid selling large amounts of unused power at a loss ....

State officials, such as S. David Freeman, former head of the Los Angeles Water and Power Department and now California's energy czar, defend the power purchases. Freeman argues that purchasing a "healthy surplus" busted the price spike of earlier this year and will protect against blackouts in coming years.

September 2001

CPUC, on September 20, 2001, suspends the right of retail end-use customers to acquire direct access service, pursuant to AB IX.

Senate Bill (SB) X2 prohibits the CPUC from raising rates for residential and small commercial customers solely as a result of the statutory end of the rate freeze. The statutory end of the transition period is March 31, 2002.

California Unit's Revenue Bond Deal Progresses, But Plan's Complexity May Cause More Delays *(WSJ, September 10, 2001)*

A $12.5 billion California Department of Water Resources power revenue-bond issue appears to be coming together, but "the plan's numerous moving parts could cause further delays," according to a veteran tax-exempt bond analyst ....

The Department of Water Resources, or DWR, has been trying since May to sell the $12.5 billion issue, but may not complete the deal until late October or early November, at best.

... There is uncertainty over the potential impact of the $12.5 billion DWR bond issue on the state of California's credit and because that credit will soon be tested.

The state of California tomorrow will sell $500 million of general-obligation bonds, securities backed by the state's full faith and credit. And on Thursday, the state will sell $5.7 billion of nine-month revenue-anticipation notes.

The DWR has borrowed some $9 billion from the state's general fund to buy power on behalf of California's three investor-owned utilities: *PG&E* Corp.'s Pacific Gas & Electric, *Edison International's* Southern California Edison and *Sempra* Corp.'s SDG&E.

The DWR has been trying since May to sell $12.5 billion in bonds backed by rate-payer revenue from electricity sales to reimburse the state and to help foot the $43 billion tab the DWR has racked up in long-term power contracts. Efforts to move all the necessary pieces into place have been mired in delays as a variety of parties essential to the sale pursued their own agendas.

Meanwhile, the California Assembly's appropriations committee last Thursday passed a bill that would set aside a portion of the rates charged to California's electric-utility customers to pay off the power revenue bonds. That bill passed the

Senate in July and now moves to the full Assembly for a vote, before being returned to the full Senate.

Nonetheless, potential litigation from one or more of the state's utilities presents a very real threat to getting the power bonds sold this year. Further delays would result in a greater debt-service burden.

In the interim, the state is scrambling to patch together short-term financing to tide it over in anticipation of being reimbursed by the oft-delayed bonds. That is the impetus behind the $5.7 billion in revenue-anticipation notes to be sold Thursday.

Vote Will Decide Deregulation's Fate—California Energy Regulators Will Decide On Instituting a Replacement for the State's Troubled Energy System *(Oregonian, September 20, 2001)*
California's Public Utilities Commission is set to vote today on a measure that could strip away one of the last vestiges of the state's failed experiment with energy deregulation, which was widely blamed for blackouts and ballooning bills ....

The PUC vote could wipe out consumers' ability to choose their electricity provider and buy power directly from retailers such as Green Mountain Energy or Enron. About 200,000 customers had switched utilities by September.

Trumpeted at its creation in 1996 as a way to stimulate competition and lower electric rates, deregulation foundered after a year of soaring wholesale electrical prices and customer bills, a utility bankruptcy and energy shortages that led to rolling blackouts.

Today, California's government is more directly involved in the power business than ever before and deregulation is dead, said PUC Commission Carl Wood ....

The expected PUC vote will continue a trend that started in January, when the Department of Water Resources started buying a third of the power needed by customers of the state's three largest private utilities—Southern California Edison, Pacific Gas and Electric Co., and San Diego Gas & Electric Co.

The utilities had faced the possibility of bankruptcy because the deregulation law didn't allow them to pass rising costs on to customers. That and the record-high wholesale prices led the three utilities to run up more than $14 billion in debt.

As their debt rose, their credit ratings fell and some wholesalers refused to sell to them. Pacific Gas and Electric filed for Chapter 11 bankruptcy in April.

Six days of rolling blackouts earlier this year cut power to more than three million customers and shut down refrigerators, ATMs and traffic signals. State regulators approved rate increases of 30 percent or higher for utility customers.

However, the threat eased after many residents followed recommendation to conserve, wholesale prices dropped and the state enjoyed an unseasonably cool summer. The last rolling blackouts were ordered May 8.

California Official Says Bond Sale Is Essential *(WSJ, September 28, 2001)*
California Treasurer Philip Angelides warned that a "freight train of fiscal chaos" is racing toward the state that can be stopped only if utility regulators clear the way for the state to sell $12.5 billion in power bonds.

California had hoped to sell the bonds in June to replenish the state general fund, which was tapped earlier this year to pay $6 billion of energy costs caused by the state's failed electricity-deregulation plan. But the sale has been delayed repeatedly. Mr. Angelides said "there's no schedule" at all anymore.

The state is fine financially for now, Mr. Angelides said, but if the bonds aren't issued by the middle of next year the state could face a budget deficit for fiscal 2003 of $9.3 billion. To close such a gap, the state might have to make big cuts to public programs, such as education, or approve a two-cent sales-tax increase, he said.

Loretta Lynch, president of the California Public Utilities Commission, said the agency has moved deliberately because it is trying to fulfill its regulatory duties and avoid legal snares that could upset the bond sale. Two rate orders believed necessary for the bond issuance will be taken up by the commission in coming weeks. More than a dozen parties, including *PG&E* Corp.'s Pacific Gas & Electric Co. unit, have said they will challenge the orders if adopted as drafted.

Some of those critics think the commission is about to take actions that are illegal. They believe the agency may be cooperating in an unconstitutional transfer of authority to the California Department of Water Resources as part of the state's effort to resolve the energy crisis. They say once the orders are passed, the state's energy consumers will be stuck with paying off the power bonds for the next fifteen years.

Pacific Gas and other utilities have criticized California's management of its power program. They fear that once the bond payments and power costs are met, they won't be left with enough money to run their companies. But Mr. Angelides counters that it is time the critics "take their energy fight somewhere else" or the state will suffer.

October 2001
CPUC, on October 2, 2001, settled "filed rate doctrine" suit and mooted the Edison MOU, retaining the objective of returning Edison to investment-grade credit worthiness through recovery of its procurement costs.

California Scrambles to Switch Strategies After Plan for Power Bonds Is Stymied *(WSJ, October 5, 2001)*
California officials are working furiously to plug a potentially big hole in next year's budget after the state's utility commission effectively undercut their plans to issue billions of dollars in power bonds.

So far, Governor Gray Davis and his team are looking at renegotiating the terms of a recent $4.3 billion bridge loan made by banks hoping to underwrite the bonds. Some state officials also hope to reopen talks on a slew of power contracts that in coming months require the state to pay billions of dollars more for electricity than the prices prevailing on the open market.

Previously, the state government planned to get out of the financial quagmire triggered by soaring electricity prices and faltering private utilities by issuing a $12.5 billion bond, to be supported by ratepayer revenues. But the California Public Utilities Commission on Tuesday refused to approve an order that would have authorized the state to be reimbursed for all its expenses with only limited public review.

The commission move, which Mr. Davis called "irresponsible," raised the prospect that California wouldn't be able to repay money it has borrowed from the state's general fund and foot the cost of continuing purchases. In addition, Mr. Davis said, it meant the state could face "the first default" in its history by failing to satisfy terms of a bridge loan calling for timely progress to be made toward the bond issuance.

State Controller Kathleen Connell yesterday played down the short-term budget threat . . . .

Ms. Connell says she now expects any bond issue to be far smaller than the one authorized by the state legislature. In the meantime, she expects the state to restructure the bridge loan, whose interest rate is expected to jump to nearly 7 percent from around 4 percent if not repaid by November 1. If the loan isn't repaid by November 1, 2002, it will carry an interest rate of the prime rate plus 2 percentage points.

She added the state may end up issuing billions of dollars in short-term notes called revenue anticipation warrants, or RAWS, to smooth over an anticipated budgetary gap in the coming fiscal year.

The genesis of that gap came in May 2000, when wholesale power prices shot through the roof in California's deregulated energy market. Since the state's two main utilities weren't allowed to raise rates, they absorbed the higher costs and slid toward bankruptcy. In January, the state assumed the duty of buying power on their behalf and tapped money from the state's general fund to foot the bill . . .

If the state doesn't repay the $4.3 billion bridge loan, interest costs on it will rise by $250,000 a day, based on rates Ms. Connell calls "usurious and outrageous.". . .

Officials also have initiated preliminary talks with some power suppliers to renegotiate terms of power-purchase contracts signed by the state earlier this year when it was desperate to rein in runaway spot-market prices.

Those contracts require the state to pay prices for electricity well above today's market prices and extend out as far as twenty years.

Dissatisfaction with those contracts is one reason the public utilities commission refused to approve a rate agreement that would have authorized the state power-buying agency to be reimbursed for its expenses.

Ms. Connell said the state has until July 2003 to fully repay the general fund before it would have to make cuts to programs. Late last month, the state issued $5.7 billion in revenue-anticipation notes, or RANs, to cover the state's immediate cash needs. She said the expected issue of revenue anticipation warrants, which can straddle fiscal years—unlike RANs—probably would be done sometime next year if the general fund hasn't been repaid.

Edison Rescue Package Approved by Federal Judge in Los Angeles (*WSJ, October 8, 2001*)

A federal court judge in Los Angeles approved a $3.3 billion financial rescue package for Southern California Edison Co., but two consumer groups opposed to the bailout said they would ask the Ninth Circuit Court of Appeals to overturn the decision.

The groups say the rescue would unfairly burden consumers with the cost of the utility's mistakes and runs counter to established practices for giving consumers a say in how rates are set.

The package was designed to settle a lawsuit brought by Edison last year against the California Public Utilities Commission in the wake of the state's energy crisis. Edison asserted in the suit that it should be reimbursed for power-procurement costs that outstripped fixed electricity rates charged to customers. Power costs, estimated at more than $3 billion, threatened to push into bankruptcy the utility unit of *Edison International,* Rosemead, California.

Utility regulators, though sympathetic to Edison's plight, repeatedly had refused to allow it to pass those costs through to ratepayers. The state's 1996 deregulation law was supposed to put Edison and other utilities at risk for fluctuations in power prices. During the first two years of deregulation, the arrangement allowed Edison to pay down billions of dollars of debt, but rising power prices after May 2000 produced enormous losses.

Under the so-called "filed rate doctrine" invoked by the utility in its lawsuit, a regulated service provider has the right to bill customers for any federally approved costs, and those collections cannot be blocked by state action. A similar lawsuit, brought by San Francisco-based *PG&E* Corp.'s Pacific Gas and Electric Co. unit, is pending in federal court against the California Public Utilities Commission. Pacific Gas and Electric, the state's biggest utility, filed for protection from creditors under Chapter 11 of U.S. bankruptcy law on April 6.

Mike Florio, a senior attorney for the Utility Reform Network, a nonprofit consumer group in San Francisco, said the terms of the Edison settlement violate at least ten prior utilities commission decisions and represent a "180-degree reversal of positions the commission has taken." He said the commission exceeded its authority and, by law, must hold public hearings in rate-setting matters.

Under the terms of the settlement approved by U.S. District Court Judge Ronald S.W. Lew, Edison will be allowed to collect at least $3.3 billion from customers through 2005 in reimbursement for past power-related expenditures. Edison also agreed that it won't pay shareholder dividends until the repayment is complete and to apply $1.5 billion of cash on hand to debt service.

Harvey Rosenfield, head of the nonprofit Foundation for Taxpayer and Consumer Rights, said, "It looks to me like Edison got every penny they wanted," and accused the state of settling the case for a price higher than what it previously had told the legislature it would accept.

In a prepared statement Friday, Edison International Chairman John Bryson applauded the settlement approval and said it represented a "workable plan ... for the utility to become creditworthy once again, to pay its obligations and to remove the state from the power business." A similar statement was issued by the utilities commission.

FERC Says California Must Pay All Bills for Power Purchases to Stabilize System (*WSJ, November 8, 2001*)

The Federal Energy Regulatory Commission ordered California's electric-grid operator to begin sending bills to the state, rather than to utility companies, for more than $ 1.6 billion of power used to stabilize the electric system ....

California assumed power-buying duties for the state's cash-strapped utilities in January, but has been picking and choosing which bills to pay; FERC says the state is directly responsible for covering the utilities' power purchases.

Thus far, California has dragged its feet on paying for "imbalance energy," the last-minute electricity purchased by the grid operator that is used to keep the electric system fully energized...

California Pays Its Grid Operator $404.8 Million for Power Purchases *(WSJ, December 7, 2001)*
California's state government made its first payment to the state's nonprofit electricity grid operator after months of wrangling and an order to do so from the Federal Energy Regulatory Commission. The money comes as a relief to power generators, which weren't sure when and if they would be paid.

The $404.8 million payment covers part of the $955 million owed to power suppliers for last-minute electricity purchases this year. The first payment covers the month of February, when California's power system was hit by high prices brought on by too much demand and too little supply . . . .

California had been reluctant to pay the high prices charged by generators, despite a FERC order in November that said the state was responsible for past-due bills on power needed to keep the lights on during that period. FERC said it wasn't fair to require generators to supply power when they would have no guarantee of being paid. The agency told power generators that it would eliminate the power-supply obligation, which could subject the state to power shortages again, if the state failed to make prompt payment once billed by the California Independent System Operator, a FERC-jurisdictional entity that runs the state's power grid.

12.11.4 February 2002

CPUC, on February 13, 2002, filed an alternative plan of reorganization for PG&E with bankruptcy court, providing for continued regulation of all of PG&E's current operations by CPUC, to become effective prior to January 31, 2003.

California Utilities Body Lifts Block on Bonds to Renew Depleted Funds *(WSJ, February 22, 2002)*
The California Public Utilities Commission lifted a major roadblock that had prevented the state from issuing as much as $11.1 billion in bonds needed to replenish public coffers depleted last year by the state's energy crisis . . . .

Under the measure, approved by a 4-to-1 vote, the state's investor-owned utilities will collect money that will be passed along to the state Department of Water Resources, which has been buying power on their behalf for a year. The bonds will be used both to repay the general fund, which supports social spending in the state, and to cover continuing power costs . . . .

For months, the commission has wrangled with the governor's office over the terms of a rate agreement between the commission and the water agency . . . .

Under the compromise hammered out by the two agencies, all electricity sold in California will be subject to a surcharge that will generate funds dedicated to bond repayment. Money from bond sales, in turn, will be used to repay the state

for $6 billion to $8 billion borrowed from the general fund last year to cover power purchases ...
California Seeks Reversal of Its Electricity Contracts *(WSJ, February 25, 2002)*
California Wants Out of Energy Contracts *(Oregonian, February 25, 2002)*
California Regulators to Ask FERC to Void Pacts *(WSJ, February 24, 2002)*
California utility regulators said they will file two complaints at the Federal Energy Regulatory Commission today asking that FERC void about $40 billion of power-supply contracts signed last year when, the state says, the energy market was being manipulated by sellers.

The complaints, to be filed under Section 206 of the Federal Power Act, provide no new evidence of market manipulation ... Those contracts obligate the state to pay double and triple today's market rate for electricity. It also comes when big independent power producers and traders are being cast as villains due to the collapse of *Enron* Corp.

> ... [It was] charged that "FERC's indifference" in 2000 and 2001 caused California's market failure and [that] the state was forced to sign high-price contracts as a result, beginning in January 2001, to keep the lights on ....

Calpine, the biggest supplier, signed deals permitting it to collect prices of $58 and $61 per megawatt hour, about double today's spot-market price that reflects slack demand due to the recession ....

Loretta Lynch, president of the PUC, said FERC's inaction in reining in a runaway wholesale market in mid-2000 "allowed gougers and gamers to come in" the California market ....

At the time the contracts were signed, critics said the state was signing too many and for time periods that were too long. In effect, they said it was creating a long-term fix for the short term problem of skyrocketing energy prices brought on by inadequate supply coupled with surging demand in the then-vibrant economy ....

In its filing this week, the state walks a rocky path. It is arguing at FERC that the contracts are neither "just" nor "reasonable" as required by the Federal Power Act. Yet within the state, it is arguing for rate-making purposes that the costs of those contracts are in fact "just and reasonable" and that retail consumers must pay to uphold them ....

California's challenge would come under a federal law that requires the commission to ensure "just and reasonable" wholesale electrical prices.
(Example of Related Actions)
California Regulators File Power Complaint—PacifiCorp Power Marketing (of Portland, Oregon) Is One of 22 Electricity Suppliers Accused of Overcharging the State in a Filing with a Federal Agency *(Oregonian, February 26, 2002)*
California regulators claim Portland-based PacifiCorp Power Marketing grossly overcharged the state of California for electricity when the two parties negotiated long-term power supply contracts during last year's energy crisis.

PacifiCorp Power Marketing, a subsidiary of Glasgow, Scotland's Scottish Power, is one of twenty-two power suppliers named in a complaint filed Monday with the Federal Energy Regulatory Commission.

The California Public Utility Commission argues that the contract prices and terms are "unjust and unreasonable" and therefore violate the Federal Power Act, over which FERC has jurisdiction.

State regulators want FERC to nullify the contracts or, as an alternative, plug in lower prices and less expensive contract terms. The commission claims that the contracts include $21 billion in overcharges.

California, through the Department of Water Resources, signed contracts paying an average of $88 a megawatt hour last year when spot prices for electricity were $300 a megawatt hour or more. But prices receded quickly in spring and summer, leaving California as well as some other electricity suppliers in a bind. FERC could undo those contracts if the federal agency determines that the prices were unjust and unreasonable. . .

Energy sellers said the complaints are without merit. Others have criticized the state for politicizing the energy crisis. Governor Gray Davis, up for reelection, has come under fire for negotiating such long-term high-priced contracts.

California Confirms Decision to Curtail Electricity Access (*WSJ, March 22, 2002*)

The California Public Utilities Commission took a step state officials say will help them sell $11.1 billion in electricity-revenue bonds to help pay back the state treasury for billions of dollars in power purchases and loans.

The commission voted 3-2 to reaffirm an earlier decision to force large and industrial electricity customers to cancel their contracts with independent suppliers, and buy directly from investor-owned utilities, or pay an "exit fee" to be allowed to maintain those contracts. The commission voted to keep September 20, 2001, as the date when such "direct access" to independent suppliers was officially suspended by the state.

State officials say the commission's suspension of direct access is vital to their ability to convince Wall Street rating agencies and investors that the bonds will be investment grade and an attractive purchase.

Push Conies to Shove on Power—A Portland-Based Marketer Challenges California's Stance That Contracts Issued Last Year During the Energy Crisis Contain Exorbitant Pricing Demands (*WSJ, March 22, 2002*)

PacifiCorp Power Marketing, caught in a fierce fight with the state of California, fought back Friday.

In a filing to federal regulators, PacifiCorp Power said its ten-year, $ 1.03 billion contract with the California Department of Water Resources is fair, legally binding and in no way excessive.

The Portland-based company is one of twenty-two companies that faced a Friday deadline from the Federal Energy Regulatory Commission to defend long-term electricity contracts signed last year with California . . . .

Two California agencies want the FERC to void the contracts or at the least force the suppliers to modify the terms. The agencies contend in a February 25 complaint

12.11 Chronology: The Crisis and Its Aftermath (to Early 2002) 385

that $45 billion worth of long-term contracts with twenty-two electricity suppliers, signed in the midst of an energy crisis, contain exorbitant pricing demands.

PacifiCorp Power counters that the complaints should be dismissed.

The back-and-forth illustrates the intensity of the squabble between energy suppliers and the state of California. For suppliers, their reputations as legitimate market players are at stake. For California, the credibility of state agencies and elected officials is on the line . . . .

The California Public Utilities Commission and the California Electricity Oversight Board filed the complaints.

The agencies said the California Department of Water Resources, authorized to purchase power on the state's behalf, forged forty-four transactions with twenty-two sellers and racked up commitments worth $45 billion . . .

California claims the contracts, all told, overcharged the state by at least $14 billion . . .

The dispute traces back to the volatile electricity markets of mid-2000 to mid-2001.

Day-ahead, or "spot" prices for wholesale electricity, soared to hundreds of dollars a megawatt hour—even exceeding $1,000 a megawatt hour—in the height of the crisis.

Early last year, when California authorized its Department of Water Resources to buy long-term power supplies, prices hovered at $500 a megawatt hour and electricity reserves were razor thin.

"We were looking at long-term contracts to stave off blackouts," said Oscar Hidalgo, a Department of Water Resources spokesman.

When the ink was dry, the state claimed success. The contracts contained electricity costs of $88 a megawatt hour, on average, officials said, a good deal compared to the triple-digit prices on the spot market.

But, last June, to the surprise of state officials and power producers alike, electricity prices rapidly fell. They dipped to less than $30 a megawatt hour during the summer, although they recently have inched up to about $45 a megawatt hour . . . .

California officials suggest a reasonable price for power rests in the $20- to $40-a-megawatt-hour range . . . .

California Power Negotiations Drag on As State Politics Heat Up *(WSJ, March 25, 2002)*

State officials here have spent almost five months getting nowhere in their efforts to renegotiate nearly $43 billion in long-term power contracts, signed at a time when spot-market prices for electricity were significantly higher than today.

Now, Governor Gray Davis and his advisers fear that the financial concerns raised by the costly contracts could evolve into a political liability for the governor as he campaigns for reelection this year.

Representatives of several of the major generators that signed multibillion dollar deals with the state say their companies' negotiators haven't talked to the state in weeks, and in one case, months. What's more, they and others say negotiations with Governor Davis's administration have been hamstrung since February 24, when the

California Public Utilities Commission filed a formal complaint with the Federal Energy Regulatory Commission, challenging the legality of the contracts . . . .

But S. David Freeman, senior energy adviser to Mr. Davis who led many of the negotiations last year, defends the PUC filing against generators . . . .

Last June, Mr. Freeman said the average price of the electricity under the long-term contracts—an estimated $69 per megawatt hour—was "a good news story" considering that the state was paying an average of $275 per megawatt hour in January 2001 on the spot market when it first got into the electricity-buying business. "We feel we've provided the major building block for licking this energy crisis," Mr. Freeman said at the time.

But the spot market has changed substantially since then, due largely to a significant fall in the price of natural gas—a key fuel for generating electricity—and to the state buying so much long-term power. The spot market price today is down to about $30 per megawatt hour.

California Electricity Managers Face Restructuring-Plan Deadline *(WSJ, April 10, 2002)*

The ISO must submit its redesign plan to the Federal Energy Regulatory Commission, which must approve it by September 30.

That is the date when FERC's efforts to mitigate electricity price increases across the West are scheduled to expire. FERC, under pressure from Western states during last summer's regional energy crisis, implemented price caps and other steps to temper exploding wholesale electricity prices.

But the ISO board made clear yesterday that it would much prefer that FERC keep the price caps and other measures in place until California can get its market in order.

The problem, ISO officials say, is that no one really knows what the state's energy market will look like in the months and years ahead, largely because it is unclear who will be responsible for buying electricity for most of the state's consumers.

In early 2001, the state Department of Water Resources started buying power on behalf of the state's financially troubled investor-owned utilities.

While state law prohibits the department from continuing to buy electricity past the end of this year, the law could be changed to extend the agency's authority or reassign it to another entity . . . .

The ISO board voted to ask FERC for an extension . . . .

California Official Sues Energy Sellers, Claims Profiteering *(WSJ, April 10, 2002)*

California Attorney General Bill Lockyer filed suit against four big energy sellers, charging them with profiteering during the state's energy crisis and claiming they could face penalties topping $ 1 billion . . . .

The suit charged "unjust, unreasonable and illegal" wholesale prices for their electricity during the energy crisis here, which bridged 2000 and 2001.

The companies deny any wrongdoing and blame California's misfortune on a badly designed market-deregulation plan that went awry . . . .

The state's latest move against power sellers comes just weeks after it filed suit seeking expanded electricity refunds of as much as $2.8 billion for power sold into the California market prior to October 2001.

12.11 Chronology: The Crisis and Its Aftermath (to Early 2002) 387

Enron's "Sham" Trading Fueled West's Power Crisis, Officials Say *(WSJ, April 12, 2002)*

Loretta Lynch, CPUC president, says: "Enron swapped the same power repeatedly among affiliates as part of a scheme to drive up the wholesale price of electricity and create turmoil in the West Coast energy market."

Power Contracts Are Renegotiated in California—California Officials Renegotiate Deals with Energy Firms *(WSJ, April 23, 2002)*

California officials and several power-generating companies renegotiated more than a third of the state's costly $43 billion of long-term power contracts, saving the state $3.5 billion, mainly in the later years of the contracts . . . .

California signed the high-cost power contracts last year when market prices far exceeded today's rates, in the wake of the state's energy crisis. State officials plan to continue negotiating to lower the cost of long-term power contracts with other energy-providing companies . . . .

In all, the state estimates it was able to cut the cost of the eight contracts to $11.4 billion from about $15 billion, providing $3.5 billion in savings. The bulk of the savings is expected to result from shortening the duration of the contracts—in one case to ten years from twenty years—and in some instances by reducing the average cost of power over the life of the contracts . . . .

When state negotiators signed long-term power contracts in June, the average price of the contracts was estimated at $69 per megawatt hour—at a time when the state was paying an average of $275 per megawatt hour on the spot market. But the spot market has fallen sharply since then, due largely to a big drop in the price of natural gas— a key fuel for generating electricity—and to the state locking up so much power in long-term contracts. The spot market price today is down to about $30 per megawatt hour.

Standoff Looms over Electricity in California *(WSJ, April 26, 2002)*

State and federal power officials are headed for a potentially divisive standoff over what California's electricity market should look like and how it should operate in coming years.

The board of the California Independent System Operator, which runs the state's power grid, late yesterday approved a sweeping redesign of the state's electricity market, a project that the Federal Energy Regulatory Commission had called for and must approve.

At the same time, though, the ISO board emphasized that the project is largely hypothetical—mainly because the agency has little idea of what the market will look like a year from now. ISO officials point out, for example, that the future operation of one of California's largest utilities is under review by the state Public Utilities Commission, while the fate of another is in the hands of a federal bankruptcy court.

As a result, the board is calling on the federal power agency to extend beyond September 30 price caps and other temporary fixes that FERC implemented last year to temper wild price swings in the Western states' energy market . . . .

Unlike last summer, California has sufficient energy largely because of expensive power contracts signed between the state and generators.

The ISO's proposed market redesign for California includes:

- A "must offer" obligation, which is designed to prohibit suppliers from withholding from the grid operator's real-time market any available nonhydropower plants. However, this provision wouldn't prohibit generators from exporting power outside the state, nor would generators be required to provide replacement energy in the event of a forced outage.
- A "damage control" price cap on supplier bids to sell power. The cap is intended to prevent against excessive market-pricing abuse. The ISO board late yesterday was still debating the size of the cap. The most controversial piece of the redesign plan would require utilities and other power purchasers to prove to the ISO that they have sufficient electricity resources, or "available capacity," to serve their load.

Power Plant Momentum Runs Out of Energy *(WSJ, May 13, 2002)*

The crisis atmosphere that gripped electricity markets countrywide heading into last summer has abated and, remarkably, regions that struggled with shortages are now wallowing in surpluses. California has plenty of power to get through the summer without a return to rolling blackouts, the state's power-grid operator reports. And New England, once bedeviled by shortages, now has enough additional electricity that power plants are likely to export the juice to other regions during peak periods this summer.

But the near-term calm belies what continues to be a troubled long-term horizon. Energy planners and players worry that a sense of complacency about the current situation is killing the momentum to resolve long-festering problems, such as inadequate transmission facilities, outdated rate structures, and lack of incentives to develop power plants before severe shortages. In other words, the absence of a crisis itself, could lead to another crisis. Analysts see problems developing in about five years, which is not that far off in the energy-planning world, or possibly sooner if the pace of plant cancellations accelerate . . . .

The radical shift from shortage to surplus results from a power-plant building frenzy, reflecting high prices and the crisis atmosphere, and slackening demand from the economic recession . . . . Developers added 48,000 megawatts—a megawatt can power about 1,000 homes—of new supply last year. Another 69,000 megawatts, committed to during the crisis, are due to come on line this year. Supplies are now projected to comfortably exceed demand for at least the next two years.

All that new capacity is scaring off investors who are worried about overbuilding. That, in turn, has prompted developers to cancel projects. Some 5,500 megawatts, enough to power 5.5 million homes, have so far been canceled this year, up from 1,300 megawatts last year. Another 37,000 megawatts in expected projects were postponed this year, the ELA reports. In New York City, the financing shortage claimed three proposed plants that would have covered about half of a projected 3,000-megawatt shortfall by 2005 . . . .

The problem, say energy planners, is now that the crisis atmosphere has abated, time-consuming efforts such as finding locations for power plants will languish, again forcing planners to play catch-up when demand does pick up.

Already, the political tide around energy issues has turned. In New England, the power-grid operator warns of an "acute" risk of failure in the undersized and overloaded transmission lines into Southwestern Connecticut. But with the supply picture so upbeat, the warning seems a hard sell. Connecticut lawmakers forced Governor John Rowland to adopt a moratorium on permitting new power lines in the region.

The California Public Utilities Commission balked at adopting so-called real-time rates after the state last year spent some $35 million to install real-time meters for commercial and industrial users. The commission's concern: lower usage by industry would reduce revenues for utilities and lead to higher rates for residential customers to recoup the losses . . . .

Trade Disclosures Shake Faith in Damaged Electricity Market *(WSJ, May 13, 2002)*
Concerns that power producers inflated the apparent size of their business with bogus trades are hammering the industry's stocks, disrupting its finances and raising new questions about the already-shaken credibility of deregulated energy markets.

The latest events, in the aftermath of the December bankruptcy-protection filing by the wholesale power industry's best-known player, Enron Corp., are likely to renew calls for greater government oversight of the freewheeling market . . . .

More broadly, the latest revelations about trading behavior suggest that the torrid growth in the three-year-old wholesale electricity market, which underpinned huge revenue growth and fat profits at these companies through much of 2000 and 2001, could have been exaggerated—no one knows by how much. The revelations also are renewing suspicions among federal and state investigators that bogus trades may have been at least partly behind electricity prices soaring as much as 46 percent in California early last year.

It's not clear how this kind of trading activity may have influenced market prices.

12.12 Comments

AB 1890 put into play what widely has been judged as a "botched attempt at deregulation." (*Business Week*, February 12, 2001) The law often has been described in less moderate terms: as "awful" (*Oregonian*, June 3, 2002); as "perfect idiocy" (*Wall Street Journal*, May 15, 2002); and as "lunacy" (*Newsweek*, January 29, 2001). California governor Gray Davis has referred to it as a "nightmare" (*Newsweek*, January 29, 2001) and as a "disaster of the first magnitude" (*Business Week*, April 23, 2001). How can it be that a law, passed unanimously by the California legislature with the backing of all interested parties, could engender such disrepute?

12.12.1 The Fatal Contradiction

AB 1890, on its face, incorporated a glaring inconsistency on the basic element of price. It established a mechanism whereby wholesale electricity prices would be unregulated, subject to the vagaries of a free market, while at the same time retail prices would be frozen at or below previously prevailing levels. Simply stated, retail prices could not respond to changes in wholesale prices.

The premise behind this arrangement was that wholesale prices paid to generators would decline. This decline would make more reasonable the margin between market-determined wholesale prices and the frozen retail rates received by the local utility. (This margin was to be retained by the local utility to recoup its prior sunk costs plus its costs incurred in making the transition required by the law.)

This scheme would work provided that wholesale prices stayed below retail rates. Everyone, it seems, assumed that this would continue to be the case. There was no preparation for the reverse condition. So when the crisis happened, when wholesale prices far exceeded retail rates, the parties were unprepared. It is redundant to comment that the utilities, the CPUC, and other government officials should have anticipated the possibility of a reversal. The fact is, they didn't. In adopting the premise that wholesale prices would decline, they had followed a will-o'-the-wisp to its bitter end.

While responsibility for the debacle must be shared by all of the contributing parties, the greatest burden must be borne by the electricity utility executives who argued strongly for the restructuring of California's electric industry and greeted it so warmly when approved by the legislature. Having governed their companies in a fully regulated environment, with all the protections engendered by the cushion of regulation, they should have been fully aware of the advantages they were losing by the restructuring as well as the hazards which such loss would entail. They seemed oblivious to the dangers which they could face. We have included this history of the crisis to drive home the point that successful leadership requires decision makers to evaluate new changes of course from all viewpoints, especially those which might pose risks.

12.12.2 Regulatory and Economic Failures

The weaknesses of AB 1890 go beyond the fatal contradiction itself. The law was also faulty conceptually in at least two respects, regulatory and economic.

Although it was touted as a "deregulation" bill, from the regulatory standpoint AB 1890 falls short of deregulating in all three phases of the electric industry, generation, transmission, and distribution. Its strongest claim to deregulation is in the generation phase. It does provide a market in which multiple generators can participate. But, it hamstrings that market by establishing the PX and ISO, quasi-government entities, through which the market is forced to function. This simply substitutes a new scheme of generation regulation for the prior method.

For transmission and distribution, and retail rates as a whole, AB 1890 mooted prior regulatory practices under which the regulatory commission adjusts regulated prices to comport with changes in costs. By imposing a long rate freeze beyond the control of the commission, the law substitutes regulation by the legislature for regulation by the commission. On this score, it is interesting to recall that the problems associated with regulation by the legislature, particularly in fixing prices, were the historical reason for the establishment of utility regulatory commissions. History was repeated by AB 1890.

From the economic point of view, the law disregards the function of price. To the economist, price is the means whereby supply and demand are brought into balance. But a constant price sends a perverse signal to consumers. Changes in costs go unrecognized. Consumers are misled. When costs are rising, constant rates give no incentive to the consumer to conserve. In this respect, AB 1890 was an anticonservation measure.

Had the rate freeze not been made a part of the statute, then retail rates could have been changed—and undoubtedly would have been changed—to reflect the higher wholesale prices which were exacted during the energy crisis. This might have prevented, and at least would have mitigated, the crisis and its aftermath.

12.12.3 *The Divestiture of Generating Capacity by California Utilities*

AB 1890 served to encourage the divestiture by California utilities of their generating capacity within the state, for which the CPUC had set a target of 50% of their fossil-fueled capacity. In the prior sections of this review, the consequent divestitures by the utilities have been sketched.

On this question, I must admit a personal bias. I believe that the rights to utility-financed generation capacity belong to the utility's customers, not to the utility. I wrote about this issue in July 1995, responding to the CPUC's "vision" for the restructuring of the electric industry[21]. The vision came well before AB 1890.

I introduced this article by saying

> The reliability and availability of electric energy to consumers depends upon there being adequate capacity in each of the component physical facilities of the electric system: generation, transmission and distribution. Under today's protocols, consumers have undiluted rights to all of the system's capacity and bear all of its costs.... But a breakup of the system ... requires that the capacity rights and corresponding rate entitlements of the respective interests be spelled out....
>
> This should temper the risks to existing customers of possible rate "bumps" in the transition process while at the same time protecting them from any capacity shortages or bottlenecks that otherwise might occur.

I urged application of the FERC natural gas algorithm

> (The algorithm establishes the principle that) capacity rights cannot be taken away from consumers that have relied upon that capacity for adequate and dependable service ....
> The resources *that are needed for load* should be classified as "reserved resources." ... The end result should be that the plants and purchase contracts so classified are the best of the generating resources, which base customer revenues have financed, operated and maintained.

---

[21] Roger L. Conkling, "Rights to Capacity: Transitional Protection for California's Existing Utility Customers," *Electricity Journal*, July, 1995

I concluded that all reserved resources should remain under utility ownership. Only surplus capacity should be divested. Also, I recommended that "any base customer desiring to buy from a nonutility generator (that is, to bypass) could do so by permanently relinquishing its call upon the utility's generating capacity."

Unfortunately, utility generating capacity has been divested without reference to whether it will be needed in the future by the utility's customers. This was a mistake, in my opinion.

12.12.4 The Issue of Long-Term Contracts

In another article of October 1998, I addressed the issue of long term contracts by utilities for power supplies, which contracts initially were prohibited by the PX. In the introduction, I said[22],

> California, self-satisfied and overconfident with its new Power Exchange (PX) spot market, seems oblivious to the fact that "it can happen here." But the state is not immune to generation shortages. Its PX provides no protection, offering only day-ahead power (at most), with no guarantee that an offer will be made and with no limit on the price.

Then I urged that California generation capacity market be established, and outlined the provisions that should govern it. In summary, it would be an *open* market, in which capacity would be traded *transparently, wilh freedom of entree* for all willing sellers and all willing buyers.

I closed with this admonition, "An electricity capacity market should be put in place before crisis strikes." And, I raised a final question, "The public policy issue is: Will California act now or will it wait until confronted with a replication of the Midwest's June debacle?"

Of course, California did wait, and when it finally gave a go-ahead for long-term power purchases by the utilities, the case for an *open, transparent* market was ignored.

I point out that my proposal came before the crisis. Had my suggestion for a generation capacity market in California been adopted prior to 2000–2001, there is a probability that the absurdly high prices for power that actually prevailed would have been reduced. This is speculation, of course, but it is based on the thought that, with more power being available to the utilities through additional long-term contracts, lesser amounts of power would have been purchased through the PX–ISO with a consequent smaller bill from these entities.

There is a reverse consequence of my proposal also. In urging that the capacity market be formed *before* the crisis, I had in mind that contracting *during* a crisis has its own dangers. Long-term contracts executed in a condition of prevailing high prices can lock in high prices in the same fashion as executing them under conditions of normal prices can secure these normal prices. This is illustrated dramatically by

---

[22]Roger L. Conkling, "A California Generation Capacity Market," *Electricity Journal*, October, 1998

the contracting experience of DWR. This agency, on an emergency basis, negotiated for huge amounts of power, against a backdrop of artificially high prices that by and large were accepted as a benchmark. These negotiations lacked transparency in an open market and the result was long-term commitments for excessive prices.

12.12.5 The Uniform-Price Auction

The PX adopted the uniform-price auction model, in which all bidders receive the price awarded to the last (the highest) bidder whose output was needed to satisfy the demand.

Since bids were ranked in merit order, starting with the lowest bid, this model means that all sellers other than the high bidder received a price in excess of their bid. In other words, all bidders received the highest price paid to any generator, regardless of the lower amount they had bid. This is in contrast to a pay-as-bid auction, in which all selected participants receive only their bid price.

Obviously, giving all bidders the highest price, disregarding their lower bids and disregarding differences in their costs, exaggerates the total bill for power. This exaggeration, I believe, was a prime mover in the energy crisis, contributing to the magnitude of the debacle. In sum, I feel that it was a grave mistake.

Many economists will disagree with this conclusion. Their disagreement arises from their acceptance of the premise, summarized by Jerry Taylor of the Cato Institute, "the most expensive sources of supply at the margin must set prices for all sources of supply, because if it does not, shortages would occur." This premise, it seems to me, rests upon the assumption of an ideal, a near perfect commodity market.

In support, Severin Borenstein adds, "This is the way all commodity markets work. Producers sell their output at the market price regardless of whether they are producing from low-cost or high-cost sources."

The California electricity market, among other reasons, differs materially from other commodity markets with respect to the unique physical characteristics of electricity, the limited number of suppliers participating, the variances in the cost of the participants, the timing of supply deliveries from hour-to-hour and from day-to-day, and the inability of participants to accumulate and store their production.

12.12.6 The Neglect of Costs

Elsewhere in this book the principle was pointed out that the validity of a price cannot be determined without a review of the supplier's costs. Stating this principle more precisely, when prices are suspect, it is necessary to examine the underlying costs of the supplier in order to reach a judgment as to whether or not the suspect price is well-grounded and fair.

Their unquestioning faith in the single-price auction led the initial framers of the California process to ignore the possibility that some prices might be out of line. They overlooked the contingency where they might have to check suspect price.

Consideration of costs of bidders did not enter into the early operations of the PX–ISO. Later, when the crisis emerged, this omission was partially corrected by the imposition of price caps by California (which essentially were arbitrary) and, still later, by the imposition by FERC of presumably cost-based, but very broad, caps. However, in both cases the actual costs of bidders were ignored.

It is unfortunate that costs did not enter the picture earlier. A simple warning at the beginning might have sufficed to put bidders on notice that a cost justification for an exceptionally high price might be called for. Granted, this would have been a detriment to some bidders, possibly leading them to refrain from entering the market. But even this result would have been preferable to the series of lawsuits and appeals to FERC for remedial action which occurred.

12.13 From Storm to Turmoil

The collapse and fall of Enron in December 2001 unleashed an ever-widening cloud of suspicion on the energy trading practices of all participants in the California electricity market. Questionable patterns of trades have been uncovered, possibly involving gaming and manipulation. Unquestionably they influenced the prices of power charged in California and in other western states.

In February 2002, the CPUC filed complaints with FERC asking that it void, as being unjust and unreasonable, some $40 billion of power purchase contracts signed earlier. In April 2002, California's attorney general filed suit in the California Superior Court against four big energy sellers, charging them with profiteering. Concurrently, power purchasers outside the state are pursuing legal remedies. Meanwhile, Department of Water Resources attempted to renegotiate the high priced contracts it signed in 2001.

This was the turmoil that followed the storm of the energy crisis.

12.14 P.S. – 2009

All's Well that Ends Well

As of 2010, it seems that the debacle of the energy crisis which began at the turn of the century has finally been played out, with all players still standing and none permanently damaged. What a game it was! But will its lesson be remembered or forgotten?

12.14.1 Pacific Gas and Electric Company

PG&E is a combination electric and natural gas utility operating in northern and central California.

PG&E emerged from bankruptcy on April 12, 2004, after being in Chap. 11 for 3 years. Its securities were restored to investment grade.

The company had revenues in excess of $14.6 billion in 2008 and assets of almost $41 billion. It served about 5.1 million electricity customers and 4.3 million natural gas customers. Its net income in 2008 was $1.34 billion, amounting to $3.63 per share.

National Energy and Gas Transmission, Inc (National Energy Group or NEGT), which had been a subsidiary of PG&E, was divorced from its parent on October 29, 2004. NEGT had been engaged in electricity generation and natural gas transportation in the United States.

In 2005, PG&E announced plans to invest $1.4 billion over the next 5 years to install nearly 10 million Smart Meters. This implements an advanced metering infrastructure program (AMI) for residential and small commercial customers to measure usage of electricity on a time-of-use basis and to charge demand-responsive rates. 1.4 million meters were installed in 2008.

The new state-of-the-art Gateway Generating Station came on line in 2008, producing electricity for almost 400,000 homes and businesses, and the company signed agreements adding 1,800 MW of new renewable resources to its supply.

12.14.2 Edison International

Edison International is a holding company whose operating subsidiaries are Southern California Edison Company (SCE), an electric utility serving retail and wholesale customers, and providing transmission service, in central, coastal, and southern California; and Edison Mission Group Inc (EMG), which supplies non-utility power generation and develops and acquires energy from independent power producers. EMG also includes Edison Capital, which furnishes capital and financial services, but has no plans to make new investments.

Assets of Edison International totaled $44.615 billion in 2008, divided as follows: Southern California Edison Company, $32.568; Edison Mission Energy, $9,080; and Edison Capital, $3,033. Operating revenues totaled $14.112 billion, of which $11.248 billion came from the utility. The net income of the consolidated company was $1.215 billion, or $3.69 per share. The utility served 4.8 million customers.

The company reports that it is expanding its wind portfolio, in 2008 having wind projects in nine states, with 962 MW in service and 223 MW under construction. Also, it is advancing its solar program. Over the past decade, it has invested hundreds of millions of dollars in its coal plants, to reduce emissions of mercury, nitrogen oxide, and sulfur dioxide.

Southern California Edison is embarking on a SmartConnect Project to install about 5.3 million meters in households and small businesses, with start of meter deployment in 2009 and completion in 2012. The total cost of the project is $1.7 billion.

12.14.3 Sempra Energy

Sempra Energy is an energy services holding company, comprising Sempra Utilities, consisting of two utilities, San Diego Gas and Electric Company and Southern California Gas Company, and Sempra Global, consisting of businesses which provide energy products and services.

Adding three zeros to each of the dollar values ($000), in 2008, Sempra had assets of $26,400, of which San Diego Gas and Electric had $9,079, Southern California Gas had $7,351, and its remaining operations had $9,970. Revenues totaled $10,758, with $3,251 originating with SDG&E, $4,768 with SoCalGas, and other, $2,739.Net income of Sempra as a whole came to $1,113, or $4.41 per share.

SDG&E had 3.4 million electric customers and 3.1 million natural gas customers. SoCalGas had 5.7 million customers. It was the nation's largest natural gas distribution utility.

In December, 2008, the CPUC approved SDG&E's Sunrise Powerlink, a 500-kV, $1.19 billion transmission line, which will improve system reliability and provide access to developing renewable-energy resources in desert areas. Also, in December, a 10-MW solar power project, employing thin-film technology, was completed.

In May 2010, a decade after the event, Sempra agreed to resolve one of the last remaining disputes from the crises. To settle accusations that a trading partner and itself had overcharged for electricity during the crisis, it agreed to pay the state of California $410 million. Sempra had been accused of devising schemes to short-circuit the proper functions of energy markets.

12.14.4 Statutory Changes

California law requires that, beginning in 2003, each electric utility must increase its purchases of renewable energy (such as biomass, wind, solar, and geothermal energy) by at least 1% of its retail sales per year, so that the amount of electricity purchased from renewable resources is at least 20% of its total retail sales by the end of 2017. In its 2005 Annual Report, PG&E stated that about 30% of its power came from renewable resources—18% from large hydroelectric facilities and 12% from qualifying renewables. The 2008 Annual Report of Edison International claims that about 40% of Southern California Edison's generation already comes from low-carbon sources and that SCE leads the nation with a renewable portfolio of about 16% of its customers' energy needs.

In September 2001, the CPUC, pursuant to AB IX, suspended the right of retail end-use customer to choose direct access service, thereby preventing additional customers from purchasing electricity from alternative providers.

The Energy Policy Act of 2005 repealed the Public Utility Holding Company Act of 1935 making electric utility industry consolidations more likely.

12.14.5 CPUC Actions

The electric rate freeze, which began on January 1, 1998, ended on January 18, 2001.

In January 2004, CPUC required the California investor-owned electric utilities to achieve by January 1, 2008 an electricity reserve margin of 15–17% in excess of peak requirements and have a diverse portfolio of electricity sources.

In December 2004, the CPUC approved each California investor-owned electric utility's long-term electricity procurement plan (LTPP), authorizing each utility to plan for and procure resources to provide reliable service to their customers for the 10-year period 2005–2014.

Revenue requirements as calculated by the CPUC are independent, or "decoupled," from the volume of sales, which eliminates volatility in revenues due to fluctuations in customer demand.

12.15 Part 3: The 2008–2009 Recession

It is agreed that the recession of 2008–2009 represents the worst economic and financial crisis to face the nation since the Great Depression.

The National Bureau of Economic Research calculates that the recession started in December 2007, lasted 18 months (the longest on record since the Great Depression), and ended in June 2009. Others have nominated an earlier starting date, October 9, 2007, the beginning of the bear market, when the Standard and Poor's 500 stock index peaked. With respect to an end date, Fed Chairman Ben Bernanke stated in mid September 2009 that the recession was "very likely over."

Home loans gone wrong seem to be a root cause. An example will illustrate a typical situation. Home values had risen substantially and promised to continue rising. A borrower having insufficient cash and poor prospects applies for a mortgage on a home he cannot afford. The bank grants the loan to expand its business, with the expectation that the value of the home will continue to rise. Further, the bank has been under pressure to be lenient in evaluating prospective borrowers so as to make homes widely available. Eventually, the borrower fails to make his payments and the bank forecloses. It has a subprime mortgage on its hands. Repeated often enough— and it was—this alone would have been sufficient to cause trouble. The activities of Fannie Mae and Freddie Mac exacerbated the difficulty because of the plethora of foreclosures which they brought to the market. These two quasi-government agencies had followed a policy of granting loans to home buyers which were beyond the borrowers' ability to repay, all in the guise of encouraging home ownership.

In many cases, borrowers owned more than the property was worth.

But the trouble was aggravated by a new feature. Generated by an exotic Wall Street invention, these subprime mortgages had been packaged into securities called CDOs, or collateralized debt obligations. These CDOs were sold as high-rated bonds. The CDOs were hedged by CDSs, credit-default swaps, which were insurance policies against a default or loss in value of the underlying CDOs. These CDOs and CDSs flooded the market. What should have been only a minor financial storm turned into a tempest.

Before turning to the chain of events just summarized, we define the terms used more fully. The CDO is a financial tool that packages individual loans into a product that can be chopped up, repackaged, and sold on the secondary market. The CDO is "collateralized" in that it typically is backed by bundles of loans, bonds, and other real assets.

A "synthetic CDO" does not hold mortgages or even mortgage-backed securities. It is a bet for or against securities held by the CDO, which holds the subprime mortgages. It can bet on the future value of these securities without actually owning them.

A CDO "squared" is a CDO made up of another CDO which itself was made up of community bank debt.

Credit-default swaps are insurance-like contracts that will rise in value if the underlying bonds, and thus the CDOs holding them, become weakened. The synthetic CDO is basically a bundle of credit-default swaps that mimic, or reference, the performance of the real bonds associated with it. Swaps can rise in value if a company starts to look as if it is at a greater risk of defaulting, and can be sold to other investors at a profit. Companies holding CDOs could offset their risk by buying CDSs.

12.16 Toxic Assets in Action: The Beginning

12.16.1 The Securitization Process in Detail

The bulk of toxic assets are based on residential mortgage-backed securities (RMBS), in which thousands of mortgages were gathered into mortgage pools. The returns on these pools were then sliced into a hierarchy of "tranches" that were sold to investors as separate classes of securities. The most senior tranches, rated AAA, received the lowest returns, and then they went down the line to lower ratings and finally to the unrated "equity" tranches at the bottom.

> But the process didn't stop there. Some of the tranches from one mortgage pool were combined with tranches from other mortgage pools, resulting in Collateralized Mortgage Obligations (CMO). Other tranches were combined with tranches from completely different types of pools, based on commercial mortgages, auto loans, student loans, credit card receivables, small business loans, and even corporate loans that had been combined into Collateralized Loan Obligations (CLO). The result was a highly heterogeneous mixture of debt securities called Collateralized Debt Obligations (CDO). The tranches of the CDOs could then be combined with other CDOs, resulting in CDO^2.
>
> Each time these tranches were mixed together with other tranches in a new pool, the securities became more complex . . . .
>
> Complexity is not the only problem. Many of the underlying mortgages were highly risky, involving little or no down payments and initially rated so low they could never amortize the loan. About 80% of the $2.5 trillion subprime mortgages made since 2000 went into securitization pools. When the housing bubble burst and house prices started declining, borrowers began to default, the lower tranches were hit with losses, and higher tranches became more risky and declined in value . . . .
>
> We examined the details of several CDOs. . .One example is a $1 billion CDO^2 created by a large bank in 2005. It had 173 investments in tranches issued by other pools: 130 CDOs, and also 43 CLOs each composed of hundreds of corporate loans. It issued $975 million of four AAA tranches, and three subordinate tranches of $55 million. The AAA tranches were bought by banks and the subordinate tranches mostly by hedge funds.

Two of the 173 investments held by this CDO^2 were in tranches from another billion-dollar CDO-created by another bank earlier in 2005-which was composed mainly of 155 MBS tranches and 40 CDOs. Two of these 155 million MBS tranches were from a $1 billion RMBS pool created in 2004 by a large investment bank, composed of almost 7,000 mortgage loans (90% subprime). That RMBS issued $865 million of AAA notes, about half of which were purchased by Fannie Mae and Freddie Mac and the rest by a variety of banks, insurance companies, pension funds and money managers. About 1,800 of the 7,000 mortgages still remain in the pool, with a current delinquency rate of about 20%.

(Kenneth E. Scott and John B. Taylor, "Why Toxic Assets Are So Hard to Clean Up," *WSJ*, July 20, 2009)

Reprinted from *The Wall Street Journal* @2009. Dow Jones & Company. All rights reserved.

12.16.2 The CDS

CDS, "credit-default swap," is an unregulated, unrecorded insurance policy issued to protect bond buyers against a bond default or a fall in the value of the bond. It was widely used to insure CDOs. The seller is not required to accumulate reserves against the possible loss in value of the CDO or other type of security which the CDS is designed to protect, as would be normal in a regulated-insurance policy.

The CDS was pioneered by AIG. Its holdings increased until they reached their height. AIG offered about $63 billion of this type of coverage backed by possibly toxic CDOs. At the outset, the CDS was an instrument for hedging, but it developed into a popular way to bet on changes in financial markets.

12.16.3 The CMBS

A typical CMBS is stuffed with mortgages on a diverse group of properties, often fewer than 100, with loans ranging from a couple million dollars to more than $100 million. A CMBS servicer, usually a big financial institution like Wachovia and Wells Fargo, collects monthly payments from the borrowers and passes the money on to the institutional investors that buy the securities.

> The CMBS sector is suffering two kinds of pain, which .... sent its delinquency rate to 3.14% in July, more than six times the level a year earlier. One is simply the result of bad underwriting. In the era of looser credit, Wall Street's CMBS machine lent owners money on the assumption that occupancy and rents of their office buildings, hotels, stores or other commercial property would keep rising. In fact, the opposite has happened. The result is that a growing number of properties aren't generating enough cash to make principal and interest payments.
>
> The other kind of hurt is coming from the inability of property owners to refinance loans bundled into CMBS when these loans mature. By the end of 2012, some $153 billion in loans that make up CMBS are coming due, and close to $100 billion of that will face difficulty getting refinanced ....Even though the cash flows of these properties are enough to pay interest and principal on the debt, their values have fallen so far that borrowers wont be able to extend existing mortgages or replace them with new debt.
>
> (Lingling Wei and Peter Grant, "Commercial Real Estate Lurks as Next Potential Mortgage Crisis," *WSJ*, August 31, 2009)

12.16.4 A Bond Called Jupiter

To illustrate the devious and convoluted patterns of the pervasive toxic security, we cite a mortgage bond referred to as Jupiter which owned 223 other bonds similar to itself, one of which owned 126 other bonds. Below these top layers were thousands of questionable individual mortgages, which had been sliced and combined into groups of varying quality.

As another example, a mortgage bond of 2006 in the amount of $36 million ended up in 30 debt pools, finally causing losses to investors of $280 million by 2008 when the bond was extinguished. This illustrates the losses caused by slicing the same bond into many other segments, which magnifies the losses manyfold.

12.17 Disregarded History

The financial faults leading to the 2008–2009 recession were not without precedent. They had been preceded by at least two other near-recent events of market turmoil which should have been a warning. The first of these followed Michael Milken's promotion of "junk" bonds for Drexel Burham Lambert in 1985. Milken built up a large market for these bonds, which collapsed in 1989. The second occurred in *1994* when two Nobel economics prizewinners, Robert H. Merton and Myron S. Scholes, went public with their claim to have discovered market models which drastically limited exposure to risk. They founded long-term capital management, which was hugely successful until 1998, when its portfolio fell 44%, losing almost $2 billion. Solomon Smith Barney lost $300 million, and Merrill Lynch lost $135 million.

12.18 Earlier Bailouts

In the same fashion as the follies of the 2008–2009 recession were foreshadowed by earlier events of a similar type, the bailouts from 2008 to 2009 also had forerunners. In 1971, Lockheed had received loan guarantees of $250 million to recover from its venture into commercial jetliners. In 1980, Chrysler had received $1.5 billion in loan guarantees to avoid bankruptcy. In the period from 1986 to 1995, savings and loan banks received $124 billion to recover from investment losses. And in 2001, following the bombings of 9/11, airlines received $5 billion for losses and $10 billion in loan guarantees. So the bailouts following the recession should not have been a surprise.

12.19 The Financial Crisis

Starting in mid-2006, housing prices started to fall dramatically. This led to home mortgage defaults, and huge losses for lenders. In 2007 and 2008 a domino effect took hold, diminishing the value of mortgage-backed bonds and the value of the financial instruments based on these bonds, such as derivatives. Banks had to write down their holds to a much lessened market value. Many banks failed, experiencing billions of dollars of losses. Citigroup had losses of $33 billion on high-risk CDOs and leveraged loans; Merrill Lynch had $26 billion and Bank of America, $9 billion. JP Morgan Chase and Co. fared somewhat better, having losses of only $5 billion.

September 2008 was the worst and perhaps the most drastic month. On September 7, Fannie Mae and Freddie Mac were nationalized. On September 14, Merrill Lynch was bought by Bank of America to avoid bankruptcy. Lehman Brothers went bankrupt on September 15. Also on September 15, AIG (American International Group, Inc.) received a $55 billion bailout. On September 22, Goldman Sachs and Morgan Stanley were converted into bank holding companies by their own actions. And on September 25, Washington Mutual was placed into receivership.

In 2006, there were about $386 billion outstanding in CDO and synthetic CDOs. In 2008, almost half of the $10.6 trillion in US mortgages were of low quality. The values of suspect toxic securities had fallen dramatically and stayed low. As an example, at auction in 2010, investors paid an average of 60 cents on the dollar for toxic CDOs which combined pieces of a $1.7 billion complex security sold by Goldman Sachs Group. As another example, a $4.2 billion CMBS underwritten by Goldman Sachs Group and Royal Bank of Scotland Group was expected to have an 11.7% loss.

The Wall Street Journal reported,

> The central bank is blamed for too vigorously spurring home buying through its low short-term interest targets, which were initially set to fight the economic slump after the dot-com bubble burst in 2001...Low interest rates around the globe, not just in the US, contributed to the housing boom that was worldwide.
>
> Subprime mortgages led to a global economic crisis in a considerable part because of securitization, in which the home loans were sliced up, packaged into securities and sold off to investors around the world.
>
> (Kara Scannell and Sudeep Reddy, "Greenspan Admits Errors to Hostile House Panel," *WSJ*, October 24, 2008.)
>
> ... aggressive financiers have manufactured what the Bank for International Settlements estimated to be $1 quadrillion worth of new derivatives (mortgage-backed securities, collateralized debt obligations, and credit default swaps) that have flooded the market.
>
> (Hernando de Soto, "Toxic Assets Were Hidden Assets," *WSJ*, March 25, 2009)
> Reprinted from *The Wall Street Journal* @2009. Dow Jones & Company.
> All rights reserved.

12.20 The Bailouts

The bailouts, and their results or lack thereof, are a story in themselves and are reserved for a different writer. However, to provide the basis for an end to this present discourse, we note the two largest bailouts which were undertaken to ease the pains of an economic recovery for the nation.

The first bailout was a $700 billion allocation, termed the Troubled Asset Relief Program (or TARP). It was designed to prevent the economy from worsening by taking toxic assets out of circulation. Initially, it was intended to function by the treasury buying toxic securities from banks and investment houses. However, the price to be paid for those securities proved to be insolvable: if the treasury paid too much, it would look like a handout; if it paid too little, it would force sellers to make enormous write-offs. So it was decided to switch from buying the toxic assets from holders, to buying holders' equity.

The American Recovery and Reinvestment Act, commonly referred to as the "stimulus," was the second major bailout. This was a massive $767 billion allocation to projects designed to jumpstart the economy. It was supposed to include only "shovel ready" projects which would create jobs. But early judgments were that it failed to rejuvenate the economy, partially, at least, because most of the dollars went into unproductive projects.

These two bailouts were not the only measures undertaken. Industry-specific bills were passed, including the cash for clunkers auto endeavor and such other financial measures as the $8,000 for home-buyer's tax credit, mortgage payment relief, and extension of jobless pay.

It is too early to evaluate the end-results of these recession-relief programs. Did they succeed in mending the economy? Only history will tell.

12.21 A Conducive Environment

A variety of diverse circumstance converged to stimulate the tempest. In addition to the unquestioning optimism that home values would continue to rise *ad infinitum*, there were other influences including the following:

1) A pervasive view among lenders, supported by government policy, that home ownership should be encouraged and promoted. This led the two home mortgage giants, Fannie Mae and Freddie Mac, to issue hundreds of billions of dollars of bonds to central banks around the world. The bonds later turned into toxic assets.
2) Confidence in the resilience of home prices was high initially. The belief encouraged mortgage underwriting because lenders assumed that borrowers living on the edge could always refinance or sell their homes for a profit if they ran into trouble. But confidence was eroded as many thousands of homeowners faced foreclosure with the fall in prices. A bond or derivative is, after all, a promise to pay someone. If there is no confidence in it, the financial system ceases to function.
3) Short-term interest rates were kept very low, stimulating borrowing.
4) Capital leverage of investment bankers rose to unduly high levels, giving them enhanced ability to purchase high-risk securities.
5) Financial institutions had to follow mark-to-market accounting, forcing them to write-off the loss in value of their risky subprime mortgages.

Then, suddenly, the import of the huge inventories of risky subprime-backed bonds which were on their books struck home to the larger US banks and investment houses. The crash was at hand. The tempest raged. At the center of the storm were CDOs, created through the process of securitization.

Heads of banks and investment houses, as well as their government regulators, were aware of the weaknesses of CDOs as financial instruments, and should have anticipated the devastation which would occur with their proliferation. Yet, none raised the alarm. In hindsight, this seems inexcusable.

However, to avoid overstatement of this crucial omission, it should be noted that there was a plausible explanation for the acceptance by some of the CDO as valid. In "The Economics of Structured Finance," (the *Journal of Economic Perspectives*, Winter 2009), Coval, Jurek, and Stafford say:

> Structured finance allows originators to satisfy the guidelines of credit rating agencies by a two-step procedure involving pooling and trenching.
> In the first step, a large collection of credit-sensitive assets is assembled in a portfolio, referred to as a "special purpose vehicle."…. Then, to manufacture a range of securities with different cash flow risks, a capital structure of prioritized claims, known as *tranches*, are issued against the underlying collateral pool. The tranches are prioritized in how they absorb losses from the underlying portfolio ….
> A central insight of structured finance is that by using a larger number of securities in the underlying pool, a progressively larger fraction of the issued tranches can end up with higher credit ratings than the average rating of the underlying pool of assets.

If the underlined conclusion was valid, it might be an acceptable excuse for the lack of alarm by those who ought to have known better. But, as experience has demonstrated, this happy academic transformation has not materialized. Subprime assets remain subprime.

12.22 Causes

As will have been clear from the foregoing discussions, it is difficult to pin down a single circumstance which can accurately describe the cause of the recession. Too many diverse factors contributed to the economic event. The following quote is a partial summary.

> Buyers bought houses they couldn't afford, believing they could refinance in the future and benefit from the ongoing appreciation. Lenders assumed that even if everything else went wrong, properties could still be sold for more than the cost and the loan could be repaid. This mentality permeated the market from the originator to the holder of securitized mortgages, from the rating agency to the financial regulator. (Phil Gramm, "Deregulation and the Financial Panic")
>
> (*WSJ*, February 20, 2009)
>
> The Steepest one-year stock market drop in 77 years, the collapse or forced sale of several big Wall Street firms and the shutdown of entire sectors of the bond market for several months at a time, combined to knock Wall Street underwriting for a loop in 2008. (Randall Smith, "Stock and Bond Insurance Shrivels")
>
> (*WSJ*, January 2, 2009)
> Reprinted from *The Wall Street Journal* @2009. Dow Jones & Company.
> All rights reserved.

12.23 The Dow from September 10 to October 10, 2008

Although greater detail on the Dow is given elsewhere, it is interesting to observe it more closely over a critical month, as has *The Wall Street Journal*,

> Sept. 10, 2008: The Dow clings to its level above 11000 as worries mount about Lehman Brothers, AIG and Merrill.
> Sept. 15: The Dow drops 504.48 points after a weekend in which Lehman and Merrill succumbed. AIG stock tumbles 60%.
> Sept. 17: Dow falls 449.36 after AIG rescue.
> Sept. 18: Smiles return, briefly: Dow soars 410.03, then 368.75 the next day. Kraft foods named to replace AIG in the Dow.
> Sept. 26: Hopes grow for government assistance.
> Sept. 29: Dow drops 777.68 after House rejects financial-rescue package.
> Oct. 3: Cheers at the NYSE after House passes the plan, but Dow still loses 817.75 on the week.
> Oct. 6: Closes below 10,000 for the first time in nearly 4 years.
> Oct. 8: Coordinated interest-rate cuts made around the world.
> Oct. 9: Relentless declines amount to a "slow motion crash."
> Oct. 10: Dow closes at 8,451.19, a 2,817.73-point drop since Sept. 10.

("Flashback to Pain," *WSJ,* Sep. 14, 2009)

12.24 The Paths of the Giants

Although the following relationships are to be found at various points throughout this report, it maybe helpful to array the major players in one summary.

> J.P. Morgan Chase
>   Absorbs Bear Stearns
>   Buys Washington Mutual
> Bank of America
>   Buys Countrywide Financial
>   Absorbs Merrill Lynch
> Wells Fargo buys Wachovia
> Citigroup posts huge losses: is buoyed by Government
> American International Group (AIG) close to bankruptcy: Government aids
> Lehman folds in bankruptcy
> Fannie Mae and Freddy Mac seized by Government
> Morgan Stanley and Goldman Sachs convert to traditional bank-holding companies

12.25 Regulation

Regulation? There was none. Control and restraint of financial markets might have prevented the credit excesses which led to the recession, but regulatory authorities remained asleep at the switch, or at least were silent. They seemed confident in their belief in non-regulation—that no interference with financial institutions was called for—and remained quiescent as the market ran amuck.

Also, there seemed to be no attention given as to the probable effects of the fashionable and widely popular exotic new financial devices which were being introduced. This proved to be a fatal flaw. Elsewhere in this book, we emphasize the necessity for accurate and thorough examination of the impacts of new policies before they are implemented. This summary illustrates what can happen when this advice is ignored.

12.26 2008 Statistics

Funds suffer $320 billion outflow in 2008, from mutual funds, a record in dollars and percentage of assets, in one of the biggest flights to safety the industry has seen.
(*Financial Times, Jan.2, 2009*)

Average share price on NYSE fell 45% from $75.01 to $41.14 (*WSJ* Jan 1, 2009) Dow closed at 8776.39, a fall of 33.8% for year. Down 38% from record of 14,165.53 of October 2007.

Total number of jobs lost in 2008, 2.5 million, most since 1945. Unemployment climbed to 7.2%.
(*WSJ* Jan. 10-11, 2009)

The Rapidly Shrinking Banking Industry
    Market caps, from March 1, 2007 to Jan. 21, 2009
        Bank of America, from 225.3 to 36.7
        JP Morgan Chase, from 170.9 to 36.7
        Goldman Sachs, from 82.1 to 25.4
        Citigroup, from 250.4 to 52

        Deutsche Bank, from 67.8 to 13.1
        HSBC, from 200.5 to 86.0
        UBS, from 123.9 to 32.8
        BNP Paribas, 96.3 to 28.2

TARP (Troubled Asset Relief Program)
    $700 billion passes by Congress during Paulson's tenure
    $350 billion released in October 2008; released in January 2009,
        went to homeowners, automakers and AIG (*Time*, June 22, 2009)

TARP allocations:
    Citi $50 billion
    BofA $45 billion
    AIG $40 billion
    JP Morgan Chase $25 billion
    Wells Fargo $25 billion
        (*Financial Times* Feb 5, 2009)

12.27 Epilogue

There is little to be gained by closing this chapter on "Matters of Judgment" with a further lecture on matters of judgment and the activities which they endorse. Suffice to say that every citizen shares in the nation's sense of social responsibility and carries a part of the nation's civic burden.

God bless our country!

12.28 Acronyms and Definitions

CDO: Collateralized debt obligations
CDS: Credit-default swap
MBS: Mortgage-backed securities
RMBS: Residential mortgage-backed securities
CMBS: Commercial mortgage-backed securities
CMO: Collateralized mortgage obligations
CLO: Collateralized loan obligations
SIVs: Structured investment vehicles—Pools of mortgages, credit card loans, and other debt created by banks but not carried on their books

Derivatives: Financial contracts whose payment terms are derived from the performance of some underlying asset or assets

Tranches: A hierarchy of security pools, or returns on the securities in the pools, which are sold to investors as separate classes of securities

Systemic risk: The chance that a problem in one part of the financial system will uncontrollably ripple to otherwise healthy parts

Toxic assets: Mostly, the investments backed by risky subprime mortgages held by larger US banks, which have lost value. Marcy Gordon observes: "They hang like shackles from the banks' feet, dragging down their balance sheets and their fortunes."

Another writer observes, "A bond or derivative is, after all, a promise to pay someone. If there is no confidence in it, the financial system ceases to function."

Market-to-market (MTM): Accounting rule that requires banks to mark subprime assets to market value, that is, to adjust their value according to prices brought by comparable securities in recent sales.

Index

A
Accounting doubts, 326–340
Acronyms and definitions of the recession, 406
Additions to standard rate forms, 291–292
Adjustment clauses, 244–245
Advertising, 175
AFUDC, 337–338
Allocation methods
  Atlantic Seaboard, 93, 96–98
  modified fixed variable, 93, 100–102
  straight fixed variable, 93, 103–104
  United, 93, 100
All-purpose rates, 253
Alternative forecasts, 195–196
Analogues, the baker, 1, 4–15, 19, 22
Application of capacity factor, 321–322
Application of diversity factor, 313–315
Application of load factor, 315–320
Arrested output, 56–57
Atlantic Seaboard method, 93, 96–98
Availability and reliability, 186–187
Average costs, 3, 29
Avoidable costs, 89

B
Base-load generating plants, 66
Beginning and causes of the recession, 400–404
Biofuels, 209
Blocking, 247–250, 268–270
Breakdown of modern rates into cost components, 202
Broad-based peaks, 306
Buildings and homes, 211–212
Bypass, 53–54

C
Capacity utilization
  bypass, 53–54
  capability of existing plant, 14–15
  dynamic plant, 33
  plant expansion, 15–17
  static plant, 31
Capability of existing plant, 14–15
Capital costs, 5
Capital-intensive industries, 25
Caps and floors, 246–247
California energy crisis, sequence of events, 339–390
  the beginning (1996) assembly bill 1890, 340
  the crisis and its aftermath (to early 2002), 356–390
  the lull before the storm (1997–1999), 342–348
  optimism reigns: no doubts (1996), 341–342
  the storm hits: the energy crisis (2000–2001), 348–355
California energy crisis, causes of the crisis, 389–393
  divestiture of generation by CA utilities, 391–392
  the fatal contradiction, 389
  long term contracts, 392–393
  neglect of costs, 393–394
  regulatory and economic failures, 390–391
  uniform price auction, 393
California energy crisis, aftermath, 394–397
  PG&E, Edison Int., and others, 394–397
  from storm to turmoil, 392
California lifeline/baseline rate, 198–201
  philosophy, 198
  pricing procedure, 200–201
  rate schedule, 198–199
Capacity factor, 321–322
Case history (1946-1950), 292–293
Case history (1991), 216

Cogeneration plant, 66
Color GREEN, 205–212
 biofuels, 209
 buildings and homes, 211–212
 landfills (methane), 209
 light bulbs, 211
 LNG, 209
 meters, 210–211
 nuclear, 210
 oil sands, 209
 politics and regulation, 212
 renewable energy, clean energy, 207–210
 solar, 208
 tidal and wind power, 209
 transmission (the grid), 210
 vehicles, 211
 wind, 208
Coincident demand peak responsibility method, 80–81
Commercial mortgage–backed securities (CMBS), 399
Commodity costs, 29
Common costs, 7, 69–70, 72–73
Company-wide cost of service, 112–113
Current accounting, 327–328
Competitive pricing, 18
Comparison of Hopkinson and Wright rates, 281–282
Constant costs, 30, 38–40
Customer charge, 262, 270–272
Cost allocation, 8
Cost allocation methods, 9
Cost and price, 11, 20
Cost approaches to rates, 100–130, 131–165
Cost apportionment, 8
Cost conditions, 29–39
 constant cost, 30, 38–40
 decreasing, 29–30, 32, 35–39
 hi-capital/low operating costs, 62–63
 increasing, 29–30, 40–42
 low-capital, high operating costs, 62–63
Cost *vs.* value, 132–133
Civic participation, 173
Classification as fixed or variable, 116–120
Classification as demand or commodity, 120–122
Class price, 151
Cost limitations, 87
Cost of service, 25–26
Costs, 2–3
Credit-default swap (COS), 399
Customer charge, 262, 270–272

D
Daily load patterns, 303
Decreasing costs, 29, 32, 37–42
Deferred income taxes, 338
Demand, 132
Demand 1/demand 2, 105
Demand charge, 105–106, 262, 283–286
Demand costs, 81–82, 89, 286–287
Demand factor, 322–323
Derived demand, 136
Direct costs, 7, 69–73
Direct demand, 136
Diminishing utility, 148
Discounted alternatives to bypass, 55–56
Disregarded history before recession, 400
Distance-related/distance-sensitive, 122–125
Distributed generation, 66
Distribution costs, 89
Diversity, 309–316
Diversity factor, 311–312
Dual fuel capability, 308
Doherty three–part rate, 287–288
Dow, Sept. 10 to Oct. 10, 2008, 404
Dubious accounting, 326–338
Duration curve, 305–307

E
Economic demand, 131–132
Economic models, 181
Edison's improvements to allocations, 79–80
Elastic demand, 137–140
Energy cost, 29
Extent of wind power, 226
Efficiency, relative, load factor, 320–321
Elements of rate design, 241–247
 adjustment clauses, 244–245
 all-purpose vs. special–purpose, 252–254
 blocking, 247–250
 caps and floors, 246–247
 changes across–the–board, 257–259
 fine print provisions, 259–260
 fish-hook blocking, 248–249
 frozen rates, 246
 inverted blocking, 247–249
 minimums, 241–243
 penalties and discounts, 245
 postage stamp *vs.* zone, 250–252
 ratchets, 243–244
 rolled-in *vs.* incremental pricing, 254–257
 seasonal *vs.* year-round, 254
 unbundling, 252–254
Energy/commodity charge, 262, 286–287

Index

F
Fine–print rate provisions, 259–260
Fish–hook rates, 248
Firm and interruptible loads (demands), 307–309
Fixed cost, 13–15, 27
Flat rates, 262–264
Forecasting assumptions, 184–185
Frequent features of rate design, 241–247
    adjustment clauses, 244–245
    minimums, 241–243
    penalties and discounts, 245
    ratchets, 243–244
Frozen rates, 246
Functionalization, 113–115
Functional division of costs, 74

G
Gauging the market analysis factors, 308–309
GREEN colored activities, 205–212
Gross and net energy, 302
Generation costs, 79
Generating options, 42–49
    peaking or firming-up plant, 46–49
    purchasing power, 50–59
    small base load plant, 42–46
Giveaways, 174–175
Government policy, 235–237
Guidelines to evaluating the forecast, 194–195

H
Handbook, tools of the trade, 301–323
Hi-capital/low operating costs, 62–63
Hopkinson rate, 272–278, 281–282
    blocked and unblocked, 274–276
    demand component, 276–278

I
Increasing cost conditions, 38, 42–43
Incremental costs, 83
Incremental pricing, 254–257
Inelastic demand, 143
Intermediate elasticity of demand, 150
Introduction to Tools, 301–324
Inverted blocking, 249–250
Issues, regulatory, 95

J
Joint costs, 8–11, 69–91, 97
Joint cost allocations
    coincident demand peak responsibility method, 74–75
    Edison's improvements, 79–80
    non–coincident demand peak responsibility method, 76
    Nordin, 78–79
    other peak responsibility methods, 77
    phantom customer, 78
    separable cost-remaining benefits method, 85–87
    simplistic methods (per customer and per unit of use), 73

L
Labeling of curves and factors, 324
Lack of conformity in accounting, 336
Landfills (methane), 209
Least-cost plans, 90
Lester special-investment three-part rate, 288–289
Lifeline/baseline rate (California), 197–201
Light bulbs, 211
Load/demand curves, 304–305
Load factor, 315–321
Long range demand forecasts, 180–182
Long-run elasticity of demand, 146–147
Low–capital/hi–operating costs, 62–63
LNG, 209

M
Marginal cost, 84
Marginal cost regulation, 212–216
    marginal cost defined, 213
    origin, 213
    termination, 216
Market analysis factors, 308–321
    diversity and diversity factor, 309–321
Marketing, 173–175
Measurement units, 177–178
    capacity factor, 321–322
    cubic foot, 177
    demand factor, 322–323
    diversity factor, 309–313
    kilowatt and kilowatt hour, 177
    load factor, 315–316
    peak requirement, 177
    therm, 177
    volume requirement, 178
Meters, 210–211
Metered commodity rates, 264–265
Metered demand rates, 265–266
Minimums, 241–243
Minimum bill, 111
Misleading accounting, 327–331
Modified fixed variable allocation method, 93, 100–102
Monopoly pricing, 149–151

N
Needle peaks, 306
Nuclear, 210
New customer rates, 254–257
Non-coincident demand peak responsibility allocation method, 76
Non-distance sensitive rates, 125
Nordin method, 78–79

O
Objective rate, 290–291
Oil sands, 209
Old customer rates, 254
One-bus one-route transit line, 318–319
Outline of utility regulation, 404
Option demand, 136–137

P
Paths of the giants in the recession, 404
Past and future forecasts, 88–89
Peaking or firming-up generating plant, 47–49
Peaking plant, 66
Peaks, needle and broad based, 306
Penalties and discounts, 245
Per-unit rate elements, 125–128
Philosophy of lifeline/baseline rate, 197
Pipeline rates for large distributors (ODL–1, 1971), 298
Planning curves
    duration, 305–306
    load, 302–303
Plant expansion, 15–17
Politics and regulation, greens, 212
Postage stamp rates, 107
Power factor, 323–324
Price, 2
Price differentials (differentiation), 152
    reasonable, 152–155
    unreasonable, 164–167
    discriminatory, 164–167
Price elasticity of demand, 137–143
Price and cost, 2, 20–22
Price regulation, 6
Pricing methods, 83–85
    incremental cost, 84
    marginal cost, 84
    total cost, 83
Pricing procedures, lifeline/baseline rates, 198–199
Predatory pricing, 168
Primer on wind rates, 217
Promotional incentive-type rates, 290
Prudence in decisions, 336

Q
Quantity discount, 11–13

R
Rate design, 238–239
Rate design, Tenneco, 112–113
    classification as demand or commodity, 120
    classification as fixed or variable, 116–120
    company–wide cost of service, 112–113
    distribution related/distance sensitive, 122–124
    functionalization, 113–115
    non-distance sensitive, 125–126
    per-unit rate elements, 125–128
    transmission sector, 121
Rate elements, 262
    customer charge, 262
    demand charge, 262
    energy/commodity charge, 262, 270–272
Rate schedule defined, 237
Rate schedule division of costs, 81–82
    commodity costs, 82
    customer costs, 81–82
    demand costs, 81
Rate schedule, lifeline/baseline rates, 198–199
Ratchets, 243–244
Rate forms and comparisons, 294–295
Rate for wind power, 224–226
Rate level changes, 257–259
Rate theory, single–part rate forms, 266–267
Rate theory, two–part rate forms, 282–287
Regulated market place, 230
    customer viewpoint, 230–231
    management viewpoint, 231–232
    public viewpoint, 232–233
Range of forecasts, 188–189
Real time pricing, 65, 204
Recession of 2008–2009, 397–398
Regulation in the recession, 404–405
Renewable energy, clean energy, 207–208
Return on equity, 5
Repression of demand, 147
Requisites for rates, 233
    California PUC, 233–234
    expert opinion, 236–237
    Federal Energy Regulatory Commission, 234
    related objectives, 236
Relative efficiency, load factor, 315–321
Relationship of load and diversity factors, 320–321

Index 411

Resource planning, 306–308
 duration curves, 307
Revenue effects of elasticity, 143–146
Rolled-in pricing, 255
Root causes of the recession, 397

S
Seasonal rates, 254
Separable cost-remaining benefits method, 85
Short-run
 demand forecasts, 178–180
 elasticity of demand, 146
Small base load plant, 42–46
Single forecast, 188–189
Single-part rates, 262–272
 blocked *vs.* unblocked, 268–270
 customer charge, 270–272
 flat rates, 262
 metered commodity rates, 264
 metered demand rates, 265
 rate theory, 266
 straight line commodity rates, 264
Season usage patterns, 303
Securitization process, 398
Solar, 208
Static plant, 33
Straight fixed variable allocation method, 93, 103–104
Straight line metered commodity rates, 264
Stimulation of demand, 147
Summer and winter usage patterns, 304
Special-purpose rates, 252
Statistics of the recession, 405

T
Tariff components, NW Natural Gas Co. (1971), 295–299
Tenneco rate design, 93, 112
Testing the forecast, 189
Tidal and wind, 209
Timed pricing, 203
Time-of-day pricing, 65
Total cost, 4, 83
Transmission (the grid), 210
Transmission costs, 82, 121
Types of rates, 261–300
 other, 292–295
 single–part rates, 260–270
 two–part rates, 272–287
 three–part rates, 287–290
Types of generating plants
 base load, 66
 cogeneration, 66
 distributed generation, 66
 peaking, 66
Types of rate classes, 152–156
 characteristics of use, 160–161
 conventional economic groupings, 157
 grade of service, 159–161
 location, 161
 tailored, 161
 type of user/use, 158
Three-part rates, 287–290
 Doherty rate, 287
 Lester rate, 288–289
 Zanoff rate, 289–290
Two-part rates, 272–287
 Hopkinson rate, 272–278
 Wright rate, 279–281
Two-part pricing, 17

U
Unbundling, 252
Unregulated marketplace, 229
Upper limit of rates concept, 133–136
Utility and general accounting compared, 333–334
Utility demand, 132
United allocation method, 93, 100
Utilization factor, 322
Utility pricing theory, 25
 cost of service, 25
 readiness-to-serve, 28
 use of service, 29
 value of service, 131–132
Utility regulation
 outline, 404
 issues, 6–7

V
Value of service, 131–132
Value approaches to rates, 162–164, 170–172
Variable cost, 27–28, 61–63
Value based rate classes, 155–156
Vehicular, 211

W
Washington Public Power Supply System (WPPSS), 140–141
Weather variations, 307
Wind, 208
Wind rates on an integrated electric system, 217–227
 balancing measures, 223
 costs, 222
 extent, 218

Wind rates on an integrated (*cont.*)
   physical specifications, 227
   planning, 219
   primer, 217
   rate, 224
Wright rate, 279–281

Y
Year-round rates, 254

Z
Zanoff three–part gas pipeline rate, 289–290
Zoning and zone rates, 106–110, 250